# THE PALGRAVE ENCYCLOPEDIA OF WORLD ECONOMIC HISTORY SINCE 1750

# THE PALGRAVE ENCYCLOPEDIA OF WORLD ECONOMIC HISTORY SINCE 1750

Graham Bannock

and

R.E. Baxter

First published 2010 by
PALGRAVE MACMILLAN

Palgrave Macmillan in the UK is an imprint of Macmillan Publishers Limited,
registered in England, company number 785998, of Houndmills, Basingstoke,
Hampshire RG21 6XS.

Palgrave Macmillan in the US is a division of St Martin's Press LLC,
175 Fifth Avenue, New York, NY 10010.

Palgrave Macmillan is the global academic imprint of the above companies
and has companies and representatives throughout the world.

Palgrave® and Macmillan® are registered trademarks in the United States,
the United Kingdom, Europe and other countries.

ISBN 978–0–230–22392–9

This book is printed on paper suitable for recycling and made from fully
managed and sustained forest sources. Logging, pulping and manufacturing
processes are expected to conform to the environmental regulations of the
country of origin.

A catalogue record for this book is available from the British Library.

A catalog record for this book is available from the Library of Congress.

10  9  8  7  6  5  4  3  2  1
19  18  17  16  15  14  13  12  11  10

Printed and bound in Great Britain by
CPI Antony Rowe, Chippenham and Eastbourne

# Contents

*Foreword*     vi
*Introduction*     viii
*Glossary*     xii
*List of Entries*     xv

**The Encyclopedia**     1

*Author Index*     543
*Subject Index*     553

# Foreword

The period since 1750 has seen the emergence and spread of sustained economic growth and the disparities and problems that have accompanied it throughout the world. This book has been conceived as a guide for students, academics and the general reader to the main elements of this period of world economic history. As of now, surprisingly, it is the only single-volume encyclopedia on the subject available in the English language.

*The Encyclopedia of World Economic History since 1750* differs from other reference books of its kind in being the work of just two people in contrast to the multi-specialist-author approach common to most encyclopedias. The advantages of the dual-author approach are, we believe, that it allows greater expository clarity, unity and readability. We have paid particular attention to clarity and readability, not, we trust, at the expense of accuracy.

A single-volume encyclopedia inevitably involves ruthless selection but we hope that everything that is really important for a general introduction to the subject gets a mention. We have tried to indicate where there is dissent and controversy and we hope academic specialists will feel that in general we have not meted out too rough a justice to their subjects. We have included entries on most of the key events and aspects of economic history. There are also entries on a number of pioneering thinkers that economic historians need to be familiar with. We have excluded contemporary economists and historians from this list both out of delicacy and on space grounds, though their work is, of course, reflected in the subject entries. We include entries for a few specific countries and regions within the limitations of space but others benefit from references in the broader entries, as the index reveals. The roots of most aspects of economic history go back earlier than 1750 and where appropriate we have also covered earlier periods.

The apparatus of the book requires some explanation because there is much more to the content than the List of Entries might suggest. The first element of this apparatus is the detailed general index which is intended to be a useful tool for the reader seeking information on a subject which is not obviously covered in the alphabetically listed main entries. For example, an important and partly still unresolved issue is the debate about the standard of living in Britain and other countries during the industrial revolutions and there is no entry on this as such. The index, however, reveals that there is coverage on this issue, giving different viewpoints, in several entries including 'The Industrial Revolution in Britain', 'Industrial Revolutions', 'Anthropometric History' and others. Similarly, there is no entry for 'British Empire' but material is to be found in several entries, including 'Britain', 'Economic Imperialism', 'India', 'South Africa' and elsewhere.

The second, and equally important element to help readers to find their way about the book is the cross-referencing system. The symbol > before a word or phrase in block capitals, thus >BIMETALLIC SYSTEM, directs the reader to another entry in which amplification or complementary information is to be found. By following these references readers can pursue an interest in a subject both intensively and extensively. The cross-referencing system also saves space because it helps to avoid repetition, though there is some of that because each entry is intended to be self-contained.

The third element is the references given at the end of every entry. These references both indicate our sources, to which we are indebted, and signpost the reader to books and articles in which things can be pursued in greater depth. The references include both elementary and advanced texts and cover articles in the learned journals as well as books. References in the text are indicated by the author's name followed by the date, thus: Jones (1999).

The fourth and final element is the glossary at the front of the book. The glossary is there to help people who are not familiar with acronyms and technical terms in economics and statistics, such as 'deflation', 'GDP',

'real terms', 'correlation'. Readers will find more elaborate definitions of these terms in '*The Penguin Dictionary of Economics*' by Bannock, Baxter and Evan Davis.

Our debts to other authors are evident in the lists of references at the end of each entry and in a sense this book is a guide to and summary of much of the literature on economic history that is accessible to the lay reader. We wish specifically to acknowledge help and encouragement from two old friends, Angus Maddison and Alan Peacock. Chris Thurman, former economist at the Brewers Society, was kind enough to read and comment on the entry on 'Beer', while Simon Dagut did the same for 'South Africa', Alan Doran for 'Accounting' and Robert Pringle for 'Central Banking' and 'Money and Banking'. We are, of course responsible for all errors and omissions. Finally, but not least, we wish to thank Françoise Bannock and Dee Baxter for their patience and forbearance in what has been a long distraction.

GRAHAM BANNOCK
R. E. BAXTER

# Introduction

In the late 1950s, I chaired a Board of Examiners for an Honours Economics examination which included a compulsory paper on Economic History. One examinee, expected to do well, instead of answering the usual three questions out of a choice of eight wrote a long essay, presumably claiming kinship with Henry Ford who, it is said, famously described history as 'bunk'. There was consternation, opinions being divided as to whether to give the paper an outright fail or to ask the student to produce a certificate claiming illness. The External Examiner advised giving the student a first-class mark, in recognition of the high quality of the writing and the persuasiveness of her arguments. After extensive discussion, and conscious of the external examiner's high reputation, we accepted his advice. The young lady returned to her native land, later wrote a much-acclaimed PhD thesis in Economics at a prestigious university and subsequently became Chair of the Economics Department of one of the best-known liberal arts colleges in the USA. (Her PhD supervisor subsequently became a Nobel Laureate in Economics!)

It may have been that her reaction was a reflection of the controversy about scope and method of economic history at the time and particularly its relation to economics. When I was in a similar position to the young American, texts on economic history were primarily descriptive and seemed to bear little relationship to the subject matter of Economics. There was no 'spin-off' either from Economics to Economic History or vice versa. One vaguely realized that confirmation of generalizations about economic behaviour lay in examination of the data, but evidence rarely bore a close relationship to the questions of interest to economists. Indeed, where it did, as in the case of the formidably learned German Historical School, it resulted in a sustained attack on the pretensions of economic analysis as a science, and led to a bitter dispute with the earlier Austrian economists, notably Karl Menger and his disciples, such as Ludwig von Mises. (The acrimonious nature of the dispute is exemplified in Menger's description of the work of the Historical School as 'historico-statistical miniature painting'.)

The very exceptions to this situation, notably in the cases of the history of money and banking and the growth in large-scale monopoly, give the clue to a major change which has brought economic history firmly into place as an integral part of economics training.

In the 19th century in the UK there was a marked increase in the documentation available largely as the result of the information demanded by governments put under pressure to take action to control business. (It is well known that Karl Marx was one of the first investigators to benefit from close study of the British Blue Books containing the evidence of public enquiries into economic condition.) Hume and Smith in making reference to economic conditions were obliged to collate data from widely disparate sources, including Classical Latin and Greek texts. A century later government reports simplified the task. The availability of decennial censuses, and later official data on the distribution of income needed in calculating the yield of actual or projected taxes, increased the opportunity to appeal to historical evidence. In the 20th century, public debate about the increased role of government in attempts to control the economy, not only by fiscal and monetary policy but by nationalization of industry, required the massive extension in information about economic trends. A statistical framework of the economy was required in order to process the data and to enable interpretation of its economic significance. When Colin Clark made the first attempt to produce comprehensive national income data for the UK in the 1930s Keynes commended him for his bravery. Nowadays, in all countries engaged in economic relations with others, the supply of such data is taken for granted and made available in a form to facilitate international comparisons of the trend in an ever-growing list of economic variables.

Statements of economic prospects and policies are festooned with tabulations displaying the quantitative nature of the expected and proposed changes in the economy. But the future cannot be divorced from the past and it soon became apparent that national and social accounting presented a wonderful opportunity for systematizing the analysis of long-term economic trends that illustrated economic and social changes – notably demographic variables and those associated with booms and slumps – incomes, prices, employment. The skills of the economist then overshadowed those of the historian in the curriculum of economic history itself.

The economists' 'takeover' was cemented by two further developments. The extension in the availability of data, although confined to what is, historically speaking, a short period of time, enlarged the list of hypotheses about economic development, notably in the fields of the causes of economic growth. One particularly crucial aspect of that development is the growth in the relative size of the public sector in maturing economies. But where economists add to their list of hypotheses, econometrists are soon found hovering, ready to evaluate their viability by statistical tests of growing complexity. (One might date the foundation of econometrics, as we know it today, as somewhere in the 1950s, when such an eminent economist as George Shackle still found it necessary to present the term in inverted commas!) Econometrians seem almost set fair to push even economists aside in having pride of place in the evolution of the study of economic history, now firmly embedded as part of the necessary equipment of the economist.

Whatever the pretensions of quantitative analysis of historical data, it makes no sense, even if one regards the economic historian's primary role as providing material for seeking to formulate and test economic models. In fact, too often the econometrist may be tempted to introduce a false precision into their analyses by how they define their variables. A prime example is found in the endeavour to identify the influences on the long-term growth in the public sector. The alternative definitions used of the 'public sector' alone make large differences to the results and may bear little reference to the governmental decision-making process.

It would therefore be wholly misleading to confine the definition of the task of economic history simply as that of acting as an upstream industry producing raw material for testing the validity of economic theories. It should be blindingly obvious that anyone wishing to understand the present state of an individual or global economy and concerned about its future development must know about its past. The potential clientele for such knowledge is wide and not confined to those who enjoy adding to their historical interest or who wish to become professional historians.

What makes this encyclopedia unique is that its authors have spent a fair proportion of their professional lives as economists in private practice, advising firms and governments, and regard economic history as an essential element in their stock-in-trade. As the saying goes, 'Geography is about maps and history about chaps'. Statistics of aggregate historical movements in saving, investment, taxation, etc. are the outcomes of decisions but merely hint at the process of decision-making by the main actors in the economy. That process entails the identification of the personal motivation for producing goods and services, the plans made to give effect to decisions and the choices about techniques that these embody, followed by the inevitable adjustments made in original estimates to take account of the uncertainties surrounding plan-fulfilment such as the unexpected actions of competitors and customers and, let it be said, of governments. The study of the nature of the 'firm', whatever its dimensions and system of ownership, not only saves the making of errors in historical interpretation; it also enhances the credibility of advice by economists to businesses.

Recently, it has had a marked effect on economic analysis itself.

The pervasive influence of Joseph Schumpeter is manifest even today – he died in 1950 – in the importance of studying entrepreneurial behaviour as the mainspring of economic change. (Curiously enough, although recognizing his mathematical knowledge as rudimentary, he helped to found and became first President of the Econometric Society!) Not only has the modelling of such behaviour been transformed but also it has prevented economic history from being, as it were, 'de-humanized' by confining it to presentation and analysis of historical movements in macro-variables. The link with the study of history in general is thereby restored. But there is a cost incurred in the return to the use of the skills required in assessing the quality of information about such behaviour. It is likely to lengthen the 'period of production' in academic study, putting the scholarly economic historian at a disadvantage in producing the evidence on which appointments and promotions in the field of economics nowadays depend.

This *tour d'horizon* of economic history may help the reader to understand what an immense task has been tackled by the authors, a task that I believe has been entirely successfully completed.

It is customary for works of this kind to be the province of senior academics who invite a list of authors, chosen because of their specialist expertise, to write one or more entries . (A recent example surrounded its general editors with an advisory board of 19 economists and employed about 300 contributors, though admittedly it is twice the length of Bannock and Baxter.) One can see the sense of such an arrangement, for it ensures careful scrutiny of entries by peer-group assessment and offers ready advertisement of the prestige of the publication. But this is not the only way of proceeding. Indeed, many contributors mean different propensities to deliver copy on time, differences over stylistic and technical matters with the editors, even widely varying degrees of intelligibility. Editors have to struggle with inevitable delay and a lack of uniformity in the quality of their submissions.

Our authors, who know each other very well, are a production force of two. Their advisory functions as economists have been their bread and butter and they have been unprotected by long-term academic contracts or an arrangement that carried the expectation of long-term employment. One might be led to expect that they would have neither the time nor inclination to familiarize themselves with the finer points of academic debate on economic history. It will soon become clear that this is not the case – to take an example at random, read the entry on 'Railways' – but in any event it would serve little purpose for them to devote space to jousting displays by rival academics. This is a work which has survived academic scrutiny with flying colours but is directed at the non-specialist reader seeking information and guidance – and that can include practised hands in economics and economic history who have confined professional attention only to particular subjects or geographical areas.

One final point of substance. I may have given the impression that the economics profession is so segmented that academics and practitioners rarely have anything to do with one another. Economists, including economic historians, frequently combine teaching and research with paid consulting. They discover that they have to develop a particular skill. They have to learn that they are not writing for their peer group. Firms of economic consultants are known to prefer to rewrite what these specialist advisers provide them with, for their directors have to guarantee that their clients receive clearly written submissions whose professional content they can both understand and respect. Our authors have, therefore, a comparative advantage in clarity of exposition which is evident in the entire spectrum of entries in the present volume.

You are invited to join me in celebrating its appearance.

ALAN PEACOCK

*Sir Alan Peacock is alleged to have retired, though holds an honorary Chair in Public Finance at Heriot-Watt University, Edinburgh. Previously, he was Reader in Economics, specializing in public finance, at the London School of Economics (1948–56), Professor of Economics at Edinburgh University (1956–62) and at York (1962–78), serving on secondment as Chief Economics Adviser to the Department of Trade and Industry (1973–6). His last full-time academic appointment was as Professor of Economics and later Vice-Chancellor of the independent University of Buckingham (1978–85). He is a Fellow of both the British Academy and the Royal Society of Edinburgh. He was knighted for public service in 1987.*

# Glossary

**Advanced (or Developed) Country**
A country classified by the United Nations as having reached a specified high level of Gross National Income per capita.

**Autarky**
A policy directed to the self-sufficiency of a country's economy and the exclusion of international trade.

**Baumol Effect**
The proposition of Professor William J. Baumol that the prices of manufactures will tend to fall relative to those of services because improvements in productivity in the latter are more difficult to achieve because they are more labour intensive.

**Bullion**
Precious metals, such as gold or silver, formed into ingots rather than into coinage.

**Cartel**
An association of producers formed for the purpose of mutually controlling output in order to exclude competition and to maintain high prices.

**Comparative Advantage**
The superior relative efficiency of an activity of an individual or country compared with other possible activities available. It is to such an activity that a country or individual should devote resources for optimum gain.

**Concentration**
The degree to which an industry is dominated by a limited number of firms; ranging from monopoly, with a single firm, to a competitive market in which each firm has an equal share.

**Convertibility**
The free exchange of a currency for another currency or gold.

**Cost Benefit Analysis**
The appraisal of an investment project by evaluating the social and financial costs and benefits throughout the prospective life of the project and calculating the net benefit to determine the project's viability in comparison to alternative investment opportunities.

**Customs Union**
An agreement between a number of countries in which all tariffs and quotas on imports are removed so that trade may pass freely between member counties, and common barriers to external trade with non-member countries erected.

**De-industrialization**
A decline in the share of manufacturing in Gross Domestic Product.

**Developing Country**
A country which has not reached the high level of Gross National Income per capita of the **Advanced (or Developed) Countries.**

**Factors of Production**
The inputs used in the processes of production which are broadly classified into Land, Labour and Capital.

**Fixed Exchange Rate**
An exchange rate, the rate at which a currency is convertible into a foreign currency, which is fixed at a particular level by government control.

### Floating Exchange Rate
An exchange rate, the rate at which a currency is convertible into a foreign currency, which is left to be determined by the market, free from government intervention.

### Gold Exchange Standard
A monetary control system in which a Central Bank will not exchange its currency for gold, as it would under the Gold Standard, but will exchange its currency for another currency whose Central Bank is on the Gold Standard.

### Gresham's Law
If two coins are in circulation in which the value of their respective bullion content differs from their face value, the dearer coin will be taken out of circulation to be melted down to extract its bullion content.

### Gross Domestic Product
A measure of the total value of all goods and services produced in an economy over a particular time period such as a year or a quarter. It is 'Gross' because it is not adjusted for the depreciation of capital and it is 'Domestic' because it excludes net income obtained from overseas. It is equivalent to Gross Domestic Income.

### Gross National Product
Gross Domestic Product plus net income earned overseas. It is equivalent to Gross National Income.

### Human Development Index
An index calculated by the United Nations which ranks countries in an order broadly reflecting their human welfare achievements. The index subsumes not only Gross National Income per capita but also such measures as death rates, life expectancy and literacy.

### Joint Stock Company
An enterprise in which contributions from investors are exchanged for a share in profits and which has the status of a legal entity. Generally it has limited liability, the financial liability of its shareholders being limited to the value of their shareholdings.

### Just-in-Time
A production system designed to minimize the capital tied up in inventories by ordering from suppliers only when there is a need in production.

### Least Developed Country
A country identified by the United Nations as having a low Gross National Income per capita, poor literacy and life expectancy and which required special international measures of support to aid its development.

### Mean
A number which is the average of two or more items in a group. An *arithmetic* mean is the sum of the values of the items in the group divided by the number of items. A *geometric* mean is derived by multiplying together the values of the items in the group and taking the root corresponding to the number of items.

### Median
The value of that item in a group for which there is an equal number of items with higher as lower values.

### Monopoly
A market in which there is only a single supplier.

### Moral Hazard
A situation in which individuals are open to the temptation to pursue a course of action from which they derive benefits but the associated costs are born by others.

### Oligopoly
A market in which there are only a few suppliers.

**Protection**
Barriers, established by a country, designed to restrict or prevent imports by such devices as tariffs or quotas.

**Purchasing Power Parity**
That exchange rate at which the expenditure on a basket of goods and services bought in one country would buy an identical basket of goods and services in another.

**Rent Seeking**
Activity which captures benefits for some at the expense of others.

**Resource Allocation**
The decisions which have to be made in order to allocate scarce factors of production between alternative uses.

**Social Welfare**
A concept of the total well-being of a country beyond that measured by Gross National Income per capita.

**Total Factor Productivity**
The relationship between output and the combined total of all factors of production. It is used as measure of changes in the efficiency with which inputs are converted into outputs and as indicator of technical progress.

**Value Added**
The total revenue earned by an enterprise from the sale of its output less the total costs it has incurred from its purchase of its inputs of goods and services used in the production of its output.

**Weighted Index**
An index of an average of the values of items in a group in which each item is multiplied by a quantity or weight reflecting its importance in the group.

# List of Entries

| | |
|---|---|
| Accounting | 3 |
| Agricultural Revolution | 8 |
| Agriculture | 11 |
| American Civil War | 15 |
| American War of Independence | 17 |
| American Westward Expansion | 23 |
| Anthropometric History | 28 |
| Anti-Trust | 29 |
| Asian Miracle | 35 |
| Automobile Industry | 38 |
| Aviation | 44 |
| | |
| Beer | 52 |
| Beveridge, William Henry (Lord Beveridge) | 56 |
| Bimetallic System | 58 |
| Britain | 59 |
| Business Cycles | 71 |
| Business Management | 75 |
| | |
| Canals | 80 |
| Capital Markets | 82 |
| Capitalism | 88 |
| Central Banking | 93 |
| Chandler, Alfred Du Pont | 102 |
| Chartism | 105 |
| China | 106 |
| Classical and Neo-Classical Economics | 113 |
| Coal | 118 |
| Coffee | 122 |
| Commercial Revolution | 124 |
| Companies | 125 |
| Concentration | 129 |
| Consumer Revolutions | 131 |
| Corporate Governance | 139 |
| Cotton and Cotton Textiles | 143 |
| | |
| Economic Development | 147 |
| Economic History | 155 |
| Economic Imperialism | 157 |
| Education | 165 |
| Electricity | 170 |
| Electronics | 176 |
| Employment of Women and Children | 183 |
| Enclosure | 188 |

English East India Company ............ 190
Entrepreneurship ............ 194

Famine ............ 199
Ford, Henry ............ 200
French Revolution ............ 203
Friedman, Milton ............ 204

Gas ............ 210
Gerschenkron, Alexander ............ 213
Globalization ............ 215
Gold ............ 221
Gold Standard ............ 226
Grain ............ 229
Great Depression ............ 232

Hamilton, Alexander ............ 238
Hammonds, The ............ 241
Hayek, Friedrich August von ............ 244

India ............ 247
Industrial Districts ............ 253
Industrial Revolution in Britain ............ 256
Industrial Revolutions ............ 262
Industrious Revolution ............ 266
Inequality ............ 268
Institutions ............ 272
International Trade ............ 273
Irish Famine ............ 280
Iron and Steel ............ 282

Jet Engines ............ 290

Keynes, John Maynard ............ 294

Luddism ............ 300

Machine Tools ............ 302
Malthus, Thomas Robert ............ 306
Marshall Plan ............ 309
Marx, Karl ............ 313
Mercantilism ............ 318
Migration ............ 322
Money and Banking ............ 326
Multinational Enterprises ............ 335

New Deal ............ 339

Oil ............ 343

Peasantry and Serfdom 348
Pedlars 349
Physiocrats 351
Poor Laws 356
Population 358
Poverty 361
Prices and Inflation 367
Productivity 372
Proto-Industrialization 377

Railways 380
Regulation 386
Ricardo, David 390
Rice 395
Road Transport 398
Rostow, Walt Whitman 406
Russia 408

Schumpeter, Joseph Aloisius 418
Seaports 421
Service Sector 425
Shipping 429
Silk 437
Silver 441
Slavery 445
Small and Medium Enterprises 449
Smith, Adam 453
South Africa 460
State, Rise of the 466
Steam Power 470
Sugar 474

Taxation 478
Taylor, Frederick W. 484
Telecommunications 486
Thompson, Edward Palmer 491
Trade Unions 492

USA 498
Usury 506

Veblen, Thorstein Bunde 509

Weber, Max 512
Wedgwood, Josiah 516
Western Europe 518
Wool and Wool Textiles 527
World War I 529
World War II 535

# The Encyclopedia

# A

## Accounting

Max >WEBER asserted that accountancy was the foundation of the rational behaviour which is the essence of >CAPITALISM. Indeed, the very word 'account' derives from the Latin for 'ratio', a reckoning. Accounts recorded on papyrus and tablets of clay and marble have survived from Babylon, Egypt and Greece. These records mostly deal with deposits and loans made by temples (relatively safe places because it was sacrilege to steal from them) or with obligations to the state and records of public expenditure. These early accounting records were often in narrative rather than tabular form and were, apparently, not normally summed to totals, perhaps because a mix of currencies was used. Bearing out Weber's contention, the first accounts in the modern sense were made by merchants.

It was in the Middle Ages that the double-entry bookkeeping system was first devised, probably in Italy in the 13th century. In this system, improved but still in use today, ledgers are used in which transactions are 'posted' under various account headings, such as 'stock', 'cash', 'capital' and 'sales'. Each item appears twice, once as a credit and once as a debit, to reflect the exchange of value represented by the transaction. The advantages of double-entry are that it facilitates economic, as opposed to purely monetary, analysis of an organization's activities over a period of time and its position at a particular point in time. Taking all the accounts in the ledger together the total of debit and credit balances should be equal. From this set of balances, the profit and loss account and the balance sheet are derived. When Fra Luca Pacioli, a Franciscan friar, published his book on mathematics in 1494, he included a section on bookkeeping and the double-entry system which, it was asserted, had been in use in Venice for over 200 years. About ten years later, the popular section on bookkeeping was published separately. The first English translation, by Hugh Oldcastle, appeared in Britain in 1543 and the double-entry system spread in Britain and Northern Europe (Morgan, 1965). By the end of the 18th century, the use of the system had begun to spread from merchants to manufacturers and others, though it had yet to reach universal acceptance.

By 1800, accountancy was beginning to be recognized as a distinct profession, though Morgan cites an estimate that there were no more than 600 accountants in England at the time. Not all of these were engaged solely in the profession, it being often a sideline for surveyors, managing agents and others. In Scotland, a Society of Accountants was formed in 1853. In England, the first among several regional societies, the Incorporated Society of Liverpool Accountants, was founded in January 1870 and one in London in November of the same year. In 1880, a Royal Charter was granted to the Institute of Chartered Accountants in England and Wales (ICAEW), which incorporated several of the existing societies into one body (Brown, 1905). The American Association of Certified Public Accountants, now the American Institute of Certified Public Accountants (AICPA), was incorporated in New York in 1887 and it was not until 1896 that an Act to regulate the profession in that state became law. This Act, which was followed by similar legislation in other states, created the status of Certified Public Accountant (CPA). Today, there is a Uniform Accounting Act and each state of the Union has a Board of Accountancy which regulates the profession and sets examinations. CPAs typically have university degrees, have passed a rigorous exam and have certain experience requirements, roughly equivalent to a minimum of one year working as an accountant. In Britain, the role of government in regulating the profession is less than in the USA and it is basically self-regulated by the associations, These, since 1974, are linked by the Consultative Committee of Accountancy Bodies (CCAB). In addition to the ICAEW there are five other accountancy associations in the UK whose members are recognized by the government as qualified to carry out audits under the Companies Acts. These include the Association of Chartered Certified Accountants (ACCA) and the Chartered Associations for Scotland and Ireland. Originally in Britain, trainee accountants were articled in an accountancy practice for five years for which a premium had to be paid to the firm. Since World War II, when universities began to offer degrees in accounting, trainees work for three years and are all now graduates.

It could be argued that British standards are somewhat more rigorous but less mechanical than those in the USA, which rely heavily upon legally backed checklists. This is not to imply that USA accounting is less advanced that that in the UK; on the contrary, many of the technical innovations in accounting have come from America. It does not seem that the associations in either country aimed at creating a 'closed shop' or any kind of monopoly, although they did achieve that as far as auditing is concerned. The motive seems to have been rather to maintain high standards and the pressure for that probably came from investors and users of accounts, as well as the profession. Membership of the associations is open to anyone who can meet the educational and work-experience requirements and the associations do not set fees.

The professionalization and general development of accounting in Continental Europe generally came later than in Britain and America. The first German accounting society was not formed until the 1930s, when larger companies were required by law to be independently audited. It was not until 1942 that a registered accounting body was established by law in France. In Japan, the statutory audit was only imposed by the occupying authorities after World War II and a professional body established under the American-influenced Certified Public Accountants Law in 1948. In China, bookkeeping was highly developed at an early stage and there was an indigenous emergence of something resembling Western double-entry systems. Even in 1905, Brown mentions, however, in neither China nor Japan were accountants recognized as a separate profession. Generally, accountancy developed alongside industrialization and in particular with the coming into prominence of the joint-stock company (>COMPANIES) and public >CAPITAL MARKETS. Just as the need for more elaborate bookkeeping systems in Italy first arose from the development of trading partnerships and the need to allocate costs and profits between the partners, so have the increasing size of businesses and demands for transparency required an increase in the number and knowledge of accountants especially in Britain and America where stock markets are so important. While audits were always important for third parties in dealing with an owner-managed company, it became much more important after the rise of the joint-stock and quoted company, where directors have a fiduciary duty to shareholders: the auditor, appointed by shareholders, oversees this. The tax authorities also rely on audits.

Matthews *et al.* (1997) estimate that the number of accountants qualified to carry out audits in Britain increased by about 8 per cent per annum between 1882 and 1911. The rate of growth fell to 3 per cent per annum in the 1930s at which it has remained (in peacetime) ever since. These are faster rates of growth than for other professions, such as medical practitioners, lawyers, scientists and teachers. They put the number of qualified accountants in Britain at 144,000 in 1990, twice as many in relation to the labour force than in the USA and vastly more than in Japan or other European countries. There are, perhaps, twice as many people working as accountants but not included in the total because they are not members of a chartered society. Matthews *et al.* also demonstrate that a very large and increasing proportion of qualified accountants (recently two-thirds) have left general practice and have been employed in business. From a sample of ICAEW members, the percentage who were company directors doubled from 4.5 per cent in 1891 to 10.3 per cent in 1991.

The exceptionally large number of qualified accountants in Britain is partly the result of the greater development of stock markets than in Germany and other European countries and Britain has also had not only relatively more publicly listed companies but also more companies of all kinds. These explanations, however, are insufficient to explain why Britain has so many more accountants than the USA. Matthews *et al.* adduce supply-side as well as demand-side explanations and they say: 'The meagre provision of management training by business and academics in Britain, left a vacuum which was filled to some extent by accountants.' Business education started surprisingly late in Britain. The Wharton Business School was founded in America in 1881 and the first business school in Germany was founded in Leipzig in 1898. The Japanese *zaibatsu* (>MONEY AND BANKING) started recruiting graduates in the 1880s and by the 1930s 70 per cent of large company presidents were graduates. As early as 1920 there were 65 business schools in the USA. In Britain the first graduate business schools, in London and Manchester, were not established until 1965. Accountancy, therefore, was the most relevant training in Britain and also sorted out some of the brightest recruits with at least some experience working as accountants. Accountancy qualifications are very demanding: according to Matthews *et al.* only some 60 per cent of those registering for articles under ICAEW make the grade, even though 90 per cent of them are now university graduates.

In the early days of the profession, insolvency work was very important. It is said that differences in the law on bankruptcy were part of the reason why the profession developed earlier in Scotland than south of the border. According to Matthews (2006), around 1900 and until the 1970s, auditing accounted for two-thirds to three-quarters of the fee income of the major accounting firms. More recently, taxation and consultancy work have grown, but in 1992 auditing was still 43 per cent of average fee income of the top ten firms. This business was to some extent driven by >REGULATION. Following the Wall Street Crash in 1929, the New York Stock Exchange introduced an independent audit requirement for listing and this received statutory support in the Securities and Exchange Act of 1934. In Britain, the 1900 Companies Act required all limited companies, public and private, to have an audit and, from 1948, this had to be carried out by a member of one of the professional associations. From 1994, audit exemptions were introduced for smaller firms. The threshold for exemption was progressively increased so that by 2004–5, no more that 20 per cent of >SMALL AND MEDIUM ENTERPRISES were obliged to have audits, though many did so. These changes were introduced in the teeth of opposition from banks and the tax authorities, but the small-firm lobby prevailed, especially since it could show that in most cases owners and managers were the same people. In Japan, audits were not compulsory until after World War II.

For many businesses, even in the last quarter of the 19th century, the preparation of annual income statements and balance sheets filed for regulatory reasons were insufficient for managing the firm. Large businesses needed to prepare monthly or quarterly management accounts. For more complex businesses with several product or service lines and significant fixed assets, managers also needed to know how to allocate overheads. This was necessary as a guide for pricing and the relative profitability of different activities. Traditional accounting, which at first focused on balance sheets and then upon income statements, had to evolve further to deal with detailed cost issues. It is generally accepted that the USA led the way in the development of cost accounting. Nonetheless, recent research has shown that pioneers of larger enterprises in the >INDUSTRIAL REVOLUTION IN BRITAIN such as Josiah >WEDGWOOD had developed quite sophisticated cost accounts (Wilson, 1995). At that time in Britain, most businesses were small scale and even large firms were very much personally controlled by their owner-managers. Johnson and Kaplan (1987), in their history of management accounting in the USA, point out that the first appearance of the new accounting systems became necessary when large, single-activity businesses such as those in >IRON and STEEL, the >RAILWAYS and in distribution (>COMMERCIAL REVOLUTION) were bringing in-house transactions which had previously been conducted in the marketplace, that is they were becoming vertically integrated. In Britain, where industries were more fragmented, market prices of intermediate products were available and elaborate cost accounting was often less necessary. As more multi-product firms emerged, and under the influence of the vogue for 'scientific management' (> TAYLOR), cost accounting continued to develop but, according to Johnson and Kaplan (1987), it was still rooted in the financial reporting system and most companies used the same system to produce both financial and management accounts.

Johnson and Kaplan argue that developments in information technology. (>ELECTRONICS), >GLOBALIZATION, shorter product cycles and innovations in production technology and organization had, by the 1970s, rendered cost accounting systems less and less effective. In the 20 years since the publication of their book, the changes they advocated have to a large extent been realized, especially in larger >MULTINATIONAL ENTERPRISES. These giant companies may have hundreds of profit centres and thousands of cost centres. The allocation of overheads used to be done by standard costing in which unit overheads are costed at levels which will cover the total at budgeted output, say by applying percentage ratios to direct labour costs. Newer systems involve the use of information automatically collected during operations and, for example, the cost of a service department is not lumped in with other overheads, but allocated to different products according to service records, such as guarantee claims (activity costing).

Another problem, among many, with which accountants have had to deal is inflation (>PRICES AND INFLATION). In times of rapidly rising prices and with assets valued in the accounts at what was paid for them or their net realizable value if this is lower (the historical cost convention), their replacement cost may be much higher than their book value. This means that depreciation provisions may be inadequate and profit overstated. In the late 1970s, following the >OIL price increases, inflation rose to high levels. In 1975 in Britain, for example, the retail price index increased by over 24 per cent compared with the previous year. The most feasible solution seemed to be either to adjust accounts for changes in the general price level (GPL) or to revalue assets to their current replacement cost (CRC). Between 1979 and 1983, companies in the USA and elsewhere were required to report their results on a CRC basis, alongside unadjusted figures. The results were regarded as often arbitrary and misleading and as inflation fell the whole issue was dropped for the time being.

Despite change in management accounting and other developments, which include increasing levels of statutory disclosure, the role of accountants in business was still very much dominated by pressures from users of accounts among the investing institutions and the public. The need for company accounts to be comparable gave rise to more and more statutory and voluntary regulation. National standards, such as those of the Accounting Standards Board (ASB) in Britain and by the Federal Accounting Standards Board (FASB) formed in 1973 in the USA, were gradually being integrated with international standards. These are set by the International Accounting Standards Board (IASB), which is based in London. IASB standards were not mandatory unless adopted by the accounting profession in each country, though the European Union proposed their adoption for all EU-registered companies. Scandals arising from fraudulent accounting in Enron and other firms led the USA to pass the Sarbanes-Oxley legislation in 2002. This required certification of financial reports by chief executives and financial officers, the prohibition of company loans to executives, tighter treatments of securities provisions for directors and other measures.

Traditionally, in smaller companies without strong internal accounting resources financial accounts were prepared and audited by the same professional firm. In larger firms draft final accounts would be prepared internally. Conflicts of interest between the accounting and auditing functions of professional firms were recognized and reflected in codes of practice and regulation. Until the 1960s, auditing meant checking and verifying against evidence all major transactions in the books and a large proportion of smaller ones. Later, partly through the influence of American practice, and generally because of cost considerations, statistical techniques were introduced. The emphasis shifted to testing the design and reliability of internal controls built into accounting systems to guard against error and fraud. Small but strictly random samples of transactions were drawn and verified as genuine and accurately recorded in all respects. With the shift to mechanical and then electronic record-keeping, and the creation of specialized accounting and auditing software, this process became more sophisticated. Clients in all but very small companies prepared their own accounts which were checked by auditors (Matthews, 2006).

An oligopoly of large auditing firms emerged. In the 1970s there were eight big firms, but 20 years later four (though one of the largest, Arthur Anderson, ceased business in 2002 in connection with the Enron case). Globally, they grew to very large size, with total revenues of about $100 billion, and they employed well over 500,000 people. They justified their size mainly on the grounds that only globally diversified firms were capable of auditing their large clients and that they had to be big enough to cope with lawsuits from shareholders and regulators. Unlimited liability used to be mandatory for auditing firms who were typically partnerships, but

later some forms of incorporation were allowed. Large accounting firms have attracted criticism because client choice was limited, they have failed to signal fraud in many corporate scandals and their consulting activities with audit clients might create conflicts of interest.

## References

Brown, Richard (ed.), *A History of Accounting and Accountants*, Frank Cass, 1905.

Johnson, H. Thomas and Kaplan, Robert S., *Relevance Lost, The Rise and Fall of Management Accounting*, Harvard Business School Press, 1987.

Matthews, Derek, *A History of Auditing: The Changing Audit Process in Britain*, Routledge, 2006.

Matthews, Derek, Anderson, Malcolm and Edwards, John Richard, 'The Rise of the Professional Accountant in British Management', *Economic History Review*, August, 1997.

Morgan, E. Victor, *History of Money*, Penguin, 1965.

Wilson, John F., *British Business History, 1720–1994*, Manchester University Press, 1995.

# Agricultural Revolution

'All history cannot furnish twenty such years of fertility and abundance as from 1730–1750 when the average prices were the lowest ever known. Another reason we assign to the fall of price, is the great improvements made in agriculture in the last fifty or sixty years.' (J. Wimpy, *Rural Improvements* (1775), quoted in Mingay, 1956)

Such was an early observation on the condition of English >AGRICULTURE in the middle of the 18th century, which had become capable not only of being able to feed an increasing population but become also able to raise >GRAIN exports from virtually nothing to 200,000 tons by 1750.

There is no doubt that >BRITAIN experienced an agricultural revolution in productivity, or at least an evolution, although there is debate among historians as to its timing and, to some extent, its causes. One view is that it occurred during the period from about the 1770s to the 1820s, and the other that there were two phases, the first before 1750 and the second in the first half of the 19th century. However, there is no doubt that, as with the >INDUSTRIAL REVOLUTION IN BRITAIN, it progressed further and earlier than other countries in Europe (Clark, 2001). It has been estimated (Allen, 2000) that, in 1500, Belgium and the Netherlands were the leading countries in Europe in the productivity of their agriculture (>WESTERN EUROPE). However, in the period up to 1750, productivity fell or at best remained unchanged throughout Continental Europe, with the exception of the Netherlands. In England, by contrast, it not only increased but also overtook the Netherlands. Agricultural productivity in Britain was 50 per cent higher than in France in 1705 and somewhat more in 1775 (Brunt, 2002). The reasons for England being ahead of other countries in the development of agriculture and, consequently, industry must be found in the way its political and social structures had developed since medieval times differently from other countries. The feudal system had been loosened early in England. For instance, the effective emancipation of the serfs (>PEASANTRY AND SERFDOM) in England took place in the 15th century, whereas traces of feudalism persisted in France until the Revolution and longer in Eastern Europe and >RUSSIA.

The timing of Britain's agricultural improvement is important for its relevance to the emergence of the Industrial Revolution and also in assessing the factors that made it possible. Some estimates suggest that agricultural output doubled from the mid-16th century to the mid-18th century, slowed in the second half of the 18th century and then increased by 65 per cent from 1800–50, and that changes in productivity matched these fluctuations in output. Improvements had a history, going back into the previous century. No single innovation seems to have been responsible for the growth in productivity, it being the result of the cumulative effects of a number of changes. The introduction of additional crops, particularly turnips and, possibly, clover, into the field rotation to replace fallow not only raised the productivity of the land directly but also, through the provision of fodder, supported more animals. In turn, the animals' manure helped to enhance yields. There were improvements in seed and livestock through selection and breeding and in the design of farm implements. The landlord–tenant relationship was often beneficial, particularly in times of stress. In the two decades before 1750, there was a severe drop in farm income and, consequently, rents, due to a fall in prices caused by excess supply. There is evidence that some landlords perceived it to be in their own interests to support their tenants by forgoing their rent payments and even supplying capital for improvements. There was an increase in farm size which would be expected to enhance efficiency. There was also some >ENCLOSURE in the early period. It is enclosure which is most emphasized as helping to raise productivity because growth was more apparent towards the end of the 18th century. It was in this period that the enclosure movement peaked through Acts of Parliament. 6.8 million acres were enclosed, of which 2.9 million acres were in the period 1793–1815, so that by the end of the century 90 per cent of farmland in Britain (England) was enclosed.

The number of people employed in agriculture in the 18th century was static at around 1.5 million and the farm acreage likewise at about 34 million acres. Against these figures, the total population of Britain (England) rose from 5.1 million in 1701 to 8.7 million in 1801. This population growth was not fed by importing food. Trade switched from exports of about 2 per cent of output in 1701 to imports of only about 5 per of output in 1801. There is no doubt that British agriculture fed the growing urban population and facilitated the Industrial Revolution by feeding its workforce and helping to underpin the demand for its output.

Throughout the 19th century, agriculture worldwide benefited from the innovations of industry. Drilling seed rather than sowing broadcast became established, which together with the horse-hoe enabled better weed control, prior to the later development of agricultural chemicals. Threshing machines were introduced early in the century and reaping machines in 1830. In 1850, clay tile pipes were invented which greatly assisted land drainage. The tractor was operating in the >USA before the end of the 19th century, although it was not until 1917 that it was mass-produced. In the 20th century, the internal combustion engine replaced the horse. Capital replaced labour as the dominant factor of production; agriculture became capital intensive. The development of new plant varieties and farming practices in the late 19th century and early

20th century also made it possible to extend >GRAIN cultivation, successfully, into areas previously commercially unattractive (Olmstead and Rhode, 2002). According to Bairoch (1973), it required 373 man-hours to produce 100 bushels of wheat in the USA in 1800, 233 man-hours in 1840, 108 man-hours in 1900, 34 man-hours in 1945/9 and 10 man-hours in 1966/70. In the Western developed countries as a whole, it has been calculated (Bairoch, 1993) that agricultural productivity increased by about 1.2 per cent per annum between 1850 and 1950 and accelerated to about 5.5 per cent per annum between 1950 and 1990, a significantly faster growth rate than industrial productivity, which grew at an estimated 3.5 per cent per annum.

After World War II, the application of new technologies to agriculture generated a 'green revolution' in the 1960s through increased yields of crops such as >RICE, wheat and maize (>GRAIN) which gave impetus to economic growth, particularly in Asia. This was made possible by the development and dissemination of improved seed varieties, investment in irrigation schemes and improved water supply and the application of fertilizers, pesticides and herbicides. In the developing countries, according to the United Nations, between 1963 and 1983, production of paddy rice increased by 3.1 per cent per annum, wheat by 5.1 per cent per annum and maize by 3.8 per cent per annum. In the following period, from 1983–93, the rates of growth slowed somewhat to 1.8 per cent per annum for rice, 2.5 per cent per annum for wheat and 3.4 per cent per annum for maize. The world experienced a continual decline in the real price of food and the elimination of the fear of recurrent world hunger (>FAMINE), but experienced a surge in the price of agricultural products in 2007 which had a severe effect on the living standards of low-income countries (>AGRICULTURE).

## References

Allen, Robert C., 'Tracking the Agricultural Revolution in England', *Economic History Review*, LII(2), 1999.

Allen, Robert C., 'Economic Structure and Agricultural Productivity in Europe, 1300–1800', *European Review of Economic History*, 4(1), 2000.

Bairoch, Paul, 'Agriculture and the Industrial Revolution', in Carlo M. Cipolla (ed.), *The Fontana Economic History of Europe*, Fontana, 1973.

Bairoch, Paul, *Economics and World History*, Harvester Wheatsheaf, 1993.

Brunt, Liam, 'New Technology and Labour Productivity in English and French Agriculture, 1700–1850', *European Review of Economic History*, August, 2002.

Brunt, Liam, 'Nature or Nurture? Explaining English Wheat Yields in the Industrial Revolution c.1770', *Journal of Economic History*, March, 2004.

Clark, Gregory, 'Farm Wages and Living Standards in the Industrial Revolution: England, 1670–1869', *Economic History Review*, LIV(3) August, 2001.

Mingay, G. E., 'The Agricultural Depression, 1730–1750', *Economic History Review*, VIII, 1956.

Olmstead, Alan L. and Rhode, Paul W., 'The Red Queen and the Hard Reds: Productivity Growth in American Wheat', *Journal of Economic History*, 62, December, 2002.

Overton, Mark, *Agricultural Revolution in England*, Cambridge, 1996.

United Nations, *The State of Food and Agriculture, 2000*.

# Agriculture

In the middle of the 18th century, agriculture was the predominant economic activity, typically employing up to 80 per cent of a country's labour force. But change was already underway in Europe and, particularly, in >BRITAIN.

Innovative ideas, many of which had had their origins back in the previous century, had begun to have an important influence on agricultural output: the replacement of oxen by horses; the improvement in the design of and invention of new implements; the introduction of crop rotation using root crops and clover in place of fallow; and >ENCLOSURE. The relative importance and the effective timing of influences such as these in relation to resulting improvements in labour productivity and land yields are subjects of debate (Allen, 1999; >AGRICULTURAL REVOLUTION). Nevertheless, by the 18th century, agriculture in Europe was beginning to come of age in the sense that it was meeting the nutritional needs of the >POPULATION.

The progress in agricultural improvement was not, however, uniform throughout Europe and, in fact, Britain made by far the most rapid advance in the application of new ideas. As a startling measure of this, by the end of the 18th century, the proportion of National Income generated by agriculture in Britain had fallen to about 32 per cent, a level which was not matched by Germany until well into the second half of the 19th century and in France and Italy not until the 20th century (>WESTERN EUROPE), by which time the share in Britain had fallen to only 6 per cent. (By comparison, according to the United Nations, about 70 per cent of the labour force was employed in agriculture in the least developed nations in 2002 and even in the somewhat more advanced developing nations the ratio was 54 per cent.) The concomitant to this was the rapid increase in the share of National Income in Britain going, first, to industry, then to services. It would appear on the face of it that the improvements in agriculture which enabled the country to feed and not to restrict a growing population (>MALTHUS) also enabled the >INDUSTRIAL REVOLUTION to flourish in Britain without hindrance. Although the numbers employed in agriculture did not begin to decline in actual numbers until the second half of the 19th century in Britain, there was a rapid fall-off in the share of the labour force devoted to agriculture because of the rapid expansion in the population. All the increase in the labour force was absorbed by the industrial and service sectors.

Improvements in communication had already considerably integrated the agricultural markets in Europe in the 18th century and >INTERNATIONAL TRADE was sufficient to influence domestic prices. Protection was in place, such as the Corn Laws in Britain which, although they were lifted during the war with France, were not finally abolished until 1846. After 1850, however, a policy of free trade spread throughout Europe; from the abolition of import tariffs on grain by the Zollverein in 1853 to similar action by Belgium in 1871. However, in the last quarter of the 19th century, with the influx of >GRAIN from North America, this policy was abandoned by all except Britain and Denmark (>WESTERN EUROPE).

In the second half of the 19th century, agricultural trade became truly international or intercontinental. The reduction in transport costs through the expansion of the >RAILWAYS and the lowering of sea freight rates (>SHIPPING), the development of refrigeration, the opening up of new lands, in North America (>USA),

Australasia and Latin America and another phase of improvements in labour productivity on the farm due to improvements in and the spread of powered machinery led to a shift in demand away from European production. As a measure of this change, the production of wheat in the USA, which accounted for 9 per cent of world production in 1850, had reached about 20 per cent by the end of the century.

The consequence of these developments was a pressure on agricultural prices. In Britain, prices fell about 40 per cent from 1873–96, a period which has been termed 'the great agricultural depression'. Elsewhere in Europe, the effect on prices was more restrained because of protection. France, for instance, raised tariffs increasingly on a wide range of agricultural products and by doing so underpinned domestic prices so that, for instance, wheat prices were up to 40 per cent higher than in Britain. This difference in policy, protection in Europe and free trade in Britain, reflected the differences in economic structure, with far less of Britain's National Income dependent on agriculture than in Europe and with far more dependency on international trade for its industrial products. The policy also kept the general price level down in Britain and so supported real incomes.

Following the end of >WORLD WAR I in 1918, an excess production of agricultural commodities began to impinge on world markets and led to a further period of weak prices. Stocks of agricultural commodities accumulated. It has been estimated that such stocks nearly doubled between 1923/5 and 1929 and rose a further 35 per cent by 1932. Such an overhang had a consequential impact on the market prices for agricultural commodities, which fell 35 per cent from 1923/5 to 1929 and a further 62 per cent to 1932. By 1937, the prices of exports of food had fallen by 15 per cent compared to 1913, in contrast to all export prices, which had risen by 9 per cent (Pollard, 1994). This decline in prices seriously affected the incomes not only of the farming communities themselves but also of those countries which were dependent on agricultural exports. Many reasons have been advanced for >THE GREAT DEPRESSION but it may certainly be argued that the decline in agricultural prices played an important part (Madsen, 2001). Governments responded in a number of ways. Measures were introduced to protect farmers from overseas competition in the form of import tariffs and quotas, and to support incomes through guaranteed prices or by restricting production. Internationally, commodity control schemes emerged covering such commodities as Rubber, >COFFEE, >SUGAR and wheat (>GRAIN).

Until the >GLOBALIZATION of markets, following the reduction in transport costs (>SHIPPING), international trade was limited both in reach and in product range. The second half of the 19th century saw major changes and by 1913 world markets had been transformed. For example, over 50 per cent of world exports of wheat came from new lands in Argentina, Australia and North America. Thanks to the development of refrigeration, over a million tonnes of meat were traded, of which one-third came from Argentina and a quarter from Australasia. A similar quantity of coffee was also exported, 60 per cent of it from Brazil. Banana exports from plantations in Latin America and the Caribbean had also increased to over a million tonnes, although in the years prior to World War I virtually all were sent to North America and Britain. Exports of >SUGAR had reached about 7 million tonnes prior to World War I, the major source being Cuba, closely followed by Indonesia.

The devastations of >WORLD WAR II led to a severe drop in agricultural production in Europe and Asia. It was not until the 1950s that cereal production reached the levels of 1934/8 in these regions. Agriculture had, however, continued to develop in North America, Australasia and Argentina. In North America, cereal production after the war was a third higher than in the late 1930s and exports increased accordingly to meet the import needs of Europe and Asia. There was considerable anxiety in the post-war period that agricultural production would fail to match the predicted expansion of the world >POPULATION and that as a consequence the future would see an increase in the frequency of >FAMINES. In the late 1960s and into the 1970s, however, what might be described as the third agricultural revolution occurred; the 'green revolution'. The development of improved plant varieties, the expansion and improvement of water supplies and irrigation, fertilizers and pesticides, led to significantly higher growth rates particularly for >RICE, wheat and maize and has been credited with averting recurrent famine, particularly in Asia. Over the last three decades of the 20th century, world agricultural output tripled in some categories and expanded in all sectors and real prices fell. Agricultural production per capita doubled in >CHINA, so that that country replaced the USA as top producer. In international trade world exports of agricultural products lagged behind that of total merchandise trade so that by the end of the 20th century it accounted for only 10 per cent of the total compared with 25 per cent in the 1960s.

In the post-war period, international commodity agreements were again considered as a means for dampening the volatility which tended to persist in the prices of primary commodities and which could adversely affect the incomes of those developing countries for which they generated significant export earnings. Agreements were made for cocoa, coffee, olive oil, rubber, sultanas, sugar, timber and wheat but in general with little success.

Export prices of agricultural products relative to manufactures fell during the last half of the 20th century and this accordingly had an adverse affect on the terms of trade of the developing countries. In spite of programmes starting in 1947 for the freeing of international trade from restrictions through the various trade negotiating rounds under first GATT and then the World Trade Organization (WTO) and ending in agreement to begin the ninth at Doha in 2001, agriculture had been virtually excluded from this process and remained heavily protected, particularly in the developed countries (>INTERNATIONAL TRADE).

In 2007/8, there was an exceptionally large increase in agricultural prices. For instance, according to the FAO, in 2007/8, compared with the average between 2002/3 and 2006/7, wheat prices increased by about 90 per cent, >RICE by 38 per cent and oilseeds by 66 per cent. The OECD/FAO identified the reasons as being partly due to the temporary effect of poor weather conditions, which cut output. In addition there was the more permanent effect of the diversion of resources to the production of bio-fuels, higher fuel prices, the increasing inelasticity of demand to price increases and some shift in tastes towards the consumption of cereals as incomes improved. Governments also reacted to sustain their home supplies by curtailing international trade. Higher food prices had a major impact on the cost of living, particularly of the urban poor. In low-income countries food could absorb 50 per cent of a household's total income. The FAO estimated that the high price of food was the major cause of the increase in the number of undernourished people by 75 million in 2007 (>POVERTY).

## References

Allen, Robert C., 'Tracking the Agricultural Revolution in England', *Economic History Review*, LII(2), 1999.

Ashworth, William, *A Short History of the International Economy Since 1850*, Longman, 1994.

Bairoch, Paul, 'Agriculture and the Industrial Revolution', in *The Fontana Economic History of Europe*, ed. Carlo M. Cipolla, Fontana, 1973.

Bairoch, Paul, *Economics and World History*, Harvester Wheatsheaf, 1993.

Food and Agriculture Organization (FAO), *Briefing Paper: Hunger on the Rise*, FAO, Rome, 2008.

Kenwood, A. G. and Lougheed, A. L., *The Growth of the International Economy, 1820–1990*, Routledge, 1992.

Landes, David, *The Wealth and Poverty of Nations*, Little, Brown, 1998.

Madsen, Jacob B., 'Agricultural Crises and the International Transmission of the Great Depression', *Journal of Economic History*, June, 2001.

OECD/FAO, *Agricultural Outlook, 2008*, FAO, 2008.

O'Rourke, Kevin H., 'The European Grain Invasion, 1870–1913', *Journal of Economic History*, 57, December, 1997.

Pollard, Sydney *Peaceful Conquest: Industrialisation of Europe, 1760–1970*, Oxford University Press, 1994.

Yates, P. Lamartine, *Forty Years of Foreign Trade*, George Allen & Unwin, 1959.

# American Civil War

The issue of >SLAVERY was at the root of the conflicts between Northern and Southern states of the Union that were to lead to the Civil War in 1861. Earlier, as with the annexation of Texas, a slaveholder state, to the Union in 1844, the slavery issue had been left to fester. Under the Missouri Compromise of 1820 Congress had acknowledged the existence of slavery in the South (which was prohibited in the Northern states), but this was repealed in 1854 by the Kansas–Nebraska Law, which admitted these two states into the Union on the basis that the acceptance of slavery would be determined by their own legislatures. The South was concerned that eventually slavery would be excluded from the new states to the west and the growth of the population in the frontier states together with a strengthening abolitionist movement in the North would threaten the long-term security of the profitable slave-based plantation system.

In 1860 South Carolina issued a declaration of its assertion of sovereignty and by February 1861 seven states, to become 11 later, had withdrawn from the Union to form the Confederacy. In March, Abraham Lincoln, elected the previous year, was inaugurated as President to face a crisis. Fort Sumner, a Federal establishment at Charleston harbour had, after a siege, fallen to South Carolinian troops. This set the stage for war in which the first major engagement at Bull Run was a victory for the Confederacy. The Union declared a blockade of the Southern ports which effectively prevented the sale of the cotton crop for foreign exchange and was to apply an economic tourniquet to the Southern economy. The Civil War, which lasted longer than anyone expected, did not end until April 1865 after Southern defeats at Gettysburg and Vicksburg and coincided with the assassination of Lincoln.

Both sides in the conflict were to claim that slavery was not the key issue; for Lincoln the war was about the sanctity of the Union and for the South it was about freedom to govern its affairs within the Union. There were other disputed North–South issues including Federal transportation projects, tariffs on imported manufactures and the use of Federal tax revenues for the expansion of the west, which were all seen as favouring the North and of little benefit to the South. Banking was another subject of contention in the antebellum period. The North wanted to charter and regulate banks at a Federal level, while the South wanted banking regulation to be left to the discretion of the states. (It was not until 1863–4, well into the war, that Federal National Banking acts could be established >BANKING). There has been some controversy about how important the tariff issue actually was. The Federal tariff was introduced by Alexander >HAMILTON, Secretary of the Treasury, in 1789, mainly for revenue purposes and had been increased from an average of about 5 per cent to 50 per cent by 1828. There was protection for some Southern products, such as raw cotton, sugar and tobacco, but tariffs on coal, wheat and manufactures, which favoured the North, rose faster. However, from 1830 tariffs were reduced substantially. In fact, although the Northern states had a growing industrial economy based on immigrant labour they were, though only to a limited extent, dependent upon the Southern (and western) states for food and markets for their products. The reverse was less true since the South was more oriented towards Europe for its exports of cotton and imports of manufactures (>USA). The contentious economic issues could have been, and indeed were being, accommodated by Congress in which the slave states had a strong position, but the slavery issue proved intractable.

While the war did result in freedom for the slaves, it was an economic and humanitarian disaster, the scars of which have still not fully healed in the Southern states. Although never seriously considered by either side, it would have been possible for the Union to have compensated slave owners for emancipation. Goldin (1973) put the theoretical costs of emancipation at between $350 million and $3.1 billion at 1860 prices, depending on whether owners were compensated in full for the market value of slaves immediately or whether the process was spread over 30 years. These costs of emancipation were much less than the costs of the war. By adding government expenditure on the army, war material and supplies to a valuation of the 2.3 million lives lost and wounded and the destruction of physical capital, Goldin and Lewis (1975) estimated the total direct cost of the war at some $6.7 billion at 1860 prices for both sides. Government expenditure was twice as high in the North and numbers killed and wounded 40 per cent greater, but this was offset by the greater physical destruction in the South, where almost all the fighting took place. The estimates for the direct cost of the war came out at roughly the same for South and North, although, with lower incomes and only 27 per cent of the combined population, the burden per capita was considerably more than twice as great for the South.

The high cost of the war put an enormous strain on public finance. This strain proved particularly acute for the South since the blockade greatly reduced revenue from tariffs and the states were reluctant to grant tax-raising powers to the Confederate government. In the end only 8 per cent of real confederate revenues came from taxation, 32 per cent from bond issues and 60 per cent by printing money. Most of the Confederate bond issues were domestic, but foreign confidence in the South was sufficient for a £3 million 'cotton-backed' loan issue in March 1863 to be five times over-subscribed. These bonds were called Erlanger Bonds after the French investment bank that underwrote the issue. There were also unbacked junk bonds issue in Amsterdam in the summer of the same year. After that, however, the defeats sustained by the Southern armies led to heavy falls in the prices of these issues and foreign debt markets were closed to the Confederacy. In the North, taxes were raised and an income tax introduced for the first time in 1861. About 25 per cent of the Federal government revenues came from taxes, 18 per cent from printing money and the rest from borrowing. Considerable use was made of issuing 'greenbacks', unbacked by gold (>GOLD STANDARD). The result of these financing pressures was inevitably inflation. Between 1860 and 1865 prices rose by 75 per cent in the North and several thousand per cent in the Confederacy, whose 'greybacks' became virtually worthless. Counterfeit money had been a chronic problem in the South.

There were, of course, other costs of the war, for example, loss of output during the hostilities compared with what it otherwise might have been. It is generally agreed that the rapid rate of economic growth experienced in the South prior to 1860 would not have continued because the overseas demand for cotton fell sharply and new sources of supply had emerged (>COTTON AND COTTON TEXTILES). Consumption in the North regained the 1860 level by the early 1870s but it took another 30 years of growth in the South to regain that level. Real wages appeared to have declined in the North and South, partly because the cessation of cotton exports led to a deterioration in the terms of trade. There was a drastic decline in agricultural income in the South both because of the break-up of the plantation system and from disease. The freed slaves did not want a wage relationship with their former masters and since there was little redistribution of land they mostly opted for a sharecropping arrangement under which the landlord received a proportion of the output while merchants provided credit in the form of goods in advance of crops. This system of sharecropping and 'debt peonage' probably resulted in the resumption of coercion and dependence and tended to deter migration to higher-paid wage jobs in the North, which were pre-empted by immigrants from Southern Europe. These post-bellum developments reduced productivity in the South as the economies of scale of the old plantation system were lost. Economic efficiency may also have been impaired by the pressures of the sharecropping system, which encouraged the new peasantry to grow its own food (>PEASANTRY AND SERFDOM: Atack and Passell, 1994).

Whether the Civil War had an adverse or favourable longer-term affect on economic growth and development in the USA is controversial, though on balance the probability is that it did not. The war did result in the ultimate supremacy of the Federal Government, it opened the way for more rapid development of the west, the Homestead Act and the raising of tariffs on imports by reducing Southern opposition (Faulkner, 1960). It was argued that the Civil War shifted the balance of power in the Union to the North and allowed the promotion of industrialization (this is the Charles Beard–Lewis Hacker thesis, see, for example, Hacker, 1940), but a more recent view as posited by Atack and Passell (1994) is that it is difficult to argue that the post-bellum slow economic growth in the South, with its over-dependence on >AGRICULTURE, can be put down to the Civil War, just as it is difficult to say that the forces underlying the long-term growth of the USA as a whole were greatly influenced by the civil conflict.

## References

Atack, Jeremy and Passell, Peter, *A New Economic View of American History from Colonial Times to 1940*, W. W. Norton, 1994.

Faulkner, Harold Underwood, *American Economic History*, Harper & Row, 1960.

Goldin, Claudia, *The Economics of Emancipation: The Economic Effects of the American Civil War*, Macmillan, 1973.

Goldin, Claudia and Lewis, Frank, 'The Economic Cost of the American Civil War: Estimates and Implications', *Journal of Economic History*, 35, 1975.

Hacker, Louis, *The Triumph of American Capitalism*, Columbia University Press, 1940.

# American War of Independence

The extended eight-year revolutionary war finally resulted in independence from Britain for the 13 colonial states by the Treaty of Paris, 1783. The first of the three great revolutions (the others were France, 1789 (>WESTERN EUROPE), and >RUSSIA, 1917), the American Revolution, like the others, removed outdated institutions and was to have profound social and economic consequences which have reverberated down the ensuing 200 years.

America had been famously 'discovered' by the Italian navigator Columbus, aided by Spain, who arrived at the Bahamas in 1492. There was an indigenous population of Indians, numbering 1 or 2 million. Columbus was followed by other explorers from several European countries, although all were, in fact, looking for a cheaper sea route to the East in place of the long and dangerous overland journey for the profitable trade in precious stones, spices, dyestuffs and other goods with India, China and Asia Minor (>COMMERCIAL REVOLUTION). Four nations sought to dominate North America: Spain, France, the Netherlands and England. In the 1520–40s, Spain succeeded in establishing itself in Central America and in the South West of America and Florida, and, with Portugal, in South America. France entered Quebec on a permanent basis in 1608 and also settled in the Mississippi valley. The Dutch founded settlements in the Hudson valley, including a village on Manhattan Island in 1623. The English concentrated initially on the eastern seaboard, with a failed attempt by Sir Walter Raleigh in 1584 and a permanent colony at Jamestown in Chesapeake Bay in 1607 that later founded a prosperous tobacco trade. All four nations had territories in the West Indies.

These early colonizations were developed by merchant capitalists, especially by the grant of government monopolies, though many colonists, such as the Plymouth Brethren, were also escaping from religious persecution. Later, individual proprietors and groups were granted or purchased land from the imperial governments.

Many new settlers were slaves or indentured servants. Two-thirds of all white immigrants to the English colonies in America between 1630 and the Revolution came under indentures (Atack and Passell, 1994). Under these leased labour contracts, the company financed transportation to the New World in return for a contract to supply labour for a fixed period of time varying, studies suggest, with the earning capacity of the immigrant (depending upon age, skill, literacy etc.) and averaging about 56 months. The immigrant population in America grew rapidly from about 2,300 in 1620 to 1.25 million by 1750 and about 2.5 million by 1775. With the population growth, output per head also grew and living standards were, on average, higher than in the home countries of the colonists. News of this reached back to Europe and stimulated further immigration. That standards of living were significantly higher in the colonies is confirmed by estimates that colonists were taller than the average for their compatriots who stayed at home (>ANTHROPOMETRIC HISTORY: >MIGRATION).

Statistics for this early period are sparse (the first national census was not taken until 1790). Atack and Passell (1994) put incomes in the American colonies at $750 per capita at 1989 prices for 1775, with growth over the previous half-century at less than 1 per cent per annum. These figures suggest that incomes were about four times higher than in the poorer African countries today. Most economic activity was farming; about 85 per cent of the labour force worked in agriculture. With ample new land being brought into cultivation there was a slow increase in capital intensity and increasing production for the market (>USA).

There has been much speculation about the importance of the economic causes of the Revolution, among them the Navigation Acts (>BRITAIN), taxation, currency problems and the American land policy of the motherland. The principles of >MERCANTILISM which underlay these policies were that the colonies should contribute to the balance of trade of the colonial power, maximize inflows of precious metals, provide key supplies, thus saving imports from outside the Empire, provide a market for its own exports and, through the exclusion of foreign shipping, promote the strength of its mercantile marine. The colonists were discouraged from developing their own manufactures which might compete with the motherland's exports. For example, the Woollen Act of 1699 prohibited the export of woollens from the colonies or between them. These principles were reflected in a series of statutes from the 1630s of which the most important were the Acts of Trade and Navigation from 1651. There were many changes to this restrictive legal framework but the general objective was to require all colonial trade within or without the Empire to be carried in English or colonial ships, while all trade had to pass through English or colonial ports. For example, exports from the American colonies to Continental Europe had to be transhipped through England. From 1660, the Act for the Encouraging and Increasing of Shipping and Navigation required not only that goods should be transported in ships largely owned and manned by the English or colonists but actually built in England or the colonies. Certain goods enumerated

in the Acts were to be exported only to England, including tobacco, sugar and, from 1706, naval stores such as tar, masts and yards. (England's own supplies of suitable timber were largely exhausted and she could not produce sugar, molasses or certain raw materials, such as indigo.) The requirement that all trade between the colonies and elsewhere had to pass through English ports raised the already high shipping costs to the colonies (though there were some exceptions).

Thomas (1965) made a detailed attempt to calculate the burden of English trade policy on the colonists. He found, after allowing for some benefits of the policies, such as cash bonuses made to the colonists for the production of some enumerated goods and protection from non-Empire competition, that the burden in 1770 amounted to less than 1 per cent of income. Although various other estimates have been made, including some higher ones (Sawers, 1992), the consensus seems to be that the purely economic burden of the Navigation Acts was slight. Walton (1971) cites Lawrence A. Harper, as arguing that it was not the exploitation of the Acts themselves but the friction generated by the frequent changes in regulations which precipitated the revolt. There was also, of course, the prospect that the burdens placed on the colonists would continue to increase in the future as they had in the past.

Distracted by its own civil war and later by the Seven Years' War with France (1756–63), little attention had been paid in Britain to enforcing the Navigation Acts and other statutes. The defeat of the French in the Seven Years' War meant that the colonists no longer feared invasion and had little need of protection from the English. At the end of the war with France the English government clamped down on the American colonies in an attempt to recoup some of the costs of that war and to meet some of the costs of the standing army in America. During the war there had been substantial illegal imports of sugar and molasses from the French West Indies by the colonists, which damaged the interests of the English sugar-producing islands. The Molasses Act of 1733, which imposed duties on this trade, had been largely evaded and the Sugar Act of 1764 halved the duties to encourage compliance, but the Act was from then on enforced rigorously. The Sugar Act was followed by the Stamp Act in 1765, requiring an excise duty stamp on legal documents and newspapers, and by the Quartering Act requiring the colonists to provide lodging for English troops. The Townsend Acts (after Charles Townsend, President of the Board of Trade) reorganized the American customs service and imposed new duties on a number of goods, including tea.

This flood of legislation stimulated resistance. In 1765 some of the colonies instigated a boycott of English goods. This hurt English manufacturers and merchants, who petitioned Parliament and both the Stamp and Sugar Acts were repealed. Encouraged by this backing down, political agitation in the colonies continued and there was a further boycott in 1768–9 in response to the Townsend Acts. This second boycott reduced imports from England by half over the two years. Again, in response to pressure from domestic business interests, Parliament repealed the duties under the Townsend Acts (except those on tea). At the same time, however, in 1770 the Declaratory Act reasserted the right of Parliament to govern the colonies and to tax them as it wished. Resistance flared up again when

the Tea Act of 1773 gave the East India Company the right to export tea directly to America from India, effectively exempting it from the Navigation Acts in this particular. The Tea Act sparked the so-called Boston Tea Party in which citizens disguised as Indians boarded ships bringing in the first supplies and dumped consignments of tea into Boston harbour. The English responded by closing the harbour to all shipping. This extreme reaction united the colonists and their representatives met at the First Continental Congress at Philadelphia in September 1774. The Congress began preparation for armed resistance. At a local level there were skirmishes between New England Militia and the English army at Concord and Lexington and in June 1775 the militia fought at Bunker Hill near Boston. The second Continental Congress, held shortly afterwards, 'adopted' the New England Militia and placed George Washington in charge. After a petition to the King, to which there was no direct response, Congress issued its Declaration of Independence, drafted by Thomas Jefferson, on the 4 July 1776.

There were two other major economic issues, in addition to trade policy and taxation, which created friction between the colonists and the motherland. (It is worth emphasizing that the relatively better-off colonists, though 'taxed without representation', were in many ways better treated than their compatriots at home. Even before some of the taxes and duties were rescinded, the colonists were lightly taxed, paying perhaps only a few per cent of the taxes borne by the English themselves.) The first of the other two points of friction was currency policy. English money circulated in the 13 colonies as well as Spanish and Portuguese money, but gold and silver coins were siphoned off to England, with which the colonies had a large commodity trade deficit. Indeed, this was mercantilist policy: to maximize the inflow of specie. There were no commercial banks and colonists were forced to rely upon merchant credit, bills of exchange, short-term treasury bills, warehouse receipts and other devices, as well as barter. Colonial state governments therefore issued their own paper money, the first being Massachusetts in 1690. Loan banks issuing paper money against the security of real property mortgages were started but these were curtailed by the application of the Bubble Act of 1720 and in 1751 Parliament passed the Currency Act, which restricted the issue of notes in New England (this Act was extended to the other colonies in 1764, though it was rescinded in 1773). These restrictions were intended to protect English creditors but were against the interests of large numbers of indebted small farmers who had an interest in a depreciating currency. In fact, sufficient paper was issued to raise the price level considerably in some colonies until the restrictions began to bite.

The other issue causing friction was land policy. Prior to 1763 the English had encouraged westward migration and expansion by the colonists to provide a buffer against the Indians and the French. Encouragement took various forms; for example land was granted to speculators on condition that they accommodated settler families. At the end of the Seven Years' War, in 1763, France ceded its territories south of Canada and from west of the Allegheny Mountains to the Mississippi River to Britain. British land policy in this year, a turning point in several respects in its relations with the colonists, changed.

A proclamation prohibited colonial governors from granting patents on western land without specific permission. There were several reasons for this; one was to pacify the Indians and thus protect the profitable fur trade, another was pressure from seaboard merchants who feared that their business would be harmed by further westward migration. Further regulations were issued in 1774 affecting land. Faulkner (1960) asserted that these changes particularly affected southern plantation owners, who were accordingly encouraged to join the patriots. The plantation owners had suffered considerably from the mercantilist restrictions and saw western land speculation as a way out of their difficulties. The Quebec Act of 1774 also ceded territory between the Ohio and Mississippi rivers to Quebec, land which three of the eastern colonies claimed as theirs, creating further friction (Atack and Passell, 1994).

The events leading up to the revolutionary war, as we have seen, moved slowly. Not all the colonists by any means were hostile to the English – probably most, including the small farmers, were little affected; some were doing well from British rule, particularly the merchants and large landowners. As a result, the revolutionary war also became a civil war and constitutional rhetoric by the patriots began to sway even those who had few economic interests at stake. Many settlers did resist the rebellion and sided with Britain, suffering accordingly; many of these left for Canada. One of the first acts of the Continental Army was an attack on Montreal and Quebec. The idea was that while Canada remained in British hands New England and New York were in danger of invasion from the north and it was hoped that the Canadians would wish to join in the revolt. This was not to be: the attack failed and the Americans had to accept that the Canadians did not wish to join them. In fact, in 1777 the British did attack from the north but were defeated at the battle of Saratoga. Having failed in the north, the British next tried to subdue the rebels in the south, but after victories in 1780 at Charleston and Camden (with help from France) the Americans finally triumphed at Yorktown in 1782. In the following year the British abandoned their efforts and negotiated the Treaty of Paris in 1783. This treaty ceded the land west of the Mississippi won from the French to the newly independent USA, giving the colonists everything they had fought for.

Alternate neglect, clamp-downs and vacillation by the British did much to precipitate the conflict. One of the most extraordinary features of the revolutionary war was that it was directed by a Continental Congress that had virtually no powers over the individual states and that it was up against Britain, the global superpower of the time with an ill-trained and -supplied army that never had more than 20,000 troops and at times as few as 3,000. As with the Confederacy in the >AMERICAN CIVIL WAR, the states were unwilling to grant taxation and other powers to a Federal body. Congress did not agree nor the states ratify Articles of Confederation until March 1781, by which time the war was almost over. Even these Articles did not give Congress power to tax but instead its expenses were to be met from funds pooled by the states, an agreement that was never implemented satisfactorily. Congress had to resort to printing money. The first issue of the Continental dollar was made in 1775 and was heavily counterfeited by the British as a matter of deliberate

policy. The states were also now free to issue more paper money. The result was highly inflationary and by 1781, according to Atack and Passell (1994), the Continental dollar was worth only 1 per cent of its original issue value and ceased to circulate. Prior to this, some states had unsuccessfully attempted to apply price controls. By 1777 the states were confiscating Loyalist property with the approval of Congress, as a contribution to the costs of the war. Much of the land in the colonies was held in large manorial estates. The large landowners were mostly Loyalists (Tories) and when these lands were confiscated some of the estates were broken up, though in many cases speculators replaced the Tories. In any event, changes in land ownership led to changes in local government. Confiscation of land, therefore, triggered important political changes and was a major element in the political and economic revolution, similar, as Faulkner points out, to the break-up of the landed estates during the French and Russian revolutions.

The short-term economic impact of the war on the colonies was probably not very great. One estimate is that the direct cost of the revolution was equivalent to about one year's national income at the time. However, there were presumably other losses of output and income compared with a counterfactual of what might have happened in the absence of the conflict. Economic losses were limited by the fact that actual armed conflict was quite localized. It seems that agriculture continued to expand – Faulkner shows that tobacco production increased by 30 per cent between 1774 and 1790. Maritime activity was not much obstructed by the British blockade, thanks to an enormous growth of privateering. Small-scale manufacturing developed to replace some imports from Britain and westward migration continued during the war. There was, however, much disorganization and a short depression followed the conflict.

After the war it still took time for the states to reach agreement on powers for the Federal institutions. In 1787 a constitutional convention altered the Articles of Confederation to allow majority voting (previously decisions had to be unanimous) and subsequently agreed, instead of further modifying the Articles, to lay down a constitution for the national government of the USA. This constitution, passed in 1787 and coming into force in June 1788, gave the Federal Government powers over taxation, the regulation of interstate commerce and asserted the sanctity of private property. Importantly, the constitution removed power from the states to issue currency and to tax imports. It is now generally seen that the constitution laid the basis for the long-term economic growth of the USA. Indeed, Beard (1986) developed the notion that economic interests predominated over other considerations in the negotiation and ratification of the constitution. This thesis subsequently aroused controversy among economic historians but later tended to be validated (Atack and Passell, 1994). In this, as in most other respects, early conclusions of economic historians on the economics of the revolution, although much deepened and filled-out, have not been radically modified by later research. It is difficult to improve upon Faulkner's judgement that the revolution was 'more than a single conflict between the economic interests of Britain and her mainland colonies; it was in many ways a revolt against a social and political system no longer applicable to conditions in America' (>ECONOMIC IMPERIALISM).

## References

Atack, Jeremy and Passell, Peter, *A New Economic View of American History from Colonial Times to 1940*, W. W. Norton, 1994.

Baack, Ben, 'Forging a Nation State: The Continental Congress and the Financing of the War of Economic Independence', *Economic History Review*, 54, 2001.

Beard, Charles A., *An Economic Interpretation of the Constitution*, The Free Press, 1986.

Faulkner, Harold Underwood, *American Economic History*, Harper & Row, 1960.

Sawers, Larry, 'The Navigation Acts Revisited', *Economic History Review*, 45,1992.

Thomas, Robert, 'A Quantitative Approach to the Study of the Effects of British Imperial Policy on Colonial Welfare: Some Preliminary Findings', *Journal of Economic History*, 25, 1965.

Walton, Gary M., 'The New Economic History and the Burdens of the Navigation Acts', *Economic History Review*, 24, 1971.

# American Westward Expansion

The westward movement in the >USA essentially began with the colonization of the east in the 17th century and it was not completed until some 300 years later. The pioneers met with resistance from Spain, which had colonized much earlier, and the French who laid claim to much of the interior but also the Indians already there and Mexico, when it achieved independence from Spain. There were also physical obstacles and internal political disagreements. The West has become an important sub-group of American economic history, first, because of the progressive settlement of 'free' land, a moving 'frontier' which it involved and, second, because the experience has influenced the whole character of American civilization, both these notions emanating from the work of Frederick Turner (1893).

At the end of the >AMERICAN WAR OF INDEPENDENCE, in the Treaty of Paris (1783), Britain ceded the lands south of Canada, east of the Missisippi River and north of Florida, to which it laid claim, to the new Confederation of American States. In 1803, President Jefferson bought the Louisiana Territory, 828,000 square miles of land west of the Mississippi, from Napoleon. Florida was acquired from Spain in 1819, Texas, newly independent from Mexico, was annexed in 1845. The Oregon Country, controlled by Britain and the Hudson Bay Company, was abandoned peacefully to American settlers by the Treaty of 1846. Territorial expansion of the USA was largely completed in 1848 with the acquisition of California and New Mexico from Mexico, which had gained its independence from Spain in 1821. As Billington (1959) puts it, the American technique adopted in all these cases was peaceful penetration followed by revolution and conquest. The stage was set for significant westward expansion by settlers, although that had, in fact, already begun, first by fur trappers and hunters and an early movement of settlers across the Appalachians (in 1790 there were already 100,000 settlers in Kentucky and Tennessee) and eventually into Texas and elsewhere. The British had at first encouraged westward migration from the eastern seaboard because it provided a buffer against the French, but later discouraged it because it was feared that further settlement would alienate the Indians, some of whom were allies and were the key to the highly profitable fur trade.

Mass transmigration from the East to California began in the 1840s and was boosted following the discovery of >GOLD there about the same time as the territory was acquired. By the end of 1848, four-fifths of the population of California were miners (Anderson and Hill, 2004). Between 1840 and 1860, 300,000 people crossed the Great Plains to California and Oregon. The trek took an average of 164 days by covered wagon from Independence, St Joseph and other places, via Fort Laramie and South Pass through the Rocky Mountains. It was a hazardous journey: disease, drowning and accidents resulted in a mortality rate of 4 per cent. By 1860, the average journey time had fallen to 116 days as better routes were found and ferries and bridges established, and there was a least one enterprising 90-mile turnpike (>ROAD TRANSPORT). By the end of the >AMERICAN CIVIL WAR in 1865, only the Great Plains between the Mississippi and the Rockies had yet to be settled. The plains were dry and treeless and, though there was grassland, there was no means of transporting produce to markets in the East. The latter problem was solved by the transcontinental railway built westward from Omaha by Union Pacific and eastwards from San Francisco by Central Pacific. Both companies were supported by Federal loans and land grants. The link between the two railways was completed on 10 May 1869, marked by a ceremony in which gold and silver spikes were driven into the track bearers. Other lines followed, to Kansas for example, and a southern track to Santa Fe and ultimately on to Los Angeles (>RAILWAYS).

In 1862, President Lincoln had signed the Homestead Act which allowed 160 acres of land free after five years of occupation and cultivation.

The acreage was increased in stages to 640 in 1916 since in the arid country 160 acres was not enough to support a family. The Homestead Act actually had a relatively small impact on the enormous amount of unsettled Federal land, though, between 1863 and 1900, 1.5 million entries were filed for homesteads. Much of the best land was obtained, one way or another, by speculators. Land policy was to prove a continuous source of disagreement, right from the start when the charters of a number of eastern and southern states claimed boundaries west of the Mississippi. By 1802 the last of these (Georgia) gave up its claims. The policy of free land was much criticized. There were concerns expressed, for example by Alexander >HAMILTON, that cheap western land starved capital from manufacturing in the East and promoted speculation and concentration of ownership. In reality, westward expansion created a market for manufactures. Fogel and Rutner (1972) show that the land policies did induce westward migration, raise GDP and redistribute income. It was more generally accepted that the provision of free land for railways and canals was a big incentive for investment. However, Atack and Passell (1994) reasoned that the value of the land grants was not a great incentive because it depended upon the economic success of the lines. They calculated that private returns on railway investment, excluding land, were about 11 per cent for the Central and Union Pacific lines – well above the returns on bonds at the time, though returns for other lines were less. Land subsidies represented only 5 per cent of the amount invested in railways between 1850 and 1880 so their impact could not have been very great. In fact, although inter-city lines in the East were profitable,

the financial structure of the railway companies made them vulnerable to economic downturns. In the mid-1870s, nearly a fifth of the nation's track fell into bankruptcy, resulting in a pause in new construction. The southern states obstructed land policy and infrastructure development. These states were against Federal expenditure in the West and North instead of in the South because they feared that the growth of the West would increase the anti-slavery movement. For example, it was not until after the Civil War that agreement could be reached on the route for the transcontinental railway. In actuality, only a small proportion of Federal land was granted free to individuals in the period up to 1904 – about 7 per cent, which was about the same as that granted for transport and less than that granted to the states for resale. Some was reserved for Native Americans and some was sold for cash, the rest being retained.

The great cattle drives from Texas to make use of the grasslands in the Great Plains and to serve the growing markets in the North and East began in 1866 and continued until about 1884. Between 1868 and 1871 a million cattle were moved. The Spanish had introduced long-horn cattle to Texas and the number grew to some 5 million after the Civil War. Branded and unbranded, they roamed free on the range. The extension of the railhead to Kansas stimulated this activity but it also stimulated enclosure and cattle raising under controlled conditions. The perfection of barbed wire also helped to bring about the end of the open-range system. According to Anderson and Hill (2004), 80.5 million pounds of barbed wire were sold in 1880 alone, enough for 500,000 miles of four-strand fencing. Anderson and Hill's book is important because it spells out in detail the elaborate institutional arrangements for property rights that rapidly evolved in a virgin land beyond the scope of Federal or state law (>INSTITUTIONS). When that law came, it was often more costly to operate and less effective than the more informal arrangements that it replaced. This is an illustration of the importance of allowing institutions wherever possible to develop bottom-up and not be imposed top-down (>ECONOMIC DEVELOPMENT). The author's theme is that the West was developed not by heroic individuals so much as by cooperative endeavour, while violence, though it existed, was certainly less than in many cities in the developed countries of today. Eighteen years before the first effective Federal Mining Law (1866), mining camps established rules for registering claims, adjudicating disputes and enforcing them in extra-legal courts. Local laws for water rights (particularly important in the case of mining) and the claiming of land, kept order before Federal law caught up with the westward-moving frontier. (The authors define 'frontier' as the margin between the time and place where resources have no value and that where they have value.) Wagon trains elected leaders and had strict rules set before departure about, for example, spreading the cost of shared equipment. Stockmen's associations compensated owners after round-ups and also registered the ownership of brands. Cattle were valued and their numbers increased unlike the case of the buffalo, where the Native Americans attributed no property rights. The result was a 'tragedy of the commons' and the number of buffalo fell from some 30 million in 1800 to a few score by the end of the

century. From a purely economic point of view the replacement of the buffalo by cattle, however, was rational because cattle were easier to control and transport, among their other qualities.

The Native American population also had their institutional arrangements. These varied from tribe to tribe and according to geographical conditions, customs and culture. Farmland was often owned in common, though allocated to individuals. There were even environmental rules such as those governing the movement of a proportion of salmon upstream for spawning. Conflicts between tribes, however, were common, and indeed it was the military skills learned in these conflicts that allowed them to hold out for so long. Anderson and Hill say that in the early days bows and arrows where more than a match for muzzle-loaded rifles (they were quicker for repeat launching) and later, when better weapons became available, the Native Americans quickly obtained them. White–Native American relationships went through three main phases. At first whites respected Native American property rights, though inevitably brought European diseases to which the indigenous population had no resistance. Whites engaged in profitable trade with them; deer, beaver and otter pelts were highly valued in Europe. In the second phase, the US government used military power to take Native American land; between 1867 and 1890, 100,000 people were moved into reservations. This change resulted from increasing demand for land from settlers, but Anderson and Hill also explain it by the release of military resources from the ending of the Mexican and Civil wars and the natural desire of the military bureaucracy to fight battles. In the third phase, from the late 19th century, Federal agencies defended and controlled Native American rights on reservations, but these had no real tribal sovereignty and the top-down treatment included attempts to 'educate' Indians to the white man's ways often with unhappy results. Today, despite financial help, including gambling and tax concessions, the reservations, as any visitor to New Mexico can see, 'remain third world islands in a sea of wealth'.

It is recognized that the frontier was closed in 1890 because there were then settlements right across the country. There was still land to be settled even after the opening up of the Oklahoma District to non-Indians in 1890 under the Homestead Act, but there was no longer a 'frontier' as such and one era in the West came to an end. The western economy has, of course, continued to grow (>USA). By 1870, Chicago was already a major manufacturing and transport centre, as was St Louis and later Kansas City. Refrigerated railway cars came into use in 1870s, there was timber processing on the Pacific coast and mining at many places in the West. This process of growth continued after the inter-war depression (>GREAT DEPRESSION), during World War II and thereafter. The term 'sunbelt' (the area below the 37th Parallel) came into use to describe the emergence of new prosperity. In 1946, the South and West accounted for 23 per cent of personal income from manufacturing, but by 1982 it was 43 per cent. By 1920, the West had automobile and aircraft plants but the South had low wages and manufacturing was mainly limited to textiles and local food and tobacco processing. This was destined to change in the post->WORLD WAR II period. California, Florida and Texas together accounted for 42 per cent of US population growth in the 1970s. Los Angeles, Houston, Dallas-Fort Worth, Phoenix and Atlanta emerged as major growth centres. California, New Mexico and other places in the West benefited from strategic decentralization during World War II and much of the resulting activity proved to be permanent. Partly because of their high unit value and low transport costs, electronics industries developed in Silicon Valley, California, Phoenix and Denver (French, 1997). In addition to lower wages and land costs and continuing lifestyle migration, the sunbelt probably also benefited from the absence of entrenched institutional rigidities which had begun to characterize the older developed regions of the USA (Olson, 1982).

From 1804, when President Thomas Jefferson sent two experienced frontiersmen, Meriwether Lewis and William Clark, to investigate the new territories which had been bought or conquered, there has developed a large literature on the West. Popularized by Western fictional stories and movies, the West holds a permanent place not only in the American imagination but also throughout the world. Movies such as *Union Pacific* (1939), *How the West was Won* (1962) and literally thousands of others have recreated the pioneering days vividly, if not always accurately. President Theodore Roosevelt was to write a four-volume work entitled *The Winning of the West* (completed in 1894) and, through his adventures in Cuba and in politics, was to be the subject of several films himself. President Ronald Reagan, former film actor in many western movies and former Governor of California, took this tradition even further. For economic historians, however, the figure of the Wisconsin historian, Frederick Jackson Turner

(1861–1932) still looms large (Turner, 1893). Turner believed not only that the Westward movement was a key element in the emergence of the US economy but also that it has left a continuing impression on the American character.

Turner has been criticized as 'too triumphalist' and for his neglect of regional, environmental issues, the role of eastern capitalists, the role of women and ethnic minorities (the Indian, Hispanics, Asian-, Mexican- and African-Americans) and much else. Subsequent research has corrected and filled out the subject and has shown that some 'truths' (such as the prevalence of violence) are not as evident as they appear, but Turner's poetic conception of the frontier has endured.

### References

Anderson, Terry L. and Hill, Peter J., *The Not So Wild, Wild West: Property Rights and the Frontier*, Stanford University Press, 2004.

Atack, Jeremy and Passell, Peter, *A New Economic View of American History from Colonial Times to 1940*, W. W. Norton, 1994.

Billington, Ray Allen, *The Westward Movement in the United States*, Van Nostrand Co., 1959.

Coman, Katharine, *Economic Beginnings of the Far West*, Macmillan, 1912.

Fogel, Robert and Rutner, Jack, 'The Efficiency Effects of Federal Land Policy 1850–1900', in William Aydelotte, Allan G. Bogue and Robert W. Fogel (eds), *The Dimensions of Quantitative Research in History*, Princeton University Press, 1972.

French, Michael, *US Economic History Since 1945*, Manchester University Press, 1997.

Olson, Mancur, *The Rise and Decline of Nations: Economic Growth, Stagflation and Social Rigidities*, Yale University Press, 1982.

Turner, F. J., *The Frontier in American History*, Henry Hall, 1893, reprint 1920.

# Anthropometric History

Anthropometrics is the use of data about the human body, such as heights of recruits into the military at different dates, as indicators of changing living standards. Biologists have established that stature reflects nutrition. Where reliable data on real incomes and expenditure budgets are not available, as is usually the case before the 19th century, data on stature have been used as proxies for living standards. Measures of real incomes present a host of technical problems, particularly in long-term comparisons of prices and hence the real value of wages over time. Stature is not subject to these problems and can also be compared across countries. Anthropometric work in economic history is fairly recent and dates only from the 1960s (>ECONOMIC HISTORY: PRICES AND INFLATION).

Studies have established a decrease in average human stature in Europe over the period of the early >INDUSTRIAL REVOLUTIONS, despite a secular trend towards increased stature over the past 200 years or so (Ewart, 2006). In the early part of this period in Europe at least, real wages seem to have been static or declining. In the >USA, however, there were declines in stature between 1830 and 1860 at a time when per capita incomes were rising strongly. These findings support the views of those who argue that earnings are not an adequate indicator of living standards in these periods or of prices paid by workers in the early stages of industrialization (>INDUSTRIAL REVOLUTION IN BRITAIN). Confirmation of the effect of environmental conditions as well as nutrition has been found in the fact that in >BRITAIN average heights were greater in rural than in urban areas, even though wages were lower. Similarly, the stature of cadets at Britain's elite military academy at Sandhurst, whose intake was drawn from the upper classes, was greater than that of ordinary working-class recruits. Although American slaves were somewhat shorter than whites, they were not subject to the general decline in heights. Steckel (1998) concluded that slave owners ensured that diets were sufficient for the work slaves had to do (>SLAVERY).

There are some limitations on the value of stature as an indicator of living standards. Environmental conditions may affect human height, as could exposure to disease. It has been argued that the fact that stature was sensitive to some elements in living standards, such as working conditions, was an advantage for anthropometric work in that these elements were not captured in wages or real incomes data. It has also been pointed out that changes in the availability of consumer goods and their prices could affect the proportion of income spent on food even where standards of living broadly defined have not changed (Leunig and Voth, 2003). CRAFTS, however, found that height was not correlated with non-income components of quality of life or with GDP per head in mid-19th-century Britain. He did not think that anthropometric data actually strengthened the case for the pessimistic view of living standards during the first industrial revolution. Leunig and Voth also make the point that height gains over time are diminishing in the advanced countries so that the value of stature as an indicator of living standards will also diminish over time.

### References

Crafts, N. F. R., 'Some Dimensions of the Quality of Life in Britain During the Industrial Revolution', *Economic History Review*, 50, November, 1977.

Ewart, Ulf Christian, 'The Biological Standard of Living on the Decline: Episodes from Germany During Early Industrialisation', *European Review of Economic History*, 10, April, 2006.

Floud, R., Wachter, K. W. and Gregory, A., *Height, Health and History: Nutritional Status in the United Kingdom, 1750–1980*, Cambridge University Press, 1990.

Komlos, John, 'Shrinking in a Growing Economy? The Mystery of Physical Stature During the Industrial Revolution', *Journal of Economic History*, 58, 1998.

Leunig, Timothy and Voth, Hans-Joachim, 'Height and the High Life', in Paul A. David and Mark Thomas (eds), *The Economic Future in Historical Perspective*, Oxford University Press, 2003.

Steckel, Richard H., 'Strategic Ideas on the Rise of the New Anthropometric History and their Implications for Interdisciplinary Research', *Journal of Economic History*, 58, 1998.

## Anti-Trust

Active monopoly, or cartel control, policy began in the >USA at the beginning of the 20th century, though it languished during the >GREAT DEPRESSION at least until the >NEW DEAL. In other countries, policies towards monopolies and cartels were benign and indeed cartels were encouraged as part of efforts towards rationalization. Cartels were also promoted in the period of rearmament that led up to >WORLD WAR II, most particularly in Germany and Japan. After the war anti-trust activities spread around the world until all the developed countries and many developing ones had active monopoly policies and there was some international cooperation in enforcing them.

Strictly speaking 'trust' is a legal form in which assets, for example, holdings in companies, are placed under the control of independent trustees. This structure was adopted by the Standard Oil Company in 1882 but the term came to be applied to any large amalgamation of companies which approach monopoly. Cartels are associations of independent producers which fix prices and curtail output. The term 'monopoly', likewise, strictly means a single seller but is commonly applied to any business which engages in anti-competitive practices. Monopolies in the strict sense of a single seller are very rare because of the existence of substitutes and some economists argue that monopoly profits will inevitably attract new competitors so that no true monopoly can endure for very long. Monopolies of all sorts have long been recognized by economists as potentially against the general welfare or, as Adam >SMITH put it, are 'injurious to the public'. It can be demonstrated that it is in the interest of a monopolist to restrict output in order to sell at prices above those in a free market. Augustine Cournot (1801–1877) and Alfred Marshall (1842–1924) extended the analysis of monopoly to markets where there were a small number of sellers. It was not until the early 1930s, however, that Joan Robinson (1903–1983), at Cambridge in England, and E. H. Chamberlin (1899–1967), in America, independently elaborated the theory of oligopoly (or imperfect or monopolistic competition). They were able to show that small numbers of firms took account of the actions of their competitors and possessed a degree of monopoly power through product differentiation. These were, in fact, the market conditions that were becoming the general rule at the time.

Not all economists have taken a hostile view of monopoly. J. B. Clark (1847–1938), in America, introduced ethics into the discussion of competitive behaviour and encouraged an influential view in the American judicial system after World War I that there were good and bad monopolies. The German Historical School (>ECONOMIC HISTORY) favoured cartels and combinations on efficiency grounds and because they helped to secure economic and social stability. For example, later on it was asserted that in Germany the trades unions could be relied upon to prevent the abuse of monopoly positions. >GERSCHENKRON also later argued that German industrialization in the 19th century had been accompanied by considerable increases in concentration, supported after 1879 by tariff protection, that was necessary for a relative late-comer to industrialization.

Joseph >SCHUMPETER made a lasting contribution to the debate on monopoly by arguing, in *Capitalism, Socialism and Democracy* (1943), that elements of monopoly were important for economic development. Monopoly profits could provide the necessary resources for research and innovation, while restrictive practices could gain time and reduce risk for the new investments that were essential to 'creative destruction'. Schumpeter's argument was a complex one and has subsequently been caricatured as meaning that monopoly always favoured innovation (which research clearly shows was not true). Schumpeter was discussing what he called 'edited competition'. He was not against state regulation, but wrote that, 'there is no case for indiscriminate "trust busting" or for the prosecution of everything that qualifies as a restraint on trade'. This economic tradition was carried into the work of the Chicago School, which argued that government intervention was often counterproductive and advocated a very light touch in competition policy. A different economic perspective on competition policy, which influenced US anti-trust policy after World War II, was the Structure–Conduct–Performance model, which held that the performance of an industry followed from its conduct which in turn was caused by its structure. A countervailing argument was that what counted was not structure but *contestibility*, that was the ease with which competitors could enter the industry. Competition policy remained controversial, though there was increasing support for the view that there should be very strict control of restrictive practices but a more pragmatic approach to the sanctioning of mergers where consumer benefits could be identified.

The Sherman Anti-Trust Act (1890) was passed during the administration of President Benjamin Harrison, following a growing number of industrial and financial combinations. Legislation allowing modern corporate structures had been introduced in many countries, including Britain, France, Germany and the USA during the 1850s and 1860s (>COMPANIES). With increasing advantages of scale and the capital investment that these required, technological developments, including those in transport and communications, as well as the opening up of global markets, there was everywhere a trend towards business consolidation (>CONCENTRATION). This process probably went even further in the USA than elsewhere at the time. There was a fear among the public that national resources, in particular, were coming under the control of a small number of 'robber barons' (though, in fact, it was the beginning of managerial capitalism in which single individuals were becoming less important). By 1873, six corporations

owned most of the anthracite deposits in Pennsylvania and, by 1882, 39 refineries of Standard Oil controlled 90 per cent of output. Public opinion, including small businesses and farmers, demanded action, which was met by the Sherman Act (>CHANDLER; Fualkner, 1960; Schmitz, 1993; >USA).

Section 1 of the Sherman Act began, 'Every contract, combination in the form of trust or otherwise or conspiracy of trade or commerce among the several States, or with foreign nations, is hereby declared to be illegal.' Section 2 explicitly banned attempts 'to monopolise or combine to conspire ... to monopolise any part of trade or commerce'. Not only were violations punishable by fines and imprisonment, but also injured parties might recover three times the damages sustained. Some objected that the Act went too far and could harm legitimate business. According to Faulkner, the framers of the Sherman Act claimed that it simply restated English common law principles. The Act had no initial effect on business consolidation, though, ironically, it was used against trade unions in the Pullman strike of 1894. The terms of the Act were perhaps too vague and the Federal government seemed to have little interest in enforcing it. However, this began to change under the administration of Theodore Roosevelt, in which a number of clarifying acts were passed and an investigative branch established in the Department of Commerce and Labor.

In 1904 the Attorney General successfully brought a suit against the Northern Securities Company, which was attempting to create a railway monopoly in the north east of the USA. Cases against the Standard Oil Company and American Tobacco were in the courts for years, but eventually, in 1911, both were successful and resulted in the breaking up of the two groups (>OIL). In these cases, the judges introduced 'rule of reason', which attempted to differentiate between good and bad combinations. Dissatisfaction with the weak impact of the Sherman Act nonetheless led to the passage of the Clayton Anti-Trust Act (1914) under Woodrow Wilson. This Act banned specific restrictive practices where they lessened competition, including price discrimination, tying agreements and resale price maintenance. The Clayton Act also introduced restrictions on cross-shareholdings and interlocking directorships. Trades unions were exempted and, at the same time, the Fair Trade Commission was created with powers to issue 'desist' orders.

The anti-monopoly Acts did not arrest the trend of business consolidation, though it did change its form by stimulating mergers and acquisitions in place of trusts. Nevertheless, there was action on other fronts and the decision in 1913 to give the Federal Reserve Board a decentralized structure (>CENTRAL BANKING) and the passing of the Glass-Steagall Act in 1933, as well as Federal and state restrictions on commercial bank branch networks, were all responses to the deep-seated fear of financial concentration (the Glass-Steagall Act required the separation of commercial and investment >BANKING). The Great Depression muted anti-trust activity somewhat; indeed, some features of the early New Deal effectively led to its suspension. However, in April 1938, Franklin D. Roosevelt, concerned by developments in Germany and Japan, delivered an important anti-monopoly speech in which he equated corporatism with fascism. He said that the liberty of democracy was not safe if private power exceeded that of government, nor was it safe if business did not produce enough employment. The Temporary National Economic Committee (TNEC) was set up to investigate the concentration of economic power and substantially increased resources were given to the Fair Trade Commission and the Anti-Trust Division of the Department of Justice. TNEC revealed extensive patent and cartel agreements with foreign companies that restricted the use of technology by American firms.

During >WORLD WAR II the enforcement of anti-trust was again relaxed, this time in the interests of defence production. The Anti-Trust Division directed attention to the pro-Nazi political activities of German cartels with which American companies had relations, thus supporting the work of the Board of Economic Warfare. Towards the end of the war the USA began to influence its allies over anti-trust and, according to Freyer (2006), this became an issue in the Anglo-USA Aid Negotiations. After the war the USA attempted to impose its model of anti-trust on Germany and Japan. In 1945, the Supreme Court upheld a judgment against Alcoa, which strengthened monopoly doctrines at home. Since foreign cartels were also involved in that case it also confirmed the extra-territorial application of the anti-trust doctrine. Freyer says that between 1945 and 1970 anti-trust enforcement was more effective than at any time in US history, though it continued to allow diversification and conglomerate mergers. The 1976 Hart–Scott–Rodino Anti-Trust Improvement Act instituted a merger notification system. In the 1980s the Ronald Reagan administration broke up AT&T, though in other respects it exerted a fairly light touch to anti-monopoly enforcement.

Within the USA, the regulation of monopolies shifted back and forth between state and Federal levels.

Twenty states enacted anti-trust statutes before the Federal Sherman Act (1890). Public Utility Commissions (PUCs) were established at state level to regulate, for example, electricity and railways. As interstate commerce expanded, however, and after the Interstate Commerce Commission (ICC) was established in 1887, states lost some of their regulatory roles and the New Deal accelerated this process. States retained some functions, notably in insurance, and also were involved in implementing Federal Monopoly law (Teske, 2004).

In the 1990s there was an intensification of anti-trust enforcement all over the world, this time with a lead coming from Europe. The European Commission (EC) of the European Union (EU) (>WESTERN EUROPE) adopted a similar, legalistic, approach as the USA (in contrast to the more discretionary, politicized approaches traditional in Britain and other European countries) but enforced stronger doctrines than the USA. The EC refused to approve a GE-Honeywell takeover because it would adversely affect competition in Europe, even though the US authorities had approved the merger. Microsoft was another example where the EC applied tougher treatment than the USA. The basis for the competition rules in the EU is embodied in Articles 81 and 82 of the Treaty of Rome (formerly 85 and 86). The first of these articles forbids cartel arrangements, except where they can be shown to be in the interests of efficiency and technical progress, and the second the abuse of dominant positions. European competition law is unique in that it controls the provision of state aids to enterprises which might result in unfair competition. There have been numerous clashes between the Commission and national member governments who wish to protect 'national champions', for example, by preventing cross-border mergers. Member states have their own national competition policies and authorities which are far from harmonized, but the Commission reserves to itself jurisdiction over large mergers and cases significantly affecting trade within the EU (Galli and Pelkmans, 2000).

Compared with the USA, Britain was very late in introducing legislation on monopolies. Britain had a long record of control of natural monopolies (>REGULATION), but before 1948 there was no general policy. Before World War II Britain promoted cartels and intervened in industrial concentration by, for example, promoting the Vickers Armstrong (armaments) merger in 1930 and producer cartels or holding companies in the coal, >IRON AND STEEL and other staple industries. Freyer mentions that, as late as 1939, the Federation of British Industries signed an agreement with its German equivalent 'to end destructive competition'. At the outbreak of war, British and German firms were party to 133 restrictive trade agreements, though government support ceased in 1940.

The Monopolies and Restrictive Practices (Inquiry and Control) Act of 1948 marked a major departure for Britain. In drafting the new Act, the British government rejected the legalistic and civil damages system of US anti-trust in favour of an administrative, pragmatic approach. The Act established a Monopolies Commission (MC) to investigate the economic effects of the structure and behaviour of the industries referred to it with a view to making judgements on whether they were in the public interest. The MC could also be asked to propose remedies. There was no helpful definition of the public interest nor did the Act attribute any virtue to competition (Allen, 1979). Leading on from the work of the MC, which had condemned various restrictive practices, the 1956 Restrictive Practices Act introduced a more judicial approach with a Restrictive Practices Court. The MC became the Monopolies and Mergers Commission (M&MC). The Resale Prices Act (1964) abolished retail price maintenance (>CONSUMER REVOLUTION). In 1973, the Fair Trading Act replaced the 1948 and 1956 Acts and established an Office of Fair Trading (OFT). The OFT could make preliminary investigations and issue desist orders or, with the approval of the Secretary of State, make references to the M&MC. The Competition Act (1998) replaced the M&MC with the Competition Commission. To a significant extent, the Enterprise Act (2002) depoliticized monopoly control procedures. Tests were laid down for determining whether arrangements were in the public interest and the Commission had powers to make decisions and implement remedies on its own initiative without reference to the Secretary of State. The OFT continued to enforce consumer and competition law and make references to the Commission.

In Japan, the Meiji regime privatized state enterprises and reduced the size of the public sector after 1880. Prominent features of the economic structure in the 1920s were the *zaibatsu*, which Allen (1972) translates literally as 'money cliques'. The ownership of these enterprises was vested in families, or groups of families, and they had close relationships with government. The four largest zaibatsu were: Mitsui, Mitsubishi, Sumitomo and Yasuda. The zaibatsu, according to Freyer, avoided involvement in cartels, at least until 1931, when the Significant Industries Control Law authorized government to create combinations. By 1932 there were 108 cartels authorized under the new law. The zaibatsu and the National Policy Companies set up by government assisted in the accumulation of capital and the industrialization of Japan in what Allen (1972) calls the 'quasi-wartime economy of the 1930s'. In 1938, the General Mobilization Law gave government almost unlimited powers of control over economic activity. A dual economy existed in which >SMALL AND MEDIUM ENTERPRISES were exploited as sub-contractors by the large combinations.

After World War II, the occupying powers attempted to impose the US anti-trust model on Japan by the Anti-Monopoly Law (1947). A Fair Trade Commission (FTC) was created to enforce the law but the Japanese were able to obtain fairly weak anti-monopoly provisions, though those on restrictive practices were fairly strong. Supreme Commander Allied Powers (SCAP) set out to build a strong trades union movement and dissolved the zaibatsu and National Policy Companies by breaking up the holding companies and major subsidiaries. After the Peace and Security Treaty (1952), which restored sovereignty to Japan, the major Zaibatsu were partially reformed, though family interests were diminished, and new groups emerged, such as Hitachi. The electric power and railway groups which emerged from SCAP's earlier denationalization measures also became centres of more diversified groups.

In 1994, the Ministry of International Trade and Industry (MITI) acknowledged that government regulation and business practices had undermined the competitiveness of the economy and served as a barrier to imports. In 1995, the Coalition Government embarked on a Deregulation Action Programme, together with tighter application of the Anti-Monopoly Law. In 1996 a new law strengthened the FTC, which was given a stronger investigations department, though at the same time the rules for smaller holding companies were relaxed. Freyer cites a Harvard study which concluded that anti-trust activity in Japan then approached US levels, although there were very few private actions.

In Germany, the Weimar Government enacted anti-cartel measures in 1923 and expanded these powers in 1930–2, but the Great Depression led to a desire for rationalization and greater acceptance of cartels. As in Japan, the Nazis enacted a Compulsory Cartel Law (1933) which authorized the Minister of Economics to establish new cartels or require firms to join existing ones. These measures later allowed the Nazis to control prices and maintain employment. Again, after the war, as in Japan, the occupation authorities imposed anti-monopoly policies on Germany but they turned out to be even weaker than those in Japan, partly because of the conflicting views of the French, British and American authorities. In a purely indigenous development, Chancellor Ludwig Erhard (1897–1977) transformed the weak anti-monopoly laws into much stronger and largely implemented ones in the Act Against Restraints on Competition (ARC) (1958). Erhard (1958) later wrote in his autobiographical account that he considered the anti-cartel measures to be an important factor in the so-called German Economic Miracle (>WESTERN EUROPE). The ARC established a Cartel Office (*Bundeskartellamt*) and an advisory body, the Monopolies Commission (*Monopolkommission*). The Act was amended in 1973 to add merger control, prohibit resale price maintenance and help protect small enterprises by allowing them to cooperate. There were further amendments to the ARC in 1999 to bring German law into conformity with EU law. The Ministry of Economics could override decisions of the Cartel Office provided it took advice from the Monopolies Commission.

## References

Allen, G. C., *A Short Economic History of Modern Japan*, George Allen & Unwin, 1946, rev. edn 1972.

Allen, G. C., *British Industry and Economic Policy*, Macmillan, 1979.

Erhard, Ludwig, *Prosperity through Competition*, Thames and Hudson, 1958.

Faulkner, Harold Underwood, *American Economic History*, Harper & Row, 1960.

Freyer, Tony A., *Antitrust and Global Capitalism, 1930–2004*, Cambridge University Press, 2006.

Galli, Giampaolo and Pelkmans, Jacques (eds), *Regulatory Reform and Competitiveness in Europe*, I, Edward Elgar, 2000.

Schmitz, Christopher J., *The Growth of Big Business in the United States and Western Europe, 1850–1939*, Macmillan, 1993.

Teske, Paul, *Regulation in the States*, Brookings Institution, 2004.

# Asian Miracle

The economic rise of East Asia (EA) (broadly defined to include >CHINA, Japan and the high-growth economies of South East Asia (SEA)) has been extraordinary. Along with the collapse of communism in Europe, the rise of Asia is the most dramatic, and unexpected, development of the second half of the 20th century. In 1999, at 26 per cent, the share of these East Asian (EA) countries in world GNP was double what it had been in 1960, while that of Europe and North America fell from 76 to

62 per cent over the same period. For value added in manufacturing, the contrast is greater still: EA accounted for 16 per cent in 1960 but 35 per cent in 1999. On another measure of economic impact, EA now accounts for over three-quarters of the world's ten largest official foreign exchange reserves (Arrighi *et al.*, 2003).

Economic expansion in EA was initiated by Japan, which achieved annual growth in GDP per capita of over 8 per cent in 1950–73. As its costs rose, Japanese producers progressively invested more in overseas output in its neighbouring countries with lower labour costs, boosting their growth. In the next period (1973–90), SEA economies, further benefiting from investment from the USA and Europe, took over the lead in Asian 'super-growth', as Japanese growth rates declined. In the following period (1990–9), as can be seen in the table below, Japan's performance was virtually static but a liberalized >CHINA grew even faster than SEA. Arrighi *et al.* liken the successive growth in these three regions to a three-stage rocket, which, the table shows, left the USA and Europe, after their post-war booms, far behind.

Percentage annual average compound growth rates in per capita GDP, selected countries and regions

|  | 1950–73 | 1973–90 | 1990–9 |
|---|---|---|---|
| Japan | 8.1 | 3.0 | 0.9 |
| SEA | 4.7 | 5.4 | 4.2 |
| China | 2.9 | 4.8 | 6.4 |
| W. Europe | 4.1 | 1.9 | 1.4 |
| USA | 2.5 | 2.0 | 2.1 |

*Source*: Adapted from Maddison, 2001.

*Note*: SEA includes Hong Kong, Malaysia, Singapore, South Korea, Taiwan and Thailand. For Western Europe data cover 1990–8. The underlined numbers are the fastest growth rates in each period and show how leadership passed successively from Japan to SEA and finally to China.

South East Asian growth was driven initially by import substitution and later by exports, the latter being much more important than for Japan. SEA is far from homogeneous and government policies have also varied. This has allowed plenty of room for disagreement about the explanation for the 'miracle'. Hong Kong, Taiwan and Singapore pursued a mostly free-market approach, though the latter did have a strong and interventionist government. Policies in South Korea were similar to those of Japan and included the use of corporate 'guidance'. Certainly protection was used, average import tariff rates for SEA were 25 per cent in 1978 and there was some state support and special incentives for industry (Dixon, 1991). The World Bank, in its early assessment, concluded that macro-economic management was 'unusually' good and that governments did the right things in terms of education and agricultural policy and other spheres. It is, however, doubtful if micro-economic intervention had a significantly favourable effect. Dixon cites a report by the Economic and Social Commission for Asia which indicated that the importance of investment incentives in the Asian region as a whole was slight or unknown, while similar critiques were made of export processing zones and other government initiatives. In this, experience in EA confirms the general outcome of government micro-industrial policies elsewhere (>STATE, RISE OF THE). Some commentators have asserted that Asian business culture is different, having been influenced by the philosophy of Confucius and other values, but it has to be explained why these ancient values did not bring growth long before. There is now an enormous economic literature on the resurgence of Asia, some of it controversial. There has been less controversy about Japan or China. The groundwork for Japanese growth was laid long ago in the Tokoguwa period, followed by the Meiji Restoration, and was based on deliberate modernization and Westernization. In >CHINA, the recent resurgence is clearly attributable to the relaxation of socialist controls, a similar development having taken place in >INDIA.

The causes of growth in SEA remain controversial, however. Krugman (1994) compared the economic surge with that earlier in the Soviet Union as being the result of the mobilization of capital and labour without improvements in efficiency. He supports this view with studies showing that increases in Total Factor >PRODUCTIVITY (TPF) in SEA have been very limited. (TFP is the residual which cannot be explained by increases in inputs and is normally attributed to technical progress.) He concluded that SEA growth being caused largely by more inputs was not therefore a miracle at all and would eventually cease as that in Russia did. Others have reached different conclusions. Some scholars have found increases in TFP in SEA countries (Maddison *et al.*, 2002). Others argue that TFP calculations do not capture administrative and organizational improvements, which can change factor proportions and which are assumed away in TFP methodologies (>PRODUCTIVITY). Gapinski and Kahn (1991) both find evidence of technical progress in SEA and agree that conventional TFP methods are misleading. That there have been major changes in the organization of production in SEA is evident from the role of foreign trade and the use of flexible production techniques imported from Japan and adopted in response to the demand generated by large merchandisers and brands

such as Wal-Mart, Home Depot, Nike and other Western-owned firms. According to Bannock (2005), these changes have taken place to a large extent through increases in numbers and employment shares of >SMALL AND MEDIUM ENTERPRISES, which have characterized all SEA countries (and China) and even in Japan and Korea whose growth performance has been mistakenly attributed solely to large firms.

Arrighi *et al.* (2003), Maddison (2001) and others all put the changes in East Asia in their long-term perspective. Arrighi *et al.* say that what has happened corresponds to the transition from British to American world hegemony. In the former case, in the 19th century, there was some convergence with Western practices in both China and Japan as these countries attempted modernization. Their motives in modernizing were partly to match Western military strength and both suffered humiliation in conflicts, China, for example, in the Opium Wars and Japan, eventually, in WORLD WAR II. In the second case, in the 20th century, a quite different pattern of combining features of both Western and Asian systems has emerged. In this process, the overseas Chinese, driven out by communist China, have played a major role by reinforcing entrepreneurship in SEA and helping, through their commercial and political networks to integrate the region through trade with the West. Arrighi *et al.* do make the point that a weakness in the EA resurgence is that it is heavily dependent upon demand from slow-growing Europe and a deficit-burdened >USA. There are signs, however, that interregional trade and cooperation are growing so that indigenous demand may support continued expansion.

All the writers who take the long view, for example Jones *et al.* (1993), draw attention to the fact that in the 14th century EA was ahead of Europe and indeed was at the forefront of world development until the 18th century. Europe was to overtake the East with its >INDUSTRIAL REVOLUTIONS but now, in the title of Jones *et al.*'s book, is *Coming Full Circle*, with a chance of restoring its former dominance.

### References

Arrighi, Giovanni, Hamashita, Takeshi and Seldon, Mark (eds), *The Resurgence of East Asia: 500, 150 and 50 Year Perspectives*, Routledge, 2003.

Bannock, Graham, *The Economics and Management of Small Business: An International Perspective*, Routledge, 2005.

Dixon, Chris, *South East Asia in the World Economy*, Cambridge University Press, 1991.

Gapinski, James M., *Economic Growth in the Asia Pacific Region*, St Martin's Press, 1991.

Jones, Eric, Frost, Lionel and White, Colin (eds), *Coming Full Circle: An Economic History of the Pacific Rim*, Westview Press, 1993.

Kahn, Haider A., *Interpreting East Asian Growth and Innovation: The Future of Miracles*, Palgrave Macmillan, 2004.

Krugman, Paul, 'The Myth of Asia's Miracle', *Foreign Affairs*, November–December, 1994.

Maddison, Angus, *The World Economy: A Millennial Perspective*, OECD, 2001.

Maddison, Angus, Rao, Prasada and Shepherd, William F., *The Asian Economies in the Twentieth Century*, Edward Elgar, 2002.

World Bank, *The East Asian Miracle: Economic Growth and Public Policy*, Oxford University Press, 1993.

## Automobile Industry

Peter Drucker wrote that, 'The automobile industry stands for modern industry all over the globe. It is to the twentieth century what the Lancashire cotton mills were to the early nineteenth century: the industry of industries' (1946). We use the term 'automobiles' to include trucks and light commercial vehicles as well as passenger cars. The industry has important backward linkages to metals, especially sheet steel, and much else, including synthetic rubber, glass, electrical and electronic and other components. The industry is a large purchaser of capital goods such as machine tools. It used to be said that there were 20,000 parts in a car, certainly more than anyone could conveniently count. Between 50 and 75 per cent of value in a car is bought-in. Practices in terms of vertical integration have varied over time but essentially motor manufacturers are designers, assemblers and marketeers of vehicles. Forward linkages are also important – to dealerships, repair stations, car parks and road building, petroleum products, insurance, vehicle testing and other services. In 1963, in a narrow sense, the motor industry accounted for 8.6 per cent of total manufacturing net output in the USA and 7.6 per cent in Britain (2.4 and 2.7 per cent respectively of total GDP) (Bannock, 1966).

Steam-driven vehicles were the grandfathers of the modern motor vehicle but because of their weight, cost and constant need for water, never achieved a mass market. The first steam-driven road vehicle was that of Joseph Cugnot (1725–1804), a French military engineer who constructed a steam wagon for towing cannon in 1760. Oliver Evans (1755–1819) patented a steam-driven carriage in the state of Maryland in 1787. The power unit which completely displaced >STEAM POWER in motor vehicles was the internal combustion engine, the principles of which were established and patented by a French engineer, Beau de Rochas (1815–1893). The first practical application of these principles was by Jean Étienne Lenoir (1822–1900), first in 1858 using coal gas and then in 1863 using petroleum and spark ignition in an engine fitted to a three-wheeled vehicle. Lenoir drove his vehicle over 50 miles on the road and apparently built it for sale. Claims are also made for the Austrian, Siegfried Markus (1831–1898), who about the same time built two cars but not for sale. Subsequently, Dr Nicolaus A. Otto (1832–1891) built a four-stroke engine of improved design in 1876. His important contribution was to realize that compressing the fuel-air mixture added greatly to the power generated. It was this design that formed the basis for liquid-fuelled engines thereafter. The first four-wheeled vehicle powered by petroleum is credited to Gottlieb Daimler (1834–1900) in 1885 but Karl Benz (1844–1929) was very close with a more advanced car and also was the first to sell one (>OIL). Daimler and Benz, although living only 60 miles apart, apparently worked quite independently at this stage, though later, in 1926, the Daimler and Benz companies amalgamated, the forerunner of Mercedes-Benz today. The Duryea was the first car marketed in the USA (1896), if we do not count steam cars. In Britain, the first was the short-lived Butler and at the same time in 1898, the Starley. The Starley was an electric-powered tricycle but the company eventually metamorphosed into the Rover Company. In France, several four-wheeled cars appeared in the 1880s after Lenoir's pioneering tricycle, including DeDion (1883), Peugeot and Panhard (1889). In Italy the first was FIAT (1899) and Bianchi (1900).

The early history of the motor car is a complex and controversial subject and the explanation of competing claims (where they are accurate, which they appear often not to be) is often that writers have different definitions in mind – 'first' can mean a tricycle or a four-wheeled car, it can mean a car built and run but not marketed. What is clear is that serious production of cars really began after 1900 and boomed from 1901–6, when various other countries entered the lists, including Russia and Hungary. At that time there were over 800 car-making firms operating, a number never exceeded before or since. The leading firms were to consolidate their position in the ensuing years and many of the major firms can trace their origins to the very late 19th or early 20th centuries. Examples are Daimler and Benz (1885), now Daimler-Chrysler (Chrysler was founded in 1923); Peugeot, now PSA Peugeot-Citroën (1889), Citroën being founded in 1919; Renault (1898); FIAT (1899); BMW (1901); Ford (1903); and General Motors (1908). Volkswagen was not founded until 1939 and the Japanese were relatively late entrants (Nissan, 1936; Toyota, 1937; Honda, 1948). The early car builders in the USA, as elsewhere, were assemblers whose production could be financed by the extensive credit supplied by their parts suppliers (Seltzer, 1973). The excess of demand over supply was such that dealers could be obliged to pay 20 per cent of the cost of a car on placing an order. As the producers prospered they could afford to integrate vertically to improve the quality and reliability of supplies. This process was carried to extremes by Henry >FORD who, by 1920, at his River Rouge plant even had blast furnaces for steel and claimed to make everything except tyres.

The early cars were very much playthings of the rich and were generally tailor-made. France led in early production and Britain was a slow starter, partly perhaps because of its population density and transport system but mainly because of restrictive legislation. The provisions of the 1861 'Red Flag Act' (originally directed at steam vehicles), which required vehicles to be preceded by a person on foot bearing a red flag, or at night a red light, to warn of the oncoming danger, was not fully repealed until 1903. Britain was still behind France in terms of vehicles produced in 1929. Between 1929 and 1937 British output doubled, while that of France declined by almost one-fifth. In 1924, France supplied about a quarter of world exports of motor vehicles but by 1937 this had fallen to 5 per cent (PEP, 1950). By 1929 the output of commercial vehicles, which had been boosted by >WORLD WAR II, accounted for about a quarter of total production in both countries. In 1929, North American production was almost nine times greater than that of Europe. By 1936, North America still led but production had fallen sharply in the >GREAT DEPRESSION. Output in France was only half that of Britain and German output had increased to give it second place in Europe after Britain. The picture was one of successive regional challenges and jockeying for position. North America held its leading position but by the mid-1960s was suffering from severe foreign penetration of its domestic market from a resurgent Europe and then, by the 1970s, both European and US makers were being challenged by Japan.

Motor vehicle production, mostly assembly, began in Japan after World War I but did not become significant until the 1930s, when the industry began to be built up behind protective tariffs. Even by 1939, when foreign assembly ceased, vehicle production in Japan amounted to only 41,000 units but it was to mushroom after World War II, especially after the mid-1960s. Servan-Schreiber wrote an influential book (1968) advocating that European industry needed more mergers to achieve bigger units of production and the adoption of US technology and managerial methods. However, it was Japan, with its lean production technique, that was to force changes in car production everywhere, including the USA. Early in the 21st century, South Korea emerged as a new world competitor producing 3.5 million vehicles in 2004. In Australia, Brazil, Malaysia and other places significant producers developed as affiliates of the big established firms. World output of motor vehicles increased from about 6.25 million in 1929 (most of it in the USA) to 64 million in 2004. In the advanced countries, car ownership was approaching saturation, creating problems of congestion and pollution.

In Britain, after World War II, car production had fluctuated about a rising trend, exceeding that of Germany until 1955 and of France until 1970. Italy's output was smaller than Britain's until 1970, though its output also began to falter from the mid-1970s. British production peaked at just over 1.9 million in 1972, while that of France and Germany continued to expand. The British industry did well in the soft markets following World War II but suffered from government restrictions on consumer spending outdated production technology, excessive product proliferation and labour problems (>BRITAIN). It failed to achieve rationalization and economies of scale or coherent leadership in a series of mergers that led to all the significant surviving indigenous firms being swallowed up by the British Leyland Motor

Corporation, later the Rover Group named after one of its distinguished elements (Bannock, 1971). British Aerospace were to acquire this group and later BMW. Ownership changes subsequently led to its dismemberment. Over a period of time Ford took ownership of Jaguar and the Land Rover division, only to resell later; BMW retained the Mini and Rolls Royce; while Volkswagen, which also owned Lamborghini and Audi, acquired Bentley. The rump of the Rover Group, the mass car division, collapsed into bankruptcy in 2005, some of its assets being sold to a Chinese company.

The history of the world automobile industry is one of continuing adaptation to changing technology and market demands. The industry as a whole has experienced long-term market growth and companies that have been able to adapt successfully to change have survived, others like Rover have been absorbed. The main successive phases of the industry from its craft origins have been fivefold. First, there was the emergence of mass-production which began in the USA around 1910 (>FORD). The second phase saw the achievement of the multi-model line and the multi-divisional structure of General Motors in the 1920s and 1930s. Before that the USA had greatly surpassed Europe in vehicle production and it was not until some time after World War II that there was a massive resurgence of European car manufacture in the 1960s to challenge the USA (Phase three), followed by the rise of Japan and 'lean manufacture' in the 1970s (Phase four). The fifth phase was the speeding up of >GLOBALIZATION. This phase might be said to have begun in earnest in the 1960s, though its roots can be traced back to the technology transfers of the early days, for example the

Otto Cycle engine and the establishment by Ford of a factory in Britain in 1911. By the 21st century, the major manufacturers had manufacturing and assembly plants around the world and a latticework of changing cross-border acquisitions, disposals and alliances.

The early history of General Motors is a fascinating story. William Durant (1861–1947) and Alfred P. Sloan (1875–1966) were the key figures in the second of the five phases in the development of the industry, just as Henry Ford was in the first. Durant, a brilliant salesman and financier, made an initial fortune through the acquisition and development of the Flint Cart Company, which had been founded in 1886. By 1900 Flint was the world's largest producer of horse-drawn vehicles. Durant, who foresaw the great future for motor cars, bought the Buick Motor Company in 1903. Exemplifying his eye for opportunity, Buick had not yet made a car at the time but had designed a powerful overhead valve engine (Madsen, 1999). By 1908 Buick produced approaching 9,000 units (Ford were then building 6,200). In that year Durant incorporated General Motors and between 1908 and 1910 brought into it 25 companies, including Buick, Olds (later Oldsmobile), Oakland (later Pontiac) and Cadillac, and some parts companies, for Durant wanted to integrate vertically. The acquisitions were largely by exchange of stock and Durant lost control of the business to a syndicate of investment banks in 1910 in a pattern he was to repeat. With Louis Chevrolet he subsequently formed the Chevrolet Company in 1913. This was another success and enabled him to regain control of the General Motors Company, which he reformed into the General Motors Corporation (GM). In 1917 the Du Pont Company, of which GM was a big customer, acquired 23.8 per cent, increased a year later to give it 26.4 per cent and joint control with Durant. In 1920 Durant lost control of GM due to his speculation in GM stock and a recession.

Alfred Sloan, who was eventually to take over from Durant, came into GM in 1918 with the acquisition of United Motors, another Durant company that owned Hyatt Roller Bearing, of which Sloan was part owner and chief executive. Durant had created the basis in GM of a vertically integrated business and advanced production methods, with models for each price range and thus the opportunity for buyers to graduate upwards while remaining customers of the corporation, concepts that would allow GM to overtake Ford, who for too long stayed with a single car model. His great skills were an ability to pick good creative managers and also to identify in which direction the next technical advances were coming from. However, he relied too much on decentralization without proper controls and was not able to secure the business financially, mainly through over-reach. Sloan separated policy formation and coordination from execution by divisional profit centre managers who were nonetheless involved in policy formation by a series of committees. He introduced strong financial controls and statistical information systems, all of which had been missing in the Durant era. In this he achieved a mid-point between the extreme centralization of Ford and the decentralization of Durant. Sloane did not believe that size was a barrier, it was a soluble management problem. His concept of coordinated policy and decentralized administration in what was later called the M-form of organization was to become standard practice in most large corporations (>CHANDLER).

Just as Sloan was to revolutionize management from the 1920s, the Japanese manufacturers were to carry out another revolution in production technique and organization in the 1970s that was to facilitate their strong incursions into both European and American market shares. In the first era, car production employed skilled workers and simple but flexible tools, in the second era of mass-production, work was de-skilled and standardized products were produced by costly, single-purpose machines. Japanese lean production combined the advantages of craft and mass-production by employing multi-skilled workers and more flexible equipment to allow products of greater variety and more responsible and more satisfying work roles. It is called lean production because it aims to use less of everything, including zero tolerance of defects and minimal inventories of parts and components, the supply of which was closely coordinated with production on the so-called 'just-in-time' basis (Womack, 1990). These techniques had diffused around the world and been combined with a shift away from vertical integration to the greater use of and coordination of suppliers. Also in the globalization phase there has been a shift towards production in low-cost countries but this has not gone as far as might be expected because lean production requires a very advanced industrial environment. It was also expected earlier that by the millennium there would only be a very small number of manufacturers remaining. This too has not happened, although there has been a considerable increase in >CONCENTRATION: there were still three or more indigenous manufacturers in Europe, the USA and Japan and new ones were emerging in Asia in the early 21st century.

Commercial vehicles (CVs) have not been given very much attention by economic historians and in contrast to the enormous literature on passenger cars there is little on trucks and light commercials or, for that matter, agricultural tractors, of which some manufacturers, for example Ford, have been important producers. This is probably because the history of CVs is very similar to that of passenger cars. Most of the once independent truck producers became part of the large motor vehicle groups. Light commercials were mostly directly derived from cars; they used the same base units or platforms, transmissions and other components. Heavy trucks were different and built in much smaller numbers. They had more powerful engines and most retained separate chassis frames. It was common for independent body-builders to adapt truck chassis for fire trucks, recovery vehicles and other specialized vehicles. An important innovation in heavy truck design was the 'fifth wheel coupling' (>ROAD TRANSPORT), which allowed the separation of tractor units from trailers and a more efficient use of equipment.

More generally, from the outset, car and CV design evolved considerably, if incrementally, mostly using technology first developed outside the industry. In 1892 Rudolph Diesel (1858–1913), a German born in France, patented the principles of the engine that bears his name. At first, diffusion of the diesel engine, which uses perhaps 20–30 per cent less fuel than the petrol unit and develops more torque (pulling power) at low engine revolutions, was slow. This was because of its more robust construction and greater weight and cost and also its greater noise and

atmospheric pollution. Subsequent development of 'clean' and quieter diesels led to increased sales and as the early 21st century progressed now powered about half of all new cars produced for Europe and virtually all trucks, though in the USA their use was vastly lower. Successive improvements in petrol engines were also remarkable. For example, improvements in fuel quality allowed increases in compression ratios yielding more power and relatively better fuel economy. Higher octane ratings were necessary for higher compression and these ratings increased by over 50 per cent as compared to 1930. There were attempts to develop alternatives to conventional reciprocating engines but they came to little. It looked as if the rotary valve Wankel engine, invented in the 1930s, would do the trick. Although the Wankel engine had great advantages, its weakness was high fuel consumption and the oil price hikes virtually finished it off. Other important innovations included automatic transmissions, which first came in in the 1930s, and integral construction. In monocoque construction a separate chassis frame was dispensed with and it become universal for cars from the 1960s, as well as for light commercials and some public service vehicles. There have also been major improvements in braking and suspension systems and in equipment such as the standardization of radios, power steering and, increasingly, air conditioning.

Since the 1960s, there were major improvements in vehicle safety brought about in the USA by Federal crash test standards and mandatory fitment of seat belts and airbags. Ralph Nader wrote an influential book in the 1950s entitled *Unsafe at Any Speed*, mainly about the GM Corvair, which helped to bring about legislative changes. These were subsequently emulated in

Europe (though some European manufacturers focused on safety standards well before the legislation). Similar developments took place with fuel economy and air quality. European fuel economy standards had always been much better than in the USA because cars were smaller, incomes lower and fuel taxes higher. In both Europe and the USA, catalytic converters were required to reduce emissions. Legislative activity in the USA began with the Clean Air Act of 1963. Serious concerns about car-related pollution arose first in California, with its famous Los Angeles smog, but became universal following the oil price rises and increasing efforts to curb global warming. Electric power for cars had been experimented with since the early days of the industry but outside specialist applications, such as milk floats and fork-lift trucks for use in factories, electric cars were held back by the weight and size of the necessary batteries. Hybrid-powered cars, which incorporate electric motors for low-speed running and conventional petroleum engines, also appeared.

### References

Altshuler, Alan (ed.), 'The Future of the Automobile, George Allen & Unwin, 1984.

Bannock, Graham, 'The Motor Industry's Contribution to the Gross Domestic Product in the UK and the USA', Economic Studies, September, 1966.

Bannock, Graham, The Juggernauts: The Age of the Big Corporation, Weidenfeld & Nicolson, 1971.

Drucker, Peter, The Concept of the Corporation, John Day, 1946.

Foreman-Peck, James, Bowden, Sue and McKinlay, Alan, 'The British Motor Industry" Manchester University Press, 1995.

Lewchuk, Wayne, American Technology and the British Vehicle Industry, Cambridge University Press, 1987.

Madsen, Axel, The Deal Maker: How William C. Durant Made General Motors, John Wiley & Son, 1999.

Political and Economic Planning, Motor Vehicles, PEP, 1950.

Rubenstein, James M., Making and Selling Cars: Innovation and Change in the Motor Industry, Johns Hopkins University Press, 2001.

Seltzer, Lawrence H., A Financial History of the American Automobile Industry, Houghton Mifflin, 1928, reprint by Augustus M. Kelley, 1973.

Servan-Schreiber, J. J., The American Challenge, Hamish Hamilton, 1968.

Sloan, Alfred P. Jr, My Years with General Motors, Doubleday & Co., 1963.

Womack, James, Jones, Daniel T. and Roos, Daniel, The Machine that Changed the World, Macmillan, 1990.

## Aviation

The aviation industry includes airlines, airports, airframe and engine production and associated activities, including missiles and guided weapons and satellite launchers (aerospace). Before heavier-than-air aircraft there were balloons and airships but, like automobiles, aviation did not get properly underway until the early 1900s. In fact, the aviation industry shares a number of features with automobile production and usage; it was initiated largely in Europe, which led in both civil and military production until the 1920s, but European producers then fell behind those in the USA (>AUTOMOBILE INDUSTRY). Though of lesser economic importance than automobiles, aircraft production is more complex but also essentially an assembly industry. Again, like automobiles, aviation has experienced a long-term expansionary trend but its very success has drawn criticism for the noise and atmospheric pollution which it creates. Here the resemblances with automobiles end because aircraft are not affordable by ordinary consumers and are therefore produced by a 'wholesale industry', one which is very dependent upon the military and strategic imperatives of government and subject to quite violent cycles in demand.

The first sustained powered flight was that of the Wright Brothers in the >USA in December 1903. A French firm, Voisin, claimed to have preceded them and was the first, in 1907, to manufacture aircraft in series production. France pioneered the use of aluminium in aircraft engines (Hispano-Suiza) (Emmanuel Chadeau's article is reproduced in Crouzet, 1993). France mounted a scheduled international airline (the Franco Roumanie, 1920–5) (see Alexandre Herlea's contribution to Trimble, 1995). Many aircraft manufacturers started up in Europe and the USA after 1908 but production of aircraft in Britain, France and Germany was much greater than in the USA before and during >WORLD WAR I. During that war, >BRITAIN's output of aircraft rose from about ten a month in 1914 to 2,700 a month in 1918. Britain had fewer military aircraft than France in 1912 but aircraft at that time were used mainly for reconnaissance and the requirement for them depended upon the size of the armies employed, which for Britain, relying mainly on its supremely powerful navy, was relatively small (Edgerton, 1991). The USA was unprepared for the war at the outset but soon expanded production capacity. The rapid shrinkage of aircraft output after the war, from 14,000 units in 1918 to only 780 the following year, in the USA was the first of the many violent fluctuations to be experienced in aviation output. Having recognized the

strategic importance of air power, governments took steps to maintain at least design capacity. Under the Versailles Treaty of 1919, Germany was not permitted to build military aircraft, though its industry maintained design offices outside the country.

F. Robert Van der Linden's chapter in Trimble (1995) argues that, in the USA, the Federal government's policy played a leading role in the creation of the air transport and production industries. After 1918, the US Post Office managed its own air-mail system but the Contract Air Mail Act (Kelly Act) in 1925 transferred this activity to private operators from 1927. The Air Commerce Act, 1926, gave the Department of Commerce authority to license pilots and to organize air navigation and regulate airlines. Investment in aviation boomed and the 1929 and 1930 Watres Bills changed the basis of the air-mail subsidies so as to encourage passenger traffic. It was in this period that the United, Eastern, American and TWA companies consolidated their oligopoly. Concern about corruption and the fact that the Post Office contracts had not been awarded on the basis of competitive tenders led to the termination of the system in 1934. The Army Air Corps were then ordered to take on the job, but it was ill-prepared and this solution was terminated after a few months. Competitive tendering was reinstated (though the same oligopolists again won most of the contracts). At the same time, airframe producers were no longer allowed to hold shares in airlines.

The first non-stop flight coast to coast in the USA was made in 1923, but Charles Lindbergh's solo flight across the Atlantic in May 1927 was the one that stimulated a stock market boom in aviation activities. US aircraft production rose to 2,552 in 1931 and reached 3,859 by 1937. An altitude record of 35,000 feet was achieved by a US-designed aircraft in 1921. US Navy flying boats carried out a stopping flight across the Atlantic in May 1919 and, in June of that year, Alcock and Brown completed a non-stop flight in a British Vickers-Vimy. Howard Hughes' Hi-Racer raised the world speed record to 352 mph in 1935 and in 1938 he completed a round-the-world flight in a Lockheed airliner in less than four days. This was a period of great international technical progress, for example: the adoption of duralumin (a copper-aluminium alloy) for all-metal stressed-skin construction (pioneered in Germany between 1914 and 1929); enclosed cockpits and pressurization (developed by the US Army Air Corps); slotted wings and flaps (1919–24); and variable pitch propellers (1923–39). French and German helicopters flew in the mid-1930s, though it was not until 1940 that Igor Sikorsky in the USA developed a helicopter that was of practical use. In Britain, Whittle patented his ideas for the >JET ENGINE in 1932 and the first report on radio detection and ranging, later known as 'radar', which was to play an important role in World War II, was published. The USA copied the European innovation of tri-motors, which allowed planes to continue to fly if one engine failed. The Ford Trimotor, the first airliner to be built in the USA and of all-metal construction, was introduced in 1926. The Boeing 247 in service in 1933 demonstrated that a twin-engined design could be more efficient than a tri-motor. The Douglas DC3, introduced in 1936, had operating costs half of those of the Ford Trimotor and set the standard for pre-war airliners. The DC3 continued in use throughout World War II and after.

The 1930s saw great interest in flying boats, these could have roomy designs, did not need airports, were sea-worthy if forced down over water and could fly across oceans in stages. Pan American ran scheduled 'Clipper' services across the Pacific. Flying boats were used in World War II but their use for passenger traffic was truncated by the emergence of long-range four-engined airliners in the 1940s and later by jet airliners, which were much more economical. The flying boat era, like that of the air dirigibles which preceded them, proved to be a dead-end, though flying in them was a golden age for air passengers.

Like the airlines, all the giant US aircraft companies were founded before World War II. Glenn Martin, for example, founded his first factory in 1912 and his career continued into the jet age. William Boeing started what was to become the Boeing Airplane Company in 1916. The National Advisory Committee for Aeronautics (NACA) was formed in 1915 to direct and actually conduct research. At this time European manufacturers were well ahead of the US industry, especially in military aircraft. No US-designed aircraft were employed in World War I and in 1918 the British de Havilland DH4 was built under license in the USA. By 1918, there were 31 aircraft manufacturers in the USA and by the 1930s, the USA led the world in commercial aircraft design and operation, being favoured by the long distances between its centres of population (Pattillo, 1998). During World War II, production by the US aircraft industry expanded from 3,623 units in 1938 to 26,289 in 1941 (74 per cent military) and 95,272 in 1944 (100 per cent for the military). Before the war, aviation was only 41st among US industries and but rose to first place in 1944 and employed over 2 million people.

In 1956, the ultimate piston-engined intercontinental airliners were introduced in the USA (the Douglas DC-7C and the Lockheed Starliner). The initial success of the British Comet, however, suggested that the future lay with jet engines and there was a need for larger aircraft. Boeing started development of wide-bodied jet aircraft in 1952 with an authorized cost of $16 billion, a considerable risk for the company. The 707 Jumbo Jet launched in 1958 and its successor the 747 in 1966 were brilliantly successful and made Boeing the world leader in large airliners at least until the emergence of the European Airbus in the 1980s.

In the late 1950s, the numbers of civil aircraft produced in the USA exceeded that of military aircraft and this was to continue even after the early 1980s when total output fell from almost 20,000 units in 1978 to under 4,000 in the mid-1980s. At that time the industry reached a new low point as both military needs, the space programme and airliner orders all declined at the same time as international competition was intensifying. By the late 1970s, two-thirds of the world airliner market was outside the USA. Nevertheless, total US aerospace sales in 1987 were $112 billion, of which missiles, space and related products accounted for $52 billion. Aerospace was still one of the country's leading industries (Pattillo, 1998).

Two major developments affecting aviation in the 1980s were the deregulation of US airlines in 1978 and the emergence of the European Airbus Industrie. From the early days until towards the end of the 20th century, the international airline industry had been cartelized and highly regulated. The International

Air Transport Association (IATA), a trade association for airlines, was founded in 1945 but was preceded by the International Air Traffic Association, which dated from 1919 when the first European air routes were established. What emerged was a system in which national control of airspace was recognized so that governments could control air services in and out of their territories. This system was much strengthened at the Chicago Convention in 1944 and there were also many bilateral agreements, which covered fares and capacity, for example, the Anglo-US Bermuda Agreement in 1946. The International Civil Aviation Organization (ICAO), an agency of the United Nations, set standards for ticketing, air navigation, accident investigation and codes for airlines and airports. In the USA, the Air Commerce Act 1926 had established Federal authority for the certification of airworthiness and the licensing of pilots. A bureau of Aeronautics in the Department of Commerce became the Civil Aviation Board (CAB), which regulated fares and routes. There were similar organizations in other countries. In Europe, most countries wanted to protect their national airlines and deregulation had different outcomes in Europe compared with the USA. Europe had twice the amount of air route mileage and there were too many unprofitable airlines. In the USA, by contrast, domestic airline capacity was kept down by regulation; there were applications for far more routes than were granted (Wheatcroft, 1956).

From 1978, under the US Airline Deregulation Act, airlines were free to choose their own routes and to set fares and in 1985 the CAB was abolished. Between 1975 and 2000, the number of domestic airline passengers grew by 225 per cent and ticket prices fell by 40 per cent. Some airlines shut down or were acquired but there was little or no increase in >CONCENTRATION because economies of scale in airline operation are limited. Deregulation was slower to come in Europe but the results were similar. Some airlines closed or had been acquired but many new low-cost airlines started and thrived. Opponents of deregulation argued that it would adversely affect safety but there has been no evidence of this. Thomas Gale, in his contribution to Moses and Salvage (1989), showed that over the periods 1971–8 and 1979–86 , the total scheduled airline accident rate in the USA halved. After 1960, global air passenger traffic grew at 9 per cent per annum, air freight at 11 per cent and mail at 7 per cent, according to estimates by Boeing. By the end of the 20th century, air transport was a big global industry, carrying 1.6 billion passengers a year and employing 3.9 million people with 1,800 aircraft and 10,000 airports.

Although only about one-third of the size of the US aviation industry, the industry in Western Europe employed, by the late 1980s, 450,000 people and exported €25 billion of goods and services (see Roger Beteille's contribution to Leary, 1995). Airbus Industrie (AI) became a credible competitor for Boeing. The collaborative European Airbus programme was initially a private sector initiative prompted by Air France, British European Airways and Deutsche Lufthansa airlines working with Sud Aviation, de Havilland and a consortium of German manufacturers. The three governments agreed to back the project in 1967. A year later the British withdrew because the British Aircraft Corporation (BAC) wanted to develop its own aircraft and Rolls Royce wanted to give precedence to the design of a high-bypass jet engine for the Lockheed L-1011 airliner. France and Germany went ahead with Hawker Siddeley Aviation (HSA), which entered the project at its own risk as a sub-contractor for a medium-haul 250-seat Airbus. Later, with a decision to build a larger aircraft, the British Government decided to support the project again and HSA became a full partner. By the end of the 1980s, Airbus Industrie had captured half of the world market and was in head-to-head competition with Boeing and McDonnell Douglas, Lockheed having exited the long-haul market in 1981. The Americans argued that competition from Airbus was subsidized by the European governments but AI countered this with the argument that Boeing's large aircraft had been subsidized by the military work for a large transport and also by the Ex-Im Bank, which financed foreign purchases of US aircraft.

The feasibility of intra-European cooperation was also demonstrated by the technical (if not commercial) success of the Anglo-French Concorde on which work began with studies by BAC and Sud Aviation in 1960. The Concorde, which flew at over twice the speed of sound (Mach 2.2) entered service in 1976 but cost escalation and rising fuel costs following the >OIL price hikes by OPEC, as well as resistance to over-flight in national air spaces on environmental grounds, prevented commercial viability and only 16 were built. There were also intra-European collaborative agreements for helicopters and for an attack aircraft which eventually became the Eurofighter (Tornado).

The British aviation industry was marked by prodigious feats of innovation but mixed commercial success and enormous, often ill-advised government interference. Miller and Sawers (1968) argued that the eventual (though not permanent) triumph of the USA over the European industry owed much to the pre-World War II existence of a competitive domestic market for commercial airliners, a market which was bigger than the military one at the time. The European market was dominated by military requirements and, in the absence of a large integrated civil market, equally dominated by governments.

Many of the subsequently famous British aircraft manufacturers started by individuals originated in the period 1908–14, for example Handley-Page (1908), Blackburn (1910), A. V. Roe (1910) and Sopwith (1911), later to become Hawker. Armament manufacturers, such as Vickers, also started designing and producing aircraft and two shipbuilders, later to become famous for flying boats, entered the industry during the same period. Military initiatives in aviation were taken well before World War I with the Balloon Factory (which was to become the Royal Aircraft Establishment). The Royal Flying Corps, which had Army and Navy wings, was founded in 1912 and merged with the Royal Naval Air Service in 1914. The Royal Air Force (RAF) emerged in 1917. Although aircraft played only a minor part in World War I, the experience convinced the military of its importance. British employment in airframe and engine manufacture rose from 49,000 in October 1916 to 268,000 in October 1918, much of it in motor car firms (Edgerton, 1991). Equivalent employment in the French industry was 180,000 at the end of World War I. In the ensuing contraction many aviation companies disappeared but it was government policy to maintain some capacity.

No major firms in Britain exited the industry between the mid-1920s and 1950. The same thing happened after World War II. Employment in the British industry grew from 13,000 in 1924 to 75,000 in 1936 and 750,000 in 1940, it then dropped to 180,000 in 1950. In both periods, government intervention was counterproductive. Policies to maintain design teams by spreading military procurement muted competition and discouraged the more efficient from investing in large-scale facilities (Hayward, 1989). A major factor in inhibiting competitive civil aircraft designs were the specialized requirements of the national airlines, which were not the same as those of world markets. This was an issue both pre-war (Imperial Airways intended to maintain communications with the British Empire) and post-war (BOAC from 1939 and BEA (1946)). Significantly, there was less government interference in engine design and production and Rolls Royce was to emerge an important producer. Rolls Royce designed the engines which were to win the 1931 Schneider Trophy Races and these units were the foundation for the brilliantly successful Merlin engines which powered the World War II Spitfire fighters.

As in the USA, the British government pressed for the substitution of metal for wood in airframes earlier pioneered in France and Germany, a policy which in one instance was happily ignored by de Havilland who were to build the all-wood Mosquito, one of the fastest and most successful military aircraft of World War II. Schatzberg (1999) demonstrates that the substitution of metal for wood in this period owed more to the association of metal with science and progress and a shift in research expenditure than to objective arguments about cost, strength and weight.

The Korean War (1950–3) gave a major boost to the British aviation industry and by 1956 employment had risen by 120,000 over 1950 levels. Six firms accounted for over 80 per cent of output but the industry continued to fall further behind that of the USA, which accounted for 80 per cent of world production by value (Hayward, 1989). Government purchasing policy led to the amalgamation of the industry into three main airframe firms (Hawker Siddeley Aviation (HSA), which had acquired de Havilland in 1960; Westland; and the British Aircraft Corporation, which included Vickers Armstrong, English Electric and others). There were two main engine manufacturers, Bristol-Siddeley and Rolls Royce. The introduction of the DH Comet jet airliner in 1952 had been a major breakthrough and presented an opportunity to surpass the Americans in this field. In-flight structural failures of the Comet tragically delayed development but the Comet 4 inaugurated scheduled trans-Atlantic jet airliner flights in 1958, three weeks before the much more successful Boeing 707. Only 112 Comets were built. The failure of the Comet effectively broke de Havilland. The VC10, another large British jet, was a successful aircraft but could not compete commercially with the Boeing 707 and Douglas DC8.

After World War II only the Vickers Viscount (a turbo-prop medium-haul airliner, of which 440 were built) was really successful. There were to be successes with military aircraft, notably the V-Bombers, the Lightning and the VTOL aircraft, but there were also failures here too. The cancellation in 1966 of the technically very successful multi-role supersonic TSR2 warplane was a major trauma for the British industry. The government cancelled the programme after £750 million had been spent in order to buy American F111s, which were cheaper. A second trauma came in 1971 with the bankruptcy and subsequent nationalization of Rolls Royce. The company was dragged down by the escalating cost of development of two engines: the RB211 for Lockheed and the RB207 for Airbus Industrie. At the same time Lockheed had to be rescued by the USA government. The British Government forced amalgamation of BAC and HSA into one nationalized entity BAe. The government denationalized BAe in 1979 and Rolls Royce was floated in 1981. By the early 21st century, BAe was a prosperous and well-diversified defence and aerospace manufacturer. It had disposed of the Rover Group (>AUTOMOBILE INDUSTRY) and felt strong enough to dispose of its stake in Airbus Industrie, which it had inherited through HSA and which was going through a bad patch with delayed development of its jumbo A380 twin-deck airliner.

Germany was prevented from rebuilding its aviation industry after World War II, although it has in part subsequently done so with collaborative pan-European projects, including Airbus. In the inter-war period German manufacturers led in various aspects of aviation. In 1942, Germany had 10,000 scientists working on aircraft and missile design and after the war it became known how advanced they were. Their findings and some of their personnel made a substantial contribution to USA and, to a lesser extent, British and probably also Russian aviation and the space programme. Japan was also excluded from aircraft production after the war, a prohibition which was not lifted until 1952. Japan was, however, able to develop airlines: JAL became a semi-government corporation in 1953 and the domestic airlines which had previously been operated by US carriers also emerged independently in the 1950s (Yamamoto, 1993).

France had an early lead in several aspects of aviation but fell back in the inter-war period. Six French companies were nationalized in 1936 and re-formed after the war into Sud and Nord Aviation. The private sector included Dassault and Breguet, which merged in 1971. The 1945–55 period saw a resurgence in the French industry, both in civil and military aircraft. The Caravelle, the first medium-haul jet airliner, was a brilliant success and 278 were built, though this success was not followed through. The Caravelle was somewhat more successful than similar British aircraft, the BAC 111 and the Trident, of which 230 and 117 respectively were produced. None of these European aircraft could compete with the DC 9 and the Boeing 727 and, by the end of the 1960s, European manufacturers had been virtually eliminated from the civil aircraft market until the emergence of Airbus Industrie. France, however, had some success in exporting military aircraft, for example, the supersonic Dassault Mirage.

## References

Crouzet, François (ed.), *The Economic Development of France Since 1870*, II, Manchester University Press, 1993.

Edgerton, David, *England and the Aeroplane*, Macmillan, 1991.

Hayward, Keith, *The British Aircraft Industry*, Manchester University Press, 1989.

Leary, William M., *From Airships to Airbus: The History of Civil and Commercial Aviation*, I, Smithsonian Institution Press, 1995.

Miller, Ronald and Sawers, David, *The Technical Development of Modern Aviation*, Routledge and Kegan Paul, 1968.

Moses, Leon N. and Savage, Ian (eds), *Transportation Safety in an Age of Deregulation*, Oxford University Press, 1989.

Pattillo, Donald M. *Pushing the Envelope: The American Aircraft Industry*, University of Michigan Press, 1998.

Schatzberg, Eric, *Wings of Wood, Wings of Metal*, Princeton University Press, 1999.

Trimble, William F. *From Airships to Airbus: The History of Civil and Commercial Aviation*, II, Smithsonian Institution Press, 1995.

Wheatcroft, Stephen, *The Economics of European Air Transport*, Manchester University Press, 1956.

Yamamoto, Hirofumi (ed.), *Technological Innovation and the Development of Transportation in Japan*, United Nations University Press, 1993.

# B

## Beer

Beer is made by fermenting malted cereal and was originally called ale, but hops were later added for preservation and flavour. Malt, the basic ingredient of beer, is made by partly germinating barley or other cereal grains, such as wheat or oats, and then halting the process by drying and kilning to produce grist, which is crushed and added to water. Making malt is to some extent a separate industry from brewing (Clark, 1998). Yeast promotes fermentation but became available in pure form only with advances in biochemistry by Louis Pasteur and others in the late 19th century. There are many kinds of beer, including bitter, which is brewed with more hops and less malt than mild, and lager, a light beer brewed over a longer period at low temperatures, while stout is a dark ale produced with roasted malt. The development of refrigeration in the 19th century facilitated the production of lager. Beers may be top-, as in traditional British beer, or bottom-fermented as in German lager. Traditionally beer was delivered in wooden casks or barrels but after World War II stainless steel or aluminium casks were developed (keg beer). Bottled beer also began to be produced in the 19th century.

Beer was produced in Egypt at least from 3000 BC, as well as in Mesopotamia somewhat later, and introduced to Britain by the Romans. In the USA, the first Virginian colonists brewed beer as early as 1587 and the first commercial brewery there was established in New Amsterdam (Manhattan) in 1612. The commercial use of hops was pioneered in Germany in the 13th century and adopted in Britain in the 15th century. In Bavaria, in 1516, the Beer Purity Law (*reinheitsgebot*) allowed the use of only pure malted barley, hops and water for brewing deep-fermented beer (yeast was permitted much later). The law survived until it was ruled a constraint on trade by the European Court of Justice of the European Union in 1987 (>WESTERN EUROPE).

The economic history of beer is essentially a story of increasing >CONCENTRATION of the ownership of production. For centuries beer was produced on a small scale at home, although beer was also produced on a larger scale in monasteries. Considerable quantities were drunk, perhaps as much as several hundred gallons per head a year. Beer was a major element in the medieval diet. Gregory King reckoned in 1695 that beer accounted for 28 per cent of English consumption. With the growth of urbanization, commercial brewers emerged and there were some 200 'common brewers' by 1700. The majority of inns and ale houses brewed their own beer. In 1700 half of all beer output in England was privately brewed and in 1850 it was still 20 per cent (Richmond and Turton, 1990). In 16th-century England there was one ale house for every 150 people. Beer consumption per head fell with the increased availability of spirits and the growing popularity of tea. Breweries got larger as the population grew and larger-scale production became technically as well as economically practicable. The number of commercial licensed breweries fell from 44,000 in 1850 to 5–6,000 in 1903. By the late 1960s this number had fallen further to less than 200.

In Britain, beer output in 1857 was some 18 million barrels (a barrel is 163.7 litres or 36 imperial gallons). Output rose to 31 million barrels by 1875, declined in the 1880s, rose again to exceed 1875 levels by 1914 and then fluctuated at a lower level throughout the 1920s. Per capita consumption and output fell sharply in the 1930s. It looked as if brewing had become a mature industry, but in the 1950s beer consumption and output started rising again. By 1974 it had reached 38 million barrels, only to decline again to about 34 million barrels in 2000. Although beer output showed little long-term growth after the 1870s, there were quite dramatic changes in the structure of the industry and in its range of products. In the 1880s the larger British brewers made use of the developing >CAPITAL MARKETS to raise capital, partly to acquire retail on-licence premises (pubs) for which licensing was quite restrictive. The number of London-quoted brewery companies rose from 17 in 1885 to 316 in 1905. The ownership of tied houses, though far from unique, was to prove to be a distinguishing characteristic of the British beer industry. With some liberalization of licensing laws from 1961, the number of tied houses, which in 1970 accounted for three-quarters of the total number of full on-licences, fell to about one-third by the 1990s, only to decline still further as the result of the forced divestment by the competition authorities in 1989.

Before World War II, the British brewing industry was, though concentrating gradually, still very fragmented and to a large extent regionalized (national companies accounted for only 25 per cent of beer output in the 1940s). Most firms were dominated by family interests, individually unprofitable pubs were kept open for social reasons and tenants of tied houses were left in place, even as they aged past their best (Hawkins and Pass, 1979). Few firms at this time had interests outside brewing and retailing and the industry seemed to be in long-term decline. The revival of beer consumption in the 1950s, together with technical changes, led to a transformation of the industry. There was a merger boom in 1959–62 and the national brewers greatly strengthened their position. They moved increasingly into the off-licence (take-home) trade and into wine and spirits. The development of keg beers, which travelled well and kept fresh for longer, led to some standardization of product. These beers increased their share of the market from 1 per cent to 17 per cent between 1959 and 1970. National beer advertising increased. As in the USA, technical change enhanced production economies of scale. These changes led to some resistance from a minority of consumers and in 1971 the Campaign for Real Ale (CAMRA) was established to promote local diversity and traditional draught beers. The campaign boosted the business of regional brewers but did not arrest the process of concentration. The share of the five largest enterprises in the industry's net output had increased from 18 per cent in 1954 to 23 per cent in 1958, 42 per cent in 1963 and 64 per cent in 1968. By 1993 just three enterprises accounted for 56 per cent of UK beer consumption.

The USA at first produced products very similar to Britain, but in the middle of the 19th century German immigrants introduced lighter lager beers, which proved more popular. Even in recent times American beer brands, for example Anheuser-Busch, including Budweiser, Coors, Miller, Pabst and Schlitz, have obvious German origins. The inter-war history of brewing in the USA was dominated by Prohibition. In the period from 1880, some states passed laws prohibiting the sale of alcohol. In 1914, the Webb-Kenyon Act prohibited the shipment of alcoholic drinks to those states which banned its sale and in 1919 the 18th Amendment of the Constitution forbade the production, transport and sales (but not the possession) of alcoholic drinks throughout the USA. Prohibition came into effect in January 1920. It was a failure which undermined respect for the law, created profitable opportunities for smuggling and racketeering and was to a large extent circumvented by making drinks at home, buying on the black market and visiting 'speakeasies'. Nonetheless, it seriously affected the brewing industry. Almost 1,600 firms in beer making were put out of business. Some firms, including large ones, survived by shifting to soft drinks and producing 'near beer' of less than the 0.5 per cent alcohol which was allowed. Beer production, which had risen from 1.8 million barrels (of 31 US gallons) in 1863 to 50.3 million in 1918 fell to 2.8 millions in 1932 (Tremblay and Tremblay, 2005).

The >GREAT DEPRESSION was a further blow to the industry but, with the repeal of Prohibition in 1933, beer output recovered. In the 1950s output growth slackened but resumed again to reach over 200 million barrels by the 1990s, after which growth slowed again. From the late 1950s it was the larger brewers which made the running. From 1960–9 the share of the four largest producers rose from 27 per cent to over 41 per cent and from 1970–89 to 86.5 per cent. By 1999, the four-firm concentration ratio in brewing was over 95 per cent. Technical change favoured concentration, though by no means fully accounted for it. A brewer with a market share of 9.9 per cent could achieve the minimum efficient scale of production (>CONCENTRATION; Tremblay and Tremblay, 2005). One producer, Anheuser-Busch, had a share of 54 per cent in 2000. Canning lines and larger brewing vessels, as well as the mechanization of other operations, helped to achieve economies. The speed of canning lines increased more than sixfold between 1952 and 2003. Other economies were found in multi-plant operation and in transport. The large national brewers also enjoyed advantages in marketing, especially with the advent of television. The rise of concentration in the USA certainly appeared to have been accompanied by higher productivity. According to Stephen Broadberry's contribution to Floud and Johnson (2004), output per person engaged in US brewing (compared with Britain = 100) was 146 in 1907, 201 in 1935, 300 in 1950 and 294 in 1968. Part of the reason for the inferior performance of Britain, apart from the smaller size of the market, must have been its more complex product offering. In fact, high concentration was general in brewing. In 1993 the three-firm concentration ratio was higher in many countries than in the USA; it was 100 per cent in New Zealand and Belgium, 92 per cent in Japan and 86 per cent in France. Britain had a relatively low three-firm concentration ratio of 56 per cent.

Beer consumption per head varied considerably between countries. In a list from *World Drink Trends*

*2003*, the Czech Republic, followed by Ireland, came top with totals of 41.8 and 39.8 gallons per capita per annum respectively. Germany came next with 32.5 gallons; Britain with 25.7 gallons came in eighth position and the USA at 11th position with 22.0 gallons (Tremblay and Tremblay, 2005). In spite of the high cost of transporting beer and the need for beer to be kept fresh, there was a degree of international trading. In the European Union, 13 per cent of beer production was exported in 2000. Ireland exported almost 25 per cent of its beer production thanks to the success of its dark beer, Guinness. Mexico, the Netherlands, Canada, Germany and Britain were also significant exporters. For the USA, exports were only 0.8 per cent, with imports much higher. Foreign direct investments in beer plant and licensing agreements between brewers to allow foreign brands to be brewed locally were solutions to the low value per unit of weight problem, though it was often difficult to achieve the same taste.

The brewing industry was the subject of considerable public policy intervention everywhere from quite early on in the interests of public health and order, >ANTI-TRUST and tax revenue. Being relatively price-inelastic, beer taxation was an important source of revenue to governments in the beer-drinking countries. Policies have varied and illegal importing from low-tax to high-tax countries was an issue. In Britain, which is a relatively high-tax country for alcoholic drinks in the European Union, the impact of excise duty, which was related to alcohol content, was magnified by Value-Added Tax (VAT) (>TAXATION) which was levied on the duty-paid price. For 1993, it was calculated that excise duty and VAT accounted for almost 32 per cent of the pub price of beer.

Regulation has a long history in the brewing and retailing of beer and other alcoholic drinks, for example, statutory licensing of ale houses was introduced in England in 1552. Concerns about health, road safety and under-age drinking have in most countries led to restrictions on opening hours, drinking and driving, the sale of alcoholic drinks to minors and other measures. In some countries the sale of alcohol has been a public monopoly. In the USA, the Alcoholic Beverage Labelling Act 1988 required warning of the health risks to appear on all packaging of drinks. High taxation was also justified on health grounds. Since there is ample evidence that moderate drinking is beneficial to health, taxes are at best a blunt instrument for controlling alcohol abuse and promoting health.

Evaluations of the impact of US anti-trust policy have been mixed. The US government dealt appropriately with price-fixing, predatory pricing and exclusive dealing contracts. However, preventing almost all mergers involving larger brewers has been misguided because it has constrained second-tier firms from growing by merger and led to their demise (Tremblay and Tremblay, 2005). Competition policy in Britain has been even more misguided. There were many investigations of beer prices in the 1960s and 1970s by the National Board for Prices and Incomes and its successor, the Price Commission. More importantly, there were major investigations by the Monopoly and Mergers Commission (M&MC) in 1969 and in 1988. Two of the continuous causes of concern have been the ownership by brewers of managed and tenanted pubs and the tendency for beer prices in pubs to increase faster than the general consumer price index and faster than the take-home price of beer. The first should not have been of concern because in the growing independent free trade beer prices were little different, allowing for differences in amenity, between brewer-owned and independent outlets. Differences in the facilities and comfort of pubs were a major element in competition between pub owners and partly the cause of the unique character of the British pub. The tendency for pub prices to rise faster than take-home prices or the price level in general was an international phenomenon and resulted from the Baumol effect (>SERVICE SECTOR); labour costs of the service element in pub prices rise faster than the manufactured cost of beer itself. Action by the M&MC to modify the tied-house system has been counterproductive. The 1989 Beer Orders forced brewers to divest estates in excess of 2,000 pubs and imposed other new regulations on the industry. The result was that ownership of pubs by the brewers was replaced by large independent pub companies, while the measures led to further concentration in brewing and higher beer prices caused, among other things, by the disruption of distribution arrangements (Slade, 1998). The Beer Orders were not revoked in their entirety until 2002. At the same time, a progressive system of beer duty was imposed favouring small brewers, similar to long-established systems in Continental Europe.

### References

Clark, Christine, *The British Malting Industry Since 1830*, Hambledon Press, 1998.

Floud, Roderick and Johnson, Paul, *The Cambridge Economic History of Modern Britain*, III, *Structural Change and Growth 1939–2000*, Cambridge University Press, 2004.

Gourvish T. R. and Wilson, R. G., *The British Brewing Industry, 1830–1980*, Cambridge University Press, 1994.

Hawkins, K. H. and Pass, C. L., *The Brewing Industry: A Study in Industry Organisation and Public Policy*, Heineman, 1979.

Mathias, Peter, *The Brewing Industry in England, 1700–1830*, Cambridge University Press, 1959.

Richmond, Lesley and Turton, Alison (eds), *The Brewing Industry: A Guide to Historical Records*, Manchester University Press, 1990.

Slade, Margaret, 'Beer and the Tie: Did Divestiture of Brewer-Owned Public Houses Lead to Higher Beer Prices?', *Economic Journal*, May, 1998.

Tremblay, Carol Horton and Tremblay, Victor J., *The US Brewing Industry: Data and Economic Analysis*, MIT Press, 2005.

## Beveridge, William Henry (Lord Beveridge)

William Beveridge, who lived from 1879 to 1963, joined the British Board of Trade as a civil servant in 1910, becoming Permanent Secretary there in 1918, and played an important part in the establishment of Labour Exchanges in >BRITAIN. In 1919, Beveridge was appointed Director of the London School of Economics, a post he held until 1937. In 1928, Beveridge and Edwin F. Gay, Professor of Economic History at Harvard University, launched a project to compile time series of prices and wages (>PRICES AND INFLATION). In 1909 he had published the first edition of *Unemployment: A Problem of Industry*; he wrote a second edition in 1930. At the request of the government, he chaired an inter-departmental committee whose report, *Social Insurance and Allied Services*, appeared in 1942. This Beveridge Report, as it became known, formed the foundation of legislation, passed between 1945 and 1948, establishing the post-war Welfare State in Britain, the essentials of which remain in place to this day. In 1944, he published *Full Employment in a Free Society*, which he saw as a sequel to his 1942 Report.

Elements of a welfare state in the sense of local or national government concern for easing the privations of >POVERTY had, of course, existed in Britain, at least, since the Poor Law Acts of the 16th century (>POOR LAWS). Progress in the widening of the scope of welfare legislation continued in the 19th and early 20th centuries in such areas as education, health and unemployment. Long before the publication of the Beveridge Report, the Poor Law system was being systemically replaced by a series of Acts of Parliament, such as the Old Age Pensions Act of 1908, the Labour Exchanges Act of 1909 and the National Insurance Act of 1911. It is wrong, therefore, to see the Beveridge Report as a document upon which the elements of the welfare state were written for the first time but rather the consolidation of previous legislation and the recognition of the responsibility of central government for the care of those in need. There is, nevertheless, some debate as to the degree of continuity between the pre-war and post-war legislation (Johnson, 1994). A national system, financed by contributions from employees and employers as well as taxes, was proposed, which would help the sick, the unemployed and the retired. The proposals were adopted by the new post-war Labour Government which passed the Family Allowance Act in 1945, the National Insurance and the National Health Service Acts in 1946, the National Assistance and Children's Acts in 1948 and the Housing Act in 1949.

Lord Beveridge had a lifetime interest in the problem of the unemployed. In fact, he himself was a notorious workaholic and other people's leisure puzzled him. 'So long as I can keep on working, I find life tolerable. But if I could not work I do not know what I would do. What do people do with their spare time, I wonder?' (Robbins, 1971). In *Full Employment in a Free Society*, he stated that, 'The central problem of unemployment between the wars in Britain was not what it had appeared to be before the first World War' (>WORLD WAR I). It was not a problem of cyclical fluctuation reducing the demand for a time, or of disorganisation of the labour market, wasting men's lives in drifting and wasting. It was a problem of general and persistent weakness of demand for labour' (Beveridge, 1944). He believed that full employment 'means having always more vacant jobs than unemployed men' (Beveridge, 1944), a view that was considerably influenced by >KEYNES' *The General Theory of Employment, Interest and Money*, which had been published in 1936, but such a view was regarded by some, including Robbins, as too dismissive of supply factors and prone to lead to inflation (Robbins, 1971). However, he did recognize the power of >TRADE UNIONS to force up wages. He suggested that a national wages policy should be drawn up by the Trades Union Congress General Council. This would be buttressed by an arbitration system which if rejected by any party to a dispute would lead to the withdrawal of all support.

In his report he suggested that, at full employment, there would be 3 per cent of the workforce out of work. This percentage was made up of 1 per cent due to seasonal fluctuations in the demand for labour, 1 per cent for the margin of change of employment incidental to progress and 1 per cent due to fluctuations in overseas demand.

## References

Beveridge, William H., *Social Insurance and Allied Services,*Report of Inter-Department Committee, chaired by William H. Beveridge, 1942.

Beveridge, William H., *Full Employment in a Free Society*, Report by William H. Beveridge, George Allen & Unwin, 1944.

Johnson, Paul, 'The Welfare State', in Roderick Floud and Donald McCloskey (eds), *The Economic History of Britain Since 1700*, I, 1700–1860 (2nd edn), Cambridge University Press, 1994.

Robbins, L., *Autobiography of an Economist*, St Martin's Press, 1971.

## Bimetallic System

>BRITAIN may be said to have begun its progress to a full >GOLD STANDARD early in the 18th century and completed it in 1821. By 1870, Australia, Brazil, Turkey and Portugal were also on the gold standard. Austria, the Netherlands and Germany were on a silver standard. Belgium, France, Italy and Switzerland were on a bimetallic standard with a fixed price ratio between >GOLD and >SILVER. However, by 1914, the gold standard or, in some countries the gold exchange standard, had spread throughout the world, with but a relatively few remaining on a silver standard. A number of reasons have been put forward as to why this switch took place and at that particular time in the 19th century.

Discussion among economists flourished vigorously at the time. It had long been recognized that with a price relative between gold and silver fixed by the monetary authority, a deviation between that ratio and that in the open market would lead to the loss from circulation of the coin of the undervalued metal because a profit could be made by melting it down and selling it on the open bullion market (Gresham's Law). On the other hand, these movements between the monetary and non-monetary markets of the two metals could, within limits, tend to redress the imbalances between the two markets. The implication, however, is that the relevant monetary reserves must be large enough in relation to the market size. This is much less likely the fewer the countries there are on a bimetallic system or having a common price ratio between the two metals. The British economist Alfred Marshall (1842–1924) proposed a solution to this problem called 'symmetallism' under which the monetary standard would not be either gold or silver but gold and silver. Convertibility would not be allowed into gold or silver but only into gold and silver combined into a single bar.

France was the pre-eminent bimetallic country in the first half of the 19th century. In 1803 its mint ratio between silver and gold was 15.5 to 1. This ratio priced gold below the market so gold circulation was limited and silver was dominant. When gold was discovered in California, Russia and Australia, the market price of gold fell and, as expected under Gresham's Law, gold flowed into France and the circulation of silver coin dropped to only about 2 per cent of the total. In 1861, the Senate was informed that 'the total lack of silver coin renders the payment of small demands difficult' (Redish, 1995). In 1878, the Latin Monetary Union, which had been set up in 1865, demonetized silver.

In the 19th century, the >USA was legally on a bimetallic system.

The Coinage Act of 1792 had set the exchange at 15 ounces of silver to be equal to 1 ounce of gold, which priced gold too low and, as in France, it left circulation. Another Coinage Act in 1834 altered the exchange rate to 16 ounces of silver to 1 ounce of gold. With the opening up of the new gold fields, again as in France, silver went out of circulation. In 1878, the Bland Act authorized the coining of $2 million in silver per month and the Silver Purchase Act was passed in 1880. The rise in price of silver, however, encouraged the Europeans to dump their surplus silver on the American market and the Act was repealed in 1893. In the context of the decline in prices of the late 19th century, a final plea was made for bimetallism. In 1896, the Democratic Presidential candidate, William Jennings Bryan, campaigned on his refusal to suffer *'mankind to be crucified on a cross of gold'*. The USA finally moved over, officially, to the gold standard by the Gold Standard Act of 1900.

A number of reasons have been proposed for the emergence of the gold standard as the internationally accepted monetary standard in the second half of the 19th century. The falling price of silver in the 1860s and 1870s, coupled with the decision by Germany to switch to gold; the transport costs of silver relative to gold in international transactions; the technical inability, until the industrial revolution produced the means, to produce the required range of coinage to cover all transactions from the large to the small (Redish, 1995, 2000).

It is also argued that the trigger was that the costs of moving from one regime to another changed. With the conclusion of the Franco-Prussian War, Germany (Prussia) benefited from a large indemnity from France granted by the Treaty of Frankfurt, which eased Germany's budget constraints. Consequently, budgetary considerations were less restrictive and Germany was able to switch to gold in 1871 (Flandreau, 1996, 2004). Scandinavia followed the German example. France was unable to support its mint ratio and abandoned the attempt in 1874.

## References

Flandreau, Marc, 'The French Crime of 1873: An Essay on the Emergence of the International Gold Standard, 1870–1880', *Journal of Economic History*, 56(4), 1996.

Flandreau, Marc, *The Glitter of Gold: France, Bimetallism, and the Emergence of the International Gold Standard, 1848–1873*, Oxford University Press, 2004.

Kenwood, A. G. and Lougheed, A. L., *The Growth of the International Economy, 1820–1990*, Routledge, 1992.

Redish, Angela, 'The Persistence of Bimetallism in Nineteenth-Century France', *Economic History Review*, XLVIII(4), 1995.

Redish, Angela, *Bimetallism: An Economic and Historical Analysis*, Cambridge University Press, 2000.

Wilson, Ted, *Battles for the Standard: Bimetallism and the Spread of the Gold Standard in the Nineteenth Century*, Ashgate, 2000.

## Britain

In 1750, Britain was on the threshold of an unprecedented shift in the very foundation of its economic and social structure which came to be referred to as the Industrial Revolution (>INDUSTRIAL REVOLUTION IN BRITAIN: >INDUSTRIAL REVOLUTIONS). It heralded an explosive break from the agrarian past not only for Britain but also for the world economy, for Britain was the first country in which it occurred and the after-shocks have reverberated down to the present day (>ASIAN MIRACLE: >GLOBALIZATION:>INDIA). It would be wrong, however, to view it as an event of a sudden 'take-off' or step-change in activity because the ground in which it was able to flourish in Britain was a long time in prep-aration and the changes associated with it took some time to play out to their fulfilment.

In 1300, Britain had reached a peak population of about 5.7 mil-lion, which, as a result of famines and plague, it failed to match again until the end of the 17th century, but thereafter the population grew rapidly and reached 9.3 million in 1800. Over these centuries productivity improved agricultural output to the extent that, from the level of bare subsistence farming in 1300, Britain was able to supply 90 per cent of the requirements of its growing, and increasingly urban, population by the 19th century. >ENCLOSURE enabled larger farm sizes with the concomitant economies of scale and improved farm manage-ment, assisted by a tenurial, rather than a peasant-based (>PEASANTRY) institutional structure. There was a drop in the acreage of land left fallow with the rotation of new crops and an increase in the numbers of livestock of better quality. Livestock output grew by four or five times compared with three times for grain. Britain avoided being mired in subsistence farming and with its surplus was able to find and develop commercial markets.

All these improvements were achieved with virtually no increase in labour. In 1300 there were about 1.2 million men working in agricul-ture and in 1800 about 1.1 million. The increase in the total population of Britain did not have to remain in agriculture and was free to go into

industry and commerce because agri-culture could meet the nation's needs not only for food but also for indus-trial raw materials and could support the demand for horses, which were required in factories and in trans-port. Between 1700 and 1850 labour productivity in agriculture increased by a factor of three and by the early 19th century British agricultural labour productivity was one-third higher than in France (>WESTERN EUROPE). In the 1760s one agricul-tural worker was able to feed one non-agricultural worker, by the 1840s one agricultural worker could feed 2.7 non-agricultural workers. Even as late as 1841, of the 1.6 million peo-ple employed in the industrial sector, about 40 per cent were employed in industries dependent on domestic agriculture for their raw materials (Wrigley, 2006) (>AGRICULTURAL REVOLUTION).

As the numbers employed in agri-culture hardly changed so, with the growth of the population, its share of the total fell rapidly. In 1700, 61 per cent of the population was employed in agriculture and 18 per cent in industry, but by 1840, 29 per cent were employed in agriculture and 47 per cent in industry (Crafts, 1994). However, there was an increase in the number of men employed in agricul-ture from 595,000 in 1770, to 628,000 in 1800 and to 971,000 in 1851, these increases being offset by the fall in the number of women and boys (>EMPLOYMENT OF WOMEN AND CHILDREN). From the 1770s to the 1860s day wages of agricultural work-ers increased by 90 per cent whereas nationally wages increased by 118 per cent and this gap gave some incen-tive to migrate to the towns rather than to stay on the farm (Clark, 2001). British agriculture, therefore, was able to frustrate the coming of what >MALTHUS postulated as the inevitability of a stationary state and the coming of the falling rate of profit feared by >RICARDO and expected by >MARX, until the transformation of the economy into an industrial one had been accomplished and a new paradigm was required.

At the beginning of the 18th century, industrial activity was centred around the household (>PROTO-INDUSTRIALIZATION). But there was an outpouring of inventions in Britain in the century which was unprecedented in its scope and influence. In order to capture the opportunities of economies of scale in production and facilitate the better management of labour and resources which the technical changes promised, there began a move into the factory system and the associated growth of urbanization. The cotton textile industry was a prime example of the changes. In the first half of the 18th century, the industry was trivial and accounted for only 1 per cent of Britain's manufactured exports, but by 1800, cotton textiles accounted for 35 per cent of total manufactured exports with wool textiles pushed into second place. Ironically, to protect the wool industry, import restrictions had been placed on imports of calico from >INDIA in 1701 and 1721, which gave the cotton textile industry room to develop (>COTTON AND COTTON TEXTILES). This it was able to do through a string of inventions such as the flying shuttle in 1733, the spinning jenny in 1770, the water frame in 1769, the mule in 1779 (and the application of >STEAM POWER to it in 1790) and the power loom in 1785. The average percentage growth of output of cotton textiles between 1780 and 1812 was about 3.4 per cent per annum and for the whole period, from 1780 to about 1860, it was 2.6 per cent per annum (McCloskey, 1994) The industry

moved into factories centred close to coal deposits and suitable water and labour supplies and so stimulated the urbanization of the North West.

In addition to the necessary development of its agriculture and the spate of inventions, Britain benefited from a progressively improving transport infrastructure, first roads (>ROAD TRANSPORT) and >CANALS and later >RAILWAYS, supported by its resources of >COAL and iron ore (>IRON AND STEEL). In the last quarter of the 18th century the growth rate of GDP about doubled, compared with earlier in the century, to about 1.4 per cent per annum and increased further to 1.9 per cent per annum in the early 19th century up to 1830. The growth rate of industry increased from 0.7 per cent per annum between 1700 and 1760, to 1.3 per cent per annum between 1760 and 1780, to 2 per cent per annum between 1780 and 1801 and to 2.8 per cent per annum between 1801 and 1831. Thereafter, the trend of the growth rate of industrial output declined until it stabilized at a growth rate of about 2 per cent per annum in the last quarter of the 19th century through to early 20th century. However, the growth in the early period was due to the use of more inputs rather than to increases in >PRODUCTIVITY. The inventions of the 18th century did not come through into higher productivity until the second quarter of the 19th century (Crafts, 1994) (>INDUSTRIAL REVOLUTION IN BRITAIN). Although the population doubled between 1780 and 1860, income per head also doubled in the period. However, the standard of living saw no real improvement until the 19th century was well advanced (>COMPANIES).

Population indeed was another aspect of the revolutionary changes taking place in Britain. At the end of the 18th century there was no particular anxiety generated by the Malthusian threat of the inevitable perils of population growth because it was thought to be stable. The first population census of 1801 delivered a shock as it revealed that population had grown by 50 per cent in the last half of the 18th century and it continued to grow apace. In the 50 years from 1681 to 1731 the population of England had increased by 6.7 per cent to 5.3 million. In the following 50 years it increased by 33.8 per cent to 7.0 million and in the following 50 years by a further 88.6 per cent to 13.3 million in 1831 (Schofield, 1994). Britain continued to accommodate exceptionally high population growth rates through the 19th century and into the twentieth century so that it had surpassed the population of France by 1900 with a population of 40.8 million (Maddison, 2003). This growth was generated by both an increase in the fertility rate and a decrease in the death rate, rather than immigration. It has been estimated that the increase in fertility was twice as important as the lowering of the mortality rate and was due to the reduction in the age at which women first married and in the number of women who never married and may be seen as an expression of confidence in a sufficient standard of living. At the same time, the improvement in and consistency of adequate nutrition together with improvements in healthcare and public infrastructure contributed to the reduction of the death rate (>POPULATION).

National indicators of the general improvement in the standard of living, however, can be misleading. The working and living conditions in the factories and the urban conurbations were such as to cause relatively high mortality from poor working conditions, pollution, overcrowded housing and inadequate public health provision, so much so that the life expectancy in the towns was considerably lower than the average. Conditions were further depressed by an increase in the cost of living during the Napoleonic War, fuelling social unrest. The general economic background was one of rising food prices and falling money and real incomes. Wheat prices in 1812 were over three times the level they had been in 1790. In contrast, weavers' wages fell by over 40 per cent between 1805 and 1815 at a time when the poorest 40 per cent of households spent 50 per cent of their income on grain foods. Absolute living standards stagnated. The standard of living of the urban factory workers fell and did not begin to recover until the second half of the 19th century (Szreter and Mooney, 1998) (>LUDDISM). There was also growing anxiety at the time about the conditions of work in the factories, particularly in respect to the employment of women and children, which led to the passing of laws regulating factory conditions. The first Act was in 1802, on the employment of pauper children in the textile factories. Further Acts followed regulating employment in textiles and the mines. In 1833, a factory inspectorate was established. In 1847 the Ten Hours Act limited the number of and specified the hours during which women could be employed, which constrained employers generally in their employment practices. An Act in 1864 reduced the number of child workers in the Potteries and in 1872 the mining industry was further regulated (>EMPLOYMENT OF WOMEN AND CHILDREN: >POOR LAWS: >POVERTY: >REGULATION).

Some measure of the regulation of trade in agricultural products had existed in England since the 14th century. In the latter half of the 17th century, reflecting the mercantilist ideas of the time, exports were encouraged through subsidy and imports controlled. There was a string of Acts of Parliament referred to as the Corn Laws. These laws were suspended for a number of years during the disruption of trade caused by the wars between 1793 and 1815. Following the end of the Napoleonic War, grain prices fell and the Corn Laws were reinstated. Imports of grain were prohibited as long as the price of the home-grown product was below 80/- (shillings) per quarter, although there was no similar restriction on exports. Adjustments were made in subsequent years, 1822, 1828 and 1842, though the protection became somewhat less severe through the reduction of import tariffs. Although, the influence of >MERCANTILISM on government policy in relation to the control of foreign trade persisted into the 19th century, Britain began to move to a free trade policy.

The Corn Laws supported the rents of landowners and incomes of farmers and rested on the argument of the need for the security of domestic production of essential foodstuffs. The laws raised the cost of living, particularly for the poor, when the poorest households in England spent about 50 per cent of their income on food derived from grain. Manufacturers became increasingly critical of the policy in so far as it generated pressure for higher nominal wages to offset the fall in real incomes. The political consequences of the >INDUSTRIAL REVOLUTION IN BRITAIN became evident as the dominance of agriculture gave way to industry. The government had reintroduced Income Tax in 1842, thus reducing the need for tariffs

as a source of revenue and import duties were reduced. The prohibition on the export of machinery was also lifted.

In 1838, an organized lobby for free trade in grain was established in the Anti-Corn Law League under the guidance of Richard Cobden and John Bright. In 1845, there was a very wet summer and autumn and a sharp drop in grain yields. At the same time blight spread throughout Northern Europe and devastated the potato crop (>IRISH FAMINE). The Corn Laws were repealed by Sir Robert Peel in May 1846 (Kadish, 1996: >CHARTISM: >INTERNATIONAL TRADE) and three years later the Navigation Acts. From 1651, a series of these Acts had applied tariffs on foreign imports and also regulated the ships which carried foreign trade. Commodities produced in Britain could only be carried in British ships and other commodities only in the ships of the country which produced them (>AMERICAN WAR OF INDEPENDENCE: >SHIPPING). By 1860, Britain had removed all protection from its international trading.

Even in the 1750s Britain had a dominant position in world trade and its pre-eminence continued throughout the 19th century. At the end of the 19th century, British exports of manufactures captured 33 per cent of the world total (Harley, 1994) and 25 per cent of British income was spent on imports, most of it on food and raw materials. Exports in 1900 were mainly of textiles, which accounted for about 40 per cent of the total, followed by iron and steel, at a share of 15 per cent, coal, at 10 per cent, and machinery, at 7 per cent. About 80 per cent of cotton textiles production was exported, 50 per cent of iron and steel and 33 per cent of coal output. While Britain's share in world exports had begun to fall in the second half of the 19th century in the face of growing competition, particularly from Germany (>WESTERN EUROPE) and the >USA, nevertheless it retained its top position until >WORLD WAR I (>BUSINESS MANAGEMENT).

Britain's position in world trade was the foundation of the regulation of international financial transactions through the >GOLD STANDARD, which was first established in Britain and then spread internationally during the 19th century. Britain had suspended the convertibility of its currency into gold during the Napoleonic War and the beginning of the setting up of a full gold standard may be put at the passing of the Coinage Act in 1816. Restrictions were lifted on international trade in gold bullion and on the conversion of coin into bullion in 1819 and the Bank of England (>CENTRAL BANKING: >CAPITAL MARKETS) was enabled to restore the convertibility of bank notes into gold at the prevailing market price of 1821. Eventually other countries joined the standard so that from about 1880 until World War I, it covered a worldwide spread of both advanced and developing countries. After its suspension during the war, Britain returned to the standard (much to >KEYNES' dismay) and eventually also about 50 other countries. However, in 1931, the Credit-Anstalt Bank of Vienna became insolvent and the consequent international loss of confidence led to short-term capital leaving Britain and it was forced to abandon the gold standard (>THE GREAT DEPRESSION).

In the second half of the 19th century, the international reduction in transport costs, technological innovation and the opening up of land in the Americas and Australia led to a shift in demand away from European agricultural produce. The consequence of these developments was a pressure on agricultural prices. In Britain, food prices fell from 1873 to their lowest in 1896 by about 42 per cent, faster than the drop in the overall price level, with a consequential fall in the real incomes of farmers, a period which has been termed 'the great agricultural depression', a drop which was more severe than that experienced in other European countries because, unlike Britain, they had pursued a policy of protection for their agriculture (>AGRICULTURE: >BUSINESS CYCLES: >SILVER).

With the growth in the population of the British Empire and in the widening of its geographical spread, British trade with the Empire became increasingly important. The British Empire accounted for 21 per cent of Britain's imports and 23 per cent of its exports by 1870, rising to 27 per cent and 35 per cent respectively in 1914 and further increased in the inter-war years to reach 36 per cent and 43 per cent respectively in 1936/8 (Alford, 1996). There has been a great deal of debate among historians concerning the costs and benefits of the British Empire (>ECONOMIC IMPERIALISM). One view holds that the markets of the Empire were a seductive and easily assessable attraction to British investors at a time when other markets were being shut out by growing protectionism and the domestic market was under attack from German and US competition (>INTERNATIONAL TRADE). As a consequence, the British Empire had a deleterious effect in that it discouraged innovation, contributed to Britain's relatively slow development in the emerging technologically advanced new industries, such as chemicals, >ELECTRICITY and >MACHINE TOOLS, and led to the persistence of old industries, such as coal, cotton textiles, iron and steel and shipbuilding. In addition, Britain had to bear a heavier burden of expenditure on defence than it would otherwise have done. Others have argued that the British economy was experiencing a declining rate of profit and funds surplus to domestic demand therefore sought opportunities in Imperial expansion. Imperial markets were not an easy option as such, although commodities in which Britain had a comparative advantage were a significant part of them. The Empire did enhance the growth of the economy in the 19th and early 20th centuries and did particularly benefit certain sectors, such as cotton textiles and railway equipment producers, and the service industries, such as banking, insurance and shipping (>INDIA). There is no doubt, however, that Britain enjoyed considerable benefits from the Empire during >WORLD WAR I. One estimate calculates that Britain's expenditure on the war amounted to £44 billion, with expenditure on the armed forces amounting to about 25 per cent of Gross National Product and that, if it were not for the financial contribution from the countries of the British Empire, it would have been 10 per cent higher than this. In addition, Britain suffered 744,000 fatalities in its armed forces and the Empire countries as many as 225,000 fatalities in the war (Edelstein, 1994).

Although, as a consequence of the international progress of industrialization, the lead enjoyed by Britain had been and was being eroded particularly by the USA and Germany, nevertheless in 1913 it yet retained its world position. Britain had a share of 14 per cent in total world merchandise exports, compared with 13 per cent for Germany and 13 per cent for the USA. Britain's GDP per capita was close that of the USA, but Germany's was 25 per cent less and other countries were even less advanced. The structure of the British economy was significantly different from that of other countries in Europe. In the years leading up to 1913, the primary sector accounted for only about 9 per cent of total employment, compared with 37 per cent in Germany, 41 per cent in France and 55 per cent in Italy. During the course of World War I, Britain continued to grow and at its close National Income was 15 per cent higher, comparable with the increase in the USA, whereas most countries in Europe suffered severe falls of the order of from 20–40 per cent. Women benefited from the opening up of opportunities for work and many men who had suffered from long-term unemployment enjoyed an improved standard of living because of the shortage of labour. However, Britain's foreign assets declined by about 15 per cent with a consequential loss of income and it had become a net debtor. Britain's merchant fleet, which had been the world's largest before the war, steadily declined in the face of the sinking of vessels during the war and never recovered (>SHIPPING: >WESTERN EUROPE: >WORLD WAR I).

After the war, Britain's Gross Domestic Product did not regain the level it had reached in 1918 until 1934. In 1921, at its lowest, it was 23 per cent below the 1918 level and unemployment was 14 per cent of the labour force. A recovery in Gross Domestic Product followed until 1929, amounting to 28 per cent, but that year heralded the > GREAT DEPRESSION. Unemployment in Britain increased from 1.5 million in 1929 to 3.4 million in 1932 but it fared relatively less badly than other leading countries because of the structure of its economy and the robustness of its financial institutions; unlike the USA and on the Continent of Europe (>WESTERN EUROPE), it suffered no bank failures. The unemployed were concentrated in the export industries of the North and West, such as coal, iron and steel, shipbuilding and cotton textiles. The economy benefited from the fall in import prices of food and raw materials. Between 1929 and 1931, wholesale prices in Britain fell by 28 per cent. The result was an increase in the real incomes of those in work. Recovery from the depression was also relatively rapid in Britain. Recovery was assisted by the abandonment of the fixed exchange rate for the pound on leaving the gold standard and so freeing the exchange rate to fall by 20 per cent. The inter-war years saw the spread of protectionism in international trade and even Britain finally abandoned its long-held free trade policy with the passing of the Imports Duties Act in 1932, with the exception of the granting of Imperial Preference for the countries of the Empire (>INTERNATIONAL TRADE). The level of output in 1929 was regained by 1934, with the economy growing at an average rate of about 3 per cent per annum until 1939, the eve of >WORLD WAR II.

During the war, attention was given to increasing the production of agriculture in order to lessen Britain's reliance on imports, which were subject to intense disruption by enemy action. Wheat and potato tonnage increased by well over 100 per cent, oats and fruit production by well over 50 per cent. By 1945, personal consumption had fallen by 22 per cent, reflecting the switch of resources to the conduct of the war. Britain lost about 19 per cent of its physical assets but human losses were small and GDP did grow, at about 2.3 per cent per annum, between 1939 and 1945,

whereas the other European countries involved in the war experienced severe falls (>WESTERN EUROPE: WORLD WAR II).

The proper course for government economic policy to pursue during the Great Depression was subject to intense debate, summed up as the difference in views between >KEYNES and the Classical economists, who argued that unemployment was a result of a misalignment between the structure of production and the structure of demand which could be eliminated by changing relative prices (>CLASSICAL AND NEO-CLASSICAL ECONOMICS: >HAYEK). >KEYNES, on the other hand, saw the problem and its solution in the deficiency of total effective demand. In practice, the argument was between expenditure on public works, even at the expense of incurring increased government deficits, or in the reduction of wages. The British Treasury, personified by Winston Churchill, the Chancellor of the Exchequer, believed that public expenditure would only divert resources from the private sector and not result in a net increase in employment.

Certain principles had been established from this debate and supported by the practical example of the central part played by government in the marshalling of resources during two world wars. It came to be recognized that high unemployment could persist, that governments had the tools of demand management to reduce it and that they had the duty to do so. These were the features of government policy by which the Labour Party was guided after the war and which dominated economic policy thinking until the 1980s. The aim of policy was low unemployment, stable prices, accelerated growth and income equality. This was to be in the context of the support of people in need though the provisions of a Welfare State. The government implemented, through legislation in the 1940s, the recommendations of the >BEVERIDGE reports of 1942 and 1944, rationalized existing practices, set up a system, financed by contributions from employees and employers as well as from taxes, to help the poor, the sick, the unemployed and the retired. An Education Act had been passed in 1944 relating to secondary schooling and the government raised the school leaving age to 16 years (>EDUCATION). Many of the policy instruments that were used in the war were continued immediately after the war, such as rationing, controls over prices and investment and import restrictions, but these were mostly abolished by the mid-1950s. However, the government also implemented its policy of nationalization (which had been written into Clause 4 of the Labour Party's constitution in 1918 and which was not removed until 1995), beginning with the Bank of England in 1946 and continuing with coal, gas, electricity, railways (including their docks), canals, long-distance road haulage, civil aviation, telecommunications and, finally, the iron and steel industry. They employed over 2 million people and together with central government accounted for 25 per cent of capital expenditure by 1950 (Millward, 1997).

By 1952, GDP was 10 per cent above and manufacturing production 36 per cent above their levels in 1946. In the 1950s and 1960s, low levels of unemployment were achieved and inflation remained restrained, benefiting from wage restraint. Between 1948 and 1958, GDP grew at 2.4 per cent per annum and the growth rate increased further to 3.4 per cent per annum in the following decade. These years spanned, however, the 'Golden Age' of world economic growth when world income grew at 3.7 per cent per annum and world trade by 6.5 per cent per annum between 1953 and 1963, rising to 5.2 per cent and 8.9 per cent respectively during the next ten years.

There were continually recurrent foreign exchange crises through the decades after the war. (The Labour Government produced, in 1965, Britain's only National Plan, the aim of which was to achieve a growth rate of 3.8 per cent to 1970 and which stated that, 'An essential part of the Plan is a solution to Britain's balance of payments problem' (HMSO, 1965)). Crude oil production was not in the Plan. It was the discovery of oil in the North Sea that eased the balance of payments problem. Crude >OIL production yielded a net surplus on foreign trade in oil from 1980, rising to a peak surplus in 1985 and then declining through the 1990s and 2000s as the fields were depleted. The effect of North Sea oil was to ease the restraints caused by the propensity of Britain to run into severe balance of payments crises which had induced 'Stop-Go' reactions in the economic policy of the government as it tried to regulate total demand in the economy through its fiscal policy. However, the downside of the effect of rising North Sea oil exports was to cause the rate of exchange to appreciate which had a detrimental effect on Britain's exports of manufactures and, consequently, a drop in employment in that sector and hastened the decline of its share of GDP. This too was in the context of a growing propensity to inflation. The post-war government had, in the early years, obtained a degree of cooperation from the trade unions for moderation in wage demands but this consensus weakened in time and attempts to impose control by imposing some kind of prices and incomes constraints and pay pauses were, in the long run, ineffectual. Inflation, which had averaged 3.8 per cent in the 1950s, increased to 7.5 per cent in the 1960s. In the 1970s, pushed up by the world increase in the price of crude >OIL in 1973, Britain's inflation rate increased further, rising to 27 per cent in mid-1975, dropping to the still-high figure of about an average of 7 per cent per annum in the 1980s to early 1990s (Cairncross, 1994).

Immediately after the war, Britain had captured about 30 per cent of the world total trade in manufactures, but this had fallen to 14 per cent in 1964 and to less than 8 per cent in the 1980s, by which time it had become a net importer of manufactures. In 1950, the GDPs per capita of Germany, France and Japan were less than that of Britain, but by 1997 they had all surpassed it. There was a decline in the share in GDP of the production of manufactures, in the share of Britain in world trade and, between 1977 and 1983, British Steel lost 61 per cent of its labour force, British Leyland 53 per cent, British Shipbuilders 28 per cent and the late 1980s saw the collapse of the coal industry (Supple, 1994). Britain had had to devalue the pound by 30 per cent to $2.80 in 1949 and again, in 1963, the pound had been devalued by a further 14 per cent to $2.40 and an application to join the European Economic Community in that year had been rejected, although it did become a member in 1973 (>WESTERN EUROPE). In 1972, the pound was finally left to float, with the dismantling of the international Bretton Woods Agreements (>KEYNES), apart from a spell from 1990 and 1992 when it attempted to fix the exchange rate against the Deutschemark within the European Exchange Rate Mechanism, but failed (>WESTERN EUROPE). It was in all a rather miserable picture and there grew up much despondent concern about the general malaise and decline of Britain in the world.

The reason for the decline was fundamentally a lack of productivity growth compared with Britain's competitors. However, some relative decline was inevitable. Britain began the post-war period with the advantage that its physical infrastructure had not suffered to the same extent as its potential European competitors (>WESTERN EUROPE) who began, therefore, from a lower base from which to develop. Moreover, during the 'Golden Age' of world growth, during which relative decline was at its fastest, there was a productivity and structural convergence between developed countries as their relative employment in agriculture declined. However, Britain's >EDUCATION system was believed by some to be inadequate and contributed to both the fall in manufacturing and the lagging behind of productivity improvements because of the lack of technical and managerial innovation and labour with relevant skills. Also, the persistent balance of payments problems and the consequential short-term preoccupations of the government led to continual switches in policy, which discouraged domestic investment (Broadberry and Crafts, 2003; Ringe and Rollings, 2000). Government economic policy did not help in that it tried to combine full employment, full capacity growth with reliance on wage restraint to contain inflation in the context of deteriorating labour relations. It was increasingly difficult to maintain the cooperation of the trade unions, who defended over-manning and restrictive practices. Nevertheless, it should not be forgotten that Britain did not decline as such; the decline was relative to others (Supple, 1994) (>PRODUCTIVITY).

This bleak view of Britain was then banished by its performance in the last decade of the 20th century and into the first decade of the 21st century. By 2007, the GDP per capita of Britain had overtaken Germany and France and was not significantly below that of Japan. In the 1980s, the Conservative Government of Margaret Thatcher instituted a number of reforms, which the New Labour Government of Tony Blair in 1997 continued. The reforms centred on the switch from a Keynesian demand-based economic policy to that centred on the control of the money supply together with the privatization of the nationalized industries and the transfer of monetary policy from the Treasury to the Bank of England (>CENTRAL BANKING: >FRIEDMAN). These reforms changed Britain from a highly regulated, nationalized, economy with very poor industrial relations, to an economy which was very open, and market-oriented and less prone to strikes. There was a switch of emphasis of welfare expenditure from people out of work to people in work and an improvement in labour relations in the context of the decline in trade union membership (>TRADE UNIONS). There is no doubt that subsequently much of the gap with competitors was closed. Some explanation of this can be found in the greater number of hours worked and higher employment, but productivity improvements still lagged behind. According to Card *et al.* (2004), the greatest productivity gains were achieved not so much by privatization as such but the process of privatization during which the industries were restructured. A negative effect of the reforms was the increase in inequality, although this was mitigated by being caused by the incomes of the people at the top rising faster than those at the bottom of the income distribution who also enjoyed increases in real incomes. A joint study organized by the National Bureau of Economic Research of the United States, the London School of Economics and the Institute of Fiscal Studies concluded that it was the reforms that explained the improved performance, although it did not push productivity up to that of the USA or the major European Union nations (>WESTERN EUROPE). (Card *et al.*, 2004)

After a recession recording a drop of 1.4 per cent in GDP in 1991, the British economy did indeed then grow close to capacity without interruption for the following 16 years, averaging a growth of 2.7 per cent per annum until 2007. The OECD, however, has warned that its international comparative studies into education reveal that the British educational performance, in spite of an expansion in expenditure by the government, yet remained below the standards set by the best performing countries. For instance, Britain ranked 17th in literacy, 24th in mathematics and 14th in science among the 57 countries in the OECD survey.

In 2007, falling house prices in the USA triggered defaults on debts in the sub-prime housing mortgage markets there, which had worldwide repercussions. The existence of opaque collateralized debt and its associated use of extensive leverage not only fed the bubble in asset prices but caused, in the subsequent collapse, a severe drought in inter-bank loans. In 2008, the crisis of confidence had spread throughout the international banking system, causing bank failures and government intervention, to the point of effective nationalization of some financial institutions in the USA and in >WESTERN EUROPE and a number of countries in Europe being forced to seek international financial assistance. House prices in Britain fell and the British Government was forced to nationalize Northern Rock, a relatively small mortgage bank. This was followed, however, by the government having to guarantee savings deposits for fear of a run on the banks, to suspend competition rules to enable bank takeovers and to inject an unprecedented amount of financial support into the banking system. The long run of years of steady growth had come to end in an uncertain future for Britain and the world economy.

## References

Alford, W. E., *Britain in the World Economy Since 1880*, Longman, 1996.

Brezis, Elise S., 'Foreign Capital Flows in the Century of Britain's Industrial Revolution: New Estimates, Controlled Conjectures', *Economic History Review*, XLVIII, February, 1995.

Broadberry, Stephen and Crafts, Nicholas, 'UK Productivity Performance from 1950 to 1979: A Restatement of the Broadberry–Crafts View', *Economic History Review*, LVI(4), November, 2003.

Cairncross, Sir Alexander, 'Economic Policy and Performance, 1964–1990', in Roderick Floud and Donald McCloskey (eds), *The Economic History of Britain Since 1700*, I, 1700–1860 (2nd edn), Cambridge University Press, 1994.

Card, David, Blundell, Richard and Freeman, Richard B., *Seeking a Premier Economy: The Economic Effects of British Economic Reforms, 1980–2000*, University of Chicago Press, 2004.

Clark, Gregory, 'Farm Wages and Living Standards in the Industrial Revolution: England, 1670–1869', *Economic History Review*, LIV(3), August, 2001.

Crafts, Nick, 'The Industrial Revolution', in Roderick Floud and Donald McCloskey (eds), *The Economic History of Britain Since 1700*, I, 1700–1860 (2nd edn), Cambridge University Press, 1994.

Edelstein, Michael, 'Imperialism: Cost and Benefit', in Roderick Floud and Donald McCloskey (eds), *The Economic History of Britain Since 1700*, I, 1700–1860 (2nd edn), Cambridge University Press, 1994.

Harley, Nick, 'Foreign Trade: Comparative Advantage and Performance', in Roderick Floud and Donald McCloskey (eds), *The Economic History of Britain Since 1700*, I, 1700–1860 (2nd edn), Cambridge University Press, 1994.

HMSO *The National Plan*, Her Majesty's Stationery Office, Cmnd. 2764, September, 1965.

Kadish, Alon (ed.), *The Corn Laws: the Formation of Popular Economics in Britain*, Pickering and Chato, 1996.

Maddison, Angus *The World Economy. Historical Statistics*, Development Centre Studies, OECD, 2003.

McCloskey, Donald, '1780–1860: A Survey', in Roderick Floud and Donald McCloskey (eds), *The Economic History of Britain Since 1700*, I, 1700–1860 (2nd edn), Cambridge University Press, 1994.

Millward, Robert, 'The 1940's Nationalisations in Britain: Means to an End or the Means of Production', *Economic History Review*, I(2), May, 1997.

Mokyr, Joel, 'Technological Change, 1700–1830', in Roderick Floud and Donald McCloskey (eds), *The Economic History of Britain Since 1700*, I, 1700–1860 (2nd edn), Cambridge University Press, 1994.

OECD, *Education at a Glance, 2008*, OECD Indicators, 2008.

Ringe, Astrid and Rollings, Neil, 'Responding to Relative Decline: The Creation of the National Economic Development Council', *Economic History Review*, LIII(2), May, 2000.

Schofield, Roger, 'British Population Change, 1700–1871', in Roderick Floud and Donald McCloskey (eds), *The Economic History of Britain Since 1700*, I, 1700–1860 (2nd edn), Cambridge University Press, 1994.

Smith, Adam, *An Inquiry into the Nature and Causes of the Wealth of Nations*

(1776), Book III, Chapter I, Ward Lock, 1812.

Supple, Barry, 'Fear of Failing: Economic History and the Decline of Britain', *Economic History Review*, XLVII(3), August, 1994.

Szreter, Simon and Mooney, Graham, 'Urbanization, Mortality, and the Standard of Living Debate: New Estimates of the Expectation of Life at Birth in Nineteenth-Century British Cities', *Economic History Review*, LI(1), February, 1998.

Wrigley, E. A., 'The Transition to an Advanced Organic Economy: Half a Millennium of English Agriculture', *Economic History Review*, LIX(3), August, 2006.

# Business Cycles

'The only cause of depression is prosperity.' *(Clement Juglar, 1862)*

Lord Overstone (1796–1883), an English banker, in 1837 defined business cycles as the 'state of trade which revolves apparently in an established cycle…from quiescence, improvement, growing confidence, prosperity, excitement, overtrading, convulsion, pressure, stagnation, and distress, ending again in quiescence' (Schumpeter, 1954).

Economic activity never runs in a continuous straight line over time, whether upwards, downwards or stationary, but traces some fluctuating wave with varying amplitude and duration. This is not to say that economic activity does not continue to grow over the span of a cycle from peak to peak or from trough to trough, even though activity may register an actual fall in the trough, rather than merely a slowing down in the rate of growth. Fluctuations in economic activity may occur around a rising trend. The economic variables exhibiting these cycles may be macro-economic, such as the Gross Domestic Product (GDP), industrial production, agricultural output, consumer or wholesale price levels and international trade. The cycles may be confined to a particular country or may be replicated internationally. Often associated with the approach of a cycle to its peak is the growth of speculation. This may be centred on an almost infinite variety of economic activities, commodities, industries, real estate or financial instruments of many kinds. Euphoric speculative booms tend to flourish on the upper reaches of the business cycle only to tip over into their inevitable depressive speculative collapses on the downward slope. Speculative manias have been a persistently recurring feature of economic activity for centuries. Kindleberger (1996) lists the many occasions where there has been an accelerating rush into a pot from which rising profits seem to be for the asking. His list starts with the spread of a currency scam of coinage debasement, referred to as the *Kipper-und Wipperzeit*, and the 'Tulipmania' speculation in Dutch bulbs in the early 17th century and continues to technology shares in 1995; to which may be added the boom in real estate asset prices in the years up to 2007. This boom occurred in the >USA and other countries and the effects of the collapse were compounded by the lack of transparency in the risks inherent in financial instruments based on sub-prime credit. This led to the freezing of inter-bank lending and a severe liquidity shortage necessitating worldwide government intervention. However, these apparently irrational, at least in their final stages, speculative excesses, although often feeding off a particular phase of a business cycle, are not necessarily an integral part of its structure.

Before the 19th century, it was, of course, recognized that economic activity may rise or fall, but emphasis was placed on particular events as the cause, such as war, pestilence or crop failure, that triggered a change of direction. In the 19th century, however, economists began to speculate that there appeared to be an inherent tendency for economies to move in a cyclical fashion. These cycles may not necessarily be generated by an exogenous event such as a poor harvest but could have an endogenously generated fluctuating structure. The >CLASSICAL AND NEO-CLASSICAL ECONOMISTS believed that an economy had an in-built tendency to a stable equilibrium and a cyclical pattern was not inconsistent with this view in so far as any deviations would be expected naturally to revert to the equilibrium position. >MALTHUS was uneasy about this and had taken issue with >RICARDO about the possibility of a persistent recession, expressing concern about the time the economy was taking to recover back to an equilibrium position from the slump following the end of the Napoleonic War in 1815.

Cycles of varying duration began to be explored from the 19th century. Clement Juglar (1819–1905), employing for the first time the mathematical analysis of time series, detected cycles of about nine or ten years. He published his results in 1862 in *Les Crises Commerciales et leur retour period en France, en Angleterre et aux Etats Unis*, and concluded that 'the only cause of depression is prosperity'. Cycles of much longer duration were found by Nikolai Kondratieff (1892–1938) (1935) in a study of prices and interest rates from the 18th century

through to the 1920s. This work was evaluated in Schumpeter (1939), in which is discussed the possibility of long waves of about 50 years. Simon Kuznets (1961) and others have identified cycles of from 14–22 years' duration and Joseph Kitchin (1923) shorter cycles of about three to five years.

Solomou (1988) found no evidence of the long Kondratieff wave in the statistical analyses of >BRITAIN, Germany, France, USA and world data, covering time series of production, investment, prices and innovation from 1856 to 1973. There was some evidence of the shorter Kuznets swings but this was mainly confined to the period before >WORLD WAR I. The world economy was rather characterized by irregular fluctuations in growth rates generated by structural changes in the world economy and the differential development between countries.

Since the pioneering work of Juglar, considerable statistical analytical work has been carried out during which the statistical bases have continuously been improved and the mathematical techniques applied have also been refined. The National Bureau of Economic Research (NBER) has compiled business cycle data for the USA from the 1850s and continues to record and publish the turning points of current cycles. The methodology and definitions used by the NBER were set out in Burns and Mitchell (1946) and on the basis of these data some scholars have concluded that recessions have become shorter in the USA after the end of >WORLD WAR II compared with the years before >WORLD WAR I. However, revisions of the historical statistical series by Romer (1994) lead to the conclusion that there was little evidence of major shifts in the pattern or the frequency of business cycles between the two periods. Romer states the average time from peak to trough to be, in fact, one month shorter before World War I compared with the period subsequent to World War II and the average loss of output from the decline is about the same. However, the experience of the USA cannot necessarily be extrapolated to that of other countries. For instance, Siegler (1998) has found evidence that in a study covering a sample of 11 countries, cyclical volatility was significantly higher in the pre-World War I period compared with the period after World War II.

The hierarchy of business cycles also includes those centred around particular industries or commodities. The textbook example is that of the 'cobweb model', which illustrates the cyclical swings that can occur in any market in which there is a lag between demand and the supply response. It is typical of agriculture, in which there is a long time interval between the planting of seed and the harvesting of crops. For instance, a poor coffee harvest due, say, to inclement weather, reduces the supply coming on to the market with the result that prices increase. Individual farmers, perceiving the lucrative returns being made, switch more land into coffee production. The problem is that they do not take into account that all farmers do this, with the result that, come harvest time, there is a glut and prices plummet. Farmers then switch out of coffee and so reduce the supply and cause an increase in prices in the next period and the cycle repeats itself. Jan Tinbergen (1903–1994) published in 1931 a mathematical model following similar principles to show how cyclical fluctuations in shipbuilding would occur because of the time lapse between changes in freight rates and the launch of additional shipping tonnage. In the post-Keynesian era (>KEYNES), there have been a number of mathematical models exploring the implications of the dynamic interactions of the macro-economic concepts such as the multiplier and the accelerator and showing how time lags may inherently generate cyclical fluctuations in the economy (Hicks, 1950). An example of a Keynesian approach to the analysis of the dynamics of cycles is given in Dow (1998), which considers a number of recessions between 1920 and 1995. Emphasis is given to shocks transmitted by falls in the level of demand through the economic system by the 'multiplier' and 'accelerator' mechanisms, which may also affect confidence. These shocks arose from, for instance, a fall in export demand, in inventory accumulation or the fiscal behaviour of government. Recovery was achieved by an increase in demand.

In addition to the statistical attempts which have been made to identify and describe a whole family of business cycles of varying duration and amplitudes and their possible interrelation, a number of explanatory theories have explored the possible organic nature of the business cycle and what the forces could be which could cause endogenous fluctuations in economic activity and what triggers or shocks may induce a change in direction. The business cycle appears to be an inherent characteristic of the free market capitalist system (>CAPITALISM). Karl >MARX believed that recessions simply reflected the 'fundamental contradiction of capitalism' (quoted in Blaug, 1978), because entrepreneurs were only interested in the production of goods for profit not for their use. The demands on the 'reserve army' of labour initially raised wages but this diminished profits, which in turn caused a drop in capital investment, a fall in demand and a drop in real wages as the 'reserve army' became larger, leading again to a rise in profits. In addition to this 'short-run' cycle, according to Marx there was also a secular trend of a continually falling rate of profit. >SCHUMPETER also believed that cycles were inherent in the capitalist system and essential for continuing long-run growth. Cycles were generated by the 'creative destruction' of 'swarms of innovations' (Schumpeter, 1939), which led to an increase in the money supply in support of new investment, which was followed by falling prices with the consequential increase in competition leading to recession.

A cycle may or may not be initiated or reversed by an external event but its behaviour may be regarded as endogenous in so far as each stage in the cycle is a function of the previous stage. Since Lord Overton's observations, several theories and ideas have been proposed to explain the motive forces in business cycles, their structure and factors which might impinge on particular cycles, it being recognized that every cycle has its own particular characteristics. A recurrent feature in these theories is the part played by investment in capital equipment, such as plant and machinery, even in those theories which emphasize the part played by money. For instance, the sequence of events may begin with the money rate at which banks lend to firms being lower than the rate of return they expect to earn from their investment in new capacity, which firms consequently expand. Eventually the money rate of interest rises as banks reach the limit of their reserves and the expected profits evaporate as the additional capacity comes on to the market, firms are forced to retrench and prices fall. The fall in prices eventually induces a lower money rate of

interest and the sequence is repeated. For >HAYEK, in the upturn there is a fall in real wages because prices rise faster than money wages and this induces firms to switch to more labour-intensive production (to more 'roundabout' methods of production). Eventually, this causes a drop in total investment. The converse happens in the recession. The trigger for change may, therefore, be inherent in the recession phase. Other candidates may be exogenous events such as the introduction of new technology, such as the >RAILWAYS in the 19th century, or a failed harvest of a critical crop or changes in expectations. >FRIEDMAN deduced from his study of the monetary history of the USA that a critical factor was a mismatch between the growth of the quantity of money and that of the economy.

In the last quarter of the 19th century, the condition of agriculture was a feature of a period which at the time was referred to as the 'Great Depression' (this expression came to be applied more appropriately to the internationally much more severe collapse in economic activity in the years between the two world wars (>GREAT DEPRESSION)). There was, throughout the world, a continual fall in the level of prices. One view is that the downturn was caused by the expansion of agriculture in North America, the lowering of transport costs (>RAILWAYS: >SHIPPING) and improved industrial technology, all of which put pressure on agricultural and other prices. The alternative view is that the prime cause of this decline was the tightening of the money supply (Capie and Wood, 1994). Economic growth was progressing faster than the supply of new gold at the time when more countries were joining the >GOLD STANDARD. In Britain, wholesale prices fell by about 40 per cent between 1873 and 1896. In France, there was a similar drop in wholesale prices. In both countries, however, there was an increase in real wages. In the USA, the general level of prices fell 16 per cent and farm prices by 28 per cent between 1870 and 1880. There were further falls in these prices of between 11 per cent and 13 per cent in the 1880s. US Agriculture, therefore, suffered particularly during this period. The recession was brought to an end with the increase in gold supplies and the recovery of confidence (>PRICES AND INFLATION: >SILVER).

Solomou and Wu (1999) explored the economies of >BRITAIN, France and Germany in the second half of the 19th century. This was a period in which >AGRICULTURE still played an important part in these countries' economies, although considerably less so in Britain. They concluded that, before 1913, weather shocks did generate cyclical effects in agricultural production in these countries, which in turn were reflected in changes in macro-economic variables. Britain was less affected than the other two countries and became less so in the period as its dependence on agriculture diminished.

## References

Blaug, Mark, *Economic Theory in Retrospect*, Cambridge University Press, 1978.

Burns, Arthur F. and Mitchell, Wesley C., *Measuring Business Cycles*, National Bureau of Economic Research, 1946.

Capie, Forrest and Wood, Geoffrey, 'Money in the Economy, 1870–1939, in Roderick Floud and Donald McCloskey (eds), *The Economic History of Britain Since 1700*, II, 1860–1970s (2nd edn), Cambridge University Press, 1994.

Dow, Christopher, *Major Recessions: Britain and the World, 1920–1995*, Oxford University Press, 1998.

Hicks, J. R., *A Contribution to the Theory of the Trade Cycle*, Oxford University Press, 1950.

Kindleberger, Charles P., *Manias, Panics, and Crashes: A History of Financial Crises*, John Wiley and Sons, 1996.

Kitchin, Joseph, 'Cycles and Trends in Economic Factors', *Review of Economic Statistics*, January, 1923.

Kondratief, Nikolai, D., 'The Long Waves in Economic Life', *Review of Economic Statistics*, 17, 1935.

Kuznets, Simon, S. 'Quantitative Aspects of the Economic Growth of Nations: Long-term Trends in Capital Formation Proportions', *Economic Development and Cultural Change*, 9, 1961.

Romer, Christina D., 'Re-measuring Business Cycles', *Journal of Economic History*, 54(3), September, 1994.

Schumpeter, Joseph A., *Business Cycles: A Theoretical, Historical and Statistical Analysis of the Capitalist Process*, McGraw Hill, 1939.

Schumpeter, Joseph A., *History of Economic Analysis*, Oxford University Press, 1954.

Siegler, Mark V., 'Real Output and Business Cycle Volatility, 1869–1993: US Experience in International Perspective', *Journal of Economic History*, 58(2), June, 1998.

Solomou, Solomos, *Phases of Economic Growth, 1850–1973: Kondratieff Waves and Kuznets Swings*, Cambridge University Press, 1988.

Solomou, Solomos and Wu, Weike, 'Weather Effects on European Agricultural Output, 1850–1913', *European Review of Economic History*, 3(3), December, 1999.

# Business Management

The organization and direction of the resources of business enterprises (and other institutions) for maximum performance, the main tasks of management, are obviously of importance to the economy. Drucker (1973) emphasizes that management, which is a practice, not a science, faces the same tasks everywhere and is therefore a generic function. This does not mean that management practices have remained unchanged through history, or that they do not differ in some respects between countries. Practices have varied over time because of changes in the scale of business and the environmental conditions they face, and also vary between countries because management is influenced by culture. Ultimately, management is about dealing with people and making decisions under conditions of uncertainty. However, various specialized skills may be involved, for example, financial management (>ACCOUNTANCY) and engineering. The essence of management is difficult to get to grips with in the abstract and perhaps this is why the subject has developed its own jargon, terminology which only a few specialist writers, the late Peter Drucker being the greatest, seem able to dispense with. Since the effectiveness of management is generally only revealed by business performance, and that is also affected by multiple external factors, there has been endless controversy about the impact of management on overall economic performance and differences between countries.

From the point of view of economic history, we can trace the relationship between management organization, time and enterprise scale in several ways. People have been organizing and managing economic activity since the beginning, but it is usual to date 'modern management' as emerging from the mercantile period (>COMMERCIAL REVOLUTION). Merchants were managers of both domestic and international trade and, until the 18th century, managed the 'putting-out system' of manufacture (>PROTO-INDUSTRIALIZATION) by placing orders for export or domestic

sale with artisans and often providing them with the necessary materials. In this they were avoiding the task of micro-management of activities by delegating it to others through the market. In fact, one of management's tasks is to decide what to do in-house and what to buy in from outside.

From the 1770s factories in >BRITAIN, owned and managed by families and small numbers of people, emerged to group workers under one roof to replace the cottage industry of the putting-out system. This raised new and more complex management issues, for example in the recruitment and disciplining of workers and in arranging flows of materials and funds. In the 19th century, beginning with >CANALS and >RAILWAYS and continuing with great industrial concerns after 1870, still more complex management issues arose. Over time, diversification and increasing scale created requirements for amounts of capital too large to be supplied by individuals. Raising the necessary funds through >CAPITAL MARKETS necessitated the splitting up of business ownership into small fractions and led to the separation of ownership and control (>CORPORATE GOVERNANCE). Increasingly, big firms were no longer owned and managed by the same people and new management systems were developed, especially after >WORLD WAR II (earlier in the >USA). All the different historical phases marked a partial transition to larger-scale firms and scale is one important determinant of types of management organization; another is the sector in which the business operates. The different management systems related to scale still run alongside one another today since there is a range of enterprise sizes from >SMALL AND MEDIUM ENTERPRISES to >MULTINATIONAL ENTERPRISES. We can classify the main types of management organization into *personal* (including mercantile), the *intermediate* (early industry) and the *managerial* (big business) (Wilson, 1995).

Personal management, whether of a trading enterprise or workshop or mine as they existed in the 18th century, is characterized by one or a small number of owners who directly manage the business. Personal management means that the owner or owners – for partnerships were increasingly common – was involved in all parts of the business with all the key personnel appointed by and reporting to him (very few women managed large enterprises in this period). There might be foremen and even a 'works manager', but the owner typically knew and communicated with all employees. It was the owner alone that devised the strategy of the business and raised the necessary funds for it. In some sectors, particularly where relatively high levels of expertise were required, as with skilled artisans, there might be sub-contracting within the firm so that a foreman or 'charge hand' would hire and manage his own people. This arrangement was very common right up to the 1890s. Personal management is only practicable in a business of limited size. In this early period there were, of course, some large businesses in which managing partners controlled quite large parts of it. Some of these large enterprises were based on state-conferred monopolies, such as the >ENGLISH EAST INDIA COMPANY, where competition and therefore organizational pressures were limited. In the early 18th century, the largest manufacturing concerns were state-owned, for example the Royal Arsenal at Chatham, described by Daniel Defoe writing in the 1720s. There were also some large landed estates which had

professional management and the management practices used in these estates are said to have been adopted elsewhere, for example, in coal mining. The vast majority of enterprises were very small and with the exception of textiles (>COTTON AND COTTON TEXTILES), where the first large private factories emerged, remained so at least until the mid-19th century. It is important to get these developments into perspective, since most enterprises in terms of numbers have always been small. In Britain by the early 21st century, 98 per cent of all enterprises employed fewer than 20 employees, though these small firms account for only 36 per cent of total employment.

Maurice Kirby in his contribution, 'Big Business Before 1900', to Kirby and Rose (1994), says that it may have been the railways which created modern corporate systems (i.e. those of salaried managers in big business) and similar conclusions have been reached for the USA. Drucker (1973) asserts that it was the great universal banks (>BANKING) which first developed these systems in Germany. Until the 1870s family ownership and management of business was particularly important. It was only from the middle of the 18th century that nepotism began to give way to the appointment of outsiders that characterized the intermediate stage on the road to big business, and, even then, the owner-managers kept a fairly tight control over the details of their business.

In the managerial, or last of the three phases, the divorce of ownership from management control is virtually complete. Professional salaried managers run the business, while the owners (shareholders) play no role in management except in the election of the boards of directors who in turn appoint the senior managers, though even then it is the management that typically propose the candidates so that the hierarchy can be self-perpetuating. A variety of organizational forms has emerged but increasingly, and especially from the 1920s, businesses were organized into divisions, each effectively a separate profit centre coordinated by committees of executives supported by a central staff (the M- or multi-divisional form). In some sectors, where product ranges were simpler and there was more vertical integration (extractive industries are an example), the firm was organized into functional departments in a centralized structure (U-form). More recently, and especially from the late 1970s, there have been pressures from shareholders, now predominantly large financial institutions, to reassert greater control over management (>CORPORATE GOVERNANCE). A consequence of these pressures in favour of 'shareholder value', combined with intensifying global competition, has been the re-emergence of flatter management structures with fewer management layers and a movement away from conglomeracy to focus on 'core activities' (>COMPANIES).

The training of the professionals engaged in managerial enterprises and the codification and diffusion of management practices has been the joint work of practitioners, consultants and a new breed of academics. Management consultancy emerged as a separate profession from the 1920s, coinciding with the spread of new forms of management in larger firms. The pace of these developments quickened in the 1960s. In 1960 only 6,000 people with MBAs graduated in the USA, by the year 2000 this number had swelled to over 100,000 and similar developments have taken place in other advanced countries.

'Scientific management', pioneered by Frederick >TAYLOR, is concerned with the study and measurement of particular work operations and locations and does not extend to the strategic element in management. This broader aspect of management is an art and not governed by science, as Drucker pointed out, though many persist in confusing the two.

The business historian Alfred >CHANDLER was to attribute >BRITAIN'S lagging economic performance after 1870 compared with the USA and Germany to the late continuance of personal and family management. This view has been much criticized. Church (1990) argued that, until World War II, family ownership and control was no more important in Britain than in the USA or Japan, and others that the identification of family ownership with economic backwardness is a misleading over-simplification since the environment for business differed between these countries (Rose, 1994). Debate about Britain's lagging performance then and later has continued until recently and it has been argued by Rubinstein (1993) that a focus on manufacturing competitiveness in this debate is anyway misleading for an economy like Britain whose competitive advantage lies in the >SERVICE SECTOR.

Cross-fertilization in management thinking between different cultures in a globalizing world has proved productive. In particular, Japanese management practices have been fairly distinctive from those in the West. The characteristics of Japanese management include: more involvement of the workforce in quality control (some of this imported by US consultants) and innovation; close attention to stock levels and material flows; and the promotion of corporate leaders by the slow upward movement of people within the firm. These different approaches seem to stem from deep-seated cultural characteristics of Japanese society, notably collectivism and the need for consensus and from the fact that as an industrial late-comer, much early technology was transferred in from abroad. For example, in Japan (and interestingly also in Germany, which has stronger collective attitudes than the Anglo-Saxon countries), engineers are more prevalent among senior management than in Britain, France or the USA, where leaders have tended to be drawn from liberally educated elites, for example, the older universities and, in France, the *Grandes écoles*. One connection between this and employee involvement is that engineer leaders are likely to spend time on the shop floor involving employees in the solution of technical problems (see the contribution by Ken'ichi Yasumuro to Brown and Rose, 1993).

Generalizations about management and its relation to economic performance need to be made and interpreted with great care. In the 1960s peaking concern about the supposed inferiority of European management systems compared with those of the USA coincided with a resurgence in the international competitiveness of European manufacturers – for example, in the >AUTOMOBILE INDUSTRY. Similarly, in the 1980s belief in the superiority of Japanese management and innovation systems compared with those of the US corporations coincided with a resurgence in US competitiveness and the collapse of the Japanese 'economic miracle'.

## References

Brown, Jonathan and Rose, Mary B. (eds), *Entrepreneurship, Networks, and Modern Business*, Manchester University Press, 1993.

Chandler, Alfred D., *Scale and Scope: The Dynamics of Industrial Capitalism*, Harvard University Press, 1989.

Church, Roy, 'The Limitations of the Personal Capitalism Paradigm', *Business History Review*, 64, 1990.

Drucker, Peter F., *Management: Tasks, Responsibilities, Practices*, Harper & Row, 1973.

Kirby, Maurice W. and Rose, Mary B. (eds), *Business Enterprise in Modern Britain from the Eighteenth to the Twentieth Century*, Routledge, 1994.

Rose, Mary B., 'The Family Firm in British Business, 1780–1914', in Maurice W. Kirby and Mary B. Rose (eds), *Business Enterprise in Modern Britain from the Eighteenth to the Twentieth Century*, Routledge, 1994.

Rubinstein, W. D., *Capitalism, Culture and Decline in Britain, 1750–1990*, Routledge, 1993.

Wilson, John F., *British Business History, 1720–1994*, Manchester University Press, 1995.

# C

## Canals

'Good roads, canals, and navigable rivers, by diminishing the expense of carriage, put the remote part of the country more nearly upon a level with those in the neighbourhood of the town. They are upon that account the greatest of all improvements. They encourage the cultivation of the remote, which must always be the most extensive circle of the country. They are advantageous to the town, by breaking down the monopoly of the country in its neighbourhood. They are advantageous even to that part of the country. Though they introduce some rival commodities into the old market, they open many new markets to its produce. Monopoly, besides, is a great enemy to good management, which can never be universally established but in consequence of that free and universal competition which forces everybody to have recourse to it for the sake of self defence.'

(Adam Smith, *'Inquiry into the Nature and Causes of the Wealth of Nations'* 1776, Chap XI, Part I)

Canal building for irrigation or transport has a long history; construction of the 1,000-mile length of the Grand Canal in >CHINA was begun in the 4th century BC; the canal lock was invented in the 14th century. However, stimulated by the need for improved transport, extensive canal building did not seriously begin until the 18th century, accelerating through the 19th and 20th centuries, particularly in Europe. Of the 90 major canals in the world in 2000, 50 were in Europe, 23 in North and South America, 13 in Asia and four in Africa. Canals have been constructed to meet three broad types of transport need: the movement of a commodity from the point of production to its market; the linking of inland river systems to widen their market hinterland; or to facilitate improvements in ocean-going shipping, such as the Kiel, Panama and Suez canals (>SHIPPING). Inland waterways offer an economical method for the transportation of bulk commodities such as coal and cereals, particularly over medium- and long-distance routes.

In >BRITAIN, a canal 'mania' followed the construction in 1761 of the Duke of Bridgewater's Worsley Canal in Lancashire for the transport of coal from the Duke's mines to Manchester. There were 1,000 miles of navigable waterways in existence in Britain in the middle of the 18th century and a further 3,000 miles of navigable waterways, most of which were canals, were developed by 1820. However, no new canals were ever again constructed in Britain, apart from the Manchester Ship Canal in 1894. By 2000, the UNECE (2004) recorded that only 191km of canals were regularly used for transport in Britain.

In transport terms, Britain enjoys the natural advantages not only of its navigable waterways but more particularly an island coastline supported throughout its length by good harbours (>SEAPORTS). Canal development in Britain was demand-based, supported generally by private enterprise and financed through joint stock companies, although schemes were subjected to constraints laid down in their respective Parliament Acts. Enterprises were also subject to the constraints of the Bubble Act of 1720 (>COMPANIES). For instance, the Duke of Bridgewater's Parliament Act for his Worsley Canal, while giving him the power to acquire land, imposed a maximum transport charge and set the maximum at which he could sell his own coal in Manchester (Odlyzko, 2004).

Canal building on the Continent of Europe, in contrast, was more influenced by government decision and supported by government finance. In Northern Europe, canals, and the navigable waterways in general, have played a more enduring role as part of the transportation system. The geography of the Continent is technically favourable to the construction of canals but also the inter-linkages of the network open up the medium and long distances favourable to the competitive carriage of bulk cargoes on waterways.

The Netherlands extended their waterway system in the 19th century with particular emphasis on improving ship access to ports. Belgium had 1,600km of navigable waterway by 1830 of which 450km were canals. In 2000, there were 836km of canals in regular use for transport (UNECE, 2004). In France, canal construction developed vigorously in the 19th century within a framework of a national plan which was drawn up in 1832. In 2000, France had 4,135km of canals in regular transport use (UNECE, 2004). In Germany, canal and waterway development began later than in other countries in Western Europe. By the middle of the 18th century, only about 750km of canals had been constructed. However, by 1914,

the length of canals and improved rivers had increased to 6,600km. In 2000, according to the UNECE (2004), there were 6,754km of navigable waterways, of which 1,238 were canals.

In the >USA, the Erie Canal was constructed by the State of New York between 1817 and 1825. It was 363 miles long and connected the Hudson River with the Great Lakes. Pennsylvania established a network of a mix of canals, rivers and roads to link Pittsburgh to Philadelphia. Eventually, a system of canals covered Ohio and parts of Indiana to afford access also to the Great Lakes. By 1850, there were about 4,000 miles of canals in the USA.

In their initial phases of development, the canals competed for the carriage of freight against transport by wagon on the roads. Canals reduced transport costs. The Bridgewater Canal in Britain reduced the price of coal in Manchester. The Iron and Steel industry of the Ruhr in Germany was assisted by the cheaper access to iron ore. When the Erie Canal opened, freight rates between New York and Buffalo fell from $100 per ton to $8 per ton (Nye and Morpurgo, 1965). As Adam Smith had shown, wheat, sheep and cattle now competed effectively against the farmers of New England. In turn, canals were faced with the arrival of the >RAILWAYS, which were inaugurated in Britain with the opening of the Stockton–Darlington Railway in 1825 and the Liverpool and Manchester in 1830, which was the first public railway. In Britain, the coming of the railways was fatal to the canals because the distances were too restricted by the geography of the country and so they lacked the competitive benefits which long hauls may have offered them. In Europe, the contrary obtained. There was significant canal investment after the advent of the railways. In France, the tonnage of freight on inland waterways grew by 73 per cent between the 1880s and 1905, on Belgium waterways by 114 per cent and on German waterways by 274 per cent (Ville, 1994). It is clear that canals and inland waterways, alongside the other transport modes of roads and railways, captured and retained their respective market niches in which they each succeeded in maintaining a competitive edge.

There has been some debate of the part played by the development of canals in the >INDUSTRIAL REVOLUTIONS. In Britain, it may be argued, canals were conducive to the industrial revolution in the sense that they could be seen to be part of the process; for instance in the transport of coal. However, a long-distance trunk canal system did not appear in Britain until the 19th century and the roads did, in fact, compete effectively in many areas of transport requirement. The Industrial Revolution in Britain took place without the advantage of either a trunk canal system or the railways. On the other hand, it has nevertheless been argued that the industrial revolution took off first in Britain because of its efficient transport system compared with that in other countries (Chartres, 1992; Szostak, 1991).

### References

Chartres, J., 'Road Transport and Economic Growth in the Eighteenth Century', in Anne Digby, Charles Feinstein and David Jenkins (eds), *New Directions in Economic and Social History*, Macmillan, 1992.

Fogel, Robert W., 'Notes on the Social Saving Controversy', in Robert Whaples and Dianne C. Betts, *Historical Perspectives on the American Economy*, Cambridge University Press, 1995.

Geiger, Reed G., *Planning the French Canals: Bureaucracy, Politics, and Enterprise Under the Restoration*,University of Delaware Press, 1994.

Kunz, Andreas and Armstrong, John (eds), *Inland Navigation and Economic Development in Nineteenth Century Europe*,Philipp von Zabern, 1995.

Nye, R. B. and Morpurgo, J. E., *The Growth of the USA*, Penguin, 1965.

Odlyzko, Andrew, 'The Evolution of Price Discrimination in Transportation and Its Implications for the Internet', *Review of Network Economics*, 3(3), September, 2004.

Pollard, Sydney, *Peaceful Conquest: Industrialisation of Europe, 1760 –1970*, Oxford University Press, 1982.

Shaw, Ronald E., *Canals for a Nation: The Canal Era in the United States, 1790–1860*, University Press of Kentucky, 1990.

Szostak, R., *The Role of Transportation in the Industrial Revolution: A Comparison of England and France*, McGill Queen's University Press, 1991.

United Nations Economic Commission for Europe (UNECE), *Annual Bulletin of Transport Statistics*, LIII, Geneva, 2004.

Ville, Simon P. 'Transport and Communications', in Derek H. Aldcroft and Simon P. Ville (eds), *The European Economy, 1750–1914*, Manchester University Press, 1994.

# Capital Markets

The term 'capital markets' may be used in a broad sense to cover all the institutions providing longer-term loanable funds, including securities markets (equities and bonds), banking, insurance companies and pension funds. There are also the money markets which deal in short-term (up to about one year) securities and other liquid instruments, including foreign exchange. In this entry we focus upon securities markets dealing in longer-term government and especially corporate stocks. In this narrower sense, the capital markets are characterized by their greater degrees of risk and a need for regulated stock exchanges to create liquidity and a focus for the provision of ownership registration, custodial and settlement systems, as well as information for investors.

The first 'modern' stock exchange began in Amsterdam, where, around 1609, shares in the Dutch East India Company were traded, although Antwerp had previously traded in negotiable bills of exchange and much earlier, in the 14th century, securities were traded in Northern Italy. After the Glorious Revolution of 1688, which brought William of Orange to the English throne, Dutch ideas and financial instruments were brought to London. A gradual financial revolution took place in which funded government debt, the establishment of the Bank of England in 1694 (>CENTRAL BANKING) and organized markets in public and private debt emerged. Development in Britain and parallel developments in France were delayed by the South Sea Bubble and the slow evolution of laws governing limited liability (>COMPANIES). By 1750, however, Britain had developed relatively sophisticated markets in public debt which enabled the government to finance its wars at a fraction of the cost of its continental rivals. That and the >TAXATION system were associated with the emergence of >BRITAIN as a powerful nation state and laid the financial infrastructure for the >INDUSTRIAL REVOLUTION IN BRITAIN. America also had its financial revolution somewhat later, in the period following the ratification of the constitution of the USA and in which the Federal government assumed liability for the debts of the states (>AMERICAN WAR OF INDEPENDENCE: >HAMILTON).

The London Stock Exchange (LSE) had informal origins in dealings of brokers meeting at coffee houses. In 1773, brokers who had dealt at Jonathan's coffee house moved to a room in a nearby alley, which constituted the first formal exchange. In the USA, the first organized stock market was established in Philadelphia in 1790. Two years later, 24 dealers agreed to meet regularly under an old buttonwood tree in Wall Street and this was the beginning of the New York Stock Exchange (NYSE). In the 19th century commercial finance was very much a local affair in both Britain and the USA. Early industrialists in Britain could borrow from local savers and county banks. Lawyers and other professionals participated in these local capital markets, though interest rates were set in London (see Larry Neal's contribution to Floud and McCloskey, 1994). In the early stages of industrial development, fixed capital requirements were low and financed mostly by mortgages and retained earnings. Stock exchanges outside London were later established in Manchester and Liverpool (1836), followed by Leeds and Birmingham. At one time there were about 25 regional exchanges in both Britain and the USA. In the USA there were regional exchanges in Boston, Cincinnati, San Francisco and elsewhere, as well as in Philadelphia-Baltimore. The Chicago Board of Trade built the world's largest market for wheat and other commodities from 1850, which also was about the time of the establishment of the American Stock Exchange (AMEX) in New York, a smaller rival to the NYSE.

In both Britain and the USA, early investors in the new exchanges preferred fixed-interest securities. The markets in government debt were maturing and included foreign government debt and, from the end of the 18th century, the unredeemable 2.5 per cent Consols. Although canal and utility enterprises were quoted on the LSE from the early 19th century, it was not until the >RAILWAY boom in the 1840s that commercial security markets took off and this development accelerated dramatically in the 1880s. In 1886, Guinness converted to a quoted company and this encouraged other brewers to float stock. At this time there were a growing number of issues from electrical engineering, chemical, cycle and motor manufacturers. However, railway stocks, especially in preference, quasi-equity form predominated, this appealed not only to investors but also to issuers who could avoid the problems of loss of control associated with pure equities.

Hannah (2007) calculates that, by 1900, 49 per cent of the market capitalization of domestic companies listed on the LSE was accounted for by railway stocks. The corresponding proportions for the Paris Bourse were 43 per cent and for the NYSE, 63 per cent. At that time, according to Hannah's figures, market capitalization of the LSE was twice that of the Paris Bourse and 50 per cent larger than that of the NYSE. The capitalization of the Berlin exchange was only half that of Paris (railways were mostly state-owned in Germany). Dimson *et al.* (2002) put the size of the US exchanges well ahead of that of London in 1900, but their figures, unlike Hannah's, presumably include the regional exchanges and foreign equities.

There were major setbacks in stock markets between the two world wars (>GREAT DEPRESSION). The British markets did not rise to the heights of Wall Street and suffered less in the downturn. The 1929 boom and crash in America was so catastrophic that the volume of trading share activity did not recover until after >WORLD WAR II. The long post-war economic boom was accompanied by a spectacular growth in stock markets with widening share ownership, the growth of >MULTINATIONAL ENTERPRISES, the expansion of government debt and >GLOBALIZATION. There has been a considerable degree of competition and consolidation among stock exchanges, which have largely ceased to be mutual organizations and become quoted enterprises in their own right. After failed attempts at a takeover by Continental European interests and NASDAQ, the LSE in 2007 was partly owned by Middle East interests (Dubai and Qatar) that have used their oil revenues to expand into financial services. LSE also merged with the Italian exchanges in 2007. In the same period the NYSE Group holding company absorbed Euronext, which in 2000 had linked the Belgian, French, Dutch and Portuguese stock exchanges. Euronext also included derivative exchanges, including the London International Financial Futures Exchange (LIFFE).

With Japan's post-war emergence as a major economic power, the Tokyo Stock Exchange (TSE), which has its origins in the Meiji period in the 1880s, has grown enormously. According to data from the World Federation of Exchanges, we can see that global securities markets have been transformed since 1900. In 2005, in terms of equity market capitalization of domestic companies, the NYSE dwarfed all other stock markets and was followed by the TSE with a third of the market capitalization of New York, the LSE, Euronext and the Deutsche Borse (DB) in that order. Following the rise of other Asian economies (>ASIAN MIRACLE),

Asian stock markets, including Hong Kong, Shanghai and Singapore, also became more important. In 2005, London had the highest ratio of market capitalization to GDP of 145 per cent (1900, 49 per cent), the NYSE ratio was 109 per cent (1900, 15 per cent according to Hannah's figures (2007)) and the DB's 107 per cent (14 per cent for Berlin only in 1900). International comparisons of stock exchanges, however, are fraught with pitfalls. For example, the US GDP ratio would be much higher if NASDAQ and regional exchanges were included. The importance of London as a financial centre is greatly understated by comparing only market capitalizations of domestic companies. London had a much larger share of the turnover of foreign equities and foreign exchange than the USA and carried out 70 per cent of trading in the secondary market for international bonds (International Financial Services, London, cited in *The Economist*, 21 October 2006).

In the last quarter of the 20th century, global securities markets became increasingly integrated, with the impact of stock market sensitive events being rapidly transmitted between countries. In this there has been a return, still perhaps not a complete return, to the 1870–1914 era when global capital markets flourished with London at the centre. In this period, industrialization was continuing and there was a convergence on the >GOLD STANDARD. Trade and foreign direct investment were promoted by improvements in communications, including >SHIPPING and >TELECOMMUNICATIONS. After 1914, the development of global capital movements was arrested and reversed by the >GREAT DEPRESSION, beggar-thy-neighbour policies and two world wars.

Controls on capital movements were widespread.

The distinguishing feature of the period 1945–71 from the point of view of the economy and capital markets, was the successful effort by governments and international organizations, including the OEEC/OECD and IMF, to rebuild the global economy after >WORLD WAR II. This was achieved by the steady dismantling of controls on trade, payments and capital movements and the introduction of a system of fixed (but adjustable) exchange rates, which ended after the USA abandoned a fixed-dollar price for gold. After 1971, there was a move to fully floating exchange rates because speculative flows following freer capital movements broke the fixed rate regimes. Governments, having lost control of their exchange rates, regulated domestic macro-economic activity with fiscal and monetary policy (>CENTRAL BANKING). These developments paved the way for the upsurge in securities markets after the 1970s.

There have inevitably been destabilizing financial crises of various kinds which have been transmitted, and largely absorbed, by the international markets. Examples of these shocks are the oil price increases in the 1970s, the Asian crisis of 1997–8, the puncturing of the dot.com boom in 2001 and the US sub-prime credit problem from 2007–8. This crisis led to widespread failures in >BANKING, precipitate falls in stock market prices on an international scale. The growing freedom enjoyed by capital markets has attracted criticism. Before 1914 and for long afterwards, securities markets were largely self-regulated, but official >REGULATION grew after the inter-war period and has been increasingly coordinated on an international scale. Self-regulation was undermined by the abuse of monopoly positions by market participants. In the USA, the >NEW DEAL had already seen a considerable extension of regulation with the Securities and Exchange Acts of 1933 and 1934, which established the Securities Exchange Commission.

There was some deregulation followed by re-regulation. The NYSE abandoned fixed commissions for securities dealing in 1975 and this was followed by similar deregulation in London (the 'Big Bang') in 1986. The opening up of foreign participation in the London markets after 1986 was instrumental in the striking recovery of London's position in global capital markets as foreign banks and other financial institutions acquired interests in or control of stock exchange companies. Another factor in the development of London as a financial centre was the emergence from the 1970s of its leading position in the Eurocurrency (Eurodollar and Eurobond) markets. (These markets deal in securities denominated in currencies other than that of the issuing country.) Corporate scandals, such as the Enron affair in the USA, led to new re-regulation, for example to improve corporate accounting transparency (Sarbanes-Oxley Act 2002). The heavy compliance costs of new regulation in the USA led to complaints that it was damaging the competitiveness of New York as a financial centre compared with London. However, London markets also carried substantial compliance costs although regulators there were perhaps more innovative than those elsewhere. The breaking down of borderlines between different activities in the financial markets led to the emergence of unitary regulators covering virtually all financial institutions in many countries, for example, the Financial Services Authority in Britain following the Financial Services Acts of 1986 and 2001.

Over the long period there have been big changes in the nature of securities traded. Governments have issued securities in which the capital value was protected from inflation, corporate bonds became more popular and securitization of credit derivatives was growing, if not fully understood. In contrast to 1900, railway securities were now of negligible importance, having been overtaken by information technology, pharmaceuticals, banking, finance and insurance and other stocks. Despite all these changes, equity securities have provided good returns to investors who held on to them for long periods. According to Dimson *et al.* (2002), over the period 1900–2000 cumulative annual returns on equities averaged about 10 per cent and bonds and bills about 5 per cent in both Britain and the USA. These returns translated to about 6–7 per cent and 1 per cent respectively in real terms.

The development of securities markets was not restricted to the core industrialized countries. Markets in developing countries were also liberalized, although with mixed success. Obstfeld and Taylor (2004) find, however, that these countries have yet to return to the scale of inward investment and capital market freedom many of them enjoyed before 1914.

Capital markets, including the securities markets, also attracted criticism on the grounds that they did not sufficiently meet the needs of industry. It has been argued that, in the 19th century, overseas investment deprived British industry of finance. Kindleberger (1984) takes the view that the problem lay more with the demand for finance than the supply and that examples could be found to demonstrate that returns on overseas investment may have been higher than in the domestic market. In 1931, in Britain, the Macmillan Committee, which included >KEYNES as a member, expressed concern about the availability of long-term finance for >SMALL AND MEDIUM ENTERPRISES, although it has been generally accepted that the Macmillan Gap was closed in the post-World War II period. Part of the solution was a major expansion in venture capital and, associated with this, the emergence of specialized second-tier securities markets with lower listing costs for smaller firms. The prime example of these second-tier markets was NASDAQ, which emerged from the US Over-the-Counter markets in 1971 to provide electronic trading services for stocks in technology companies and other growth businesses. NASDAQ (which stands for National Association of Securities Dealers Automated Quotation System) subsequently expanded enormously to deal in large as well as smaller companies in rivalry with the NYSE. LSE also had a second-tier market, the Alternative Investment Market (AIM). AIM had less demanding entry requirements than the main market and benefited from tax concessions for unlisted securities and venture capital investment. Established in 1995 to replace the Unlisted Securities Market (USM), it proved very successful and attracted foreign as well as British flotations. There were similar, though less successful, markets in Japan and in most European countries. Whilst there were inevitable difficulties in obtaining finance for early-stage innovative companies (>USA), it can hardly be said that the securities markets failed to back new technologies as the dot.com boom around the millenium demonstrated. There also seems to be little justification for the view that stock markets were 'short-termist' and tended to undervalue companies investing heavily in research and development.

Overall, securities markets have come a long way from their beginnings in the government debt markets of the 18th century. There was probably general agreement among economic historians that the financial sector, including both securities markets, banks and other financial institutions, preceded >ECONOMIC DEVELOPMENT. This was obviously true for the early >INDUSTRIAL REVOLUTIONS in Europe but also for the USA, Japan and other countries (Sylla, 2002). On a global scale, international capital mobility helped to smooth shocks, as it did with the aftermath of the oil crises of the 1970s, and allowed capital to flow to locations where returns were highest. Competition between securities markets helped to improve the availability and reduce the cost of capital for enterprise. For a discussion of bank-based and securities market-based financial systems, see >BANKING and for the separation of ownership from control in corporate finance that has been associated with widening share ownership, see >CORPORATE GOVERNANCE.

## References

Baskin, Jonathan Barron and Miranti, Paul J. Jr, *A History of Corporate Finance*, Cambridge University Press, 1997.

Dimson, Elroy, Marsh, Paul and Staunton, Mike, *Triumph of the Optimists: 101 Years of Global Investment Returns*, Princeton University Press, 2002.

Floud, Roderick and McCloskey, Donald (eds), *The Economic History of Britain Since 1700*, I, 1700–1860 (2nd edn), Cambridge University Press, 1994.

Hannah, Leslie, 'The Divorce of Ownership from Control from 1900 Onwards: Recalibrating Imagined

Global Trends', *Business History*, 49, July, 2007.

Kindleberger, Charles P., *A Financial History of Western Europe*, George Allen & Unwin, 1984.

Obstfeld, Maurice and Taylor, Alan M., *Global Capital Markets: Integration, Crisis and Growth*, Cambridge University Press, 2004.

Sylla, Richard, 'Financial Systems and Economic Modernisation', *Journal of Economic History*, 62, June, 2002.

# Capitalism

This is the social and economic system in which resources are allocated by markets and privately owned producers motivated by profit, employing free labour. There are no economies for which this definition holds in a pure sense, since everywhere the state owns some of the means of production and the operation of market forces is muted by >REGULATION and market imperfections. That this 'imperfect' capitalism is now accepted as the universal norm is illustrated by the falling out of use of the term 'the mixed economy' to describe an intermediate position between the market and the planned economy. Capitalism, like its opposites socialism and communism, is an ideological rather than economic concept, though it is useful as a synonym for 'market economy'. With the virtual demise of communism, all economies are now capitalistic to some degree. >CHINA combines political communism with a regulated market economy. Moreover, although widely used in economics and economic history, capitalism is rarely defined – >SCHUMPETER, in his famous book, *Capitalism, Socialism and Democracy* (1942), for example, does not take the trouble to define what he means by 'capitalism'.

Modern capitalism has evolved through a series of revolutions – commercial, consumer, industrial and post-industrial – from medieval times onwards. Max Weber (1981), writing in the tradition of the German Historical School (>ECONOMIC HISTORY) traced this evolution comprehensively over the whole sweep of history up to his time. Weber recognized that, in the sense of market exchange and profit seeking, capitalism has existed in some form since the earliest times (though it was possible that there were forms of agrarian communism in the first stages of human settlement). There were plantations producing for the market using slave labour in Carthage and in the Roman Empire, there was production for the market for the landowner's profit under the manorial system and there were merchant and regulated artisanal enterprises under the guilds.

For Weber, *modern capitalism* began only with the emergence of free labour and with minimal regulation of markets, though within a strong framework of law for example governing property rights. Other conditions for modern capitalism identified by Weber were: mechanization; the use of paper instruments to represent share rights in enterprise and property ownership; the penetration of the system to cover the provision of everyday wants by enterprises; and, crucially, the use of 'rational capital accounting'. For Weber, rational >ACCOUNTING seems to mean the use not only of double-entry bookkeeping and balance sheets, but also the ex-ante calculation of risk and potential profit and the ex-post calculation of profit or losses. It is the extreme rationality of capitalism in this way which distinguishes it from earlier systems. According to Weber, the conditions for modern capitalism were not present until the middle of the 19th century. Although he does not explicitly say so, Weber thus clearly placed the beginnings of modern capitalism with the >INDUSTRIAL REVOLUTION IN BRITAIN. Adam >SMITH, who has been referred to as the intellectual father of capitalism, described its origins and features and was to provide the basis for the theoretical justification of the market system (>CLASSICAL AND NEO-CLASSICAL ECONOMICS). Smith, however, did not actually use the term 'capitalism', which did not come into use until the 1850s.

It was the Industrial Revolution and in particular the poor working and living conditions in the early British factories described by Engels (1820–1895) that generated the ideological movement against capitalism and in favour of socialism (although there were other roots of socialism in a broad sense). The most powerful critic of capitalism proved to be Karl >MARX (1818–1883). Marx and Engels (1967), in their *Communist Manifesto*, did not use the term capitalism either, although they refer to capitalists (the bourgeoisie) and both Marx and Smith lay great emphasis on the role of 'capitals'. The *Manifesto*, which contains most of the key ideas that the authors were to develop later, interpreted economic history in terms of class conflict ('lord and serf, guild master and journeyman, in a word, oppressor and oppressed'). For Marx, the economic system based on private ownership of the means of production (capitalism) inevitably led to the exploitation of the working class, immiseration and alienation, accelerated by a falling rate of profit and increasing scale, to war and to the eventual overthrow of the system by the proletariat and its replacement by communism.

After Marx, Lenin, J. A. Hobson and others continued the Marxist tradition by criticizing the tendency to monopoly in capitalism and by asserting, as hinted by Marx, that the system inevitably resulted in the exploitation of the poorer developing countries (>ECONOMIC IMPERIALISM). Early writers, both Marxist and non-Marxist, were interested in the source of the immense amounts of capital absorbed by the industrial revolution as it went on. For Marx it came from the capture of the surplus value of the working class over and above their means of subsistence and he traced this process of accumulation back to the dispossession of small landowners. Others emphasized the profits made in the >COMMERCIAL REVOLUTION and the influx of bullion from the Spanish colonies. Some have argued that >SLAVERY and other forms of colonial exploitation provided both capital and markets for industrialization. Today, the explanation of the accumulation of capital is more of a natural process of the gradual development of >CAPITAL MARKETS and the use of reinvested profits. After >KEYNES, we also assume that on certain assumptions, and through the multiplier effect, investment itself generates the incomes and savings necessary to support it.

Marx was very vague about what communism would mean in practice and might well have been surprised that it was adopted in >RUSSIA after 1917, not as he expected in an advanced economy such as Britain. >CHINA, after a civil war, became communist in 1948, another country in which capitalism had yet to develop fully. Russian communism was extended mainly by conquest rather than emulation and communist control continued until its demise in Europe in the 1980s.

Paradoxically, the end of communism in >WESTERN EUROPE has not silenced the critics of capitalism, indeed it seems to have strengthened the view that capitalism must be regulated (>REGULATION). Marx was not alone in predicting that capitalism could not endure. Joseph >SCHUMPETER argued that the inherent instability of capitalism, together with rising wealth, would lead to its peaceful transformation into a form of socialism which would retain some of its best features.

There is a long line of defenders of capitalism, from Smith onwards. Friedrich >HAYEK argued that state-controlled, planned economies inevitably lead to totalitarianism, while Milton >FRIEDMAN wrote a powerful defence of capitalism (*Free to Choose*), which, like Hayek's *The Road to Serfdom*, became a bestseller. Some people would argue that the whole theoretical apparatus of modern economics is a defence of capitalism, though there are plenty of those within the profession who maintain that, left to themselves, markets do not guarantee either efficiency or equity (the justification for state intervention). Historians have probably been more hostile to capitalism than economists, Hayek certainly thought so (Hartwell, 1977).

J. K. Galbraith (1908–2006) criticized the private affluence and public squalor which resulted from capitalism and argued that the free market ideal had long since been lost to rule by giant corporations. Keynes had earlier argued that 'laissez-faire' (a term introduced by the >PHYSIOCRATS) was dead and that the inherent instability of capitalism meant that it could not be left to the free play of market forces. Polyani (2001) argued that there never had been a free market system; economic affairs had been regulated from feudal times and that

continued regulation was absolutely necessary to maintain social stability and thus allow the economic system to function.

Marx was wrong in most of his predictions: communism did not turn out to be an efficient way of ordering the economy and, as Hayek argued, it resulted in totalitarianism. Communism was not adopted in the advanced countries and, where it was adopted, communism was not led by the proletariat nor was the ensuing order managed by it. There has been no secular decline in profit or immiseration of the workforce living standards, for all have risen dramatically over 200 years or so of modern capitalism – this is why communism never took hold in the developed capitalist economies.

Capitalism today has evolved from the situation in the mid-19th century when labour was fairly mobile, there was free trade and a reasonably stable monetary and exchange rate regime under the >GOLD STANDARD. At that time the neo-classical model of competitive markets was a closer approximation to reality than it is today. Among the major changes that have taken place in the advanced countries since then are: an enormous increase in the role of the state in the economy (>STATE, RISE OF THE); a parallel increase in >REGULATION which, among other things has reduced factor mobility, especially in labour markets; a continuing increase in the scale of enterprises (>CONCENTRATION); enhanced international capital mobility and expanded trade both within and between trading blocs (>INTERNATIONAL TRADE). There has been a continuance of the process of >GLOBALIZATION with a major role for >MULTINATIONAL ENTERPRISE. In addition, there has been a major change in the rise of the

>SERVICE SECTOR, while manufacturing, following >AGRICULTURE, has shrunk relatively in terms of total output and employment. There have also been recessions and >BUSINESS CYCLES (one of the few of Marx's predictions not falsified by events). Capitalism has proved to be prone to fluctuations; indeed Schumpeter argued that this was an integral part of its advance. His view was that instability was the very essence of capitalism and that 'gales of creative destruction' caused by new activities were necessary for the system to advance. None of the downturns has proved to be as deep or as protracted as that of the >GREAT DEPRESSION, which led, after >WORLD WAR II, to the creation of a set of international organizations, like the International Monetary Fund and the Organization for Economic Cooperation and Development, aimed at preventing a recurrence of the protectionism and monetary instability which plagued the inter-war period. A fixed exchange rate regime was introduced after the international conference at Bretton Woods in 1944. The ensuing so-called period of managed capitalism broke down in the 1970s after a 20-year 'Golden Age' and was replaced by a system of market-determined exchange rates with an increasingly powerful role for >CENTRAL BANKING after a prolonged period of inflation and unemployment (stagflation). This new regime, however, again broke down under a banking crisis and a stock market crash in 2008 (>BANKING: >CAPITAL MARKETS).

One of the most important features of the way capitalist economies have developed is that there has been a separation of ownership and control among the larger enterprises. Unlike in the early 19th century, the directors and senior executives of these large enterprises no longer own a significant proportion of the equity share capital in the businesses they manage. Typically, the managers own just a few per cent or even less, while the majority of the shares are owned by large financial institutions such as insurance companies, banks and pension funds. Moreover, the shares of companies are widely dispersed among these institutions in the interest of minimizing risk so that none has more than about 5 per cent or so of the equity in any individual company. The effect has been that managers are not subject to close shareholder control and can be largely free to pursue their own interests, subject to the threat of takeover by other companies. Corporate governance has become a major issue, with regulations or codes of conduct to require shareholder approval for certain management actions and the appointment of non-executive directors to watch over shareholder interests (>COMPANIES: >CORPORATE GOVERNANCE). Berle and Means (1967) were the first to document the trend towards the separation of ownership and control and the process has continued. For example, Scott (1986) found that in Britain in 1976, for the 100 largest enterprises 20 financial institutions held over half the shareholdings. In no case, however, could any single institution be said to exercise control, even taking into account the fact that a company can be effectively controlled with less than 50 per cent of the equity. Scott found that the general picture was not radically different in Japan and in the USA, although Britain had more state- and more foreign- and family-controlled enterprises than the other two countries. There were also many links between companies. In Britain all but four of the top 20 financial institutions were themselves members of the top 250 companies and over three-quarters of that 250 had interlocking directorships. So contemporary capitalism is incestuous, though there is no reason to think that it is conspiritorial. The dispersal of the ownership of much of business into financial institutions does, however, go some way to fulfil Schumpeter's prediction that capitalism would evolve into socialism. Peter Drucker memorably described the process as 'pension fund socialism'.

Despite commonality in many respects, for example, in terms of >CONCENTRATON of ownership and the rise of the state, there are nonetheless some significant differences in structure and institutions between advanced capitalist countries. Manufacturing and producer goods are relatively more important in Germany, services in Britain and consumer goods in Italy, for example (Boltho *et al.*, 2001). These differences can be attributed to the workings of comparative advantage and path dependence. Other differences seem to reflect deeper institutional characteristics. For example, the importance of stock markets (as measured by total market capitalization as a percentage of GDP) is greater in the USA and Britain than in the Continental European economies, while banking plays a more important role. Sigurt Vitols, in his contribution 'The Origins of Bank-based and Market-Based Financial Systems' in Streeck and Yamamura (2001), calculated that, in 1976, the proportion of banking system assets in total financial system assets was 63.6 per cent in Japan, 74.3 per cent in Germany and only 24.6 per cent in the USA. He also found that the proportion of securitized assets in total financial assets was 22.9 per cent in Japan, 32.0 per cent in Germany and 54.0 per cent in the USA. There are also major differences in corporate governance systems, training systems, labour market and other institutions between these countries. These differences have led commentators to distinguish between the Anglo-Saxon model of capitalism and the Japanese and Continental European models (although there are major differences, for example between Japan and Germany, for example, in the weight and structure of >TAXATION). Writing of an earlier period, Alfred >CHANDLER characterized the USA and German models respectively as 'competitive managerial capitalism' and 'cooperative managerial capitalism'. Over time the differences between advanced capitalist systems have tended to converge somewhat but important differences remain. The German and Japanese economies showed more rapid growth for long periods of the post-World War II period, but their performance relative to Britain and the USA has weakened more recently and pressures in a globalizing economy to conform more closely to the Anglo-Saxon model are apparent. Whether or not social and political forces will allow more rapid convergence of capitalist systems, and indeed whether or not that is ultimately desirable, remains to be seen.

A further interesting aspect of comparative capitalist systems is the role of >SMALL AND MEDIUM ENTERPRISES (SME). Among SME, owners and managers are usually the same people and the access of these firms to external sources of finance is more limited. Marx and Weber both did not regard small firms as an important part of the emerging capitalist system and their implication was that small firms, including what Marx called the petit bourgeoisie, would disappear. This has not happened in either the Anglo-Saxon or the cooperative models: indeed the quantitative role of SMEs tends to be greater in the latter. In all countries, moreover, it is becoming increasingly clear that small and large firms play complementary roles in the capitalist system (Bannock, 2005).

Perhaps the most important characteristic of capitalism and the reason for its survival lies in its ability to adapt and change. Capitalism has accommodated enormous changes in the volume of world trade and payments, in structure and ownership and in the role of the state in the economy. It has also coped with numerous shocks, such as the oil price increases of the early 1970s. Despite all this, the system has delivered enormous increases in living standards since the early 19th century (>ECONOMIC DEVELOPMENT). New products, services and technologies have throughout provided a basis for increased output and >PRODUCTIVITY. Baumol (2002), as did Schumpeter, places innovation as the driving force behind capitalist advance and argues that the essence of competition in the free market system is not in price but in innovation. It is true that the deep recession of the 1930s appears as a large blot on the record of capitalism but the consensus among economists now is that the extent of that depression was the result of macro-economic policy errors and not a symptom of irremediable deep-seated faults in the capitalist system. The world economy faces further major challenges in the future, the greatest of which are the need to restore some stability to the system and to help the poor countries of the developing world to participate fully in global advance.

### References

Bannock, Graham, *The Economics and Management of Small Business: An International Perspective*, Routledge, 2005.

Baumol, William J., 'The Free Market Innovation Machine: Analysing the Growth Miracle of Capitalism', Princeton University Press, 2002.

Berle, A. A. and Means, G. C., *The Modern Corporation and Private Property* (1932), Harcourt Brace (new edn), 1967.

Boltho, Andrea, Vercelli, Alessandro and Hiroshi, Yoshikawa (eds), *Comparing Economic Systems: Italy and Japan*, Palgrave, 2001.

Hartwell, Ronald Max, 'Capitalism and the Historians', in Fritz Machlup, *Essays on Hayek*, Routledge & Kegan Paul, 1977.

Machlup, Fritz, *Essays on Hayek*, Routledge & Kegan Paul, 1977.

Marx, Karl and Engels, Friedrich, *The Communist Manifesto* (1848, in English 1850), Penguin, 1967.

Polanyi, Karl, *The Great Transformation: The Political and Economic Origins of Our Time* (1944, rev. edn 1957), Beacon Press (new edn), 2001.

Schumpeter, Joseph A., *Capitalism, Socialism and Democracy* (1942), Harper Brothers, 3rd edn, 1950.

Scott, John, *Capitalist Property and Financial Power: A Comparative Study of Britain, the United States and Japan*, Wheatsheaf Books, 1986.

Streeck, Wolfgang and Yamamura, Kozo (eds), *The Origins of Non-Liberal Capitalism: Germany and Japan in Comparison*, Cornell University Press, 2001.

Weber, Max, *General Economic History* (trans. Frank 1927), Transaction Publishers, new edn, 1981.

## Central Banking

The core functions of contemporary central banks are to be the lenders of last resort to the banking system as a whole and to conduct monetary policy aimed at achieving price stability. Central banks act as bankers to the government and to commercial banks, issue bank notes, arrange international payments and oversee domestic payments systems and manage foreign reserves. Central banks are responsible for the stability of the financial system (that is, they guard against systemic breakdown) and many still supervise banking systems. Most countries have a central bank, although a few have currency boards which tie the value of their domestic currency to a foreign currency, such as the Hong Kong Currency Board, which pegs the Hong–Kong dollar to the – US dollar. There is a school of thought, with origins in the 19th century and continued in more recent controversies about the role of the money supply in inflation (>MONEY), which believes that central banks could be dispensed with altogether by a move to 'free banking'. This would mean requiring banks to issue their own currencies and provide convertibility for their notes and deposits against some real asset. There are some early precedents for free banking in North America and elsewhere and its advocates argue that it would distance monetary policy from government influence and achieve both price and systemic stability without the need for a central bank. A central bank, however, would be able to provide the same theoretical benefits if it simply operated according to fixed rules, as indeed the Bank of England more or less did during the >GOLD STANDARD, expanding or contracting credit according to movements in bullion. There does not seem much prospect that free banking will be adopted today, but Capie *et al.* (1994) say that it might come back into consideration if the recent trend towards central bank independence does not result in lasting price stability.

Today there are over 160 central banks in the world of which only 18 were established before the 20th century. The total number rose steadily up to the year 2000 but has since fallen as the European Central Bank (ECB) has taken over the core functions of most national central banks within the single currency area of the enlarging European Union (EU) (CBP, 2005a) (>WESTERN EUROPE). Since 1930 there has also been a central bank for central banks, the Bank for International Settlements (BIS), headquartered in Basle and which, among other functions, sets international capital adequacy standards for commercial banks (>BANKING).

The early central banks were private and chartered by government, as in the case of the earliest, the Bank of Sweden (1668), the Bank of England (1694) and the central banks of France, Finland and the Netherlands (founded respectively in 1800, 1811 and 1814). The First Bank of the United States (1791) was also a private bank, designed and advocated by Alexander >HAMILTON, but it was not to survive as the basis for the present Federal Reserve System (see also below). In some other countries, such as Germany, where the Bundesbank (1957) can trace its origins to the Prussian Bank (1846) and the Reichsbank (1876), and in Japan where the Bank of Japan was founded in 1882, central banks were created and substantially owned by governments    (>GERSCHENKRON argued that the establishment of state banks was necessary for the late industrializers). Except in the case of the Scandinavian central banks, where commercial banks were not developed and where these institutions were established to help develop a commercial banking system, the early central banks existed alongside commercial banks and competed with them in note issues. The early government-owned banks also engaged in private banking though like all of the early central banks, part of their *raison d'être* was to provide finance for government, particularly war finance. Indeed, the prime motive for the establishment of the Bank of England was the need for finance for the war with France. In most cases, around the beginning of the 20th century central banks withdrew from commercial banking and the private banks accepted, in return as it were, the leadership of the central bank in controlling the credit creation process through open market operations and as lenders of last resort. This process was slower in Continental Europe and the >USA than in >BRITAIN. (Open market operations are buying and selling government securities and other instruments to augment or diminish the cash reserves of the commercial banks and therefore their ability to expand or contract credit.)

Many central banks started with a high degree of independence but wars and the government's need for funds resulted in closer relations. Later, during the period of the >GOLD STANDARD, the central banks again enjoyed a high degree of freedom from government interference and the function of maintaining price stability, as opposed to convertibility, had yet to emerge as a discrete activity (it was taken for granted in countries adhering to the gold standard). From >WORLD WAR I, when the emphasis on economic management grew, and under the influence of the >GREAT DEPRESSION, government pressures grew further and there was much tighter regulation of the commercial banks. In the USA, unlike other countries, regulation of the banks preceded the establishment of the central bank, the Federal Reserve System, in 1914. The individual states had regulated banks but there were bank panics and failures and the 'Fed' was created in response to this.

After >WORLD WAR II the trend towards state control continued. The Banque de France was nationalized in 1945 and the Bank of England in the following year. There was some nationalization of commercial banks and quite rigorous exchange controls were introduced or maintained in most countries. After the >OIL price shock of the early 1970s, the breakdown of the system of fixed exchange rates and the cessation of dollar convertibility into >GOLD, the central banks ran into a difficult and challenging era. The emergence of stagflation (recessions combined with inflation) led to unsuccessful attempts to curb inflation (>PRICES AND INFLATION). The end result of the various experiments, particularly in the Anglo-Saxon countries, which included, in addition to money supply control, exchange rate and inflation targeting, has been a trend towards greater central bank independence. In effect, governments were forced to adopt more market-friendly approaches by giving the central banks the freedom to do their job. At the same time banks tended to lose responsibility for commercial bank supervision in favour of unitary financial services authorities; Australia, Germany, Japan and other countries now have universal regulators of this type. For example, the Bank of England Act 1998 conferred on the central bank sole responsibility for the determination of interest rates, previously exercised by the Treasury, but the bank no longer supervises the commercial banks nor does it manage the government debt issue, though it has retained responsibility for the stability of the financial system as a whole. It does not set the inflation target.

The trend towards central bank independence and the focus of their objectives on the primary aim of ensuring price stability are of great importance. Independence is not easily defined since governments inevitably have influence over their central banks. If we define independence as freedom to change interest rates without reference to government, as Capie *et al.* (1994) do, then the Federal Reserve Board, the Bank of England and the ECB are independent on the basis of experience, while the People's Bank of China (see below) is clearly not. Some banks have legal independence in this sense but not de facto independence: this is quite common in developing and some transition countries, where central bank governors have been dismissed when the government disagrees with policies of the central bank. For these reasons academic studies have adopted multiple definitions of independence and treat it as a question of degree. Thus, a central bank is regarded as more independent if the government does not appoint the governor. The length of the term of governor appointment and whether or not the central bank is free to set its own short-term policy goals or targets are also taken as indicators of independence. Stanley Fischer, in his contribution, 'Modern Central Banking', to Capie *et al.* (1994), reviews the empirical evidence on central bank independence and finds that among the industrialized countries, greater degrees of independence are associated with lower inflation. This relationship, however, does not extend to a larger sample, including developing countries, which Fischer explains as being the result of cases where legal independence may not preclude political interference.

The trend to independence grew out of the lessons learned from the 1970s, the most turbulent and disastrous decade in monetary history since World War II until the events following the credit crisis in 2007–8. The 1970s had witnessed a near total loss of monetary control in many core OECD countries, the main exceptions being Germany and Japan (hence the great rise at the time in the prestige of the Bundesbank, which in turn served as a model for independent central banks elsewhere and in the European Union). The 1980s saw a sea change in economic doctrine and especially broad acceptance that ultimately inflation was a monetary phenomenon. The change is associated among economists particularly with the work of Milton >FRIEDMAN. It became accepted that any attempt to drive unemployment below a certain point (the so-called natural rate) by stimulatory policies resulted not just in inflation but in accelerating inflation. British inflation reached 25 per cent at an annual rate, an unprecedented collapse in the value of money for countries that had historically been stable, such as Britain and the USA. All this was part of the abandonment of the link which existed in the Bretton Woods system in which the dollar was fixed to gold and other countries fixed, if adjustable, to the dollar under an international monetary policeman, the International Monetary Fund.

It is not historically true to say that monetarism failed; a particular narrow interpretation of monetarism failed, but the broad lesson, which is that monetary policy can control inflation, was accepted. This had been denied in the 1960s and early 1970s, periods of stagflation, in favour of a cost-push doctrine of inflation. It has come to be understood that >TRADE UNIONS, oil prices and similar pressures could not have caused inflation without an accommodating monetary policy. Everything that has happened in central banking in the past 30 years stemmed from and has depended on the crucial change that took place in attitudes to the money supply in the late 1970s. Central bank independence is simply a pragmatic way of giving central banks the freedom to interpret the changed attitudes in their own way without interference from governments. There are still some problems to be resolved. Inflation targeting is now the most widely used model of monetary policy decision-making. But now this is coming under pressure from the difficulty of dealing with asset price bubbles. How to measure inflation – the cost of living – is another growing problem. The inflation target in these circumstances often means inflation-forecast targeting; but if the forecasts are driven partly or mainly by anticipated asset price movements, this means policy itself is at the mercy of forecast future events. Despite these strains developing in the current orthodoxy, it is still working fairly well in most countries, though there is a big contrast between success in OECD and other core countries in achieving relative price stability and in many developing countries high inflation rates continued, often linked to exchange rate crises (>PRICES AND INFLATION).

An important function of central banking is that of managing the national foreign reserves which may be needed for market operations to influence the exchange rate and to provide a contingency against unforeseen developments. Sometimes (as with the European Central Bank (ECB)) (>WESTERN EUROPE), the reserve management is conducted by the central bank in full independence of governments. Elsewhere, the policy decisions are taken by the Treasury, as in Britain, with the central bank acting as an agent or advisor. Reserve portfolios, which are not predominately in cash but in securities of the foreign countries concerned, are a very important source of income for many central banks. Recently there has been a huge rise in global reserves to over $4 trillion, as countries and central banks aim to accumulate more reserves to provide a cushion against external shocks, especially as confidence in the IMF's capacity to come to their assistance in a crisis diminishes. Much of these reserves are held by Asian countries and in many cases they are to a large extent held in dollar-denominated assets, the acquisition of which helps to provide their exporters with some protection against a falling dollar which would make these countries less competitive.

To illustrate and give more depth to some of the general points made above, we go on to review the structure and functions of five major central banks. Of these, the most recent is the European Cenral Bank (ECB), established only in 1998 and now subsuming the 12 national central banks of the European Union (EU) that have adopted the euro currency (>WESTERN EUROPE). The national EU central banks continue to operate; for example, they hold the ECB's minimum reserve requirements for the commercial banks in the current accounts of those banks with their national central bank and they have important roles in implementing the ECB's monetary policy decisions. These national banks now support the ECB's monetary policies instead of formulating their own. The EU members that have not joined the euro system are the long-established members, Britain, Sweden and Denmark, and ten new members in Eastern Europe and the Mediterranean, the latter are expected to adopt the euro later. The non-euro countries are represented in a General Council consisting of the president and vice president of the ECB and the governors of the central banks of all EU member states. The ECB itself has an executive board and a Governing Council comprised of the full-time members of the executive board and the governors of the 12 national banks, which are now effectively regional branches of the euro system. The ECB has the sole right of note issue and sets monetary policy. The sole objective of the ECB is to maintain price stability, which it has interpreted to mean annual increases of below, but close to, 2 per cent in the medium term in the Harmonized Index of Consumer Prices. This gentle inflation target is regarded as a precaution against deflation. The ECB conducts open market operations in conjunction with a marginal lending facility and, as mentioned, requires credit institutions to hold minimum remunerated reserves (Issing, 2004).

The European Central Bank has full political independence in its pursuit of price stability and endeavours to operate in a transparent way with the publication of information about its decisions and the reasons for them. The Bank pays considerable attention to the evolution of the money supply, probably more than other central banks, and uses reserve requirements rather than relying solely on interest rates. Until 2007, the ECB was successful in achieving its target, but in 2008 euro-area inflation rose to unprecedented levels. There remain concerns about a one-size-fits-all policy for economies as varied as those of the euro area, particularly since the public sector accounts for approaching half of GDP, which means that macroeconomic adjustments may bear heavily on the private sector. This,

in conjunction with the freedom of member countries to set their own fiscal policy, has resulted in some states having difficulty in abiding by the Growth and Stability Pact which restricts public deficits to 3 per cent of GDP. The bank argues that the relatively poor growth performance of Europe is explained not by its own policies but by institutional rigidities, including the inflexibility of labour markets. The ECB is not responsible for banking supervision or for regulating other financial institutions; these functions remain with national authorities within the overall framework of European directives.

Also relatively recent is the People's Bank of China (PBC), founded in 1948 (>CHINA). This was just before the establishment of the People's Republic, after the victory of the communists over Chiang Kai-shek in the long war which ended in 1949. The PBC was formed from a consolidation of the state-owned commercial banking system. In 1983, the State Council, the governing body of China, decided that the PBC should formally function as a central bank. In 1995 the Bank of China Law confirmed the central banking functions. The PBC's commercial banking activities had been earlier spun off into separate state-owned banks. From 1998 everything started changing with the Deng reforms to open up the economy. From that time, the role of the central bank has evolved from being an instrument of state planning towards the modern conception but the process is still far from complete. At present the bank has nine regional offices and over 2,000 sub-branches. In 2003, the PBC's supervision of the commercial banks and other financial institutions was transferred to a new body, the China Banking Regulatory Commission.

The Governor of the PBC is appointed by the President of China. The bank formulates and implements monetary policy 'under the guidance of' a standing committee of the State Council. The bank monitors the money supply, sets interest rates and operates as a lender of last resort with open market operations. The PBC imposes reserve requirements on the commercial banks, which, incidentally, have large non-performing elements in their loan portfolios thanks to lending to loss-making state-owned enterprises. The PBC is responsible for the note issue, manages the state treasury, maintains payment and settlement systems and is responsible for the stability of the financial system. The PBC also, through its affiliate, State Administration of Foreign Exchange (SAFE), holds the gold and foreign exchange reserves which total over $700 billion, the second largest in the world after Japan. The exchange rate has been pegged to the US dollar since 1994 and in 2005 a small adjustment was made to the rate in a new system which is based not just on the dollar but on a basket of currencies. This action may have been a response to growing US concern about China's surging exports and under-valuation of the currency but in the short run is not expected to make much difference. The latest exchange rate reform might have far-reaching effects in the longer term if it does indeed lead to greater flexibility (as the IMF and USA want) but further changes are likely to be very cautiously made. The fixed exchange rate with the dollar has allowed the central bank to keep control of the money supply, which has given China greater monetary stability than it has known for a 100 years.

As already mentioned, the US Federal Reserve System was not founded until 1914. There were two predecessors: the First Bank of the United States (1791–1811) and the Second Bank of the United States (1817–37). Both banks issued their own notes and acted as Federal government banks, but their 20-year charters were not renewed through opposition from the anti-Federalists, who feared too much power was being given to the centre and away from the individual states. From 1841, central banking functions were performed by the Independent Treasury and from 1863 there was a National Banking System under which the commercial banks had to fully cover their note issues by holdings of Treasury debt and to meet reserve requirements. The result was a very inelastic money supply and there were frequent banking panics (Capie *et al.*, 1994). A particularly severe banking crisis in 1907 led to investigations which culminated in the establishment of the Federal Reserve System in 1914. The Federal Reserve Act of 1914 created 12 reserve banks, which now have 25 branches, under a Federal Reserve Board located in Washington. The system is owned by the member banks but, since the 1935 Banking Act, the Chairman and board members are appointed by the President of the USA.

The 'Fed' as it has come to be called, is responsible for banking supervision and systemic stability but not the issue of currency notes or exchange rate policy, which is handled by the US Department of the Treasury. The Fed is also responsible for bank clearance and sets reserve requirements for the commercial banks. However, in the complex US system of financial regulation, there are other federal bodies involved in bank regulation and there are also regulators at state level. Monetary policy, which is operated mainly through open market operations, is determined by the Federal Open Market Committee, which consists of seven members of the Reserve Board and five Federal Reserve Bank presidents, one of which is always president of the Federal Reserve Bank of New York. Since the Monetary Control Act 1980, all US banks are members of the Federal Reserve System. The independence of the Fed partly depends upon the character of its chairman, but is helped by the long-term appointment of the governors (14 years, chairman four years) and the fact that the system is not dependent upon Congress for funding, since it earns a surplus and in fact pays a dividend to the Treasury.

The Fed has been very successful in constraining inflation while promoting economic growth since the 1980s in particular, but is considered to have failed to take appropriate action both during the 1930s recession and in the 1970s. In these two periods, the Fed lost control of the money supply, in the first case by allowing it to fall too much and in the second to rise too much, causing accelerating inflation. In the 1930s the Fed had ensured that the commercial banks had plenty of cash but apparently allowed for insufficient further expansion of the money supply on the grounds that it did not have enough resources to do so without jeopardizing its own viability. Tim Congdon has drawn parallels in this with the lack of effective action by the Bank of Japan in the prolonged recession in that country since the 1980s (Congdon, 2004). There are two other examples of inappropriate central banking action in the earlier history of banking in the USA with which parallels have also been drawn with the 1930s – though, of course, such errors have not been confined to America. There

was criticism of the actions of the First Bank of the United States shortly after it was established in 1791. The Bank's role at this time has recently been established by new research (Cohen, 2000). The bank initially provided needed credit expansion, but unfortunately a William Duer and his associates were speculating heavily in securities, forcing up prices which peaked in late January 1792. The collapse of the bubble in March of that year (the Panic of 1792, which was to result in the imprisonment of Duer for debt) seems to have been aggravated if not precipitated by the withdrawal of credit by the First Bank. According to Cohen the Treasury under Hamilton took timely action and purchased securities and the bank followed. A crisis was therefore avoided. The Panic of 1792 was not followed by a depression, however, unlike the Panic of 1819, as Cohen points out, in which the Second Bank of the United States was also accused of an unduly abrupt curtailment of credit.

Because of the central role of the dollar in the world monetary system, as well as because of their strong personalities and abilities, the two giants of 20th-century central banking are Paul Volcker, who was chairman of the Federal Reserve Board from 1974–87, and Alan Greenspan, who succeeded him up to appointment of Ben S. Bernanke in February 2006. Volcker's demonstration, beginning in October 1979, that if you let interest rates rise high enough a central bank can control inflation and Greenspan's successful management of interest rates in the long inflation-free boom in the USA in the 1990s and into the millennium are key epochs in the modern history of central banking. However, Greenspan is now being criticized for keeping interest rates too low at the expense of asset inflation and the severe credit crisis which emerged in 2007–8.

The Bank of Japan (Nippon Ginko) was founded in 1882, 50 per cent owned by government. Prior to 1876 in Japan, commercial bank notes, convertible into silver, circulated alongside the government issue which was not convertible. From 1885 the bank started to issue its own notes, which together with the government issues became convertible into silver (the gold standard was not adopted by Japan until 1897). In 1942 during World War II, the bank restructured and government ownership increased to 55 per cent (Capie *et al.*, 1994). Since 1997 the bank has had 32 branches and 14 local offices and had an increased degree of autonomy. Although the Minister of Finance has powers to override the bank's decisions, this power has never been exercised. The Bank of Japan today is the sole bank of issue and its objective is to pursue price stability. It sets interest rates, acts as a lender of last resort and conducts open market operations. The bank manages government finances and settlement services as well as international financial transactions and is responsible for the stability of the financial system. It no longer regulates the banks or financial services, this now being the function of the Financial Services Agency.

The Bank of England, which covers the whole of the United Kingdom, was founded in 1694 under government charter and by public subscription. It was authorized to issue bank notes and in 1844 became the sole bank of new issue. Explicit open market operations to support its discount rate began in 1847 and its role as lender of last resort in the 1870s. At the time, the bank was concerned to support convertibility into gold without an explicit objective of price stability.

The bank was nationalized in 1946 and became the statutory authority for the banking system. In May 1997, the bank became operationally independent over monetary policy, but supervision of the banks became the responsibility of a new unitary authority, the Financial Services Authority (FSA), from 1998. The bank, like virtually all central banks, remains responsible for the effectiveness and stability of the financial system as a whole. Monetary policy decisions are taken by the bank's Monetary Policy Committee (MPC), which consists of the governor (appointed by the government for a five-year term), the two deputy governors, two executive directors of the bank and four non-executive members appointed by the Chancellor of the Exchequer for three-year terms. The bank no longer manages the government debt issue. It acts as a banker for government and commercial banks (which do not have significant reserve requirements) and continues to be the lender of last resort with open market operations to support the discount rate. The bank also manages the reserves as agent for HM Treasury. The post-1997 arrangements are generally considered to have been very successful and steady growth has been achieved with a moderate level of inflation around the targeted level of 2 per cent, but the record has been sullied by the 2007–8 credit crisis and >BANKING failures.

### References

Capie, Forrest, Goodhart, Charles, Fischer, Stanley and Schnadt, Norbert (eds), *The Future of Central Banking: The Tercentenary Symposium of the Bank of England*, Cambridge University Press, 1994.

CBP, *The Central Banking Directory 2005*, Central Banking Publications, 2005a.

CBP, *How Countries Supervise their Banks, Insurers and Securities Markets*, Central Banking Publications, 2005b.

Congdon, Tim, 'New Light on the Fed's History', *Central Banking*, February, 2004.

Cohen, David J., 'The First Bank of the United States and the Securities Market Crash of 1792', *Journal of Economic History*, December, 2000.

Issing, Otmar, *The ECB and the Euro: The First Five Years*, Institute of Economic Affairs, 2004.

# Chandler, Alfred Du Pont

The most frequently cited American business historian, who lived from 1918 to 2007, Chandler's works trace the structure and organization of the large corporations which began to emerge in the second half of the 19th century. Although he wrote much else, Chandler's reputation is primarily based on three major books. In *Strategy and Structure* (1962), he describes in detail how the structure of four major companies (Du Pont, General Motors, Standard Oil and Sears Roebuck) changed to meet the challenges posed by new strategies for growth and diversification (demonstrating that 'structure follows strategy'). *The Visible Hand* (Chandler, 1977), for which he was awarded the Pulitzer Prize, broadened the approach to cover the evolution of American big business as a whole and its reciprocal influences for technology and economic growth. The last of the trilogy, *Scale and Scope* (Chandler, 1989) broadened his field still further to cover leading corporations in the USA, Germany and Britain. These books were preceded and followed by journal articles and many other books. Early on, for example, Chandler wrote two full-length biographies of businessmen

*Henry Varnum Poor* (1956) and *Pierre S. du Pont* (1971) (to whom Chandler was not related, despite his second Christian name, Du Pont). More recently Chandler produced two books, global in scope but on industrial sectors: *Inventing the Electronic Century* (Chandler, 2002) deals with electronics and *Shaping the Industrial Century* (Chandler, 2005) with chemicals and pharmaceuticals.

The Chandlerian view of the big business universe first set out in the trilogy has been filled out and extended over the years. In essence, this view is that, from the 1880s, the development of the railway, steamship, telegraph and cable networks led to recurrent waves of technological innovations. These innovations transformed businesses in both new and existing industries into high-volume capital-intensive activities. These developments in the 'Second Industrial Revolution' (>INDUSTRIAL REVOLUTIONS) were not restricted to the centres of the first industrial revolution and brought increased productivity and economic growth. The new giant enterprises which emerged were necessary to raise the capital and to monitor and coordinate production and distribution on an ever-increasing scale. These corporations were handling increasingly complex activities, were often vertically integrated and, as time went by, diversifying into new fields using related skills and technologies. Economies of scale and scope, including learning and skills development, allowed expansion beyond national boundaries and the diffusion of technology by exports, licensing and overseas manufacture, all contributing to economic growth. World War I, the >GREAT DEPRESSION of the 1930s and World War II slowed the process, but from 1950 there was a dramatic period of catch-up (the 'Golden Age').

The evolution of business required major changes in structure and organization. Before 1920, Chandler established, large companies were centralized functionally (U-form >BUSINESS MANAGEMENT) but, as mentioned, the skills and knowledge for one set of products began to be applied to others, while domestic and territorial expansion also increased the pressure for organizational change. By the mid-1920s the multidivisional structure (M-form) was being adopted by the largest diversified companies. After 1940 this type of structure spread rapidly. Chandler, particularly in his later works, emphasizes the interactive complementarity between physical capital investment and intangible investment in knowledge and organization. The large corporations, in his view, have been central to economic growth through capital accumulation, knowledge augmentation via R&D and organizational learning and as cores of networks of enterprises (Chandler *et al.*, 1997).

In *Scale and Scope* (1989) Chandler argued that Britain was slow to exploit the second industrial revolution and, in particular, failed to make the necessary 'three pronged investments' in production, distribution and corporate structures. Unlike the US model of 'competitive managerial capitalism' and Germany's 'cooperative managerial capitalism', Chandler characterized the British system in the period covered in the book, 1880–1940, as 'personal capitalism'. He argued that the managerial hierarchies of leading British large firms were less developed and, even where entrepreneurs recruited substantial management teams, founding families and their heirs continued to play a large role in top management decisions. Critics, notably Church (1990, 1993), pointed out

that family control was equally prevalent in the American and German economies and even more extensive in Japan than in Britain. It was also stressed that differences in business environments could explain many more of the differences in strategies adopted than differences in family control (>ENTREPRENEURSHIP). For example, British producers did not need to build extensive distribution networks because they already existed. Chandler was to reply to these critics that what was important for his thesis was not the degree of family ownership but the depth of the managerial hierarchy: British management teams were demonstrably much smaller than those in the more rapidly growing economies of the USA and Germany (Chandler, 1990). In a recent study, Hannah (2007), however, shows that ownership was already substantially divorced from control in leading businesses in Europe (>CORPORATE GOVERNANCE). At that time, in the >USA corporations were dominated by 'plutocratic family owners, such as the Vanderbilts and the Rockefellers. Britain, partly as a result of listing requirements for large 'free-floats' at the London Stock Exchange (>CAPITAL MARKETS), was in fact an early pioneer of dispersed stock ownership and it took decades for America to catch up.

In his earlier work, Chandler wrote as if it was only giant firms that mattered (>SMALL AND MEDIUM ENTERPRISES). In his later books, he acknowledges that 'other forms of enterprise have also been essential to economic progress' especially in the labour-intensive and service industries with which he was little concerned (Chandler *et al.*, 1997). In his concentration on giant enterprise he writes in the tradition of the later >SCHUMPETER and

>GERSCHENKRON, but Chandler was also influenced by Max >WEBER and the business sociologist Talcott Parsons of Harvard.

The brilliance and depth of Chandler's historical research is universally recognized but the questions of whether the American way is the one way applying to all converging economies, whether corporate scale is decisive in a dynamic sense and whether Americanization is the same thing as >GLOBALIZATION remain controversial. Though they leave it open, the authors of Chandler and Mazlish (2005), writing in their introduction about the roles of >MULTINATIONAL COMPANIES, do not think that Americanization in the sense of homogenization is taking place and they also accept that alternative forms of productive organization are compatible with success in the global economy. Chandler *et al.* (1997) provided evidence that there are striking differentials between the organizational structure of firms between the early and later industrializers, as well as within the latter group. It does not seem that large enterprise size is a decisive factor in economic development. Bannock (2005) reviews the literature on that subject and concludes that it is equally possible to argue that small as well as large firms have everywhere played a major active role in >ECONOMIC DEVELOPMENT, while large and small firms in fact play complementary roles.

Like those of Gerschenkron, not all of Chandler's generalizations have been upheld but such paradigms are necessary to stimulate new thinking. Chandler may be said to be the first to draw general conclusions on the relationships between organizations and growth on the basis of massive empirical research and in so doing to give order and form to the multiple available facts of business history. Unintentionally (by his own admission), Chandler has had a major influence on management education. Some of his contributions, notably on the links between knowledge accumulation, business organization and economic development are relevant to the central issues of >ECONOMIC HISTORY and economic theory. His work, especially in international comparisons, has also stimulated creative work by others, even in areas which he himself was not much interested, such as labour force skill formation (see, for example, Lazonick (1993) and Lazonick and O'Sullivan (1997)).

Chandler, who graduated from Harvard, did wartime service with the US Navy and returned to Harvard after the war to gain a PhD in History. After over 20 years at MIT and Johns Hopkins University, he returned to Harvard in 1971 as Isador Professor of Business History.

## References

Bannock, Graham, *The Economics and Management of Small Business: A International Perspective*, Routledge, 2005.

Chandler, Alfred D., *Strategy and Structure: Chapters in the History of American Industrial Enterprise*, MIT Press, 1962.

Chandler, Alfred D., *The Visible Hand: The Managerial Revolution in American Business*, Harvard University Press, 1977.

Chandler, Alfred D., *Scale and Scope: The Dynamics of Industrial Capitalism*, Harvard University Press, 1989.

Chandler, Alfred D., 'Response to the Contributors to the Review Colloquium on Scale and Scope', *Business History*, 64, Winter, 1990.

Chandler, Alfred D., *Inventing the Electronic Century: The Epic Story of the Consumer Electronics and Computer Science Industries*, The Free Press, 2002.

Chandler, Alfred D., *Shaping the Industrial Century: The Remarkable Story of the Evolution of the Modern Chemical and Pharmaceutical Industries*, Harvard University Press, 2005.

Chandler, Alfred D. and Mazlish, Bruce (eds), *Leviathans: Multinational Corporations and the New Global History*, Cambridge University Press, 2005.

Chandler, Alfred D., Amatori, Franco and Hikino, Takashi (eds), *Big Business and the Wealth of Nations*, Cambridge University Press, 1997.

Church, Roy, 'The Limitations of the Personal Capitalism Paradigm', *Business History Review*, 64, 1990.

Church, Roy, 'The Family Firm in Industrial Capitalism: International Perspectives on Hypotheses and History', *Business History*, 35(4), Winter, 1993.

Hannah, Leslie, 'The Divorce of Ownership from Control from 1900 onwards: Recalibrating Imagined Global Trends', *Business History*, 49, July, 2007.

Lazonick, William, *Business Organisation and the Myth of the Market Economy*, Cambridge University Press, 1993.

Lazonick, William and O'Sullivan, Mary, 'Big Business and Skill Formation in the Wealthiest Nations', in Alfred D. Chandler, Franco Amatori and Takashi Hikino (eds), *Big Business and the Wealth of Nations*, Cambridge University Press, 1997.

# Chartism

A movement of the working class in >BRITAIN in the early 19th century. Its Charter sought universal male suffrage, equal parliamentary constituencies, secret ballots, annual elections to parliament, the abolition of the property qualification for Members of Parliament and the payment of salaries to Members of Parliament. The Chartists' demands were presented to parliament in the form of petitions carrying over a million signatures.

The Reform Act of 1832 had widened the franchise but only to the property-owning middle classes. The size of the electorate in England and Wales rose only to 650,000; the mass of the working classes was excluded. The Factory Act of 1833, while restricting the employment of children to some degree, still allowed children over 14 to be worked 12 hours a day (>REGULATION). Demands for a ten-hour day were rejected. (>EMPLOYMENT OF WOMEN AND CHILDREN). In 1834, the Poor Law Amendment Act (> POOR LAWS) introduced a regime in workhouses which was designed explicitly to punish, in the belief that people were responsible for their own poverty. Trade unionists were liable to be transported (>TRADE UNIONISM). The political context was unsurprisingly perceived to be anti-labour. The movement was given impetus when the economy slumped into a recession which saw a fall in GDP of over 7 per cent between 1839 and 1842.

The Charter was drawn up in 1838 by the London Working Men's Association, which had been founded by William Lovett two years earlier. Mass meetings were organized. The spread of support for Chartism was greatly assisted by Fergus O'Connor through his Great Northern Union and his *Northern Star* newspaper, and a National Charter Association was formed in 1840.

Support for the movement, however, began to fade in the 1840s with the return of economic prosperity. Moreover, legislation became somewhat more enlightened. In 1846, the Corn Laws, which were seen to raise the price of corn for the benefit of the rich at the expense of the poor, were repealed and in the following year the Poor Law Commission was abolished. There was a revival of Chartism in an industrial recession in 1848 and a petition was made to parliament, but the movement finally collapsed.

## Reference

Royle, E., 'Chartism', in Anne Digby and Charles Feinstein (eds), *New Directions in Economic and Social History*, Macmillan, 1989.

# China

The largest and longest-lived political unit in the world, Chinese civilization has a much longer history than that of any of the other great empires, including those of Rome and Egypt. Its territory has not, of course, been constant, even in relatively recent times, for example, parts were ceded to Russia and France in the 19th century and Japan occupied much of Manchuria in 1931, while Taiwan split off after the civil war. Generalizations about China are inevitable, but it is a vast country that exhibits great regional and local variety. In his 1985 presidential address, 'The Structure of Chinese History', William Skinner identified eight physiographic macro-regions. These regions he asserted, although affected by the dynastic cycles of growth and decline, had cycles of their own, usually out of phase with one another (except in the general stagnations of the 14th and 15th centuries). Most of these regions are roughly the size of France. It is important to note, however, that, despite the variety, for most of its history from pre-modern times, and certainly from the Ch'n Dynasty from 221 BCE to 206 BCE, China has had a common written language and a unified imperial structure (with interruptions), with common weights and measures and extensive internal commercial trade. In the 6th century, Emperor Yang Guang built granaries and canals to bring supplies to the capital. This was the precursor of the Imperial system of waterways which was fully developed a few hundred years later (Powelson, 1994). In the 1790s, the state granaries, built to even out fluctuations in harvests, reached a peak level of 3 million tonnes. The dynasties, ever fearful of usurpation, put the maintenance of social stability very high in their priorities (Richardson, 1999).

Between the 10th and 15th century, China was richer on a per capita basis than Europe and in terms of the volume of internal trade and the size of the economy. China was also ahead of Europe in inventions but did not pursue them; world firsts included the manufacture of paper, metallurgy, >STEAMPOWER, chain drives, the compass, gunpowder, >SILK, fine porcelain and the water clock. China had printing 600 years before Gutenberg in Europe and sailing ships of advanced design. Maddison (2007a) describes how Chinese ships in the early 15th century differed from European or other Asian ones. The big ships had 15 or more watertight compartments (not introduced in the British Navy until 1795), multiple masts and bamboo-slatted sails that permitted precise reefing and furling and confined damage of torn sails to relatively small areas. These ships were far larger than any in Europe and were up to 400 feet long.

The first, and still debated, question in the economic history of China is why, with it great advantages and progress, and apparently on the verge of industrialization, did it stagnate from the 15th century, while Europe and much of the rest of the world was to forge ahead from the 17th century. This is the so-called 'Needham question', after Joseph Needham (1900–1995) who was responsible for major works on science, technology and medicine in China. East Asia was also the first non-Western region to follow Europe into industrialization, though it was Japan that achieved this initially, not China (>ASIAN MIRACLE). On Maddison's estimates, GDP per capita in China was about $450 in the 10th century, compared with $400–425 in Western Europe at the time. By 1500, Chinese income per capita had levelled out at $600, where it remained until the 19th century, while that in Europe rose from about $800 in 1500 to $1243 in 1820 and $2,087 in 1870. Over the period 1820–1950, Chinese per capita incomes fell from 90 to 20 per cent of the world average.

Before getting into more detail about some aspects of China's long-term economic development, it is helpful for the reader to fix in the mind the major phases of growth and decline in that history. There are considerable difficulties in the way of this, mainly because of uncertainties about the output of the dominant agricultural sector. Richardson (1999) wrote that, 'It is still not possible, and it may never be possible, to offer a definitive quantification of the trend experience of the Chinese economy prior to the

**Population and GDP per capita, China 1000–2003**

|  | Population (thousands) | GDP/Capita $ |
|---|---|---|
| 1000 | 59,000 | 450 |
| 1500 | 103,000 | 600 |
| 1600 | 160,000 | 600 |
| 1700 | 138,000 | 600 |
| 1820 | 381,000 | 600 |
| 1870 | 358,000 | 530 |
| 1913 | 437,140 | 552 |
| 1950 | 546,815 | 548 |
| 1973 | 881,940 | 838 |
| 2003 | 1,288,400 | 4,803 |

*Source*: Maddison, 2007a.

*Note*: GDP data are at 1990 purchasing power parities.

1950s.' More recently, Maddison (2007b) has, however, produced some benchmark estimates (see table). He delineates five phases in the transformations of the Chinese economy from the first millennium to the present time:

(i) Innovation and growth in the period 960–1280 (the Sung dynasty and pre-modern peak) in which per capita income rose by a third at a time when the population doubled and incomes were significantly higher than those in Western Europe.

(ii) A 'long period of mediocre progress and setbacks' from the 14th to 18th centuries during which population rose and fell but per capita incomes were roughly maintained, despite periods of crisis and depopulation. This was achieved by more intensive agriculture and the expansion of dry crops in the North. It was towards the end of this period, though, that economic leadership passed to industrializing Europe.

(iii) From 1840–1950, China was wracked by civil war and conflict, including foreign intrusions. Per capita incomes fell over this period. There were severe famines in 1876–9 and 1928–9, which killed millions.

(iv) In the Maoist period (1950–78), as a whole and despite disastrous episodes, industry grew and incomes per capita doubled by 1973. The 'Great Leap Forward', which included the reorganization of farming on a collective basis, caused 20–30 million deaths by famine in 1958–62.

(v) In the recent period, after the reforms of 1978, incomes grew rapidly to reach almost six times their 1973 level by 2003. China overtook Germany in 1982 and in 1992 it overtook Japan. Maddison calculates that China will overtake the USA by 2015 in aggregate, though not in per capita, terms.

Economic data, poor throughout all the first four periods, improved after 1950. However, Maddison and Wu (2008) give their reasons for doubting official Chinese data, which they consider overstate growth. From 1978–2003, the official GDP data indicate a growth rate of 9.59 per cent, which the authors revise down to 7.85 per cent.

Chinese history has been characterized by political strife and internal and external wars, as well as long periods of relative stability. The Zenith of pre-modern economic activity, as already mentioned, came under the Sung Dynasty (960–1279), which was able to reunify much of China after the decline of its predecessors, the Tang (618–907). However, the Sung were forced to retreat to the South by nomadic incursions in 1127 (Southern Sung), before they achieved real stability. Maddison shows that a major shift took place in the distribution of population in this period, three-quarters of Chinese under the Tang had lived in North China, mainly on dry crops like wheat and millet, but by the end of the 13th century, under the Southern Sung, three-quarters lived South of the Yangtse River, with its rice-based agriculture. The Sung bureaucracy promoted irrigation, early ripening seeds and new crops, such as cotton, and promulgated the best-known agricultural techniques with printed handbooks. There were considerable advances in industry; Deng (2000), for example, cites authorities indicating that annual iron production in China during Sung times was estimated at 150,000 tons. Even under the Tang, which introduced tea planting, and subsequently under the Yuan (1271–1368) and Ming (1368–1644) dynasties, governments promoted agriculture, including sorghum and New World crops (maize, potatoes, peanuts and tobacco). The bureaucracy was therefore helpful to agriculture (which it saw as promoting stability), but was oppressive towards entrepreneurial activity. There were wars and arbitrary confiscations and the only mitigating factor, Powelson (1994) points out, was the inability of the central authorities to fully restrict and control the activities of the people in its vast territory, something which is still true today. Although land was privately held, rents and taxes probably absorbed much of the investable surplus (although this is open to dispute).

During the Yuan (Mongol) Dynasty, between 1271–1368, which followed the conquering of South China by the Mongols (Yuan) under Kubla Kahn, there was initially much destruction. It was at this time that Marco Polo (1254–1324) visited China and for a while served the Emperor. The Mongols, installed a dual Yuan-Chinese administration and were eventually absorbed by the Chinese and their culture. The Ming Dynasty which followed the Yuan endured for 276 years. Initially continuing the fairly open policies of the Yuan, it authorized exploratory voyages to India, Africa and the Middle East (the Portuguese came to China in 1514, followed by the Spanish and the Dutch). The bureaucracy did not approve of these external contacts, however, and after a while virtually prohibited overseas trade and greatly reduced the size of the fleet. Foreign exploration was stopped and, from 1500, anyone building a ship with more than two masts was liable to a death penalty. The later Ming and Yuan regimes were inward looking and quite uninterested in developments outside China. The early Manchu period which followed the Ming and was the last of the Imperial dynasties, again saw much destruction of life and property, as well as depopulation caused by epidemic disease, repeating a similar experience in the 14th century and which was to recur again in the 19th century. By 1670 there was some relaxation in isolationism under the Manchu (Ch'ng) Dynasty (1644–1912) and it was the Manchu that introduced the Factory System. This allowed foreign traders but regulated them closely, limiting them to dealings only with the government. Many writers cite the official response to gifts of scientific instruments and other wonders brought from George III to the Chien-lung Emperor in 1793 by Lord Macartney: 'there is nothing we lack. We have never set much store on strange or ingenious objects, nor do we need any more of your country's manufactures'. Although the British did quite well out of the Factory System, this lack of appetite for imports led them to start smuggling in opium to finance more trade in tea and silk, for which there was a substantial demand in Europe. This precipitated war with the Manchu in 1840, which was soon ended by British gunboats and rifles.

The Opium War and the later Anglo-French attack and looting of the Summer Palace in Peking (now Beijing) in 1858–60 are among the less glorious episodes of Western colonial history (>ECONOMIC IMPERIALISM). Not satisfied with the highly regulated Factory System, the colonial powers (including the USA) forcibly increased their grip upon Chinese trade. After the Opium War, under the Treaty of Nanking (1842), the Factory System was ended and replaced with five Treaty Ports, and Hong Kong was leased to Britain. Similar treaties were made by China with the USA, France, Holland and Germany. After further wars, the Treaty of Tientsin (1858) extended the treaty system to 11 new ports, some on waterways inland. Ultimately, there were 92 treaty ports and 19 countries enjoyed treaty privileges. The ports were given rights to manufacture in 1895 and, surprisingly, the system lasted until 1943.

The direct economic impact of the foreign commercial intrusions was strongly positive though the impact of the treaty ports on the Chinese economy as a whole is difficult to assess. The ports did help in the establishment of a modern industrial sector and stimulate foreign investment, particularly in the early railway developments in the late 1890s. The foreigners, in their enclaves, had little direct contact with producers and consumers in the interior and found it necessary to deal with Chinese intermediaries for the distribution of imports and the acquisition of goods for export. It has been estimated, according to Richardson, that as an indicator of indigenous activity, as much as 70 per cent of all Western shipping in the China trade may have been financed by Chinese merchants. Foreign military intrusions, particularly those by Japan, another Asian nation which proved that economic development was not only the preserve of the West, did, however, have a catalytic effect. Shanghai, at the mouth of the system of waterways and the centre of the Treaty Ports arrangements, accounted for 70 per cent of China's foreign trade in the early 1870s and almost 50 per cent still in 1931. Shanghai's population rose from 230,000 in the 1840s to 3.6 million by 1938.

According to Ma (2008), the lower Yangtse region (the administrative provinces of Jiangsu and Zhejiang), an area 86 per cent of the size of Britain and with a population of 60 million in the 1930s, had a per capita GDP some 50 per cent higher than China's national average in 1753. The growth of incomes in the region between the 1910s and the 1930s was comparable to that of Japan and her colonies. Shanghai alone produced 41 per cent of national manufacturing output in that period, or 48 per cent, if Japanese-controlled Manchuria is excluded. Ma's estimates, which he admits like all those for early China, are highly speculative (being based on tax revenue-regional income differences), imply considerably higher levels of per capita income than Maddison's. Ma argues that the international settlement in the Shanghai area was a 'European-style city-state under the rule of Western business elites and provided effective public security and private property rights for both Chinese and foreign business within its jurisdiction' (2008). This underlines the fact that >INSTITUTIONS in the rest of China were not conducive to economic development. The relative stability and political autonomy of the lower Yangtse region was in stark contrast to the battleground of warlords and factions in much of the rest of China at the time.

The Ch'ing regime fell in 1911 after 70 years of internal conflict and foreign intrusions. After the collapse, and for almost 40 years, China was governed by the military of the KMT/ Nationalists. The autonomy and dynamic prosperity of Shanghai came to an end with the full-scale Japanese invasion in 1941 and the triumph of the Communists in 1949. These events, as Ma puts it, led to 'Shanghai capitalists' massive exodus to colonial Hong Kong [which] brought that city capital, industrial skills, entrepreneurial vision and... a 10–15 year start in industrialization over many other Asian countries' (2008). The lower Yangtse was to resume its prosperity in the reform period after 1978, which led to China's amazing resurgence.

The Maoist period, which began with the establishment of the People's Republic in 1949, was accompanied by the centralized controls, propaganda and expropriation familiar from that in >RUSSIA earlier. China once again closed in on itself, resisted all foreign influences, especially from America, and, from 1960, fell out even with Russia, which had given it initial help. Despite disastrous economic and social experimentation (the Great Leap Forward, 1958–60, and the Cultural Revolution, 1966–76), economic performance improved over the past. Incomes almost doubled between 1950 and 1973. Industry's share of GDP rose from 8 to 30 per cent, exceeding that of agriculture by 1978. >PRODUCTIVITY growth was very poor and China grew more slowly than the world as a whole, while its share of world trade fell. China also benefited from investment and entrepreneurship from the diaspora of overseas Chinese, good macro-economic management and foreign trade. The state sector has been privatized only to a limited extent (mostly for smaller state enterprises) but is, with some exceptions, being allowed to wither away. The number of state-owned enterprises has declined from 114,000 in 1996 to 34,000 in 2003; the non-state sector accounted for two-thirds of China's GDP in 2003 (Garnaut et al., 2005).

The reforms in 1978 decentralized the economy: in agriculture, the peasantry regained autonomy in the use of land; in industry small-scale activity under private and private/ local authority ownership resumed, especially in rural areas. Maddison (2007b) says that the average size of enterprises in the non-state sector fell from 112 to 8 employees by 1955. There is general agreement that the rapid growth of the Chinese economy has been driven by smaller firms. Their number (firms with less than 200 employees) rose from 344,000 in 1978 to 8 million in 1996, when their share in output amounted to 66 per cent (Wang and Yao, 2002). Productivity in the private sector rose sharply and the volume of exports rose by 15 per cent per annum from 1978–2006. GDP per capita shot up from $838 in 1973 to $4,803 in 2003. China was more successful in abandoning its command economy than the former USSR: in 1950 its income per capita was only 16 per cent of the Soviet's, but by 2003 it was 89 per cent. China's relatively better performance is attributed by Maddison, in addition to the scope it had for catch-up, to the priority given to agriculture and the fact that it did not disintegrate as the USSR did, but grew with the reintegration of Hong Kong and Macao (>ASIAN MIRACLE: >RUSSIA).

The accounts of the economic history of China are studded with unanswered questions, speculations and disputes, especially about the Needham question: why did the economy rise under the Sung and why did it fail to match European industrialization? The extraordinary thing is that until very recently the research has been led and dominated by Western scholars who face masses of information but linguistic problems in accessing it. Research by Chinese scholars in the command economy was over-influenced by Marxism and ideology and, while much work has apparently been done in Japan, little of this has been translated into English (Deng, 2000). In a much-cited book, Pomeranz (2000) argues that incomes in the lower Yangtse were high, even by European standards in the 18th century. His thesis is that China failed to industrialize because of lack of land and other natural resources, especially >COAL, to which Europe had ample recourse, both domestically and from the New World. Ma (2008), to the contrary, argues that coal did not constrain Shanghai-based industrialization; at first it was imported from England, then Japan in the late 19th century and from North China when railways were completed in the 20th century. Eric Jones (2003) doubts if European industrialization was constrained by natural resources since technical progress was reducing these constraints. Jones is in general, and rightly, very sceptical of monocausal explanations for economic development and believes that multiple factors are always at work.

An interesting line of research discussed by Hamilton and Wei-An Chang in Arrighi et al. (2003) establishes important continuities between the late Imperial economy and the rapidly developing capitalism of Taiwan and mainland China. Development, not only in late Imperial times, but also recently, has been concentrated in >SMALL AND MEDIUM ENTERPRISES and in rural areas. Hamilton and Chang argue that throughout this period it has been the distribution sectors which have driven the structure of the economy, not, as predominantly in Europe, the production sectors. The result was that peasants moved into 'handicrafts' – small-scale production of textiles, for example – and it was this, along with continuing agricultural advance, which allowed the doubling of population in the long 18th century (1700–1840) and internal growth in trade in grain, cotton, silk and tea, without any decline in per capita incomes. Hamilton and Chang (Arrighi *et al.*, 2003) cite Pomeranz as saying that China's internal trade rivalled that of Europe as late as the late 18th century. There was, however, little apparent technological advance: the >PROTO-INDUSTRIALIZATION in rural areas did not lead to factory systems. Hamilton and Chang refer to the thesis of Mark Elvin, in his book *The Pattern of the Chinese Past* (1973). Elvin's view was that population pressures created a 'high-level equilibrium trap' in which population density diminished wages and reduced demand to the point where there was no incentive to centralize production as occurred in Europe. Hamilton and Chang's answer, by contrast, is that the existence of a complex distribution system meant that small-scale production could be and was efficient and competitive. They demonstrate this by showing that cotton textiles produced in cottage industries had a thriving export trade and were well able to compete with imports from Europe. In 1850, virtually all peasants were able to wear cotton, which did not exist in China 500 years earlier. The argument is that the traditional vertically integrated production system of the West is not the only form of efficient capitalism and flexible production systems with external economies of scale are a viable alternative. The same argument has been advanced in a more general way by Piore and Sabel (>INDUSTRIAL DISTRICTS). As mentioned, production in China has been distribution-led and concentrated into small-scale units in the countryside. Western brand-name retailers, such as Home Depot, Wal-Mart and Nike have played an important part with the active participation of the Chinese diaspora. The distribution-driven system prefers dealing with small firms because it gives the merchant function bargaining power. Hamilton and Chang conclude that: 'Young girls make cloth on single spindle looms a century ago or that women (and often men too) in households gather around the dining table to assemble computer parts does not indicate economic involution or capitalistic ineptitude' (Arrighi *et al.*, 2003). (By 'involution' is meant growth without development – where the marginal product of additional labour inputs is below subsistence.) We might add that this system does not depend solely on low labour costs but, as Piore and Sabel (1984) have shown, can be upgraded with more sophisticated technology as living standards and labour costs rise. For some commodities where systems are production- and not distribution-driven, such as steel and in the >AUTOMOBILE industry, China, of course, has already developed large-scale units. Even in Imperial times there were some large state-initiated undertakings in ceramics, iron making and mining.

## References

Arrighi, Giovanni, Hamashita, Takeshi and Seldon, Mark (eds), *The Resurgence of East Asia: 500, 150 and 50 Year Perspectives*, Routledge, 2003.

Deng, Kent G., 'A Critical Survey of Recent Research in Chinese Economic History', *Economic History Review*, February, 2000.

Elvin, Mark, *The Pattern of the Chinese Past*, Methuen, 1973.

Garnaut, Ross, Song, Lingang, Tenev, Stoyan and Yao, Yang, *China's Ownership Transformation*, International Finance Corporation, 2005.

Jones, Eric, *The European Miracle: Environments, Economies and Geopolitics* in the History of Europe and Asia, Cambridge University Press, 2003.

Ma, Debin, 'Economic Growth in the Lower Yangtse Region of China in 1911–1937', Journal of Economic History, 68(2), June, 2008.

Maddison, Angus, Contours of the World Economy, 1–2030 AD: Essays in Macro-Economic History, Oxford University Press, 2007a.

Maddison, Angus, Chinese Economic Performance in the Long Run, 960–2030, OECD, 2007b.

Maddison, Angus and Wu, Harry X., 'Measuring China's Economic Performance', World Economics, 9(2), April–June, 2008.

Piore, Michel J. and Sabel, Charles F., The Second Industrial Divide: Possibilities for Prosperity, Basic Books, 1984.

Pomeranz, Kenneth, The Great Divergence: China, Europe and the Making of the Modern Economy, Princeton University Press, 2000.

Powelson, John P., Centuries of Economic Endeavour: Parallel Paths in Japan and Europe and their Contrast with the Third World, University of Michigan Press, 1994.

Richardson, Philip, Economic Change in China c.1800–1950, Cambridge University Press, 1999.

Skinner, William, 'The Structure of Chinese History', Journal of Asian Studies, 1985.

Wang, Yueping and Yao, Yang, 'Market Reforms, Technological Capabilities and the Performance of Small Enterprises in China', Small Business Economics, February–May, 2002.

# Classical and Neo-Classical Economics

The publication of Adam >SMITH's An Inquiry into the Nature and Causes of the Wealth of Nations in 1776 met with instant success; by 1800, the book's fame was widespread not only in >BRITAIN but throughout Europe and in the >USA and it had been translated into many languages. It was upon this work that Economics was founded as a subject for study in its own right and eventually matured into an academic and professional discipline with the stature of a science through its development in what came to be called the Classical period of economics of the 19th century. Adam Smith's work had become available and internationally debated at a time of unprecedented upheaval and change. Europe had become engulfed in the French wars (>WESTERN EUROPE). There were harvest failures, restrictions on international trade, rising prices and problems of finance to the extent that the Bank of England suspended the guarantee of gold payments on its banknotes (>GOLD STANDARD). The industrial revolution was in the process of fundamentally changing the structure of the British economy (>INDUSTRIAL REVOLUTION IN BRITAIN). There were a multitude of problems urgently seeking solutions in the field of political economy for which answers were sought for practical policy-making. The leading practitioners in seeking solutions to these problems developed new arguments and theories from the comprehensive foundation set out with such clarity in the Wealth of Nations, many of the themes from which persist in Economics to the present day.

Adam Smith had viewed political economy as a part of moral philosophy and as a human activity governed by the divine will. In the Theory of Moral Sentiments (quoted in Deane, 1978), he had argued that, 'The happiness of mankind as well as of all other rational creatures, seems to have been the original purpose intended by the Author of nature when he brought them into existence'. He believed that, provided people acted within the precepts of the natural law, human motivations would lead towards the best outcomes. Although individuals may be selfish as well as altruistic, on the whole they were, at heart, sociable and reluctant to antagonize others. Although throughout his work he was therefore disposed to emphasize the benefits of allowing the markets to act freely without government interference, nevertheless he did not advocate unconstrained 'laissez-faire'. He believed government action was needed in many areas in order to offset the actions of interest groups which would otherwise run counter to the interests of society as a whole. In addition, government must ensure the security of the country, the maintenance of justice and the development of >EDUCATION. Government should also, he believed, be responsible for the infrastructure of the country as it could not be profitably left to private business. The belief in the efficacy of free markets with only the lightest necessary touch of government remained at the core of classical economics, persisting into the 21st century with Milton >FRIEDMAN, in particular, an effective proponent who linked the belief in free markets with democratic political freedom (Friedman, 1962).

To Adam Smith, labour was the fundamental measure of value. The true value of any commodity was the amount of labour which it could command in the market. Labour was the source of all wealth and the growth of a country's national income came from the increase in the labour supply and improvements in labour productivity. In the long run, the wages of labour would determine their number. If wages fell to or below subsistence, the birth rate would decline and the death rate increase and vice versa as wages increased above subsistence level. In addition to the specialization of labour, the accumulation of capital was necessary to generate economic growth. Capital

made available the sums necessary for the employment of labour and it arose from the savings generated from the profits earned on the capital employed. Its accumulation encouraged an increase in population, and in the specialization of labour, commensurate with the growth in the size of the market for the goods and services produced. This accumulation of capital was generated by savings, which were assumed to be spent and not hoarded. This continued increase in capital investment, however, would lead to a fall in the rate of profit as the economy approached a limit governed by its natural resources, real wages rose and competition between capitalists increased. There was, therefore, a natural tendency of an economy towards the point at which a limit on resources would lead to a stationary state. >RICARDO also held a labour theory of value. The value of a commodity, he argued, was determined by the amount of labour which was embodied in its production. In long-run equilibrium and perfect competition, the relative exchange values of different commodities were equal to the relative quantities of labour embodied in their production (>MARX). The early Classical economists, therefore, took the view that it was essentially the costs of production that determined market prices; a view which prevailed until the 'Marginal Revolution' in economic theory emerged in the last quarter of the 19th century.

The Bank of England (>CENTRAL BANKING) had suspended the convertibility of sterling banknotes into gold in 1797 and the market price of gold rose from the mint parity of £3.89 per ounce to £4.60 per ounce in 1809 (>GOLD STANDARD). Ricardo argued that the currency had depreciated because of the excessive issue of banknotes by the Bank of England and not by the disruption of trade or poor harvests. What would become the essence of the classical quantity theory of money (>FRIEDMAN: >KEYNES) was clearly stated by Ricardo in 1810 in the *High Price of Bullion, a Proof of the Depreciation of Bank Notes*:

'However abundant may be the quantity of money or of bank-notes; though it may increase the nominal prices of commodities; though it may distribute the productive capital in different proportions; though the Bank [of England], by increasing the quantity of their notes, may enable A to carry on part of the business formerly engrossed by B and C, nothing will be added to the real revenue and wealth of the country...There will be a violent and an unjust transfer of property, but no benefit whatever will be gained by the community.' (*The High Price of Bullion*, quoted in Deane, 1978)

Ricardo insisted that changes in the quantity of notes or coin in circulation only affected financial markets and the general level of prices and had no affect on the real economy except in the very short run. Henry Thornton (1760–1815) had already, in his *Enquiry into the Nature and Effects of the Paper Credit of Great Britain*, which was published in 1802, suggested that an increase in the money supply *could* stimulate economic activity and had drawn attention to what became know as people's liquidity preference which could increase in times of uncertainty and cause a drop in money in circulation with a consequential dampening of economic activity. Ricardo, however, won the day and Thornton's leads in monetary economics were not followed through until the turn of the century.

In contrast to Adam Smith's *Wealth of Nations*, the study and criticism of which formed the foundation of his own work, Ricardo saw the distribution of National Income between labour, land and capital, rather than its total level, as the major concern of his analysis. In a letter to Thomas >MALTHUS, he said that political economy 'should rather be called an inquiry into the laws which determine the division of the produce of industry amongst the classes who concur in its formation' (quoted in Roll, 1973). His method was to construct a theoretical model of the economy on simplified assumptions in order to reveal those laws and, in so doing, he helped to launch Economics along a path to its acceptance as a serious discipline comparable with those in the natural sciences. Factors influencing the growth of the total National Income did not receive attention because Ricardo accepted Say's Law (J. B. Say (1767–1832)).

Malthus disagreed with Ricardo on the validity of Say's Law, which postulated that there could be no continuing deficiency of aggregate demand in the economy because the supply of goods and services generated the means to acquire them. For every buyer there was a seller. He insisted that it was possible for an economy to suffer from a persistent deficiency of effective demand and a general unsaleable glut of products (>KEYNES). Malthus felt justified in this view because he worried about the continuation of the recession in >BRITAIN following the end of the war with France in 1815. However, Malthus' analysis suffered from not having the intellectual rigour of that of Ricardo. As Robert Torrens, a contemporary of his put it: 'As presented by Mr Ricardo, Political Economy possesses a regularity and simplicity beyond what exists in nature: as exhibited by Mr Malthus, it is a chaos of original and unconnected elements' (quoted in Blaug, 1978). It may be said that the consequence of Ricardo was that the progress of economics through the 19th century was more concerned with micro-economics, that is, in the problems of the consumer and of the firm, rather than with macro-economics, that is, the problems of the monetary variables and economic aggregates that influence and comprise the National Income.

The Smith/Ricardian theories dominated economic thought in the first half of the 19th century and with refinements were comprehensively set out by John Stuart Mill (1806–1873) in his *Principles of Political Economy with Some of Their Application to Social Philosophy* in 1848. This work was so successful that it survived as a text for students of economics until the end of the century. Mill's work marked the peak of the Classical period in economics, with probably the last purely Classical work being *Some Leading Principles of Political Economy Newly Expounded* by J. E. Cairnes, which was published in 1874. Thomas Carlyle (1795–1881), who believed in an hierarchical structure of society in which the low must be guided by their betters, criticized the fundamental assumption of Classical economics that the inherent motivations of individuals lead to improvement and the common good. Great men made history; they were not made by it. The description of economics as the 'dismal science' first appeared in 1849 in Thomas Carlyle's *Occasional Discourse on the Negro Question*. Economics was anarchy with a constable (Levy, 2002: >MARX: >SLAVERY).

In the last quarter of the 19th century, three publications appeared independently which applied the principles of marginal analysis and optimization to the problems of the behaviour of consumers and firms using mathematical tools such as the calculus and brought into play the concept of utility. These publications marked the end of the Classical period and the beginning of the neo-Classical period in economics. William Stanley Jevons (1835–1882) published his *Theory of Political Economy* in 1871, in which he postulated that the ratio at which one commodity was exchanged for another was the ratio of their marginal utilities. Carl Menger (1840–1921), again in 1871, published *Principles of Economics*, in which he also proposed a theory of value based on marginal utility. In two volumes in 1874 and 1877, Marie Esprit Léon Walrus (1834–1910), in his *Elements of Pure Economics*, argued that commodities were exchanged at a price at which the marginal utilities of the people making the exchange were equal. Moreover, he argued that the utility (satisfaction or usefulness) of a commodity to an individual diminished the more of the commodity he or she possessed. Walrus applied mathematical techniques to demonstrate how the demand for and the supply of a commodity was brought into balance. The consequence was that the determination of value was no longer seen as dependent on labour or the cost of production but on utility or satisfaction.

It was, however, Alfred Marshall (1842–1924) who brought economics up to date in a new comprehensive structure in his *Principles of Economics*, published in 1890, a book which surpassed that of J. S. Mill in its success as a textbook and in the longevity of its influence in the field of micro-economics. The early Classical economists had derived the market price of a commodity from its cost of production, for instance, the amount of labour used to supply it. On the other hand, the marginalists had emphasized the unique determinant to be utility. The essence of Marshall's neo-Classical economics was the determination of an equilibrium by the simultaneous and mutual influence of various factors in a market. The quantity and price at which a commodity was exchanged was determined not only by the marginal utility of the consumer but also the marginal costs of the supplier of the commodity. The market price was where the rising graph of the schedule of supply crossed over the falling graph of the schedule of demand, the result of the consumer attempting to maximize utility and the producer attempting to maximize profits. From such a structure could be determined in theory the optimum allocation of resources in the economy.

Such comprehensive reformulation as had been achieved in the field of micro-economics was not, however, made in that of the macro-economics of the determinants of the National Income. Macro-economics was still strongly conditioned by the early classical economists. If there was unemployment in the economy this was due to the stickiness of wages and relative prices. The national income was determined by the level of employment which in turn depended on the level of real wages. The economy had an inherent long-run tendency to full employment, given flexibility in wages and relative prices. The quantity of money determined the price level and the rate of interest brought into balance savings and investment.

>KEYNES published *The General Theory of Employment, Interest and Money* in 1936, which revolutionized the macro-economic theory applicable to conditions of mass unemployment, which he saw as the deficiency of effective demand rather than the stickiness of prices or wages. In the *General Theory*, savings and investment were brought into balance by changes in the level of national income. Expenditure on public projects would be desirable if only because they assisted in generating a more optimistic outlook among businessmen and therefore encouraged them to look for new investment opportunities.

The quantity theory of money, which was central to Classical macro-economics, postulated that changes in the supply of money had a direct influence on prices. Keynes rejected this and argued that the quantity of money would increase total output if there were spare capacity. There was no direct link between money and prices as assumed.

Milton Friedman was an economist who was fully in sympathy with and took his guiding principles of free markets and minimum government from the Classical tradition. To Friedman, the joy of Classical economics was that it was in complete accord with his natural love of individual liberty. From the earliest days, Classical economists had shown that an economy would not descend into chaos, if government left individual citizens to go about their business with the minimum of controls. Moreover, he agreed with Adam Smith that economics considered as:

'a branch of the science of a statesman or legislator, proposes two distinct objects: first, to provide a plentiful revenue, or subsistence for the people, or, more properly, to enable them to provide such revenue or subsistence for themselves; and secondly, to supply the state or commonwealth with a revenue sufficient for the public services.' (*Wealth of Nations*, 1776, introduction to Book IV)

## References

Blaug, Mark, *Economic Theory in Retrospect*, Cambridge University Press, 1978.

Deane, Phyllis, *The Evolution of Economic Ideas*, Cambridge University Press, 1978.

Friedman, Milton, *Capitalism and Freedom*, University of Chicago Press, 1962.

Levy, David M., *How the Dismal Science Got Its Name: Classical Economics and the Ur-Text of Racial Politics*, University of Michigan Press, 2002.

O'Brien, D. P. O., *The Classical Economists*, Clarendon Press, 1975.

Roll, Eric, *A History of Economic Thought*, Faber and Faber, 1973.

Schumpeter, Joseph A., *History of Economic Analysis*, Oxford University Press, 1954.

Smith, Adam, *An Inquiry into the Nature and Causes of the Wealth of Nations* (1776), with an Introduction by Dugald Stuart, Ward Lock, 1812.

# Coal

Coal deposits, unlike >OIL and natural gas, are distributed widely throughout the world. Coal is present in over 80 countries, although proportionately more is located in the Northern Hemisphere. Nevertheless, in 2000, it is estimated that the >USA: >RUSSIA: >CHINA and Australia accounted for over 60 per cent of World coal reserves of 1 trillion tons (International Energy Agency, 2000). World reserves have an expected life of 200 years. Coal was the energy source which powered the >INDUSTRIAL REVOLUTION in Europe (>WESTERN EUROPE) and the USA in the 19th century and its abundant availability influenced the direction of industrial expansion through the application of steam as the characteristic motive force of the

period. It would be wrong to conclude from this, however, that the timing of a country's 'take-off' was necessarily determined uniquely by its exploitation of its coal resources, but, nevertheless, progress was handicapped in those countries with little or no coal. Countries such as Spain, Austria, Hungary and Italy had to rely on imports and while >RUSSIA had substantial deposits they were late to be developed. For instance, in the late 19th and early 20th centuries the price of coal in Italy was twice as expensive as in France and between three and four times higher than in Britain, because of high transport costs. This high cost discouraged investment in those steam-based activities which were the dominant technologies of the time (Bardini, 1997). Britain, on the other hand, was remarkably well endowed for its size with coal resources and as it was the first country to experience the Industrial Revolution (>INDUSTRIAL REVOLUTION IN BRITAIN), so it was to the fore in the rapid development of its coal deposits.

Coal had been available in Britain for centuries. London, for instance, relied on coal shipped coastwise from Tyneside in the North East from the 14th century. An indicator of the growth in production, in fact, could be the statistics of coastal shipping from Newcastle-upon-Tyne, which record shipments of coal totalling 111,000 tons per annum in the late 16th century, rising to 298,000 tons per annum in the early 1620s to 412,000 tons per annum in the late 1650s (Coleman, 1977). Britain, because of its geography, had the benefit of a long coastline with enumerable harbours which its coastal >SHIPPING could exploit. Nevertheless, transport costs were a constraint on the distribution of coal inland until the coming of the >CANALS and >RAILWAYS. However, in the 18th century, there were developments that opened up opportunities for coal in markets in which wood and charcoal had been dominant. In 1709, Abraham Darby successfully heated a blast furnace with coke for the production of pig iron and the process was refined by John Smeaton in 1762 so that, thereafter, coke became the dominant fuel. Other technical improvements in the >IRON AND STEEL industry helped the market for coal, such as Benjamin Huntsman's crucible steel process using furnace coke in 1740 and Henry Cort's puddling furnace in 1784, subsequently improved by James Neilsen in 1829. The other major early market development was the arrival of the steam engine, exemplified by James Watt and Matthew Bolton's technical and financial success in making steam engines established by the end of the 18th century. The first railway was opened in Britain in 1825 from Stockton to Darlington. In 1827, the Dutch sailed the first steamer across the Atlantic, followed in 1837, by I. K. Brunel's 'Great Western' (>RAILWAYS: >SHIPPING: >STEAMPOWER).

Coal production in Britain passed the 10 million tons level in the 1780s, compared with 3 million tons in the 1680s (Coleman, 1977). By the mid-19th century, coal production in Britain had reached 56 million tons. With the exception of Belgium, which was producing 8 million tons of coal by the 1840s, other European countries lagged behind Britain in the exploitation of their coal resources. Britain was able to take advantage of this and its export markets flourished as industry began to develop on the European Continent. About 90 per cent of the coal deposits in Western Europe were located in Britain and Germany and most of the rest in Belgium, France and the Netherlands. British exports passed 1 million tons in 1837 and 12 million tons by 1870 (Saul, 1960). By the end of the 19th century, Britain was still the world's largest producer of coal, but production in other countries was rapidly gaining ground, particularly in the USA and Germany. In 1896/1900, it has been estimated that Britain accounted for 35 per cent of the world total production of 595 million tons, a drop from the 44 per cent achieved in 1881/5. In this period, the USA share was 26 per cent. By the early 20th century, the respective shares had been reversed and the USA was the lead producer with 43 per cent of the total world production. In spite of the growth in international competition, coal still accounted for 13 per cent of British exports at the turn of the century and on the eve of World War I accounted for almost a half of world exports (Yates, 1959). However, Britain was falling behind technically. There were a large number of small firms in the industry, which had need of rationalization; capital investment in new technology consequently was inadequate. The industry was also having to mine progressively more difficult seams (Supple, 1994). By >WORLD WAR I, over 50 per cent of production in the USA was machine-cut, compared with only 8 per cent in Britain. This deficiency was materially rectified during the inter-war period and some rationalization was achieved. The number of mines was reduced from 2,000 in 1913 to 1,900 in 1938 (Supple, 1994) and employment fell from a peak of 1,084,000 in 1923 to 674, 000 in 1938. However, the increase in international competition and the world recession resulted in excess capacity. The industry was labour intensive and the wage bill accounted for up to three-quarters of the cost of production. Wages and hours worked came under pressure and this, together with unemployment which affected up to 24 per cent of miners, combined to produce a state of distress and social unrest in the mining communities (Supple, 1994) (>KEYNES). An attempt was made by the government to engineer some rationalization of the industry through the Coal Mines Act of 1930, with limited success. A more thorough solution was looked for in 1947 when the government nationalized the industry and merged 800 mines into the National Coal Board (later renamed British Coal Corporation) and which, at its peak, employed 716,500. The industry was returned to the private sector by the Coal Industry Act of 1994. By the end of the 20th century the British industry had considerably diminished, production having fallen to 31 million tons, and dropped further to 18 million tons by 2006.

In Western Europe, the major location of coal resources, comparable to Britain, was in Germany (Prussia). The mines in Prussia were not, however, seriously developed until the opening of the >RAILWAYS. Coal production in 1846 was only about 3 million tons, a level Britain had reached in the 17th century. With the opening of the first state railway through the Saar for the transport of coal in 1847, the industrialization (>INDUSTRIAL REVOLUTION) of Germany was given impetus and new mines were dug, particularly in the Ruhr. By 1860/4, production of hard coal in Germany had reached 16 million tons, just under 20 per cent of the output of Britain; by 1900/4, it had expanded to just under 50 per cent and by World War I it was over 60 per cent, at 169 million tons (Ashworth, 1994). This rapid growth was, however, overshadowed by the rapidity with which

the coal resources of the USA, which is estimated to have 25 per cent of the world total (International Energy Agency, 2000), were brought to the market in the late 19th century. As for Britain and Germany, coal was an essential source of power for the industrial growth of the USA and the statistics of coal production afford a good indicator of the expansion of the US economy. On average in the years 1860/4, the US production of coal was similar to that of Germany. By the 1880/4 period, it had surpassed the German output level by over 70 per cent, by the 1900/4 period it had surpassed British production by 24 per cent and in the period just before World War I, production had reached 477 million tons, compared with a British output of 275 million tons.

The US experience contrasts with that of Russia, which also has substantial reserves of coal, accounting for about 16 per cent of the world total. Industrial development came later in Russia than in the countries of Western Europe and the major exploitation of the coalfields could not be achieved until the railway network had been established. Coal output from the Ukraine then grew vigorously (>RAILWAYS). Coal production rose from about 1 million tons per annum in the 1870s to 36 million tons just prior to World War I. During the First Five Year Plan period of >RUSSIA, coal production was lifted from 35 million tons in 1927/8 to 64 million tons in 1932. The Second Five Year Plan period achieved substantial increases in output per miner and an increase in production to 128 million tons by 1937 (Nove, 1992).

The world energy market, however, in the 20th century saw the arrival of energy sources in competition to coal and also changes in technology, which had an adverse effect on the market for coal. >OIL had been discovered in the USA in 1859 and the internal combustion engine arrived by the end of the century. In 1882, Thomas Alva Edison initiated the new industry of >ELECTRICITY generation. Although Britain had more of an incentive to continue to fuel its ships by coal compared with the USA because of its lack of domestic supplies of oil, nevertheless it opted in 1911 to switch its navy to oil. The US Navy also at the same time did likewise. The Emergency Shipbuilding Programme established by the Shipping Act of 1916 also chose oil for all new ships it commissioned (Gibson and Donovan, 2001). Oil-burning ships steadily replaced coal worldwide. Electric light replaced gas light, electric traction replaced the steam train, and electricity, oil and, later, natural gas replaced coal in domestic and industrial heating. Oil firing replaced coke in furnaces. In 1950, coal (including lignite) accounted for 60 per cent of the total world consumption of energy, liquid fuels 29 per cent, natural gas 10 per cent and hydro-electricity 1 per cent. In the 1950s, oil became cheaper than coal with the development of low-cost oil in the Middle East and this accelerated the switch to oil. By 1972 the share of coal/lignite in total world energy consumption had fallen to 31 per cent and that of oil had risen to 46 per cent, natural gas to 20 per cent; hydro-electricity and nuclear energy made up the remainder. The change was, however, checked by the quadrupling of oil prices by the Organization of Oil Exporting Countries (OPEC) in the 1970s and coal also benefited from the long-term growth of the electricity supply industry. Coal became dependent on two markets, electricity and the coke ovens of the iron and steel industry. The International Energy Agency (IEA) estimates that in 1980, in the member countries of the Organization for Economic Cooperation and Development (OECD), 66 per cent of total coal use was accounted for by the electricity industry and 21 per cent by coke ovens. World coal output rose, as a consequence of the growth in electricity demand, through the second half of the 20th century. In 1950, the USA accounted for 32 per cent of the world total coal production, and Russia and Britain 14 per cent each; by the end of the century China was the major producer, accounting for 37 per cent, the USA for 23 per cent, India 8 per cent and Australia 5 per cent, which was the major exporter.

## References

Ashworth, William, *A Short History of the International Economy Since 1850*, Longman, 1994.

Bardini, Carlo, 'Without Coal in the Age of Steam: A Factor-Endowment Explanation of the Italian Industrial Lag before World War I', *Journal of Economic History*, 57(3), September, 1997.

Coleman, D. C., *The Economy of England, 1450–1750*, Oxford University Press, 1977.

Gibson, Andrew and Donovan, Arthur, *The Abandoned Ocean: A History of United States Maritime Policy*, University of South Carolina Press, 2001.

International Energy Agency, *World Energy Report 2000*, OECD, 2000.

Nove, Alec, *An Economic History of the USSR, 1917–1991*, Penguin, 1992.

Saul, S. B., *Studies in British Overseas Trade, 1870–1914*, Liverpool University Press, 1960.

Supple, B., 'The British Coal Industry Between the Wars', in Anne Digby, Charles Feinstein and David Jenkins (eds), *New Directions in Economic and Social History*, Macmillan, 1992.

Yates, Lamartine P., *Forty Years of Foreign Trade*, George Allen & Unwin, 1959.

# Coffee

Coffee is obtained from the berries of a tree which could grow to 7 metres or more, although, in practice, it is kept pruned to a height of 1 or 2 metres. The tree takes about six years to reach maturity and can continue to be profitable for up to 40 years. There are broadly two varieties which are grown commercially, *caffea arabica* and *caffea canephora*. The latter is referred to as *robusta*. The coffee tree was first domesticated in Ethiopia, from where it spread in the 16th century throughout the Ottoman Empire. In the 17th century the Europeans began to take an interest and began coffee cultivation in the East Indies. From 1652, when the first coffee house was opened in London, coffee had a significant impact on the social and business life of the City. By 1714, there were over 500 coffee houses in London, each one attracting men with specific interests such as merchants, booksellers, stock-jobbers, clergymen, the most famous, perhaps, being Lloyds Coffee House in Lombard Street where marine insurers gathered (Porter, 2000). Ironically, tea was soon to replace coffee in >BRITAIN and it fell to the countries in Continental Europe to sustain demand.

Coffee was introduced by the Dutch into the East Indies in the 17th century. Coffee production continued to spread through European colonies in the 18th century, particularly successfully by France into the Caribbean, where towards the end of the century Haiti became the world's top producer, until the rebellion of the plantation slaves there in 1791 destroyed the plantations. In the 19th century, production spread through Latin America; and Brazil became the top producer. In the 1830s, coffee had replaced >SUGAR and cotton (>COTTON AND COTTON TEXTILES) as Brazil's leading export commodity (Williamson, 1992). It has been estimated that, in the second half of the century, Brazil accounted for about 50 per cent of total world exports, with Java (Indonesia) accounting for about 20 per cent. Coffee at this time became responsible for as much as 60 per cent of the foreign exchange earnings of Brazil (Bulmer-Thomas, 1994). In the early 20th century, prior to >WORLD WAR I, Brazil had increased its share to 60 per cent and Java (Indonesia) had fallen to 2 per cent, behind Colombia, Venezuela and other countries in Latin America.

In the second half of the 20th century, the trend of production was flat from 1960 to the late 1970s but from the 1980s production was on an upward trend in Latin America and Asia, though not in Africa. The >WORLD BANK has estimated that total production rose from 60 million bags to about 115 million bags in 2000/1. In the latter year, the total share of output of Brazil, Colombia and Vietnam accounted for 60 per cent of the total. (Although coffee was introduced into Vietnam in 1857, output did not become significant until the 1970s.) World production, therefore, grew at an average annual rate of 3.3 per cent over 20 years. Demand, however, grew relatively less strongly.

According to the World Bank, prices dropped from 1970–2000 at an annual average of between 3 per cent and 5 per cent, partly because of the tendency to excess supply, but also because of improved productivity, the entry of low-cost producers and the response of producers to price spikes. As with many other agricultural commodities, coffee is inherently liable to experiencing volatile fluctuations in prices. The classic sequence is that a price spike, for instance, caused by a temporary drop in production because of adverse weather conditions, encourages planting. When these plantings reach maturity, in the case of coffee in about six years, they swamp the market, by which time production has recovered in any case from the interruption due to weather. Moreover, the newly planted coffee trees have a continuing productive life of up to 40 years. There is consequently a reluctance to destroy these trees and switch to another product, even if that were feasible. Prices fell in real terms by the end of the 20th century to their lowest levels in 100 years. This caused hardship to the estimated 20 million households that relied on coffee for their livelihood (Lewin *et al.*, 2004).

There have been a number of schemes designed to stabilize the market. A coffee valorization scheme was set up in Brazil in 1906 designed to regulate the market through stock levels. The scheme lasted until World War I. In the face of a decline in world prices of coffee in the 1920s, Brazil reintroduced the valorization scheme. Producers were supported financially to offset their loss of liquidity. This activity led to further overproduction, not only in Brazil but also in other countries. It also escalated Brazil's foreign debt (Williamson, 1992).The scheme was abandoned and an attempt made to pursue an international solution. In the context of the decline in prices in 1931 (>GREAT DEPRESSION) from 25 cents per pound to 8 cents per pound, there was an international agreement to destroy excess production during the period 1930–7. However, the scheme was terminated because Brazil refused to continue to destroy its production. It had found that it was losing market share because of the problem of free-loaders; other countries failed to carry out their promises.

After World War II, an International Coffee Agreement, including both producers and consumers, came into force in 1962 which was designed to control prices by fixing export quotas for each producer. Surpluses were stockpiled or sold to non-members of the agreement. Agreements were regularly renewed after the initial five years. The 7th International Coffee Agreement was signed in 2007 by 77 exporting and importing countries and came into force in 2008, with the aim of promoting a sustainable expansion of the coffee sector, but it did not include the manipulation of market prices as previous Agreements had attempted to do.

### References

Bulmer-Thomas, Victor, *The Economic History of Latin America Since Independence*, Cambridge University Press, 1994.

Clarence-Smith, William Gervase and Topik, Steven (eds), *The Global Coffee Economy in Africa, Asia and Latin America, 1500–1989*, Cambridge University Press, 2003.

Lewin, Bryan, Goivannucci, Daniele and Varangis, Panos, 'Coffee Markets: New Paradigms in Global Supply and Demand', World Bank, Agriculture and Rural Development Discussion Paper 3, 2004.

Porter, Roy, *London, A Social History*, Penguin, 2000.

Roseberry, William, Gudmundson, Lowell and Kutschbach, Mario Samper (eds), *Coffee, Society and Power in Latin America*, Johns Hopkins Press, 1995.

Williamson, Edwin, *The Penguin History of Latin America*, Penguin, 1992.

Yates, Lamartine P., *'Forty Years of Foreign Trade'* George Allen & Unwin, 1959.

# Commercial Revolution

New sea routes to the East and the discovery of America stimulated the European economies and led to a major shift in trade from the Mediterranean to the Atlantic from the 16th century. The commercial revolution was one of several, which, with changes in agriculture and transport, have created the modern world (>INDUSTRIAL REVOLUTIONS:    >CONSUMER REVOLUTION). In the Middle Ages, European trade with the East (including Arabia, China, India and Asia Minor) was, if limited in volume, of considerable importance for Royalty and the better off. Imports from the East included not only drugs, plants, spices and precious stones, but also dyestuffs, carpets, cutlery and >SILK, but in return the Europeans had to pay in gold and silver which created a scarcity of these precious metals. The overland routes to and from the East were long and often dangerous and there were no contiguous sea lanes – only those across the Arabian Sea into the Persian Gulf or the Red Sea (via Baghdad, Cairo and other cities), all of which required costly transhipments onto caravans. The Italian cities of Venice, Pisa and Genoa captured much of the Mediterranean end of the trade with the East. All this was to change with the discovery of new routes to India via the Cape of Good Hope and the discovery of America, which shifted trade to the Atlantic (Faulkner, 1960).

The commercial revolution is perhaps not emphasized as much by contemporary economic historians as earlier ones and has been overshadowed by the Industrial Revolution 200 years later, of which it was an important precursor (Hammond, 1926; Knowles, 1930). The new sea routes brought down the cost of oriental goods and the flow of bullion from the Spanish possessions in South America pushed up the general level of prices in Europe, increasing the profits of enterprise. This was because wages and rents lagged behind the rise in prices – facts noted by Adam Smith writing in 1776. Faulkner wrote that 'all the influences tending to the development of merchant capitalism and economic imperialism were accentuated' (1960) by the commercial revolution (>ECONOMIC IMPERIALISM). Among other things, the revival of trade hastened the decline of the guilds and, indeed, led to the tendencies to >GLOBALIZATION which persist to this day.

Hammond (1926) pointed out that the more distant trade opportunities required larger ships and bigger capitalized trading companies and this in turn stimulated the development of stock-jobbing, >BANKING and >CAPITAL MARKETS. The deep-sea routes were pioneered by the Portuguese, the Spanish and later the Dutch, followed by the English. Banking was more advanced in Holland and Italy than in Britain at the time and, as Hammond wrote: 'The part played by England in the Industrial Revolution of the eighteenth century was played by the Dutch in the commercial revolution that preceded it and helped bring it about' (1926). Navigational innovations by the Portuguese and others and larger ships were only among the first technological advances stimulated by the commercial revolution which were eventually followed during and after the Industrial Revolution by revolutions in transport (including the >RAILWAYS and >SHIPPING) and >TELECOMMUNICATIONS.

Note that Hammond does not say that the commercial revolution caused the Industrial Revolution but simply that it helped bring it about. This is also the contemporary view. Knick Harley, in his contribution, 'Trade, Discovery, Mercantilism and Technology', to Floud and Johnson (2004) acknowledges that the institutional developments during the commercial revolution supported the subsequent revolution in industry (>INSTITUTIONS). He also notes that the leading industries (coal, textiles and metalworking) grew by selling worldwide. Exports and incomes in England were also correlated with the growth of trade: the percentage of the national income derived from exports doubled during the 18th century. He goes on to argue, however, that trade was as much a response to technological development and industrial expansion as a cause of it (>INTERNATIONAL TRADE).

### References

Faulkner, Harold Underwood, *American Economic History*, Harper & Row, 1960.

Floud, Roderick and Johnson, Paul, 'Industrialisation 1700–1860', in Roderick Floud and Paul Johnson (eds), *The Cambridge Economic History of Modern Britain*, I, *Industrialisation, 1700–1860*, Cambridge University Press, 2004.

Hammond, J. L. and Hammond, Barbara, *The Rise of Modern Industry* (1925), Methuen (2nd edn), 1926.

Knowles, L. C. A., *The Industrial and Commercial Revolutions in Great Britain during the Nineteenth Century*, Routledge, 1930.

# Companies

Firms, enterprises, businesses or companies (the terms are frequently used interchangeably) are the basic units of >CAPITALISM. These organizations bring together the financial, physical and human resources needed to engage in producing, buying and selling. Their structure is determined by the legal form they adopt, be it a *sole-proprietorship*, a *partnership* (>SMALL AND MEDIUM ENTERPRISES) or an *incorporated limited liability company*. The limited company as we know it today dates only from the second half of the 19th century, though it has long and involved antecedents. Because the company is so central to the workings of the free market economy, its history and impact are dealt with at many points in this book. This entry deals mainly with the early evolution of the corporate legal form.

The earliest form of business enterprise was the sole proprietorship. Partnerships were used by the early Italian banks and trading companies and before that by most of the early civilizations (Mesopotamian, Phoenician, Greek and Roman, for example). The *commenda* or commercial partnership was in widespread use in the western Mediteranean from at least the 13th century. According to North (1990), these partnerships had Jewish, Byzantine and Muslim origins and often featured limited liability for the partners, or some of them, from third-party claims. The *commenda* is therefore the root of the joint stock company in which ownership is divided into equity shares and which was to evolve eventually elsewhere in Europe, starting, probably, in Portugal. Much of the early impetus for the development of partnerships came from the needs of distant trade. A merchant or a prince needed to provide capital for land caravans or ships where he might or might not accompany the trip. His liability might be limited to the capital he put in, while another of the partners might be a ship-owner who would also share in the profits but bear the loss of his ship if it went down. Families were important in partnerships since family members were less likely to cheat each other, though the partnership might well include non-family members. Another root of the modern company was in the medieval guild corporation. In regulated companies which followed the guilds, individual merchants were granted monopolies in return for financial support for the sovereign. Later, state-chartered companies with similar characteristics to regulated companies emerged with legal personalities and a joint stock form (>ENGLISH EAST INDIA COMPANY). One of the earliest English chartered joint stock companies was the Muscovy Company founded in 1553 for trade with >RUSSIA.

In the early 18th century, the French and British governments hit upon the idea that the chartered joint stock companies could be used to restructure their large debts resulting from the wars and competition between the two countries (>WESTERN EUROPE). This financial innovation included the exchange of long-term state debt obligations held by the public for equity shares in the companies. This practice, according to Baskin and Miranti (1997), was known as 'engraftment', appropriately enough because graft was certainly exercised in the later stock promotion of the companies and their management. The advantages of the debt exchange included lower debt servicing and administration costs for government and less onerous repayment terms, as well as, for the companies, a means of credit expansion for business development. The Bank of England pioneered this form of financial engineering but was

followed on a large scale by France through the Banque Royale and the Mississippi company (Compagnie des Indes) of John Law, a Scotsman in exile. In >BRITAIN, the South Sea Company, which at its founding in 1711 outbid the Bank of England for another round of refinancing, gained some dubious trading monopolies in Latin America. The monopolies were intended to make the company's equity shares more attractive but in a second, larger, round in 1719, it mainly relied on making exaggerated claims for its prospects and inflating the market value of its shares. This was achieved by issuing fewer shares than authorized so as to give a premium over the par values of the government debt it was taking in, and making sales at 10–20 per cent margins. These measures gave the new holders the prospect of an immediate capital gain and led to a scramble for the stock, which spread to a boom in other companies' shares in canals and insurance and a 'bubble mania'. At first, the early apparent success of the French operations (which were soon to plunge in disarray) also encouraged investors who were actually exchanging solid annuities for the soon to be debased currency of South Sea stock. The famous Bubble Act of June 1720 was not intended to curb the boom but to protect the South Sea Company from competition by placing restrictions on the formation of new chartered joint stock companies and even disenfranchising some existing ones that had strayed from their original, authorized, purpose.

The Bubble Act, described by many at the time as 'unintelligible', did not achieve its purpose (Shannon, 1954). The boom was punctured in the late summer of 1720, the South Sea Company failed and was effectively nationalized. The collapse left investors with large losses, though it did not bring down the financial system as did the collapse in France, where the currency was undermined. The magnitude of the bubble in Britain can be illustrated by the path of the share price, which rose to £950 by early July only to fall to £170 by October. The Bubble Act was not repealed until 1825 through pressures from the same kind of rent-seeking interests that had led to its enactment in the first place (Harris, 1997). The significance of the Bubble Act drawn by some writers is that it delayed the development of modern limited liability companies until the second half of the 19th century. This view has been challenged by others who argue that capital requirements during the early part of the >INDUSTRIAL REVOLUTION IN BRITAIN were still quite modest and could be met in most cases by various forms of partnerships. That this view is more nearly correct is supported by the fact that more flexible forms of business structure actually developed earlier in Continental Europe, where industrial development was slower, and, as we shall see, in the USA. In France, for example, limited partnerships were available from the 1820s (*commandites par action*), while, according to Kindleberger (1984), Sweden, as in >CENTRAL BANKING, was ahead of Britain and achieved generalized incorporation as early as 1848.

The repeal of the Bubble Act, although it did not achieve generalized incorporation, did encourage the formation of joint stock companies in Britain, many of these being conversions from partnerships. Partnership law at the time was unsuitable for large enterprises (which required large numbers of investors). There was no public register of partners and the law required that in any suit

against the partnership third parties bringing a claim had to list the members and all their particulars in detail for it to succeed. This was virtually impossible where the largest partnerships had very many individual members, some of whom might be abroad, with the members changing all the time. There were also difficulties in the way of partners internally seeking remedies from the partnership. The Partnership Act, fully reforming the law was not enacted until 1890 by which time incorporation was easily available. Parliament moved slowly in the reform of company law because of concerns aroused by past and continuing company frauds. The Registration Act of 1844 required commercial partnerships of more than 25 members to register and to file balance sheets (extended to cover banking in the Joint Stock Banking Act of 1845) but this act did not confer automatic limited liability on registration; this did not come until 1856. Further Acts over the period 1855–62 eliminated the need for Acts of Parliament and extended limited liability to all companies. In the years between 1856 and 1862, large numbers of limited liability companies were incorporated, though most businesses remained unincorporated, as indeed they are today. The limited liability system continued to be extended in the period 1866–83 and the laws on fraud were tightened. The mandatory registration requirements of the 1844 Act were replaced by a voluntary system, though they were restored in 1900.

As already mentioned, the development of free incorporation in the >USA moved somewhat faster than in Britain, though a general requirement to file financial statements was not fully implemented until the 1930s (>NEW DEAL). In the early years following independence, the states continued to follow the British practice in granting corporate charters by special acts of legislation, but gradually this requirement was eliminated and replaced with 'free incorporation'. Connecticut was the first state to have a general incorporation statute (for non-bank corporations) in 1816. Other states followed and by 1850 free incorporation prevailed throughout the country. Bank incorporation continued to require state charters until the late 1930s. The early non-bank charters did not automatically confer limited liability for shareholders, though Court decisions up to the 1850s generally held that limited liability was implicit in the charter. After 1850 no special act was required and limited liability was automatic (Kroos, 1974). Echoing the situation in Britain at the same time, Kroos says that, 'Limited liability though important was not the cardinal consideration in incorporating, for about the same number of corporations were formed in the less lenient states as in the most lenient' (1974). What was important was that enterprises could raise more capital than under partnerships, a critical factor for banks, canals and railway companies. Between 1790 and 1860 thousands of special franchise corporations were authorized by state legislators, half of them in the 1850s. Apparently, the laws allowing these creations were essentially indigenous and owed little to English Law (Hurst, 1970).

In the last quarter of the 19th century, the modern corporate form of business organization spread around the world. In India and Africa it came through colonization (>ECONOMIC IMPERIALISM), while in Asia primarily out of a desire for modernization on Western lines. Early Japanese business was organized in guild associations of individual merchants and merchant houses (to which the great *zaibatsu* owed their origins), which were effectively family partnerships (though not all members were necessarily of the same blood line). Even in these early days the family merchant houses seem to have a legal personality. With the Meiji Restoration (1868), guilds were abolished and replaced with trade associations. From the 1890s more modern businesses tended to join the newly formed Chambers of Commerce and Industry. As in Europe, from the early 1870s state-chartered companies were authorized in Japan. In 1878 the system of national charters was changed so that local governments could authorize joint stock companies (Hirschmeier and Yui, 1975). In the 1890s general incorporation laws on Western lines were passed in Japan.

With the complete emergence of free incorporation and limited liability in place of partnerships and chartered companies, there were few restrictions on the extension of the corporate form. Companies had three important characteristics: they had a legal personality distinct from their owners, the liability of those owners was limited to the value of their equity and these shares were freely transferable. The way was set for higher levels of investment, the emergence of giant companies, including >MULTINATIONAL ENTERPRISES, and, especially from 1900, the development of >CAPITAL MARKETS that would facilitate further corporate expansion and the widening of their ownership. This last, by leading to the increasing separation of business ownership and control, would create the possibility of agency problems in which the interests of managers and owners might diverge. The same developments would also lead to mergers and trusts and monopoly issues and all of this would require governments to reassert controls over many aspects of corporate behaviour, so company law has continued to evolve (>CORPORATE GOVERNANCE: >ANTI TRUST).

Unincorporated enterprises predominated at the turn of the century in all major countries in terms of numbers of firms. For example, in Britain, in 2001, 62 per cent of all private sector enterprises were sole proprietorships, 15 per cent were partnerships and 23 per cent were incorporated. In the USA, in 1997, according to business tax returns, 73 per cent of non-farm businesses were proprietorships, 7 per cent partnerships and 20 per cent corporations. Whether or not enterprises incorporate is very much a function of size – almost all firms with more than 100 employees were incorporated (>ACCOUNTING: >BUSINESS MANAGEMENT: >CHANDLER: >CONCENTRATION: >ENGLISH EAST INDIA COMPANY: >ENTREPRENEURSHIP: >REGULATION: >SMALL AND MEDIUM ENTERPRISES: >TAXATION: >USURY).

### References

Baskin, Jonathan Barron and Miranti, Paul J.,*A History of Corporate Finance*, Cambridge University Press, 1997.

Harris, Ron, 'Political Economy, Interest Groups, Legal Institutions and the Repeal of the Bubble Act of 1825', *Economic History Review*, November, 1997.

Hirschmeier, Johannes and Yui, Tsunehiko, *The Development of Japanese Business, 1600–1973*, George Allen & Unwin, 1975.

Hurst, James Willard,*The Legitimacy of the Business Corporation in the United States*, University Press of Virginia, 1970.

Kindleberger, Charles P., *A Financial History of Western Europe*, George Allen & Unwin, 1984.

Kroos, Herman E., *American Economic Development* (3rd edn), Prentice Hall, 1974.

North, Douglass C., *Institutions, Institutional Change and Economic Performance*, Cambridge University Press, 1990.

Shannon, H. A., 'The Coming of General Limited Liability', *Economic History*, II(6) (1931), reproduced in E. M. Carus-Wilson (ed.), *Essays in Economic History*, Edward Arnold, 1954.

Wilson, John F., *British Business History, 1720–1994*, Manchester University Press, 1995.

## Concentration

The extent to which a small number of firms account for a large proportion of output, sales or some other measure of economic importance has also been discussed elsewhere in this book (>ANTITRUST: >CORPORATE GOVERNANCE). The issue of corporate 'bigness' is also the mirror-image of >SMALL AND MEDIUM ENTERPRISES. In the long run, concentration increased up to 1970s, though it has levelled off since in an aggregate sense. >MARX foresaw the increase in concentration, which he termed 'the centralization of capital', and that this would mean fewer capitalists, though he failed to predict the limits of the process and wrongly expected it to be accompanied by increased exploitation of workers, in fact the reverse has been true.

By the 1960s, although there were thousands of companies, a mere 100 accounted for about 40 per cent of total profits and assets in manufacturing in both >BRITAIN and the >USA. A hundred and thirty years earlier, apart from the >RAILWAYS and a few multiple retailers, there were very few giant enterprises. As early as the late 1920s, Berle and Means (1967) concluded that ownership and control of most large corporations had passed from the owner-managers to financial institutions and management by salaried staff that owned only a tiny proportion of the shares of the companies they ran. >CHANDLER argued that increased concentration was necessary and inevitable as the capital requirements of new technologies and markets increased dramatically in the latter part of the 19th century. Chandler also showed how new, decentralized corporate structures emerged from the 1920s to deal with the managerial challenges of increasing scale. There is, of course, a possibility that concentration could reduce competition and innovation (>ANTI-TRUST). Some writers, notably >SCHUMPETER, have believed that large scale is necessary for innovation, while others that concentration has advanced beyond the point at which it can be justified by economies of scale and scope. The wide range of firm sizes which has persisted in all market economies, however, suggests that large and small firms play complementary roles (Bannock, 2005).

The trends in concentration seem to have been universal though the pace of change has varied. *Aggregate concentration* (the share of a limited number of large firms in total output) had grown faster in the USA than in Europe, with the possible exception of Germany, and certainly faster than in France, up to 1909. From the 1920s, concentration in Britain speeded up and equalled or exceeded that of the USA by the 1960s. Much of the increased concentration was the result of horizontal and conglomerate mergers, especially in the USA and Britain where the greater development of stock markets facilitated mergers (>CAPITAL MARKETS). Aggregate concentration rose over the whole period 1909–68 interrupted only by World War II. There was then a plateau of stability until the early 1980s, followed by a sustained decline. The latest data suggests that the decline has levelled off. It has been suggested that the decline in concentration resulted from restructuring in response to the pressures of international competition, especially from Asia. How much of the increase in aggregate concentration in the past was the result of mergers, as opposed to internal growth, is controversial but probably approached half (Hannah, 1976; Prais, 1976). Quite apart from the 'real' causes of mergers, such as economies of scale, managerial aggrandizement and the drive for monopoly control, there is an interesting autonomous factor at work. It can be shown that, on certain assumptions, random growth factors will themselves lead to increased concentration because of the differential effect of given increases and contractions on large and small firms. This was propounded by a French engineer, Gibrat, in 1931, though it is not clear whether or not it has practical significance (Hannah and Kay, 1977).

*Market concentration* (or concentration ratio, the share of the, say, four top enterprises in a specific product market), is much used in the execution of competition policy (Blair, 1972). There are many difficulties in defining markets for this purpose and, in practice, even greater difficulties in making comparisons of concentration ratios over time because of changes in coverage. Studies of market concentration in the post-World War II period suggest relatively slow increases in the USA but much faster increases in Britain. As examples of the results, we have seen that concentration in British retailing (>CONSUMER REVOLUTION) and >BANKING is very high and in both the USA and Britain concentration is high in >BEER and the >AUTOMOBILE INDUSTRY. However, in the motor industry and also >IRON & STEEL, actual competition has been transformed by the vigorous entry of overseas producers. Deregulation and technological development have had similar effects in >AVIATION and >TELECOMMUNICATIONS.

### References

Bannock, Graham, *The Economics and Management of Small Business: An International Perspective*, Routledge, 2005.

Berle, A. A. and Means, G. C., *The Modern Corporation and Private Property* (1932), Harcourt Brace (new edn), 1967.

Blair, John M., *Economic Concentration: Structure, Behaviour and Public Policy*, Harcourt Brace, 1972.

Hannah, Leslie, *The Rise of the Corporate Economy*, Methuen, 1976.

Hannah, L. and Kay, J. A., *Concentration in Modern Industry*, Macmillan, 1977.

Prais, S .J., *The Evolution of Giant Firms in Britain*, Cambridge University Press, 1976.

Schmitz, Christopher J., *The Growth of Big Business in the United States and Western Europe, 1850–1939*, Macmillan, 1993.

# Consumer Revolutions

Developments in distribution and retailing have been influenced by a great many factors including population change, urbanization, levels of income, transport, the structure of the service and manufacturing industries, international investment, regulation and lifestyles and culture. Historically, there have been various forms, from itinerant traders and open markets to fixed shops, chain stores, shopping malls and superstores, as well as cooperatives, mail order and franchising. It is difficult to apply the term 'revolution' to any stage of these developments because, although varying in pace, change has been continuous since at least medieval times when shops were controlled by guilds. Also old forms have always continued alongside innovations so that no form of retail distribution has ever disappeared altogether, For example, the earliest forms of retailing, open markets and itinerant traders still exist today in much of the world (>PEDLARS).

It is convenient, for the purposes of this narrative, to discuss three periods of historical change that have been identified by economic historians, even though it needs to be borne in mind that development has been continuous and that the very existence of some of these 'revolutions' is controversial. This applies particularly to the first consumer revolution, which is supposed to have occurred in Britain and other countries before the early >INDUSTRIAL REVOLUTIONS. The second consumer revolution, perhaps the only one that really justifies the term, began about 1850 in >BRITAIN and the >USA and saw the emergence of chain stores, as well as what was to become a flood of manufactured and packaged goods. Some historians have distinguished another consumer revolution, particularly in the inter-war period in the USA, which was characterized by the spread of cars and other durable goods and the beginnings of self-service supermarkets. These developments were to intensify and spread around the world in the third consumer revolution after >WORLD WAR II. This third phase saw the rise of a true age of mass consumption. These developments took place to some extent in all the advanced countries though the pace of change varied.

The first consumer revolution is poorly documented. Davis (1966) put the critical point in the slow early evolution of retailing in London in the reign of Elizabeth I (1558–1603). At that time, population was growing, there was an increase in the number of wealthy people and new goods were becoming available from abroad (>COMMERCIAL REVOLUTION). Jefferys (1954) asserted that the general shape of retailing in Britain differed in the mid-19th century only in degree from what it had been in the previous century. Others, including Clapham (1930), found that the number of shopkeepers had grown rapidly in the 18th century, as well as the number of middlemen. He made it clear that the growing needs of London, especially for fuel and food, required a complex system of distribution. Fixed shops in the 18th century were mostly in towns and there were general stores in country areas selling a wide variety of goods. The vast majority of people were very poor – village labourers, outworkers and a growing number of factory workers – and these used open markets. Weekly or even daily markets in town and country were where growers sold their own food. There were also fairs which dealt in a range of produce, including imported food, artefacts and materials. The fixed shops in the 17th and early 18th centuries tended not to have window displays (plate glass and bow windows were unusual before 1750) and none of these outlets seem to have had fixed and displayed prices. Jefferys (1954) points out that there were few trades in which the retailer was not called upon to do some processing. Grocers, for example, cured and cut bacon, washed dried fruit and blended tea as well as packaging it. Retailing was therefore a skilled trade and the necessary skills were acquired through formal apprenticeships or from family members (shops were managed by owners, generally living on the premises). According to Davis (1966), specialist wholesalers began to appear in the 18th century, though the majority of provincial shopkeepers bought goods from London stores, some of which evolved into wholesalers. By the early 19th century, wholesalers employed travelling salesmen to supply country shops. Itinerant traders were important, both in town and country, and some offered a range of items including second-hand clothing in which there was a large market from 1700. As urbanization and factory production grew, some of the needs of the new working class were met by company shops and some workers were paid by vouchers for use in these stores (truck). Captive retailing of this kind could be and was abused by employers and in England a series of Acts from 1749 regulated the practice culminating in the Truck Acts 1831–71, which made it illegal.

Maxine Berg's contribution, 'Consumption in Eighteenth and Early Nineteenth Century Britain' in Floud and Johnson (2004) points to the apparent contradiction between the revisionist views of some economic historians that aggregate consumption grew only slowly in the late 18th and early 19th centuries and the evidence of social and cultural historians of a consumer revolution in tastes, shopping and the ownership of consumer goods. Other writers have discussed the same contradiction, for example, De Vries' >INDUSTRIOUS REVOLUTION, while still others have speculated about the role, if any, of changes in domestic demand in triggering the >INDUSTRIAL REVOLUTION IN BRITAIN. Historically, services have always preceded manufacturing; it was merchants who organized the putting-out system, for example (>PROTO-INDUSTRIALIZATION). Demand and supply are inextricably linked, as Alfred Marshall (1842–1924) (>CLASSICAL AND NEO-CLASSICAL ECONOMICS) illustrated with his analogy of them being equivalent to the two blades of a pair of scissors in determining price. Export demand played a large part in certain industries, such as >COTTON AND COTTON TEXTILES. In these cases exports were supply-driven by offering competitive advantages in price and quality. To explain Berg's contradiction in terms of exports is to say that the industrial revolution, initially at least, was only confined to these industries (another subject of controversy). Certainly part of industrialization was to substitute mass-produced goods for the costly luxuries consumed by the rich – >WEDGWOOD's mission, for example was to bring forth cheaper fine china goods previously imported from Asia for a wider market (Berg, 2005). Mokyr (1999) devotes considerable space to a discussion of the role of domestic and export demand in the industrial revolution. He concludes that demand was not a central factor in economic change in the 18th century, though he does not deny that there were big changes in distribution.

These issues become clearer in the 19th century, for which better data are available including information on the consumption of commodities drawn from indirect taxes. Between 1840 and 1886, for example, the consumption of tea rose five times, that of ham and bacon rose from tiny levels in 1840 to 12lbs (imperial pounds of weight) per capita and butter from 1lb to over 7lbs. We also know from a variety of sources that in this period incomes were rising rapidly and that there were major changes in

distribution from 1850–1914, and this was the second consumer revolution in which the pace of change accelerated. There were several reasons for changes in distribution. The British population doubled from 20–40 million between 1851 and 1911. The practice of self-sufficiency had largely ended with >ENCLOSURE and the growth of industry and urbanization. Imports of cheaper food were increasingly available. Producer/retailers found it more difficult to survive in increasingly urban areas because of difficulties in keeping in contact with customers and the extension of factory production to many of their products, such as footwear, and rising rents in high streets to which more modern retailing was moving. W.H. Smith (books, magazines and newspapers) and Singer, a producer of sewing machines, were among the first of the multiple retail organizations, but it was not until the 1870s that multiple outlets emerged in the main consumer goods trades and especially for those selling imported food. According to Jefferys (1954), in 1875 there were 257 firms and 11,645 branches and by 1920, 471 and 24,713 respectively. Over this same period, the number of firms with 25 or more branches increased from 10–180. The two decades before 1914, therefore, saw the emergence of giant retail firms with near-national networks. It is interesting to note that these large-scale national retailers emerged before similar developments in most areas of British manufacturing: another instance of services preceding manufacture. In fact, the national chains were integrating vertically into manufacture and in a few cases into overseas sources of supply, such as plantations. Examples of these early chains are the Maypole Dairy, Lipton Ltd and Boots Pure Drug Co. Manufacturers were also integrating vertically into retailing; Singer has already been mentioned.

Despite this early sign of >CONCENTRATION in retailing, there was still a place for >SMALL AND MEDIUM ENTERPRISES which offered personal service, longer opening hours and credit, which the multiples did not yet offer. However, the independents had to change and adapt. Skill levels continued to decline and the practice of living over the shop began to give way to 'lock-ups'. The very important cooperative movement also started to grow vigorously in the 19th century. The origins of this movement were earlier – the Oldham Cooperative Supply Company was founded in 1795. The principle of cooperatives was that consumers should share in the margins of the enterprise by means of dividends in proportion to their volume of purchases as well as by fair prices and high standards of quality. Behind this, as Martin Purvis, in his contribution to Benson and Shaw (1992), wrote, was, 'a belief in the redeeming power of collective effort to transform a corrupt and competitive world into a more equitable co-operative commonwealth'. These ideological beliefs led some cooperative retailers to extend their activities to production, housing and education. According to Purvis, the experience of cooperatives stores was similar to that of the independents, that is, there were many failures but also successes. From Rochdale in 1844, retail cooperative societies spread all over the country. Cooperative Wholesale Societies were founded in England (1863) and Scotland to facilitate purchasing but not all co-ops became members. By 1913 there were 1,500 local retail cooperative societies in Britain with a total of 2.9 million members. By 1939, membership of co-ops had grown to 8.5 million. Although at one time co-ops accounted for 25 per cent of milk sales, 20.5 per cent of groceries and 19.5 per cent of bread and flour, they were not able to make much of a national impact in other areas, except in meat, coal and footwear. There were weaknesses which became more important over time. As Michael Winstanley, in his contribution to Kirby and Rose (1994), says, 'unlike the nationally controlled multiples, the cooperative movement was federal with power vested in individual societies whose leaders were democratically accountable to local shareholders' and there were tensions between the concerns of business management and the ideology of the lay members. The cooperative movement did not prove able to compete fully with the other multiples in the third consumer revolution after World War II. By 1985 its share of total retail sales had fallen to about 5 per cent, perhaps half of its peak level in the inter-war period, and was to decline further.

Jefferys (1954) estimates that the share of multiples in total retail sales went from 3–4.5 per cent in 1900 to 7–10 per cent in 1920, for co-ops from 6–7 per cent in 1900 to 7.5–9 per cent in 1920 and from 1–2 per cent in 1900 to 3–4 per cent in 1920 for department stores. Department stores began as successful drapery and clothing outlets, then diversified into other ranges and bought up adjacent properties. This reflected a desire to expand on a single site and avoid the complications of multiple-site management, but later, purpose-built stores appeared, for example, Gordon Selfridge's famous store in Oxford Street, which opened in 1909. These stores were definitely up-market and designed to appeal to the growing middle class of merchants, government officials and the like.

The department stores were the first to promote shopping as a pleasant, entertaining experience, with cafés, toilets, hairdressing and other facilities. A major boost to the growth of multiple food stores came from the increased availability of cheaper, imported food and improved transport as rail and tramways increased the mobility of customers in urban areas (>RAILWAYS). Food supply areas were transformed by the railway. In the 1840s railway companies began to organize the carriage of fresh fish. The price of fish brought from Hull to Manchester, for example, fell by as much as 70 per cent and the volume sold rose from three to 80 tons per week (Benson and Shaw, 1992). Britain cut the duties on imported meat and abolished them altogether in 1846. After 1870 refrigeration led to imports from South America, Australia and New Zealand. The growing availability of mass-produced non-foods, such as furniture, shoes and clothing from the 1880s and new electrical goods towards the outbreak of World War II, further stimulated retailing. More stimulus came from media promotion and the growing availability of credit. Hire purchase (HP, or instalment-buying) grew rapidly. By 1891 there were some 1 million HP agreements in force mainly for the middle class; poorer people used independent shop credit. Smaller enterprises remained dominant. Jefferys (1954) estimated that it was only in footwear, milk and furniture that independents accounted for less than 50 per cent of sales at the beginning of World War II. Although multiples were to move forward decisively after the war and especially after 1970, for the time being independents accounted for over 80 per cent of sales, not only in the traditional fields of fish, fruit and vegetables,

printed media, tobacco and confectionery, but also they had captured a similar position in the new consumer durables which developed rapidly in the inter-war period. It was estimated that from 1901–31 there were declines in the number of independent retailers relative to the human population in some sectors, notably in food and other staples which had suffered from competition from multiples. However, there were increases again from 1921, though not back to 1901 levels or above in most trades (Ford, 1936).

Part of the explanation for the relatively slow growth of multiples in the first half of the 20th century was the existence of Resale Price Maintenance (RPM) in which manufacturers set minimum prices at which their products should be sold with breaches enforced by refusal to supply. There were collective agreements between manufacturers and retail organizations to maintain RPM, which had originated in the 1890s, but it began to break down in the 1950s and was largely abolished by the Restrictive Trade Practices Act (1956) and the Resale Prices Act (1964). The growth of suburbanization also checked the expansion of multiples for faster-selling items such as food.

The third consumer revolution in Britain began in the 1950s when wider car ownership led multiple stores to begin developing supermarkets with car parks on the edge of town centres. From the mid-1970s, superstores or hypermarkets selling an increasingly wide range of goods appeared and from the early 1990s this expansion accelerated. The number of stores operated by Tesco, the largest operator, grew from 379 in 1990 to 639 in 1999 and for Sainsbury, from 291 to 405. In 1995 the three largest operators accounted for 54 per cent of national grocery sales (Competition

Commission, 2000). Competition between the large groups was intense and from the 1980s there was consolidation in the second division by merger, culminating in the acquisition of Safeway by Morrisons, a successful multiple from the North of Britain, to create the fourth largest group. In the late 1980s the large multiples ceased to deliver to their stores directly but instead to Regional Distribution Centres (RDCs). RDCs allowed a reduction in the number of individual deliveries and by shortening delivery times allowed the release of floor space previously used for storage in the branches. Bar coding and electronic point-of-sales systems linked to the RDCs allowed further efficiencies in store replenishment and reordering from suppliers. The latest development is the installation of equipment to allow customers to checkout their own purchases, which virtually completes the long transition from skilled proprietor-service to customer self-service. Other developments have included a move back by the multiples into the high streets where they began with mini- or convenience stores and the extension of operations abroad. This internationalization goes back to the 1960s but in terms of the number of investments it tripled in the 1970s and more than doubled again in the 1980s, broadening to include not only Europe and North America but also the Far East (Burt, 1993).

The growth of the multiples has attracted criticism continuously from the second half of the 19th century when the trend started. Independent retailer interests called for protection from the 'unfair' competition from the big retailing units. These complaints have so far resulted in no significant action in Britain. Between 1979 and 1989, according to numbers of registrations for VAT, there was only a small decline in the number of retailers. In this period, retailing and agriculture were the only major industry sectors to show a decline, though the number of wholesalers increased substantially. Cost savings have been largely passed on to consumers and British retailing has been showing substantial increases in labour productivity in contrast to the USA, where it seems to have been fairly static, at least until fairly recently (Wrigley, 1989). Concern about the role of large retailers has widened, culminating in a series of inquiries by the competition authorities. Many believe that continued growth of the largest multiples may eventually result in diminished competition and choice but also that their bargaining power over manufacturers has become counterproductive. Many countries have taken action to curb the growth of multiples from the early days of their expansion. Bavaria introduced a special tax on large shops in 1899, for example, and this was followed by similar measures elsewhere. The USA and other countries have taken action against retailing mergers (>ANTI-TRUST). The Robinson-Patman Act (1936) made it illegal to sell goods to retailers at different prices unless justified by differences in the cost of supply; in other words, unjustified price discrimination between large and smaller buyers was banned. Italy and Japan went further by introducing restrictions on large store openings; for example, by Japan's 1937 Department Store Law and the 1973 Large Scale Retail Store Law. Restrictive shop licensing was introduced in Italy early on in the Fascist period. In 1987, only 'two per cent of total retail food sales in Italy were made in hypermarkets compared to 17 per cent in Spain, 18 per cent in Belgium and Germany and 40 per cent in France' (Jonathan

Morris in Alexander and Akehurst, 1999).

Thus, although the broad shape of the developments in Britain that we have described have been paralleled elsewhere, retail structures are not the same everywhere and the pace of change has varied from country to country. Consumer cooperatives, for example, were still much more important in the Britain than in Germany or most other European countries in 1961. Many of the innovations in retailing and retailing technology in the third consumer revolution have come to Europe from the USA. For example, the concept of single-price (variety) stores was imported from the USA in the inter-war period. This was not so for department stores, which seem to have emerged more or less simultaneously in New York, Paris and London. Multiple stores may have been a British first, but America took the lead in many respects from the beginning of the 20th century. Despite this, multiples in the USA were not to achieve the same dominant position that they have in Britain, presumably because of the continental scale of the country. It was also no doubt geography that favoured the enormous development of mail order in the USA to supplement country stores in the 1890s. Montgomery Ward was founded in 1872 and Sears Roebuck in 1895. The widening of car ownership (>AUTOMOBILE INDUSTRY) forced the mail order houses to open retail outlets in cities, which led to lower prices and enabled them to sell to urban as well as rural customers (Faulkner, 1960).

Instalment buying in the USA developed rapidly for 'big ticket' items in the 1920s and 1930s and manufacturers such as General Motors, as well as financial institutions, became increasingly involved in the provision of credit. In 1922–9, 75 per cent of car purchases were on credit. As mentioned at the beginning of this entry, some economic historians count the developments of the 1920s, especially in the USA, as constituting another consumer revolution, this time in consumer durables. At the start of the 1930s, 40 per cent of Americans already owned a radio, 30 per cent a vacuum cleaner and 24 per cent a washing machine. Chain stores led this growth: there were only 500 such stores in 1900, but 8,000 in 1914 and as many as 50,000 in 1920. American economic historians place considerable emphasis on the growth of leisure activities in this period. By 1927, according to Thompson (1994), 56 per cent of families had cars and this and rising incomes led consumers to enjoy more tourism and to see movies. There were 40 million moviegoers in 1922 and twice that number at the end of the decade. Other forms of entertainment, including spectator sports and vaudeville, gained wider audiences. Amusement parks, such as Coney Island, New York, developed on the edge of cities, promoted in part by urban transport operators. Advances in printing had already been made in the 1890s and permitted an explosion in media and advertising. The *Ladies' Home Journal*, aimed at middle-class women, for example, had a circulation of 850,000 as early as 1910.

The >GREAT DEPRESSION in the 1930s and World War II interrupted the growth of what came to be called 'consumerism', but after the war growth and innovation resumed. By the 1970s, 70 per cent of American consumers had a credit card. The continued diffusion of car ownership led to a rapid expansion in out-of-city-centre supermarkets and shopping malls and franchised retail operations, including fast food. Food retailing at these supermarkets was boosted by virtual saturation in ownership of refrigerators. All these developments had started before the war but accelerated. Television became the dominant form of entertainment and second only to print media for advertising. In television and in other respects America was far ahead of Europe and Japan. In 1961 there were 306 television sets per thousand of the population in the USA, 220 in the Britain, about 100 in Germany and Japan and only 55 in France and Italy. In most of these aspects of consumerism, Europe was soon to follow America and innovation has continued. Today in all the advanced countries a rising proportion of retail activity has moved onto the internet, although it has yet to displace conventional outlets and indeed these are participating fully.

Although there are signs of convergence, the structure of retailing continues to differ considerably between countries. Kiyohiko G. Nishimura and Lionello F. Punzo's contribution to Boltho *et al.* (2001) presents data showing that, in 1994, establishments with one to nine employees accounted for 49.4 per cent of retail sales in Italy, 43.5 per cent in Japan and only 8.6 per cent in the USA. Although these figures may not be fully comparable, the differences are striking. The structure of retailing in the UK is much closer to that of the USA than to the Italian pattern and in fact is even more concentrated. Nishimura and Punzo say that the conventional view that Japan and Italy have too many 'momma and poppa' outlets and are inefficient is an oversimplification. The different structures may reflect rational adaptation to local conditions (including regulation) but also differences in tastes. Italian consumers, for example, seem to prefer the convenience and personal service which characterize their smaller stores, as well as, in the case of food, placing a high value on

freshness which is a consequence of a greater use of local sources of supply by small local stores and daily instead of weekly shopping habits, which are becoming the norm in the USA and Britain. If there were not differences in tastes the perceived 'inefficiencies' would not be expected to persist, especially in the European Union which has virtually free trade and capital movements. The authors also show that sales per worker are much lower in smaller than larger stores in all three countries, while net output per employee in retailing is about 30 per cent lower in Italy compared with the USA and even lower in Japan. We might add here that even though these comparisons are made at purchasing power parities, this does not mean that total factor productivity is necessarily lower since small shops employ much less capital per worker (>PRODUCTIVITY). International comparisons of retail structures raise interesting questions. Nishimura and Ponzo argue that in Italy and Japan the relative functions of manufacturers and retailers give a greater role (for example, in after-sales service) to manufacturers whose bargaining power is greater than in the more retailer-oriented structures where supermarkets, especially in Britain, have the upper hand. Retail distribution has tended to be neglected by economic historians but, given its economic importance – well over a fifth of employment in most advanced countries – this may be expected to change.

## References

Alexander, Nicholas and Akehurst, Gary (eds), *The Emergence of Modern Retailing 1750–1950*, Frank Cass, 1999.

Benson, John and Shaw, Gareth (eds), *The Evolution of Retail Systems c.1800–1914*, Leicester University Press, 1992.

Berg, Maxine, *Luxury and Pleasure in Eighteenth Century Britain*, Oxford University Press, 2005.

Boltho, Andrea, Vercelli, Alessandro and Hiroshi, Yoshikawa (eds), *Comparing Economic Systems: Italy and Japan*, Palgrave, 2001.

Burt, S., 'Temporal Trends in the Internationalisation of British Retailing', *International Review of Retail Distribution and Consumer Research*, 3(4), 1993.

Clapham, J. H., *An Economic History of Modern Britain: The Early Railway Age, 1820–1850* (2nd edn), Cambridge University Press, 1930.

Competition Commission, *Supermarkets: A Report on the Supply of Groceries from Multiple Stores in the UK*, 2000.

Davis, Dorothy, *A History of Shopping*, Routledge, 1966.

Faulkner, Harold Underwood, *American Economic History*, Harper & Row, 1960.

Floud, Roderick and Johnson, Paul (eds), *The Cambridge Economic History of Modern Britain, Volume I Industrialisation 1700–1860*, Cambridge University Press, 2004.

Ford, P., 'Decentralisation and Changes in the Number of Shops, 1901–1931', *Economic Journal*, 46, 1936.

Jefferys, J. B., *Retail Trading in Britain 1850–1950*, Cambridge University Press, 1954.

Kirby, Maurice W. and Rose, Mary B. (eds), *Business Enterprise in Modern Britain from the Eighteenth to the Twentieth Century*, Routledge, 1994.

Mokyr, Joel (ed.), *The British Industrial Revolution: An Economic Perspective* (2nd edn), Westview Press, 1999.

Thompson, Grahame (ed.), *The United States in the Twentieth Century: Markets*, Hodder & Stoughton, 1994.

Wrigley, N., 'The Lure of the USA: Further Reflections on the Internationalisation of British Grocery Capital', *Environment and Planning*, 21(3), 1989.

# Corporate Governance

Who manages companies, how managers are appointed and remunerated and who watches over them, as well as the relationships between companies and their employees and the public at large, were not prominent issues for the general public when most companies were small and managed by their owners. There were, of course exceptions even as long ago as the early 18th century; think for example, of the South Sea Bubble (>COMPANIES), and, of course, there was rising concern about how businesses treated their employees during the >INDUSTRIAL REVOLUTIONS. What brought corporate governance into prominence was the great growth in the size of companies that came about from the end of the 19th century, when capital requirements rose sharply. Ownership in very large businesses became increasingly dispersed among large numbers of people and a new class of salaried professional managers emerged. These managers were not owners of the business they ran and their interests might diverge from those of the owners (the agency problem). The process of the separation of ownership from control first became evident in the >USA, where the capital requirements for >RAILWAYS, utilities and other great companies in the third quarter of the 19th century (though Hilt (2008) puts it earlier). At that time, amalgamations in successive merger waves necessitated the issue of securities in amounts too large for individuals to retain or to gain control of these enterprises. 'Managerial capitalism' had really arrived by the 1920s in the USA and was to follow elsewhere in the industrialized world.

Berle and Means (1967) were the first to document and quantify the separation of ownership and control in the big corporations. They found that by the end of 1929, the 200 largest non-financial corporations accounted for 49.2 per cent of the assets of all non-financial companies. Management owned only a few per cent of the stock in these firms, often less than 1 per cent and rarely more than 5 per cent. Because stock ownership was so widely dispersed, managers were virtually free of control by shareholders. Moreover, industries were becoming more concentrated as the share of the leading firms was consolidated through internal growth and mergers to create oligopolistic conditions across swathes of the economy (>CONCENTRATION). The process of concentration continued until the 1960s, by which time the 100 largest enterprises in both the USA and >BRITAIN accounted for about half of net output or assets in manufacturing. There was then a levelling off in the growth of concentration and even some reduction. The big corporations had grown too large and too diversified for effective management in the face of competition from abroad. There was a trend towards selling off unwanted subsidiaries and a refocusing on core activities and 'shareholder value'. These trends were common to all countries but there were important differences, nonetheless. For example, in Japan, where large companies also dominated many industries, large and small companies functioned in a dual economy with small subcontractors absorbing fluctuations in economic activity and offering little security and much lower earnings for their employees, who did not participate in the 'life-long employment' system practiced by large firms.

There were also differences in systems of corporate governance: broadly speaking, in Germany and Japan, although there had been a separation of ownership and control, shareholdings were less dispersed than in the Anglo-Saxon countries,

but were to a large extent held in blocks by banks and other financial institutions or by other commercial and industrial companies. In East Asia, outside Japan, family ownership remained important (Morck, 2005). In Italy, banks played a relatively small role; instead shares in corporate groups were controlled in a pyramidal structure by founding families and by the state, which acquired its stakes during the crises of the 1930s (>GREAT DEPRESSION). At that time there was de facto nationalization of almost a quarter of the Italian economy (Boltho et al., 2001). These differences are deeply rooted in cultures and history. In the Anglo-Saxon countries, the monitoring role associated with banks in Germany and Japan was left to market forces. Bad managements were under the threat of takeovers from more successful groups.

Governance arrangements in Germany and Japan are far from the same, but in their effects are closer to each other than to those of the USA and Britain. The Anglo-Saxon countries also do not have identical arrangements: for example, in Britain until quite recently many large firms had few external (non-executive) directors, whereas in the USA the majority of directors tend to be non-executive (Toms and Wright, 2005). By contrast with the USA and Britain, and for that matter with Japan, Germany has a two-tier board system: a supervisory board (*Aufsichsrat*) and a management board (*Vorstand*). This system has been mandatory since the corporate law reform of 1884. According to Cheffins (2001), professional managers were taking over in large German companies from the beginning of the 20th century, but shareholdings did not become dispersed as in Britain and the USA. The crises of the inter-war period saw continued conglomeration and cartellization of larger enterprises and the beginnings of corporate shareholdings by the banks. This process continued after World War II. Between 1950 and 1995 ownership by banks and insurance companies in Germany increased from 3 to 22 per cent of market value and inter-firm holdings rose from 22 to 42 per cent, while family and individual ownership fell from 42 to 17 per cent. Corporate ownership by financial institutions and large holding groups (*Konzern*), therefore, has been closely intertwined in Germany. The German system of corporate governance also includes mandatory works councils and representation of trade unions on supervisory boards (co-determination). Banks are represented on 10 per cent of supervisory boards but housebanks are intimately linked into the system through their holdings of proxy voting powers under shares deposited with them (>BANKING). Finally, companies in Germany are required to take account of the wider public interest in their activities. Corporate law reforms in 1965 did strengthen shareholders' rights (for example, in terms of disclosure and profit distribution and weakened the public interest requirement), but Streeck and Yamamura (2001) conclude that the basic 'constitutional logic' of corporate governance in Germany has been maintained throughout the post-war period.

In Japan, the Commercial Code introduced by the Meiji government at the end of the 19th century did not lay down formal systems for corporate governance other than giving shareholders strong powers. In the inter-war period, inter-corporate holdings increased under the *zaibatsu* and bank holdings also increased. After World War II, US forces of occupation disbanded the *zaibatsu* and family ownerships of big corporations were virtually eliminated. However, horizontal links were built up under new groupings of cross-holdings (*keiretsu*), in part organized by banks, which took it upon themselves to perform a monitoring function of the firms in their group. Similar attempts by the Allies in Germany to impose Anglo-Saxon corporate governance systems also failed (Buck and Tull, 2000). Corporate law reforms in Japan in 1950 went against the global trend by actually limiting the power of shareholders meetings to recall managements through requiring a two-thirds majority. Today, according to Streeck and Yamamura (2001), only about one-third of large Japanese companies have outside directors on their boards. Company directors tend to emerge by rising through the ranks. Employees also have a strong influence in Japan. Since 1946, there have been statute-based works councils but there are no legal provisions requiring employee representation on the (unitary) boards. Employee influence is strengthened by a general presumption that employers must exercise responsibility in their relations with their employees and we have already mentioned the life-long employment system, which is a manifestation of this.

The economic consequences of different forms of corporate governance have long been controversial. >CHANDLER argued that Britain's late adoption of American patterns of governance explained its relatively slower growth. Controversy has also raged over the alleged failure of 'hands-off' banking in Britain to facilitate industrial investment and modernization (>BANKING). Roe (1994) has emphasized the role of legal factors in preventing the emergence of strong financial institutions to temper the power of management in the USA. He cites passive insurance companies which, for half a century, were prohibited from owning the stock of companies, the legal separation of commercial and investment banking, legal obstacles to interstate banking leading to the fragmentation of commercial banking and fiscal >ANTI-TRUST and other legal restrictions on inter-corporate holdings. Behind these legal barriers to German and Japanese types of governance, Roe (1994) identified enduring populist distrust of financial power which originated in the political interests of small farmers and a desire to curb the power of the 'robber barons' in the early inter-war period (>NEW DEAL). Undoubtedly, legal forces have helped to shape the US system, but in Britain, where commercial banks face few restrictions but have still adopted hands-off attitudes and where, for example, competition law has been more passive than in the USA, essentially the same system of governance has emerged. It can be argued that in both countries the listing rules of stock exchanges have had just as much, and generally a prior influence on governance. From early in the 20th century, the New York Stock Exchange saw itself as the guardian of the financial quality of its listed companies. This regulation of listed companies is also helping to erode differences in systems of governance. When German and Japanese companies seek listings abroad, which they increasingly do in an era of >GLOBALIZATION, for example, to facilitate capital raising or acquisitions in New York or London, they have to conform to the listing rules and become more responsive to shareholder requirements.

There are also some pressures the other way for convergence of the two types of governance systems. Recent failures in corporate governance in the USA and the Britain, as evidenced not only by scandals such as the Enron case but also by evidence of excessive executive remuneration unrelated to corporate performance, have led to more activism on the part of institutional shareholders. Their shareholdings are not large enough for them to intervene directly, though there have been cases where institutions have banded together but they have pressed for voluntarist and legal measures to improve governance. In the USA, recent efforts to improve governance go back to the Report of the National Commission of Fraudulent Financial Reporting in 1987 and have culminated in the Sarbanes-Oxley Act (2002) and other legislation (>REGULATION). In Britain, there have been successful attempts to gain acceptance for codes of conduct (the Cadbury Committee Code, 1992, and the Combined Code, 1999). These codes emphasize shareholder accountability, the separation of the roles of the chief executive and the chairman and the appointment of non-executive directors. Reforms in corporate law are also underway in Britain.

Although there are some signs of international convergence in governance systems, the German and Japanese systems do remain very different from the Anglo-Saxon model. The French, Italian and other variants also remain different but are slowly moving in the same direction. The European Commission is also attempting to create a single market in financial services against strong national resistance (>WESTERN EUROPE). At different times, the German and Japanese systems of governance have been held to be superior to the Anglo-Saxon model but it is doubtful if these systems in themselves have been central to differences in economic performance in the long run. In the latest banking crisis, beginning in 2007–8, European banks have proved somewhat more robust than those in Anglo-Saxon countries because they have been less exposed to securitized mortgage and other assets.

### References

Berle, A. A. and Means, G. C., *The Modern Corporation and Private Property* (1932), Harcourt Brace (new edn), 1967.

Boltho, Andrea, Vercelli, Alessandro and Hiroshi Yoshikawa (eds), *Comparing Economic Systems: Italy and Japan*, Palgrave, 2001.

Buck, Trevor and Tull, Malcolm, 'Anglo-American Contributions to Japanese and German Corporate Governance after World War II', *Business History*, April, 2000.

Cheffins, Brian R., 'History and the Global Corporate Governance Revolution: The UK Perspective', *Business History*, October, 2001.

Hilt, Eric, 'When did Ownership Separate from Control? Corporate Governance in the Early Nineteenth Century', *Journal of Economic History*, September, 2008.

Morck, Randall K. (ed.), *A History of Corporate Governance Around the World: Family Business Groups to Professional Managers*, University of Chicago Press, 2005.

Roe, Mark J., *Strong Managers, Weak Owners*, Princeton University Press, 1994.

Streeck, Wolfgang and Yamamura, Kozo (eds), *The Origins of Non-Liberal Capitalism: Germany and Japan in Comparison*, Cornell University Press, 2001.

Toms, Steven and Wright, Mike, 'Divergence and Convergence with Anglo-American Corporate Governance Systems: Evidence from the US and UK 1950–2000', *Business History*, April, 2005.

## Cotton and Cotton Textiles

Cotton, which had originated in >INDIA, reached Europe in the Middle Ages and cotton textile manufacture spread from Italy through the continent to >BRITAIN, where production began in Lanchashire early in the 17th century. Manufacture was then based on the putting-out system, by which merchants organized the distribution of the fibres, the spun yarn and the woven fabric among out-workers operating manually.

Cotton is the industry that exemplifies most vigorously those changes in manufacturing enterprise that came to be referred to as the Industrial Revolution (>INDUSTRIAL REVOLUTION IN BRITAIN). As in other industries, Britain was the world leader. The industry was insignificant in Britain at the beginning of the 18th century, importing less than 500 tonnes of raw cotton. Exports accounted for only 1 per cent of total manufactured exports in the first half of the 18th century (>WOOL AND WOOL TEXTILES). In the last decade or so of the century, however, there was a great change. Cotton textiles leaped to first place in British manufactured exports by 1800, capturing 35 per cent of the total and pushing wool textiles to second place at 22 per cent, compared with the 85 per cent wool had enjoyed at the beginning of the century (Floud and McCloskey, 1994).

British demand had previously been met by imports of printed cotton cloth (calico) from India but, by Acts of Parliament of 1701 and 1721, such imports had been restricted to protect the domestic wool textile industry. This encouraged a substitution of the importation of cotton textiles by raw cotton and the consequent establishment of a new industry free from any of the constraints of traditional methods. A series of inventions and the application of water and later steam power yielded substantial improvements in labour productivity. In 1733, John Kay (1704–1780) patented the flying shuttle; in 1770, James Hargreaves (1720–1778) the spinning jenny; in 1769, Richard Arkwright (1732–1792) invented the water frame. In 1779, Samuel Crompton (1753–1827) introduced the mule, which was converted to steam power in 1790 and, in 1785, Edmund Cartwright (1743–1823) patented a power loom. These developments, which required investment in fixed assets, led to the reorganization of the industry into factories located appropriately for the availability of supplies of suitable coal and labour. Lancashire became the centre because, in addition to coal and labour supplies, its damp climate helped the processing of the cotton fibres and the county had available supplies of soft, lime-free water.

The improvement in productivity led to a very significant drop in the real price of cotton textiles. There is some discussion about the size of this price decline based on the derivation and interpretation of the available trade statistics. This discussion is in the context of the extent to which the demand for British exports played a role in the British Industrial Revolution in comparison to the evident supply-side changes in the British economy (Esteban, 1997, 1999; Harley, 1998).

The switch from manual to machine spinning was accomplished in Britain by 1820, although the transformation of weaving took longer. Compared to Britain, development in Continental Europe was hampered by the Napoleonic Wars and the Continental blockade, which retarded the diffusion of British technology, in spite of the

smuggling of Crompton mules and steam engines into Belgium. The Continental industry, particularly spinning, found it hard to compete after the war. In 1800, Britain consumed 25,000 tonnes of raw cotton per year. By 1835, this had increased to 144,000 tonnes per year, compared with 68,000 tonnes consumed by the whole of Continental Europe (including >RUSSIA). Meanwhile, the cotton textile industry was established in the >USA in New England, where it was protected by import tariffs (Irwin and Temin, 2001); the USA became the world's second largest producer by the 1840s. Even so, Britain produced three times the output of its American competitor. In 1846, over 65 per cent of the world total of cotton spindles was located in Britain. The consumption of cotton in Continental Europe did not surpass British levels until the 1880s.

The cost reductions achievable from the technological change in the methods of production could be utilized commercially because of the worldwide demand for cotton textiles. In 1813, the monopoly enjoyed by the >ENGLISH EAST INDIA COMPANY was repealed and, as a result, imports of cotton goods were free to enter India. British exports of cotton manufactures to India increased from 1 million yards in 1813, to 51 million yards in 1830. This trade continued to expand through the 19th century and accounted for about 20 per cent of British exports of cotton goods. Nevertheless, British exports were diversified geographically. Over 50 per cent of cotton manufactures were exported to Europe and the Mediterranean countries. Europe was the dominant destination for yarn, taking 76 per cent of the total in the early 1840s.

Another technological improvement came at an opportune time for the industry. Europe had obtained its raw cotton from India and the Middle East but these sources could not have met the increased demand for the quality of staple required. In the late 18th century, the cultivation of cotton was introduced into the USA. It was grown to good quality but it was costly to separate the seeds of the plant from the fibre. However, in 1793, Eli Whitney designed a mechanical gin which enabled the separation to be done by the turning of a set of teeth embedded in a drum. The USA rapidly became the world's leading supplier of raw cotton. Cotton production in the USA was based on plantations in the southern states from Virginia to Texas which were worked by slave labour (>SLAVERY). Production increased from 5 million pounds in the 1790s to 60 million pounds in the early 1800s, 400 million pounds in 1845 and 1,000 million pounds in 1850. The productivity of the plantations was significantly advanced by the development of new cotton strains there (Olmstead and Rhode, 2008). During the Civil War, Europe switched to India, Egypt and Latin America for its supplies. However, although the plantation system did not survive, the USA was able to recapture its market after the war, though world demand growth had entered a slower phase. Throughout the 19th century and early 20th century, the USA exported on average about 60 per cent of its cotton output.

In the second half of the 19th century Japan developed its cotton textile industry to such effect that by 1920 it accounted for over 10 per cent of its National Income and it replaced Britain as the top exporter in the 1930s. After World War I, synthetic fibres began effectively to compete and developing countries to expand their own domestic

industries. Demand for raw cotton fell in Europe but particularly in Britain. From just before World War I to the 1950s, imports of raw cotton into Britain fell by 60 per cent. The British industry was decentralized into separate companies specializing in the various operations such as spinning, weaving and finishing. The responsibility of selling finished products was left to independent merchants. With new technology in the inter-war period, slower demand growth and more competition, such a structure was less beneficial and hampered investment decisions.

The USA diverted more cotton to the supply of its own industry so that exports fell from 2 million tonnes (out of total world export of 3 million tonnes) to 792, 000 tonnes (out of a total world export of 2.6 million tonnes). India raised its imports from 13,000 tonnes to 118,000 tonnes in this period. Similarly, Japan increased its imports from 310,000 tonnes to 486,000 tonnes, thereby exceeding imports into Britain. In the same period Brazil and Mexico, together, increased their exports from virtually nothing to 469,000 tonnes. Japan was replaced by >CHINA as the dominant producer and exporter of cotton and cotton textiles in the last quarter or so of the 20th century. According to the International Cotton Advisory Committee, China produced 4.4 million metric tonnes of cotton in 2000 compared with the US production of 3.7 million tones, out of a world total of 19 million tonnes. China's net exports, however, were minimal whereas net exports from the USA amounted to 1.5 million tonnes.

The developed countries' concern for employment in their own industries in the face of competition from low-cost competition from the developing countries led to the Multi-Fibre

Arrangement in 1974, which permitted the imposition of import quotas. The agreement was periodically renewed until 1991. There then followed a transitional period of ten years during which protection was gradually phased out. From 2005, textiles were no longer given special treatment under the general rules of multilateral international trading. Exports of textiles from China increased rapidly so that it had doubled its share of the world total to 22 per cent between 2000 and 2006 (>INTERNATIONAL TRADE: >WESTERN EUROPE).

## References

Badiane, Ousmane, Ghura, Dhaneshwar, Goreux, Louis and Masson, Paul, 'Cotton Subsidies in West and Central Africa', World Bank Policy Research Working Paper 2867, 2002.

Esteban, Javier Cuenca, 'The Rising Share of British Industrial Exports in Industrial Output, 1700–1851', *Journal of Economic History*, 57, December, 1997.

Esteban, Javier Cuenca, 'Factory Costs, Market Prices, and Indian Calicos: Cotton Textile Prices revisited, 1779–1831', *Economic History Review*, LII(4), 1999.

Floud, Roderick and McCloskey, Donald (eds), *The Economic History of Britain Since 1700*, Cambridge University Press, 1994.

Goodman, Jordan and Honeyman, Katrina, *Gainful Pursuits, The Making of Industrial Europe, 1600–1914*, Edward Arnold, 1988.

Harley, C. Knick, 'Cotton Textile Prices and the Industrial Revolution', *Economic History Review*, LI(1) 1998.

Irwin, Douglas A. and Temin, Peter, 'The Antebellum Tariff on Cotton Textiles Revisited', *Journal of Economic History*, 61(3), 2001.

Jenkins, David (ed.), *Cambridge History of Western Textiles*, Cambridge University Press, 2001.

Mokyr, Joel (ed.), *The British Industrial Revolution: An Economic Perspective*, Westview Press, 1993.

Olmstead, Alan L. and Rhode, Paul W., 'Biological Innovation and Productivity Growth in the Antebellum Cotton Economy', *Journal of Economic History*, 68(4), December, 2008.

Pollard, Sydney, *Peaceful Conquest: Industrialisation of Europe, 1760 –1970*, Oxford University Press, 1981.

Rose, Mary B. (ed.), *The Lancashire Cotton Industry: A History since 1700*, Lancashire County Books, 1996.

# E

## Economic Development

The subject of economic development deals with the process by which economies grow. It also concerns why some countries are richer than others and what the policy implications of this are. In this entry we merely outline this large subject, a central preoccupation of economic history. Some aspects of economic development are dealt with in more detail in many other entries, such as those for individual countries and regions, for related processes such as >INDUSTRIAL REVOLUTIONS, the >COMMERCIAL REVOLUTION and for basic elements in economic growth, such as >PRODUCTIVITY and >POPULATION. Innovation is very important >USA. We begin with a brief discussion on how economic growth is measured, then sketch the path of world economic growth over time. Then we look at the ideas on the sources of growth and why growth rates differ between countries. Finally, we summarize the history of policies adopted by the advanced countries for promoting growth in the poorer parts of the world (Development Economics).

Economic growth is usually measured by changes in the volume of Gross Domestic Product (GDP), or some other national accounting aggregate such as GNP which includes net income from abroad. GDP adds up the value of domestic outputs of goods and services, not including intermediate products, and for these purposes is adjusted for inflation to allow meaningful comparisons in 'real terms' over time. For international comparisons, further adjustments are necessary since the conversion of national data into a common currency at current exchange rates can be misleading. This is because these rates are affected by capital movements and reflect only exchange traded goods and services. Instead of market exchange rates, purchasing power parities (PPPs) produced by international organizations such as the OECD and UN are now used to ensure that the units of measurement employed reflect actual purchasing power in terms of the same basket of goods in each country (Maddison, 1995). In practice, different PPPs are not used in an historical series but rather a benchmark year is taken and extrapolations are made back and forwards on the basis of national data on real product for the other years. There are, of course, technical problems with this procedure arising from the use of weighted index numbers for prices and outputs (different results may be obtained depending upon the choice of years used in weighting). Also inflation (>PRICES AND INFLATION) may be overstated and output understated where price indices are not adjusted for changes in quality (a passenger car in 1998 incorporates much improved performance and features compared with another of 40 years earlier at the same price). However, this understatement may be partly or wholly offset for the purposes of assessing welfare by the fact that environmental conditions (pollution and traffic congestion, for example) are not allowed for in official estimates of the national product. Moreover, income distribution may vary over time so that for all these and other reasons changes in real GDP may not accurately reflect changes in the well-being of the average consumer (>POVERTY).

Bearing in mind these caveats, the available long-run data compiled by Maddison (2001) show quite remarkable increases in world output per capita from about 1820–1998. Per capita output rose over eightfold over this period. Prior to 1820 the increase was much less: about 50 per cent according to Maddison's earlier data (1995) for the period 1000–1820. Between 1820 and 1998 there was also a large increase in population (fivefold). Maddison (2001) points out that over the long period there has also been a dramatic increase in life expectancy, especially after 1820. In the year 1000 an infant could expect to live for only about 24 years on average; at the end of the period the figure was 66 years (higher in the advanced countries) and still rising. This meant that people are enjoying increased wealth for longer and longer periods.

In 1820 (and indeed earlier) the countries of Western Europe and the USA, which were undergoing or about to undergo industrial revolutions, had output per capita of about twice that of Eastern Europe and Asia. The leading countries were also growing much faster than the others from 1500–1820 and their growth accelerated in the period 1820–70 and began to spread to Eastern Europe and >RUSSIA. Between 1870 and World War I, growth rates quickened still further and, with the growth of international trade and investment, spread to Latin America and Japan and Africa. In the period between the world wars, which included the >GREAT DEPRESSION, growth slowed (though not in Africa nor in Russia) (Maddison, 2001).

Between 1950 and 1973 was a golden age for Europe as it began to make up the gap in output and productivity with the USA, while Japan moved ahead even faster (twice as fast as Europe) (>WESTERN EUROPE). The rest of Asia, especially South East Asia and >CHINA, also grew rapidly in this period as did Latin America. Between 1973 and 1998 the leading countries as well as Latin America, Africa and Japan slowed down. The Eastern European countries which gained freedom from communist rule around 1990 also slowed down, though by 1995 they were growing vigorously. In this final period growth in China and the rest of Asia speeded up, a development of considerable importance. There was a surge of growth in East Asia (>ASIAN MIRACLE) from about 1960 as countries like Malaya, Singapore, South Korea and Taiwan industrialized rapidly. Today some of these countries have nearly caught up with the European leaders and from about 1990 growth in China and >INDIA has also surged as the result of some relaxation in regulation. By 1998, GDP per capita in Western Europe was still more than double that in much of the rest of the world, though it was exceeded by that of Japan. The >USA, which had overtaken Europe in the middle of the 19th century, was still ahead of Europe by a substantial margin. Incomes in what Maddison (2001) calls 'other European offshoots' (such as Canada and Australia) are also high, indeed higher than in Western Europe. Africa, much of Latin America and much of Asia remain very poor.

Given the paucity of data pre-1820 especially, there are differences among scholars over some of these findings. Some historians question the general view shared by Landes (1998) and Maddison (2001) that Europe was already relatively rich before the industrial revolution. Bairoch (1993) says: 'it is probable that before the upheavals of the Industrial Revolution, the average country in the future Third World was probably not poorer than a similar region in the future developed world'. He did not think this was surprising, 'since before the Industrial Revolution no country or region could be really rich. The world's average standard of living was not far off from the minimum level.' Snooks (1993), on the other hand, denies 'the conventional wisdom that the long-run rate of economic growth in Europe was very slow before 1700 and non-existent before 1500'. His answer to the objection raised by Landes (1998) that backward extrapolation of growth rates would soon bring incomes too low for human survival does not allow for the different categories of consumption included in the per capita income data and also the impact of great waves of change with historical downturns, often violent, on growth rates. Those who backward-extrapolate growth rates need to realize the scope for improvement in the supply of non-perishable items, such as housing and transport, which could explain growth beyond irreducible minima of subsistence. In relation to a more recent period, there has been controversy over the growth path of national income during the 18th and 19th centuries in Europe. >GERSCHENKRON and >ROSTOW believed that there were a succession of take-offs, or upward kinks or spurts in the growth figures, at the time of the early >INDUSTRIAL REVOLUTIONS. Recent research, now widely, but not universally, accepted, suggests that the path of growth was

smoother than previously thought. The notion that there were spurts of growth, either before or after the >AMERICAN CIVIL WAR has also been challenged (>RUSSIA).

Thinking by economists and historians on economic development has a long history. The earliest economists, for example, Quesnay and the >PHYSIOCRATS in the 18th century, thought that economic development was hampered by a mass of regulation – interestingly an echo of a current preoccupation (>REGULATION). Adam >SMITH deserves the main credit for putting economic development on the map. Smith saw the operation of markets, the division of labour and the accumulation of capital as the sources of rising income per head. >RICARDO was more interested in the division of production between the elements of society and this view, not common to all of the Classical economists, was the dominant concern of the neo-Classical economists and the 'Marginal Revolution' (>CLASSICAL AND NEO-CLASSICAL ECONOMICS). At the same time, there was a reduction in interest in history and dynamic change and an emphasis on deductive rather than inductive methods. Both Ricardo and >MALTHUS saw limits to growth, the first through using up of the most fertile land and the second through the tendency for population to press on the means of subsistence. Although there was some basis for these views in the circumstances of the time, they were wrong because they ignored the impact of technical advance and other factors, such as the opening up of new lands and foreign trade, in overcoming diminishing returns. >MARX, who did appreciate the impact of technology and trade, from a different perspective also foresaw a falling profit rate, which in his case would lead to the collapse of the capitalist system rather than the stationary state envisaged by some of the Classical economists. >SCHUMPETER, with a truer analysis of historical developments, did construct a more dynamic model of capitalism putting technological change at the centre of the system, though he also took a gloomy view of the outlook for sociological reasons.

Modern theories of growth were next rooted in the work of Harrod, Domar and Robert Solow, who modelled growth in abstract terms involving a number of variables, including output, labour and capital in an attempt to generate equilibrium growth. They did not ignore the impact of technology but were not able satisfactorily to incorporate changes in it within their models. Technological progress was assumed to be wholly or largely exogenous and capital accumulation subject to diminishing returns as the best projects were taken up first. An important implication of these models was that all countries would converge to a steady rate of growth. From the 1950s, thinking on economic growth was to be revolutionized by the discovery that by no means all of economic growth could be explained by changes in the quantities of labour and capital. Once these inputs were accounted for and adjusted for quality, a large unexplained residual remained which could only be explained by technical progress. This advance in what came to be called 'growth accounting' was identified, more or less simultaneously, in 1956 by M. Abramovitz, an economic historian, and J. W. Kendrick and R. M. Solow (Drukker, 2006).

In a book covering US economic growth from 1929–69, Denison (1974) calculated that, of annual real income growth of 3.2 per cent over the period, 1.31 per cent was accounted

for by the growth of labour inputs and 0.52 per was attributable to capital inputs, leaving a residual of 1.52 per cent, or almost half, accounted for by technical progress and other causes such as increasing returns to scale. This residual (total factor productivity (TFP) >PRODUCTIVITY) has been increasing over time. N. F. R. Crafts, in his contribution, 'Long-term Growth', to Volume II of Floud and Johnson (2004), shows for Britain, between 1951 and 1973, the composition of output growth of 2.8 per cent as follows: capital 0.95 per cent; labour negative at $-0.35$ and TFP 2.20, a residual approaching four times that for 1924–37 shown by his earlier figures for Britain. Maddison, in his contribution, 'Explaining the Long-term Economic Performance of Nations, 1820–1989' to Baumol et al. (1994), makes an important distinction between the proximate and the ultimate causes of growth. The ultimate causes of growth explain *why* some countries invest more or make technological improvements and involve institutions and other factors which are inherently difficult, if not impossible, to quantify. The ultimate causes have traditionally been the province of historians, but, given their importance, economists and economic historians are now increasingly concerned with them.

International comparisons of growth have suggested that there has been no general convergence of long-run growth rates around a steady rate of growth. Measuring convergence is not a simple matter and results depend upon the time period chosen and the countries included, as well as upon how convergence is defined (does it mean the catching up of countries on the leaders or on a narrowing in the variation between productivity in a group of countries?). As we have seen, in the 18th and 19th centuries the rapid advance of Britain, the USA and other European countries widened the gap between their output per capita and the rest. Between the latter part of the 19th century and the mid-20th century there was some convergence in the range and variation of output per capita in the rest of the world, though none caught up with the USA. Baumol *et al.* (1994) had earlier coined the term 'convergence club' to denote the tendency for some countries to approach but not to eliminate the US lead. Since 1970, new members have joined the rich-country – club, including some newly industrialized countries in East Asia. Other countries seem to be on the way, though there is no overall tendency for convergence to include, for example, most countries in Africa and Latin America, at least as yet.

The 'new growth theory', which dates from the 1970s and 1980s, has been influenced by Douglass North and other neo-institutionalists (>INSTITUTIONS) and by Abramovitz (1986) and Romer (1994). Stages of growth theories, such as that of >ROSTOW, are now out of fashion. The essence of the new growth theory is that technological change, the main driver of modern economic growth among the advanced countries, is not exogenous or 'manna from heaven', but endogenous. This implies, as indeed is a fact, that backward countries cannot be expected to catch up with the leaders in some automatic way but that growth is determined by the way institutions and incentives are structured and barriers to growth eliminated. The further implication of this view is that appropriate public policies, for example, on >EDUCATION and research, can make a difference and by favouring innovation help to ensure that the diminishing returns postulated in earlier theories do not

set in. That said, exactly what these appropriate policies are and what impact they have had in the past is controversial (>THE STATE, RISE OF THE), as well as what causes can be attributed where long-term economic growth surges or falters (see, for example, >ASIAN MIRACLE and >ENTREPRENEURSHIP).

Despite the redundancy of stages of growth theories, it can be observed that different levels of income per capita are associated with substantially different economic structures. At the present time, countries at higher stages of development (with higher levels of income per capita) have a larger proportion of their population living in urban areas, a lower proportion of GDP generated in agriculture and a higher proportion in services. Industrialization first becomes more important as development proceeds and then declines again as countries reach the advanced stage of the 'post-industrial society'. There is also a general tendency for GDP per capita growth to decline with development, though this does not necessarily mean, as we have seen, that systematic convergence takes place.

Developing countries (or Third World or Less Developed Countries (LDCs), all euphemisms for poor countries) are ones that have not reached the stage of significant industrialization .These countries are characterized by large informal sectors (up to 80 per cent of the labour force) dominated by subsistence agriculture and low-productivity artisanal activities and are largely unregulated and untaxed. There is also a very much smaller formal sector mainly in urban areas (extractive industries apart) and consisting mostly of large state-owned and foreign enterprises. Arthur Lewis (1915–1991) analyzed this dual economy and concluded that the very large reserve of labour in the informal, or traditional, sector kept urban wages low. Wages and purchasing power would remain low until urban industrialization absorbed the surplus labour, at which point the economy would be explainable by conventional economic theory. In fact, this did not happen, or only rarely; the formal sectors have imported capital-intensive technology and urban centres have swelled with the unemployed and informal activities. In practice, the informal sector suffers from numerous barriers which prevent expansion into the formal sector, including lack of skills and education, lack of capital or access to it and, above all, high thresholds of regulation and taxation in the formal sector (Bannock, 2005).

Other ideas have been influential in development thinking in the past. Ragnar Nurkse, who earlier on had been an economist at the League of Nations, and others were in favour of measures to promote total demand so that expansion in all sectors would result, giving balanced growth – simply promoting a few leading sectors would lead to imbalanced growth and shortages of inputs for those sectors. These 'big push' theories were criticized by Albert Hirschman. He argued the opposite: unbalanced growth was needed so that bottlenecks would emerge, creating opportunities in sectors linked to the leading ones for investment by entrepreneurs. Raul Prebisch, an economist at the UN Economic Commission for Latin America, argued that poor countries had become trapped into supplying raw materials for the advanced countries at the expense of their own industrialization so that the terms of trade moved progressively against them. The policy implications of Prebisch's notions were for governments to

stimulate and grant tariff protection to domestic industry in a policy of import substitution. Policy was influenced in this way in several countries in Latin America. The need for infant industry protection is a recurrent theme in economic history. Modern proponents are able to argue that most industrialized countries, including Britain, the USA and Japan enjoyed protection in the early stages of their industrialization.

The Lewis model of development, described by him in an article in 1954, may have helped to influence thinking already prevalent in development circles that LDCs needed capital inflows and technology embodied in direct investment from the advanced countries. This thinking was that poor countries lacked the savings and investment to grow which resulted in a vicious circle of underdevelopment. Wartime experience and the apparent success of communist planning in Russia and elsewhere led to the belief that development could be planned with foreign technical and financial help. However, attempts to fill the savings and investment gap in the 1950s and 1960s did not lead to sustainable growth. In the 1970s and 1980s, the focus of international aid efforts turned successively to programmes to finance improvements in health and education and then to the role of macro-economic management and the furtherance of the market economy. It became clear that macro-economic liberalization through 'economic structural adjustment' programmes (ESAPs – freeing-up of interest rates and price controls and privatization of loss-making state-owned enterprises to reduce budget deficits) were not in themselves sufficient to trigger systematic growth, although with some positive results the ESAPs often harmed the poor and were generally unpopular. Only in Eastern Europe, and after considerable initial disruption and chaos, were policies of these kinds ultimately to be followed by success, or appeared to be, and this clearly owed much to the inherited higher standards of social and economic infrastructure and the capacity of these countries to resurrect pre-communist-era institutions, such as property registers and property rights. It is to these institutional factors that bilateral and multilateral donors such as the World Bank are now devoting more attention.

There is an enormous literature on economic development policy dating from World War II, much of it now very much outmoded. A few writers, including economic historians such as Douglass North, anticipated and indeed stimulated the new trends in development thought. The late Peter Bauer (1915–2002) argued as long ago as the 1950s that there could be no vicious circle of underdevelopment in the sense of lack of savings. If that were so then the now developed countries would never have developed. Towards the end of his life, Bauer wrote: 'Poverty or riches and personal and social satisfaction depend on man, on his culture, and on his political arrangements. Understand that and you understand the most important causes of wealth or deprivation' (2000). Hernando de Soto has written two influential books (1989, 2000) showing how the advanced countries had to reform their legal structures and regulations as a precondition for development by breaking down restrictive 'mercantilist' (>MERCANTILISM) institutions like the guilds and the establishment of modern property rights. He shows that people in the informal sector in LDCs are not culturally predisposed to work outside the law since they set up their own institutions even though forced to operate outside the formal legal system. Moreover, de Soto demonstrates that the poor do in fact save but that this saving is embodied in property such as dwellings on common land to which they have no legal title and cannot therefore be used as collateral for borrowing; these savings therefore are effectively sterilized. De Soto calculates in the latter of his two books (2000) that the value of savings in LDCs far exceeds, perhaps by a factor of 40, the sum total of foreign aid in the post-World War II period.

Recent developments in the use of cross-section analysis by the World Bank and various other organizations and individuals provide statistical support for the importance of regulation and other institutional factors in economic development, such as the cost and effectiveness of judicial systems for enforcement of business contracts. These studies show that across large numbers of countries, heavier regulation is associated with larger informal sectors, more corruption, lower productivity and more unemployment. While evidence accumulates that economic development is associated with institutional change, it is not clear whether improved institutions precede or follow the beginnings of better economic performance. Prime among the institutional barriers are arrangements that divert the energies of the most able in society to rent-seeking – behaviour that improves the welfare of someone at the expense of someone else. The removal of rent-seeking historically has required the diffusion of power and competition (Powelson, 1994). How is this to be achieved but by domestic forces within a strong state providing a stable legal framework? Institutions by definition are not easily changed and the will to change them must be present. Without powerful internal forces, external assistance cannot be very effective. The resurgence of economic growth in Asia recently owed little or nothing to foreign assistance, though foreign ideas and precedents will have helped. Landes (1998) confirms that 'History tells us that the most successful cures of poverty come from within.'

Happily, some progress is being made in reducing poverty through economic growth. The World Bank's estimates show that, despite a big increase in population, the proportion of the world's population living on less than a dollar a day fell on a worldwide basis, from 40.4 per cent to 21.1 per cent in the past two decades. The most striking features of the World Bank estimates are the lack of progress in Latin America and the slipping back in Sub-Saharan Africa, which is now the largest region of poverty in the world. East Asia and the Pacific, which was the poorest region in 1981, has seen a spectacular surge forward as industrialization in the region, including China, has lifted large numbers out of poverty. South Asia, thanks to a surge in growth in India, has made slower but still significant progress. At a higher level, there has also been progress after the early chaos following the end of communist rule. Finally, also at a relatively high level and thanks to oil revenues, the Middle East and North Africa have also made progress. A dollar a day is a very low threshold of poverty, of course; much of the world continues to suffer abject deprivation and there is a long way to go before this will be remedied (>POVERTY).

## References

Abramovitz, Moses, 'Catching Up, Forging Ahead and Falling Behind', *Journal of Economic History*, 46, 1986.

Bairoch, Paul, *Economics and World History*, Harvester Wheatsheaf, 1993.

Bannock, Graham, *The Economics and Management of Small Business: An International Perspective*, Routledge, 2005.

Bauer, Peter, *From Subsistence to Exchange and other Essays*, Princeton University Press, 2000.

Baumol, William J., Nelson, Richard R. and Wolff, Edward N. (eds), *Convergence of Productivity: Cross National Studies and Historical Evidence*, Oxford University Press, 1994.

De Soto, Hernando, *The Other Path: The Invisible Revolution in the Third World*, I. B. Tauris, 1989.

De Soto, Hernando, *The Mystery of Capital: Why Capitalism Triumphs in the West and Fails Everywhere Else*, Bantam Press, 2000.

Denison, Edward F., *Accounting for United States Economic Growth 1929–1969*, Brookings Institute, 1974.

Drukker, J. W., *The Revolution that Bit its own Tail: How Economic History Changed our Ideas on Economic Growth*, Transaction, 2006.

Floud, Roderick and Johnson, Paul (eds), *The Cambridge Economic History of Modern Britain*, Cambridge University Press, 2004.

Landes, David S., *The Wealth and Poverty of Nations: Why Some are so Rich and Some so Poor*, W. W. Norton, 1998.

Maddison, Angus, *Monitoring the World Economy 1820–1992*, OECD, 1995.

Maddison, Angus, *The World Economy: A Millennial Perspective*, OECD, 2001.

Pomeranz, Kenneth, *The Great Divergence: China, Europe and the Making of the Modern Economy*, Princeton University Press, 2000.

Powelson, John P., *Centuries of Economic Endeavour: Parallel Paths in Japan and Europe and their Contrast with the Third World*, University of Michigan Press, 1994.

Romer, Pau, 'The Origins of Endogenous Growth', *Journal of Economic Perspectives*, Winter, 1994.

Snooks, Graeme Donald, *Economics Without Time: A Science Blind to the forms of Historical Change*, Macmillan, 1993.

# Economic History

The study of the subject matter of economics, that is, the production, distribution and consumption of wealth, in a historical context. This means that, as pointed out by John Clapham in his inaugural lecture as Professor of Economic History at Cambridge in 1929, economic history is a borderline study. The subject does not only overlap with history and economics but with other disciplines, including anthropology, geography, demography, sociology and much else. The history of the subject is one of repeated stimuli, incursions and colonizations from these adjoining territories. Cross-border traffic has enriched the subject, which has a more dynamic focus than much of economics. Economic history is primarily about how the material life of humanity has changed over time and what has caused these changes.

The Classical economists did not compartmentalize; their field was *political* economy: Adam >SMITH'S *Wealth of Nations* is full of economic history. This changed with David >RICARDO and J. S. Mill and further still after Alfred Marshall. Marshall was interested in, and wrote about, economic history but economics in neo-Classicism was essentially deductive and abstract (>CLASSICAL AND NEO-CLASSICAL ECONOMICS). Before Marshall, economics and economic history were both taught and studied in faculties of history and moral philosophy as largely distinct subjects from one another. Within those faculties, some historical economists struggled for independence, that is, for the right to teach economic theory and economic history together and were critical of both Classical and the emerging neo-Classical economics. Thomas Edward Cliffe Leslie (1827–1882)

was an early member of the English Historical School, as it came to be called, and was followed by Thorold Rogers, William Cunningham, James Ashley and Arnold Toynbee (>INDUSTRIAL REVOLUTION IN BRITAIN), who were among the important founders of economic history in Britain. The members of the English Historical School of economics were mostly politically committed reformists who were concerned that free trade and 'laissez-faire' had not benefited the mass of the population (>HAMMONDS). They argued that deductive economics was too abstract and of little relevance to contemporary conditions. They were not to prevail, however; the work of W. S. Jevons (1835–1882) in Britain and the French economist Leon Walras (1835–1910) was to carry the critique of Classical economics further into the deductive, mathematical path it has followed ever since.

The English Historical economists were influenced by, and to some extent anticipated by, the German Historical School, founded by Wilhelm Roscher and Karl Knies in the early 1840s and carried on by Gustav von Schmoller and others. The influence of the Germans on the English Historical School was limited by the fact that little of the German work was available in English. A different path was taken by the Austrian, Carl Menger (1840–1921) who had more in common with Jevons and Walras (though he was not an advocate of mathematical methods). Menger engaged in a protracted and bitter controversy with Schmoller over deductive versus inductive methods (the *'Methodenstreit'*, or struggle over method) . This debate was ultimately sterile since deductive results inevitably have to be tested against inductive material if they are to be of value: this is the essence of scientific method. Despite the later attempts by >SCHUMPETER, historical economists were never able to arrive at satisfactory theoretical propositions solely by induction.

It is difficult to trace all the antecedents of modern economic history in a short compass (a fuller account would include the early French economists, such as the >PHYSIOCRATS, and the later ones in the 'Annales School' from the 1930s, including Marc Boch and Fernand Braudel (Drukker, 2006). Karl >MARX also placed dynamic economic developments at the heart of his interpretation of history. Some of the early struggles between the study of economics and history were also to take place in the USA, where economics and economic history are no longer clearly separated. The first chair in Economic History in the English-speaking world was not in Britain but in the USA, where W. J. Ashley, an Englishman, was appointed to the chair of Economic History at Harvard in 1892. The first chair in Economic History in Britain was not founded until 1910 and was occupied by George Unwin. The second was in 1921 at the London School of Economics, with Lilian Knowles, a student of Cunningham. Cambridge followed with the third chair, which was that of John Clapham (Kadish, 1989).

In the mid-1950s, a new wave of ideas involving the application of economic theory and econometrics in economic history began to enter the field from the USA. At first it seemed that the New Economics, as it was called (and later Cliometrics), would reabsorb economic history into economics (Fogel, 1957) and, to a large extent, this did happen in the USA. A sub-branch of economic history, >ANTHROPOMETRIC HISTORY, which draws conclusions about living standards from data on human heights, also emerged as part of the New Economic History. Despite some very important and creative work in Europe, for example by N. F. R Crafts, the New Economic History movement was essentially American, though it soon influenced economic history everywhere. New Economic History was not to remove the boundary between economics and economic history but to revitalize and enrich the subject by challenging some long-held views (such as those on >SLAVERY, the >RAILWAYS, the >AMERICAN CIVIL WAR, >PRODUCTIVITY and the >INDUSTRIAL REVOLUTION IN BRITAIN). Douglass North, a pioneer in cliometrics, re-established institutional economics by demonstrating the importance of deeply embedded institutional factors for economic change (>INSTITUTIONS). Transaction-cost economics, initiated by Ronald Coase in the 1930s and developed by Oliver Williamson, also stimulated the development of business history (>BUSINESS MANAGEMENT).

All these and other influences have widened the field for economic history by supporting the subject's long tradition that many of the influences on economic development are too complex and interconnected to be explained solely by econometric modelling. Economics and economic history have now turned full circle from the political economy of the Classical economists to the New Economic History and now a recognition that institutional and cultural factors (to a large extent unquantifiable) are indispensable in any explanation of >ECONOMIC DEVELOPMENT. The separate identity of economic history now seems well established, though some economic historians, perhaps after a century or more of buffeting of the subject by other disciplines, still seem to feel unsure of this.

## References

Cliometric Society, *Two Pioneers of Cliometrics: Robert W. Fogel and Douglass C. North, Nobel Laureates of 1993*, Cliometric Society, 1994.

Drukker, J. W., *The Revolution that Bit its own Tail: How Economic History Changed our Ideas on Economic Growth*, Transaction, 2006.

Fogel, R. W., 'The Reunification of Economic History with Economic Theory', *American Economic Review*, 55, 1957.

Kadish, Alon, *Historians, Economists and Economic History*, Routledge, 1989.

# Economic Imperialism

The exertion of political and economic control over subordinate peoples and their territory is more ancient even than the abandonment of a nomadic for a settled life. The term 'imperialism' itself did not come into use until the second half of the 19th century, but the whole known history of the world has been characterized by the wax and wane of empires. The Islamic empires of India and the Middle East, the Greek and Persian empires and the dynasties of China are well-known cases of empires, even though perhaps the most mentioned today are those of the Romans and Venetians. Much of the early history of ancient empires is lost. For example, long before the West Europeans discovered the New World, it is believed that the Phoenicians and the Vikings had preceded them and Mongoloid tribes had penetrated South America.

Modern imperialism has its roots in the competitive treaty and conquest of overseas territories by Europeans and was pioneered by the Portuguese, who had the advantages of location on the Atlantic seaboard, and, for the time, advanced ship design, navigation and seamanship. Portugal developed a thriving trade in spices from the East, established themselves in the Azores in 1492 and in Brazil, Angola and Mozambique very early in the 16th century. The Dutch developed into a strong power after their independence from Spain and from 1600 until the early 19th century had the highest income per capita in Europe, though British GDP excluding Ireland was absolutely larger, being twice theirs in 1700 (Maddison, 2001). Spain financed Columbus's voyage to Barbados in 1492 and later spread north and south from there. The Dutch Republic displaced Portugal in the trade with the east and, among other things, established a small colony in New Amsterdam, now Manhattan in New York, in 1625. The Dutch were peaceably ousted from Manhattan by the British who by this time laid claim to most of the eastern seaboard of North America. All four of these countries had territories in the West Indies. The early explorations and trading ventures were initially made by private merchant adventurers but from 1600 state-chartered trading companies were formed by the Dutch, English and French among others (>ENGLISH EAST INDIA COMPANY). These companies employed force of arms when necessary. The English East India Company, chartered by Queen Elizabeth I, was later to play a major role in the conquest of India by Britain.

These beginnings were part of the first phase of 'modern' imperialism, say between 1500 and 1776. In this *first mercantilist phase* (>MERCANTILISM) colonies were largely seen as promoting the self-sufficiency of the mother country, for example, by supplying tropical or other produce, which could not be raised at home, and precious metals. In the case of England, in particular, legislative measures were soon taken through the Navigation Acts, to ensure that colonial trade was conducted through home ports and ships (>AMERICAN WAR OF INDEPENDENCE). A subsidiary objective of colonization came to be to provide space for the peoples of the colonizers, for example, for the French in Canada or later the British in Australasia (from the 1840s) and South Africa. Knowles (1921) distinguishes between the colonial empire of the second phase, where 'racial expansion' was a motive, and the trading empire of the first phase, where the objective was to improve the balance of trade. The trading empires, at least in Britain, were considered more important and of these, the West Indian islands were the most favoured. Knowles says this explains why Britain did not make more effort to hold onto the 13 colonies of the American seaboard. Defeating the French, Spanish and Dutch was seen as a higher priority. The Continental colonies in America were regarded as merely a strip of coastline and the forthcoming great expansion of that territory westward was not foreseen.

The loss of the American colonies from 1776 ushered in a *second phase, of drift*, in modern colonialism lasting until the 1860s or later. The colonial empires of the Portuguese, Spanish and Dutch came under strain from emerging British hegemony. From 1830, for example, the Spanish Empire in the Americas largely disappeared as a consequence of the Napoleonic Wars and the emergence of independence movements in Latin America and incursions by the USA. Knowles (1921) says that the loss of the American colonies resulted in

a major change in English colonial policy and initiated this period of drift. If the colonies were going to seek independence as soon as they developed, might not England be better off without them? This view was reinforced by the changing position of >SLAVERY, the trade in which was abolished in 1807 and in the existing British possessions in 1833. This created friction with the colonists in the West Indies and in South Africa who did not feel they were adequately compensated for their loss of control over the labour supply. The same considerations affected attitudes to the colonies in West Africa which had been the source of the slave trade and withdrawal from them was at one time officially contemplated. Certainly, in the period from 1776 to the 1860s the imperialist drive weakened. The >INDUSTRIAL REVOLUTIONS and nation-building preoccupied Britain. The distinction between trading and colonial empires tended to disappear in the second phase as emigration and settlement became more important, at least for Britain. >GOLD was discovered in Australia in 1851 and gold and diamonds in >SOUTH AFRICA in the 1860s, important economic events for these countries.

The *third phase, renewed imperialism* (1860–1914), saw the colonization of much of Africa and parts of the Far East. In this phase, burgeoning industrial power in Belgium, Germany, Japan and >RUSSIA, whose Siberian railway brought another power to the Far East, entered the frame, changing the balance of power and placing Britain under threat. >RAILWAYS, >SHIPPING and >TELECOMMUNICATIONS were transformed. Britain consolidated its hold over >INDIA and rivalry between Britain and France led to the British occupation of Egypt in 1882 (with the excuse that political stability of a major creditor justified it). This was followed by the 'scramble for Africa' in which the French retaliated by expanding its possessions in Africa and Germany followed suit. Before the 1880s, apart from coastal outposts and fuelling stations, there were no European possessions in Africa apart from Algeria, which had been invaded by the armies of the King of France in 1830. The Conference of Berlin, brokered by Bismarck in 1885, tried to lay down some agreed rules. The scramble involved Belgium (the Congo) and later Italy (Tripoli, present-day Libya, as well as territories in East Africa) in addition to Britain, France and Germany. The Portuguese remained in Angola and Mozambique. Britain occupied much of West Africa and extended its foothold in Cape Colony (at the expense of the Dutch, who had first settled there in the 1650s), ultimately to embrace present day South Africa, Rhodesia (Zambia and Zimbabwe) and Kenya (>SOUTH AFRICA).

Michael Edelstein, in his contribution, 'Foreign Investment, Accumulation and Empire 1860–1914' to Floud and Johnson (2004), says that many historians have described the third phase as the age of high imperialism. In fact, he calculates that, as far as the British Empire was concerned, the amounts of territory acquired between 1815–64 and 1865–1914 were roughly equivalent. The motives though were different. He points to: the changed balance of power; higher tariff levels among the other newly industrialized countries; a possible slowing of investment opportunities at home; and political instability in the independent regions of Africa, as well as domestic political considerations. Certainly, powerful new players emerged in the field. From 1803, when Commodore

Perry opened up Japan, that country modernized rapidly and embarked on war with China (1894–5) and then Russia (1904–5). The defeat of Russia by the Japanese was experienced as a traumatic event in Western circles as it showed that an Asian people could threaten European and American hegemony. Britain, Germany and France were also active in Asia. At the end of the Opium Wars (1839–42), Britain had obtained Hong Kong, while Britain and other European countries concluded treaties with >CHINA, giving them ports under consular supervision. France grabbed much of North West Africa and occupied Cochin China, Cambodia and other countries to form French Indo-China. Even the USA, despite its vow to abjure imperialism, in 1848 took over from Mexico a large part of its territory and in the Spanish-American War (1898) was ceded Cuba, the Philippines, Guam and Puerto Rico. The >USA nevertheless managed to exclude European powers from further aggrandizement in Central and South America (the Monroe Doctrine), thereafter contenting itself largely with commercial expansion.

The *fourth phase, between the wars* (1914–44), saw Germany's colonies parcelled out among the victorious combatants after the Treaty of Versailles (1919) and the League of Nations (1920–46) attempted vainly to bring order to international affairs. The fourth phase saw Britain trying to rationalize its rambling empire, develop Imperial Preference and turn the Empire into a coherent Commonwealth of Nations. Imperial Preference, tariff structures favourable to empire countries, was introduced from 1931 after the abandonment of Free Trade (>INTERNATIONAL TRADE). At its apogee, the British Empire was the largest the world had ever seen, occupying over one-fifth of the global landmass and with a population of over 400 million. Unlike previous great empires, the British was not contiguous, thanks to its sea power and improving communications, but spread over every continent (Carrington, 1950). By 1900, European empires, not counting Russia, occupied 35 per cent of the earth's surface (Crouzet, 2001).

The *fifth phase, decolonization* (1945–2000), saw the dismantling of imperial controls, including those of Russia in Eastern Europe. Italy lost its colonies during >WORLD WAR II and it is not practicable to list all the divestments of the other powers here. Examples of British divestments are: India and Pakistan (1947), Palestine (1948), the Gold Coast (Ghana) in 1957, Kenya and Northern Rhodesia in 1963, Fiji 1970 and several Carribbean islands in the decade ending 1983. Over a lengthy period, beginning in 1945 and ending in 1963, the Netherlands gave up its possessions in the East Indies to an independent Indonesia. The Portuguese ceded independence to Angola and Mozambique, after fighting involving South African and Cuban troops, but hung onto East Timor until 1976. French sovereignty in Indo-China, Morocco and Tunisia ended in 1954 and, after a traumatic struggle, because it was counted as a *Departement* of France, Algeria gained independence in 1962.

The five phases of modern imperialism delineated above are simply a narrative/analytical device and some events do not fit into the spans of dates given. For example, Egypt gained its independence from Britain as long ago as 1922 and Canada became a self-governing dominion in 1867; Australia, New Zealand and >SOUTH AFRICA achieved this status between 1900 and 1910, foreshadowing the fifth, final phase.

A distinction was made by Knowles (1921) between trading and colonial empires which included settlement. Modern writers have made further distinctions of which the most important is that between formal and informal empires (Robinson and Gallagher, 1953). Formal colonization, whether by annexation and military occupation or by settlement, is not the only way of influencing a country in the interests of the imperial power, there are also informal methods not involving direct rule: by treaty, by trade, investment and other economic links. There is also the important distinction between settlement on a significant scale and other types of imperialism. With settlement, the settlers bring with them their cultures and >INSTITUTIONS which can have a lasting impact on the pace of growth to advanced country status, as in the USA. Many economists and sociologists have argued that differences in legal systems, commercial cultures and religions can help to explain differential economic performance, indeed this is now the prevailing view among economic historians (>ECONOMIC DEVELOPMENT: >WEBER). It is interesting that the former French, Portuguese and Spanish territories have not, at least until recently, enjoyed the same degree of development as some of the British dominions or North America. However, the differences in inherited legal systems, such as the Napoleonic Codes, did not prevent the economic development of France, or much later Spain and Portugal. It also seems true that development has been vastly slower in some colonial territories where institutions ossified long ago. In many of the former European territories in Sub-Saharan Africa, for example, some out-dated laws from the colonial inter-war period or earlier still remain in force.

As we have already indicated, imperialism is a vast subject. Its impact is also covered briefly in some of the country entries in this book, for example, >SOUTH AFRICA, and related issues such as the >AMERICAN WAR OF INDEPENDENCE and >SLAVERY. In the remainder of this entry we concentrate upon three topics which have aroused controversy among economic historians, namely: Marxist views on imperialism, the motivations and mechanisms of empire and the costs and benefits of colonization for both the colonizers and the colonized.

To put it simply, >MARX argued that, at its advanced stage, capitalism is subject to crises which lead to a search for new markets, colonialism and war. The crises arise as a result of over-production or under-consumption due to the exploitation of labour which leaves the working class with insufficient means to purchase increasing output, from a falling rate of profit and from the centralization of capital (the tendency towards monopoly). These ideas, as Robbins (1940) clearly showed, were not fully developed by Marx himself. They were, instead, adopted by others, including J. A. Hobson and Rosa Luxemburg, in a somewhat different form. Marx, although pessimistic about the long run, did apparently believe that capitalism would spur economic development in the subjugated imperial economies, notably British India. Lenin, in his book, *Imperialism: The Highest State of Capitalism* (1915), took a more straightforward view and argued that modern imperialism was the result of a clash of financial interests (finance capitalism) competing for the construction of international

combinations. Robbins (1940) found that Lenin's theory did have intellectual coherence unlike that of Marx and the others, but did not think that imperialism could explain past cases of conflict, such as World War I. Other more recent writers in the Marxist tradition, like Baran (1957), took the view that capitalism destroyed indigenous forms of development and would immiserate less-developed economies by siphoning off the investable surplus, leaving these countries dependent upon the capitalist mother countries. At first, this seemed to be what was happening, but dependency theories have been falsified by the emergence of strong indigenous economic growth in newly industrialized countries (>ASIAN MIRACLE). Successors to the Marxist theories of dependency, particularly in Latin America, also argued that exports to more-developed countries could not promote indigenous growth and that the only solution was to build up indigenous industry behind tariff barriers, pursuing a policy of import substitution (>ECONOMIC DEVELOPMENT).

Kuznets (1955) put forward the hypothesis that there was a trade-off at low levels of income between economic growth and reducing inequality so that, as seems to have happened in the >INDUSTRIAL REVOLUTION IN BRITAIN and also in the industrializing USA, inequality would first increase and then diminish once the necessary capital accumulation had taken place (the rich save more than the poor). The Kuznets hypothesis would certainly, if well founded, have been a powerful answer to the dependency theories, though there is only conflicting evidence in favour of it. However, Marxist theory has been disproved in several other ways, not least by the demonstration that indigenous growth has been possible in East Asia (>ASIAN MIRACLE). In East Asia there was also low equality and rapid growth, while in some parts of Latin America there have been low rates of growth with very high inequality. In a recent study of a region in Brazil, Frank (2001) found that export-led growth raised per capita income above the Brazilian average and when export growth faltered, so did income growth. In any event, trade between underdeveloped and advanced capitalist countries was not predominant in the exports and imports of the developed world at the end of the 19th century. Foreman-Peck (1983), citing data from A. W. Flux published in 1899 for the period 1892–6, shows that, for Britain, colonial trade was 22 per cent of exports (though 33 per cent of imports) and very much less for other imperialist powers, for example, less than 10 per cent for both exports and imports for France and less than 1 per cent for Germany. Moreover, this trade was concentrated among a few colonies; for France, two-thirds was with Algeria and Tunisia, while India dominated British trade. Foreman-Peck concludes that trading patterns were a cause not a consequence of colonization: the powers staked claims to countries where their nationals already had a trading interest.

Some authors have argued that financial assets accumulated through slave trading and other exploitative practices were crucial to the funding of the industrial revolution (Williams, 1944). This view, which retains some popularity among African historians, has been rejected by mainstream economic historians, basically on the grounds that the resources involved were relatively small. Pomeranz (2000), however, without actually endorsing the Williams' view, does give

it serious consideration. He argues that the capital requirements of the early industrial revolution were actually quite low – railways, for example, developed later – so that, at the margin, additional resources generated by colonialism could have been significant, especially since at that time depreciation on investments might have been high. He estimates that 'super-profits' from the Empire could have been enough to double the amount available for investment after depreciation at the low growth rates of the time. Colonial sources of cotton were certainly important for Britain and Pomeranz (2000) identifies the ability to overcome physical resource constraints, such as the availability of sufficient land in the New World and energy (coal) with the technology of the time, not income levels, as the main reasons why Europe developed industrially before >CHINA.

Overall, it seems extremely improbable that the industrialization and enrichment of >WESTERN EUROPE was at the expense of the subjugate economies: one has only to consider that Spain and Portugal gained much in precious metals and trade but did not at that time develop, whereas Germany, which had few colonies, developed most. The Dutch probably did benefit considerably from their colonies in the East Indies from 1830 to the 1860s but they were not to industrialize fully until later.

Contemporary discourse among economic historians on imperialism has been much influenced by the thesis of Cain and Hopkins (1993). Their massive and widely welcomed study, *British Imperialism*, which introduced the concept of 'gentlemanly capitalism', rejects the views not only of the Marxists but also more mainstream views that emphasize strategic and competitive explanations for imperialism. They argue that non-manufacturing interests of finance and services, not physical exports of goods, were the driving force in British imperialism, downplaying the role of manufacturing interests. They say, no doubt correctly, that the role of the >SERVICE SECTOR in the British economy has been neglected and point out that, although British manufacturing may have declined relatively from the 19th century, this was not true of the service sector, with the result that in 1914 Britain was still a major power. They also point, among other things, to the role of the service sector in improving productivity, for example, by reducing transaction costs in shipping, foreign exchange and bill discounting. Gentlemanly capitalists were the powerful class which emerged from the fusion of the landed aristocracy and the financial/commercial bourgeoisie over a long period from the Glorious Revolution in England in 1688. It was this group which provided the originating motives and driving force behind British imperialism, both in the formal and informal empires. The Cain and Hopkins thesis has been criticized on a variety of grounds, as large generalized interpretations of history inevitably are. The downplaying of manufacturing neglects the contribution of technological advance in shipping and communications, as well as the fact that financiers and industrial enterprises were also linked by investments overseas, for example, in mining and food processing, in addition to the motives of politicians and civil servants to promote, through empire the interests of industrialists (Dumett, 1999).

The scale of the benefit which the imperial countries gained from their empires is controversial. The difficulty, as always, lies in establishing the counterfactual: what would have happened had there been no empire? For the European countries with smaller empires and with the possible exception, already mentioned, of the Dutch, for a period, the gains from empire in the later periods were probably small and even negative. (In the first phase this might not have been so, the Iberian colonizers, particularly Spain, gained enormously from their colonies in terms of trade and inflows of precious metals.) Dormois (2004) for France, writing of the period after the 1890s, asserts that the gains from colonization were scanty and/or short-lived. Davis and Huttenback (1986) and O'Brien (1982), writing on both the British and other European empires, have taken a similar view. Gains or losses were very small in relation to the whole imperialist economies in any event, though these gains might have been largest for Britain, which had the largest empire. Edelstein, on the basis of complex calculations based on alternative counterfactual assumptions, concludes that benefits from trade and investment were largely negated by government transfers and amounted to as little as 0 in 1870 and 1 per cent in 1913. These calculations did not take account of the benefits to Britain of the contributions of the Empire to >WORLD WAR I.

Offer (1993) has taken a contrary view to these conclusions, at least for Britain. He criticizes the methodology of Davis and Huttenback (1986) and earlier work by Edelstein than that cited above. In these studies Davis and Huttenback used a sample of company accounts, while Edelstein's used samples of securities of various kinds. Offer (1993) concludes that the returns to overseas investment (which were higher than domestic returns because of political risk) represented a rational choice by British investors, especially since a premium in defence costs was being incurred by taxpayers to minimize the risk. Offer also argues that large deductions of defence costs on Empire to arrive at net gains were inappropriate. Given its role in the world economy and the changing balance of power, Britain would have had heavy defence costs even if it had no empire as such. At 2.95 per cent of national income, British defence expenditure in the period 1870–1914 was well covered by the overseas investment premium over domestic returns of 4 per cent of national income. Offer says, at the outset of his article (1993), that although the New Economic History (>ECONOMIC HISTORY) has 'striven to demonstrate the rationality of controversial institutions such as American slavery and British entrepreneurship, in the debate over imperialism, however, the presumption of irrationality has a long lineage'. We may add, as Offer does, that the British people have derived considerable 'psychic' benefit from the Empire and that the contribution of the colonies and dominions to both world wars was irreplaceable, at least in the early stages of these conflicts before the USA joined in.

The divestment of informal and formal empires after World War II, by which time costs clearly exceeded benefits, does not negate past rationality. Circumstances had changed. Krozewski (1993), for example, argues that in the late 1940s and early 1950s the Empire served a purpose in supporting the Sterling Area for which political control was necessary. As Britain's economic position recovered after the war and its trade with Europe and America grew, the importance of the Sterling Area and with it the colonies diminished. The former empires have continuing cultural as well as economic significance and British cultural and educational establishments continue to benefit from the links with the now independent overseas territories. But it is worth noting that regrets, if not apologies, for some of the excesses of the imperial past, not only slavery, but also in other respects, continue to emerge, as, for instance, Belgium in the Congo, Japan in Manchuria, the Dutch in the East Indies, the British in Kenya over the Mau Mau uprising and of the French use of violence and torture in the final stages of colonization in Algeria.

Systematic analyses of the net benefits of colonialism to the colonized of the kind made for Britain are lacking. The implication of the dependency school that colonialism arrested or frustrated indigenous development have, as we have seen, been largely rejected. However, as Landes (1998) points out, the colonists did little to prepare the colonized for independence; they did not teach them much. The imperialists, particularly the British and French, did leave valuable infrastructure, not subsequently well maintained. Their trade also benefited some local interests. The problem of the counterfactual is especially difficult and we have no way of knowing what would have happened had the colonized been left alone. Post-independence experience suggests that there would have been only very muted indigenous development, if any, in many countries. >INDIA is a possible exception. Until the 1850s the British discouraged industrial development in the interests of its own exports, but thereafter it promoted communications and manufacturing to maximize remittances to London helping to provide the basis for the indigenous development which had already started. Elsewhere, economic performance among former territories was very mixed. It actually regressed in most African countries, which have been plagued by political instability (arguably partly because colonial boundaries cut across more natural ones). Zimbabwe is a tragic example of failed independence. Progress in Latin America has also been mixed and pervasive growth elusive. Some countries in East Asia, by contrast, have developed rapidly, though it is doubtful if the colonial legacy has had much to do with that. North America and the settled dominions have, as already mentioned, developed extremely well and this must owe much to the institutions left behind by the colonizers.

### References

Baran, Paul, 'The Political Economy of Growth', *Monthly Review Press*, 1957.

Cain, P. J and Hopkins, A.G., *British Imperialism 1688–2000*, Longman, 2002.

Carrington, C. E., *The British Overseas: Exploits of a Nation of Shopkeepers*, Cambridge University Press, 1950.

Crouzet, Francois, *A History of the European Economy, 1000–2000*, University Press of Virginia, 2001.

Davis, L. E. and Huttenback, R. A., *Mammon and the Pursuit of Empire: the Political Economy of British Imperialism, 1860–1912*, Cambridge University Press, 1986.

Dormois, Jean-Pierre, *The French Economy in the Twentieth Century*, Cambridge University Press, 2004.

Dumett, Raymond E. (ed.), *Gentlemanly Capitalism and British Imperialism: The New Debate on Empire*, Longman, 1999.

Floud, Roderick and Johnson, Paul (eds), *The Cambridge Economic History of Modern Britain*, II, *Economic Maturity, 1860–1939*, Cambridge University Press, 2004.

Foreman-Peck, James, *A History of the World Economy: International Economic Relations Since 1850*, Wheatsheaf Books, 1983.

Frank, Zephyr L. 'Exports and Inequality: Evidence from the Brazilian Frontier 1870–1937', *Journal of Economic History*, 67, March, 2001.

Knowles, L. C. A., *The Industrial and Commercial Revolutions in Great Britain during the Nineteenth Century*, Routledge, 1921.

Krozewski, Gerold, 'Sterling, the 'Minor' Territories and the End of the Formal Empire, 1939–1958', *Economic History Review*, May, 1993.

Kuznets, Simon, 'Economic Growth and Income Equality', *American Economic Review*, 45(1), 1955.

Landes, David S., *The Wealth and Poverty of Nations: Why Some are so Rich and Some so Poor*, W. W. Norton, 1998.

Maddison, Angus, *The World Economy: A Millennial Perspective*, OECD, 2001.

O'Brien, Patrick K., 'European Economic Development: The Contribution of the Periphery', *Economic History Review*, 35, February.

Offer, Avner, 'The British Empire 1870–1914: A Waste of Money?', *Economic History Review*, May, 1993.

Pomeranz, Kenneth, *The Great Divergence: China, Europe and the Making of the Modern Economy*, Princeton University Press, 2000.

Robbins, Lionel, *The Economic Causes of War*, Macmillan, 1940.

Robinson, Ronald and Gallagher, Jack, 'The Imperialism of Free Trade', *Economic History Review*, 2nd series, 6, 1953.

Williams, Eric, *Capitalism and Slavery*, Russell and Russell, 1944.

World Bank, *Doing Business in 2004*, World Bank, 2003.

# Education

Education is the process by which knowledge is transmitted to individuals throughout a community and from one generation to another. This transmission may be formal or informal and requires an environment or culture that facilitates the necessary transactions. At the very heart of education is its root meaning of the enabling to flourish talent which would otherwise remain latent.

Education, whether informal or formal, is generated by perceived attainable objectives sufficiently powerful to surpass the costs and sacrifices required whether by the individual or the state. For an individual, the time he or she spends on education is time in which income could otherwise be earned and is therefore forgone. Education, accordingly, would be expected to grant the individual additional knowledge, skills and abilities which would yield an income sufficiently higher than he or she would otherwise earn, to recompense the loss of earnings, perhaps augmented by the less tangible benefits of possessing a wider understanding that knowledge might bring. For the state, the incentives may range from the inculcation of a desired cultural attitude in its population to the transmission of knowledge and the training of its actual or potential workforce appropriate to the current and expected demands of the economy. Education, therefore, may be directed to improving general abilities, such as social understanding and behaviour and the propensity to learn. In addition, education may have more emphasis on the gaining of technical skills specific to particular areas of activity or requirement. At the extreme, there would be no point in the state teaching a person reading and writing, if his or her job did not require it. The education process may, in addition, attach as it were a signal to individuals which indicates to prospective employers the extent of their ability to absorb further training and therefore at what cost.

The operation of incentives on the output of education and the means of transmission of knowledge, however, are influenced by the cultural environment and different views on the best means by which knowledge may be imparted. Literacy, for instance, may be regarded as more or less important as to whether a person's productivity is best improved by enhanced communication skills giving access to written instruction or whether the time would be better spent in on-the-job training. There has been a continuing tension between the concept of education as a programme for broad, liberal, cognitive training to prepare a student for the unforeseen challenges of life or for the acquiring of skills specific to particular occupations in which he or she is likely to be seeking to earn a living.

Prior to the spread of the regulation of education by state governments in Europe, the transmission of education was left to individual initiative, the apprenticeship system and religious and secular private institutions. The growth in the interest of the state in the encouragement of education in Europe began in the 18th century. Prussia was the first to introduce a compulsory eight years of primary schooling in 1763. In France, artillery schools were set up in the 1720s and the École des Ponts et Chaussées and the École du Génie in the 1740s and, in 1794, the École Polytechnique. These schools were science-based, originally practical, technical subjects for the training of the military, but they developed into a wider field of technical application for students going into other fields, including business. In >BRITAIN education was left more to the private sector, relying on other providers, such as the Royal Society, which was founded in 1662, and the Society of Arts in 1754 and similar institutions throughout the country.

In the 19th century, with increasing state investment, the literacy rates in >WESTERN EUROPE improved substantially. For instance, in 1850, the literacy rate (as a percentage of the adult population) in Belgium was 53, in France 58 and in Britain 62 and by 1900, these rates had risen to 81, 83 and 97 respectively. However, this progress was not general. By 1900, Italy and Spain had a literacy rate of 52 and 44 respectively, although Italy in particular improved its rate rapidly thereafter. The serious laggard in Western Europe was Portugal, which had a rate of only 22 in 1900 and by as late as 1980 only 78, that is, 22 per cent of the adult population was illiterate. There was a similar pattern in school enrolment rates with Italy, Spain and Portugal, considerably behind the rest of Western Europe. Whereas, Italy made considerable progress in the first decades of the 20th century, Portugal lagged behind with a rate per 1,000 of population of 64 by 1930 compared with 116 for Italy and 95 for Spain (Tortella, 1994).

The 20th century saw the expansion of secondary education enrolment rates, particularly in the first half of the century, followed by the tertiary education sector in the second half. At the beginning of the 20th century, with the exception of the >USA, secondary schooling was very limited worldwide but had become widespread by the end of the century. In the tertiary sector, in 1960, the percentage of 20–24 year-olds in university or equivalent education was 32 per cent in the USA, compared with only 9 per cent in Japan and Britain and 6 per cent in Germany. By 1980, these rates had risen to 57 per cent in the USA, 30 per cent in Japan, 28 per cent in Germany and 20 per cent in Britain (Floud and McCloskey, 1994).

There was a different emphasis in education placed in the USA and in European countries in relation to the content of the curricula and the method of delivery. The American system was more egalitarian, with a mix of academic and technical subjects compared with many European countries, which tended to early separation of pupils into different fields of study, with university education reserved for an elite. In Britain, there persisted a preference and emphasis on the perceived benefits of a Classical education. In Germany, pupils were separated into studies appropriate to their ability and their prospective employment in blue- or white-collar work, or for university. Apprenticeships and on-the-job learning was more prevalent in Europe than in the USA. In the USA, the period from 1910–40 saw the expansion of the public high school, followed by college education after >WORLD WAR II. The USA had pulled far ahead of the European countries in secondary and tertiary education by the 1950s. Thereafter, education provision in Europe and many other countries converged on that of the USA. Education in the 20th century had come to be generally seen as a prerequisite for economic and social development (Goldin, 2001).

'A man educated at the expense of much labour and time to any of those employments which require extraordinary dexterity and skill, may be compared to one of those expensive machines. The work which he learns to perform, must be expected, over and above the usual wages of common labour, will replace to him the whole expense of his education, with at least the ordinary profits of an equally valuable capital.' (Smith, 1776)

Investment in education, and through education in human capital, came to be seen as having a comparable effect on economic growth as investment in physical capital. Adam Smith viewed the attraction of education from the point of view of the individual. A person would seek out and devote time to develop skills if a sufficient return to himself in the form of enhanced income made it worthwhile. Government-funded investment in education developed because it was expected to enhance a country's economic growth in a similar way to expenditure on research and development through technological progress. Many studies have sought to measure the extent in practice that economic growth could be attributed to education with varying success. Education is one of a multitude of factors which influence economic growth; it is difficult to define precisely and therefore to measure statistically and its effects are played out fully only over a long time from one generation to the next (Mokyr, 2005).

In 1979, Sandberg postulated the idea of 'the Impoverished Sophisticate' in which education yielded an advantage for future growth prospects and he subsequently showed that there was a correlation between the levels of literacy in various countries in 1850 and their per capita national income in 1970. The poor, high literacy countries grew the fastest and the low literacy countries grew the slowest (Sandberg, 1982). Further studies of late 19th century data indicated that education was a contributor to real wage growth, although >GLOBALIZATION was a more important factor in convergence among the countries of Europe and the USA. This relationship between literacy rates and economic growth also emerges in the different rates of development between the southern and the northern countries of Europe in the first half of the 20th century. By 1980, the southern countries had stemmed their relative decline and high rates of literacy were achieved, with the exception of Portugal, which still lagged behind. O'Rourke and Williamson (1997), in an analysis of the growth rates of 32 countries during the period from 1870–1914, showed that, for the 15 most advanced countries at the time, the state of education did not have any influence but poor education did seem to be a significant contributor to the poor growth in Spain and Portugal and good education to confer some benefit to Scandinavian growth.

The part played by education in the rise and fall of the economic growth of >BRITAIN relative to other countries following the second half of the 18th century has also attracted the attention of scholars. The >INDUSTRIAL REVOLUTION took place for the first time in Britain and caused a major transformation in the economic prosperity of the country. In 1700, the Gross Domestic Product of Britain was 45 per cent below that of France, 26 per cent below that of Italy and 21 per cent below that of Germany. By 1820, Britain had pulled ahead of all other countries and its GDP was as much as 60 per cent above that of Italy and 35 per cent above that of Germany. It was even 2 per cent above that of France, in spite of the fact that the latter's >POPULATION was 47 per cent higher. By the 1870s, Britain had lost its world lead to the USA and by the early 20th century had dropped behind Germany (Maddison, 2003).

Formal education in Britain in the 18th century was sparse and of poor quality, although the male literacy rate was 60 per cent compared with 47 per cent in France in the 1780s, but there is a suggestion that there could be a threshold of literacy required for economic take-off to be accomplished and this could have been reached by Britain by the 1740s. Mokyr (2005) has argued that Britain benefited in the 18th century from a culture in which the people with the theoretical knowledge could communicate closely with those with the practical skills. As well as personal contact, there developed a flourishing media of printed material with an increase in the circulation of newspapers, the expansion of lending libraries and cheaper books. The French attributed the growth of Britain as due to the intimacy between the *'savants'* and the *'fabricants'*. In spite of the lack of formal schooling, knowledge was relatively easily attainable and there were sufficient incentives to tap it and put it into practice. By the 1870s, however, this casual scenario in Britain became less effective as scientific and engineering knowledge became more sophisticated and whole new applications emerged to form new industries such as the >ELECTRICITY: >AUTOMOBILE and chemical industries. According to the Institute of Civil Engineers in 1870, 'The education of an engineer is effected by a simple course of apprenticeship to a practising engineer. It is not the custom in England to consider "theoretical" knowledge as absolutely essential' (quoted in Mokyr, 2005). There emerged in Britain an intellectual resistance to technological expansion and an aversion to formal education as a transmitter of practical skills. The privately financed public schools in Britain persisted into the second half of the 20th century in an education based on the Classics, rather than practical, vocational or professional skills; a view carried over in the state-funded grammar schools. Even the Education Act of 1944 failed to address the problem. The top 20 per cent of students at 11 years were chosen to go to a grammar school by public examination and only 2 per cent into technical schools. Many relied on part-time education in polytechnics. In the 1980s, two-thirds of Britain's industrial workers had no vocational qualification. In Germany only one-third were without a vocational qualification. Similarly, in the tertiary education sector, Britain fell behind other countries. Between 1960 and 1980, the proportion of people between 20 and 24 years of age at university or the equivalent rose in Britain from 9 per cent to 20 per cent, compared with from 6 per cent to 28 per cent in Germany and from 32 per cent to 57 per cent in the USA. Britain, however, spent proportionally more per student, although with apparently little effect (Floud and McCloskey, 1994). Britain's cultural bias against engineering, industry and practical skills led to an educational provision from an economic point of view little short of disastrous in the period between 1950 and 1980, according to Aldcroft (1990).

By the end of the 20th century, more attention was being paid worldwide to vocational training, with a mix of some academic study in vocational courses, and widening the opportunities for university-level study for vocational students. The prospect was opened up of raising the status of vocational studies to give them the cultural acceptability that been enjoyed by academic studies. In 1996, an OECD report expressed the hope that the distinction between the two, and the tension between them which had persisted for so long, would vanish (Stern, 1996).

Early in the 21st century, the French were still worrying about the *savants* and the *fabricants*. Nicolas Sarkozy, the President of France, conscious of the recent falling-behind of French economic growth, said 'too much time is spent on doctrine, theory and abstraction and not enough on practical applications' (reported in *The Economist*, 15 December 2007).

## References

Abramovitz, Moses and David, Paul A., 'Technological Change and the Rise of Intangible Investments: The US Economy's Growth-Path in the Twentieth Century', in *Employment and Growth in the Knowledge-based Economy*, OECD, 1996.

Aldcroft, Derek H., 'Education and Britain's Growth Failure, 1950–1980', in Gabriel Tortella (ed.), *Education and Economic Development Since the Industrial Revolution*, Generalitat Valencia, 1990.

Floud, Roderick and McCloskey, Donald (eds), *The Economic History of Britain Since 1700*, III, 1939–1992, Cambridge University Press, 1994.

Goldin, Claudia, 'The Human-Capital Century and American Leadership: Virtues of the Past', *Journal of Economic History*, 61, June, 2001.

Maddison, Angus *The World Economy. Historical Statistics*, Development Centre Studies, OECD, 2003.

Mokyr, Joel, *The Gifts of Athena. Historical Origins of the Knowledge Economy*, Princeton University Press, 2005.

O'Rourke, Kevin H. and Williamson, Jeffrey G., 'Around the European Periphery 1870–1913: Globalisation, Schooling and Growth', *European Review of Economic History*, 1(2), August, 1997.

Sandberg, L.G., 'Ignorance, Poverty and Economic Backwardness in the Early Stages of European Industrialisation', *Journal of European Economic History*, 11, Winter, 1982.

Smith, Adam, *An Inquiry into the Nature and Causes of the Wealth of Nations* (1776), Ward Lock, 1812.

Stern, David, 'Human Resource Development in the Knowledge-Based Economy: Roles of Firms, Schools and Governments', in *Employment and Growth in the Knowledge-based Economy*, OECD, 1996.

Tortella, Gabriel, 'Patterns of Economic Retardation and Recovery in South-Western Europe in the Nineteenth and Twentieth Centuries', *Economic History Review*, XLVII(1), February, 1994.

Williamson, Jeffrey G., 'Globalisation, Convergence, and History', *Journal of Economic History*, 56(2), June, 1996.

# Electricity

>COAL, through the generation of steam, had empowered the >INDUSTRIAL REVOLUTIONS and had subsequently yielded to the economic and technical superiority of >OIL in the early 20th century. These energy sources played a fundamental part in >ECONOMIC DEVELOPMENT through the 19th and 20th centuries. The emergence of scientific understanding of the phenomena of electricity and their commercial applications, however, not only enabled a greater flexibility between, and greater variety in, the sources of energy but also in their delivery to the point of need. Moreover, electricity made possible the opening up of a cornucopia of new technologies from the telegraph to the computer chip and nuclear power.

Electricity was born in scientific enquiry pursued as intellectual challenge, rather than financial gain per se. Before electricity could find its commercial applications, a body of theory supported by practical experiment had to be established. The early entrepreneurs had to have a grasp of the scientific literature before they could get down to business.

The electricity industry has three aspects: generation, distribution and load (demand), and before the industry could mature each of these three had to meet the requirements of the other two.

Static electricity was known to the classical Greeks; the word electric being derived from the Greek for amber, which if rubbed could generate a spark. A current of electricity, however, was not achieved until 1800, in which year Alessandro Volta (1745–1827) demonstrated a battery from which a current flowed through a conductor from its positive anode to its negative cathode. Thus was born the first generator.

Michael Faraday (1791–1867) showed for the first time that if a coil of wire is rotated between the two poles of a magnet, an electric current passes. As the coil rotates the strength of the current fluctuates and reverses. Faraday, therefore, discovered the principles of the dynamo and the electric motor. Unlike Volta's battery, which produced direct current, Faraday's dynamo produced alternating current.

Another discovery was to have an important significance for electricity distribution. In 1836, Nicholas Callan (1799–1864) invented the induction coil. He found that if a current was passed through a coil with a few turns round an iron core, when the current was interrupted current was transmitted, through a secondary coil with a larger number of turns round the iron core, even though the coils were not connected. Putting this discovery together with that of alternating current, which was interrupted as it reversed direction, the basis was established for the transformer, which could raise and lower the voltage of alternating current economically, unlike direct current.

The first commercial applications for electricity, generated by battery, was for the telegraph, for which systems were established by the middle of the 19th century, and electroplating, which developed also about the same time. However, it was not until the second half of the century that a substantial demand emerged which initiated the explosive growth of the industry and its entrenchment in economic development.

In 1855, a substance called 'rock oil' was found to be suitable, as kerosene, for use in lamps for lighting and far superior to the animal and vegetable fats currently used. It proved to be a viable competitor to coal >GAS for illumination, particularly in that it was not confined to urban areas. It was in this market that electricity was to find a sufficient load to enable it to flourish. Sir Humphry Davy (1778–1829) had demonstrated in 1807 how electricity could be transformed into light by passing a current through a carbon rod and creating an arc to a second carbon rod. Arc lamps were found suitable for large establishments such as railway stations but they were very cumbersome and not suitable for domestic houses. The solution was found in the incandescent filament lamp.

It has been calculated that as many as 20 incandescent lamps were invented between 1809 and 1878 but they all failed because of their short life (Hughes, 1993). The solution was found by Thomas Alva Edison (1847–1931) in the >USA, who was granted a patent in 1879, and, about the same time, by Joseph Wilson Swan (1828–1914) in >BRITAIN. Edison, however, unlike Swan, viewed his filament lamps as part of a system and it was the system as a whole that Edison understood to be the key to technical and commercial success:

'It was not only necessary that the lamps should give light and the dynamos generate current, but the lamps must be adapted to the current of the dynamos, and the dynamos must be constructed to give the character of current required by the lamps, and likewise all parts of the system must be constructed with reference to all other parts, since, in one sense, all the parts form one machine, and the connections between the parts being electrical instead of mechanical. Like any other machine the failure of one part to cooperate properly with the other part disorganises the whole and renders it inoperative for the purpose intended. The problem then that I understood to solve was stated generally, production of the multifarious apparatus, methods and devices, each adapted for use with every other, and all forming a comprehensive system.' (Edison's public testimony, quoted in Hughes, 1993)

Edison formed a number of companies which reflected his understanding of the electricity industry as a business. The Edison Electric Light Company of 1878 intended to facilitate his research and sale of licences; the Edison Electric Illuminating Company of New York was for the operation of his electricity network based on a central generating station; and other companies were established for the production of dynamos and cables. In September 1882, commercial operation began from a central station on Pearl Street, New York City, which distributed electricity over a square mile. Edison was not, however, by any means parochial and had an international reach and the consequences of his activity offer a good example of technology transfer. Edison's systems were transferred to London and Berlin. The English Electric Light Company established a central station on Holborn Viaduct

in London in April 1882, in fact a few months before the opening of Pearl Street. In 1884, Stadtische Elektrizitats-Werke began operations in Berlin and by 1886 operated two central stations there.

Edison's system was based on direct current and in 1886 it came into competition with a single-phase alternating current system introduced into the USA by George Westinghouse (1846–1914). Direct current was inefficient if it were distributed over a few miles because of its loss of power. Alternating current was able to avoid this by the use of transformers to change the voltage at which the current was transmitted. The competition between alternating current and direct current systems become known as the 'battle of the currents'. The weakness of alternating current was that no motor was available that was suitable for the single-phase alternating current at the time. In 1885, George Westinghouse bought the rights to the alternating current polyphase dynamo, transformer and induction motor from their inventor Nikola Tesla (1856–1943), which enabled his system to meet the demands not only for lighting but also for motor power. Although Westinghouse experienced financial failure himself, his system eventually prevailed technically. (The problem of the loss of energy from the transmission of direct current over long distances was not solved until the development of mercury-arc valves by Uno Lamm (1904–1989), which were first used for a major project in 1954 and subsequently employed for the 35-mile electricity transmission linking Britain and France across the English Channel.)

By the beginning of the 20th century, the electricity supply industry had solved the major problems of generation, distribution and load. It had begun to encourage new consumer goods to overcome the poor load factors associated with the narrow demand of lighting. New consumer products such as electric ovens, kettles and radiators were on the market by 1900, heralding the future expansion of durable consumer white goods and, in transport, electric traction. Electrification spread rapidly throughout the major developed nations in the early 20th century. In 1907, electricity accounted for 10 per cent of the total power used in British industry; by 1912 it had risen to 25 per cent. In 1904, electrification had reached 32 per cent of the engineering, shipbuilding and vehicles industry in the USA and this had doubled by 1909 (Byatt, 1979). By 1907, 48 per cent of engineering firms in Berlin had replaced steam power with electricity (Goodman and Honeyman, 1988), and in German industry as a whole between 20 per cent and 24 per cent had been electrified by that time (Byatt, 1979). The penetration of electricity in Japan rapidly matched the levels of Europe and the USA. It has been estimated that electric motors claimed about 52 per cent of the power requirements in Japanese industry by 1920 (Landes, 1998). The electrification of >RUSSIA lagged considerably behind. A plan had been presented at a Party Congress in Moscow in 1920 during which a map was displayed with light bulbs, showing the expected course of progress, but in order to keep the bulbs alight a significant area of Moscow had to be disconnected. Electrification grew rapidly in the 1930s but even in 1940 only about 4 per cent of Russia's collective farms had electricity (Nove, 1992).

By the end of the 19th century the electricity industry in the USA was dominated by two firms, General

Electric (which had been formed by a merger of Edison General Electric and Thomson-Houston) and Westinghouse. In Germany, Siemens and Halske, which had been established in 1847 in the telegraph and cable-laying business, eventually developed a dynamo which became a market leader. The company became the major supplier of electrical equipment throughout Europe. However, in 1883, Emile Rathenau set up the Deutsche Edison-Gesellschaft (DEG) and, in 1887, the Allgemeine Elektrizitats-Gessellschaft (AEG). The USA and Germany dominated the new electrical industry which had sprung up for the production of the whole range of equipment for the power stations, the transmission and distribution systems and the lighting, power and traction requirements of the final user. They dominated Europe. For example, at the end of the 19th century, 70 per cent of the electrical installations in Italy were run by Siemens and Halske. Four companies, therefore, controlled the world electrical industry: in the USA, General Electric, whose sales revenue in 1912 was £17.8 million, and Westinghouse, whose sales revenue in 1913 was £8 million, and, in Germany, Siemens, whose sales revenue was £23.6 million in 1913, and AEG, whose sales revenue in 1913 was £22.6 million. In Britain, also, the Americans and Germans generally dominated the market, except in cable making, which had two entrenched companies, British Insulated Wire and Callenders (Goodman and Honeyman, 1988; Byatt, 1979).

A surprising characteristic of the early period was the relatively slow take-up of electricity in Britain; surprising considering it was the first country to have a public supply from a central station. This relative sluggishness was not conducive to the vigorous development of a domestic British industry for the production of electrical equipment. There is a view that the problem lay in the conservatism of British engineers in the adoption of the polyphase distribution system and the induction motor and their indifference to turbine development (Goodman and Honeyman, 1988). However, the Institute of Electrical Engineers (IEE) at the time refuted this, following the view of their president that 'Larger areas of supply and fewer generating centres in an area are necessities-it is recognised that the secret of economic working is to generate on a large scale and to distribute over a large area at the appropriate high voltage' (Hughes, 1993). When the IEE presented its opinion to the President of the Board of Trade, it was doubted whether the problem was entirely due to statutory regulation: 'there was a large number of strongly established interests which produced a very strongly developed instinct of conservatism' (Hughes, 1993).

In 1913, London had 65 electricity undertakings, 70 generating stations, 49 different distribution systems, ten different frequencies, 32 voltage levels for transmission and 24 for distribution and 70 different tariffs. In 1911/12, the average capacity per generating station was 4,670kw, compared with 37,000kw in Chicago and 23,000kw in Berlin. The load factor was 24.9 per cent, compared with 41 per cent in Chicago and 33.1 per cent in Berlin, because as much as 61 per cent of output was for lighting. In spite of the fact that coal was 36 per cent more expensive in Berlin, electricity in London cost 23 per cent more (Hughes, 1993).

Electricity reached Britain at a time when municipal socialism was fashionable in politics and local government expected to control the public utilities within their jurisdiction. In 1882, the Electric Lighting Act was passed. Under this Act, the consent of the relevant local authority had to be given before an electricity network could be set up and the local authority was empowered to purchase the assets after 21 years at their individual value rather than as a business. In the next four years no schemes were started because of the lack of investors. It took a further Electric Lighting Act in 1888 to put things right. This extended the period before which the local authorities could purchase the assets to 41 years and adjusted the valuation to the worth of the business as a going concern. There then followed a revival of business. The problem was, however, not just of legislation. Proposals were often met with objections, supported by local authorities, from vested interests, such as the gas undertakings, and the industry developed piecemeal. After >WORLD WAR I, further Electricity Acts were passed and, in 1926, the Central Electricity Board was formed and the industry was restructured onto a limited number of large stations interconnected by a national grid.

After World War II, global electricity output continued to grow rapidly, consistently faster than the demand for energy in total, thus increasing its market share. Between 1960 and 1970, it grew at about 7 per cent per annum in the OECD member countries, the following ten years at about 4 per cent per annum and in the remaining years of the century just under 5 per cent per annum (International Energy Agency, 1982, 2000). Electricity had consolidated its supremacy as the dominant energy in final demand, benefiting from its exclusive markets, economies of scale and its flexibility in the use of its primary fuel.

The primary energy source for the industry from its beginning has been coal, but hydro also played an early part, particularly in Italy and France because of the relatively high price of coal coupled with the development of high voltage transmission which enabled the economic transfer of energy to the centres of demand. In the 1950s and 1960s, coal began to be seen as a dirty fuel, >OIL became cheaper than coal and the need was also recognized to take advantage of electricity's flexibility by lessening the dependence on a single fuel source. This situation encouraged the development of oil-fired power stations and nuclear energy. Coal lost market share. Its share of power generation fell from about 40 per cent in 1971 to about 32 per cent in 1980, oil rose from 21 per cent to 26 per cent over the same period and nuclear energy rose from 3 per cent to 10 per cent. The market had responded to the change in relative prices, the demands for security of supply and the environment. After the large increases in oil prices in the 1970s, coal was rehabilitated. The share of coal in the OECD total electricity production was back to 40 per cent in 2000. More remarkably, nuclear power increased its share to 24 per cent by 2000, second to coal as the most important source of energy for electricity generation.

Electricity was produced for the first time from nuclear energy in the USA in 1952, but the first commercial nuclear power stations were the British Magnox reactors. The first was commissioned in Britain in 1962 and a further six were built, the last being commissioned in 1971. By 1965, Britain accounted for 50 per cent of world output of nuclear electricity, having being

spurred on by the search for alternative energy sources by the Suez Crisis of 1956. However, the Magnox reactors were not economic and less efficient than the water-cooled reactors developed in the USA. After 1965, Britain invested in another design, the advanced gas-cooled reactors, but were incapable of getting them commissioned on time and within budget. The first was not commissioned until 1985, nearly 20 years late, because it had to be rebuilt. In 1978, authorization was given to the purchase of a US-designed pressurized water reactor. Britain, therefore, finished up with four different designs, which was not conducive to efficiency. In contrast, France based its programme on the pressurized water reactor design. Progress in the installation of nuclear energy plants throughout the world in the last half of the 20th century, has been stimulated by fears of disruption in oil supplies, as happened following the Suez Crisis in 1956 and the Gulf War in 1991 and major increases in the price of oil, such as the OPEC rises in the 1970s, and retarded by fear of the consequences of failure in nuclear plant, such as the failure of a pump at Three Mile Island, near Harrisburg, USA,in 1979 and the explosion at Chernobyl, in Ukraine, in 1986. However, nuclear energy expanded during the course of the last half of the 20th century. According to the International Energy Agency, nuclear energy accounted for 5 per cent of total OECD electricity generation in 1974; this share rose to 11 per cent by 1980. By 2004, nuclear energy had increased its share to about 23 per cent in the OECD countries. France, in particular, persistently pursued a policy favourable to nuclear energy so that nuclear plants accounted for about 79 per cent of the electricity generated in 2004.

## References

Bowers, B., *The Origins of the Electricity Supply Industry*, Institute of Electrical Engineers, 1973.

Burdon, I., *Developments in UK Electricity Supply, 1947–2000*, Institute of Electrical Engineers, 2000.

Byatt, I. C. R., *The British Electrical Industry, 1875–1914*, Clarendon Press, 1979.

Cory, B., *High Voltage Direct Current Transmission Developments, 1945–1955*, Institute of Electrical Engineers, 1980.

Goodman, J. and Honeyman, K., *Gainful Pursuits: The Making of Industrial Europe, 1600–1914*, Edward Arnold, 1988.

Hannah, L., 'The Economic Consequences of the State Ownership of Industry, 1945–1990', in Roderick Floud and Donald McCloskey (eds), *The Economic History of Britain Since 1700, Volume III*, Cambridge, 1994.

Hughes, Thomas P., *Networks of Power: Electrification in Western Society, 1880–1930*, Johns Hopkins University Press, 1993.

International Energy Agency, *World Energy Outlook*, OECD, 1982, 2000.

Jones, J., *Empires of Light: Edison, Tesla, Westinghouse, and the Race to Electrify the World*, Random House, 2003.

Landes, David, *The Wealth and Poverty of Nations*, Little, Brown, 1998.

Licht, W., *Industrialising America: The Nineteenth Century*, Johns Hopkins University Press, 1995.

Lilley, S., 'Technological Progress and the Industrial Revolution 1700–1914', in Carlo M. Cipolla (ed.), *The Fontana Economic History of Europe*, Fontana, 1973.

Marland, E. A., *The History of the Power Transformer*, Institute of Electrical Engineers, 1973.

Minchinton, W., 'Patterns of Demand, 1750–1914', in Carlo M. Cipolla (ed.), *The Fontana Economic History of Europe*, Fontana, 1973.

Nove, A., *An Economic History of the USSR, 1917–1991*, Penguin, 1992.

Storaci, M. and Tattara, G., 'The External Financing of Italian Electric Companies in the Interwar Years', *European Review of Economic History*, December, 1998.

# Electronics

Innovations in electricity, chemistry and the internal combustion engine drove the second industrial revolution in the late 19th and early 20th centuries. In the same way, but to a greater extent, innovations in the single area of electronics have been central to the third industrial revolution (dubbed the 'Information Age'), which began late in the 20th century and is still underway (>INDUSTRIAL REVOLUTIONS). The electronics sector produces devices which move electrically charged sub-atomic particles (electrons) through gaseous or solid materials to actuate consumer and industrial equipment. The industry is normally described as having two segments: first, components, including transistors, integrated circuits (ICs) and microprocessors, and, second, the consumer and industrial products which incorporate the components, such as TV sets and other radio and video systems, process control equipment and computers. The roots of all this go back very much earlier than the 1950s, when the electronics industry as such emerged, for example, to the telegraph (>TELECOMMUNICATIONS), and to the development of radio technology by Marconi and others towards the end of the 19th century. Electronics is very much a science-based industry, perhaps the first truly so, and some of the developments in the basic science of electro-chemistry and what is now called solid-state physics go back even earlier. In practical terms, modern electronics has been made possible through the successive invention of four related devices: the vacuum tube or valve; the transistor; the integrated circuit, as well as the process innovations which made them possible.

Vacuum tubes, or thermionic valves, allowed electrons to pass between two electrodes sealed within a vacuum, like an electric bulb, to rectify and amplify radio signals. These valves were developed in Britain, Germany and the USA around 1900, based on research in the late 19th century. The rapid extension of sound radio in the 1920s and 1930s led to the mass-production of valves, for example, by Telefunken, Siemens and Philips in Europe and General Electric (GE) in the USA, which had been producing light bulbs since the 1890s. Early modern vacuum tubes replaced spark transmitters (crystal sets) in radios but were later to find a host of other uses. The Radio Corporation of America (RCA) was partly spun out of GE in 1921 and acquired the Marconi Wireless Company of America from its British shareholders. This was encouraged by the US Navy, concerned that the technology of ship-to-shore communications should be in US hands. GE, Westinghouse and AT&T (>TELECOMMUNCATIONS) were among RCAs shareholders. RCA was to become a leading producer of radio and, from 1941, TV sets, but eventually failed as a result of unsuccessful attempts in the 1960s to diversify away from consumer electronics into computers and other products (Chandler, 2002).

There were many deficiencies in vacuum tubes for electronics producers, they took up a lot of space, were costly to manufacture, generated a lot of heat and tended to blow or burn out. They were used in the first US digital computer in 1946 and for many years after that. The crucial breakthrough in replacing valves with solid-state devices was made by Bell Laboratories in 1948. AT&T, which owned Bell Labs, was facing increasing demand for long-distance telephone traffic and the need to expand the equipment in its exchanges to cater for it. Bell had been carrying out research in solid-state physics since the 1930s and the Director of Research (Mervin Kelly) suspected that the solution to the heavy costs of valves lay with a solid-state device. That solution emerged in late 1947 in the form of the transistor, a device for which William Shockley and colleagues at Bell Labs were credited. The transistor performs the basic function of a tiny valve in a sandwich of silicon (a semiconductor), giving greatly reduced size and weight, with lower operating voltages and enormously greater robustness and reliability. The conductivity of semiconductors (silicon or germanium was usually used) can be controlled precisely by adding traces of impurities (Mowery and Rosenberg, 1998). Influenced by anti-trust considerations, AT&T made the technology of transistors available to all comers at nominal rates and, where appropriate, in exchange for cross-licensing of patents with others. One of AT&T's licensees, Texas Instruments (TI), produced the first commercially successful transistor in 1954, considerably improving on AT&T's design. TI followed this by the innovation of integrated circuits in 1961.

The integrated circuit (IC) was the second great advance in electronics after the transistor. ICs combine a number of transistors on a single silicon chip, thus reducing the number of connections, still further reducing cost and increasing reliability. It proved possible to increase the number of transistors per IC from a few to over 100 million three decades later. The layout of the circuits was done by photo-lithography, and later, in 1959, Fairchild, the inventors of ICs, developed the planar process which greatly reduced the cost of production. Transistors and ICs permitted a high degree of miniaturization: while the base of a valve might occupy several square inches, transistors occupied millionths of an inch. In 1964, Gordon E. Moore observed that the complexity of integrated circuits was doubling every year and that costs were falling at the rate of 28 per cent for each doubling (Moore's Law, Robert N. Noyce in a special issue of *Scientific American*, September 1977, reproduced in Forester, 1981). According to Mowery and Rosenberg (1998), the value of IC production rose from under $100 million in 1962–5 to $312 million in 1968, while the average cost per IC fell from $50 to $2.33 per circuit.

One of the characteristics of the early development of US information technology was that the liberal treatment of inventions and the diffusion of knowledge and personnel, which allowed the development of new start-ups and competition. For example, William Shockley left Bell in the early 1950s to found Shockley Semi-Conductor Laboratories in what was to be known as Silicon Valley. Eight of Shockley's team in turn left in 1957 to join the Fairchild Camera and Instrument Corporation. Another characteristic of the semiconductor industry was the early importance of government R&D funding and demand for product. The robustness of semiconductors and their speed of operation were critical for military and aerospace requirements (>AVIATION). The military also always required a second source of supply, which further increased competition and information diffusion. According to Mowery and Rosenberg (1998), between 1955 and 1958, the government absorbed 36–9 per cent of output, rising to a peak of 45–8 per cent in 1959–60, before falling back to 8–12 per cent in 1960–77

as civilian demand mushroomed. Unlike in computers, universities were not important contributors to the development of semiconductors, which were mainly the result of research in private corporations.

The vertically integrated producers of electronic systems for office equipment, consumer products and other electricals, such as RCA and GE, were still important, but by 1975 the dominant producers of semiconductors and components were new firms, such as Fairchild and Intel. It was Intel, a 1968 spin-off from Fairchild, which first commercialized the microprocessor, the third great step in the development of the electronics industry. Microprocessors, which effectively put a computer on a single silicon chip, together with Dynamic Random Access Memory chips (DRAMs), the fourth step, revolutionized mainframe production and made possible the desk-top computer, which emerged in the late 1970s. These components found a diversity of other applications in consumer electronics, process industries and major durables like >AUTOMOBILES.

By this time, commercial mainframe computers were well established, though IBM did not use ICs in its mainframes until 1969. The company, which was to become the world leader in computers, had its origins in the electro-mechanical punched card tabulators, which first appeared in the 1880s (though the Jacquard Loom of 1804, a programmable silk loom, had a healthy lead in the use of punched cards). A company, CTR, had been formed in 1911 based on mergers, including Herman Hollerith's Tabulating Machine Company; it was renamed IBM in 1924. It was led by Thomas J. Watson, who had previously worked at NCR. IBM did well out of the >NEW

DEAL, which increased the demand for data processing. By the late 1940s the company held 90 per cent of the punched card machine market, which accounted for 85 per cent of its revenues. Watson's son, Thomas J. Watson Jr, pushed his reluctant father into the computer business with the IBM 701, which appeared in 1952 following completion of a machine for the government (McCraw, 1998). The 701 was not the first mainframe computer, even in the USA. The ENIAC (Electronic Numerical Integrator and Computer), developed by J. Prosper Eckert and John W. Mauchly at the University of Pennsylvania, is generally considered to be the first electromechanical digital computer. It was largely funded by Army Ordnance to compute ballistic tables for artillery. By modern-day standards, ENIAC, like all the very early computers, was massive – it weighed 33 metric tonnes and contained 18,000 vacuum tubes. It was hard-wired, that is, it had to be reconfigured for new uses and did not have the general purpose software available today. John Von Neuman, a mathematician, whose work was to influence much subsequent computer architecture, advised the ENIAC team and together they designed its successor, the UNIVAC (1951), which did have stored software programmes, though a British team at Manchester University were first with this. In 1946, Eckert-Mauchly set up a corporation to develop computers but it was not successful and it was bought out by Remington-Rand, which later marketed the UNIVAC. In 1949, another computer was designed at MIT for the US Navy, the Whirlwind; its importance was that it led to the development of magnetic core memories. Meanwhile, the civilian market for computers grew and IBM successfully launched a series of models against competition from

Sperry-Rand (as it was to become) and others. These were mostly vertically integrated companies that had major positions in office equipment and consumer electronics, though in the 1950s new challengers came onto the horizon.

In 1964, IBM introduced the 360 series after a major investment which amounted to three times its 1960 total revenues. The new product replaced its existing disparate series of machines with a modular approach using a common operating system and a new line of peripherals. It also began IBM's backward integration into component production. The 360 set the industry standard and led to competition from 'plug compatibles' such as those of Control Data. IBM began to rely more heavily on its overseas operations, including R&D in which it also invested heavily abroad. McCraw (1998) describes the 360 as 'the most successful big-ticket product introduction in American business since the Model T Ford'. By 1969, IBM's foreign revenues were 35 per cent of the total and by 1990, 61 per cent. By the mid-1960s IBM had 75 per cent of the computer markets in West Germany, Italy and France, 50 per cent in Britain and 40 per cent in Japan, a market which most US producers had difficulty in penetrating. (IBM had been in Japan with its punched card machines before World War II and managed to regain control of its assets there after the war.) With the 360 series, IBM's sales were growing at almost 30 per cent a year. They reached $2.5 billion in 1965 and $7.5 billion in 1970. In 1971, when Watson Jr retired, IBM had become the world leader in mainframe computers, with 62 per cent of the market, and remained in that position for 30 years (Bresnahan and Malerba, in Mowery and Nelson, 1999).

In 1952, the USA >ANTI TRUST authorities had filed suit against IBM and the 1956 consent decree required the company to offer its equipment for sale as well as for lease. Another suit in 1969 led IBM to unbundle its software and services from hardware. Competition from overseas grew and the innovations in semiconductors described above were to change the computer scene fundamentally. The availability of ICs allowed the entry of new computer producers, notably DEC, with new minicomputers having a wide variety of uses, including research and the monitoring and control of processes in, for example, petro-chemicals. DEC introduced its enormously successful VAX series in 1970. There were also other manufacturers, such as Hewlett-Packard, that diversified into minicomputers.

The advent of microprocessors made possible the next major development, which was micro- or personal computers (PCs). IBM entered this market in 1981. It was not the first and there are various competing claims, but credit for the first serious commercialization of PCs goes to Steve Jobs and Steve Wozniak, two 20-year-olds who grew up in Silicon Valley. Their business was incorporated in 1977 and in the same year they introduced Apple II. In the interests of speed, IBM departed from its usual policy and outsourced its PC's operating system software to another youthful outfit called Microsoft, while Intel supplied the microprocessor. The IBM PC was spectacularly successful and rapidly set the industry standard with more than 200 clone suppliers by 1986. There were significant start-ups like Compaq and Dell, which exploited new distribution channels and undercut IBM's prices. According to McCraw (1998), by the mid-1990s, Microsoft/Intel were a feature of more than four-fifths of

the world's 176 million PCs. IBM suffered badly from the intense competition and made a heavy loss in 1993. It was forced to downsize substantially, though it was to recover again later in the 1990s.

One of the interesting features of the growth of the information technology industry in the USA is that it started in the east of the country, especially around Boston Route 128, but by the 1960s a heavy concentration of IT activity arose in the San Francisco Bay area to the west. This >INDUSTRIAL DISTRICT has been called Silicon Valley since the early 1970s. As usual in economic history, however, there were some signs of related activity there as far back as the 1920s, when Litton Industries produced vacuum tubes and magnetrons. According to Lecuyer (2006), there had been a large amateur radio community there based on shipping communications. The Valley has Sanford University, a clean environment suitable for the demanding conditions in electronics and is a pleasant and, originally, inexpensive place to live for the entrepreneurs attracted there. The Valley has developed a special culture of it own, with flat managerial hierarchies, extensive use of stock options and manufacturing firms in which designers, physicists and production engineers are mixed together in single units instead of separated into R&D and production establishments. The area also has an exotic mix of financiers, including specialized venture capitalists, suppliers, publicists and consultants. According to Chandler (2002), three of the most successful 1967–9 start-ups (National Semiconductor, Advanced Micro Devices (AMD) and Intel) contributed to the creation of more than 200,000 new technology jobs in the region in the 1970s, more than quadrupling local technology employment.

Developments outside the USA followed a different path. Throughout the second half of the 20th century, the USA remained at the frontier of basic electronics technology in componentry, though not necessarily in terms of production technique. The Japanese electronics industry, which certainly vied with that in America, was built upon technology licensed from the USA and initially upon consumer electronics in which it was to achieve lasting supremacy, at least until the emergence of other Asian producers. Sony, for example, obtained one of the first US licenses to produce transistors in 1953 and in the 1960s led the way in the production of integrated circuits in Japan. It produced colour TV sets and in the 1970s introduced the Walkman. Sony took the lead in CD and CD ROM diskette technology in the 1980s and again in the 1990s with videodiscs (DVDs), and produced video games from 1993. Sony famously lost out to Matsushita (JVC) in videocassette recorders (VCRs – the Betamax/VHS battle), but recovered and by 1985 Japanese manufacturers were world leaders. Matsushita and Sony both acquired Hollywood film studios to secure content. Unlike Sony, Matsushita, started by Konosuke Matsushita in 1918, engaged heavily in original equipment manufacture (OEM) for other producers. Using licensed technology and alliances with US firms, a partly different set of Japanese electronics manufacturers moved on from consumer electronics to mainframe computers. Notable among these were Fujitsu, NEC and Hitachi. From 1984, Fujitsu were also producing minicomputers. These companies exported plug-compatible mainframes, often on an OEM basis, to European firms and later extended into the PC market. By 1996, Fujitsu was the third largest PC

manufacturer in the world. Sony did not successfully enter the PC market until 1985.

It was characteristic of the major Japanese electronics firms that, despite government attempts to encourage concentration, there were quite a few of them, six at least for most products. Competition was a factor to which Porter (1990) attributed much of the strength of the Japanese economy at the time. The Japanese firms were also mostly vertically integrated – producing components as well as end products. As elsewhere, but more successfully than in Europe and in a different way from the USA, government support was important – through high tariffs, public purchasing, particularly in telecommunications and in funding R&D. The Ministry of International Trade and Industry's (MITI's) Very Large Scale Integration (VLSI) project for integrated circuits assisted Japanese manufacturers in their capture of the world DRAM market by the 1980s. This successful Japanese challenge caused a great deal of heart-searching in America and almost destroyed many firms, with even Intel making heavy losses though it remained in the lead in microprocessors. However, Japanese dominance in DRAMs was reversed by 1992. This was achieved, among other things, by separating design from production through sub-contracting to 'silicon foundries', especially in emerging countries in East Asia. There was also a Semi-Conductor Trade Agreement in 1986 to set a floor under prices. By 1994, Intel was the largest IC producer in the world, though NEC, the Japanese firm, came second (R. N. Langlois and W. E. Steinmueller's contribution to Mowery and Nelson, 1999). Overseas sub-contracting, also practised by the Japanese firms, as time went by led to the growth of very significant semiconductor industries in Taiwan, Singapore and Korea (Samsung and Hyundi). Korea was to emerge as a major challenger to Japan in semiconductors and later in consumer products. Other countries in the Pacific basin, including >CHINA are following.

Europe had contributed to the early science, inventions and innovations in the electronics field. Most accounts of the early development of electronic computers ignore British achievements during and immediately after the war. The ENIAC was the first computer to be publicized (in 1946) but, in fact, the universities of Manchester and Cambridge in England also built computers quite independently of the US work. According to Mike Hally (2005), the Manchester machine was 'the world's first stored programme electronic digital computer' in 1948. Manchester was followed immediately by Cambridge and, a few years later, a commercial machine using similar technology was built by J. Lyons & Co. for the administration of its fine tea and cake shops. Before all this, in 1943, the secret code-breaking centre at Bletchley Park had a computer named Colossus, ten of which were ultimately built, though all were destroyed along with all the records after the war. This computer used punched tape and, in its second version, had 2,500 valves (Ferry, 2003). Nothing much seems to have come from these pioneering British efforts and the early indigenous manufacturers, such as ICL and Ferranti, are now largely forgotten.

By the 1990s, indigenous European electronics innovation had been largely eliminated except in cooperation with Japanese and American companies, though Philips in the Netherlands and Siemens in Germany retained some technological independence. This was not for lack of government support and encouragement. Both the French and British governments made the mistake of encouraging mergers between disparate and largely unsuccessful local producers. Although the national champions in these two countries did initially achieve some volume of production, they were not able to achieve what Chandler (2002), in his detailed historical review, calls 'integrated learning bases', capable of continuing innovation, though Philips and Siemens did better. In France, where the consumer electronics industry was nationalized in 1992, Thomson was briefly the fourth largest producer of consumer electronics in 1998 after Matsushita, Sony and Philips. Machines Bull, a French office equipment firm, established in 1932, developed digital computers in the 1950s with NEC, had been nationalized in 1981 but sunk with heavy losses after 1996. As Chandler (2002) writes, Cap Gemini Sogetti in France and SAP in Germany were very successful in IT services and software, perhaps partly because of the existence of unique European needs for tailored services. In Italy, Olivetti, a typewriter producer established in 1911, had an early success in IT products in the 1980s and early 1990s but was unable to sustain it.

From the early 1980s, the world electronics industry was being further boosted by the development of networking within corporations and institutions using workstations connected to mainframes and minicomputers with network-server technology. The necessary software was initiated by new or recent start-ups (Apollo and Sun Microsystems). CISCO, another start-up established in 1984, led in the production of the necessary routers and other switching hardware. First, public and then private networks between computer systems led to the emergence of the internet. Back in 1957, during the Cold War, the US Department of Defense had been concerned that the communications system might not survive a first nuclear strike. It set up an agency, the Advanced Research Project Agency (ARPA). Subsequently, in the late 1960s, ARPANET was developed for networking the computers in various public institutions and universities. It was later supplemented by private networks but initially was specifically excluded from commercial activity. A civilian part of the network was spun out and privatized in 1994. The first prototype for the World Wide Web was written at the European Centre for Nuclear Research (CERN) by Tim Berners-Lee in 1990 and the other essential element in the use of the internet, as we know it today, was the development of browser software to navigate the Web. This innovation was made at the University of Illinois and commercialized by a start-up, Netscape Communication Corporation, in 1994. The anti-trust suits against Microsoft originated in its attempt to capture the browser market by incorporating its own internet explorer as a free feature in Windows, the dominant PC software. The availability of e-mail communication and easily locatable websites led to an explosion of internet usage in the 1990s and not only in demand for hardware and software but also for newly created services, such as eBay (1995) and Google (1998). Financing was readily available and an over-inflated boom in new dot.com companies was arrested by a stock market collapse in technology stocks in 2000. IT products and internet services are transforming industry, commerce and daily life, though their precise effects on >PRODUCTIVITY remain controversial.

## References

Chandler, Alfred D., *Inventing the Electronic Century: The Epic Story of the Consumer Electronics and Computer Science Industries*, The Free Press, 2002.

Ferry, Georgina, *A Computer called Leo*, HarperCollins, 2003.

Forester, Tom (ed.), *The Microelectronics Revolution*, MIT Press, 1981.

Hally, Mike, *Electronic Brains: Stories from the Dawn of the Computer Age*, Granta Books, 2005.

Lecuyer, Christopher, *Making Silicon Valley: The Innovation and Growth of High Tech, 1930–1970*, MIT Press, 2006.

McCraw, Thomas K. (ed.), *Creating Modern Capitalism*, Harvard University Press, 1998.

Mowery, David C. and Nelson, Richard (eds), *Sources of Industrial Leadership*, Cambridge University Press, 1999.

Mowery, David C. and Rosenberg, Nathan, *Paths of Innovation*, Cambridge University Press, 1998.

Porter, Michel E. *The Competitive Advantage of Nations*, The Free Press, 1990.

# Employment of Women and Children

In the agricultural economy of Britain before the industrial revolution (>INDUSTRIAL REVOLUTION IN BRITAIN), women were active in a range of occupations centred on home, farming and small local workshops, in which they allocated their time between paid work, depending on the demand for their labour, and the unpaid work of the care of their family and household, although the >AGRICULTURAL REVOLUTION of the 18th century reduced the demand for their paid labour. The Industrial Revolution brought with it tensions in the position of women in the labour force which would yet be moving towards some sort of resolution into the 21st century.

Within his capabilities, a man decides on his choice of work depending on the balance between the benefits he gains from it and the alternative value he places on his leisure time. A woman, in addition, must take into account her alternatives of having children and caring for them. Her decision not only affects her choice of work but is also interrelated with the male response to her decision. The participation rate of women in the labour force, therefore, is not only dependent on the demand for their labour but also on male income, the lower that is the higher the implicit cost of her leisure and consequently the lower the market wage she will accept. The Industrial Revolution created a variety of paid new occupations in factories but evidence suggests that the participation rate of women in the workforce, after fluctuating in the early 19th century, then declined (Horrell and Humphries, 1995). While women did find new opportunities in growing industries, they were constrained by a strong institutional and ideological antipathy against such employment. The concept of the family wage arose, not only implying that a man should earn enough to support a wife and family but that it was necessary, therefore, for a woman to be paid only the 'customary' wage rate rather than the market rate. An institutional bias emerged in men's favour against equality of pay between men and women for the same work. As incomes rose in the 19th century, the proportion of the female contribution to family income fell. However, evidence suggests that the fall in women's wages relative to those of men was likely to have been caused by a fall in demand rather than wage discrimination as such, because employment on offer was restrained and women were discouraged from paid work. In 1844, Lord Shaftesbury, in the British House of Commons, expressed his view that the employment of women should be discouraged because they would otherwise neglect their domestic duties, be less obedient than they should be to their husbands and take on work which ought to be his, an attitude which was to persist – widely.

Not only was woman's place in the home but, if she was allowed to work, it was thought she would take jobs away from men. This ideology became entrenched in the >TRADE UNIONS and the professional associations, which women found difficult to overcome, so that even young women, themselves, grew up accepting this. The recruitment of women into the labour force was limited by this attitude and the female labour force was further marginalized because the education necessary to widen the skill base of women was lacking as a consequence. In the 19th century, the textile industry and domestic service dominated female employment and, in spite of the growth of employment in education, health and clerical work, domestic service remained the major employer of women in Britain into the inter-war years of the 20th century (>SERVICE SECTOR). According to the British Census, the participation rate for all women in 1861 was 42 per cent but it declined thereafter and it did not regain this level again for 100 years. The participation rate for married women was much lower, averaging about 9 per cent in the first few decades of the 20th century.

While, from necessity, women were in paid employment in a wide range of occupations during >WORLD

WAR I at an unprecedented level, it was not until >WORLD WAR II that a major and permanent shift occurred throughout the developed economies in female employment, the emergence of which has been termed a 'social revolution'. Central to this was the continuing change in the structure of economies with the rise of the >SERVICE SECTOR and the relative decline of manufacturing. The percentage of the working population employed in services in Britain increased from about 43 per cent in 1901, to about 50 per cent by 1950 and to about 80 per cent by the turn of the century, a shift which benefited women. A similar rate of change was experienced by the >USA.

After World War II, the female labour force in the USA was 2.7 million higher than before the war and in Britain it was higher than pre-war by 600,000. In 1955, the female participation rate in the USA was 38 per cent, compared with that of Britain of 46 per cent and ranging among the other countries of Western Europe between Italy, of 27 per cent, and Denmark, of 49 per cent. The war had helped to change attitudes and the second half of the 20th century saw considerable progress towards the employment of women, supported by equal pay and equal rights legislation in the USA and >WESTERN EUROPE. Internationally also some progress was achieved in the treatment of employed women, through the continuing initiatives of the International Labour Organization (ILO) from its original Charter of 1919 to the 'Declaration on Fundamental Principles and Rights at Work' in 1998.

The International Labour Organization (2008) reported that the average female participation rate for all countries in 2007 was about 49 per cent compared with the male participation rate of about 74 per cent. The female participation rate increased over the previous ten years for most regions (though fell in East and South Asia and Sub-Saharan Africa) and over the same period the service sector replaced agriculture as the major employer of women. In East Asia, the difference between the male and female participation rates was 13 percentage points and in the developed economies, including the European Union, it was 15 percentage points. In other regions of the world, however, the difference was over 40 percentage points. Women, moreover, were more likely than men to be in vulnerable employment, which the ILO defined as those working on their own account and contributing family members. Workers in these activities were at greater risk from market fluctuations and they lacked access to the protection of the employment benefits of the formally employed. Inequality in earnings also persisted. In the European Union the gap between male and female earnings remained at about 15 per cent in 2006, having improved by only 1 per cent since 2000, due to the attraction of women into specific occupations and in particular into part-time employment, 76 per cent of which were women, and into temporary employment (Commission of the European Communities, 2008). The existence of prejudice limiting the access of women to particular occupations and preventing their achieving the commanding heights of industry or politics encouraged calls for employment quotas in their favour. However, while discrimination no doubt exists, it has been argued that women have a different set of opportunities and preferences than men against which to make their life choices and it would be wrong to assume the inequality of treatment between the sexes because women's pattern of occupation differed from that of men. Even though they have the ability and opportunity to become chief executives, they may choose not to (Pinker, 2008). A study carried out by Guiso in 2008 indicated a more insidious effect of the difference in cultural attitudes between men and women. Examination results have, in general, shown that boys surpass girls in mathematics and girls surpass boys in reading, but the Guiso study found that girls match boys in maths in those countries with the closest equality between the sexes and yet girls still retain their edge at reading. The implication of this could be the reason why women are attracted more to some occupations, such as the media and publishing, than others; they are optimizing their natural comparative advantage.

The employment of children has also undergone considerable improvement over the past century or so, although, as with women, there still existed an imbalance of progress between different regions of the world at the beginning of the 21st century.

In pre-industrial agricultural societies, children worked (and still work) within the family on farming or household activities, as domestic servants or in small local workshops. It was not until the Industrial Revolution that they were employed in factories and in the mines for wages, although most were still employed in the traditional activities in the middle of the 19th century. From the early years of the Industrial Revolution in Britain, children from just a few years of age worked not only in the textile industry but also in >COAL mining. The historians John and Barbara Hammond (>HAMMONDS) went so far as to claim that the employment of children was the foundation of industry (Hammond and Hammond, 1917), somewhat of an exaggeration, although children played an important though varying role in the industrialization of Europe. For instance, in the labour force of the textile industry in 1833 in Manchester 22.3 per cent were children under 14 years of age and in Glasgow 35.6 per cent. In the middle of the 19th century, 13 per cent of the labour force in the British coal industry was under 15 years of age. Similar percentages were found in Europe and the USA at the time. The US Census in 1870 recorded 750,000 children between ten years and 15 years of age working in industry, a number which omitted those at work on the farm, and in 1880 about 17 per cent of children under 16 years of age were in work. Only seven states by that time had made illegal the employment of children under 12 years of age. By 1900, there were about 1.8 million children working for wages in the USA (Mofford, 1997). The trade unions argued against child labour, as they did against female labour. In an echo of Lord Shaftesbury, Samuel Gompers, the President of the American Federation of Labor, in a speech in 1888, put the unions' argument: 'don't you know that the child is employed because its labour can be had cheaper than that of a man?...if the father is not discharged, some other child's father often is...it is bad from an economic point of view to send young children out to work' (quoted in Mofford, 1997).

In Britain, at the end of the 19th century, the pattern of work shifted and children worked more in the service sector, so that, for instance, in the early 20th century 25 per cent of boys under 15 years of age worked as messengers (Cunningham, 2000). In the 19th century, in Europe and the USA, children brought home a significant contribution to the family income. In Britain between 1787 and 1865 the proportion of family income earned by children was greater than that earned by women. As the earnings of the male head of the household fell as he became older, the children's proportion of the family income increased to about 33 per cent in the USA and to about 40 per cent in >WESTERN EUROPE. In France, it has been estimated that children's average share of family income rose from about 10 per cent in 1907 to about 18 per cent in 1914, as the share from women's work declined from about 12 per cent of total family income to about 5 per cent (Cunningham, 2000). In 1889/90, a Budget Survey of the US Commissioner of Labor found that about 30 per cent of family income was from children's work and another survey by the US Department of Labor in 1917/19 estimated that the share from children's earnings in family incomes had fallen to 23 per cent (Moehling, 2005).

The prevalence of child labour remained a serious international problem through into the 21st century. In 2007, the International Labour Organization (2007) estimated that there were over 200 million children working between the ages of five and 17 years of age, of which 126 million were involved in hazardous occupations. There were 122 million working children in the Asia/Pacific region, 49 million in Sub-Saharan Africa and 5.7 million in Latin America and the Caribbean. About 70 per cent were employed in agriculture and 10 per cent industry. The ILO, however, did record that there had been a drop of 20 million in working children of from five and 14 years of age between 2000 and 2004.

Child labour had, however, virtually disappeared from the developed nations by the middle of the 20th century and the reasons for this change have been much debated by scholars. In the 18th and 19th centuries child labour was regarded in a positive light in industrializing European and North American societies and it was even thought to be a characteristic of industrialization that there would be an increase in the demand for child labour. The income of children was considered by some as a proper contribution to the prevention of the family from falling into poverty and even to keep children from idleness. In contrast to this attitude in Western societies was that of Japan, which saw children as a pleasure to be enjoyed and indulged in. In fact, one of the reasons for the change in Western societies may be the change in the view of children from a producer good whose value was their potential as a source of family income to that of children as a consumption good to be nurtured for their inherent parental satisfaction. As real incomes increased, so diminished the pressing daily need to find enough food, clothing and shelter for the family, enabling a longer view to be taken for the welfare of the children.

There was also, in the 19th century, growing anxiety about the conditions of work which led to the passing of laws regulating factory conditions. The first, albeit limited, Act was in Britain in 1802, on the employment of pauper children in the textile factories. Further Acts followed regulating employment in textiles and the mines. In 1833, a factory inspectorate was established. In 1847 the Ten Hours Act limited the number of and specified the hours during which women could be employed which constrained employers generally in their employment practices. An Act in 1864 reduced the number of child workers in the Potteries and the mining industry was further regulated in 1872. In the USA, Massachusetts introduced the regulation of child labour from 1836 and most states had imposed limitations on child labour before World War I. The Fair Labor Standards Act 1938 set minimum ages for employment in hazardous and non-hazardous work and whether during or outside school hours. The National Industrial Recovery Act in 1933 also included regulations relating to child labour. France limited working hours of children by law from 1841 and in 1848 limited all workers to 12 hours per day, but ineffectively because there was no inspectorate until an Act of 1874. In Prussia, child protection was adopted in 1839 but widely evaded.

It has been argued that the enactment of a string of regulations affecting child labour throughout the industrializing nations of which the above are samples was a powerful force in removing children from the mines and the factory floor and shifting them to the less harsh service industries. On the other hand, the Acts, themselves would not have been possible without the cultural change in the attitude of society to child employment, which also in itself could only perhaps have been possible with the growth in real incomes. Moreover, evasion of the regulations was not unknown and it may also be argued that it was the introduction of compulsory >EDUCATION that finally tipped the balance. This was because truancy was easier to police than the evasion of factory regulation; schooling put children out of harm's way and it also had the effect of conditioning the mindset of parents as to the appropriate age for a child to go out to work.

## References

Commission of the European Communities, *Equality between Women and Men*, Brussels, 2008.

Cunningham, Hugh, 'The Decline of Child Labour: Labour Markets and Family Economies in Europe and North America Since 1830', *Economic History Review*, LIII(3), August, 2000.

Goldin, Claudia, *Understanding the Gender Gap: An Economic History of American Women*, Oxford University Press, 1992.

Guiso, Luigi, Monte, Ferdinando, Sapienza, Paola and Zingales, Luigi, 'Diversity: Culture, Gender and Math', *Science*, 30 May, 2008.

Hammond, J. L. and Hammond, L. B., *The Town Labourer 1760–1832: The New Civilisation*, Longmans Green & Co., 1917.

Horrell, Sara and Humphries, Jane, 'Women's Labour Force Participation and the Transition to the Male-Breadwinner Family, 1790–1865', *Economic History Review*, XLVIII(1), February, 1995.

International Labour Organization, 'The End of Child Labour: Millions of Voices, One Common Hope: From Child Labour to Education', *World of Work*, 61, December, 2007.

International Labour Organization, *Global Employment Trends For Women*, March, 2008.

Moehling, Carolyn M., ' "She Has Suddenly Become Powerful": Youth Employment and Household Decision in the Early Twentieth Century', *Journal of Economic History*, 65(2), June, 2005.

Mofford, Juliet H., *Child Labor in America*, Discovery Enterprises, 1997.

Pinker, Susan, *The Sexual Paradox: Troubled Boys, Gifted Girls and the Real Differences Between the Sexes*, Atlantic Books, 2008.

# Enclosure

The erection of boundary fences, hedges or walls around open land for agricultural development. The land subject to enclosure was of three types: land operated under the open field system, common land and waste land. In the open field system of farming, the land was held by individual tenure but farmed jointly. Common land was that over which local people could exercise their rights of use freely, such as for the grazing of their animals and gathering of wood. Although enclosure occurred throughout Europe where the three-field system was practised, it was in Britain that it had the most impact.

In Britain, there were two ways to achieve enclosure: by mutual agreement or by Act of Parliament. Enclosures initially took place in the 15th and 16th centuries and by the beginning of the 17th century about a half of the land of England had been enclosed, generally by mutual agreement. The driving force had been a movement out of arable farming into sheep. A consequence had been a lack of employment in the villages, because sheep husbandry was less labour intensive, and emigration to the towns. The first parliamentary Enclosure Act in 1603 attempted to address this problem. Enclosures continued throughout the 17th century and the 18th century but the use of Acts of Parliament became more frequent. In total, 6.8 million acres of Britain were enclosed by Acts of Parliament but as many as 2.9 million acres were thus enclosed in the short period from 1793–1815. This second major phase of enclosure was driven by rising agricultural prices caused by the disruption of trade following the wars with France and the American Colonies (>GRAIN). This inflation caused a fall in the real incomes of landlords because of the stickiness of rents of long leases in money terms. The Enclosure Acts offered a means for renegotiating rents. By the end of the Napoleonic War about 90 per cent of English agricultural land had been enclosed.

The second major phase of enclosure yielded further agricultural improvement (>AGRICULTURAL REVOLUTION). Enclosure enabled a better, more market-responsive, allocation of land to be achieved because field management was more flexible. The rents on enclosed land rose to twice those of unenclosed land. On enclosure, there was considerable expenditure on fencing, hedging, boundary wall construction, on buildings and local roads. In the short run, therefore, enclosure generated an additional demand for labour. Although the demand for labour fell in line with improved efficiency in the longer run, enclosure, itself, did not cause the surplus of labour that emigrated from the villages to the towns. This was primarily due to the growth of >POPULATION. However, the work available did become more seasonal and there was less work available for women. Moreover, enclosure did remove a useful source of real benefit that the common land had supplied and reduced the numbers of small landholders >AGRICULTURE: >HAMMONDS.

## References

Burnett, John, *Idle Hands, The Experience of Unemployment, 1790 to 1990*, Routledge, 1994.

Coleman, D. C., *The Economy of England, 1450–1750*, Oxford University Press, 1977.

Mingay, G. E., *Parliamentary Enclosure in England: an Introduction to its Causes, Incidence and Impact, 1750–1850*, Longman, 1997.

Moselle, Boaz, 'Allotments, Enclosure, and Proletarianisation in Early Nineteenth Century England', *Economic History Review*, XLVIII, 1995.

Turner, M. E., 'Parliamentary Enclosures: Gains and Costs', in Anne Digby and Charles Feinstein (eds), *New Directions in Economic and Social History*, Macmillan, 1989.

# English East India Company

A group of London merchants at the close of the year 1600 received a charter from Elizabeth I, granting them the monopoly of British trade with the East Indies (defined as the region east of the Cape of Good Hope and west of the Magellan Strait) and they formed the East India Company (EIC). From that charter developed in its time the largest commercial enterprise in >BRITAIN, one of the world's first multinational companies and the British imperium in >INDIA. The company found that the Portuguese and the Dutch were already established in their prospective markets. In 1602 the Vereenigde Oost-indische Compagnie (VOC), the Dutch equivalent to the EIC, had been formed by the amalgamation of competing Dutch East Indies traders. Although the Portuguese authority was in decline, the Dutch proved formidable opponents. They expelled the Portuguese from Ceylon and also gained control of the spice trade. The most valuable spices, such as cinnamon, cloves and nutmeg were found in the Banda and Moluccas Islands between Celebes and New Guinea over which the Dutch gained the ascendancy against both the Portuguese and the English. The EIC, therefore, having been thwarted by the Dutch, was driven to turn its attention to >INDIA from where it could trade Indian silk and cotton goods for the spices which were initially the trade that most interested them. Throughout the 17th century,

it set up over 20 trading posts, or 'factories', and at Madras, Bombay and Calcutta the Company established regional executive centres of administration called 'presidencies', each with its own governor.

The EIC directors were clear as to their company's objective; it was not just to trade but to maximize its profits and to brook no rivals who might attempt to frustrate its purpose. In 1689, the EIC board in London, passed the following resolution:

'The increase of our revenue is the subject of our care, as much as our trade; 'tis that must maintain our force when twenty accidents may interrupt our trade; 'tis that must make us a nation in India; without that we are but a great number of interlopers, united by His Majesty's royal charter, fit only to trade where nobody of power thinks it their interest to prevent us.' (Quoted in Landes, 1998)

In the 18th century as the power of the Mughal Emperor declined so correspondingly did the regional authorities in India begin to exert their independence and the Europeans to insinuate their influence in the ensuing redistribution of power. The French formed an alliance with the *nawab* of the Carnatic and a number of conflicts with the EIC occurred. In 1751, French and Indian troops laid siege to Arcot but it was defended successfully by an EIC servant named Robert Clive (Baron Clive of Plassey, 1725–1774) who proved to have considerable military talent for fighting in the particular Indian conditions with the support of the EIC's *sepoys*. He was appointed governor in 1755. In the following year, Siraj-ud-Duala, the *nawab* of Bengal, captured Calcutta but Clive retook the town and defeated Siraj at Plassey in June 1757. Clive made his own appointee *nawab* of Bengal, Bihar and Orissa and the EIC received all their future land taxes. In 1765, the Mughal Emperor accepted the EIC as the ruler of Bengal. Although French ambitions in India were frustrated by the fall of Pondicherry in 1761, they continued to cooperate with Indian princes against the EIC. Hyder Ali Khan, the Sultan of Mysore and subsequently his son, Tipu, helped by the French, waged war on the EIC through the last decades of the 18th century. In 1799, Richard Wellesley (Marquess, 1760–1842), who had became governor-general in 1798, invaded Mysore and Tipu was killed in its capital of Seringapatam. The EIC annexed part of Awadh in 1801 and the Punjab and Sind in the 1840s. It was not until after the Indian Mutiny in 1857 that the British government finally took control completely out of the hands of the EIC. (>INDIA)

Throughout its history, the EIC built up a considerable military capability, so that by early in the 19th century it had an army of about 300,000 men, of which Europeans numbered about 40,000. All the commissioned ranks were British. Its army fought not only throughout India and Afghanistan but also against Napoleon in Egypt. The EIC also controlled a large fleet of armed merchant ships. In its early years, the EIC constructed and refitted its own ships at its shipyard at Dartford in London. Their design was such that it was difficult to distinguish them from the Royal Navy's warships. In 1681, the EIC owned 35 ships of sizes from 100–775 tons and between 1682 and 1689 built 16 ships of sizes from 900–1,300 tons. However, the company later stopped building or buying vessels in Britain in favour of hiring what tonnage it needed. The EIC entered into contracts of service with ship-owners which guaranteed that their ships would be employed and in rotation with others to ensure a fair division of its business. A ship typically made four voyages with the EIC before it was considered unfit for the East Indies trades. They carried exceptionally large numbers of crew, compared with other trades, because of piracy in the Indian Ocean and the lack of naval protection and consequently the need to be well armed, with up to 28 guns. For instance, for ships of comparable tonnage, the crew numbers were three times larger on an EIC ship than on one trading to the West Indies. The EIC, however, did continue to build ships in India, including galleys and frigates in support of its commercial interests (>SHIPPING). (Gardiner, 1995).

The EIC imported tea, spices, silk, indigo and saltpetre, but by the late 17th century cotton textiles made up a half of the company's total imports into Europe. At that time, it was recognized that India produced the finest quality cotton goods, but it was the EIC which created a market for these in Europe and was ahead of the Dutch in this early example of aggressive marketing. 'Calicoes are a commodity whereof the use is not generally known, the vent must be forced and trial made into all ports' (quoted in Chaudhuri, 1978; Landes, 1998). The EIC imported about 221,500 units of cotton textiles into Britain by 1625, 578,000 by the 1670s and 707,000 units by the 1680s. The Dutch were slow to realize the market potential and never imported more than half that traded by the EIC. From 1658–89 EIC paid an annual average dividend of over 20 per cent and a 100 per cent bonus per share in 1682 (Coleman, 1977).

The imbalance of commodity trade was met by the export to India of bullion. Acts of Parliament in 1701 and

1721 limited the import into Britain of printed cotton cloth in order to protect the domestic wool textile industry and encouraged a switch from imported cotton textiles to raw cotton. By the 1790s, India supplied most of the indigo imported into Britain or re-exported, over a half of the raw silk, a wide range of cotton materials and high-quality saltpetre. In 1813, the monopoly of the Indian trade enjoyed by the EIC was repealed and, as a result, cotton textiles were free to enter India. British exports of cotton manufactures to India increased from 1 million yards in 1813, to 51 million yards in 1830 (>COTTON AND COTTON TEXTILES). It was the EIC's >CHINA trade, in which the company continued to retain its monopoly until the Charter Act of 1833, which had become particularly profitable. The consumption of tea had been growing steadily through the 18th century in spite of its high price and was given a great boost by the Commutation Act of 1784 by which the ad valorem rate of tax on tea was reduced from 119 per cent to 12.5 per cent. Within a year, the sales of tea by the EIC rose from 6.5 million pounds to 16.3 million pounds and increased its shipping tonnage needs threefold. From 1814, the EIC's profit on this trade was reported to average over £1 million a year (Philips, 1940). While the EIC was a producer of opium in India, it avoided directly flouting the Chinese ban on shipment but left this illicit trade to independent agencies, thereby profiting from it albeit indirectly (Webster, 2006).

Sources of revenue other than those arising from trade were those which the EIC accrued from its political and military activity in India. As the company extended its influence with the Mughal Emperor and local and regional authorities in India, it gained extensive advantages such as rights of tax collection and exemption from customs duties. The company did not fail to exploit these gains to the full.

'The English, building on an imperial firman exempting them from customs duties, took all manner of merchants under their protection and sold them passes, while levying upon agents and representatives of the Nawab (of Bengal) and taxing land transfers and marriages in the area under their control.' (Edwardes, *The Battle of Plassey*, quoted in Landes, 1998)

The defeat of the *nawab* at the battle of Plassey yielded the EIC compensation which eventually totalled at about £1 million, which Landes (1998) calculates as equivalent to about $1 billion in 1990s dollars; Robert Clive personally gaining about $140 million in today's dollars. Following the battle of Plassey, the rich revenues of Bengal were in the hands of the EIC.

Surplus revenues arising in India were converted into commodities, referred to as the 'Investment' and exported to London where they were auctioned off. After the deduction of expenses and the EIC's dividends, the profits of these sales were used to finance the supply of manpower, military equipment, manufactures and bullion for shipment to India.

The growth in power of the EIC during the 18th century led to the government in London increasing its hold over the company. The Judicature Act 1773 created a Supreme Court in Calcutta through which appeals could reach the Privy Council in London. The Regulating Act 1773 strengthened the legal rights of the government in Indian affairs. A Supreme Council was established in London, some members of which were appointed by the government. The governor-general of Bengal was made the prime authority over the Bombay and Madras Presidencies and Calcutta the headquarters of EIC administration in India (James, 1997). The India Act of 1784, shifted administrative control to the government, although the EIC was able to retain its monopoly. Although the governor-general had complete authority in India, he was responsible to a Board of Control whose president was given the status of a member of the Cabinet. The EIC dividend was fixed at 8 per cent, which was raised to 10.5 per cent by the Act of 1793. By the Charter Act 1813, the EIC lost its monopoly of trade with India. By the Charter Act of 1833, the EIC lost its monopoly of trade with China and ceased to be a trading company. The company continued to administer India but as an agent of the government and under a governor-general appointed by the government.

It would seem difficult if not impossible to regulate affairs in India from Britain because of the distance, time and risks involved in sailing around the Cape of Good Hope and the EIC was presented with a potentially intractable problem of management in the control and discipline of its servants who were acting as its agents at the other side of the world. The company succeeded in this by the application of both a carrot and a stick. The carrot was that the EIC allowed its servants to trade on their own account in Asia and this accorded them the opportunity to accumulate considerable wealth. They in effect ran their own businesses with the added advantage of having the authority, facilities and the protection of the company in support of their private operations.

They were paid a salary and had the prospect of promotion but it was the greater opportunity of trading profits as they gained experience which was important. It was a high-risk employment. Death accounted for nearly 80 per cent of those who left the EIC's service in the first five years of contract. Profit from trade, therefore, was their motivation rather than prospects for promotion. Experience and therefore time was vital. The EIC, also, provided the channels through which servants could transfer money to England. It was the freedom to trade on their own account and the wealth that could be made which provided the incentive necessary to sustain the supply of EIC servants. The stick was the threat of dismissal if they failed to meet the directors' objectives or failed to follow their instructions. The EIC benefited from the expertise that its servants gained and the cash flow generated by the private accounts (Hejeebu, 2005). In the second half of the 18th century, as the government exerted more influence over the EIC, its servants were prohibited from trading on their own account. As a result, independent 'agency houses' were established which received deposits from EIC servants and invested them in trading activities. They also became the conduit for the transfer of funds to London (Webster, 2006).

## References

Bowen, H. V., *The Business of Empire: The East India Company and Imperial Britain, 1758–1833*, Cambridge, 2005.

Chaudhuri, K. N., *The Trading World of Asia and the English East India Company, 1660–1760*, Cambridge University Press, 1978.

Coleman, D. C., *The Economy of England, 1450–1750*, Oxford University Press, 1977.

Gardiner, Robert (ed.), 'The Heyday of Sail', *Conway's History of the Ship*, Conway Maritime Press, 1995.

Hejeebu, Santhi, 'Contract Enforcement in the English East India Company', *Journal of Economic History*, 65(2), June, 2005.

James, Lawrence, *Raj, The Making and Unmaking of British India*, Little, Brown, 1997.

Landes, David, *The Wealth and Poverty of Nations*, Little, Brown, 1998.

Philips, C. H., *The East India Company, 1784–1834*, Manchester University Press, 1940.

Webster, Anthony, 'The Strategies and Limits of Gentlemanly Capitalism: The London East India Agency Houses, Provincial Commercial Interests, and the Evolution of British Economic Policy in South and South East Asia, 1800–1850', *Economic History Review*, LIX(4), November, 2006.

# Entrepreneurship

Under >CAPITALISM, the function of the entrepreneur is to recognize consumer needs and put together the resources and people to meet these needs through the firm. This is an essential function – these things do not happen by chance and risks are involved so that successful entrepreneurs have to be rewarded by profit as well as by the intangible satisfactions of creation. It comes as a surprise, therefore, that for much of the history of economic thought, there has been little explicit analysis of the role of the entrepreneur – that role has simply been taken for granted. This was not always so; it seems that the term 'entrepreneur' (someone who undertakes things), together with the concept of the uncertainty he faced, was first introduced into economics by Richard Cantillon (1680–1734), an Irish banker living in France, and developed by Jean-Baptist Say (1767–1832), who distinguished between profit as a return to capital and profit as a reward to the entrepreneur. The British Classical economists did not distinguish between the capital provider and the entrepreneur or otherwise explore the subject Later, economics ceased to be political economy and became more abstract, more mathematical and ahistorical with the development of marginal and equilibrium analysis (>CLASSICAL AND NEO-CLASSICAL ECONOMICS). In this evolution the special function of the entrepreneur was lost. In fact, in neo-Classical economics, under its assumptions of perfect competition there was no place for the entrepreneur at all. It was assumed that all information was instantly available to firms and prices and quantities of output adjusted automatically through competition among large numbers of producers. The later emergence of theories of monopolistic competition did not change this situation.

Alfred Marshall (1842–1924), straddling the old political economy and the neo-Classical schools and with a deep interest in >ECONOMIC HISTORY, did assign importance to the entrepreneurial function which he saw as one of the factors of production. He recognized that firms tended to decline as the ages of their founders increased and emphasized the importance of the 'watchful eye' of the owner-manager for business efficiency. However, he did not fully deal with the information-searching function of the entrepreneur or the transitional change in entrepreneurship with the emergence of giant companies. T. A. B. Corley (in 'The Entrepreneur: The Central Issue of Business History', in Brown and Rose, 1993) quotes Kenneth Boulding as writing that with the further development of neo-Classicism by 1950 economists had turned the firm 'into a strange bloodless creature without a balance sheet, without any visible capital structure, without debts and engaged apparently in the simultaneous purchase of inputs and sale of outputs at constant prices'. Attitudes to entrepreneurship were already changing, however; Frank Knight, who published *Risk, Uncertainty and Profit* in 1921, emphasized the risks and uncertainties faced by entrepreneurs. >SCHUMPETER, in his *Theory of Economic Development* (1911 (1934)), was way ahead of his time and now perhaps is the best-known writer on the subject; he placed the entrepreneur at the centre of the capitalist system. There were also the other neo-Austrians (notably Friedrich von >HAYEK (1899–1992), I. M. Kirzner and H. L. Leibenstein), with their focus on the information-acquisition process and the role of the entrepreneur in taking advantage of opportunities for arbitrage. Mark Casson (1982) has attempted to integrate these various strands into a unified theory which identifies the use of judgement as the key characteristic. His definition is: 'an entrepreneur is someone who specialises in taking judgemental decisions about the coordination of scarce resources' (1982). Casson assumes that the entrepreneur is motivated by profit, but accepts that this is not the whole story.

The entrepreneur is a constant figure in economic history, right from the adventuring merchants of the >COMMERCIAL REVOLUTION to the pioneers of early industrialization such as Josiah >WEDGWOOD and James Watt (>STEAM POWER). Later figures are the 'robber barons' of the late 19th century, from J. P. Morgan (>USA) to Henry >FORD. A present-day well-known example is Bill Gates, the founder of Microsoft. These are the big names, but are not the large numbers of founders of less innovative businesses such

as hairdressers or corner shops also entrepreneurs? They also fall within Casson's definition and Schumpeter recognized that there are various types of entrepreneurs (even including a few government officials), though only a few initiate the 'gales of creative destruction' which he saw as fundamental to the progression of the capitalist system (Schumpeter, 1934, 1942).

Numerous questions arise and those that have particularly interested economic historians include the following. What determines the supply of entrepreneurs and can shortfalls in this supply and in its quality explain the way Britain appeared to fall behind other countries after the 1860s? Is the role of the innovative function of the entrepreneur declining with the continued growth of giant corporations? The consensus on the supply of entrepreneurs is that it is elastic: to be sure, not all adult members of the population have the potential to start and grow a business, but at any given time the number who come forward will depend upon the market opportunities for profit which, in turn, will depend upon the pace of economic change and technological development. The pace of change in turn will be affected by entrepreneurial activity, so the relationships are not simple ones. Push as well as pull factors will be at work. Recession may see a reduction in employment opportunities forcing some to choose self-employment as the only alternative (Storey, 1994). Foreman-Peck (1985), in a study of the regional pattern of firm foundation in Britain in the 1920s, found that areas with high incomes and rising populations were likely to have higher new firm formation rates. He and others also noted that small firms breed more small firms. This suggests that employees in small firms gain valuable information about the opportunities and issues in entrepreneurship from the more varied work experience in small firms and the proximity of owner-managers as role models. Within the range of human abilities, therefore, as Foreman-Peck puts it: 'entrepreneurs are not a particular number of clearly identified people. Their number as well as their performance will vary with circumstances' (1985). Other writers have reached similar conclusions about the variability of the entrepreneurial population, for example, Baumol (2002). Schumpeter reminds us that entrepreneurs may not only create wealth, they may also competitively destroy it and effect social change: 'In fact the upper strata of society are like hotels which are indeed always full of people, but people who are forever changing' (Schumpeter, 1934). A good illustration of all these points is the way in which the dot. com boom which ended in 2002 was accompanied by the appearance of a large number of new entrepreneurs, funds were raised and money made or lost and some traditional activities moved onto the World Wide Web, while other new ones appeared.

There has been a long-running debate about the relative decline of >BRITAIN compared with other advanced countries (a decline which in itself is a matter for dispute). It has been argued that following the 1850s anti-industrial sentiments appeared in British society, permeating educational institutions to create a 'cultural *cordon sanitaire* encircling the forces of economic development – technology, industry and commerce' (Wiener, 1981). Part of this supposed cultural change was reflected in the gentrification of entrepreneurs who, once wealthy, put their money into land while they and their heirs withdrew from the economic fray. In other words, the decline was attributable to

a failure of entrepreneurship, a view reinforced and extended to the contemporary period by popular writers such as Anthony Sampson *(The Anatomy of Britain*, 1962) and Corelli Barnett (*The Collapse of British Power*, 1972). D. H. Aldcroft (1964) attributed British decline not so much to cultural change as to deficiencies in education and in the financing of industry, a prevalence of small family businesses and the disadvantages experienced by Britain as a first mover in industrialization (>INDUSTRIAL          REVOLUTIONS). Landes (1969) attributed the overtaking of Britain in the 19th century to 'amateurism and complacency', that is, to social and institutional deficiencies in Britain. These views have aroused    considerable    controversy and have been rebutted, for example, by Rubinstein (1993) on the grounds that industrialism was the wrong target and that Britain's comparative advantage lay in services and finance and no longer in manufacturing, as was recognized by the Thatcher Government in the early 1970s. More recently Thompson (2001) has produced    compelling    arguments that although limited gentrification did occur it was a sign of success and upward social mobility and had little discernable impact upon Britain's economic performance. McCloskey and Sandberg (1971) argue that the Victorian entrepreneurs did not fail but took rational decisions based on the opportunities open to them (>EDUCATION).

Another interpretation of Britain's perceived entrepreneurial failure came from the American business historian Alfred >CHANDLER. In summary, his thesis was that it was the large managerial enterprise on the American model which 'played the most fundamental role in the transformation of Western Economies' (Chandler,

1990). The surpassing of British growth by America and Germany was to be explained by the relatively slow adoption by Britain of the multidivisional corporate form of organization in which salaried mangers make decisions in a heirarchy based on merit, not ownership or personal connections. The British had failed to make the necessary investments in large-scale organizations for production and marketing. Chandler's 860-page *Scale and Scope* (1990) followed two other detailed studies of American business history and economic development. In this book, he labelled the American system as 'Competitive Managerial Capitalism', the German system as 'Cooperative Managerial Capitalism' and the British as 'Personal Capitalism'. Chandler's thesis met with heavy criticism from economic historians in Britain on a variety of grounds (see, for example, Church, 1990, 1993, and Hannah, 1991). They argued that Chandler had not demonstrated the link between organizational form and economic performance, that the USA did not have fewer family-managed businesses than Britain or Germany, while he had not taken into account of the different environment in which British entrepreneurs operated. For example, Britain had highly developed distribution systems at home and abroad, which had not existed in the USA. Chandler's book is also primarily about industrial companies, not the service and financial sectors in which Britain excelled. Today it has become clear that neither successful German nor Japanese large companies were closely modelled upon American management practices. Perhaps most important, Chandler ignored altogether the role of >SMALL AND MEDIUM ENTERPRISES in economic growth, a role which economists have only recently begun to explore.

It will be noted that Chandler's hotly disputed views are really about the desirable, as he would see it, diminution of the role of the individual entrepreneur in favour of salaried managers. The later Schumpeter, significantly after his move from Europe to the USA, had predicted in *Capitalism, Socialism and Democracy* (1943) that innovation would increasingly be the work of teams of specialists who would turn it into routine; 'figuring out' would take over from intuition. This view would be ascendant for a long time but a more balanced and realistic view is now emerging. While it is true that much of the innovation in large companies can be described as a collective activity, individuals and small companies remain prominent in radical innovations and in about half of the economic system (at least in terms of employment). As Jonathan Brown and Mary Rose emphasize in their introduction to Brown and Rose (1993), individuals, whether labelled as entrepreneurs or executives, may still dominate large corporations and have a major effect upon business performance – for good or ill.

One of the reasons for the downplay of entrepreneurship in an increasingly mathematical mainstream economics is that the whole subject is not readily amenable to quantification. Business historians are aware that entrepreneurs are a heterogeneous group. Many attempts have been made by sociologists and economists to isolate the personal characteristics which are associated with success in entrepreneurship. Storey, reviewing 18 such studies, concluded that: 'Prior to start-up, the identikit picture of the entrepreneur whose business is likely to grow is extremely fuzzy' (1994). For the America, at least in the 17th to 19th centuries, there is evidence of a rags to riches syndrome

(Sarachek, 1978). Recent biographies of business leaders in Britain often reveal early school-leaving, elements of eccentricity and also a degree of 'social marginality', which helps to explain why immigrants appear to be over-represented among entrepreneurs. It is also becoming clear that entrepreneurs do not work alone, they are dependent on networks of finance, information and trust, and exploring these networks is a lively preoccupation of business historians (Brown and Rose, 1993).

One of the trickiest aspects of the analysis of entrepreneurship is that of where entrepreneurship stops and purely administrative functions begin. In this sense, since all business-people exercise many different functions, whether defined in terms of Casson's use of judgement in coordinating scarce resources or Schumpeter's forces for change, the term 'entrepreneur' is actually an abstraction, even though he or she is the 'soul of the machine' (Bannock, 2005) and absolutely fundamental to the workings of capitalism (>BUSINESS MANAGEMENT).

## References

Aldcroft, D. H., 'The Entrepreneur and the British Economy 1870–1914', *Economic History Review*, 17, August, 1964.

Bannock, Graham, *The Economics and Management of Small Business: An International Perspective*, Routledge, 2005.

Baumol, William J., *The Free Market Innovation Machine: Analysing the Growth Mechanism of Capitalism*, Princeton University Press, 2002.

Brown, Jonathan and Rose, Mary B. (eds), *Entrepreneurship, Networks, and Modern Business*, Manchester University Press, 1993.

Casson, Mark, *The Entrepreneur: An Economic Theory*, Martin Robertson, 1982.

Chandler, Alfred D., *Scale and Scope: The Dynamics of Industrial Capitalism*, Harvard University Press, 1989.

Church, Roy, 'The Limitations of the Personal Capitalism Paradigm', *Business History Review*, 64, 1990.

Church, Roy, 'The Family Firm in Industrial Capitalism: International Perspectives on Hypotheses and History', *Business History*, 35 (4), Winter, 1993.

Foreman-Peck, J. S., 'Seedcorn or Chaff? New Firms and Industrial Performance in the Inter-War Economy', *Economic History Review*, 38, August, 1985.

Hannah, Leslie, 'Scale and Scope: Towards a European Visible Hand', *Business History*, 33, 1991.

Landes, David S., *The Unbound Prometheus: Technological Change and Industrial Development in Western Europe from 1750 to the Present*, Cambridge University Press, 1969.

McCloskey, Donald M. and Sandberg, Lars G., 'From Damnation to Redemption: Judgements on the late Victorian Entrepreneurs', *Explorations in Economic History*, 9, 1971.

Rubinstein, W. D., *Capitalism, Culture and Decline in Britain, 1750–1990*, Routledge, 1993.

Sarachek, Bernard, 'American Entrepreneurs and the Horatio Alger Myth', *Journal of Economic History*, 38, June, 1978.

Schumpeter, Joseph A., *The Theory of Economic Development: An Enquiry into Profits, Capital, Credit, Interest and the Business Cycle* (1911), in English, Harvard University Press, 1934.

Schumpeter, J. A., *Capitalism, Socialism and Democracy* (1942), George Allen & Unwin (rev. edn), 1954.

Storey, David J., *Understanding the Small Business Sector*, Routledge, 1994.

Thompson, F. M. L., *Gentrification and the Enterprise Culture, Britain 1780–1980*, Oxford University Press, 2001.

Wiener, Martin J. *English Culture and the Decline of the Industrial Spirit 1850–1980*, Allen Lane, 1981.

# F

## Famine

Famine leads to death through the insidious weakening of the immune system caused by the lack of nutrition and the consequential susceptibility of the population to disease. The >AGRICULTURAL REVOLUTION which manifested itself in >BRITAIN in the 18th century and subsequently spread throughout Europe, marked the beginning of the end of endemic famine in >WESTERN EUROPE. Britain had its last famine in 1709/10. That is not to say that the devastating effect of repeated crop failure would not occur, as it did in the collapse of the potato crop that gave rise to the >IRISH FAMINE of 1846–52 and it was not until the last quarter of the 19th century that Western Europe no longer had to endure another famine. The >INDUSTRIAL REVOLUTION, following on from that in agriculture, had made this possible together with the expansion of >INTERNATIONAL TRADE (Mokyr and O'Grada, 2002).

When >MALTHUS published *An Essay on the Principle of Population, as it Affects the Future Improvement of Society* in 1798, there was concern that there must be a resolution between the tendency of the >POPULATION to grow and the limitations of resources available to satisfy it. The population was controlled between the reduction of the birth rate caused by the drop in the amount of food available per head, on the one hand, and, on the other, an increase in the birth rate in time of plenty. At the extreme, if families did not exercise restraint, famine and disease would effect the necessary adjustment. As economies grew in the 19th century, not only did their agricultural output per head increase but also improvements in intra-country, inter-country and inter-continental transport and distribution opened up markets which had been isolated by high transport costs or lack of market information. A harvest failure in one area would raise prices in that market and this would encourage arbitrage, attracting a supply to make up the deficiency of the harvest (>GRAIN).

Success in the elimination of famine in Western Europe was not emulated in other countries. In >CHINA, there were famines between 1876 and 1879 and between 1928 and 1929. As a result of collectivization, famine killed over 20 million people between 1958 and 1962. In >INDIA, millions died of famine between 1896 and 1867 and an estimated 1.5 million died of famine in Bengal in 1943/4. A drought in >RUSSIA resulted in falls in the grain harvests in 1920 and 1921 of up to 54 per cent below average and millions died of hunger as a result. In the years 1931/3, a further major famine occurred through collectivization and the commandeering of produce from the peasants for distribution to the urban centres, resulting in the deaths of from 7–10 million. By the last quarter of the 20th century, recurrent famines were confined to Sub-Saharan Africa, although there was a severe famine in North Korea between 1995 and 1999 (Davies, 1994; Nove, 1992: Jones *et al.*, 1993) (>MIGRATION: POPULATION).

Agricultural output may always be susceptible to exogenous shocks caused by natural disasters such as drought or flood. The consequences may be mitigated or may be exacerbated by maladministration. The adjustment of supply to the disequilibrium of the market may fail because of inadequate transport infrastructure. It may also fail to the extent that high prices encourage speculation and local hoarding. Moreover, the high prices particularly exclude the poorest from the market. As mentioned above, it is not by actual starvation that famine kills but by disease and it is the poor who are the less well nourished and therefore already the most vulnerable.

### References

Davies, R. W., 'Changing Economic Systems: An Overview', in R. W. Davies, Mark Harrison and S. G. Wheatcroft (eds), *The Economic Transformation of the Soviet Union, 1913–1945*, Cambridge University Press, 1994.

Jones, Eric, Frost, Lionel and White, Colin (eds), *Coming Full Circle: An Economic History of the Pacific Rim*, Westview Press, 1993.

Mokyr, Joel and O'Grada, Cormac, 'What Do People Die of During Famines? The Great Irish Famine in Comparative Perspective', *European Review of Economic History*, 6(3), 2002.

Nove, Alec, *An Economic History of the USSR, 1917–1991*, Penguin, 1992.

# Ford, Henry

After two false starts, Ford founded the Ford Motor Company (FMC) on 16 June 1903. By then he was already 40 but the company was to become the largest in the world until the late 1920s, when it was overtaken by the less personalized General Motors (GM). GM was created by William C. Durant and brought to efficiency by Alfred P. Sloan. Ford's Model T car, introduced in 1908, pioneered standardized mass-production and the assembly line, high wages and mass durable-good consumption (a combination later labelled 'Fordism'). Ford was to be seen as the embodiment of the Second Industrial Revolution (>INDUSTRIAL REVOLUTIONS). Near to foundering in the >GREAT DEPRESSION, the Ford Motor Company has survived until today as one of the 'big three' US automotive companies, and still with a relative of Henry Ford at the helm. Ford was to be seen as different from some of the other spectacular big businessmen of the era (the 'robber barons' such as Jay Gould, Andrew Carnegie, John D. Rockefeller and J. P. Morgan) and was both populist and mostly popular, despite his great wealth, racism and ruthlessness towards his colleagues (>USA).

Henry Ford, who lived from 1863 to 1947, was born near Dearborn in Michigan. His father was a prosperous farmer and the son was brought up with strong Victorian moral values. From an early age, Henry loved tinkering with clocks and machinery and became an expert mechanic. In 1879 when only 16, but with the support of his parents, he moved to Detroit and found jobs in a machine shop, a shipyard and eventually the Edison Illumination Co., becoming Chief of Engineering by 1893. In his spare time he built a two-cylinder petrol engine and installed it in a 'carriage', as cars were then called, making several successful trial runs. Ford was not alone in developing a car; this had already been done in France and Germany and by the time, in 1899, Ford developed his second improved car, which seemed ready for production, there were many American competitors (>AUTOMOBILE INDUSTRY). Between 1900 and 1908, according to his latest biographer (Watts, 2005), 501 auto companies were formed in the USA. There were also competing technologies, including >STEAM POWER and electric cars, as well as bicycles. Around the turn of the century some of the companies which were to leave a lasting imprint on the history of the automobile were founded in addition to Ford, including Buick (1903) and Olds (1899) which were also to be absorbed into GM.

Ford resigned from the Edison company to help found the Detroit Motor Company, his first venture in car making, but progress was slow. He had difficulties in developing his second car and had no control over the direction of the business. In January 1901, Detroit Auto was dissolved though it was immediately resurrected by some of its investors to evolve into the Cadillac Motor Company, also later a component of GM. Ford started again with a second company, the Henry Ford Automobile Company, in November 1901 but his shareholders fell out over policy – most wanted to make an expensive car, Ford a cheaper one – and this second firm was also dissolved in less than a year. Ford's third attempt, the Ford Motor Company, founded in 1903 and in which he had a 25 per cent share, was a brilliant success. Ford got the backing of a prosperous Detroit coal dealer along with others, including the Dodge Brothers. In 18 months after incorporation, the new firm had paid dividends equal to the value of the whole issued stock. To gain publicity, Ford entered and won several car races with specially constructed machines, piloting some himself. In five years Ford had bought out some of the other

shareholders and gained a majority control of the company. In 1913 FMC produced 182,000 cars, including the famous Model T; half of the US total output. In 1910 FMC had opened a new factory at Highland Park and it was there that the assembly line was introduced in which workers in fixed positions had cars and components at various stages of build brought to them. It is said that Ford arrived at this notion by observing local meat-packing factories that featured moving conveyors.

After a lawsuit with the Dodge Brothers, his own shareholders, he was able to gain total control of the company. He achieved this with support from some financial institutions and possibly by allowing rumours to develop that he was going to form a new company, thus depressing the prospects of FMC and reducing the value of the shares. Freed from outside interests, Ford pushed ahead with plans to build an enormous new integrated plant at River Rouge, which had good rail access. The new plant had its own blast furnaces and foundry, among other things, and the idea was to eliminate problems with suppliers. Early in 1914, Ford announced a doubling of the standard wage to $5 a day plus bonuses and a reduction in working hours from nine to eight, with the introduction of three shifts instead of two. This was an astonishing development for the time. Ford believed that higher wages would reduce labour turnover and increase the purchasing power of workers. He also had a paternalistic belief in siding with his employees. In fact, labour turnover did not fall very much, perhaps because of pressures arising from the pace and monotony of work on the assembly line, but also because Ford chose to extend his paternalism to authoritarian attempts to control workers' personal conduct. A Sociological Department was established to discourage drinking and encourage regular saving and even 'clean well conducted homes' (Ford gave up on this department in 1921). Ford continued with his policy of reducing the selling price of the Model T, which went down from $850 in 1908 to $600 in 1912, $440 in 1920 and $290 in 1924. Production expanded from 585,000 in 1916 to 750,000 in 1914 and 2 million by 1923.

Ford's wealth and success led him into political activity. He also wrote or had ghosted several books (Ford, 1923). Against American participation in >WORLD WAR I, he sent a 'peace ship' to Europe. He travelled in the ship himself but deserted it when it became clear that there was no support for the venture. He supported Woodrow Wilson for the Presidency in 1916 and himself unsuccessfully stood for the Senate the following year. In 1933 he refused to co-perate with F. D. Roosevelt's >NEW DEAL, though after Pearl Harbor he was to abandon neutrality and also publicly retracted his earlier anti-Semitism. During >WORLD WAR II, FMC manufactured trucks, tanks and aircraft, producing 425 Liberator bombers a month by 1944. The 1920s and 1930s were turbulent times for Ford. There were labour incidents (Ford did not recognize unions until 1941) and in 1932 there was a major riot outside the plant. Harry Bennett, FMC's head of Security and Labour Negotiation, was knocked out by rocks thrown by demonstrating unemployed workers. Following police intervention there was gunfire, reportedly from both sides, and four people were killed.

With the depression and broadening tastes, it became clear that Ford's single-product policy was inferior to that of GM, which had a wider range of cars in various price brackets. In 1927,

the River Rouge plant was closed for six months to retool for a new model. Henry Ford's autocratic management was largely responsible for the company's slow adoption to new trends (he did not cease to play an active role in management until 1945 when he was 82). He had lost most of his better executives, some of which had loyally remained with him from the early days. It was not only product policy that was the problem; GM adopted a different approach to management structure (the 'M' Form), which was more appropriate for the giant enterprises which the leading motor enterprises had become (>CHANDLER). GM overtook Ford in production in 1929 and from 1925–86 the profit performance of GM exceeded that of FMC (McCraw, 1998).

Henry Ford was much affected by the death in 1943 of his talented son, Edsel, whom he had dominated. Henry himself was to die from a cerebral haemorrhage in 1947. The company's post-war revival began in 1945 when Henry Ford II, Edsel's son, became chief executive officer. Although FMC overtook Chrysler to return to second position in 1950, GM remained ahead in sales. Today, all three of the major US automobile manufacturers are in trouble from foreign competition and a high cost base.

## References

Ford, Henry with Crowther, Samuel, *My Life and Work*, Doubleday, 1923.

McCraw, Thomas K. (ed.), *Creating Modern Capitalism*, Harvard University Press, 1998.

Seltzer, Lawrence H., *A Financial History of the American Automobile Industry*, Houghton Mifflin, 1928, reprint by Augustus M. Kelley, 1973.

Watts, Steven, *The People's Tycoon: Henry Ford and the American Century*, Alfred A. Knopf, 2005.

# French Revolution

The French Revolution was influenced by the ideas of the Enlightenment which preceded it – the belief in reason, progress, liberty and toleration. The American revolution influenced France in at least two important ways: first, its ideas were clearly transferable; second, out of enmity for Britain, France had supported the Americans at a cost which pushed its already shaky finances to the edge. It was his need for help in salvaging the French Treasury that motivated the King, Louis XIV, to summons meetings of the Three Estates, which had not met since 1614. The King's Ministers of Finance, successively Turgot, Necker and Colonne, under the influence of the >PHYSIOCRATS were already groping their way towards reforming the very inequitable tax system and especially towards the establishment of a national land and gross income taxes – neither the Church nor the nobility effectively were taxed. The existing *Parlements* would never have approved such radical measures and this was why the Estates General was called. The deputies from the Three Estates, who were elected locally, did not, as is commonly supposed, comprehensively reflect social classes. For example, the Third Estate consisted two-thirds of bourgeois commoners, including landowners and lawyers, but not a single peasant (nor a woman) was included. The 300 members of the First Estate were nobles and military men, the 300 members of the Second Estate, representing the Church, were mostly parish priests. The Third Estate, which had 600 members, soon seized control, declaring in June 1789 that it was the National Assembly, though it invited the members of the other states to join it.

The Assembly considered that the first priority was to establish a Constitution, not deal with the financial and economic crisis (agriculture was severely depressed). But things soon developed into insurrection. The state prison of the Bastille in Paris was stormed by a mob on 14 July 1789 and there were uprisings in the countryside. Spurred by the street violence, the National Convention (as it became) was to pass 11,250 Decrees in three years including, after the August Declaration of the Rights of Man, the abolition of serfdom, craft guilds and internal customs duties and the prohibition of monopolies, including chartered >COMPANIES. Private property was declared inviolable (though this was soon breached by state confiscations). In 1792, France became a Republic. Agreement could not be reached on tax reform and the printing of paper money (the Assignats) was the main motor of the increasingly desperate path of the revolutionary governments towards inflation, the aggravation of the subsistence crisis and ultimately domestic and external violence. This is Aftalion's (1990) economic interpretation of the revolution. The Assignats were supposed to be backed by prospective revenues from the sale of property confiscated from the Church, émigrés and others, but eventually, despite being granted the status of legal tender, became virtually worthless. The state financed itself mainly in this way and by plunder from foreign territories in the Revolutionary Wars.

In the face of continuous pressure from the mob over the shortage of food, the authorities introduced more and more counterproductive regulation against hoarding and speculation. Maximum prices were imposed on grain and other necessities and ration cards were introduced. Violence was appalling, not only in the execution of Louis XIV and Marie-Antoinette in 1793 and many members of the aristocracy and others, but even leaders of the Committee of Public Safety, Danton and Robespierre, were guillotined. There was also savage repression of royalist uprisings. In 1794, according to Davies (1996), the Republican Army shot, guillotined and burned, tens of thousands of loyalists in the Vendée and drowned others in hulks sunk during the night and reloaded with more victims the next day.

The consequences of the French Revolution, however favourable for institutional cleansing in the long run (>INSTITUTIONS), unsurprisingly were very unfavourable in the short run. Agricultural output only recovered to its 1789 levels in 1800, but industrial output had still not recovered by then, partly because of loss of foreign markets, but also because industry was deprived of capital which state demands were crowding out. The relative profitability of investing in agriculture instead of industry was enhanced by lower land prices following the sales of confiscated property. There is evidence that industrialists deferred projects, for example, the use of coking coal for >IRON AND STEEL, until after the period of disruption. It could be argued that French industrialization was put back many years. In the longer term France and much of the rest of Continental Europe benefited from the ending of feudalism and the removal of other out-dated restrictions. Certainly the French peasantry gained from the removal of feudal dues and became the full owners of their lands and, in some cases, acquired new ones. Some, however, have argued that the Revolution slowed the rate of rural emigration and ensured the survival of too many small-scale farms.

## References

Aftalion, Florin, *The French Revolution: An Economic Interpretation*, Cambridge University Press, 1990.

Davis, Norman, Europe: *A History*, Oxford University Press, 1996.

# Friedman, Milton

Milton Friedman, who lived from 1912 to 2006, was born in New York in 1912, the only son, with three sisters, of Sarah and Jeno Friedman who had met after emigrating to the USA when still in their teens from Carpatho-Ruthenia, which was at that time a part of the Austria-Hungarian Empire. The family was poor but Milton won a scholarship to Rutgers University from where he graduated in 1932 with a degree in Economics, which he followed with a masters degree from the University of Chicago in the following year. It was here that he met Rose Director, a fellow student, whom he married six years later. After a year at Columbia, he returned to Chicago. In 1935 he moved to Washington to work at the National Resources Committee on consumer budgets, then, in 1937, at the National Bureau of Economic Research to help Simon Kuznets with the analysis of professional incomes (Friedman and Kuznets, 1946). Both these studies were to form the foundation of his *Theory of the Consumption Function* (1957). During >WORLD WAR II, he worked at the US Treasury and at Columbia University on war-related projects. In 1946, he returned to Chicago, where he stayed until his official retirement in 1976. He was then appointed a senior research fellow at the Hoover Institution at Stanford University, where he was free to continue his research work until his death in 2006. In 1951, he was awarded the John Bates Clark

Medal by the American Economic Association. In 1976, he received the Nobel Prize in Economics 'for his achievements in the fields of consumption analysis, monetary history and theory, and for his demonstration of the complexity of stabilization policy'.

Barry Goldwater appointed Friedman his chief economic adviser for his 1964 presidential campaign, recognizing their mutual commitment to a political philosophy of minimum government and maximum individual freedom. In 1968, Friedman was appointed to a committee to provide economic advice to Richard Nixon before his election as President and Nixon gave him the opportunity on a number of occasions during his presidency to put his views, albeit not always successfully. However, it was with President Ronald Reagan that Friedman had the closest affinity. Friedman had helped Reagan in the 1970s when he was Governor of California and he had confirmed that he would have his support in his campaign for the Presidency. Friedman was appointed to a committee to offer economic policy advice to Reagan on becoming President but with a somewhat different outcome compared with the Nixon administration. According to Friedman in his memoirs, 'Once in office, Reagan acted very much along the lines that we recommended' (quoted in Ebenstein, 2007).

Milton Friedman was an economist who was fully in sympathy with and took his guiding principles of free markets and minimum government from the Classical tradition (>CLASSICAL AND NEO-CLASSICAL ECONOMICS). To Friedman, the joy of Classical economics was that it was in complete accord with his natural love of individual liberty. From the earliest days, Classical economists had shown that an economy would

not descend into chaos if government left individual citizens to go about their business with the minimum of controls. Moreover, he agreed with Adam >SMITH that economics considered as:

'a branch of the science of a statesman or legislator, proposes two distinct objects: first, to provide a plentiful revenue, or subsistence for the people, or, more properly, to enable them to provide such revenue or subsistence for themselves; and secondly, to supply the state or commonwealth with a revenue sufficient for the public services.' (Smith, *Wealth of Nations*, introduction to Book IV,)

Friedman also believed, with >KEYNES, that it was ideas that shaped practical political decisions, although he disagreed with him that new ideas necessarily took a long time to permeate through to politicians and government officials. He vigorously pursued an active campaign of the dissemination of his ideas not only to politicians and government officials but also to the general public. He believed that there was an intimate link between economics and political structure:

'A society which is socialist cannot also be democratic... I know of no example in time or place of a society that has been marked by a large measure of political freedom, and that has not also used something comparable to a free market to organize the bulk of economic activity.' (Friedman, 1962)

The fundamentals of his approach were established early and set out in his essay 'The Methodology of Positive Economics' (in Friedman, 1953). Keynes's father, John Neville Keynes, in his *The Scope and Method of Political Economy* (1891), had emphasized the difference between positive and normative propositions in social studies. The former relates to what is or what can be and the latter allows value judgements as to what ought to be. Economics and economists, as economists, should be concerned only with the former. Friedman emphasized this in the context of his belief that the ability to make successful predictions must play a central part for economic theory to be meaningful. He was critical of the complex econometric models which had been developed in the wake of the Keynesian revolution. However, while he certainly did not become part of that revolution and was a severe critic, nevertheless he did not repudiate Keynesian theory but through his criticism and strictures made and inspired important contributions to the development of economic theory and the application of economics to practical affairs.

A central feature of Keynes's macro-economic model was the aggregate consumption function and the related savings variable which assumed that as incomes increased so did the proportion of income which was saved. Friedman saw how Keynes's structure could be improved through his *permanent-income hypothesis* (Friedman, 1957). If consumers have fluctuating income, they do not necessarily spend in step with it but will tend to relate their expenditure to their average long-term income to keep their consumption stable. If they have a good year, they increase their savings, if they have a low-income year they reduce their savings. A large short-run increase in household incomes, therefore, does not lead to a large increase in expenditure. He concluded that only the permanent proportion of current consumption is a function of, and only of, the permanent proportion of income. In other words, current consumption

is a function of current income and expectations of future income.

A further attack on Keynes came with Friedman's revival and reformulation of the quantity theory of money in his *Studies in the Quantity Theory of Money.* (Friedman, 1956). The quantity theory of money, which was central to Classical macro-economics, postulated that changes in the supply of money had a direct influence on prices. Its elements were summed up by M = kPY where M is the demand for money, k is the velocity of circulation of money, P is the price level and Y is total output. Keynes rejected this on the argument that k was not constant but variable and an increase in the quantity of money would increase total output if there was spare capacity, so there was no direct link between money and prices as assumed. Friedman, while accepting that k could change, believed that it did so in a stable and predictable way. Further, he argued that if there was unemployment in the economy this was due to structural imbalances between the various sectors and the expansion of total demand would not in the long run be effective.

A. W. H. Phillips, the Tooke Professor of Economics, Science and Statistics at the London School of Economics, published an article in *Economica* in 1958 entitled 'The Relation between Unemployment and the Rate of Change of Money wage rates in the United Kingdom, 1861–1957' which concluded that there was a significant relationship between the percentage change in money wages and the level of unemployment, the graphical representation of which became known as the 'Phillips Curve'. The implication of this was that there existed a trade-off between unemployment and inflation. Friedman disputed this with his concept of the 'natural rate of unemployment'. In his Presidential address to the American Economic Association in 1967, he defined this as,

'the level of unemployment which is consistent with equilibrium in the structure of real wage rates. At that level of unemployment, real wage rates are tending on the average to rise at a 'normal' secular rate, i.e., at a rate that can be indefinitely maintained so long as capital formation, technological improvements, etc. remain on their long term trends.'

Any attempt to reduce unemployment below this level through higher inflation would be bound to fail as it is a feature of the institutional framework of the labour market. Friedman also believed that people behave rationally. Businessmen might be encouraged to increase employment as inflation widens the gap between their prices and their wage bill. However, as inflation persists workers come to expect it and demand wage increases in line with their expectations and by so doing restore the original lower margins. There might be a temporary reduction in unemployment but it would inevitably rise back up again to the natural rate in spite of higher inflation, leading to what was subsequently called 'stagflation'.

Keynes was concerned with the conditions that prevailed in the years of the >GREAT DEPRESSION' and had concluded that the quantity theory of money was inadequate as a guide to policy in those conditions and recommended the fiscal solution of government expenditure in order to increase economic activity. Friedman believed that the subsequent neglect of monetary in favour of fiscal policy was to be regretted and set about the

task of proving that money does matter and to persuade economic policymakers that it does, a task which he pursued with enormous energy, enthusiasm and success.

In Friedman and Schwarz (1963), the authors had constructed and analyzed a time series of money supply in the USA from 1775 but concentrated on the period after 1867. This study Friedman used to refute Keynes's argument that monetary policy was ineffective in times of Depression. On the contrary, Friedman argued that the 'Great Contraction' in the USA between 1929 and 1933 was as severe as it was because of the large fall in the stock of money because of the inept policy of the Federal Reserve Bank. It was, he insisted, the mismanagement of the monetary system that produced it and not a failure of the capitalist market system which people had come to believe. 'The Great Contraction is tragic testimony to the power of monetary policy – not, as Keynes and so many of his contemporaries believed, evidence of its impotence' (quoted in Burton, 1981) (>GREAT DEPRESSION).

Friedman was sceptical of the ability of government to control economic activity through 'fine tuning'. Through his research, he identified various lags that occurred that could disrupt the effectiveness of policies intended to stabilize fluctuations in the >BUSINESS CYCLE. He described three areas in which such delays occurred, which he called 'observation-lag', 'decision-lag' and 'effect-lag'. As a result, he advocated that economic policy should aim to allow the quantity of money to grow at a steady long-run rate of, for instance, 3 per cent per annum (Friedman, 1959). He agreed with Alan Blinder, a vice-chairman of the Federal Reserve Bank, that inflation was always and everywhere primarily a monetary phenomenon.

Reflecting his belief in minimum government, Friedman argued that the international rates of exchange of currencies should be left to be determined by the market, believed in the freeing of domestic and international markets from restrictions and subsidies (>INTERNATIONAL TRADE) and the privatization of enterprises owned or controlled by the government. He vigorously advocated the freedom from government intervention and the restoration of freedom to individuals to operate in the market as they wished, and listed government involvement in many activities (in Friedman, 1962) which he thought was not justified. These included government price support in agriculture and controls on outputs, rents, prices and wages, legal minimum wage rates and maximum prices, and publicly owned and operated toll roads (>ROAD TRANSPORT). He supported the introduction of school vouchers in order to widen parental choice in education.

Friedman was not only a professional theoretical and applied economist of the first rank but an extremely active, lively and effective communicator, not only in the USA but also internationally. His avocation was to take his ideas not only to the makers of policy but also to the general public. He firmly believed in the importance of ideas in influencing political action. For 18 years he had a column in *Newsweek* and he and his wife wrote *Free to Choose*, based on his successful television programme, which was published in 1980 and became a bestseller. He continued writing to the end; just a month before his death he published an article in the *Wall Street Journal*. President Ronald Reagan proved especially sympathetic to his ideas and Prime Minister Margaret Thatcher (>BRITAIN) also willingly heard him. The tide of Keynesian in the form of the predominance of fiscal policy and the government control over the economy in the post->WORLD WAR II years was reversed in favour of monetarism. Attempts to control the quantity of money, however, failed because of the practical difficulty of tying down what proved to be an elusive concept, particularly exacerbated by the >GLOBALIZATION of markets and the consequential greater internationalization of money flows. Generally, however, success in controlling inflation was achieved by central bank (>CENTRAL BANKING) control directly targeted at the price level through the rate of interest rather than through fiscal policies.

Milton Friedman expressed some doubts about the stability of the currency zone set up by some members of the European Union when they adopted the euro as a common currency in 1998 under a European Central Bank. He was concerned that the structural inflexibilities, for instance, in and between the labour markets of the member countries under a single monetary policy would be put under severe stress in the event of a serious recession. (>CENTRAL BANKING: >WESTERN EUROPE)

## References

Burton, John, 'Positively Milton Friedman', in J. R. Shackleton and Gareth Locksley (eds), *Twelve Contemporary Economists*, Macmillan, 1981.

Ebenstein, Lanny, *Milton Friedman, A Biography*, Palgrave Macmillan, 2007.

Friedman, Milton, *Essays in Positive Economics*, University of Chicago Press, 1953.

Friedman, Milton, 'The Quantity Theory of Money- A Restatement', in Milton Friedman (ed.), *Studies in the Quantity*

*Theory of Money*, University of Chicago Press, 1956.

Friedman, Milton, *Theory of the Consumption Function*, National Bureau of Economic Research General Series, 63, Princeton University Press, 1957.

Friedman, Milton, *A Program for Monetary Stability*, Fordham University Press, 1959.

Friedman, Milton, *Capitalism and Freedom*, University of Chicago Press, 1962.

Friedman, Milton and Kuznets, Simon, *Income of Independent Professional Practice*, National Bureau of Economic Research, 1946.

Friedman, M. and Schwarz, A. J., *A Monetary History of the United States, 1867–1960*, National Bureau of Economic Research, Studies in Business Cycles, 12, Princeton University Press, 1963.

Keynes, J. A., *The Scope and Method of Political Economy* (1890), Cosmo Publications (new edn), 2004.

Smith, Adam, *An Inquiry into the Nature and Causes of the Wealth of Nations* (1776), Book IV, Ward Lock, 1812.

# G

## Gas

Although it had been shown in France how manufactured gas could be used for lighting, it was developed commercially in >BRITAIN. The first practical installation of a lighting system using manufactured gas (coal-gas) was built in 1805 by its inventor, William Murdock, to light the cotton mills of Phillips and Lee in Salford. A system was also installed in the same year by Samuel Clegg for the cotton mill of Henry Lodge at Sowerby Bridge, Halifax. Gas lighting arrived in London in 1807. >THE INDUSTRIAL REVOLUTION IN BRITAIN spurred the development of the necessary demand, technology, materials and capital investment by which the new business could grow in the early 19th century. It was reported that 'it was common practice on the part of the largest mill owners to make their own gas' (Falkus, 1967) and other organizations, such as >RAILWAY companies, also did so. The 19th century was the century of light.

The first company to be set up specifically to produce and distribute gas was the Gas Light and Coke Company, London, in 1812. Other companies followed swiftly, introducing gas lighting progressively first into the largest and then into the smaller towns. By 1846, there were few towns except for the smallest that did not have a gas undertaking in Britain. The >USA and Europe followed. Gas light reached Baltimore in 1816 and New York in 1825. Paris was illuminated in 1819 and gas light spread through the largest towns in Europe until it had become generally established by the 1860s.

In Britain, virtually all the suppliers of manufactured gas that were established in the first half of the century were privately owned but thereafter municipal ownership became common. By the end of the century, about 35 per cent of the total output of gas from authorized undertakings were from enterprises that were owned by local authorities. In Germany, in comparison, about 80 per cent of the industry was operated by municipalities. The consumption of gas per consumer in Britain was on average less for the municipally owned enterprises than for the privately owned. This has been attributed to the generally lower prices charged by the municipal operations which attracted relatively more poor households into their networks. However, it has been argued that, nevertheless, there is little evidence that the business objectives differed materially between the different sectors. Evidence suggests that the managers of municipal undertakings were just as profit-conscious as their private counterparts. The transfer of any surpluses from a municipal business to the local authority did not seem to have any effect that differed materially from the distribution of dividends by private companies (Millward, 1991).

Some British government regulation was imposed on the industry. In 1847, the Gas Clauses Act restricted dividends to 10 per cent but it was not effectively enforced. From the 1870s, private companies were subject to a scale in which a specified dividend percentage could only be exceeded if prices were below a fixed price level by a certain amount. The municipal undertakings were subject to controlled maximum prices.

As the industry expanded it was able to achieve a continuing reduction in prices through economies of scale and the benefits accruing from the reduction of the costs of its inputs. For instance, the price of iron retorts fell from about £20 per ton in 1817 to £12 per ton in the 1820s to £7.5 per ton in the 1830s (Falkus, 1967). Consequently, the price of gas fell and continued to do so. Between 1825 and 1900, the price of gas in London dropped by about 85 per cent, compared with a drop of about 40 per cent in wholesale prices (Goodall, 1993). The gas market was also facilitated by technical improvements such as the installation of credit meters from the 1830s and coin-in-the-slot meters in the 1890s. In 1885, the incandescent gas mantle was invented by Baron Von Welsbach (1858–1929) of Austria. When they were first marketed they gave out four times as much light per cubic foot of gas as the burners they replaced and by the mid-1890s this had been raised to nine times.

Lighting was effectively the sole use of coal-gas throughout the 19th century and it had no rival in this use until the coming of >ELECTRICITY to London and New York in 1882. When Edison was designing his network, he specifically aimed to be competitive with town gas at $2.25 per thousand cubic foot. Lighting from manufactured gas was relatively more expensive in the USA compared with Britain because the enterprises were smaller and inputs, such as coal, were more expensive. This was true also in other countries. Britain was unusual in that gas lighting remained cheaper than electric lighting until >WORLD WAR I.

An industry with lighting as its only demand has a very poor load factor and with the threat from electricity aimed at that demand, it was necessary for the industry to open up new applications for its product and to spread the load more evenly over the day. Although gas stoves had been available since the 1830s, they had not been able to compete with the coal and wood burning ranges. However, by the 1880s, the falling price of gas had made appliances a more economical proposition and the industry launched a marketing campaign intended to increase the penetration of domestic appliance ownership. The companies in the USA began to sell appliances but the undertakings in Britain pursued a more vigorous policy of hiring out appliances such as cookers, water heaters and gas fires below cost to promote the use of gas away from the lighting peak. The industry succeeded. In the first two decades of the 20th century it achieved a rate of growth of just under 3 per cent per annum and lighting had fallen to 35 per cent of the total load by 1913, to be replaced by electricity completely during the inter-war period. In the second half of the 20th century, manufactured gas was finally replaced by natural gas.

Natural gas first came on to the market as a competitor to manufactured gas in 1883 in the USA when Robert Pew established a supply in Pittsburgh. Robert Pew sold his business to the Standard Oil Company, which set up a Natural Gas Trust in 1886. By 1911, there were 176 plants in the USA processing natural gas but the business was constrained by the technical difficulty of transmitting gas by pipeline the long distances required to transport it from the producing fields to the consumers. It was not until the 1920s that high-pressure steel pipes were developed which eliminated the high losses which had been experienced by the use of the old cast iron pipes. Natural gas had a technical superiority over coal-gas in that it gave a cleaner burn, it required no storage facilities and had better security of supply. Until a market was found for it, the >OIL industry had treated it as a value-less biproduct and had flared it off. It had, therefore, a very favourable cost base compared with manufactured gas. Manufactured gas production in the USA continued to grow, however, finally reaching a peak in 1947, after which it declined as natural gas replaced it in the market. Moreover, natural gas was also increasingly seen as an alternative to oil in many industrial as well as domestic and commercial uses, particularly in the production of electricity. In the second half of the 20th century, the energy markets had suffered a series of shocks; such as the rapid escalation of oil prices in the 1970s, the explosion in the nuclear power plant at Chernobyl in the Ukraine in 1986, the serious spillage of oil into Prince William Sound in Alaska in 1989 and the perceived risk to supplies of the concentration of oil supplies in the Middle East. Natural gas came to be seen as an attractive alternative. Indeed, as early as 1942, President Roosevelt wrote to his Secretary of the Interior, ' I wish you would get some of your people to look into the possibility of using natural gas...an enormous amount of natural gas is lying idle in the ground because it is too far to pipe to large communities' (quoted in Yergin, 1992). During the war, two major pipelines, called 'Big Inch' and 'Little Inch', had been constructed to shift oil across the country and in 1947 these were sold to the

Texas Eastern Transmission company for natural gas. Los Angeles was also linked by pipeline to natural gas in New Mexico. Natural gas was clean and certainly cheap. According to the OECD, the price of natural gas per barrel of oil equivalent in 1950 delivered to the consumer was 40 per cent less than the well-head price of oil. This low price persisted in real terms until the 1970s as they were entrenched into the federal government's regulatory system. This had the effect of encouraging the demand for natural gas but it discouraged the opening up of new supplies. The policy was eased with the passing of the Natural Gas Policy Act in 1978. Natural gas consumption in the USA grew between 1960 and 1980 at just under 3 per cent per annum and by the latter year electricity production accounted for 13 per cent of its use and the rest of industry 31 per cent (International Energy Agency, 1982).

There were similar developments in >WESTERN EUROPE in the second half of the 20th century. In the 1950s, Italy was the largest consumer and producer of natural gas, which accounted for 40 per cent of domestic energy production based on deposits in the Po valley. Production in France grew in the 1950s with the discovery of deposits at Lacq in the south west of the country, which was connected to Paris and other cities by a 1,930 km pipeline. However, it was the discovery of a major natural gas deposit at Groningen in the Netherlands in 1959 and several major gas fields in the southern North Sea in the 1960s which transformed the European gas market as it had that of the USA. In 1950, the USA accounted for 98 per cent of the total production of natural gas of the member countries of the OECD; by 1980 this had fallen to 67 per cent as Western Europe increased its share to 23 per cent

(International Energy Agency, 1982). Natural gas had replaced manufactured gas; the conversion of appliances in Britain was completed by the late 1970s.

The major development in the world natural gas economy in the second half of the 20th century was, however, the discovery of major fields in >RUSSIA in Western Siberia and the Urals. By 1980, Russia possessed 35 per cent of the world's proven reserves of natural gas (International Energy Agency, 1982). By the end of the 20th century, Russia was the world's largest producer, accounting for 26 per cent of the total, and was the world's largest exporter, accounting for 37 per cent of the total, its major markets being found in Western Europe (United Nations, 2002).

## References

American Petroleum Institute, *Petroleum Facts and Figures*, 1959.

Byatt, I. C. R., *The British Electrical Industry, 1875–1914*, Clarendon Press, 1979.

Dewhurst, Frederic J., Coppock O. John and Yates, Lamartine P., *Europe's Needs and Resources: Trends and Prospects in Eighteen Countries*, Macmillan, 1961.

Falkus, M. E., 'The British Gas Industry before 1850', *Economic History Review*, XX(3), December, 1967.

Goodall, Francis, 'Appliance Trading Activities of British Gas Utilities, 1875–1935', *Economic History Review*, XLVI(3), August, 1993.

Hughes, Thomas P., *Networks of Power: Electrification in Western Society, 1880–1930*, Johns Hopkins University Press, 1993.

International Energy Agency, *World Energy Outlook*, OECD, 1982, 2000.

Millward, Robert, 'The Market Behaviour of Local Authorities', *Economic History Review*, XLIV(1), February, 1991.

Porter, Roy, *London, A Social History*, Penguin, 2000.

United Nations, *Energy Statistics Yearbook*, 2002.

Yergin, Daniel, *The Prize: The Epic Quest for Oil, Money and Power*, Simon & Schuster, 1992.

# Gerschenkron, Alexander

Generally accepted as a seminal thinker in the study of economic history, Gerschenkron, who lived from 1904 to 1978, was born in >RUSSIA but his entrepreneurial family had to flee from the Bolsheviks in 1920 during the civil war. They moved to Austria where Gerschenkron completed his education and married. As a liberal academic from a Jewish family he and his parents were again uprooted by the political union of Austria and Germany (*Anschluss*). Leaving his wife and parents in England, Gershenkron accepted an offer of a junior post at Berkeley, an opportunity he used to complete a book on the economic basis for Hitler's rise to power (*Bread and Democracy in Germany*, 1943). After four years in Washington in the State Department and the Office of Strategic Services, where be became an expert in Russian affairs, Gerschenkron finally came to rest at Harvard, where he remained as a professor until his retirement in 1974. Gerschenkron's work on the history of European industrialization included in-depth research, not only on Russia but on Bulgaria, Italy and other countries. In a project for the RAND Corporation he was able to demonstrate that Soviet statistics on industrial output were inflated by technical choices on weighting of index numbers. Gerschenkron is best known for his concept of relative backwardness with its implications for the pace of economic development.

In analyzing industrialization, Gerschenkron argued that in countries that were economically backward (as, in the 19th century, Germany and particularly Russia were in comparison to Britain) long periods of slow growth were followed at a turning point marked by a 'spurt' in industrial growth, the degree of the acceleration being a function of the extent of economic backwardness. The more backward the country, the greater the discontinuity. Plant sizes were also larger and there was an emphasis on producer goods so as to incorporate state-of-the-art technologies from more advanced countries. The state would also play a greater role in making up for (substituting for) the necessary elements missing from the economic environment, such as the availability of finance and entrepreneurial and commercial standards. This thesis certainly seemed to fit the cases of Germany (>WESTERN EUROPE) and Russia, where there was an emphasis on steel making, machine tools and other basic industries, as well as a greater role for the state than in the earlier British development. Britain had no need for state-sponsored universal banks, for example, like Germany (>BANKING), since its industrialization was more gradual and could be financed from wealth accumulated from agriculture and trade.

Unlike >ROSTOW, whose stages of growth theories he criticized, Gerschenkron measured his spurts in terms of industrial, not total output or national income. Not only was total output impossible to measure with any accuracy during the 19th century but also by the time industrial output had grown to the point where it significantly affected the total, the spurt was probably over – a point reiterated by N. F. R. Crafts much later when he showed that the growth sectors in the >INDUSTRIAL REVOLUTION IN BRITAIN accounted for only a tiny proportion of total output during the period 1760–1830. Stages of growth theories involving prerequisites for take-off ,as in the case of Rostow's, were criticized by Gerschenkron on the grounds that all countries did not go through the same phases and, as indicated, some prerequisites could be and were substituted for. These stage theories, Gerschenkron asserted, were defeated by history, though, in fact, his own findings on turning points could not be corroborated by Crafts, Leybourne and Mills in Sylla and Toniolo (1991) (>INDUSTRIAL REVOLUTIONS). Gerschenkron was not at all dogmatic about his model (though his prose sometimes suggested this) and emphasized the importance of specific country explanations of development. Indeed, he says in the final page of his 1962 collection, that, having stimulated more work, his model might be superseded by new hypotheses as new research was undertaken.

Gerschenkron was much admired for his mastery of foreign languages and his general erudition: his 1962 collection, for example, includes articles on Russian intellectual history and novelists, as well as on the mathematics of index numbers. Several of the participants in his Harvard workshops, for example Donald McCloskey, Paul David and Peter Temin, were to become well-known economic historians in their own right and pioneers in the new quantitative >ECONOMIC HISTORY.

## References

Dawidoff, Nicholas, *The Fly Swatter: How my Grandfather Made his way in the World*, Pantheon, 2002.

Gerschenkron, Alexander, *Economic Backwardness in Historical Perspective*, Harvard University Press, 1962.

Gerschenkron, Alexander, *Continuity in History and Other Essays*, Harvard University Press, 1968.

Gerschenkron, Alexander, *Europe in the Russian Mirror: Four Lectures on Economic History*, Cambridge University Press, 1970.

Sylla, Richard and Toniolo, Gianni (eds), *Patterns of Industrialisation: The Nineteenth Century*, Routledge, 1991.

# Globalization

The expression 'globalization' did not reach the academic or business literature until towards the end of the 20th century. It first appeared in a business context in an article entitled 'The Globalization of Marketing' by Theodore Levitt in 1983, shortly before he became editor of the *Harvard Business Review*. In this article, Levitt criticized companies for their failure to appreciate the way that technological changes had affected international communications and travel in such a way as to open up new opportunities for international mass marketing and sales. Nevertheless, globalization itself was hardly new; although there is some disagreement about the timing of its origin historically. Much of this disagreement may be attributed to differences in the definition of globalization. The word itself implies comprehensive intercommunication and the interplay of transfers of resources of some kind on a world scale. These inter-connections could be accomplished through trade flows (>INTERNATIONAL TRADE), >MIGRATION, direct foreign investment and transfers of capital or technology but any agreement on a strict definition of the term may depend on the method used to identify the timing of a transmission from a pre-globalized period to a globalized one (Bordo *et al.*, 2005).

It could be argued that globalization began when trade first extended its reach throughout the Euro-Asian landmass at a level significant enough to impinge on the economies of the trading countries as exemplified by the kind of international merchandise trades that flourished at the time of the Roman Empire:

'Even Northern Italy, Gaul and Spain began with some success... to imitate the products of oriental industry. Innumerable merchant ships ploughed the Mediterranean, great commercial expeditions explored new rivers and coasts, and pushed as far as remote India and China in search of silk and pearls, of rice... and taking with them in addition to the gold and silver which these very remote countries accepted in payment for their goods, the few products of the Mediterranean such as wine, which were consumed there.' (*The Empire at the Death of Marcus Aurelius (AD121–180), A Short History of Rome*, by Guglielmo Ferrero and Corrado Barbagallo, 1919)

On the other hand, trade may not be considered to have been potentially truly global until ocean-going vessels had been developed capable of connecting the Americas and Africa with Europe and Asia. This was not achieved until after the discoveries of Christopher Columbus and Vasco da Gama in the 15th century. Adam >SMITH firmly believed that 'The discovery of America, and that of a passage to the East Indies by the Cape of Good Hope, are the two greatest and most important events recorded in the history of mankind' (*An Inquiry into the Nature and Causes of the Wealth of Nations*, Book IV, Chapter VII, Part III, 1776).

Flynn and Giraldez (2004) placed the timing of the birth of globalization somewhat later in 1571 and more precisely on the establishment of the entrepôt of Manila through which the Americas were first directly connected commercially to Asia. They argued that in addition to these linkages, the timing of the arrival of globalization did not necessarily depend on a high volume or value of the flows of trade but the impact these flows had subsequently on the economies of the countries which were opened up to this new trade. For instance, they pointed out the importance of the repercussions which the arrival of horses, cattle, >SUGAR, >COFFEE and wheat (>GRAIN) had on the economies of the Americas and the reverse flow of trade from there into the Old World of corn, potatoes, beans and other plants. For instance, the cultivation of American maize, the sweet potato and the peanut induced an agricultural revolution in >CHINA in the 17th and 18th centuries sufficiently powerful to support a surge in the growth of China's population. Moreover, because these crops required less labour in their cultivation than the existing food crops such as >RICE, labour could be redirected to the production of other commodities such as tea, sugar and silk for export. The introduction of new crops, such as the potato, originating from the Americas also had a similar importance in sustaining the high density of the population of Japan. They argued that in so far as price convergence gives a clue to globalization this criterion was also met. The price of >SILVER which was a dominant commodity traded at the time, converged between the markets of Europe and Asia in the 17th century, after having been about twice as expensive in China as it had been in Europe. The insatiable demand for silver by China, supplied from America through Manila, was the engine of the intercontinental expansion of trade in the 16th century and

the trigger for the start of globalization. On the other hand, it could be argued that this convergence of the price of silver was simply a result of arbitrage and had little impact itself on the structure of the economies of the trading countries. An alternative definition of globalization is that which is based on evidence of a reduction of barriers of whatever description between intercontinental economies and the impact of this liberalization had on the allocation of resources within the trading countries themselves.

This approach to the definition of and the uncovering of the origin of the start of globalization is derived from the theory of international trade which has been developed from the Law of Comparative Cost of David >RICARDO into the Heckscher–Ohlin Principle by Eli Heckscher (1949) and Bertil Ohlin (1933) and subsequently refined by Paul Samuelson (1948). Ricardo's Law of Comparative Cost, subsequently coming to be referred to as the Law of Comparative Advantage, revealed in what way mutually beneficial trade was generated between countries depending on their relative costs of production of different commodities. Heckscher and Ohlin showed that these differences in relative costs reflected the differences in the factors of production (such as land, labour and capital) with which the various countries were endowed. Countries would export those commodities which were intensive in those factors of production in which they were relatively well endowed and import those commodities which were intensive in those factors in which they were relatively poor. Samuelson further demonstrated that as free trade tended to bring commodity prices in the countries trading into line so also it did the incomes of the factors of production used in their production. Free international trade in commodities had the same effect as the free international mobility of the factors of production such as labour and capital. Any barriers to trade would block the convergence of the prices of the commodities traded and therefore the tendency to the equalization of the incomes of the factors of production. Globalization may be defined as the progressive reduction of the barriers to international exchange whether of merchandise trade, which itself stimulates further trade and impinges indirectly on factors of production, or of the actual international transfer of factors of production directly, such as of capital and labour, leading to the tendency to convergence of the prices of the commodities traded and the incomes of the corresponding factors of production. There is a general agreement among economists that free trade and by implication the wider reach of globalization, rather than protectionism, is necessary for the optimum allocation of resources and for the achievement of maximum economic growth and consequently the maximization of economic welfare worldwide, a view persisting in the tradition of >CLASSICAL AND NEO-CLASSICAL ECONOMICS since Adam Smith (>INTERNATIONAL TRADE: >INEQUALITY).

As Heckscher pointed out:

'It must be emphasised that without the change in the proportions of the factors of production that occurs as a result of migration or population growth, differences in factor prices in various countries will persist, and the factors of production of the world as a whole will not be used to their best advantage.' (1949)

O'Rourke and Williamson (1994) explored trade over the period from 1870–1913 during which there was a major expansion of exports of grain from the >USA to >BRITAIN, as a result of which the relative price of grain fell in Britain and increased in the USA. At the time, the relative factor endowments of the two countries were mirror images of each other, Britain having a relatively plentiful supply of labour but relatively little land, whereas the USA had an abundant supply of land and little labour. In the USA wages were high and rents were low in 1870 and the reverse was true in Britain. O'Rourke and Williamson's estimates confirmed that the convergence of prices arising from the opening up of trade was a powerful influence on the narrowing of the factor price gaps between the two countries. In other words, they concluded that the predictions of the Heckscher–Ohlin theory of the relationship between trade and factor incomes could be substantiated. The reduction in through-transport costs over land as well as across the Atlantic Ocean triggered the flow of grain from North America to Europe. Some European countries raised tariff barriers but Britain kept to a free trade policy and so its economy was brought into closer contact with the USA as transport costs fell. O'Rourke and Williamson (2002) proposed that any definition of globalization should encapsulate this interrelationship between the reduction of barriers to trade, the convergence of prices and the consequential impact on the relative prices and therefore incomes of factors of production. In the context of international merchandise trade a necessary indicator of globalization was the convergence of the prices of commodities internationally. This convergence impacts on to the structure of trading economies to affect their allocation of resources and the distribution of incomes.

Given their definitional require-ments, O'Rourke and Williamson concluded that globalization did not begin until the 19th century. There was no transport revolution or price convergence of significance before the 19th century. Thereafter, mer-chandise trade increased in response to a reduction in import restrictions and reduced transport costs follow-ing the >SHIPPING and >RAILWAY revolutions and as a result there was a tendency for prices to converge.

Three periods of economic growth among the most advanced countries of the world at the time occurred after the mid-19th century. In the first period, up until World War I, not only was there a rapid growth in world merchandise trade but there were also large international move-ments in capital and labour and a technological revolution in transport (>SHIPPING: >RAILWAYS). In addi-tion, in 1866 the first trans-Atlantic cable was laid which would even-tually lead to the internet and the prime example of globalization in a particular field with its total elimina-tion of international interconnect-ing technical barriers. In this period, there was some convergence of mar-kets. In the second phase, between World War I and World War II, con-vergence stopped and even reversed as protectionism became widespread. In the third phase, after 1950, con-vergence among the advanced coun-tries resumed, together with rapid economic growth encouraged by the removal of constraints on interna-tional exchange (>INTERNATIONAL TRADE). >MIGRATION, as well as the reduction in barriers to merchandise trade, was the major engine driving the convergence of markets up to 1914 and the implication is that the con-straints which were imposed on these transfers between the two world wars effected the reversal of convergence.

Real wages in the New World were higher than in the Old World by 136 per cent in 1870 but this difference had dropped to 100 per cent in 1895 and to 87 per cent in 1910 (O'Rourke and Williamson, 1994). Migration from the Old World to the New World contributed to the narrowing of the gap between real wages between the two areas from 1870–1913. The implications of globalization are that as convergence takes place between countries the incomes of the fac-tors of production are changed and consequently the distribution of income. In the late 19th century and early 20th century, the New World exported land and other resource-intensive merchandise in exchange for labour and labour-intensive mer-chandise from the Old World. The ratio of wages to rents consequently fell in the New World and rose in the Old World.

Williamson (1996) estimated that real wages among those countries of European origin that are now in the Organization of Economic Cooperation and Development (OECD) converged at about 1 per cent per annum between 1870 and 1913 and somewhat faster at 1.2 per cent per annum in earlier years of the period from 1870–90. In Europe, a number of countries drove the over-all rate of convergence. Between 1870 and 1900, real wages in Denmark rose from 54 per cent to 85 per cent of those in >BRITAIN; in Ireland from 73 per cent to 89 per cent: in Sweden from 42 per cent to 82 per cent; in Norway from 42 per cent to 65 per cent. On the other hand, in Portugal real wages fell from 48 per cent of those in Britain to 42 per cent and in Spain from 76 per cent to 48 per cent. Williamson concluded that countries, such as Spain and Portugal, that had imposed high barriers to trade by their protectionist policies were likely to fail to converge. In general, the different rates of convergence could be attributed to the extent to which particular countries embraced globalization (O'Rourke and Williamson, 1997).

In addition to trade, the migrations of the 19th century also contributed to convergence, possibly by as much as 70 per cent of the convergence in real wages seen between 1870 and 1910, between the Old World and the New. It has been estimated that without migration the wage gap between the USA and Britain would have doubled between 1870 and 1913 instead of falling by 20 per cent. Similarly, two-thirds of the reduction in the real wage gap between Ireland and Britain was a result of emigration between 1851 and 1911. These developments would have had an influence on income distributions. Emigrants were predominantly unskilled. Accordingly, the relative price of unskilled labour would have risen in the source countries following emigration and fallen in the receiving countries. In the source countries, therefore, the incomes of skilled workers would have fallen relatively to those of the unskilled. The reverse would have been true in the receiving countries such as the USA.

Evidence suggests that commodity price convergence and relative factor price convergence in the period between 1870 and 1940 was particularly strong in the less developed countries on the periphery of those of the advanced Atlantic group. The transport revolutions in shipping and railways and the opening of the Suez and Panama canals had as major an effect on the trade routes of the Third World countries as they had on those across the Atlantic. For instance, the tramp charter shipping rate for rice from Rangoon to Europe fell 74 per cent to 18 per cent of the price of rice

in Rangoon between 1882 and 1914 and the freight rate for coal between Nagasaki and Shanghai fell by 76 per cent between 1880 and 1910. This fall in transport costs was coupled with the removal of trade restrictions. Japan emerged from isolation and opened up its markets from 1858, with the consequence that its international trade rose to 7 per cent of national income from zero. In 1842, >CHINA opened its ports following a treaty with Britain with a limit of 5 per cent placed on import tariffs. Siam (Thailand), Korea, India and Indonesia also all became and stayed liberal in regard to their trade policy. There was, therefore, in these countries no movement in the late 19th century or early 20th century towards protectionism as there was in Europe and North America, which could have offset the effects of the lowering of transport costs in these Third World countries. As between the North Atlantic economies so in the Third World periphery, commodity prices converged. Evidence suggests that this convergence led to the predicted movements in relative factor prices. Land-poor countries such as Japan, Korea and Taiwan experienced an increase in their ratio of wages to rent, whereas in countries which were relatively well endowed in land, such as the southern cone of South America, wage rental ratios fell. These movements to convergence were in relative factor price ratios. Growth in real incomes in absolute terms in these Third World countries, nevertheless, fell considerably behind the growth in real incomes in the more advanced countries in the period (Williamson, 2002).

In the second half of the 20th century, globalization, after being stagnant or even receding between the two world wars, accelerated, encouraged by the further lowering of transport costs stimulated by technical change (>SHIPPING), the lifting of restrictions on international capital flows, the liberalization of trade through several rounds of tariff reductions negotiated through GATT and later the World Trade Organization (>INTERNATIONAL TRADE) and the development of information technology. The period was noted for the rapid growth of countries in East Asia such as Malaya, South Korea and Taiwan initially and later of China and India (>ASIAN MIRACLE: >ECONOMIC DEVELOPMENT). The countries of Asia narrowed the gap between their GDP per head and that of the advanced countries of the Organization of Economic Cooperation and Development. China and India also opened up their economies from the end of the 1970s with spectacular results. Between 1980 and 2000 China grew by 10 per cent per annum and India by 6 per cent per annum. Considerable progress was accordingly made in the second half of the 20th century towards the reduction of >POVERTY through economic growth, particularly in the countries of Asia. The average incidence of poverty has been estimated in >INDIA to have fallen by 0.7 per cent per annum between 1957 and 1992, in >CHINA by 1.6 per cent per annum and in South East Asia by 1.4 per cent per annum. By contrast, the lack of economic growth in Sub-Saharan Africa in the second half of the 20th century was accompanied by increasing poverty in the region. In 1960, 11 per cent of the world's poor lived in Africa but in 1998, 66 per cent did so (>POVERTY).

There is clear evidence that those countries which in the past have opened up their economies to globalization have achieved faster economic growth than those countries which have remained closed. Nevertheless, it is also clear that globalization either indirectly through trade or directly through the actual migration of people or capital causes shifts in the allocation of resources in response to new patterns of supply and demand and therefore induces changes in the distribution of incomes (>INEQUALITY). Therefore, while it may be argued that globalization raises a country's real incomes in total, nevertheless, there are in the short-run losers as well as gainers. However, there is no need to throw the baby out with the bath water. There are economic benefits from globalization which should be more than sufficient for the gainers to compensate the losers and still remain better off. Nevertheless, the voices raised against globalization became more vociferous in the late 20th century. Many argued that globalization caused the corruption of indigenous national cultures by the incursion and spread of foreign mores, led to the exploitation of the weak and even the loss of sovereignty because decisions affecting one economy were made in others. Globalization, it was also argued, bred uncertainty and made the world more unstable because of the ease and rapidity with which enormous amounts of liquid capital were free to shift from one centre to another.

Many objections and anxieties were swept into the term globalization which did not belong there because the perceived losses either were unfounded because, for instance, they could be adjusted or prevented by government aid or action or because they were the result of other forces, such as technical change (Bhagwati, 2004). Technical change has played the central role in the growth of globalization from the shipping and railway and telecommunication innovations of the

19th century, through to the further innovations in transport, logistics, information technology and the repercussions of the internet in the 20th century. It could be argued, therefore, that globalization at the end of the 20th century was the continuing fall-out from the big bang of the >INDUSTRIAL REVOLUTION IN BRITAIN in the 18th century. Everyone was then taken by surprise, as Carlo M. Cipolla put it in *The Fontana Economic History of Europe*.

It is not globalization as such that makes people nervous, it is what the industrial revolution continues to spawn.

### References

Bhagwati, Jagdish, *In Defense of Globalization*, Oxford University Press, 2004.

Bordo, Michael D., Taylor, Alan M. and Williamson, Jeffrey G. (eds), *Globalisation in Historical Perspective*, University of Chicago Press, 2005.

Carlo M. Cipolla (ed.), *The Fontana Economic History of Europe*, Fontana, 1973.

Flynn, Dennis O. and Giraldez, Arturo, 'Path Dependence, Time Lags and the Birth of Globalisation: A Critique of O'Rourke and Williamson', *European Review of Economic History*, April, 2004.

Heckscher, Eli F., 'The Influence of Foreign Trade on the Distribution of Income', *Ekonomisk Tidskrift* (1919), reprinted in *Readings in the Theory of International Trade*, American Economic Association, 1949.

Ohlin, Bertil, *Interregional Trade and International Trade*, Cambridge University Press, 1933.

O'Rourke, Kevin H. and Williamson, Jeffrey G., 'Late Nineteenth-Century Anglo-American Factor-Price Convergence: Were Heckscher and Ohlin Right?', *Journal of Economic History*, December, 1994.

O'Rourke, Kevin H. and Williamson, Jeffrey G., 'Around the European Periphery 1870–1913: Globalisation, Schooling and Growth', *European Review of Economic History*, 1(2), August, 1997.

O'Rourke, Kevin H. and Williamson, Jeffrey G., 'When did Globalisation Begin?', *European Review of Economic History*, 6(I), April, 2002.

Samuelson, Paul A., 'International Trade and the Equalisation of Factor Prices', *Economic Journal*, LVIII, June, 1948.

Smith, Adam, *An Inquiry into the Nature and Causes of the Wealth of Nations* (1776), Book IV, Chapter VII, Part III, Ward Lock, 1812.

Taylor, Alan M. and Williamson, Jeffrey G., 'Convergence in the Age of Mass Migration', *European Review of Economic History*, 1(I) April, 1997.

Williamson, Jeffrey G., 'Globalisation, Convergence, and History', *Journal of Economic History*, 56(2), June, 1996.

Williamson, Jeffrey G., 'Land, Labour, and Globalisation in the Third World, 1870–1940', *Journal of Economic History*, 62(1), March, 2002.

# Gold

Herodotus in his *Histories* records that Croesus let Alcamaeon have as much gold as he could carry on his own and he loaded himself up so much that he could hardly stagger along under its weight. Croesus was so amused by the sight that he doubled the quantity. That, said Herodotus, was how the family of Alcamaeon got wealthy and could run a four-horse chariot.

Croesus, the last king of Lydia, reigned from 560 BC to 546 BC. Lydia was a country whose capital, Sardis, was near to the present-day Izmir in Turkey. It had the good fortune of having a rich source of alluvial gold and electrum (a natural alloy of gold and silver) washed down into the Pactolus River, which ran through the country. Lydia has been credited with the earliest minting of official coinage in about 700 BC, using electrum, although gold bars were used in Egypt in 4000 BC. Croesus, as well as gold, also used silver for coinage for low values with a silver to gold ratio of 10.1 parts of silver to 1 part of gold (Bernstein, 2000) (>BI-METALLISM: >SILVER).

Gold, of all minerals, has peculiarly attractive characteristics. It has a fine, colourful lustre. It is virtually indestructible so that all gold that has ever been recovered, estimated by the World Gold Council to be about 125,000 tonnes, still exists somewhere, on land or at the bottom of the sea. It is malleable and may be easily worked into intricate design. Moreover, it is scarce but not too scarce and is spread, albeit irregularly, throughout the world. It may be relatively easily recovered from alluvial, placer, deposits flushed downstream and extracted by panning or it may require considerable investment to mine it from reefs which may lay, as in >SOUTH AFRICA, over 3 km deep. The passion and excitement that stimulated the overjoyed Alcamaeon echoes throughout its history down to the lust for it which drove men in the rush to get to the gold finds of the 19th century, in spite of the hardship they had to endure. The Lydian coinage too may trace its successors throughout history to the gold lodged in the exchange reserves of the central banks (>CENTRAL BANKING) and the International Monetary Fund in the 21st century. Gold's qualities were summed up on the edge of the gold guinea introduced in >BRITAIN in 1664, around which was engraved 'Decus et Tutamen' (Adornment and Security); rightly or wrongly the summation of the sources of gold's reputation reflected in the dual role of gold as a monetary means of exchange and store of value on the one hand and as a decorative commodity on the other. Gold, however, never had it completely all its own way but had to meet with the fluctuating contending advantages of >SILVER, in its monetary uses at least, until the wide acceptance of the >GOLD STANDARD in the 19th and 20th centuries.

Until the Roman Empire, the supply of gold was sufficient to meet the financial needs of the states which succeeded each other in the hegemony of Asia Minor, Europe and the Mediterranean but then there began to be a deficiency which the Romans could not meet by production and which led to the debasement of the coinage. There was a long period of inflation which Diocletian set about correcting by both reforming the currency, which he completed in 301, and by imposing maximum prices on agricultural and industrial goods. In 312, Constantine began a further reform of the coinage which included the issue of a new gold coin called the *solidus* which survived for centuries, as the *bezant,* as an internationally acceptable medium of exchange. With the decline of the Byzantine Empire, gold coinage of various kinds fluctuated in popularity with the rise and fall of the nations striking them. By the 13th century, European sources of gold were again insufficient and reliance had to be placed on trade; a major source was developed by these means from the Gold Coast of West Africa (>SOUTH AFRICA). However, by the 15th century there was a severe lack of monetary gold and a consequential fall in prices (>PRICES AND INFLATION).

In the 15th century began the exploration, discovery, plunder and mining of the precious metals of South America with a consequential unprecedented increase in the amount of gold and silver in Europe. There was a long period of persistent inflation beginning in the last quarter of the 15th century and lasting until the mid-17th century. This was not caused solely by the inward flood of gold (and silver), the arrival of which did not exactly coincide with the period of inflation. The influx of gold from Brazil, for instance, did not reach Portugal until the 18th century. Other influences were the debasement of coinage both by governments and individuals, by clipping and the speed with which gold was spent to finance the wars, which themselves disrupted production and markets. It was from this period, however, that the first thoughts were articulated on the relationship between money and prices by Jean Bodin in his *Les Six Livres de la Republique* in 1576, which were eventually developed into the quantity theory of money of >CLASSICAL AND NEO-CLASSICAL ECONOMICS (>FRIEDMAN).

In 1664, Britain issued a new gold coin, called the *guinea*, which was one of the first coins to be struck by machine and which was to have a milled or lettered edge to prevent clipping. Britain completed a major re-coinage in 1696 and technically was on a bimetallic standard of gold and silver (>BIMETALLIC SYSTEM). However, the silver/gold ratio was set higher than that in France and silver tended to leave circulation. In 1717, the price of the gold guinea was fixed at 21 shillings of silver and the price of gold was at £3.17s.10½d (£3.89375) per ounce and Britain was effectively on a gold standard rather than a silver or bimetallic standard. In 1817, the gold sovereign was issued at a value of £1 or 20 shillings and the guinea was withdrawn. Convertibility into gold at the Bank of England was suspended during the Napoleonic War but fully restored in 1821 and Britain remained on the >GOLD STANDARD until it was suspended again in

>WORLD WAR I, to be briefly restored between 1925 and 1931.

During the 16th century and into the 18th century, the extraordinary influx of precious metals into Europe and the perceived benefits this influx appeared to bestow on the recipients led to much discussion at the time about the appropriate policies for governments to pursue. The central axiom of the mercantilist philosophy, which these ideas came to be called, was that the accumulation of gold and silver was essential for a state to have power and international influence. A strong state was that which had a well-stocked treasury. Governments, therefore, were advised to prohibit the export of bullion or promote a surplus on the balance of trade. If exports of commodities exceeded imports of commodities, it would follow that there would be a net inflow of gold and silver to pay for the excess and the stock of money in the economy would rise (>MERCANTILISM). These views were severely criticized by Adam >SMITH.

Among the Classical economists there was an assumption that there was feedback at least in the long run between gold production and the price level. Inflation lowered the real price of gold and raised production costs which led to a drop in production. This fall in the supply of monetary gold (and silver) in turn exerted a downward pressure on inflation.

By these means the flow of gold into the world monetary system was regulated. The same influence on the price levels of individual states of the flow of gold between them was at the heart of the Gold Standard of the 19th and early 20th centuries. The exploitation of the gold discoveries of the 19th century, however, launched an unprecedented volume of gold on to world markets which had relatively little to do with the gold price as such but more to do with the economic development at their locations and the existence of the infrastructure there, which enabled the necessary resources to be assembled. There was, therefore, a divergence of views about the extent to which gold was or was not price elastic, although the majority of the US Gold Commission reporting in 1982 believed it was price elastic:

'Under the gold standard, a rise in the purchasing power of gold ultimately increased the rate of growth of the US monetary gold stock by raising the rate of world gold output and inducing a shift from non-monetary use to monetary use of gold. Movements in the purchasing power of gold thus preceded long-term movements in the monetary gold stock.' (US Gold Commission, quoted in Eichengreen and McLean, 1994)

At the beginning of the 19th century, world gold output was running at an average of about 15 tonnes per year during which time Brazil, Colombia and >RUSSIA were the major producers. Gold had been known to exist in the Urals as far back as the age of Croesus but the deposits were not seriously exploited there or in Siberia until the early 19th century. Russian output from the Urals reached 5 tonnes per year in 1830 and, in Siberia, 11 tonnes per year by 1842. As a result of these developments, Russia accounted for about 60 per cent of world output of gold in the 1840s. (Bernstein, 2000; Eichengreen and McLean, 1994). In January 1848, gold was discovered in California on the American River, at a sawmill being constructed for J. A. Sutter; the first of the major gold rushes of the 19th century began and gold production reached unprecedented heights. Before that time,

during the whole of the long history of gold production, it has been estimated that a total of 10,000 tonnes had been extracted. Since that time, production has reached over 112,000 tonnes, 90 per cent of the 125,000 tonnes ever produced (World Gold Council).

By the end of 1848, there were 10,000 men at the find in California but the news was spread quickly through the media and by the end of 1849, a further 81,000 people arrived in California, of whom 42,000 came across the prairie and the rest by sea to the little port of San Francisco, some by tran-shipment across Panama and others around Cape Horn, mainly from the US East Coast but as many as 16,000 from Europe. In the following year, the inflow grew even more when 36,000 people arrived by sea and 55,000 overland (Morrell, 1968). Gold output in California expanded rapidly and reached a peak of about 93 tonnes in 1853; the >USA became the world's leading gold producer, accounting for about 46 per cent of the average annual world production of about 181 tons in the 1850s, replacing Russia, whose share dropped to 14 per cent (Eichengreen and McLean, 1994). In 1896, gold was discovered in Alaska at the Throndiuck or Klondike River, a tributary of the Yukon, generating another gold rush. Between 1899 and 1901 output had reached a peak. In the decade and a half before World War I, the average annual output of gold in the USA had reached about 132 tonnes, almost 60 per cent higher than in the 1850s, but the USA had lost it pre-eminent position to South Africa.

In 1851, gold was discovered in Australia, in a tributary of the Macquarie River in New South Wales and at Ballarat and Bendigo in Victoria, followed by other finds. By 1852, the rush to these finds had reached Europe and the influx reached about 15,000 people a month (Morrell, 1968), with most coming from Britain. By 1861, the population of Victoria had risen to 540,000 of whom about 110,000 were miners. In the 1860s, the average production of gold per year in Australia reached about 62 tonnes, Australia being second to the USA as a major producer with 36 per cent of the world total. In 1893, gold was also discovered at Kalgoorlie in Western Australia. Output in Australia reached a peak in 1903 of 119 tonnes.

The development of the diamond mines of Kimberley in South Africa in the 1880s greatly assisted the search for gold with a number of finds leading to the discoveries of the Witwatersrand in the Transvaal in 1886. The Rand, however, was totally different from the alluvial deposits which could be relatively easily worked by individual miners. Gold lay in reefs of low-grade ore up to 3 km deep which could only be exploited by machinery and companies with the capital required for the necessary investment. A new process called 'cyanidation' was invented that sufficiently lowered the costs of extracting the gold from the ore as to make exploitation economic. Gold production rose to 14 tonnes in 1889 and to 120 tonnes in 1898, when output was disrupted by the Boer War. Between 1890 and 1899, the average annual gold output in South Africa was 62 tonnes, and 171 tonnes in the following decade, propelling South Africa to the top of the table with 33 per cent of world output. South Africa continued as the world's top producer with on average about 40 per cent of the world total with a peak year in 1970 of over 1,000 tonnes, three-quarters of the world total (World Gold Council).

The extraordinary tonnage of gold produced from these discoveries enabled the monetary system of the >GOLD STANDARD to spread from Britain throughout the international community and to be maintained through the 19th century until its collapse in the 1930s. The demise of the gold standard was not, however, the end of the role of gold as an international medium of exchange. At the international conference held at Bretton Woods in New Hampshire, USA, in 1944, which led to the setting up of the International Monetary Fund and the World Bank, a system of exchange rates was agreed which set rates fixed to the dollar but the dollar itself was tied to gold at a fixed price of $35 per ounce a price which was raised to $38 by the Smithsonian Agreement in 1971. However, in 1973, the USA abandoned the dollar link to gold, and international exchange rates were left to float freely, opening a period in which, for the only time in history, currencies had not been linked in some way to gold. In spite of these developments, gold retained its unique place in the world's monetary system. Gold remained an important asset in the official reserves of central banks (>CENTRAL BANKING) and in the International Monetary Fund's holdings in which it amounted to 3,217 tonnes in 2007.

Throughout its history, gold has been the sanctuary to which people have fled in times of trouble. In the international tumult of the 1970s occasioned by the dramatic increase in three years of the price of a barrel of >OIL from $1.8 to $11.65, which lowered economic growth and generated an inflation of prices in double digits in some countries, the demand for gold caused its price to rise from $110 to $850 an ounce in three weeks at the beginning of 1980 to fall again to $300 in 1981. A new peak was reached in March 2008 at a price of $1,030 an ounce, again in a time of uncertainty following sub-prime mortgage crisis in the >USA in 2007.

## References

Bernstein, Peter L., *The Power of Gold: The History of an Obsession*, John Wiley, 2000.

Eichengreen, Barry and McLean, Ian W., 'The Supply of Gold under the pre-1914 Gold Standard', *Economic History Review*, XLVII(2), 1994.

Gold Commission, *Report to the Congress of the Commission of the Role of Gold in the Domestic and International Monetary Systems*, 1982.

International Monetary Fund, 'Gold in the IMF', Factsheet, April, 2007.

Morrell, W. P., *The Gold Rushes*, Adam and Charles Black, 1968.

Mundell, Robert A., 'The International Monetary System in the 21st Century: Could Gold Make a Comeback?', St Vincent College, Letrobe, Pennsylvania, 1997.

World Gold Council, www.gold.org

# Gold Standard

A domestic or international monetary system in which the values of the currencies in circulation are fixed in terms of a specified weight of >GOLD. The >CENTRAL BANK of a country on the gold standard must be ready to exchange its currency for gold on demand at the specified rate. In addition to bank notes, gold coins also form part of the currency without any legal hindrance to their being convertible into gold bullion and both gold coins and bullion may be freely imported and exported. The quantity of money in the economy is determined by the country's stock of gold (>MONEY AND BANKING)

The gold standard was first established in >BRITAIN and then spread internationally during the 19th century. Britain had suspended the convertibility of the currency into gold during the Napoleonic War and the beginning of the setting up of a full gold standard may be put at the passing of the Coinage Act after the war in 1816. The sovereign, with a face value of £1, was issued in 1817, with its gold content valued at the rate of £3.17s.10½d (£3.89375) per ounce. This was the gold price that prevailed in the previous century. Restrictions were lifted on international trading in gold bullion and on the conversion of coin into bullion in 1819 and the Bank of England was enabled to restore the convertibility of bank notes into gold at the prevailing market price in 1821. By that year, the transformation to a full gold standard had been completed by Britain.

It was some time before other countries followed the example of Britain. The Latin Monetary Union of Belgium, France, Italy and Switzerland had a >BIMETALLIC SYSTEM of gold and silver, as did the >USA. Germany, Latin America and countries in Asia were based on silver. There has been debate as to whether the bimetallic system had an inherent weakness because of the difficulty of holding a fixed rate of exchange between the two metals and this encouraged a move to the gold standard. (Flandreau, 1996). For instance, in the USA, the Coinage Act of 1792 had set the exchange at 15 ounces of silver to be equal to 1 ounce of gold but the market price of silver fell. As a result, gold coins went out of circulation because more silver coins could be purchased with the gold content of gold coins than could be at their face value. Another Coinage Act in 1834 altered the exchange rate to 16 ounces of silver to 1 ounce of gold. However, by the middle of the century, the opening up of new gold fields had depressed the price of gold to the point at which silver went out of circulation. The convertibility of bank notes was restored in the USA in 1879, after lapsing during the Civil War (>AMERICAN CIVIL WAR), and the USA finally went, officially, on the gold standard by the Gold Standard Act of 1900.

The decline of the bimetallic and silver-based monetary system was encouraged in favour of gold by the recommendation of a European Conference in Paris in 1867. In 1872, Germany replaced the silver thaler with the gold mark. The Latin Monetary Union stopped minting silver coins in 1878. By 1880, Belgium, Denmark, France, Italy, the Netherlands, Norway, Sweden, Switzerland and, in effect, the USA had joined Britain on the gold standard. These countries were followed after 1890 by Argentina, Austria/Hungary, Ceylon, Japan, Mexico, Peru, >RUSSIA, Siam and Uruguay. >INDIA and the Philippines opted for a gold exchange standard by which they linked their currencies not to gold directly but to sterling and the US dollar respectively. Some other countries, such as El Salvador, >CHINA and Honduras, stayed on a silver standard. The gold standard, therefore, was operated by a wide geographical spread of both advanced and developing countries from about 1880 until 1914, the outbreak of >WORLD WAR I.

The Classical view (>CLASSICAL AND NEO-CLASSICAL ECONOMICS) of the gold standard was that it was an automatic mechanism that continuously adjusted the quantity and flows of international money to maintain a path of stable equilibrium in international exchange rates and prices. If prices rose, say, in Britain, British exports to, say, the USA, fell and imports from the USA rose. The British balance of payments with the USA worsened and sterling depreciated against the dollar. Both sterling and the dollar were, however, under the gold standard, convertible into a fixed quantity of gold. If sterling fell relative to the dollar by an amount greater than the cost of transporting gold across the Atlantic, it would pay traders to convert sterling into gold in Britain and ship it to the USA and buy dollars with it there. This outflow of gold from Britain lowered the stock of gold backing for the domestic currency and forced a reduction in the quantity in circulation. This reduction in the quantity of money reduced domestic prices, thereby reversing the initial rise.

This view of the operation of the gold standard is very questionable in terms of how the gold standard worked in practice but also whether it was responsible for achieving the stability in prices claimed for it. There has been debate as to whether prices and incomes were more stable during the period of operation of the international gold standard, although there did seem to have been fewer balance of payments crises and major exchange rate adjustments, at least among the developed countries (Eichengreen, 1985; Eichengreen and McLean, 1994).

The gold standard was not left by the central banks to operate automatically. The rate of interest was often altered for policy reasons, sometimes contrary to the direction required for balance of payments equilibrium. Moreover, it would be wrong to suppose that the rules by which the gold standard was applied did not differ significantly between countries. For instance, in Germany, Britain and the USA, the central banks were obliged to convert bank notes into gold on demand, whereas in Belgium, France and Switzerland, they were not. In Finland, Japan, Norway, Russia and

Britain, a part of the bank note issue, called the fiduciary issue, was exempt from gold backing, and, therefore, could be increased without a corresponding increase on the stock of gold. On the other hand, in, for instance, Belgium, the Netherlands and Switzerland the whole of the bank note issue was controlled by a given ratio to the stock of gold. Prices were not as flexible as the Classical theory implied. Prices and wages rose more easily than they fell. Finally, the theory is a theory of visible trade and overlooks the major part played during the period by international capital flows.

The efficiency of the gold standard must be considered in the context of the period during which it was most fully in operation, that is, the 30 years or so before World War I. The most outstanding feature of that period was the dominance of Britain in international trade and of London in international finance. Britain had a persistent surplus on the current account of the balance of payments. Although there was an increasing deficit on visible trade, this was more than offset by a surplus on invisibles. Sterling was the leading currency for the settlement of international debts. Because of confidence in the stability of sterling, there were no destabilizing short-term financial flows across the exchanges, gambling on exchange rate movements. This confidence in sterling held firm during the period in spite of the fact that the total money supply in Britain expanded without any commensurate increase in the stock of gold; bank notes and bank deposits accounted for 90 per cent of the increase in the money supply.

The surplus on the British balance of payments was a major source of considerable flows of investment capital in overseas markets.

Often, developing countries such as Australia, Latin America, Canada and the USA had persistent balance of payments deficits on current account but these were financed by inward flows of capital from Britain and other countries of Europe and these flows helped to achieve a general stability in exchange rates. However, it has been argued that this stability did not extend to the poor countries because in time of recession and a fall in the demand for the exports of the developed countries, investment capital was withdrawn which exacerbated the balance of payments problems of the less developed countries in a recession. At least for the more advanced countries, the gold standard appears to have been, for the stability of exchange rates and balance of payments equilibrium, an important influence but in the context of the rapid economic growth of the time and unwavering confidence in sterling, which was rooted in the predominance of Britain as a trading nation (Bayoumi et al., 1996). The gold standard was suspended during the World War I (1914–18). After the war, Britain lost its dominant world role and sterling its central part in international finance.

The USA returned to gold in 1919, Germany in 1924 and Britain in 1925. Eventually, about 50 countries returned to a gold standard of some kind. There was, however, a shortage of gold; a conference in Geneva in 1922 recommended a gold exchange standard in order to ameliorate this shortage. By a law of 1928, the Bank of France was required to accept only gold in payment of debts, a policy which put an added strain on the international system by further exaggerating the unequal distribution of the available gold which already existed. Eventually, the USA and France together held 60 per cent of the world gold stock.

In 1931, the Credit-Anstalt Bank of Vienna (>GREAT DEPRESSION) became insolvent and the consequent loss of confidence led to a run on the German mark and a rise in interest rates. Short-term capital left Britain in spite of an increase in bank rate there and central banks, losing confidence in the currency, switched out of sterling into gold, forcing Britain off the gold standard. By the end of the following year, 32 countries had left the gold standard, leaving only Belgium, France, the Netherlands, Switzerland and the USA. In 1933, the USA abolished gold convertibility, marking the effective end of the international gold standard system.

The failure of the international gold standard during the period between the first and the second world wars was only partly due to the shortage of gold and its poor distribution. There was growing reliance on a mix of foreign currencies in international reserves. Speculative short-term capital flows between countries had a destabilizing effect on balance of payments and exchange rates. The very existence of the gold exchange system played a part in generating these movements in so far as for a country to be seen to be possibly forced to abandon gold led to a flight of capital from it. Countries on the gold standard were seen to be more credit-worthy (Bordo and Rockoff, 1996). It may be also that governments after World War I gave higher priority to policies for the regulation of domestic incomes and prices, compared to the achieving of balance of payments stability, which had been more their concern in the earlier period (>BIMETALLIC SYSTEM).

## References

Bayoumi, T., Eichengreen, B. and Taylor M. P. (eds), *Modern Perspectives on the Gold Standard*, Cambridge University Press, 1996.

Bordo, Michael D. and Rockoff, Hugh, 'The Gold Standard as a "Good Housekeeping Seal of Approval"', *Journal of Economic History*, 56(2), 1996.

Eichengreen, Barry (ed.), *The Gold Standard in Theory and History*, Methuen 1985.

Eichengreen, Barry, *Golden Fetters: The Gold Standard and the Great Depression, 1919–1939*, Oxford University Press, 1992.

Eichengreen, Barry and McLean, Ian W., 'The Supply of Gold under the pre-1914 Gold Standard', *Economic History Review*, XLVII(2), 1994.

Ferderer, Peter J. and Zalewski, David A., 'To Raise the Golden Anchor? Financial Crises and Uncertainty During the Great Depression', *Journal of Economic History*, 59(3), 1999.

Flandeau, Marc, 'The French Crime of 1873: An Essay on the Emergence of the International Gold Standard, 1870–1880', *Journal of Economic History*, 56(4), 1996.

# Grain

European grain prices began to rise in the middle of the 18th century, after a period of decline, and increased by two or three times in particular years towards the end of the century and remained high until the end of the Napoleonic War in 1815. This resulted in a significant drop in the real incomes of the poor. After the end of the war, prices fell and measures of trade protection were introduced in an attempt to maintain domestic prices. Protection in Europe was eased by different countries at different times from the mid-19th century until the early 1870s (>INTERNATIONAL TRADE). In >BRITAIN output of grain increased by over 100 per cent between 1750 and 1850 (Floud and McCloskey,

1994), an increase achieved through increases in factor productivity (>AGRICULTURE).

With the development of the >RAILWAYS, intra-continental freight rates fell, re-enforcing the unification of the European grain market reflected in the narrowing of price differentials between the different countries. But it was not until the second half of the 19th century that the development of the steamship began to bring down the high cost of intercontinental transport and so gave the newly exploited extensive farmlands of North America competitive access to the European markets (> SHIPPING). The production of wheat in the >USA, which accounted for 9 per cent of world production in 1850, reached about 20 per cent by the end of the century.

In 1870, wheat prices were about 60 per cent higher in Liverpool than in Chicago and 20 per cent higher than in New York, reflecting the premium required to cover both the domestic rail freight costs and the trans-Atlantic shipping costs (Foreman-Peck, 1995). Between 1869/71 and 1890/2 freight rates between Chicago and New York fell by about 55 per cent and the shipping freight rate from New York and Liverpool by a similar amount. North America was able to realize the potential of its abundant supply of good agricultural land with which it was relatively well endowed compared with Europe (>GLOBALIZATION). The result was the transformation of the European market, which was no longer insulated from the availability of cheap grain from North America, and individual countries reacted in different ways, broadly related to the stage they had reached in economic development and the structure of their domestic agricultural markets. Britain and Denmark maintained free trade. France and Germany reintroduced protection and this restrained the effect on prices in their domestic markets. Between 1870/1874 and 1909/1913, the price of wheat in real terms declined in Britain by 35 per cent compared with 22 per cent in France; the price of barley in Britain fell by 25 per cent, in France by 13 per cent and in Germany by 8 per cent (O'Rourke, 1997). In Britain, because of its relatively small proportion of the labour force employed in agriculture, the negative effect of the reduction in rents and farmers' incomes was offset by the improvement in the general increase in real income.

There was an unprecedented increase in the world output of grain. Wheat production, for instance, during the period 1909/14 was over 100 per cent more than the average in 1871/80. Accordingly, the world price of wheat fell by 50 per cent between 1871/1880 and 1889/99 and was still below the 1871/1880 price level in 1909/1914. In Britain, Denmark, the Netherlands, Germany and Italy, there was a consequential shift to dairy products and meat (Pollard, 1994).The geographical distribution of international trade also changed substantially. Britain became the world's largest importer of wheat. >RUSSIA, the traditional supplier of grain to the European market, temporarily lost share to North America. By 1909/13, however, Russia was the main world exporter of wheat, accounting for 24 per cent of the total, followed by the USA at 15 per cent and Argentina at 14 per cent, slightly more than Canada (Yates, 1959).

In the post->WORLD WAR I period during the 1920s there was a number of agricultural crises in Russia, culminating in a very serious >FAMINE in 1921/2. Grain exports fell to about

25 per cent of their pre-war level. Production of grain recovered subsequently so that by 1928 it had been restored to the pre-war level. This achievement was reversed, however, by the collectivization of farms by the state, which led to a further collapse in the harvest and famine in 1932/3 (>RUSSIA). This was against a background of a general world overhang of excess grain production. The increase in production occasioned by the extension of the area under cultivation and improvement in yields was faced with a weakening in the demand for cereals in favour of other foodstuffs as incomes increased worldwide. This led to grain prices dropping faster than those of manufactures. The US government passed the Smoot-Hawley Act in 1931 to protect farm income by raising import tariffs to very restrictive levels (>GREAT DEPRESSION). Attempts were made, unsuccessfully, to limit price fluctuations by commodity control schemes. A scheme for wheat established in 1933 tried to control prices through quantitative restrictions on production but failed (>AGRICULTURE).

The devastations of >WORLD WAR II led to a severe drop in agricultural production in Europe and Asia. It was not until the 1950s that grain production reached the levels of 1934/8 in these regions. In North America, cereal production after the war was a third higher than in the late 1930s and exports increased accordingly to meet the import needs of Europe and Asia. In 1953/4, Canada was the major exporter of wheat, accounting for a third of the world total, followed by the USA with 28 per cent, Argentina with 11 per cent and Australia with about 10 per cent. In the post-war period, international commodity agreements were again considered as a means for dampening the volatility of prices but without success.

With economic recovery in Europe and the establishment of the European Common Market of the six countries of Belgium, France, Germany, Italy, Luxembourg and the Netherlands (subsequently becoming the European Union and expanding to 27 member states by 2008), the international trade in grain, as in other agricultural products, was transformed. The EEC (EU) set up the Common Agricultural Policy (CAP) which was designed to establish self-sufficiency in agricultural through the protection of its farmers from international competition by a system of price support and export subsidies. The European Union was not alone in this, the USA and Japan being also heavily protectionist with regard to agriculture. According to the Food and Agricultural Organization (FAO), the share of world exports of wheat originating in North America fell from about 70 per cent in the early 1960s down to 40 per cent by 2000. By comparison, exports of wheat from France rose from about 3 per cent to 15 per cent. The granting of export subsidies by the developed countries and the improvements in agricultural productivity in grain production in those countries made grain relatively cheap on export markets. As a result, the surplus grain production of North America and Europe arrived at the ports of the developing countries at a price against which they could not compete. As an example of this, according to the FAO, the share of imports of wheat into the developing countries of Africa rose from 6 per cent of the world total in 1970 to 20 per cent in 2000 (>RICE).

## References

Bairoch, Paul, *Economics and World History*, Harvester Wheatsheaf, 1993.

Davies, R. W., Harrison, Mark and Wheatcroft, S. G. (eds), *The Economic*

*Transformation of the Soviet Union, 1913–1945,* Cambridge University Press, 1994.

Floud, Roderick and McCloskey, Donald, *The Economic History of Britain Since 1700,* Cambridge University Press (2nd edn), 1994.

Foreman-Peck, James, *A History of the World Economy,* Harvester Wheatsheaf, 1995.

O'Rourke, Kevin H., 'The European Grain Invasion, 1870–1913', *Journal of Economic History,* 57, December, 1997.

Pollard, Sydney, *Peaceful Conquest: Industrialisation of Europe, 1760–1970,* Oxford University Press, 1994.

Yates, P. Lamartine, *Forty Years of Foreign Trade,* George Allen & Unwin, 1959.

# Great Depression

There had been a previous period which was referred to as the 'Great Depression' which lasted for several years from 1873 (>BUSINESS CYCLES) but this title has since been inherited by the period between >WORLD WAR I and >WORLD WAR II. During this time there was a deep and rapid collapse in national and international economic activity which had had no precedence in history and which in good fortune has not since been approached in such severity. There were serious declines in output, prices, investment, profits and >INTERNATIONAL TRADE and there was a failure of financial institutions. A consequence was the loss of employment and hardship for many millions of workers. The >USA and Germany, of the major industrialized nations, were the most affected. For instance, between 1930 and 1938 the average industrial unemployment rate in the USA was 26 per cent, (compared with 8 per cent between 1921 and 1929), in Germany 22 per cent (compared with 9 per cent),

15 per cent in >BRITAIN (compared with 12 per cent) and 10 per cent in France (compared with 4 per cent) (Temin, 1991). The US Department of Commerce has estimated that the real GNP of the USA reached a low in 1933 which was 30 per cent below that of 1929 and it did not reach the 1929 level again until 1939 (Vernon, 1994). A remarkable feature of the Depression in the USA was the rapidity of the collapse. Industrial production fell by 22 per cent in the six months from June to December in 1929. Car production, which was at 660,000 units in March, fell to only 92,500 units in December 1929 (Kindleberger, 1996). Between 1929 and 1931, wholesale prices in Britain fell by 28 per cent, in France by 24 per cent, Germany by 17 per cent and in the USA by 24 per cent (League of Nations, quoted in Clavin, 2000). Between 1929 and 1932 world exports fell by about 27 per cent in real terms (and as much as 43 per cent in current prices) (Maddison, 1995). World trade did not regain the level reached in 1929 until after World War II. Developing countries which relied heavily on the export of primary commodities, particularly to Britain, France, Germany and the USA fared particularly badly, the prices of primary products of countries in Latin America showing a drop of over 50 per cent. As a consequence, the GDP of Chile, for instance, fell, between 1929 and 1932, by about 36 per cent and that of Cuba by 33 per cent (Bulmer-Thomas, 1994).

In 1922, Germany had stopped the payment of war reparations and as a result France had occupied the Ruhr. There was a rapid hyper-inflation of prices in Germany. In January 1923, a US dollar exchanged for 7,260 marks but by December the value of the mark had plummeted to the point at which a dollar exchanged for 4,210 billion marks. The German stock market crashed in May 1927 and the discount rate was raised to control a capital outflow. The revision of the reparation agreements concluded by the Young Plan in 1929 effectively constrained the credit that the Reichsbank could advance to the German government. Mutual distrust persisted between Germany and its wartime opponents with arguments over a German–Austrian Customs Union and Germany's frontier (Ritschl, 1998 )

In August 1929, the Frankfurter Allegemeine Bank failed, along with a number of lesser banks. In Austria, in November 1929, the Bodencreditanstalt Bank failed and merged with the Credit Anstalt, to become the largest private bank in Austria but this too failed in May 1931 and also the Vienna Mercur Bank. As a consequence, German banks by July 1931 began to suffer heavy withdrawals. The Danatbank, the second largest in Germany, failed and the Reichsbank had to abandon convertibility and came off the >GOLD STANDARD. In the following year Germany defaulted on its foreign debts (Schnabel, 2004). (There were also bank failures in France and the USA but not in Britain.) Industrial production in Germany fell by 39 per cent between 1929 and 1932, after which it recovered to reach its 1929 level again in 1936. Industrial unemployment in Germany rose from 13 per cent in 1929 to a peak of 44 per cent in 1932 (Clavin, 2000). In September 1930, the NSDAP (the National Socialist German Workers' Party) increased the number of seats it held in the Reichstag from 12 to 107 and increased its representation further to 37 per cent of the vote in 1932. Hitler became Chancellor in January 1933, marking the end of the Weimer Republic. At the time,

there was a prevailing view among the German public that the cause of their hardship was that they were hamstrung by the demands of the reparations settlement (>WESTERN EUROPE).

In the USA, industrial production began its decline in 1929 and the stock market crashed in October. A fall-off in domestic consumption coincided with a drop in export demand. Herbert Hoover's election platform had included a promise to help out farmers from the effects of the fall in world agricultural prices. Accordingly, in spite of protests from many economists, he signed the Smoot–Hawley Act in 1931 which raised relatively high US import tariffs even higher, so encouraging international protectionism (>INTERNATIONAL TRADE). In December 1930, the Bank of the USA failed and between August 1931 and January 1932 a total of 1,860 bank failures were recorded. In June 1932 there were further bank collapses in Chicago and in October in the mid- and far West. When Britain was forced to come off the >GOLD STANDARD in September 1931, there followed speculation in the USA against the dollar inducing the Federal Reserve Bank to raise interest rates from 1.5 per cent to 3.5 per cent, which Milton >FRIEDMAN and Anna Schwartz claimed was 'the sharpest rise within so brief a period in the whole history of the System, before or since' (Friedman and Schwartz, quoted in Ferderer and Zalewski, 1994). The USA also left the gold standard and President Roosevelt, having obtained authority to fix the price of gold in April 1933, allowed the dollar to devalue and it fell by 100 per cent against the pound sterling during the rest of the year. Stability returned with the passing of the Gold Reserve Act in 1934 which set the price of gold at $35 per ounce. In 1939, however, the GDP per capita in the USA was still about 3 per cent below that of 1929 (>NEW DEAL).

Unemployment in Britain increased from 1.5 million in 1929 to 3.4 million in 1932 but it fared relatively less badly than other leading countries because of the structure of its economy and the robustness of its financial institutions; unlike in the USA and on the Continent of Europe, it suffered no bank failures. The unemployed were concentrated in the export industries of the North and West, such as coal, iron and steel, shipbuilding and cotton textiles, and its economy benefited from the fall in import prices of food and raw materials. The result was an increase in the real incomes of those in work. It was the international banking crises that forced Britain to come off the gold standard in September 1931 because of the outflow of funds from the Bank of England as foreign banks tried to meet their obligations. Recovery from the depression was also relatively rapid in Britain. The level of output in 1929 was regained by 1934, whereas in the USA, although it reached that level in 1937 it fell again and France did not manage to reach it until after World War II (Baines, 1992).

The isolation and the defining of the various causes that could have initiated the Great Depression, the reasons for its proliferation through the world economy, its persistence and whether and how it could have been avoided have exercised scholars since contemporaries struggled to elucidate the correct policy prescriptions at the time to the present day (Parker, 2007).

The development of economic theory in the tradition of >CLASSICAL AND NEO-CLASSICAL ECONOMICS through the 19th century had focused more on the motivation and interrelation of consumers and producers – the micro-economics of society. There was an underlying presumption in Classical economic theory that, although economies might be cyclical (>BUSINESS CYCLES), they had an in-built tendency in the long run towards a stable equilibrium. >MALTHUS had started a hare by suggesting the possibility of a persistent economic downturn in his idea of 'gluts', but he was unable to kill the hare. He had no supportable theory to sustain his ideas against the powerful logical structures of >RICARDO. (>KEYNES went so far as to claim 'If only Malthus, instead of Ricardo, had been the parent stem from which nineteenth-century economics proceeded, what a much wiser and richer place the world would be today'(Deane, 1978).) However, Keynes's view of the neo-Classical economics at the time of the Great Depression was unduly negative. The shift of emphasis from micro- to macro-economics was underway, although a fully integrated theoretical model upon which policies could be convincingly placed did not reach fruition until 1936, when Keynes published his *The General Theory of Employment, Interest and Money.*

Two major issues of the time, were the efficacy of expenditure on public works to alleviate unemployment and the advantages or otherwise of reducing wages. There still persisted in some quarters, notably in the British Treasury, the view that government expenditure on public works did not increase employment because it merely diverted resources from the private sector, although A. C. Pigou, the Professor of Political Economy at Cambridge University at the time, refuted this argument in his book *Wealth and Welfare* in 1912. Moreover, in his book *Unemployment*, published in the following year, he showed how employment would be created by public expenditure financed by a rise in taxation, thereby preserving a balanced budget which was considered to be a necessary virtue. By the beginning of the Great Depression, most economists agreed that government expenditure could reduce unemployment. A considerable number of economists in the USA, centred on the universities of Chicago and Columbia, confirmed their support for government expenditure even if it led to a budget deficit. There were, however, eminent economists, both in the USA and Britain, who disagreed, although their disagreement became muted by the extent of the economic collapse. In particular, >HAYEK argued that unemployment was a result of a misalignment between the structure of production and the structure of demand which would be eliminated by changes in relative prices as the economy freely readjusted towards equilibrium. (Lionel Robbins (1971) (Lord Robbins), the Professor of Economics at the London School of Economics, who was influenced by Hayek, regretted his disagreement which he had with Keynes on this matter in 1930 and put it down to a 'fundamental error of perspective', not appreciating the new situation that had arisen from the vast deflation that had occurred.) Nevertheless, the views of economists failed to permeate through to those responsible for policy decisions. The British Chancellor of the Exchequer asserted in 1929, 'Very little additional employment and no permanent additional employment can, in fact, and as a general rule, be created by State borrowing and State expenditure' (Winston Churchill, quoted in Blaug, 1978). Roosevelt, in 1932, criticized the Republicans for running a budget deficit. Another contentious area of economic policy was whether or not a reduction in wages would raise employment, which Keynes considered to be the Classical view falsely derived from the perspective of individual firms. However, many economists in Britain argued that while in theory wage cuts could have a reflationary effect, nevertheless it was considered to be impractical politically. In the USA, there was no argument, because money wages dropped considerably without affecting employment, unlike in Britain where money wages were constant. Blaug (1978) concludes that the neo-Classical economists of the time had various solutions to the economic collapse but it took Keynes's *General Theory* to produce the theoretical model needed to support the practical policies that their ideas indicated. At the time of the onset of the Great Depression at the end of the 1920s, therefore, there were conflicting ideas about the proper course of action to take in the event of such a large contraction in economic activity among professional economists, but even where there was agreement among them, their views had not penetrated the thinking of practical politicians and their advisors.

There have been a number of views expressed of the cause of the Depression internationally and in particular countries. A 'monetarist view' was that which was argued by Friedman and Schwartz (1963), that the depression in the USA was caused by a contraction in the money supply between August 1929 and March 1933, coupled with the inept policy of the Federal Reserve Bank which, for instance, raised rather than lowered interest rates (>CENTRAL BANKING). They claimed that the stock market crash in October 1929 and movements in foreign exchange rates and international capital flows were less important. A 'Keynesian view' was that the money supply fell because there was a drop in aggregate demand following the fall in consumption and investment. Others have argued that the US stock market crash was important because it led to a severe credit constraint by the banks and a loss of confidence. A further contributor was the fall in primary commodity prices which triggered an international liquidity crisis at a time when there was no central bank with sufficient resources and authority to offer or organize support as the Bank of England had pre-war. Kindleberger (1996) points to the collapse of the Kredit Anstaldt Bank in Austria in May 1931 as the critical event as it triggered a number of debt defaults, exchange controls and a fall in international trade. The American decision to enact the Smoot–Hawley tariff inspired a competitive protectionist era which inhibited a revival.

There is a body of opinion that the origins of the Great Depression lay in >WORLD WAR I and the conflicts in Europe that gave rise to it and which were not resolved until after >WORLD WAR II and the setting up of the European Union and international institutions such as the International Monetary Fund and the World Bank. In particular, the settlement following the end of World War I failed to address the needs for the reconstruction of the devastated economies of Europe and left a hangover of mutual suspicion, exacerbated by the question of reparations that bedevilled any attempt to arrive at a consensus on economic matters of international concern in the inter-war years. Germany, in particular, was caught between the external demands for reparations and its domestic needs for reconstruction and renewed economic development. The extensive revision of national

boundaries in Europe also imposed added burdens by distorting interregional trade flows. Into this post-war landscape was introduced the pre-war gold standard, which Eichengreen (1992) argues to be the prime suspect as the cause of the catastrophe. The strength of the gold standard pre-war was that it benefited from international cooperation and credibility, both of which lost their lustre in the post-war distrust. Credibility, at least initially, was strong. Indeed, there was such universal faith in the efficacy of the gold standard that it held the seeds in itself of the economic collapse. It was firmly believed that the re-establishment of the gold standard, even in its adjusted form as the gold exchange standard, after the war was the only way to prevent disaster. The problem with the system was that it was asymmetric between creditor and debtor countries. As debtor countries experienced an outflow of gold, they were forced to deflate in order to maintain the rate of exchange of their currency; on the other hand no action was forced on to the creditor countries to cause them to reflate. The net result was an international trend to deflation which was accentuated by the fact that the distribution of gold reserves was heavily biased to the USA and France. A financial crisis as that which hit the Austrian Credit Anstaldt Bank in May 1931 inevitably produced fear and uncertainty caused both by the short-run alarm of possible losses from a devaluation of currencies and the long-run belief that the collapse of the gold standard itself would lead to even worse economic turmoil. In these kinds of circumstances entrepreneurs lose the will to invest. In early 1931, Austria, Germany and Hungary abandoned gold, followed by Britain in September and several other countries before the end of the year. Evidence shows that those countries which had never been part of the gold standard system (such as Spain) or left the regime relatively early fared better than those that remained. Their prices stabilized and began to recover. Also, these countries had higher rates of recovery in industrial production (Bernanke, 2004; Eichengreen, 1992) (>INEQUALITY).

## References

Baines, D., 'Recovery from the Depression in Great Britain, 1932–1939', in in Anne Digby, Charles Feinstein and David Jenkins (eds), *New Directions in Economic and Social History*, II, Macmillan, 1992.

Bernanke, Ben S., *Essays on the Great Depression*, Princeton University Press, 2004.

Blaug, Mark, *Economic Theory in Retrospect*, Cambridge University Press, 1978.

Borchardt, Knut, *Perspectives on Modern German Economic History and Policy*, Cambridge University Press, 1991.

Bulmer-Thomas, Victor, *The Economic History of Latin America Since Independence*, Cambridge University Press, 1994.

Clavin, Patricia, *The Great Depression in Europe, 1929–1939*, Macmillan, 2000.

Deane, Phyllis, *The Evolution of Economic Ideas*, Cambridge University Press, 1978.

Eichengreen, Barry, *Golden Fetters: The Gold Standard and the Great Depression, 1919–1939*, Oxford University Press, 1992.

Ferderer, J. Peter and Zalewski, David A., 'Uncertainty as a Propagating Force in the Great Depression', *Journal of Economic History*, 54(4), December, 1994.

Friedman, Milton and Schwartz, Anna Jacobson, *A Monetary History of the United States, 1867–1960*, Princeton University Press, 1963.

Kindleberger, Charles P., *Manias, Panics, and Crashes: A History of Financial Crises*, John Wiley and Sons, 1996.

Maddison, Angus, *Monitoring the World Economy 1820–1992*, OECD, 1995.

Parker, Randall E., *The Economics of the Great Depression: A Twenty-First Century Look Back at the Economics of the Interwar Era*, Edward Elgar, 2007.

Ritschl, Albrecht, 'Reparation Transfers, the Borchadt Hypothesis and the Great Depression, 1929–1932: A Guided Tour for Hard Headed Keynesians', *European Review of Economic History*, 2(1), April, 1998.

Robbins, L., *Autobiography of an Economist*, St Martin's Press, 1971.

Schnabel, Isabel, 'The German Twin Crisis of 1931', *Journal of Economic History*, 64(3). September, 2004.

Temin, Peter, *Lessons from the Great Depression*, MIT Press, 1991.

Vernon, J. R., 'World War II Fiscal Policies and the End of the Great Depression', *Journal of Economic History*, 54(4), December, 1994.

Winch, David, *Malthus*, Oxford University Press, 1987.

# H

## Hamilton, Alexander

Hamilton, who lived from 1755 to 1804, was appointed by George Washington as the first Secretary of the Treasury of the USA in 1776. Hamilton held this position from the end of the >AMERICAN WAR OF INDEPENDENCE until his resignation in 1794. He was instrumental in the establishment of sound public finances and many institutions that helped to establish the rule of law and a culture of capitalism in the new Republic. His latest biographer writes that, 'If Washington was the father of the country and Madison the father of the Constitution, then Alexander Hamilton was surely the father of the American Government' (Chernow, 2004). Hamilton's role impinged on four principal aspects of the early economic history of the >USA: public debt and the currency; >TAXATION; >CENTRAL BANKING; and the development of manufacturing. Hamilton had already expounded his basic views on federal government in a series of essays compiled by himself and James Madison to help persuade New Yorkers to ratify the Constitution. Beginning in 1787 the 'Federalist' essays ended up as a large two-volume book. To present times, these essays have been cited by the Supreme Court in its interpretations of the constitution.

Hamilton's views were elaborated after he obtained office in four early reports for Congress. In the first report, on 'Public Credit' (January 1790), he proposed that Federal foreign and domestic debt incurred by the Confederation to its allies, France and Spain and to Holland, as well as the debts of the states, should be consolidated by the issue of new Federal securities; in other words the government would be assuming the debts of the states. The combined total of these debts was, for the time, the huge amount of $79 million (Faulkner, 1960) The foreign debt was to be repaid in full and domestic debt funded at a lower interest rate than the original but also at par capital value. This proposal inevitably led to speculation and political mayhem since the state debt was circulating at much-depressed levels (although in fact the speculation brought down interest rates to good economic effect). A political deadlock over the assumption of the state debt (much of which was held in the South) was resolved by Hamilton through a deal with Thomas Jefferson, its leading opponent, to locate the national capital at Washington on the River Potomac. Hamilton's position over the refinancing plan (which included a sinking fund to pay off the debt) was based on his belief that sound public finances were important for the development of capital markets. There was also the political motivation that the holders of the new issues would be inclined to support the new federalist government. Actually most of Hamilton's economic proposals had the political motive of strengthening the Federal government, something not lost on his anti-federalist opponents, led by Jefferson.

Hamilton's second report (December 1790) recommended an excise tax on whiskey and other domestic spirits. The only major sources of Federal government revenue at the time, apart from land sales, was the import tariff introduced in 1789 and with Hamilton's support subsequently increased in 1790, 1792 and 1794. The excise tax also met with bitter opposition, particularly in rural areas. However, the excise seemed preferable to other sources of revenue such as a land tax and Hamilton again prevailed. The tax took effect in July 1791, enforced by inspectors. There was to be a Whiskey Rebellion in 1794 but this was suppressed, though Jefferson, again an opponent, was to abolish the excise after he became President in 1800 and the Republicans triumphed over the Federalists (and were to remain in power for 20 years).

Hamilton's third report, also in December 1790, proposed a national bank. The USA still did not have a uniform currency and its citizens were making do with a limited supply of state-chartered commercial bank notes, IOUs and various foreign coins (>MONEY AND BANKING). Under the new Constitution, the states were not permitted to issue money. Hamilton knew that the country needed a central bank which could act as the Federal government's banker, issue bank notes, extend credit, expand the money supply and handle foreign exchange (>CENTRAL BANKING). His recommendations were modelled on the Bank of England, with the difference that the First Bank of the United States, as it came to be called, had one-fifth of its stock held by the government to safeguard the public interest. Again there was controversy with the Republicans and some critics feared that the bank would favour the already powerful

position of the northern merchants and financiers at the expense of the indebted agrarian community, particularly in the South. There were also disputes about the location of the new bank. Hamilton wanted it to be in Philadelphia, already a thriving centre of commerce. His opponents wanted the bank in Washington fearing that a more northerly location would lead to a revision of an agreement that the national capital should be in the South. The dispute led to a rift between Hamilton and Madison who, with Jefferson, argued that there was no power under the Constitution to create a central bank. Hamilton was able to persuade President Washington not to veto the bill as requested by the anti-federalists. His argument was that the Constitution gave Congress the right to pass any legislation deemed 'necessary and proper' to exercise the powers that were specifically listed (the doctrine of implied powers). The bill to charter the Bank of the United States was passed by Congress in January 1791. Shortly afterward, Hamilton produced yet another report on the mint which was necessary for Federal coinage. He opted for a >BIMETALLIC SYSTEM in which the coins would be in both gold and silver. The Coinage Act of 1792 laid down that both foreign and domestically minted coins were accepted as legal tender. The value of gold coins was fixed at 15 times as much by weight as silver and the government undertook to exchange one for the other on this basis. This was to create problems since the market value of the two metals did not remain constant and in practice only gold or silver coins circulated most of the time (Atack and Passell, 1979). Hamilton had thus prevailed over his critics but when the US Mint was established in 1792 it was put under Jefferson, the

Secretary of the State Department, and not under the Treasury as Hamilton had wished. Located from the start in Philadelphia with the provisional seat of government, the mint remained there when the government moved to Washington, DC, in 1800. There was a scramble for the stock of the Bank of the United States (which Hamilton had ensured would be a profitable institution) when the public subscription opened in July 1791. The market value of the stock, issued at $25, rose to over $300 but a month later fell back sharply and stabilized in September.

The First Bank was permitted under its charter to operate branches in all states. This gave it a competitive advantage over the state-chartered banks which could operate only in their home state. The bank also had a large financial base because the government kept its cash there. The bank was generally a net creditor with the commercial banks and gradually began to police the growing number of smaller commercial banks. The bank's 20-year charter, however, failed to be renewed by a narrow margin in 1811 because of concerted opposition from the Republicans and the state-chartered banks. The absence of a central bank weakened both the banking system and public finances and there was a run on the banks in 1814. Accordingly, Congress changed its mind and the Second Bank of the United States was chartered in 1816, though later this bank did not have the government's full support under Andrew Jackson, who became President in 1829. Jackson split the government's banking business among other banks and thereafter the Second Bank barely survived until its charter expired in 1836. The USA was then left without a central bank until, following more bank crises, the Federal Reserve was established in 1914 (>CENTRAL BANKING).

Hamilton's fourth major report that we describe here was his famous 'Report on the Subject of Manufactures' (December 1791). At the time, the USA had a largely agricultural economy and relied on imports, especially from Britain for a wide range of industrial goods. The President was concerned that the USA was so dependent on other countries for key manufactures, including military supplies, and Congress asked for a report. 'Manufactures' was a landmark in the history of US economic policy because it marked an active approach and a willingness to protect domestic industry. Hamilton's report made a sophisticated case for manufacturing, rejecting the view of the French >PHYSIOCRATS that agriculture was the sole source of wealth. He pointed to the scope for productivity gains from the division of labour and the use of machinery and to the first-mover advantages that other countries had in establishing industry. Hamilton advocated moderately higher import tariffs and subsidies ('bounties') on some 20 products (Irwin, 2004).

The anti-federalists were against promoting manufacturing: 'manufactures are founded in poverty' wrote Benjamin Franklin, 'for it is the multitude of poor without land in a country and who must work for others at low wages or starve, that enables undertakers to carry on manufacture' (quoted by Licht, 1995). Thomas Jefferson and James Madison even feared that manufacturing could lead to despotism over a landless poor and favoured a society of independent farmers (>USA). None of these distinguished people were against mechanization (Franklin was a scientist and inventor), as Licht emphasizes, but they were against the predominance of large enterprise. More particularly, they were specifically against subsidizing manufacturing which they held was unconstitutional. Irwin (2004) explains that Hamilton's proposals were never debated by Congress as a package. However, while his proposals for subsidies were not implemented at the time, his tariff recommendations were all passed within six months of the appearance of the report. From his later history it is clear that Hamilton was not a protectionist and did not believe in state planning of industry. He believed in the market system. (As a young man he had predicted that in the long run the colonies would overtake Britain in economic power.)

Hamilton had a colourful, if tragic, life that was full of achievement. He was born a British subject on Nevis in the West Indies. Deserted by his father, he was brought up and apprenticed by a respected merchant. His education at King's College, New York, was financed by public subscription on the island of his birth. He fought in the Revolutionary War, was active in the politics of the new Constitution and had the confidence of George Washington (he drafted Washington's valedictory address that was published, not spoken, in 1796) and remained in the President's cabinet until Hamilton's resignation in 1794. He was a fervent believer in the need for a strong Federal government and financial stability, both of which he was instrumental in achieving. Among other things, Hamilton also founded the Customs Service and US Coastguard and the military academy at West Point. Hamilton acquired many enemies and endured unsubstantiated attacks for his supposed pro-British sentiments and for taking personal advantage of his position in government (he never

became rich and for much of his later life supported his family through his legal practice). Hamilton's death was caused by a pistol duel, in which he was defending his honour, at the age of 49. This last episode was given added poignancy by the fact, according to Chernow (2004), that Hamilton had no intention of killing his opponent and threw his first shot in the air.

### References

Atack, Jeremy and Passell, Peter, *A New Economic View of American History from Colonial Times to 1940*, W. W. Norton, 1994.

Chernow, Ron, *Alexander Hamilton*, Penguin, 2004.

Faulkner, Harold Underwood, *American Economic History*, Harper & Row, 1960.

Irwin, Douglas A., 'The Aftermath of Hamilton's Report on Manufactures', *Journal of Economic History*, September, 2004.

Licht, W., *Industrialising America: The Nineteenth Century*, Johns Hopkins University Press, 1995.

# Hammonds, The

John Lawrence Hammond (1872–1949) and his wife, Lucy Barbara (1873–1961), were politically engaged social historians who made important contributions to the study of the >ENCLOSURE movement and the >INDUSTRIAL REVOLUTION IN BRITAIN. They were principally concerned about the bad impact of these developments upon working people as, in the latter case, was Arnold Toynbee, Charles Dickens, the novelist, and others, a tradition continued until recently most notably by E. P. >THOMPSON who, like the Hammonds, wrote 'history from below'.

The Hammonds are best known for their trilogy which began with *The Village Labourer* (1911). That book dealt with enclosure and the condition of the agricultural worker including the Labourers' Revolt (or Swing Riots) of 1830 in the South of England which culminated in nine men hanged and 457 transported to the colonies for their part in the revolt. The Hammonds recognized that enclosure was necessary for what we now call the >AGRICULTURAL REVOLUTION but believe it was done without taking into account the consequences for the poor. They argued that a minimum wage should have been set to enable agricultural workers to share in the increased prosperity of their sector which resulted from enclosure. *The Village Labourer* is a lament for the ruination of the yeoman class of England which, before enclosure and the industrial revolution, had not only varied sources of income from labouring, domestic industry (>PROTO-INDUSTRIALIZATION) and self-sufficiency, but also some participation in the affairs of their village. The medieval system, although it kept the poor in their place, explained the Hammonds, at least gave them protection and conferred rights and participation which could be enforced in the Manorial Courts, some of which were still functioning at the beginning of the 18th century. These rights were removed by a government in which the workers had no participation. (It was not until the Reform Act of 1832 that voting was extended from landowners to the propertied middle class (though not women), and not until 1918 that all adult males were enfranchised and even then most women did not have a vote (>CHARTISM)). By the end of the 18th century, the Hammonds pointed out, Parliament was controlled by the aristocracy and employers and local affairs were also dominated by the Justices of the Peace (the same people). The Hammonds describe vividly the legal reinforcement of the loss of access to common lands resulting from enclosure. For example, offenders against the Game Laws (1740–1828) and the Malicious Trespass Act (1820) for poaching or taking firewood from a hedgerow could be sentenced to hard labour or worse if they could not pay heavy fines.

The second volume of the trilogy, *The Town Labourer* (1917), is about the industrial revolution and its effect upon the social and economic conditions of working people. This book argued that the industrial revolution gave violent birth to a new and brutal civilization in which workers paid the price for economic progress and this sparked a debate which continues to this day (>INDUSTRIAL REVOLUTION IN BRITAIN: >INDUSTRIAL REVOLUTIONS). The trilogy was completed with the publication in 1919 of *The Skilled Labourer.* This book is largely about the doomed efforts of domestic outworkers, such as handloom weavers, to arrest the degradation of their trade under the advance of machinery and factories (>LUDDISM).

*The Rise of Modern Industry* (1925) written for use in extra-mural education, is the best introduction to the Hammonds' thinking, summarizing, and at some points extending, the trilogy and setting the social and economic changes of the 18th and 19th centuries in their long-term perspective. The book is particularly good on the role of the >COMMERCIAL REVOLUTION which preceded the industrial revolution. It points out that ancient Rome and the Venetian Empire had >CAPITALISM and foreign trade (pillage in the former case) but these economic activities were based exclusively on goods and services for the elite. True capitalist large-scale manufacture was only possible when it was applied to production for the mass of the population and this is what the English pioneered. (This was not a contradiction of the Hammonds' thesis since they were concerned with the short-term impact of the necessary changes on workers.) Some of material in this book still retains the power to shock the modern reader, particularly the sections on child labour and >SLAVERY. The Hammonds show how workhouse children were often hired out ('apprenticed') to mill owners a long way from where they had grown up, while later, former handloom weavers were given factory jobs only on condition that their children also worked at the mill. *The Rise of Modern Industry* is shorter than most of the Hammonds' earlier output and provides a good illustration of the sweep, power and rhythm of Lawrence's prose. Lawrence was the most fluent writer of the two, while Barbara concentrated more on research; however, in his excellent (and the only) full biography of the Hammonds, Weaver (1997) says that the couple were unique in the extent of their fused identity.

Much of the Hammonds' writings created controversy. They were accused of peddling socialist propaganda though, as Weaver puts it: 'the Hammonds were not Fabians; they were not even socialists... they were members of that Hobsonian-cum-Keynesian circle that brilliantly navigated the narrow space between liberalism and social democracy in the first half of the century' (1997). The Hammonds were fighting against the temper of the time, which they believed was that all that mattered was economic progress. The

*Rise of Modern Industry*, as with most of the Hammonds' books, ends on an optimistic note, however, with the statement that by mid-century 'civilisation begun slowly to raise its head above the smoke', citing factory laws and inspections of industrial premises, a Civil Service using 'educated men on terms which preserved their independence and self-respect' (Hammond and Hammond, 1926) and more permissiveness towards >TRADE UNIONS as signs of a widening appreciation of a need for progressive social policy.

Most weighty among the criticism of the Hammonds were those of J. H. Clapham, who in the first volume of his economic history of Britain, without specifically referring to the Hammonds, lamented 'the legend that everything was getting worse for the working man, down to some unspecified date between the drafting of the People's Charter and the Great Exhibition' (1926). Clapham claimed, as economic historians do now, that the industrial revolution was more gradual and more localized than the Hammonds implied and that, with the important exception of the cotton handloom weavers, wages rose between 1780 and 1850. Lawrence Hammond's response was that statistics on wages were not an adequate measure of the human condition. Later, Lawrence was able to catch out Clapham on a technical point: the latter had used unweighted arithmetic averages which concealed the fact that for 60 per cent of workers wages were below the averages he arrived at. Clapham was to acknowledge these points in the second edition of his book in 1930.

Lawrence Hammond's journalistic output was formidable. He edited *The Speaker: The Liberal Review*, wrote for *The Nation* and, in particular, for the *Manchester Guardian*, with which he had a virtually unbroken association from 1918, when he represented the paper at the Paris Peace Conference. Lawrence did military service and worked for the Civil Service Commission but spent most of his life as an independent writer. The Hammonds, who met at Oxford University where Barbara was to get a Double First, the first woman to do so, married in 1901. They both suffered from ill health. Lawrence died in 1949, aged 76, but Barbara outlived him and died at the age of 88.

### References

Clapham, J. H., *An Economic History of Modern Britain: The Early Railway Age, 1820–1850*, Cambridge University Press, 1926.

Hammond, J. L. and Hammond, Barbara, *The Village Labourer, 1760–1832: A Study of the Government of England Before the Reform Bill*, Longmans Green & Co., 1911.

Hammond, J. L. and Hammond, Barbara, *The Town Labourer 1760–1832: The New Civilisation*, Longmans Green & Co., 1917.

Hammond, J. L. and Hammond, Barbara, *The Skilled Labourer 1760–1832*, Longmans Green & Co., 1919.

Hammond, J. L. and Hammond, Barbara, *The Rise of Modern Industry* (1925), Methuen (2nd edn), 1926.

Weaver, Stewart A., *The Hammonds: A Marriage in History*, Stanford University Press, 1997.

# Hayek, Friedrich August von

A very important figure in 20th-century economic and political thought, Hayek, who lived from 1899 to 1992, was not an economic historian, though he wrote, particularly in his early days, in German, on the history of money and prices and has deeply influenced writers, and indeed events, in economic history. He saw himself as an economist but also wrote in a wide range of other disciplines, including the history of ideas, scientific method, psychology and the intellectual process. As an economist, he made major contributions in capital theory, monetary theory and the theory of business cycles. He is best known, however, for his work in political philosophy to which he increasingly devoted himself after 1933 from when his economics began to be overshadowed by that of >KEYNES. Hayek again came into prominence in the 1960s and 1970s and he was awarded the Nobel Prize in economics jointly with Gunnar Myrdal (1898–1987), something of a compromise between conflicting schemes of thought. Hayek's biographer Ebenstein (2001) cites Milton >FRIEDMAN as noting that major changes in social and economic policy are preceded by tides of intellectual opinion and wrote of three tides: 'the rise of laissez-faire (the Adam Smith tide)','the rise of the welfare state (the Fabian tide)' and 'the resurgence of free markets (the Hayek tide)'. This is a measure of the esteem in which Hayek is held by his fellow economists.

Three basic sets of ideas are central to Hayek's thought. The first is that the market economy creates *spontaneous order* by bringing about ends not willed by individual participants (as originally argued by Adam >SMITH). Hayek criticized what he called Constructivism (Rationalism) for holding in error that because man created human >INSTITUTIONS, a powerful individual or government can redesign them for the better. He was also against the view that we can know and measure what is important in economic affairs. This leads to his second basic idea which is that in the market economy the key information is dispersed (*the division of knowledge*) among large numbers of individuals and communicated only by prices and profits that guide activity, >ENTREPRENEURSHIP being a search function to establish economic activities by trial and error. The third basic notion follows from the first two and is that effective central control or planning of an economy, and thus socialism, is a rational impossibility and must lead to pervasive economic control and loss of liberty (Machlup, 1977). This was what had happened with National Socialism in Nazi Germany. This was the theme of his bestselling polemic, *The Road to Serfdom* (Hayek, 1944). Hayek was not an advocate of pure laissez-faire; he believed, for example, in the rule of law, advocated a minimum income for all and the regulation of monopoly and working conditions. He did not even believe that >CAPITALISM was always more efficient than socialism (as it was not in the 1930s), but the loss of liberty which ultimately follows socialism was his primary concern.

Like >SCHUMPETER, though for somewhat different reasons, Hayek was very much against the ideas Keynes put forward in *The General Theory*. Hayek's theory of >BUSINESS CYCLES was based on the view that unemployment was caused by real factors, basically a mismatch between investment and demand at micro-level and that boosting aggregate demand before the necessary structural changes were brought about, which Keynes advocated, would result in accelerating inflation. Although Keynes may have been right in the special case of the 1930s, Hayek appears to have been vindicated by the inflationary experience of the 1970s. Key passages from Hayek's long-running critiques

of Keynes dating from the 1930s onwards are conveniently assembled in Hayek's *A Tiger by the Tail* (1972).

Hayek was a prolific writer, though his technical material is heavy going. This does not apply to *The Road to Serfdom*, nor to his many essays and some of his lectures. The essays contain fascinating insights into a wide range of matters. For example, 'Two Types of Mind', in Hayek's *New Studies in Philosophy, Politics, Economics and the History of Ideas* (1978), distinguishes between the 'verbal' or 'memory type' and the less conventional, intuitive or 'puzzler type' of mind. The puzzler reads or listens to other people's arguments but cannot reproduce them from memory; rather he has to incorporate them unconsciously in his own scheme of thought. Hayek saw himself in the puzzler category and thought socialists tended to be of the verbal type. A constant theme of Hayek's is that what is important cannot necessarily be measured and that the error of macro-economics is to assume that what can be measured is what is important. This means, of course, that the unmeasurable, such as the infinite number of dispersed price and supply demand relationships in an economy, could not be empirically determined.

Hayek was born in Vienna in 1899, the son of a professor of Botany. After brief military service, which ended in 1918, he enrolled as a student of the university of the city of his birth to study in the faculty of law, which then included economics. He was greatly influenced there by Friedrich von Wieser (1851–1926), who succeeded Carl Menger (1840–1921) as Professor of Economics at the University of Vienna and, after he graduated, by Ludwig von Mises (1881–1973). After his second degree in 1921 and a stay in New York, where he learned about statistics and quantitative economics from Wesley Clair Mitchell (1874–1948), Hayek became the first director of the Austrian Institute for Business Cycle Research modelled on Mitchell's National Bureau of Economic Research. From 1931–50, Hayek held the Tooke Chair in Economics and Statistics at the London School of Economics, where he became friendly with Lionel Robbins (1898–1984). Hayek became a naturalized British subject in 1938. From 1950–62 he was a professor at the University of Chicago, returning to Europe at the German University of Freiburg. He retired in 1969, but taught as a visiting professor at the University of Salzburg in Austria. He died in 1992, just short of his 93rd birthday.

## References

Ebenstein, Alan, *Friedrich Hayek, A Biography*, University of Chicago Press, 2001.

Hayek, F. A., *The Road to Serfdom*, George Routledge & Sons, 1944.

Hayek, F. A., *A Tiger by the Tail*, Institute of Economic Affairs, 1972.

Hayek, F. A., *New Studies in Philosophy, Politics, Economics and the History of Ideas*, Routledge & Kegan Paul, 1978.

Machlup, Fritz, *Essays on Hayek*, Routledge & Kegan Paul, 1977.

# I

## India

The forces of the >ENGLISH EAST INDIA COMPANY (EIC), led by Robert Clive, defeated Siraj-ud-Duala, the *nawab* of Bengal at Plassey in 1757. As a consequence, the EIC captured the lucrative land revenues of Bengal and was confirmed as its ruler by the Mughal Emperor in 1765. The EIC's influence grew and it became the dominant power in India. By the annexation of Bengal and Bihar in 1757 and other territories, concluding with the annexation of Awadh in 1856, about 60 per cent of the area of what constitutes today the three countries of Bangladesh, India and Pakistan fell under the direct control of the EIC. Although the remaining Indian principalities were free, they were only nominally so. The British government began to constrain the EIC's activities in the early 19th century and finally took complete control in India in 1857, which it held until Independence in 1947.

As in the India of the Great Mughal, agriculture was the major economic activity and was one of the major sources of taxation revenue throughout the colonial period. The British inherited an administrative revenue collection system constructed roughly on three levels. At the bottom level were individuals, families or whole villages that had rights to cultivate land; above these were those who had a right to collect tax from the cultivators of the land; and at the top were those who had the authority to grant the right to collect taxes. Below them all were agricultural labourers. Because of the intricate complexity of the mix of rights and obligations, the buying and selling of land was in effect impossible in practice and no effective economic market for land existed. As the Mughal authority declined, it was forced to give away more and more taxation rights. Under the Mughal, it is believed that the tax regime was such as to extract from the land all surplus, down to subsistence level for the peasants and artisans working on the land. The major share of this revenue went to the Emperor and a few families (Roy, 2006).

The British restructured the taxation system based on rights to property, so that, for instance, peasants were give title to the land which they cultivated with the sanction that their land was forfeit if the rent for which they were responsible remained unpaid. Unlike the situation under the Mughal Emperor, the cultivators of the land had the potential of making a profit, thus opening up the possibility of there developing a land market. However, the actual administrative arrangements chosen to implement these aims were influenced by the prevailing structures in the different regions and the changing political perceptions of the British as their control spread through South Asia. On taking over Bengal, the EIC found established there a group of powerful agents of the Mughal, called *zamindars*, who had hereditary fiscal and taxation authority, whose presence, the company decided, would be politically wise to accept. A permanent settlement was made in the

1790s which gave the *zamindars* perpetual rights in land, subject to their meeting their taxation obligations. The tax demand was fixed forever at the levels returned in 1789/90, a year of high tax revenue and based on the *zamindars* retaining 10 per cent of what they collected from rent. The *zamindars* became landlords and the peasant cultivators of the land paid rent to these landlords rather than taxes. Tax revenues were de-coupled from fluctuations in the harvests. The permanent settlement, however, while it did lead to a market in land, did nothing to encourage the development of agriculture in so far as the *zamindars'* income came from rent and they had little incentive to invest for profit. Between 1799 and 1810, the *zamindars* were given freedom to raise rents. Investment in land in Bengal became increasingly attractive in the course of the 19th century as the price of land rose. *Zamindars* accumulated wealth but seldom invested in agricultural improvements. *Zamindar*-type settlements were also introduced in other regions in Central, Northern and South West India. After 1820, a different, *ryotwari*, system was applied in the North West, West and South regions of India. The *ryot*, or cultivator, entered into a contract directly with the government to pay tax at a given rate for a specified number of, generally, 30 years. The tax revenue was fixed at nine-tenths of output in 1820 adjusted to two-thirds in 1833. The idea was to eliminate the intermediaries and encourage the efficient cultivator as well as to create a market in land. In practice, the tax rates were set too high and caused distress, possibly aggravated by agricultural depression reflected in the decline in prices in the 1830s (Tomlinson, 1996). The tax rates were lightened by a reassessment in the 1840s. The

areas governed through the *zamindar* system and the areas governed by the *ryotwari* system developed differently. In the former, the *zamindars* were expected by the government to be responsible for investment in infrastructure; in the latter, the government took that responsibility. Roy (2006) suggests that this might perhaps have been one of the reasons for the lower investment in irrigation in the *zamindar* areas. The EIC used these taxation revenues to meet local expenditure and to buy commodities which were exported to England, where they were sold at auction. Revenues from these sales were used to pay expenses and the EIC's dividends, referred to as the 'Home Charges', and the remaining profits financed the supply of manpower, military equipment, manufactures and bullion for shipment to India.

Originally attracted by the spice trade, the Portuguese, followed by the Dutch and finally the British joined in the thriving maritime trades of the Indian Ocean and the Indonesian Islands. Indian cotton textiles were traded for spices and the latter shipped to Europe together with tea, silk, indigo and saltpetre. However, the EIC quickly realized the potential for the high-quality cotton textiles which were produced in India and opened up the market for them in England, successfully establishing this trade in the 17th century. Cotton textiles, along with grain, became the major Indian export in the 18th century, based on the Punjab, Gujarat, Caromondel and Bengal regions. Exports had became very important for specific regions, although at that time probably made up less than 2 per cent of total National Income. The imbalance of commodity trade was met by the export to India of bullion. By the 1790s, India supplied most of the indigo imported into Britain or re-exported, over a half of the raw silk, a wide range of cotton materials and high-quality saltpetre but, early in the 18th century, Britain limited the import of printed cotton cloth in order to protect its domestic wool textile industry which encouraged a switch from imported cotton textiles to raw cotton. In 1813, the EIC's monopoly of the Indian trade was repealed and, as a result, cotton textiles were free to enter India, leading to a rapid increase in British exports. This trade expanded through the 19th century and amounted to about 20 per cent of Britain's total exports of cotton textiles. While the EIC was a producer of opium in India, it avoided directly flouting the Chinese ban on shipment by leaving this illicit trade to independent agencies, thereby profiting from it, albeit indirectly. Early in the 19th century this trade accounted for 24 per cent of total Indian exports, second only to cotton textiles, which had a 33 per cent share. By the second half of the century, these two commodities had given way in importance to raw cotton, raw jute, tea and leather. India exported agricultural commodities and imported textiles, machinery, metals and intermediate goods (>COTTON AND COTTON TEXTILES). The international trade of India grew rapidly through the 19th century and up to World War I, so that it has been estimated that the proportion of trade in total National Income rose from between 1 per cent and 2.5 per cent in 1835 to over 20 per cent in 1913, with exports growing at an average of over 5 per cent per annum between 1858 and 1913. There was also a change in the direction of Indian trade, with the share of exports and imports with Britain and China falling as trade shifted to Japan and the >USA, although Britain

still retained the highest share up to 1940 (Roy, 2006).

Agriculture enjoyed a period of rising incomes between 1865 and 1910 from 15.5 million rupees to 25.4 million rupees and more land was brought under cultivation. Land became an attractive investment and the price per acre rose in the period by about 4 per cent per annum. But in the mid-1920s incomes fell back with the collapse of world agricultural prices and had not fully recovered by 1940 (>AGRICULTURE). There was no change in the acreage sown between 1910 and 1940 and the average yield was either static or falling. Although the percentage of the labour force employed in agriculture remained at about 70 per cent, the sector's share of the National Income fell from 51 per cent in 1900 to 40 per cent in 1946. This was against the background of an acceleration in the growth of the population and a fall in the availability of food (net imports plus production) from 18.8 ounces per capita in 1910/14 to 14.4 ounces per capita in 1940/4 (Roy, 2006).

>FAMINES were endemic. There was a serous loss of life in 1770 when a third of the population of Bengal perished, in 1876/8 during which 4 million died in Bombay and Madras and in 1896/7 when 5 million died. The last major famine was in 1943/4 when 1.5 million people died in Bengal. (The Board of Enquiry into the latter argued that, although it was triggered by a shortage of >RICE following a failure of the harvest, it was compounded by the rise in prices, inflated by speculation, so that the rural population could not afford to buy food and the physical distribution of available supplies from surplus areas by the government was incompetent.)

In the mid-18th century, the handicraft sector in India had an established international market and produced about a quarter of world manufactures but the >INDUSTRIAL REVOLUTION IN BRITAIN completely changed both the overseas and the domestic markets to which the Indian producers had to adjust. Before competition from Britain made itself felt, it has been estimated that between 4 million and 5 million people were employed in the handicraft sector in India. In the first half of the 19th century, there was little overall impact, but between 1850 and 1880 there was a large drop in employment in the sector, which did not recover its previous levels until World War I. The relatively large drop in employment, however, did not entail a commensurate drop in earnings, as hand-spinning was a part-time and low-income activity. Moreover, the lower cost of imported textiles had a favourable effect on the cost of living generally and on the costs of the remaining producers in India. The loss of employment was somewhat offset by growth in the expanding export markets in agriculture.

The British government enticed British investors into the development of the railways in India by a guarantee of a minimum return on capital. By 1869, a total of 4,225 miles of railway track had been laid, 25,000 miles by 1900 and 40,000 miles by 1946. The corresponding demand for steel, engines and wagons and coal was met by imports from Britain and did not generate any significant domestic support industry for these inputs. From 1865 to 1941, 12,000 engines were imported from Britain and only 700 produced in India. Technical improvements in >SHIPPING and the opening of the Suez Canal caused a revolutionary lowering of ocean freight rates (>GLOBALIZATION) so that, for instance, British coal was competitive with Indian coal until World War I. The railway, together with its following telegraph network, brought some integration into India with a reduction in commodity price fluctuations, some narrowing of the differences in development between regions and enhancement of India's connections with foreign markets. This investment in communications failed, however, to trigger any significant industrial response in the Indian economy in spite of the fact that India had begun tentatively to industrialize from about 1870 with manufacturing increasing its share of National Income. In 1947, however, over 50 per cent of manufacturing industry was still in small-scale activities and the percentage of the labour force employed in industry, including transport and communications as well as manufacturing, did not change from about 12 per cent between 1901 and 1951. In 1947, less than 2 per cent of the labour force was employed in large-scale modern industry and the emphasis was still on textiles, which contributed about 30 per cent to total manufacturing output and employed a similar percentage of the workforce (Tomlinson, 1996). The rise in the value of land in the second half of the 19th century, together with a banking system which inhibited the release of its value into other, riskier, enterprises, could have been a factor in delaying the growth of investment in India in new industrial enterprises. It has been estimated that land accounted for 25 per cent of total national wealth in 1860, rising to 50 per cent in 1913 (Rothermund, 1993).

Given the international lead in the quality and low cost of its textile products in the 17th century and, in the 19th century, the (government-supported) investment in the railway network and in communications, there has been much debate as to the reasons for the failure of an industrial revolution to appear in India and no 'take-off' in industrial expansion occurring, and the extent to which this failure was due to colonial subjugation.

One view was that the EIC's activities in meeting its 'Home Charges' caused a 'draining' away of resources which, had they been retained, would have helped to stimulate economic development in India, although there have been differing views on which financial flows between India and Britain might be considered to measure the size of such a drain. One view was that it was only those payments made to meet the 'Home Charges' which could be regarded as unrequited and these amounted to less than 2 per cent of the value of exports at the end of the 19th century and less than 1 per cent by 1913. Another view was that it consisted of the whole of the British balance of payments surplus with India (Tomlinson, 1996). In the financing of its growing world balance of trade deficit, Britain certainly benefited considerably from the position of India within the international trade and payments system. Before >WORLD WAR I, India had a balance of payments surplus with the world as a whole but a deficit with Britain. Saul (1960) estimated that India financed more than 40 per cent of Britain's total deficit with the world in 1910/11. Moreover, at a time of an increase in protectionism among Britain's trading partners, India's market remained free to British exports and Indian exports to other countries were less affected by trade barriers than British exports and thus yielded a further, indirect, benefit to Britain (>INTERNATIONAL TRADE).

It has also been argued that there was a persistent shortage of capital for investment in industry because of the imposition of the British of its legal and administrative system on existing Indian custom and practice for the collection of tax revenues. This led to bias in favour of the ownership of land. More generally, the Indian economy became imbued with the commercial philosophy of the trader because of the nature of the activities of the EIC and the British government. Globalization had encouraged this by exploiting the structure of the factor endowments of India, which had a comparative surplus of land and a shortage of capital and skilled labour. This gave rise to a distrust of business, which initially even influenced Indian government policy after independence (Rodrik and Subramanian, 2004).

These views accorded with the Marxist idea that economic development was teleological in that, as Karl >MARX said in the introduction to *Das Kapital*, 'The country that is more developed industrially only shows to the less developed, the image of its own future.' Colonialism frustrated this potential.

The contrary view was that the people of under-developed countries were naturally averse to work, lacked ambition and were reluctant to take risks. They endured cultural and institutional conditions which inhibited change. This viewpoint may have suffered from a distortion of perspective. With low standards of living, bordering on malnutrition, in a country in which famine was hardly unknown, it might not be thought surprising that people found it difficult to find the energy to work, let alone to work at some new unknown venture. Landes (1998) argues that before the EIC there was evidence of the lack of technical innovation in India at the handicraft level as shown by the limited tools that were used and in shipbuilding in which the Europeans employed metal spikes but the Indians still used ropes and glue. It was globalization that caused the shift to agriculture and this would have happened without colonialism (>ECONOMIC IMPERIALISM).

Following Independence, the Indian government placed emphasis on a strong centrally directed autarkic policy stance reflected in an economic planning structure and the first five-year plan for 1951–66. (Economic policy within the framework of five-year plans continued to be the chosen method for the conduct of economic policy through to the tenth five-year plan for 2002–7.) In the 1950s and 1960s, economic policy was aimed at lifting the share of industry in the country's national income through import substitution, with direct intervention conducted through pervasive government regulation. Protective barriers to trade to exclude foreign competition were imposed and government industrial investment expenditure was concentrated in heavy industry. This policy was a success in its aims in the first plan period and into the second and it achieved a rate of growth of over 2 per cent per annum in GDP per capita (Maddison, 2003). However, growth was brought to a halt by a severe drought in 1965/6 and the following recession lasted until GDP recovered its 1964 peak in 1969. The economic policies achieved their purpose in so far as there was growth in the output of industries such as steel and machine tools but this was not matched by the cotton textile industry, which suffered from a lack of improvement in productivity. There was also an expansion in agricultural output but this was due to an increase in the cultivated area, there being no improvement in yields. Following the drought of

1965/6, agriculture recovered with the 'Green Revolution', benefiting from improved plant varieties with higher yields and greater expenditure on fertilizers and irrigation projects, which were sufficiently successful to make India self-sufficient in food products (>AGRICULTURE: >RICE).

From 1970 to 1980, GDP per capita slowed to an average of 0.8 per cent per annum, compared with 1.4 per cent per annum in the previous decade. A fall in the rate of growth was experienced throughout industry, including steel, pig iron, cement, automobiles and an actual decline in the output of cotton textile mills, which was offset by a continuing growth in the handicraft sector. There was a rate of growth in GDP in the three decades following independence of about 3.5 per cent per annum, which became known as the 'Hindu Rate of Growth', while the population was growing at 2.2 per cent per annum. The period was characterized by a heavy government presence in the economy through protectionist policies, regulation of industry and price controls. The effect was to encourage domestic industry but because of the lack of competition it lapsed into acceptance of high costs and poor quality and fell behind best international standards.

In the 1980s, the government introduced some liberalizing measures to shift the balance away from state to entrepreneurial decision-making by easing government regulation. Rodrik and Subramanian (2004) argue that this represented an important shift in the attitude taken by the Indian government towards the private sector, to which it had been previously hostile under its socialist ideology, and set the groundwork for the more thorough-going liberalizing measures of the following decade. It resulted in a growth rate of 5.5 per cent per annum in GDP between 1980 and 1991 but it was supported by a deficit-financed fiscal expansion which led to a balance of payments crisis in 1991. In the following years, the government pursued a policy of exposing the domestic economy to international competition by lowering trade barriers and further reduced government controls, with the result that the high rate of growth in GDP continued through the 1990s, achieving a rate of 5.8 per cent per annum with further improvement to an average rate of growth of 7.4 per cent per annum from 2000–8. India experienced rapid growth in businesses such as information technology, telecommunications and outsourcing and developed successful international corporations, such as Tata Steel of India (>IRON AND STEEL). There was a decline in the share of agriculture in GDP but the switch in activity was to services rather than industry. The share of services in GDP rose from 37 per cent in 1980 to 48 per cent in 2000, whereas there was little change in that of industry (World Bank, 2008).

The increase in the rate of growth in the last decades of the 20th century enabled India to reduce the incidence of poverty by 50 per cent and to increase the expectation of life from 54 years to 63 years. But, in spite of these improvements, 20 per cent of the population remained undernourished and in some rural areas the incidence of poverty was as low as that of the world's most under-developed nations. About 75 per cent of the poor lived in rural areas and in spite of the development of industry and services, the 2001 census showed that agriculture still employed 58 per cent of the labour force of 235 million, though it contributed only 25 per cent to National Income (World Bank, 2006) (>ECONOMIC DEVELOPMENT).

At Independence, the population India was 346 million and by 2000 it had reached 1,264 million. Such growth in population, together with such gains as were made in economic efficiency, enabled India to become the fourth largest economy in the world.

## References

James, Lawrence, *Raj, The Making and Unmaking of British India*, Little, Brown, 1997.

Landes, David, *The Wealth and Poverty of Nations*, Little, Brown, 1998.

Maddison, Angus *The World Economy. Historical Statistics*, Development Centre Studies, OECD, 2003.

Myrdal, Gunnar, *Against the Stream, Critical Essays in Economics*, Macmillan, 1974.

Rodrik, Dani and Subramanian, Arvind, 'From "Hindu Growth" to Productivity Surge: The Mystery of the Indian Growth Transition', National Bureau of Economic Research, Working Paper No.10376, March, 2004.

Rothermund, Dietmar, *An Economic History of India from Pre-Colonial Times to 1991*, Routledge, 1993.

Roy, Tirthankar, *The Economic History of India, 1857–1947*, Oxford University Press, 2006.

Saul, S. B., *Studies in British Overseas Trade, 1870–1914*, Liverpool University Press, 1960.

Tomlinson, B. R., *The Economy of Modern India, 1860–1970*, Cambridge University Press, 1996.

World Bank, *India Inclusive Growth and Service Delivery: Building on India's Success*, Development Policy Review, May, 2006.

World Bank, *World Economic Outlook*, April, 2008.

## Industrial Districts

'The Concentration of Specialised Industries in Particular Localities' was the title of Chapter X in Alfred Marshall's *Principles of Economics* (1890) (>CLASSICAL AND NEO-CLASSICAL ECONOMICS). In the previous chapter of that book, Marshall also introduced the distinction between the internal economies of a firm that can arise as production increases and external economies that may be gained from the concentration of firms in the same trade in a particular area. These external economies may take the form of the ready availability of skilled labour or other specialized inputs, such as intermediate products as well as, we should say today, specific services such as waste treatment, testing laboratories, design facilities and specialized sources of finance. In his later *Industry and Trade* (1919) Marshall wrote that, 'Sheffield and Soligen have acquired industrial "atmospheres" of their own; which yield gratis to the manufacturers of cutlery great advantages, that are not easily to be had elsewhere: and an atmosphere cannot be moved' .

Though some of the examples of industrial districts in Britain which Marshall cited have largely disappeared or been absorbed into large firms, others have emerged, such as the agglomeration of electronics companies near Cambridge and the M4 motorway corridor. Most industrialized countries seem to have had, and continue to have, industrial districts (often now referred to as 'clusters') of which the best-known examples include Silicon Valley and the Boston cluster in the USA, metal working in Wurttemberg in Germany and the small export-oriented manufacturers of ceramics, leather and other goods in Northern Italy. External economies are not confined to manufacturing and, for example, as Marshall pointed out, are also to be found in retailing. Retail customers may wish to reduce search costs by going to an area where there is a choice of shops for particular types of goods, such as up-market fashions in Bond Street or books in the Charing Cross Road in London. Sometimes retail and craft manufacturing trades may be found together, as in the case of jewellery in Hatton Garden in London and West 47th Street in New York.

Because external economies are more important for small firms than for large companies, for which these economies may be more easily internalized, most industrial districts are composed mainly of small firms. A growing body of literature sees small firms using *flexible production* in decentralized districts or regions as an alternative form of industrial capitalism to the centralized model of large firms. In flexible production, firms use multipurpose machines and skilled labour to produce goods for markets where tastes change and evolve and where quality and variety are more important than low price (Piore and Sabel, 1984; Sabel and Zeitlin, 1997; Herrigel, 1996; Scranton, 1997). This decentralized view contrasts with the traditional, centralist, views rooted in Adam >SMITH and developed by >MARX, >SCHUMPETER and >CHANDLER to postulate a single trajectory from small to large enterprise with division of labour leading over time to large-scale production as the sole means for raising productivity. Herrigel (1996) includes >GERSCHENKRON in this train of thought and argues that, contrary to the traditional view, forms of centralized and decentralized industry structures have co-existed on a regional basis in Germany from the beginning.

Implicit in the decentralized viewpoint is the observation that in industrial districts and flexible production (which go together) there are to be found differences in institutions, in government, and particularly local government, as well as private collective endeavours. In Goodman and Bamford (1989), for example, the contributors show that in the case of Italy, for example, in Emilia-Romagna, community spirit and institutions encouraged by trade unions and local authorities in the early 1980s had modulated excessive price competition in favour of competition in quality and also pressures for the exploitation of labour, reproducing, in effect, the roles of earlier guilds (>TRADE UNIONS). Revisiting Emilia, Rinaldi (2005) found that, after some decline, the regional economy had regenerated its competitive advantage and returned to higher growth rates in the 1990s, along with changes in governance and structure.

The contributors to Sabel and Zeitlin (1997)provide a rich array of cases of cooperative action, for example, the collective purchase of costly centrifuges for cream and cheese production by Danish dairy producers. This evidence of social homogeneity giving rise to cooperation seems to be particularly characteristic of Continental European industrial districts: the availability of cooperative wine storage and bottling facilities for vintners, for example, is commonplace in France, Germany and Italy. Dedicated institutions and a cooperative spirit may be necessary in some industries to prevent cutthroat competition from leading to concentration in industrial districts and their destruction (as apparently happened in the Sheffield cutlery district though not in Soligen in Germany, where there was more community spirit). In Britain, industrial districts may be less common than elsewhere. Nonetheless there is at least one documented case in England where, despite fierce and sometimes unethical competition, market forces did not frustrate cooperative action. Carnevali (2004) shows that in the Birmingham jewellery district in 1887 and in the depths of a depression (because of a depression), over 200 manufacturers joined to form the Birmingham Jewellers and Silversmiths Association to regulate trade and lobby on its behalf.

Herrigel (1996) and Piore and Sabel (1984) (Scranton's (1997) and some others' accounts stop in the 1920s) show that in a wide range of countries the persistence of flexible production in industrial districts raises important questions about the evolution of industrial structures and indeed the long-term significance of the >INDUSTRIAL REVOLUTIONS. It would be misleading though for a focus on the decentralized model to lead to an underestimation of the complementarity of >SMALL AND MEDIUM ENTERPRISES and large firms. The increased market fluctuations and pressures since the early 1970s, as noted by Piore and Sabel (1984), have resulted in some resurgence of flexible production but they have resulted in a more general increase in the numerical importance of small firms, partly as pricing pressures have led large firms to concentrate on core activities ('downsizing') and make greater use of bought-in intermediate products and services. Given the economic generational impact of smaller firms and decentralized industry and the role of industrial districts in 'high technology' enterprise, many governments have endeavoured to promote industrial districts, often by promoting science parks, though the results have been mixed. Most of the existing districts seem to have arisen spontaneously (as in the case of Cambridge and Silicon Valley, although both benefited from proximity to higher educational and research establishments). There may be some exceptions: Sophia-Antipolis near Nice in France, for example, does appear to owe its original existence to public initiative.

## References

Carnevali, Francesca, 'Crooks, Thieves, and Receivers': Transaction Costs in Nineteenth Century Industrial Birmingham', *Economic History Review*, August, 2004.

Goodman, Edward and Bamford, Julia (eds), *Small Firms and Industrial Districts in Italy*, Routledge, 1989.

Herrigel, Gary, *Industrial Constructions: The Sources of German Industrial Power*, Cambridge University Press, 1996.

Piore, Michel J. and Sabel, Charles F., *The Second Industrial Divide: Possibilities for Prosperity*, Basic Books, 1984.

Rinaldi, Alberto, 'The Emilian Model Revisited Twenty Years After', *Business History*, 47, April, 2005.

Sabel, Charles F. and Jonathan Zeitlin (eds), *World of Possibilities: Flexibility and Mass Production in Western Industrialisation*, Cambridge University Press, 1997.

Scranton, Philip, *Endless Novelty: Specialty Production and American Industrialisation, 1865–1925*, Princeton University Press, 1997.

## Industrial Revolution in Britain

The significant shift towards machine manufacture which started first in Britain in the 18th century and later in other countries (>INDUSTRIAL REVOLUTIONS). Industrialization involved not only the adoption of powered machinery but changes in organization, a shift in >POPULATION from >AGRICULTURE into towns and later a sustained increase in wealth and income. Industrialization was to have profound social and political as well as economic consequences.

In >BRITAIN, the period of the industrial revolution, after Ashton (1948), is generally put between about 1760 and 1830. It was in this period that a number of inventions enabled the transformation of the >IRON AND STEEL making, textile and chemical sectors and it is these that define the industrial revolution (>COTTON AND COTTON TEXTILES). It is misleading, however, to view these particular developments as outside the more general context of a relatively rich, expanding economy benefiting from the >AGRICULTURAL REVOLUTION which was still continuing and a growing overseas trade and empire which provided necessary supplies, such as raw cotton, and markets to supplement domestic demand (>CONSUMER REVOLUTION: >INTERNATIONAL TRADE). It would be wrong also to ignore the necessary social, scientific and technical groundwork for industrialization stretching back to the Middle Ages, or to imagine that the process had much more than got underway by the 1830s (>EDUCATION: >PEASANTRY AND SERFDOM).

For example, Thomas Savery (1650–1715) built a steam pump as early as 1698, but it was James Watt's (1736–1819) development of the steam condenser and the use of cogs and gears that made it possible to replace water power in the cotton and other industries. >STEAM POWER was the key development in the industrial revolution but its full impact was not felt until much later. By 1833 half of all textile mills were still worked by water power. >MACHINE TOOLS which allowed the accurate mass-production of further machines did not emerge until the 1820s, and the revolution in transport that came with the >RAILWAYS and the steamship (>SHIPPING) did not really get underway until about 1840.

Another set of key inventions were those in cotton spinning. These started early with the flying shuttle in 1733, but it was not until 1764 that spinning could be mechanized with James Hargreaves' (1720–1778) spinning jenny. The early cotton machinery was made of wood and powered by water. From 1785, when steam power came to be applied to spinning and weaving, the end of the cottage system came into sight (>PROTO-INDUSTRIALIZATION). The wool industry, in which Britain led the way before the industrial revolution, was mechanized later and it was not until about 1840 that cotton and wool manufacture had become essentially a factory industry (>WOOL AND WOOL TEXTILES).

Although the mechanization of textiles was more spectacular and involved many more people, it was the iron and steel industries which were the first to industrialize in factories. Iron production was declining at the beginning of the 18th century, mainly because of a shortage of wood for the charcoal then needed. Early inventions enabled the use of >COAL in blast furnaces, and puddling and rolling made more efficient the production of high-quality bar iron, much of which had been imported until the 1790s. The use of coal instead of charcoal meant that iron production could move away from the wooded areas and into the coalfields near which most iron ore was located. Iron, coal and water power were all available in South Wales, the North East and North West and large iron works developed in these places. Between 1790 and 1796 the production of iron almost doubled. The increased demand for coal stimulated the development of steam power for pumping water and hoisting coal out of deeper mines. Steam engines required more accurate engineering and machining methods, and the demand for machinery increased the demand for coal and iron. Increased output of textiles stimulated other inventions, which made possible developments in industrial chemicals, for example, for bleaching and pottery. Many of the key figures in the industrial revolution, Richard Arkwright (1732–1792), Matthew Boulton (1728–1809), John Kay (1704–1764), James Watt, Josiah >WEDGWOOD and John Wilkinson (1728–1808), for example, played a role in several of its developments, and indeed worked together in some of them. Wedgwood promoted canals and turnpikes as well as in transforming the pottery industry. Matthew Boulton, a pioneer in hardware manufactures, partly financed Watt's development of the steam engine, which was made possible by Wilkinson's ability as a cannon founder to cast and bore iron cylinders to high standards of accuracy.

There were three other important elements in addition to technological change in the industrial revolution. The first was the growth in population. The population of England, for example, only rose from about 5.1 to 5.8 million from 1701–51, but by 1801 it was about 8.7 million and by 1856, 17.7 million. Net >MIGRATION was not responsible. This rapid growth was also not solely the result of a fall in the death rate, though this did fall, especially after 1825, but also of a rise in the birth rate, notably between 1801 and 1825. The increase in population favoured the industrial revolution, but it was neither a prime cause, nor a result of it (population was increasing elsewhere in Europe). However, industrialization and improved productivity in agriculture did confound the beliefs of Classical economists that decreasing returns in agriculture would place a limit on population expansion (>CASSICAL AND NEO-CLASSICAL ECONOMICS: >MALTHUS). Industrialization also saw a major shift in the distribution of population towards the North. If we leave aside the metropolitan counties of London, the three most densely populated counties in 1700 were Gloucester, Northampton and Somerset, the manufacturing areas of the West. By 1881, the top three were Lancashire (textiles), Durham (coal and iron) and Stafford (pottery).

The second other element in industrialization was the expansion of the transport system. Depending heavily on local markets and local sources of supply of materials and water power, Britain could make do with a road system, in many places little improved since Roman times, and river and coastal shipping. As output in factories increased, overseas and domestic markets grew and the new districts in the North and West developed, improved transport became urgently necessary. This was provided by roads and canals, with railways coming later. From 1750, the Turnpike Acts shifted responsibility for maintenance and new roads from adjoining parishes to the users, via tolls. The first canal, which opened in 1757, cut the cost of transporting coal from the coalfields of Lancashire to Liverpool by 75 per cent (>CANALS: >ROAD TRANSPORT).

The third element was a growing separation between political and economic power encapsulated in the phrase 'laissez-faire' (though Britain was not a laissez-faire state in the literal sense and the positive role of the state was not unimportant (>STATE AND ECONOMIC DEVELOPMENT: >MERCANTILISM)).

The scientific revolution of the 16th and 17th centuries helped to open up minds and stimulate empirical inquiry but science seems to have been less important in the 18th century than technological progress achieved by practical trial and error. This remains controversial, since many of the famous engineers, ironmasters and industrial chemists were Fellows of the Royal Society, which Ashton took to reveal the close relations between science and practice, but it remains difficult to trace cause and effect between the two in the period 1760–1830 (>EDUCATION). Not all the important technical developments involved powered machinery, the cotton handloom is an example, or were restricted to the so-called 'growth industries'. Improvements in hand technology, such as the development of bone china, an innovation in pottery, and coach springs for road vehicles, vital for the transport industry, were also very important. These and similar non-powered developments and improvements in organization encouraged expansion in the output of thousands of small enterprises which predominated in numerical terms in all industries, including cotton.

Two important questions are raised by the industrial revolution. Why did it take place in Britain first and was there a social price to pay and, if so, who paid it?

The answers to these questions remain controversial. Britain, though in the shadow of Spain in the 16th century and the economic inferior of Holland and France in the 17th, emerged in the 18th as a relatively prosperous country compared with say, Germany which, weakened by the 30 Years' War (1618–1648), was in 1800 still an agglomeration of over 300 states separated by tolls and tariffs. Spain was no longer a great power and the Dutch Republic was in decline. France, with more than three times the population of its British rival, had a larger industrial base and its manufacturing may have grown at a similar rate to Britain's in the 18th century (Crouzet, 2001). The question therefore really becomes, why did Britain's industrial revolution precede that of France (>WESTERN EUROPE)?

The answer is that Britain, stretching back to medieval times, had greater personal freedom and mobility and distinctively different social, economic and legal systems, especially in terms of property rights, not only from Asia but also to a lesser degree Continental Europe and it is these institutional differences that count in >ECONOMIC DEVELOPMENT. These differences, earlier >ENCLOSURE of farmland and better techniques, including the greater use of animal power, allowed a faster growth in agriculture in Britain than in France, which helped to develop the necessary capital and labour resources for industrialization (>AGRICULTURAL REVOLUTION). Britain's level of skills in some artisan technologies seem to have been superior to those of France and its sea power was a key to its success in rivalry with France abroad. In addition, Britain had better coastal transport and ample supplies of coal conveniently located near waterways and sources of iron ore. It was not until after the French Revolution in 1789 that France could begin to modernize and it was this political revolution that was to speed up development elsewhere. Indeed, it has been said that 19th-century development was the product of French ideas and British techniques. It is worth pointing out here that >SLAVERY and colonization were probably not crucial to the British industrial revolution (>ECONOMIC IMPERIALISM). As Mokyr (1999) argues, other non-imperial nations were early industrializers and without American slavery the British cotton industry's supplies of raw material would have been curtailed.

The reason why the industrial revolution took place in Europe and not elsewhere was also probably to do with the superiority of its agriculture and its political systems, which provided, not only in Britain, relatively greater freedom for individual initiative and scope for personal wealth accumulation within the framework of law. Also important were rationality, freedom from superstition and other social factors. Europe was, by international standards, relatively wealthy and that wealth was more evenly distributed. In Britain and France real income per head in the 1750s was higher than in many countries of the Third World in the early 21st century. The identity of political, religious and economic power in earlier civilizations had not prevented remarkable technical advance from which Europe benefited. Gunpowder, various mechanical inventions, the compass, paper and probably printing, came to Europe from >CHINA, where they had been developed from 618 onwards. Muslim civilization, via the early Greeks, had brought mathematics, astronomy and medicine to Europe; but none of these early civilizations achieved industrialization, something which still eludes much of the Third World today (>ECONOMIC DEVELOPMENT).

Controversy continues over the social price paid in Britain (and indeed elsewhere) for industrialization. As industrialization proceeded there was increasing concern about the working and living conditions of the poor in factories and towns. There were a number of official inquiries into health, children's employment and other matters from the early 1830s. Frederick Engel's book, *The Condition of the Working Class in England*, was first published in German in 1845 and in English in 1887. Engels compared the conditions for industrial workers unfavourably with those of workers in the agrarian period and he and >MARX were to assert that exploitation of workers was inevitable under >CAPITALISM. Arnold Toynbee (1852–1883) also took a very unfavourable view of the consequences of industrialization. Beatrice (1858–1943) and Sidney Webb (1859–1947) and J. L. and B. >HAMMOND did likewise. Since the 1950s, with the work of E. J. Hobsbaum, E. P. >THOMPSON and others, historians have also taken a pessimistic view in what has become an exceptionally long-running debate about living standards. These more recent writers criticized measures of living standards based on real incomes alone as inadequate and drew attention to other factors such as hours of work, health and safety at work and >INEQUALITY.

There was certainly abuse and exploitation of workers in the 19th century. Fear of the results of social and economic change led to social stress and the emergence of >TRADE UNIONS, >LUDDISM and an extension of state >REGULATION of industry and the environment. From the 1830s, the Factory Acts led to major improvements. Conditions in cities were appalling by modern standards, with severe problems of disposing of the dead and sewage. Conditions in the towns compared unfavourably with those in rural areas; studies of people's heights in rural and urban areas confirm that living standards generally were superior (>ANTHROPOMETRIC HISTORY). Living standards overall degenerated during the early period of the industrial revolution. Average

living standards, as measured by real wages, are now believed not to have improved significantly until the mid-1850s. However, much of the romantic perception of cottage industry (in which children were probably made to work longer than they later did in factories, while textile workers slept, ate and worked in damp and filthy conditions) has given way to a more realistic assessment. Conditions in factories were probably better than those in much of domestic industry and the position of women was better, though, cut off from their farming activities, families became more vulnerable to acute economic hardship.

Studies of the 18th and the early 19th centuries are hampered by the lack of adequate data. There are, for example, data on wages for some sectors but average hours worked and price levels to convert money wages into real earnings are difficult to estimate. Moreover, the level of wages might not be a good indicator of household as distinct from individual incomes (>INDUSTRIOUS REVOLUTION). There is also controversy about the levels of National Income and rates of economic growth during the industrial revolution. The general thrust of recent research has been to smooth out the earlier impression of an upward kink in economic growth during the period (>INDUSTRIAL REVOLUTIONS). New estimates of population growth, price changes and incomes have led to a revision of earlier views. Crafts, in Floud and McCloskey (1994), reports an annual percentage industry output growth of 1.3 per cent from 1760–80 compared with 0.7 per cent in 1700–60 and 2.0 and 2.8 per cent respectively in 1780 – 1801 and 1801–31. Earlier estimates had shown slower growth in 1760–80 and much faster expansion in the later periods.

The new estimates have triggered continuing controversy, though the new figures do not alter the long-standing view that there was a fundamental shift to industrialization between 1760 and 1830. In detail, however, the differences between old and new estimates reveal a difference between those who see the industrial revolution as a more or less pervasive change and those who see it mainly restricted to a few industries, notably coal, cotton, some engineering trades and iron and steel. This *is* important because higher output and productivity growth outside the 'growth sectors' has implications for income levels and the role of domestic consumption and exports in total demand. In support of the revisionist view, Estaban (1997) has shown that the export share of industrial output rose continuously between 1723 and 1851, a phenomena that could not be explained solely by cotton, even though half of its sales were abroad. Temin (1997) demonstrates that many sectors contributed to exports. The trade figures show that Britain had a comparative advantage in a wide range of sectors, implying that productivity growth was not confined to a small number of sectors. This debate is bound up with the parallel debates on the standard of living and the concept of the industrious revolution. It is likely that the impact of the industrial revolution did extend outside the large factories and impacted also on the host of smaller firms which persisted throughout the period, although data on their output and productivity is hard to find. A further factor in the debate is that the growth industries were largely confined to the Midlands and North of the country. Some economic historians have argued that the industrial revolution, not only in Britain, was essentially a regional phenomenon.

One of the defining characteristics of the industrial revolution was a shift of the labour force out of agriculture and into manufacturing. While a declining relative contribution of agriculture to the national income of England and Wales has been confirmed in the new estimates (45 per cent in 1770 down to 20 per cent in 1851), it is now believed that manufacturing, mining and construction contributed little more as a percentage of the total in 1801 than in 1770 – it was the share of commerce, transport and the rest which rose from 31 per cent to 43 per cent over the period. The overall share of investment in the national product also rose less than was earlier believed, at least up to 1830, though there was heavy investment in mineral-based industries and, of course, in transport. Even so, investment probably doubled from 6–12 per cent of National Income over the period 1760–1830. Financing increases in fixed and working capital does not appear to have been a constraint, even though general limited liability structures and public equity securities markets were little developed compared with earlier periods (>CAPITAL MARKETS). Much of the necessary finance came from families, friends and business partners, while regional banking developed rapidly (>MONEY AND BANKING).

### References

Ashton, T. S., *The Industrial Revolution, 1760–1830*, Oxford University Press, 1948.

Berg, Maxine and Hudson, Pat, 'Rehabilitating the Industrial Revolution', *Economic History Review*, 45, 1992.

Coleman, D. C., *Myth, History and the Industrial Revolution*, Hambledon Press, 1992.

Crafts, N. F. R. and Harley, C. K., 'Simulating the Two Views of the Industrial Revolution', *Journal of Economic History*, 60, 2000.

Crouzet, François, *A History of the European Economy, 1000–2000*, University Press of Virginia, 2001.

Deane, Phyllis and Cole, W. A. *British Economic Growth, 1688–1959: Trends and Structure*, Cambridge University Press, 1969.

Engels, Frederick, *The Condition of the Working Class in England*, Panther, 1845, English trans. 1887.

Estaban, Javier Cuenca, 'The Rising Share of British Industrial Exports in Industrial Output, 1700–1851', *Journal of Economic History*, 57, 1997.

Floud, Roderick and McCloskey, Donald, *The Economic History of Britain Since 1700*, I, 1700–1860 (2nd edn), Cambridge University Press, 1994.

Hudson, Pat , *The Industrial Revolution*, Edward Arnold, 1992.

James, John A. and Thomas, Mark (eds), *Capitalism in Context*, University of Chicago Press, 1994.

King, Steven and Timmins, Geoffrey, *Making Sense of the Industrial Revolution*, Manchester University Press, 2001.

Macfarlane, Alan, *The Origins of English Individualism*, Basil Blackwell, 1978.

Mathias, Peter, *The First Industrial Nation*, Routledge, 1983.

Mokyr, Joel (ed.), *The British Industrial Revolution: An Economic Perspective* (2nd edn), Westview Press, 1999.

Pollard, Sydney, *Peaceful Conquest: Industrialisation of Europe, 1760–1970*, Oxford University Press, 1981.

Temin, Peter, 'Two Views of the Industrial Revolution', *Journal of Economic History*, 57, 1997.

# Industrial Revolutions

From the middle of the 18th and into the final quarter of the 19th centuries, the economies of a number of Western countries experienced an initial and what was to be a continuing shift towards machine manufacture. These industrial 'revolutions' were to be accompanied by shifts of resources from agriculture to industry, important social changes and, ultimately, higher levels of sustained economic growth. The importance of these changes, though not widely appreciated at the time, was such that they amounted to a turning point in civilization to which the roots of many of the features of the present globalizing world can be traced.

Although now common currency and as such probably irreplaceable, the term 'industrial revolution' is not an entirely satisfactory one because it suggests an event instead of what in reality were quite long, drawn-out processes without definite start and finish dates. For that reason, and because data for the 18th and 19th centuries are unreliable, although we give dates in this exposition they cannot be regarded as other than rough indications in most cases. Moreover, no two industrial revolutions were identical. For example, industrial exports were an important dynamic and imports a key source of raw material supplies in the >INDUSTRIAL REVOLUTION IN BRITAIN and also in Japan and later in the industrialization of East Asia (>ASIAN MIRACLE), but not in the cases of >RUSSIA or the >USA. British industrialization was led most prominently by >COTTON AND COTTON TEXTILES, those of >RUSSIA and Germany were dominated by heavy industry, while in France an important role was taken by the manufacture of luxury goods. Although it might be said that one of the characteristics of all these revolutions was the emergence of large factories, much output and certainly the majority of industrial employment, was in >SMALL AND MEDIUM ENTERPRISES (and still is today). Economic historians have unearthed all kinds of surprising facts to demonstrate the contrasts between the popular view of 'dark satanic mills' (which did, of course, exist) and actual evolutionary change. In the 1820s, for example, when the British industrial revolution was in full swing, more was invested in public houses than in factories (King and Timmins, 2001) and N. F. R. Crafts (2000) calculated that, in 1780, the two drivers of the revolution in Britain, cotton and >IRON AND STEEL, at that stage contributed only 3 per cent of the National Income. Findings of these sorts have led to major revisions of earlier views of industrial revolutions and not only for Britain.

Crouzet (2001) accepts that the French industrial revolution, compared with Britain's, was relatively slow. The growth of GNP in the 19th century was long thought to have stagnated and it was in fact slower than that of many countries; however, this was mainly because of a stabilization in the population from mid-century. In per capita terms, French growth was close to that of Britain though GNP per capita was well below British levels. Crouzet says that by 1860, France was the second in the world but it was not an industrial nation since half of the labour force was still in agriculture. After 1900, France was industrializing rapidly with new industry, for example, in motor vehicles and aircraft but this development was cut short by >WORLD WAR I. The pattern of early French industrialization was also very different from that of Britain. In Britain, the industrial revolution began with basic industries such as steel and cotton and developed downstream. In France industrialization began in labour-intensive consumption goods industries, especially luxury goods, and developed upstream, for example, into silk mills

and chemicals. To some extent this was also true of other Continental European countries, for example, Switzerland. Jeff Horn (2006) argues that Britain was able to control and exploit its labour force to a greater extent than France, thanks to the emergence of revolutionary politics in the 18th century and that this forced France to take a somewhat different route to industrialization At one time it was thought by economic historians that France suffered from failures of >ENTREPRENEURSHIP and excessively fragmented industry, though it does not seem that the average size of plants was very different in the two countries.

The industrial revolution in Britain was first analyzed explicitly by Arnold Toynbee (1969) in lectures delivered in Oxford in 1880–1 though not published until 1864. Toynbee was not the first to use the term 'industrial revolution'; this is credited to a French diplomat, Louis Guillaume Otto in 1799 (Crouzet, in Teich and Porter, 1996). These revolutions can perhaps be recognized once well underway, but their defining characteristics and therefore their precise timing are in practice not easily established. Both Alexander >GERSHENKRON and Walt >ROSTOW thought that industrial revolutions were characterized by spurts or take-offs in industrial and economic growth. Later scholars have thrown doubt on this. Crafts, Leybourne and Mills, in Sylla and Toniolo (1991), using sophisticated statistical analysis were unable to identify kinks in the industrial growth curves of a number of early industrializers, including Austria, France, Germany, Hungary and Russia. They did find an upward discontinuity in trend growth in Britain (1760) and in Italy (1890). Crafts' recent work for Britain (Crafts and Harley, 2000) and that of several scholars for other countries have found that overall industrial growth has generally been slower than was earlier supposed, mainly because the weight of the rapidly expanding sectors was so small. Recent research for the USA does not suggest that there were spurts of growth either before or after the >AMERICAN CIVIL WAR.

Stearns (1993), in his valuable international overview, distinguishes three global periods of industrialization: 1760–1880; 1880–1950; and 1950s to the present. The industrial revolution in Britain, now generally taken to be between 1760 and 1830, was undoubtedly the first. Britain was followed by Belgium and France (though there is controversy about the latter, see below). Other very early industrializers included the American northern >USA, from about 1800, and Austria and Germany in the 1830s (>WESTERN EUROPE). The Netherlands, which at the end of the 18th century had been the richest country in Europe and relatively highly developed in financial and commercial terms, was a surprisingly late industrializer: some writers put its initial phase at the end of the 19th century, around 1890 and perhaps only a little earlier than Italy. Hungary, Sweden and Switzerland, probably in that order, had their industrial revolutions between 1860 and the middle 1880s. Spain seems to have been a special case with the turning point being attributed by some scholars to various times in the 100 years following 1850. Some British dominions, notably Australia and Canada, were industrialized before 1880, though primary activities, agriculture and mining have remained important.

The second of Stearns' periods (1880–1950) was indelibly marked by the rise of Russia and Japan. Both were different from one another and from the earlier industrializers which gave them inspiration. Japan's industrialization from the 1880s to the 1950s was a virtually continuous process which carried it into the front rank of industrial countries. Russia had two goes at it, once in the late Tsarist period and another after the political revolution of 1917. Russia could also be said to have begun a third phase of industrialization from the Stalinist 1930s. Some scholars write of second and third industrial revolutions in this way in this and in other cases. William N. Parker, in Teich and Porter (1996), distinguishes a first, light-industrial phase in New England from 1800 and a second phase in Pittsburg–Cleveland from 1850. As in America and Britain, industrialization was usually concentrated in particular sectors and regions, followed many decades later by even more profound and widespread changes, and it is this process of diffusion and even acceleration that may be referred to as second or third industrial revolutions. Such second revolutions have been distinguished in the >USA and in >WESTERN EUROPE and indeed a third in the 1920s with the spread of electrical technologies (>ELECTRICITY). A fourth revolution began after World War II in >ELECTRONICS. These examples bring out the point that industrialization is a process and not an event, as mentioned above, though the initial phases have received the most attention in economic history.

The process of world industrialization continued in Stearns' third phase (1950 to the present), for example, in the newly industrialized countries of East Asia from about the 1960s (>ASIAN MIRACLE). As Stearns(1993) points out, however, from after about 1880, and particularly since >WORLD WAR II, it becomes increasingly difficult to apply the term 'industrial revolution' in its original sense of a first breakthrough because most countries had industrial sectors in some degree. Some countries, >SOUTH AFRICA and Brazil today, for example, have dual economies with a quite advanced manufacturing sector but also large proportions of the population languishing in traditional subsistence or petty trading activities. >CHINA and >INDIA also have dual economies in this sense, though both are now industrializing rapidly. Levels of income per capita are not a criteria that can be used unambiguously to indicate industrialization. Some >OIL-producing countries have national incomes per capita, however unequally distributed, as high as those of the developed countries. The advanced countries have long since entered a post-industrial era in which economies are dominated by the >SERVICE SECTOR and are even experiencing de-industrialization as manufacturing, attracted by lower labour costs, increasingly shifts to developing countries, a kind of industrial revolution in reverse (>ECONOMIC DEVELOPMENT).

The economic literature on industrial revolutions is now very large. A number of trends in this literature can be identified. As already mentioned, the notion of sharp discontinuities in industrial or overall economic growth at the beginning of industrialization has been partly discredited. Some writers, notably Pollard (1981), have focused increasingly on sectoral and regional issues while others have emphasized that technical advance and economic growth were more even than previously thought and, just as important, that its roots are being pushed back in time. Several writers have identified an industrial revolution of sorts in medieval Europe (Gimpel, 1976).

There was not anywhere, perhaps, a sudden break with old ways. In many countries, certainly among many if not all the earlier industrializers, market-oriented household economic activity preceded factory industrialization (>PROTO-INDUSTRIALIZATION). Despite considerable variety, most industrial revolutions do seem to have certain features in common: shifts out of agriculture into industry and towns with an >AGRICULTURAL REVOLUTION to make this possible and to accommodate a rising >POPULATION; important legal and social developments (>INSTITUTIONS); and organizational and technological change in industry (the former preceding the latter in many cases, while some developments, particularly more recently, were imported from other countries). In much of the earlier literature the industrial revolutions were seen primarily as supply-led phenomena but rising domestic consumption of capital and consumer goods were parallel and possibly prior developments. The nature, timing and extent of the >CONSUMER REVOLUTIONS which must have accompanied industrialization are attracting increasing interest by economic historians but, because of a lack of data, remain controversial.

A common feature of all industrial revolutions seems to have been an early deterioration in worker conditions and living standards. This raises the question, if real wages deteriorated initially, as they may have done in the >INDUSTRIAL REVOLUTION IN BRITAIN, how could consumers have purchased the rising output from the new factories (Berg and Hudson, 1992)? The answer to this may be that it was an increasingly affluent middle class that led the consumer revolution, if in fact there was one, or more likely that households had more earners than before, particularly women (>INDUSTRIOUS REVOLUTION). Toynbee may have been the first to draw forceful attention to the evils of industrialization in Britain, but Charles Dickens and numerous other novelists and historians were also to do so, not only in Britain but elsewhere. There was considerable mass suffering in Japan, Russia and the USA during early industrialization, for example, even if living standards were to rise a few decades later. Industrial revolutions were to have profound social and political as well as economic consequences (>CAPITALISM: >REGULATION). Among these consequences were major changes in the international balance of power (>ECONOMIC IMPERIALISM). It is not surprising that there has always been intense interest in the causes of industrialization and how it might be promoted (>STATE, RISE OF: >ECONOMIC DEVELOPMENT).

### References

Ashton, T. S., *The Industrial Revolution, 1760–1830*, Oxford University Press, 1948.

Berg, Maxine and Hudson, Pat, 'Rehabilitating the Industrial Revolution', *Economic History Review*, 45, 1992.

Coleman, D. C., *Myth, History and the Industrial Revolution*, Hambledon Press, 1992.

Crafts, N. F. R. and Harley, C. K., 'Simulating the Two Views of the Industrial Revolution', *Journal of Economic History*, 60, 2000.

Crouzet, François, *A History of the European Economy, 1000–2000*, University Press of Virginia, 2001.

Deane, Phyllis and Cole, W. A. *British Economic Growth, 1688–1959: Trends and Structure*, Cambridge University Press, 1969.

Engels, Frederick, *The Condition of the Working Class in England*, Panther, 1845, English trans. 1887.

Estaban, Javier Cuenca, 'The Rising Share of British Industrial Exports in Industrial Output, 1700–1851', *Journal of Economic History*, 57, 1997.

Floud, Roderick and McCloskey, Donald, *The Economic History of Britain Since 1700*, I, 1700–1860 (2nd edn), Cambridge University Press, 1994.

Gimpel, Jean, *The Medieval Machine: The Industrial Revolution of the Middle Ages*, Victor Gollanz, 1976.

Horn, Jeff, *The Path Not Taken: French Industrialisation in the Age of Revolution, 1750–1830*, MIT Press, 2006.

Hudson, Pat , *The Industrial Revolution*, Edward Arnold, 1992.

James, John A. and Thomas, Mark (eds), *Capitalism in Context*, University of Chicago Press, 1994.

King, Steven and Timmins, Geoffrey, *Making Sense of the Industrial Revolution*, Manchester University Press, 2001.

Macfarlane, Alan, *The Origins of English Individualism*, Basil Blackwell, 1978.

Mathias, Peter, *The First Industrial Nation*, Routledge, 1983.

Mokyr, Joel (ed.), *The British Industrial Revolution: An Economic Perspective* (2nd edn), Westview Press, 1999.

Pollard, Sydney, *Peaceful Conquest: Industrialisation of Europe, 1760–1970*, Oxford University Press, 1981.

Stearns, Peter N., *The Industrial Revolution in World History*, Westview Press, 1993.

Sylla, Richard and Toniolo, Gianni (eds), *Patterns of Industrialisation: The Nineteenth Century*, Routledge, 1991.

Teich, Mikulas and Porter, Roy (eds), *The Industrial Revolution in National Context*, Cambridge University Press, 1996.

Temin, Peter, 'Two Views of the Industrial Revolution', *Journal of Economic History*, 57, 1997.

Toynbee, Arnold, *Lectures on the Industrial Revolution in England* (1884), David and Charles Reprints, 1969.

# Industrious Revolution

From the mid-17th century to the early 19th century, De Vries (1994) argues, new consumption possibilities encouraged people to work longer hours and enjoy less leisure. De Vries puts this 'industrious revolution' in terms of changes in household-based resource allocations that increased both the supply of marketed commodities and labour and the demand for market-supplied goods. Households were turning from domestic production for subsistence (in which women and children participated) and increasingly producing for the market. At the same time, it seems, there was also an increase in the pace of work as the marginal utility (>CLASSICAL AND NEO-CLASSICAL ECONOMICS) of money income rose as it became possible to purchase a wider variety of commodities outside the household. De Vries argues that this industrious revolution helps to explain the paradox that wealth (as shown by probate assessments) and apparently consumption rose even though real wages were declining or stagnant (>INDUSTRIAL REVOLUTION IN BRITAIN). From 1800, and especially after 1850, women and children tended to withdraw from the paid labour market which, along with technological developments, forced up wages and promoted more capital-intensive modes of production. The concept of the industrious revolution has its origins in the thesis that industrialization in factories was preceded by a process of >PROTO-INDUSTRIALIZATION (household production for the market), which undoubtedly did occur in many, if not all, industrializing countries.

Several writers have shown that there was a >CONSUMER REVOLUTION accompanying the >INDUSTRIAL REVOLUTIONS in which households began to purchase more goods in the market. Unlike information on wages, which is copious if not always reliable or comprehensive, we have little information on household income, time spent working or expenditure patterns in this period. This lack of data has led to criticism of the industrious revolution thesis. Nonetheless the De Vries (1994) concept has become quite widely accepted, not only by economic historians but also by others. As well as the shift of work to factories, the reallocations of household resources brought bad as well as good social consequences. De Vries points to the effect on courtship and marriage, illegitimacy, an increase in binge drinking to relieve tension and, of course, reductions in leisure time.

An eventual partial withdrawal of women from the labour force that followed the industrial revolution as rising male wages allowed their return to the household did not last (>EMPLOYMENT OF WOMEN AND CHILDREN). De Vries points out that from the 1960s in Europe and the USA there was a second industrious revolution with a steep rise in female labour force participation: in the >USA that participation rose from 14 per cent in 1940 to 60 per cent in 1990. There was also in this period an increase in teenage labour force participation, despite increasing school attendance and, in many countries, more second jobs. De Vries says that the household is now rarely a site for production, though in fact about half of >SMALL AND MEDIUM ENTERPRISES are home-based and teleworking is quite extensive in some countries. As for the 18th and 19th centuries, the concept of the industrious revolutions helps to resolve the paradox of stagnant or declining individual real wages in some countries, and particularly in the USA, in the face of very high levels of consumption. This well-documented recent experience increases the credibility of the concept of the industrious revolution, which is a valuable addition to the economic historian's toolbox even though it may lack complete historical empirical validation.

### References

Clark, Gregory and Werf, Ysbrand Van der, 'Work in Progress?', *Journal of Economic History*, 58, 1998.
De Vries, Jan, 'The Industrial Revolution and the Industrious Revolution', *Journal of Economic History*, 54, 1994.
Voth, Hans Joachim, 'Time and Work in 18th Century London', *Journal of Economic History*, 58, 1998.

## Inequality

Inequality is not >POVERTY. People in the bottom strata of a society may not necessarily be poor compared with their opposite numbers who live in a society in which income or wealth is more evenly divided between them. Inequality may breed resentment and therefore disharmony and should be closely watched for that reason, but it is not a synonym for poverty. It may be defined in a number of ways, restricted to particular levels of society, particular countries or across a number of countries and it may be measured in a number of different ways. Inequality is generally concerned either with the distribution of personal income within a society or with the distribution of personal wealth and may or may not span a person's lifetime. This view contrasts with that of functional distribution which was the concern of the Classical economists, following >RICARDO, who were exercised about how the National Income was distributed between the

factors of production of land, labour and capital with the classes of society being identified with these. This may have yielded views on how and why the total income of a functional group of this kind fluctuated and on its share of the total, but did not throw any light directly on the distribution of the group's share among the individuals making up the group (>CLASSICAL AND NEO-CLASSICAL ECONOMICS).

A person's success or otherwise in attracting income or wealth is determined by inheritance and investment in assets which assist in producing income. The inheritance is not only the property and financial assets which are bequeathed but also personal characteristics such as intelligence, physical health and personality, together with the culture of the parental home and country. Okun (1980) quoted a study which showed that the sons of parents in the top 20 per cent earned 75 per cent more than the sons of those in the bottom 20 per cent. According to Jäntti *et al.* (2006), the intergenerational male earnings mobility in various countries differed significantly. Moreover, generational mobility was lowest in the >USA and highest in the Nordic countries, with >BRITAIN in between. The reason Britain registered lower than the Nordic countries was because of its lower downward movement from the top to the bottom. The main factor influencing the results for the USA was the low mobility from the lowest group to a higher. In the USA, it appeared to be most likely for the sons of poor parents to stay poor compared with the other countries studied.

Investment is not simply in financial assets but also in education and training suitable for earning a living. One person may earn more than another because he or she prefers to work excess hours in exchange for leisure or chooses work which has a higher than usual risk. A partner may chose to stay at home to look after children or chose to go out to work and pay for child care. Inequality in incomes is ingrained into the fabric of a society. In particular, people have inequality of opportunity because of their initial endowments and they may not be able to escape the inequality of outcomes. Inequality of opportunity is more pernicious when it exists not in the natural endowment of inheritance but outside in society as a whole, such as racial and sexual prejudice that prevents people from gaining their own potential. When it is said that every man or woman is born equal, what is meant is that every man or woman born should expect to be treated equally. Concern about inequality arises from the recognition that people may be dealt a poor hand in their initial inheritances and the just society should adjust the balance in so far as it might be practical and for the common good. Hence, for instance, the supply of free >EDUCATION by the state. For a society to be stable and coherent, it must retain a common culture and, therefore, constrain any tendency to the extremes of inequality of wealth and income (>EMPLOYMENT OF WOMEN AND CHILDREN).

Inequality may be measured by incomes earned, by consumption expenditures or the wealth owned by individuals or households and before or after tax and financial and other transfers, such as social security payments. The data may be considered for a specific year or over a whole lifetime. In so far as it is economic welfare which people seek to maximize, simple money income or wealth may not be a sufficient surrogate. Families not only vary in size but also by age

range from children to grandparents; a person's needs will vary depending on age, background and health; current income may be financed by past savings; non-financial benefits may be enjoyed such as an owner-occupied house.

In the USA, there was a significant fall in income inequality during >WORLD WAR II but, thereafter, for a number of years, there was little change, although there was considerable growth in real incomes throughout all ranges of income. In 1974, the average family income after tax was about $14,000 and the median was $12,000 as the distribution was skewed. The bottom 11 per cent of families had an average income of about $5,000 and the bottom 20 per cent of the population were in families with an average income below $7,000. The top 20 per cent had average incomes above $18,000 and the top 5 per cent had an average income of about $28,000. The top 20 per cent of families had about the same share of income after tax as the bottom 60 per cent (Okun, 1980). These figures were very similar to those for Britain at about the same time. In 1976/7, the top 20 per cent of households accounted for about 39 per cent of total after tax income compared with 36 per cent of the bottom 60 per cent. The degree by which government taxation policy had succeeded in shifting the spread of income may be seen in that, prior to tax, the top 20 per cent earned 42 per cent of total income compared with only 33 per cent of the total earned by the bottom 60 per cent (Royal Commission, 1980).

Tracing the degrees of inequality in income and wealth over the past to make comparisons between countries presents intractable problems of data availability and scholars have exercised considerable ingenuity in order to construct databases of acceptable creditability. At the same time, it is beneficial to be able to compare the degree of equality of income or wealth between one country and another or between one time period and another and a variety of measures have been applied which summarize the distributions in a simple statistic. Up to nine different measures of this nature have been used, each of which has it own advantages and disadvantages (Sala-i-Martin, 2002), but the most common is the Gini coefficient. The lower the value of this statistic the more evenly spread is the distribution, with a value of zero indicating perfect equality in the distribution. The higher the value, up to its maximum of unity, the more unequal the distribution.

Simon Kuznets, in 1955, found some evidence that the distribution of income was influenced by economic growth. Income inequality increased as an economy moved into the early stages of development and then, after reaching a peak, it began to decline. An inverted U was traced (>POVERTY). There appeared to be some indication of this in the changes in income distribution in Europe and the USA (>WESTERN EUROPE). These have followed two separate phases, before >WORLD WAR I and after. In the early period, there seemed to have been a deterioration in equality of incomes but after the war, there was, as in most developed countries, a clear reduction in income inequality. These results were not universal and accurate determination of degrees of inequality of income or wealth are fraught with data problems for early periods. There was a view that increasing inequality not only reflected growth but also encouraged it. This was based on the observation that the savings rate of the rich was higher than that of

the poor and that the resulting additional savings were translated into investment for growth. This idea fell out of favour in so far as it was clear that it was far too simplistic a view of the factors which generated economic expansion (>ECONOMIC DEVELOPMENT).

Williamson (1991), in a study of British inequality from the end of the 18th century to the second half of the 20th century, had concluded that there was some confirmation of the Kuznets curve in the British experience. He estimated that there was a considerable rise in inequality between 1815 and the 1860s. For instance, he calculated the Gini coefficient for employed male workers as rising from 0.29 in 1827 to 0.36 in 1851, with a drop to 0.33 in 1881 and 1901, a plateau on the Kuznets curve. After World War I, income inequality fell considerably. However, other studies have led to revisions of the data which have resulted in doubt being thrown on the validity of these results for Britain, suggesting that there may not have been any increase in inequality during the 18th and 19th centuries. Moreover, a different picture also emerged if inequality was measured by lifetime consumption rather than annual income so that changes in life expectancy may be taken into account. Jackson (1994) estimated that the inequality of lifetime consumption fell slightly in the 18th and 19th centuries, followed by a rapid decline in the 20th century, generated by the fall in the death rate.

Studies for the USA indicated that income inequality increased from the end of the Civil War to a peak in 1916, fell during World War I, to renew its upward movement so that it surpassed its 1916 peak by 1929. McLean (1991) argued the case that there was an increase in income inequality during the >GREAT DEPRESSION rather than a fall as had previously been determined and that the peak was in 1933 and not 1929. Thereafter, income inequality declined until the 1950s. In the second half of the 20th century, however, there was a considerable deterioration in income equality in the USA, particularly after 1980; although part of this deterioration may have been offset by the fall in the relative prices of the goods typically bought by the poor (Goldin and Katz, 2007).

A study by Sala-i-Martin (2002) of 125 countries between 1970 and 1998 tabulated the degree of income inequality worldwide and found that, on a number of measures, world income inequality fell overall in the these three decades. Although inequality changed little or increased in the 1970s, it declined considerably in the 1980s and 1990s. The Gini coefficient, for instance, in 1978 was 0.657 and by 1980 had risen slightly to 0.662. In 1990, however, it had fallen to 0.654 or by 1.2 per cent. By 1998 it had dropped further to 0.633 or a drop of 3.2 per cent. The ratio of the average income of the top 20 per cent of the population to that of the bottom 20 per cent was 40 in 1970, 45 in 1980, 41 in 1990 and 39 in 1998.

However, a different dispersion emerges for the worldwide ownership of wealth (defined as the ownership of physical and financial assets net of debt), rather than income. In the year 2000, it has been estimated that the top 10 per cent of the world adult population owned 85 per cent of the world total of household wealth and the bottom 50 per cent of the population owned about 1 per cent. The ownership of wealth per head ranged from $181,000 in Japan, $144,000 in the USA and $127,000 in Britain to $1,400 in Indonesia and $1,100 in >INDIA. The more advanced countries generally had a larger share of world wealth than of world Gross Domestic Product. The study calculated that whereas income distributions within countries ranged from a Gini coefficient of from about 0.35 to 0.45, that for the distribution of wealth within countries ranged typically from about 0.65 to 0.75. The USA, however, returned a Gini coefficient for the distribution of wealth at a high of 0.8, compared with Japan, which recorded a Gini coefficient of 0.55. The distribution of wealth across the world as a whole recorded a Gini coefficient of 0.89 (Shorrocks *et al.* 2006) (>PRICES AND INFLATION).

## References

Asian Development Bank, *Poverty, Inequality, and Human Development*, Key Indicators, 2005.

Goldin, Claudia and Katz, Lawrence F., 'Does China Benefit the Poor in America?', WP 13568, National Bureau of Economic Research, December, 2007.

Jackson, R. V., 'Inequality of Incomes and Lifespans in England since 1688', *Economic History Review*, XLVII(3), August, 1994.

Jäntti, Markus, Roed, Knut, Naylor, Robin, Björklund, Anders, Bratsberg, Bernt, Raaum, Oddbjorn and Eriksson, Tor, 'American Exceptionalism in a New Light: A Comparison of Intergenerational Earnings Mobility in the Nordic Countries, the United Kingdom, and the United States', Discussion Paper No. 1998, Institute for Study of Labour, Bonn, January. 2006 (Acrobat file).

Kuznets, Simon, 'Economic Growth and Income Equality', *American Economic Review*, 45(1), 1955.

McLean, Ian W., 'The Distributional Impact of the Depression in the United States.', in Y. S. Brenner, Hartmut Kaelble and Mark Thomas (eds), *Income Distribution in Historical Perspective*, Cambridge University Press, 1991.

Okun, A. M., 'Equality and Efficiency', Brookings Institute, 1975, extract in A.B. Atkinson (ed.), *Wealth, Income and Inequality*, Oxford University Press, 1980.

Royal Commission on the Distribution of Income and Wealth, *An A to Z of Income and Wealth*, HMSO, 1980.

Sala-i-Martin, X., 'The World Distribution of Income (estimated from individual country distributions)', NBER Working Paper No. 8933, 2002.

Shorrocks, Anthony, Davies, James, Sandström, Susanna and Wolff, Edward, 'World Distribution of Household Wealth', World Institute of Development Economics Research of United Nations University, December, 2006.

Townsend, P., 'The Development of the Research on Poverty', reprinted in A. B. Atkinson (ed.), *Wealth, Income and Inequality*, Oxford University Press, 1980.

Williamson, Jeffrey G., 'British Inequality during the Industrial Revolution: Accounting for the Kuznets' Curve', in Y. S. Brenner, Hartmut Kaelble and Mark Thomas (eds), *Income Distribution in Historical Perspective*, Cambridge University Press, 1991.

# Institutions

Established forms of law, accepted practice and organization which govern social and economic relationships. Sociologists classify institutions into economic, political, cultural and kinship (family and human relations) (Mitchell, 1968). Mitchell reviews various interpretations of the term; all agree that an institution is an established way of behaving, but this definition covers a wide range of phenomena, for example, the money economy, funerals, folk dancing and democracy. The term is used to apply both in an abstract sense and to concrete organizations, such as financial institutions and the judiciary.

'Culture' is also a set of established practices but also refers more to the products of learned traditional or intellectual endeavour, including their artefacts. Sociologists, as in Mitchell, have defined culture as 'that part of human action (and its products) which is socially as opposed to genetically transmitted' (Jones, 2003). The terms 'culture' and 'institutions' therefore may overlap.

Economic historians and economists make much use of the term 'institutions' and there is general agreement that institutions affect economic performance, but institutions are rarely defined. An exception is Douglass North whose definition of institutions is: 'rules of the game in society or, more formally...the humanly defined constraints that shape human interaction. In consequence they structure incentives in human exchange, whether political, social or economic.' He goes on to say, 'Institutional change shapes the way societies evolve through time and hence is the key to understanding historical change' (North, 1990). Jones draws the distinction between institutions and culture in that the former 'can be created or abolished by a conscious act of will; they are essentially creations of politics and power'. 'The term culture', he continues, 'is best applied to values and patterns of customary behaviour, which at least in the short term are harder to invent, induce or abolish' (2003). Jones also says that most economists believe that culture has little or no significance for economic performance because it adjusts to economic imperatives. There is clearly some truth in this. For example, Germany and to a lesser extent France, at one time in the post->WORLD WAR II period, were generally held not to have an 'equity culture' in the sense that their publics were little interested in buying and selling shares in companies, unlike those in Britain and the USA. This changed quickly, however, from the 1980s as money-making opportunities were created by the privatization movement, which had spread from Britain, and the emergence of livelier second-tier stock markets for smaller companies. The ultimate evidence for the change in the culture of equity were the unsuccessful attempts by the French (Euronext) and German stock exchanges in 2004–5 to take over the London Stock Exchange (>CAPITAL MARKETS). Nevertheless, Jones maintains that the persistence of French culture in Quebec and the 'messy relations between Islam and Christendom' (2003) show the enduring importance of culture (he might have cited other examples, such as the persistence of authoritarian regimes in Russia or the slowness of business transactions in Mediterranean Europe). Friedrich >HAYEK held that institutions evolve only slowly over time and, as a result of multiple human interactions, attempts by governments to change them quickly can only result in a loss of liberty.

Because institutions are held to be important in economic performance, and perhaps because they are inherently difficult to handle quantitatively, the economics of institutions are becoming a major preoccupation of economic history. The World Bank (2003) has, however, made some progress using cross-section analysis to study the impact of institutions on >ECONOMIC DEVELOPMENT. The interest in institutions in economics has roots in England in the works of Richard Jones (1790–1855) and others and in the German Historical School (>ECONOMIC HISTORY) and flourished in the USA in the 1920s, though interest waned in the 1930s.

In America, institutional economics was initiated by Thorstein Bunde Veblin (1857–1929) to whom institutional economics was an attempt to apply the evolutionary ideas of Charles Darwin to the analysis of society. Veblin was followed by Wesley Clair Mitchell, John Rogers Commons and J. M. Clark (Backhouse, 2002). Institutional economics experienced a revival in the work of John Kenneth Galbraith (1908–2006), Gunnar Myrdal (1898–1987), Douglass North and Mancur Olson (1932–1996). Although there are variations between the approaches of the various members of the institutional tradition, they all have in common a revolt against neo-Classical economics and stress processes and evolution rather than statics and equilibrium (>CLASSICAL AND NEO-CLASSICAL ECONOMICS).

## References

Backhouse, Roger E., *The Penguin History of Economics*, Penguin, 2002.
Jones, E. L., 'The Revival of Cultural Explanation in Economics', *Economic Affairs*, December, 2003.
Mitchell, Duncan G. (ed.), *A Dictionary of Sociology*, Routledge & Kegan Paul, 1968.
North, Douglass C., *Institutions, Institutional Change and Economic Performance*, Cambridge University Press, 1990.
World Bank, *Doing Business in 2004*, World Bank, 2003.

## International Trade

Trade between sovereign countries is essentially subject to the same motivational forces, such as the strength of demand and the availability of supply, as the exchange of goods and services within countries and shares, by some measure, similar constraints. International trade is, however, particularly burdened by the comparatively longer distances and costs of transportation and the influence of government policies. International trade on a truly extensive global scale had to await the development of the ocean-going sailing vessel and the opening up of the trade routes interconnecting Europe, the Americas and Asia in the 16th century. Adam >SMITH judged the opening up of the great deep-sea ocean routes as the major advance in world economic development and recorded his optimism for the continued benefits into the future of what became known as >GLOBALIZATION.

Early deep-sea trade was characterized by the export of particular commodities which had no effective substitutes in the receiving countries, such as pepper and other spices, silk, silver and, later, sugar and raw cotton. An exceptional trade was the export of cotton textiles from >INDIA, which made up over half of the total imports into Europe of the British >ENGLISH EAST INDIA COMPANY from the late 17th century. Many of these commodities also had a high value relative to their bulk, which helped them to bear the high transport costs. There has been some debate as to the importance of the declining costs of intercontinental transport and the removal of protectionist barriers as generators of the expansion of deep-sea world trade in the 17th and 18th centuries. It has been argued that because there was no international convergence of commodity prices during the period, the physical and commercial reduction of barriers to interchange on a continental scale could not itself explain the growth in trade. O'Rourke and Williamson (2001) postulate that European demand and the meeting of that demand in Asia and the Americas with the appropriate supply were the major sources of the dynamic impetus. They estimate that up to 65 per cent of the growth in trade could be attributed to the increase in European demand.

The rapid growth in the volume and the diversification of the commodity composition of international trade, particularly along the ocean-going intercontinental routes, had to await the >INDUSTRIAL REVOLUTION and the technological changes in transportation both in >SHIPPING and >RAILWAYS. In the 18th century world trade grew on average by about 1.3 per cent per annum. In the following 19th century it grew by as much as 3.5 per cent per annum and by a similar rate in the 20th century, although world Gross Domestic Product (GDP) grew only at about 1.5 per cent per annum between 1820 and 1913, compared with about 3 per cent per annum between 1913 and 2000. The proportion of global production traded internationally accordingly grew rapidly in the 19th century (Maddison, 1995; O'Rourke and Williamson, 2001: World Trade Organization, 2001). There were considerable fluctuations, however, within these periods. Between 1820 and 1870, the rate of growth in trade averaged about 4.2 per cent but this rate fell in subsequent decades to an average of 2.7 per cent per annum between 1891 and 1901. It again recovered to 5.6 per cent per annum between 1911 and 1913. The ratio of international trade to world output was 11 times higher in 1913 than it had been in 1800 and its volume per capita was 25 times higher than in 1800, in spite of the fact that output per capita had increased only just over twofold (Kenwood and Lougheed, 1992).

Europe, and particularly >BRITAIN, dominated international trade in the 19th century. Between 1820 and 1850, the growth in the volume of exports from Britain averaged 4.9 per cent per annum. While Britain's share in world exports, thereafter, fell against the growth in exports particularly from Germany and the >USA, nevertheless it retained its dominant position until 1913. Exports from Europe (including >RUSSIA) accounted for 59 per cent, North America 14.8 per cent and Asia 11.8 per cent of the world total in that year. An important feature of the export trade of Britain and Spain was the trade with their colonies. In 1892/6, for instance, exports to her colonies accounted for 33 per cent of Britain's total export market and for Spain 24 per cent. However, for the other countries of Europe it was not particularly significant and for Germany, which was the most rapidly developing country in Europe, it was trivial (Foreman-Peck, 1994). The pattern of trade which emerged during the 19th century was of a dominant Europe exporting the manufactured products of its industrialization in exchange for primary commodities from the rest of the world. During the period the composition of the manufactured goods traded showed a relative decline in textiles in favour of metal manufactures, chemicals and other manufactures. Nevertheless, in spite of industrialization, the share of primary commodities in world trade total stayed virtually constant between 1876/80 and 1913 at around 63 per cent, although there were major shifts in the mix of commodities in this group. Trade in ores and iron and steel gained share and food and raw materials lost share. The relative drop in demand from the developed countries was balanced by a relative growth in trade between the developing countries (Kenwood and Lougheed, 1992; Yates, 1959).

Trade recovered after >WORLD WAR I to reach a peak in 1929 after growing at 5.7 per cent per annum from 1924. However, World War I resulted in a dislocation from the past. It was a European war and it accelerated the rate at which other countries entered into the international market and competed with Europe (>WESTERN EUROPE). With the removal of European products from foreign trade during the war, industries in other countries were left free to develop, entrench their positions in their domestic markets and extend their reach internationally. The European share in total world output fell from 43 per cent in 1913 to 34 per cent in 1924 and its share of international trade fell to 50 per cent of the total (Pollard, 1981). The repercussions of the >GREAT DEPRESSION led to the collapse of world trade in the following years. Between 1929 and 1932 world exports fell by about 27 per cent in real terms (and as much as 43 per cent in current prices) (Maddison, 1995). World trade did not regain the level reached in 1929 until after >WORLD WAR II. In the 1950s and 1960s world trade grew rapidly, averaging 6.4 per cent per annum and 7.5 per cent per annum respectively. In the following two decades average growth fell to 4.6 per cent per annum and to 4.1 per cent per annum. The rate of growth fell further before picking up to finish the century with a growth of 11.5 per cent in its final year (Maddison, 1995; World Trade Organization, 2001).

In the second half of the 20th century the growth of international trade was multiregional. The developed countries expanded their intra-trade through the diversification of the range of commodities traded;

exchanging among themselves manufactured final products both finished and semi-finished in apparent defiance of the theory that it is the differences in countries' factor endowments that stimulate trade. The developing countries also benefited from this world trade growth and, in fact, their share of the total of world trade increased from 20 per cent in 1960 to 33 per cent by the end of the 20th century. The fastest-growing region was Asia, which increased its share of merchandise exports from 13.6 per cent in 1948 to 26.7 per cent in 2000, at the expense of loss of share by North America, which dropped from 27.3 per cent to 17.1 per cent (>ASIAN MIRACLE). The countries of Western Europe increased their share of exports from 31.5 per cent in 1948 to 39.5 per cent in 2000. The commodity composition of trade between World War I and World War II had been relatively stable in broad terms. The share of manufactures, for instance, in the total was the same in 1937 as it was in 1913 at about 36 per cent. In contrast, in the 50 years between 1950 and 2000, while the total volume of merchandise exports grew at an average annual rate of 6.4 per cent, manufactures grew in this period by an average annual rate of 7.8 per cent. As a result, by 2000, manufactures claimed about 75 per cent of total world merchandise exports. Agriculture was not party to this expansion, its annual rate of growth recording only 3.6 per cent, and its share fell to about 10 per cent. International trade in commercial services, such as transport, tourism, insurance and banking grew at an annual rate of 6 per cent per annum in the last decade of the 20th century, a rate similar to that of merchandise exports, and reached 20 per cent of total trade. The leading exporter of

commercial services in 2000 was the USA, with 19 per cent, followed in second place by Britain, with 7 per cent (World Trade Organization, 2001; World Bank, 2005) (>ECONOMIC DEVELOPMENT).

Following Adam >SMITH, the Classical economists (>CLASSICAL AND NEO-CLASSICAL ECONOMICS) believed that international trade should be free from government interference on the same principles upon which they argued for freedom in domestic markets. They refuted the >MERCANTILISM doctrine of the 17th and 18th centuries that recommended that governments should pursue policies, such as the imposition of subsidies and restrictions on imports, for the encouragement of a surplus on the balance of trade with a view to the accumulation of precious metals.

The case for free trade was reinforced by >RICARDO in his 'Law of Comparative Costs', in which he demonstrated that a country could benefit from trade by exploiting differences in the comparative costs of production. Countries were able mutually to benefit from trading even if one country's costs overall were greater than its trading partner. It was the comparative costs of production which were the significant costs. A country could profitably import a commodity from another country even when it could produce it cheaper at home. The theory was developed further by Eli F. Heckscher in 1919 and Bertil Ohlin in 1933 into what became know as the Heckscher–Ohlin Principle. This postulates that the differences in comparative advantage between countries exist because of the differences in their relative factor endowments. The commodity composition of a country's trade would reflect its mix of factors. For instance, in a country with a large pool of labour but little capital, wages would be relatively low and it would export labour-intensive goods and import capital-intensive ones.

There has been a strong consensus among many economists that Adam Smith's position on the benefits of free trade was the correct one in that it was the optimum policy for achieving maximum economic welfare internationally. Nevertheless, protectionism has persisted, albeit sometimes strongly and other times less so. There have always been arguments in favour of protection in particular special cases. Adam Smith, himself, supported the British Navigation Acts (>SHIPPING). From 1651, a series of these Acts applied tariffs on foreign imports and also regulated the ships which carried foreign trade. Commodities produced in Britain could only be carried in British ships and other commodities only in the ships of the country which produced them. Adam Smith argued in favour of these Acts on the ground that they safeguarded an industry that was vital for defence. He also supported a countervailing tax on an imported commodity to bring it into line with a tax on a competitive domestic product and import tariffs in retaliation against foreign countries that impeded other countries' exports.

Alexander >HAMILTON, who was the USA's first Secretary to the Treasury between 1789 and 1795, disagreed with Adam Smith's advocacy of minimum government. In his 'Report on Manufactures' in 1791, he argued that it was necessary for the government to support manufacturing industry by subsidy and import controls to encourage its growth. He believed that the country should be self-sufficient in manufactures and that support was required until industry was securely established.

Friedrich List, who encouraged the setting up of the custom union, the *Zollverein,* which was established by the German states between 1834 and 1867, approved of Alexander Hamilton's ideas and supported the infant industry argument for tariff protection in his *The National System of Political Economy,*which was published in 1841. Support for embryonic industry, the requirements for national defence or self-sufficiency were not the only arguments that came to be brought into play in favour of protection but others also, such as the need to sustain domestic employment, to improve the balance of payments, protect international reserves and to maintain wages.

The Mercantilist influence on government policy in relation to the control of foreign trade persisted into the first half of the 19th century in Britain as well as in the rest of Europe, but Britain then began to move to a free trade policy. In 1842, import duties were reduced and the prohibition on the export of machinery lifted. Britain had controlled trade in agricultural products since the 15th century and imports of grain were regulated through a series of Corn Laws. After the Napoleonic War, imports were banned if the domestic price fell below 80 shillings (£4) per quarter. A shift of influence from the landowners to the new industrialists, who were anxious about the policy's effect on wages, led to a powerful free trade movement. In 1845, there was a very wet summer and autumn and a severe drop in the grain harvest. There was also a blight which spread throughout the potato harvest in Europe (>IRISH FAMINE). The Corn Laws were repealed in 1846 to be followed three years later by the repeal of the Navigation Acts. Thereafter, Britain pursued a programme of reducing its restrictions on foreign trade and the process was virtually complete by the 1860s. Restrictions were also eased in other countries, particularly through a series of treaties. The Anglo/French Cobden–Chevalier Act of 1860 was followed by a number of others which France made, such as with Belgium and the German *Zollverein* in 1862 and with a number of others through the 1860s. The Anglo/French treaty of 1860 had included a 'Most Favoured Nation' (MFN) clause by which what was granted to one country had to be accorded to others in order to avoid discrimination and this had the effect of extending free trade throughout Europe. This was free trade's golden age but it did not last. France, Germany, Italy, Russia and Switzerland all began to implement tougher tariff protection in the 1870s. Most new tariffs which were introduced in Europe at this time were specific. This meant that, because international prices fell during the last quarter of the 19th century, the tariffs became increasingly restrictive in their effect (>WESTERN EUROPE).

Government policy in the USA, from the Tariff Act of 1816, was protectionist and continued to be so until the Tariff Act of 1833, after which tariff restrictions became increasingly easier. The need for revenue, however, led to a substantial increase in tariffs during the Civil War (>AMERICAN CIVIL WAR) and the average tariff rate rose to 47 per cent in 1864. In 1875, the average level of import tariffs on manufactures in the countries of Continental Europe was between 9 per cent and 12 per cent. In the USA, the comparable average was between 40 per cent and 50 per cent. High tariff levels persisted in the USA until the Underwood–Simmons Tariff Act in 1913, which carried through major revisions to the tariff schedules and led to a drop to an average rate of duty of only 16 per cent (Bairoch, 1993).

Protectionism became more widespread, stronger and deeper after World War I. Industries in Australia, India, Japan and in Latin America which had benefited from the lack of competition from Europe lobbied successfully to be protected from it after the end of the war. European countries increased their tariffs or introduced tariffs for the first time. Other forms of protection were also introduced such as quotas and import licensing. By 1939, 28 countries had imposed quotas or licenses, of which 19 were in Europe (Kenwood and Lougheed, 1992). Even in Britain, the McKenna Act of 1915, which imposed tariffs of one-third on specified manufactures, was extended after the war. In 1921, Britain passed the Safeguarding of Industries Act and the Dyestuffs Importation Act, which imposed tariffs on listed products and in some cases banned their importation. The last traces of free trade were eliminated in Britain by the Imports Duties Act of 1932, which imposed a general import duty of 10 per cent, except on imports from the British Empire and some commodities which were admitted free. In the USA the Fordney–McCumber Tariff Act 1922 and the Smoot–Hawley Tariff Act of 1930 raised tariff barriers to their highest ever. The latter induced considerable retaliation from the USA's trading partners. By the end of 1931, 25 countries had increased their import duties against exports from the USA (Bairoch, 1993). A number of international conferences in the 1920s advocated a return to free trade without success. The League of Nations in 1942 commented on this period:

'The international conferences unanimously recommended, and a great majority of Governments repeatedly proclaimed their intention to pursue, policies designed to bring about conditions of freer and equal trade; yet never before in history were trade barriers raised so rapidly or discrimination so widely practised.' (Quoted in Findlay and O'Rourke, 2005)

Given that it was so widely considered that there were undoubted benefits to be gained from pursuing policies in which the impediments to free trade should be kept to a minimum, it might be wondered why there was so much opposition in practice. Lionel (Lord) Robbins, in his *Politics and Economics*, gave his view:

'changes in the conditions of international supply and demand might involve damage to the position of particular groups and, in any case, impediments to trade might imply benefits. The interest of organised producers therefore frequently might point to restriction: and if this was so, there was no reason to suppose that they would refrain from pressing this interest. ... The interest of producers is almost always more active than that *of* consumers.' (1963)

After >WORLD WAR II, there was a concerted international effort to head off any possible return to protectionism. In October 1947, the General Agreement on Tariffs and Trade (GATT) was signed and the first of a series of trade negotiations was launched, the aim of which was to reduce international trading barriers. The eighth, the so-called Uruguay Round, begun in 1986 was concluded in 1993. GATT was replaced in 1995 by the World Trade Organization (WTO) under whose auspices, agreement was reached at Doha in 2001 to begin a ninth round but was suspended in

2008. These trade negotiations were generally successful in reducing tariffs on manufactured goods but less progress was made for agricultural products. Agriculture was not brought into the multi-trading rules of GATT until the Uruguay Round. Agriculture remained heavily protected particularly in the European Union (>WESTERN EUROPE), the USA and Japan, such as seriously to distort international trade. The Organization for Economic Cooperation and Development (OECD) estimated that in 2001 farm subsidies as a proportion of farm incomes were 21 per cent in the USA, 35 per cent in the European Union and 60 per cent in Japan. In the second half of the 20th century, alongside the attempt through GATT and the WTO to achieve agreement multilaterally, there had become established Regional and Bi-lateral Trade Agreements (RTAs) beginning with the European Coal and Steel Community in 1952 and the European Economic Community in 1958, which merged to form the European Union in 1967. The number of these RTAs proliferated in the last decade of the 20th century, jumping from 50 in 1990 to 230, with a further 60 under negotiation and trade between participating members accounted for 40 per cent of total world trade (World Bank, 2005).

The international institutions established as a result of the Bretton Woods conference in 1944 were strongly influenced by the principles in favour of free trade in spite of exceptions which were made, such as the need to protect infant industries particularly in the developing countries and the tacit abandonment of the Most Favoured Nation Clause in RTAs, and much success was achieved in reducing tariff levels. Nevertheless protection remained the rule rather than the exception in spite of the theoretical arguments against it.

In the light of the strong growth in world trade in the last few decades of the 19th century and up to World War I, there is little evidence that the increase in protectionism in the period had a general dampening effect on growth. That is not to say that damage was not done to specific trades. Wool exports from Britain, for instance, lost markets in the USA and Europe. In other cases, it is difficult to separate out the effect of protection from the growing competition from the development of new industries in countries such as the USA and Germany. Tariff protection for their iron and steel manufactures, for instance, shortly became irrelevant as their own industries matured. Without protection, on the other hand, completely free trade could be destructive. As Bairoch (1993) pointed out, textiles manufactures accounted for about 65 per cent of the total exports of >INDIA before the 19th century. After the English East India Company lost its monopoly in 1813 and the Indian market was opened up, there was a vast increase in cheap cotton textiles from Britain which overwhelmed the domestic Indian textile industry.

Many studies have failed to confirm that there was any evidence that protectionism diminished growth either in the period up to 1913 or during the inter-war years. On the other hand, many studies have concluded that there was a positive relationship between free trade and growth in the late 20th century. Clemens and Williamson (2001) argued that the paradox might be explained by the fact that tariff barriers had fallen to their lowest for a century and a half thanks to the international determination to avoid competitive protectionism.

## References

Bairoch, Paul, *Economics and World History*, Harvester Wheatsheaf, 1993.

Capie, Forrest, *Tariffs and Growth*, Manchester University Press, 1994.

Clemens, Michael A. and Williamson, Jeffrey G., 'A Tariff-Growth Paradox? Protection's Impact the World Around, 1875–1997', Working Paper 8459, National Bureau of Economic Research, September, 2001.

Findlay, Ronald and O'Rourke, Kevin H., 'Commodity Market Integration, 1500–2000', in Michael D. Bordo, Alan M. Taylor and Jeffrey G. Williamson (eds), *Globalisation in Historical Perspective*, University of Chicago Press, 2005.

Foreman-Peck, James, 'Foreign Trade and Economic Growth', in Derek H. Aldcroft and Simon P. Ville, *The European Economy, 1750–1914*, Manchester University Press, 1994.

Kenwood, A. G. and Lougheed, A. L., *The Growth of the International Economy, 1820–1990*, Routledge, 1992.

Lamartine Yates, P., *Forty Years of Foreign Trade*, George Allen & Unwin, 1959.

Maddison, Angus, *Monitoring the World Economy 1820–1992*, OECD, 1995.

O'Rourke, Kevin H. and Williamson, Jeffrey G., 'After Columbus: Explaining the Global Trade Boom, 1500–1800', Working Paper 8186, National Bureau of Economic Research, March, 2001.

Pollard, Sydney, *Peaceful Conquest: Industrialisation of Europe, 1760–1970*, Oxford University Press, 1981.

Robbins, Lionel (Lord Robbins), *Politics and Economics*, Macmillan, 1963.

World Bank, *Global Economic Prospects: Trade, Regionalism, and Development*, 2005.

World Trade Organization, *International Trade Statistics*, 2001.

## Irish Famine

The >POPULATION of Ireland grew rapidly in the last half of the18th century to about 5 million in 1800. The increase continued through the early 19th century and reached just over 8 million by 1841, although the rate of increase steadily declined. By the Census of 1851, the population had fallen to 6.6 million and was to continue to decline until, by the Census of 1951, the population touched 4.3 million. In 1801, at the time of the Act of Union with >BRITAIN, Ireland accounted for about a third of the total population of Britain but by the end of the 19th century for only one-tenth (>MIGRATION).

What became known as the Great Irish Famine of 1846–52 was triggered in September 1845 when blight reached Ireland from the Continent of Europe and destroyed half of the potato crop. By the following year, the infestation had spread throughout the country and in 1847 only a minimum acreage was planted. More seed was sown in 1848 but the harvest failed yet again. There was, therefore, four years of failure of a crop that was the staple diet of the poor, particularly in the west of the country. It has been estimated that the ensuing famine was the cause of the deaths of about 1 million people, over 10 per cent of the total population. The incidence varied across the country, the counties in the west losing as much as 25 per cent of their total number of inhabitants. The potato crop had on occasion failed before but not as to be regarded as so unreliable as to be likely to fail through so many harvests as it did. There had been no comparable famine in Ireland since 1740 or in England since the 17th century. It occurred in a country that was part of the Britain, which was the most advanced industrialized nation in the world at that time (>INDUSTRIAL REVOLUTION IN BRITAIN).

The potato had been introduced into the diet of the poor in Ireland at the end of the 18th century; vegetables and grain were displaced by it and it became the dominant food. In 1845, 2.2 million acres were cultivated for potatoes, compared with 3.5 million acres for grain (O'Grada, 1993). (In England and Wales, at about the same time, the acreage down to potatoes was 0.4 million and the acreage down to grain was 7.2 million.) The average size of farm was less than 10 acres, compared with over 100 acres in England. Ireland was underdeveloped comparatively. It has been estimated that average per capita income was half that of Britain. The introduction of the potato into the diet made economic and nutritional sense. In spite of their relative poverty, the indices of physical health, such as the expectation of life and the recorded heights of recruits to the forces, implied a dietary standard equal if not superior to that of other European countries. Moreover, the potato had long proved itself a reasonably safe crop. It was this very reliability that led the farmers and cottiers into a trap in which they were so vulnerable.

Not only did potatoes account for far too high a proportion of the diet, which could not be supplemented easily and quickly with substitutes, but also there was too much dependence on one variety to the detriment of resistance to disease. It was a crop which was costly and difficult to store and transport. Nevertheless, the arrival of blight in Ireland was cruelly timed. If it had arrived later, the development of >MIGRATION would have eased the pressures on and assisted the transformation of agriculture in Ireland, particularly in the west.

Economists, such as Nassau Senior who had written with Edwin Chadwick the report leading to the Poor Law Amendment Act 1834

(>POOR LAWS), persuaded the British government that state interference would exacerbate the problem and that if the market were left to operate freely, a satisfactory equilibrium would be reached (>CLASSICAL AND NEO-CLASSICAL ECONOMICS). Therefore, no controls were placed on the export of grain or on its use in distilling and pleas for the distribution of grain to the poor were rejected. However, public works were introduced in 1847 which gave employment to up to 700,000 people and public soup kitchens were installed which served up to 3 million people. In 1847, the government passed the responsibility of assisting the poor to the administrators of the Irish Poor Law. The government aggravated the disaster by insisting that any state aid should be matched locally from the rates. Many farmers were forced to throw their tenants off their land in an attempt to avoid bankruptcy. Over 20 per cent of farms were sold. It has been estimated that the total amount spent on relief amounted to no more than 0.3 per cent of the Britain's GNP. The economists were right in theory. For instance, the Irish trade in grain was reversed; exports fell from 485,000 tons in 1845 to 87,000 tons in 1846 and in 1847 743,000 tons were imported and 123,000 tons in 1848. It was, however, a long-run theory, not a short-run theory; adjustment came too late. Moreover, there was not only an absolute shortage of food, which needed to be addressed quickly, but also the country was relatively poor and there were insufficient funds locally to finance the gap (>FAMINE).

### References

Mokyr, Joel, *Why Ireland Starved: A Historical and Analytical History of the Irish Economy, 1800–1850,* HarperCollins, 1985.

O'Grada, Cormac, *Ireland Before and After the Famine, Explorations in Economic History, 1800–1925,* Manchester University Press, 1993.

O'Grada, Cormac, *Black '47 and Beyond: The Great Irish Famine in History, Economy and Memory,* Princeton University Press, 1999.

Woods, Robert, *The Population of Britain in the Nineteenth Century: Studies in Economic and Social History,* Macmillan, 1992.

# Iron and Steel

Despite competition from plastics, aluminium and other materials, iron and steel remain the most widely used of metals and, fortunately, the materials for making them are also widely found. About 5 per cent of the earth's crust is iron, from which steel is made. Steel is a very strong material, is versatile and can be easily recycled. Much of production in the older producing countries, over half in the >USA, is made from scrap. Steel products have a multiplicity of uses: for cars and car parts, girders and reinforcing bars used in construction, for containers, fasteners and tools, for example. Iron is never found as a metal, except in meteorites, but with oxygen in a chemical combination and with impurities which have to be removed by smelting in a furnace to obtain usable iron and then with further processing to produce steel (Gale, 1967). The evolution of the iron and steel industry is a story of innovation and the changing fortunes of the many suppliers. Britain, which first discovered how to mass-produce the metals in the 18th and 19th centuries, was, at the end of this period, giving up its first place in Europe to Germany and, by this time, the USA was producing more than both of these countries. After >WORLD WAR II, Japan became the world's leading producer. Japan was eclipsed later on by China, with other emerging countries in pursuit of what had become a global market, not only in steel but in the raw materials needed to make it. The latest challenge is that steel production is inherently environmentally dirty and all producers are now struggling to achieve cleaner production, especially in the advanced countries.

The basic products of the industry are wrought iron, cast iron and steel. They are distinguished from one another by their carbon content, the processes involved in their production and their different qualities. Wrought iron is ductile, resistant to corrosion and has only a small amount of carbon (about 0.05 per cent). Cast iron was traditionally produced by reheating and 'fining' wrought iron and increasing the carbon content to 3–4 per cent. Cast iron is very strong in compression but weak in tension. Once produced, cast iron can be machined (>MACHINE TOOLS) but cannot be forged, pressed or rolled, as wrought iron and steel can. Steel, the last of the three basic types of product, can be made by melting wrought or cast iron and scrap, removing impurities and adding or taking away carbon. Steel has a very much lower carbon content than cast iron and a much higher one than wrought iron. Various materials can be added to steel during production to give it special qualities. For example, manganese can be added for toughness and resistance to abrasion. Stainless steel, which has a very high resistance to corrosion, contains about 18 per cent nickel and 8 per cent chromium.

Iron was known to many earlier civilizations, for example in >CHINA and among the Egyptians and the Romans, though the quantities produced by the latter two were very small and mostly reserved for tools and weapons. As already mentioned, it was in Britain that most, but not all, of the basic innovations were developed that allowed the mass-production of iron and subsequently steel. In early times, iron was made by simply heating iron ore in a fire and hammering it to get rid of the slag. Later, in the Middle Ages, this was done in furnaces with charcoal, which is a crude form of carbon first produced by heating wood in an airless container, such as a pit, to drive off the volatile substances. The iron ore was crushed and mixed with marl and lime to bind it together before placing it in the furnace. After heating, the resulting lumps of iron were subjected to several reheatings and hammerings to produce 'blooms'. Leather bellows, powered by hand or water power, were used to raise the necessary heat. Trip hammers, powered by water and subsequently steam, reduced the physical labour involved in iron production somewhat. Iron was produced in this way until the 17th and 18th centuries near forests all over Britain and indeed Continental Europe, mostly making malleable iron in small quantities.

The next step was the blast furnace, which came to Britain, probably from Flanders, around 1500, in which pre-heated air was blown through the furnace. At first blast furnaces used charcoal and later, as will be explained, coke, to smelt the iron in a way that raised the temperature to melting point so that the liquid iron could be tapped and run off into sand to make 'pigs'. (Coke is coal with the gases burned off; it has the advantage of allowing more combustible material to be stacked in the furnace and is cheaper, but contains less pure carbon than charcoal.) Timber became in short supply in the South East of England (>BRITAIN) and its use had to be regulated. Forests had been cut down for agricultural reasons and for shipbuilding and this led to a migration of furnaces and forges away from the Sussex Weald, notably to Wales and the West Midlands. Around 1600 the Weald was a considerable centre of industry. More than half of English blast furnaces were located there and the region produced not only iron but also glass, textiles and timber products (Hudson, 1992). The Weald, with its proximity to London, was an original centre for iron making and the production of cannon. The first cannon was cast there in 1543. Before 1500, Sussex may, or may not, have developed a blast furnace before Continental producers did, and before that innovation is thought to have come across the Channel. Ashton (1951) refers to the discovery of a slab of cast iron in Sussex used as a grave-slab that must have been produced in an earlier period.

The demand for iron was increasing and the adoption of the blast furnace made an increase in output possible. Blooms of iron were also being imported from Sweden, Norway, Spain and Russia. However, massive increases in output could not be achieved until ways could be found of using mineral fuels instead of costly charcoal. The use of coke in England was pioneered by Abraham Darby at Coalbrookdale in Shropshire in 1709. Coke was not widely adopted for 50 years because most ores had a high phosphoric content and the use of coke did not, at first, produce iron of as good a quality as charcoal. It so happened that the local ore for Coalbrookdale was fairly good for what Darby was doing; he pioneered

the use of cast iron for such things as firebacks and hollowware. He also, from 1718, specialized in castings for Newcomen engines (>STEAM POWER). Darby was not the first to produce coke itself, that was credited to a Captain Buck who had taken out a patent as early as 1627. About 1750, his son, the second Abraham Darby, was able to make pig iron of a quality that was good enough for users of bar iron in forges. He did not take out a patent for his process because he believed it should be available for other ironmasters in the social interest.

A further major advance was made in 1740 by Benjamin Huntsman (1704–1776), who used coke in a reverberatory furnace to reheat 'blister' steel to melting point and produce 'crucible steel' of high quality. A reverberatory furnace is one in which the flames do not play on the metal, while blister steel is produced by 'cementation', that is, heating wrought iron covered in charcoal and hammering it to spread the carbon through the metal. Twenty years later, John Seaton (1724–1792) replaced bellows with water-powered blowing cylinders, later to be powered by steam engines. The next, and one of the most important advances, was made by Henry Cort (1740–1800) who, from 1784, went beyond Darby to show that coke could also be used to produce bar iron as well as pig, dispensing with the use of charcoal as well as hammering. This removed the bottleneck of turning pig iron from the blast furnace into wrought iron (Mokyr, 1990). Cort built on the work of others, but was probably the first to perfect the process of heating pig iron in a coke-fired reverberatory 'puddling' furnace. His furnace had holes in the door through which bars were thrust to stir the molten metal. The resulting lumps of iron were then reheated and hammered into blooms and slabs which, after further reheating, were passed through grooved rollers to produce bar iron. This process transformed the iron industry in England by producing fifteen tons of bar iron in the time previously required for a single ton, though it placed great physical demands on the workers in the foundry. Cort patented his inventions in 1783 and 1784 but placed them as security for a loan. He lost the patents to the government because the source of the loaned funds was public money, though it was not Cort's fault. In the ensuing case, his partner, Samuel Jellicoe, went bankrupt. Cort died in poverty in 1800, though his methods had made fortunes for other ironmasters. In 1829 James Nielson in Scotland made it possible to use local black-band iron ore deposits by using blast furnace gases to pre-heat the air inside. This reduced the fuel requirement by a factor of three and raised temperatures sufficiently to use anthracite and other fuels.

The work of reducing the cost of iron and steel making was done by many hands. Sir Henry Bessemer (1813–1898) was the next to make a big advance. In 1856 he revealed the details of the soon-to-become famous Bessemer Converter and obtained a patent in 1855. In the USA, William Kelly (1811–1888) independently made the same invention and got a US patent for it in 1857. The Bessemer Converter turned pig iron from the blast furnace directly into steel without reheating or other processing. This removed the second bottleneck, which was that of turning wrought iron into steel and it took only 20–40 minutes, very much faster than puddling. It did require the rarer non-phosphoric ore to be used and Bessemer steel was somewhat brittle, though it was more suitable for locomotive rails and boiler plates than the wrought iron that was currently being used for these purposes.

By 1869, the Siemens–Martin Open Hearth process was developed in Britain and Germany by the Siemens family and Pierre-Emile Martin (1824–1915), a Frenchman. This process used the regenerative principle in which waste gases were employed to add heat at a considerable saving in fuel. Scrap iron was added to facilitate the process of decarburization and it produced better quality steel than Bessemer, though again non-phosphoric ores were needed. The great advantage of Siemens–Martin over Bessemer was that checks on quality could be carried out during steel making and adjustments made where necessary.

The last of the great transforming inventions was the Gilchrist–Thomas process (Sidney Gilchrist Thomas (1850–1885) and Percy Gilchrist (1851–1935)) in 1878, which added limestone to the molten metal to combine with the phosphorous from the ore so that the phosphoric slag (a useful source of fertilizer) could be drawn off. To prevent the slag eating away the walls of the furnace these were lined with special bricks. The flux plus lining innovation could be used in Bessemer Converters as well as in Open Hearth, these processes, producing what is known as basic, as distinct from acid steel. The new processes, according to Landes (1996) brought down the cost of steel by 80–90 per cent between the 1860s and the mid-1890s. Landes points out that Gilchrist and Thomas were among the last of the great tinkers of the revolution in steel making (though in fact Gilchrist was a chemist in a steelworks). Thomas was a clerk in a police court, Cort was a Navy agent, Huntsman was a clockmaker and Bessemer a general-ist inventor.

Even in 1805, pig iron output in Britain was only about 250,000 tons though this was a big increase on the 30,000 tons or so it produced in 1760. Thereafter output continued to grow to over a million tons in 1835–90 and over 8 million tons by 1880–4. Deane and Cole (1969) estimated that, in 1871, the gross value of iron and steel output was 11.6 per cent of GNP. It should be noted that the real growth of the industry and some of the innovations that made it possi-ble lay outside the usual boundaries (1760–1830) of the >INDUSTRIAL REVOLUTION IN BRITAIN. Iron making was actually only a small part of the Industrial Revolution, much less important than cotton, although iron and steel were vital for the later phases in industrial devel-opment which followed.

Pig iron production in Britain peaked at 10.6 million tons in 1913, a level not to be reached again until 1952. Until the 1870s, Britain had a large export trade to the >USA, but lost it as American domestic production grew. The USA had non-phosphoric ore which was found, with anthra-cite, south of Lake Superior, though later steel making was to move south and east. Bessemer Converters were rapidly introduced from the 1850s but after 1906 they were just as rap-idly supplanted by the Open Hearth process. By 1913 steel output in the USA was four times as great as in Britain, which from 1885 cut back on Bessemer development to concentrate on high-quality steel produced in Open Hearth, particularly acid Open Hearth (Allen, 1959). In 1913 the USA, Germany and Britain, in that order of magnitude, accounted for 87 per cent of the world's pig iron. It has been argued that Britain's failure to keep up with Germany and the USA marked a deficiency in entrepreneurship. Indeed, some attributed Britain's rela-tive decline in steel and other indus-tries to a general cultural malaise. These views have been strongly criti-cized. Chandler (1989) took the view that British plants were too small, that personal ownership had failed to give way to managerial hierarchies and that owners failed to make the neces-sary investments in production and marketing. Britain's relative decline in iron and steel, however, was enhanced by the lack of suitable domestic ore, by the rising cost of coal from 1880 as the more accessible seams were exhausted and by the inevitable fact that much of its plant was older than that of its competitors. As Pollard wrote : 'It is evident that a small island with only limited resources could not go on forever producing almost half of the world's output of iron and steel' (1992). He went on to argue that not all the entrepreneurs in the industry could be said to have failed. The most recent view is that British entrepre-neurs made rational choices based on the opportunities open to them (>ENTREPRENEURSHIP).

We have devoted considerable space to the early British endeavours because it was the innovations made then and built upon in other countries which made possible the enormous increase in steel production that was to come later. To be sure innovation has con-tinued, though at a slower pace. From the 1890s the electric furnace was used for special steels, especially in countries with ample water power. Oxygen steel making (BOS) has vir-tually replaced both Siemens and Bessemer. BOS involves the injection of oxygen into molten steel and origi-nated in Austria in 1952. Continuous casting developed in the USA. In this process, molten steel is solidified directly into billets and strip by pass-ing through rolls, bypassing the ingot stage altogether. In 2006, continuous casting accounted for well over 95 per cent of European and US steel production. Companies using electric arc furnaces (EAF) are producing certain steel products solely from scrap. These 'mini-mills' are very efficient and offer serious competition to integrated producers, which continue to produce finished steel through all stages of the process from iron ore onwards. The >GREAT DEPRESSION hit the steel industries hard. Iron and steel capacity in Britain and the rest of Europe was about 50 per cent higher than in 1913, though output for much of the 1920s and 1930s was below the pre-war level. After 1924–5 there was some recovery in world output but not significantly in Britain until 1936–9, when rearmament boosted production.

By 1900, the US steel industry had become more concentrated (>CONCENTRATION) than either the British or German industries. Mostly as a result of mergers, two companies produced one-third of the country's steel and had bought up ore and coal mines. These two companies, Andrew Carnegies' company and Federal Steel, merged to form US Steel, which, by 1917, had assets four times greater than those of Standard Oil. US Steel did not reorganize to take advantage of its potential economies of scale and allowed competitors to emerge. The company diversified into oil and gas and eventually, in 1986 changed its name to USX Corporation. In the 1960s competition was growing and also from the 1950s, mini-mills were eating into the market shares of the integrated producers. By the late 1970s, import penetration in the US market was consistently over 15 per cent. By then the European Economic Community (EEC) (>WESTERN EUROPE), which had earlier accounted for two-thirds of US imports, was down to 25–30 per cent, while imports from Japan accounted for 30 per cent of imports. International trade in raw materials was growing and this dissipated the advantage US Steel had in owning mines. In 1950, 15 per cent of the iron ore used in the world was internationally traded; by 1980 this proportion had risen to 50 per cent (Auerbach, 1988). For a time the larger US steel producers benefited from the managerial efficiencies described by Chandler (1989), but these too were dissipated and even reversed. As Auerbach (1988) explains, the emerging Japanese competition showed that despite lack of raw materials it is possible to build a world-leading industry in the new era of international trade in commodities and steel products. With government support, the Japanese developed and partly financed new sources of coal and ore overseas, developed large bulk carriers and built ultra-modern steel plants in deep-water locations to facilitate the import of materials and export of product. Auerbach demonstrates that by 1980, the US industry, and to a lesser extent the EEC, was paying significantly more than Japan for raw materials, whereas in 1960 it had been the other way around. The large US integrated producers had suffered from innovative competition from the mini-mills, but Japanese success was based upon plants operating at hitherto unprecedentedly large scales of output and integration. As in the >AUTOMOBILE INDUSTRY, Japanese producers were demonstrating that they, not the USA, were now the leaders in managerial – if not technological – innovation. From the 1960s, Japan was, to use Auerbach's phrase, 'the battering ram of the new competition' and, as we show below, was to be followed by other countries. Government sponsorship of the industry in Japan, which dates back to the 1850s, was very important in the 1930s when Japan was rearming. The Yawata steelworks was founded and operated by government in the early 1900s. In 1934 Yawata was merged with six other companies to form Nippon Steel, which was to become the largest single producer in the world (Allen, 1965). How important the Ministry of International Trade and Industry (MITI) was to the development of the industry after the 1970s is less clear.

Just as surprising as the Japanese phenomenon, has been the more recent development of competitive steel industries in newly emerging countries – South Korea, >CHINA, >INDIA and Brazil, for example, and the persistence of significant output from some older producing countries with relatively high labour costs, such as Germany (number 6 in the world rankings in 2006), Italy (number 9) and France (number 13). The US industry experienced something of a resurgence based on its large home market and innovation after the 1980s. According to Cyert and Fruehan (1996), in the early 1960s, the Japanese required 15–30 labour hours per ton of steel, but by the 1970s this had been reduced to five hours per ton. In the USA, >PRODUCTIVITY stagnated from the 1960s to the 1980s, but labour input by early in the millennium was later reduced for integrated producers to four hours per ton for many products and to less than two hours for EAF producers. This brought US costs into parity with Japan, though, despite lower productivity and because of very low wages, South Korea and other low-cost producers can market steel at very competitive prices. Except for some higher grades of steel the product is now very much a commodity and buyers are very price-sensitive.

By 2006, Britain had fallen to number 17 in the world rankings in terms of crude steel production and it has had a chequered history since World War II. Although steel output grew roughly in line with GDP from 1950 to the oil price increases in 1973, when, like all energy-intensive industries in Europe, the steel industry experienced increased costs and a downturn in demand. The industry in Britain had been nationalized in 1950, denationalized three years later only to be taken back into public ownership in 1967 and finally privatized in 1986. These oscillations in ownership were facilitated by holding company structures which left the former 14 private companies as operating units, though in 1970 the British Steel Corporation (BSC) reorganized the industry on a product basis. Since 1953, the European Coal and Steel Community (ECSC) promoted free trade in steel among its six members but until 1988 had production quotas which did little to promote competition, though efforts were made to reduce excess and outmoded capacity. Britain had not joined the ECSC at the outset but effectively became a member when it became part of the European Community into which ECSC had been absorbed in 1967. A remarkable turnaround in the British steel industry was achieved while it was in public ownership (but under threat of a return to the private sector). In 1999, British Steel was merged with the Dutch steel company Hoogovens to form Corus, which in turn was taken over by Tata Steel of India in 2007.

### References

Allen, G. C., *British Industries and their Organisation* (1933) , Longmans (4th edn), 1959.

Allen, G. C., *Japan's Economic Expansion*, Oxford University Press, 1965.

Ashton, T. S., *Iron and Steel in the Industrial Revolution* (1924), Oxford University Press (rev. edn), 1951.

Auerbach, Paul, *Competition: The Economics of Industrial Change*, Basil Blackwell, 1988.

Chandler, Alfred D., *Scale and Scope: The Dynamics of Industrial Capitalism*, Harvard University Press, 1989.

Cyert, R. M. and Fruehan, R. J., *The Basic Steel Industry*, US Department of Commerce, 1996.

Deane, Phyllis and Cole, W. A. *British Economic Growth, 1688–1959: Trends and Structure*, Cambridge University Press, 1969.

Floud, Roderick and Johnson, Paul, *The Cambridge Economic History of Modern Britain*, III, *Structural Change and Growth 1939–2000*, Cambridge University Press, 2004.

Gale, W. K. V., *The British Iron and Steel Industry, A Technical History*, David & Charles, 1967.

Hudson, Pat, *The Industrial Revolution*, Edward Arnold, 1992.

Landes, David S., *The Unbound Prometheus: Technological Change and Industrial Development in Western Europe from 1750 to the Present*, Cambridge University Press, 1969.

Mokyr, Joel, *The Lever of Riches, Technological Creativity and Economic Progress*, Oxford University Press, 1990.

Pollard, Sidney, *The Development of the British Economy*, Edward Arnold, 1992.

# J

## Jet Engines

The first aircraft to be powered by jet engines were developed by the Germans and the British during >WORLD WAR II. As usual, there were long antecedents to the use of gases as a means of propulsion: Hero of Alexandria around AD 60 designed a sphere which rotated by steam escaping from nozzles; the Chinese in medieval times invented and developed rockets; and in 1794 John Barber of Nuneaton, England, designed and patented what has been described as a recognizable turbine (Golley and Gunston, 1987; Jones, 1989). Steam-powered turbines for stationary use were developed in the late 19th century in France, >BRITAIN, Germany and Switzerland (>STEAM POWER); but it was not until the 1920s and 1930s that serious work began on the use of turbine principles for aircraft. A Frenchman, Maxime Guillaume, patented a design for a turbo jet in 1921 but did not get to a working prototype; the first to do this was Frank Whittle in 1937, closely followed by the German, Hans Ohain, who was actually the first to design a jet engine for an aircraft that flew.

In a jet engine, although there are various types, the basic principle is that air is compressed, mixed with fuel and then ignited to drive the turbine. The thrust of high velocity gases out of the back of the engine provides forward motion. In a *ramjet,* first developed in France, it is the forward motion initiated by rockets that compresses the air; in a *turbojet* an axial or centrifugal compressor does that job. In a *turboprop* the turbine power is used to drive a propeller which pulls the aircraft along. The turboprop was used to exploit the relatively low weight, fuel tolerance and smoothness of the turbine but being propeller driven meant that it was subject to the height limitations that affect all such aircraft since air becomes thinner with altitude and gives less for the propeller to bite on. Turboprops were used for medium-distance flights where, in the early stages of development, jets were uneconomic as, for example, in the very successful Vickers Viscount airliner (>AVIATION). Since the Wright brothers' first flights, aircraft had been propeller driven by reciprocating piston engines but the jet engine offered great advantages: fewer moving parts; less vibration; use of a cheaper fuel (kerosene); and, very importantly, less limitation on altitude where air offers less resistance. In this inter-war period, at first it was not thought that jet engines could be made to work. This was because of restrictions imposed by high operating temperatures under continuous burning, requiring heat-resistant materials not then available, and problems of efficiency arising from energy losses in the turbine and the compressor. Frank Whittle, then a young pilot officer in the Royal Air Force (RAF), thought these problems could be solved and in 1930 patented the design of a turbo jet that he believed would work. Initially, however, he was unable to get a manufacturer to invest in the necessary development.

Only a little later and apparently unaware of Whittle's patent, Hans Ohain, a student at Gottingen University in Germany, came to similar conclusions as Whittle. In 1936, Ohain was introduced to Ernst Heinkel, the plane maker, who engaged him to work on his ideas for a turbo jet. Ohain therefore had already gained backing but Whittle, an impoverished engineering student at Cambridge, sponsored by the RAF, lacked the necessary £5 to renew his patent, which lapsed in January 1935. The Air Ministry was approached but declined to help. However, Whittle was able finally to get backing from a merchant bank; with their support he was able to patent some improvements to his original ideas and found a company in 1936, Power Jets, to make the engine. The Air Ministry took a shareholding in this company.

The subsequent story of the parallel developments in Britain and Germany is a fascinating one told by Jones (1989). In Britain money was very tight. Power Jets had a capital of only £20,000, the Air Ministry was very cautious and slow about making funds available, while private investors were inhibited by the government's presence in the company. The Air Ministry was never happy with Whittle and his creative band of engineers at Power Jets, just as the German government were not wedded to the unconventional Heinkel. The British Air Ministry consistently declined to allow Power Jets to manufacture anything other than prototypes. Development of Whittle's design was sub-contracted first to British Thomson Houston (BTH), a company which built turbines, and later to Rover and then Rolls Royce (>AVIATION). When work was sub-contracted in this way, Whittle had no control and felt that the two

terrestrial companies, which in particular had no experience in aviation work, were unsuitable. Worthy of mention is the role of Dr Alan Arnold Griffith at the Royal Aircraft Establishment (RAE), who improved turbine and compressor blade design and anticipated the development of turboprops but did not at the time appreciate that the jet flow was all that was necessary to power aircraft. RAE's work on gas turbines, however, was suspended between 1930 and 1937 but started again after Whittle gave his prototype engine a first test run in April 1937. Despite this success, there were many technical problems left to solve with the Whittle power unit. Until mid-1939 it seemed touch and go whether the Ministry would continue funding work at Power Jets, though by then other manufacturers were working on their own jet engines. For example, Metropolitan-Vickers were working with RAE on their axial-flow design and DeHavilland were brought in under government jet engine contracts in 1941.

Whittle's test run had been the first jet to run on liquid fuel, although Ohain had run his engine on hydrogen a few months earlier. In June 1937 Von Braun's rocket plane, also a Heinkel, made its first flight and on 27 August Ohain's Heinkel 178 made the first jet-powered flight in secrecy on the Baltic coast, unknown to the British. By 1938, several German manufacturers were working on jet-powered aircraft and engines for the government and Heinkel was sidelined. It was Messerschmitt in 1940 that won a contract for the production of a jet fighter. The Me 262, with a BMW engine, was 200 mph faster than the best propeller fighters. The mass-production of jet aircraft by the Germans was delayed because it was believed that priority should be given to the mass-production of conventional aircraft, particularly bombers. The Me 262 in basic design and performance was superior to its later British equivalent (see below) but was unreliable and crashed frequently; it was said that the fighter killed more Germans than the enemy.

In Britain, the first jet aircraft to fly was the Gloster E28 in May 1941, powered by a Whittle engine. The E28 was to evolve two years later into the Gloster Meteor, the British competitor to the Me 262. The first Meteor, which flew in March 1943, was powered by a de Havilland jet engine; production aircraft followed from July 1944, though these versions had Rolls Royce Whittle engines. The Meteor was to see service intercepting V1 flying bombs (which were launched by rocket and had intermittent ramjets), but the Meteors were not allowed to fly behind enemy lines for security reasons. Jet aircraft arrived too late to affect the outcome of the war. There were no battles between Meteors and Me 262s during the war, although Messerschmitts did shoot down a number of American bombers (>WORLD WAR II).

Whittle's W2B26 engine had been redesigned by Rover as a straight-through design (Whittle's original engine incorporated a reverse flow to save length), but both engines were further developed by Rolls Royce: the Whittle layout became the Welland and the Rover one the Derwent, the acknowledged parents of all modern jet engine designs. De Havilland were to develop the Vampire fighter and later the Comet, the world's first jet airliner.

By 1939, the >USA had made major advances in civil >AVIATION and piston engine development had been raised to an advanced degree. American airlines at the time were flying almost twice as many passenger miles as the European. There was no widespread interest in the potential for jets but the US government could appreciate their military implications and was aware of British developments by 1941. The General Electric company (GE), which had done a lot of work on superchargers and turbines, was selected to develop a US jet engine and Bell Aircraft to develop the airframe. Information between Britain and the USA was freely exchanged and in 1941 a complete Whittle engine was sent to GE in a Liberator aircraft; several British personnel were to follow to give advice, including Whittle himself. By 1942, GE had engines running and the Bell P59 Airacomet prototype fighter flew in October of that year. By 1945 GE had flown turboprop aircraft and in 1947 the rocket-powered Bell X1 was the world's first aircraft to exceed the speed of sound. With the tragic failure of the DH Comet, America was to take the lead in jet aircraft. The US industry was supported by the federally funded National Advisory Committee for Aeronautics (NACA), whose laboratories and testing facilities made a material contribution (see Virginia P. Dawson's chapter, 'The American Turbojet Industry and British Competition: The Mediating Role of Government Research', in Leary, 1995). America also benefited from German as well as British technology; the Germans had several developments underway at the end of the war, including swept-wing aircraft.

The variously called turbofan, bypass or ducted-fan engines were the major post-war innovation in jet engines. Fan jets were quieter and more economical. The first fan jet was the Rolls Royce Conway (1951), followed by GE (1958) and Pratt and Whitney (1960). The fan jet had been anticipated by Whittle in his

1936 patents and was actually under development when the Power Jets team was broken up. The jet engine was not merely a technical, but also an economic success. By the 1960s, apart from greater speed and range, the fuel costs of jet aircraft were 25–30 per cent lower than those for the piston-engined aircraft, which were largely supplanted for all but short hauls (Miller and Sawers, 1968). Whittle himself was never to receive enough funding to develop all of his ideas himself. Resistance from competitive manufacturers who had more clout with the Air Ministry was probably mainly responsible for this. Effectively, Power Jets was nationalized in 1944. In 1948 Whittle retired from the RAF at the age of 41. He was awarded £100,000 that year and knighted but ceased to work on jet engines. Whittle was bitter about the frustrations he experienced in developing the jet engine (see his autobiographical account, Whittle, 1953). The multiplicity of contemporary projects in various countries (which included the Soviet Union and Hungary), as well as in Germany, suggest that knowledge was advancing to the point where the jet engine could have emerged simultaneously elsewhere, a regular feature in innovation. For long controversial, the story of the jet engine is now settling down to a more balanced account.

The latest study by Nahum (2004), which is commendably brief and easy to read, gives more credit than hitherto to the British Air Ministry. Nevertheless, Whittle was the pioneer. In his assessment for the Royal Commission on Awards to Inventors in 1946, Harold Roxbee Cox, Lord Kings Norton, wrote: '[Whittle's] name in the annals of engineering comes after those of Watt, Stephenson and Parsons only for reasons of chronology or alphabetical order' (cited by Jones, 1989). The jet engine eventually enabled military aircraft and the Anglo-French Concorde to travel at supersonic speeds.

## References

Golley, John and Gunston, Bill, *Whittle, The True Story*, Airlife Publishing, 1987.

Jones, Glyn, *The Jet Pioneers: The Birth of Jet Powered Flight*, Methuen, 1989.

Leary, William M. (Ed.), *From Airships to Airbus: The History of Civil and Commercial Aviation, Volume 1, Infrastructure and Environment*, Smithsonian Institution Press, 1995.

Miller, Ronald and Sawers, David, *The Technical Development of Modern Aviation*, Routledge & Kegan Paul, 1968.

Nahum, Andrew, *Frank Whittle: Invention of the Jet*, Icon Books, 2004.

Whittle, Sir Frank, *Jet*, Frederick Muller, 1953.

# K

## Keynes, John Maynard

John Maynard Keynes was born in June 1883 in Cambridge, England, the son of John Neville and Florence Ada (née Brown) Keynes. He had a younger sister, Margaret Neville, who was born in 1885 and a younger brother, Geoffrey Langdon, who was born in 1887. His father was a Fellow of Pembroke College, Cambridge, between 1876 and 1882 and University Lecturer in Moral Sciences until 1911. He published, in 1884, a very successful textbook *Studies and Exercises in Formal Logic* and, in 1891, the *The Scope and Method of Political Economy*, with which Alfred Marshall, who was Professor of Political Economy at Cambridge, was very impressed and which became a minor classic (>FRIEDMAN). Keynes's mother Florence had been educated at Newnham College, Cambridge, having won a scholarship. John Maynard was educated at Eton from 1897–1902 and from there went on to King's College, Cambridge, to study for the Mathematics Tripos. After he had graduated in 1905, he planned to sit the Civil Service Examinations and attended lectures given by Alfred Marshall. Marshall was sufficiently encouraged by his work to hope that he would opt for a career as an economist rather than as a Civil Servant. He had responded to one of Keynes's essays, 'this is a powerful answer. I trust your further career will not cease to be an economist' (quoted in Moggridge, 1992). He won a fellowship at King's in 1909 by his work on the philosophy of the theory of probability, which he published later as *Treatise on Probability* in 1921.

There were two major influences on his life as a student at Cambridge. He was very sociable and joined a number of clubs and debating societies and played golf and bridge. He was bisexual and had several male affairs. In 1903, he was elected to the Cambridge Conversazione Society, called the Apostles, which had flourished at Cambridge since 1820. Keynes's contemporaries in this group included the novelist E. M. Forster (1879–1970), biographer Lytton Strachey (1880–1932) and publisher and editor Leonard Woolf (1880–1969). The group was also joined by more senior members from the Cambridge establishment and in particular G. E. Moore (1873–1958), who was to replace Neville Keynes as University Lecturer in Moral Sciences and to be appointed Professor of Moral Philosophy and Logic in 1925. In 1903, G. E. Moore had published *Principia Ethica* in which he had stressed the need to be sure of the right understanding of the question you ask before you attempt to answer it and that an action should be performed only if it results in more good effects in the world than any available alternative:

'By far the most valuable things, which we know or can imagine, are certain states of consciousness, which may be roughly described as the pleasures of human intercourse and the enjoyment of beautiful objects...It is only for the sake of these things – in order that as much of them as possible may at some time exist – that anyone can be justified in performing any public or private duty; that they are the raison d'être of virtue, that it is they...that form the rational ultimate end of human action and the sole criterion of social purpose.' (*Principia Ethica*, quoted in Moggridge, 1992)

Moore's philosophy had a profound influence on the evolving moral and philosophical beliefs of Keynes and his fellow Apostles.

In 1906, Keynes passed the Civil Service examinations and entered the India Office and served in the Revenue, Statistics and Commerce Department. He resigned in 1908 on accepting a lectureship in Economics at Cambridge. He was appointed editor of the *Economic Journal* in 1911. Keynes accepted the post of Second Bursar to King's College in 1919 and First Bursar in 1924 in which position he was given a generally free hand in the investing of the college's funds. He also took a keen interest in financial speculation in stocks, commodities and foreign exchange on his own account, and acquired a good reputation in these activities. He became Chairman of the National Mutual Life Assurance Society in 1921 and a board member of the Provincial Insurance Company in 1923. In the 1920s, he was also involved in three investment companies. After a shaky start in the 1920s, the performance of his personal portfolios improved. His net worth rose from £7,815 in 1929 to a peak of £506,522 in 1936, afterwards falling to £200,000 in the ensuing slump and rising to £411,238 in 1945, following the stock market fall of 40 per cent from 1936–40 and the subsequent rise of 60 per cent to 1945 (Moggridge, 1992).

Keynes's love of society, which he had embraced among the group of Apostles in Cambridge, shifted to London with the informal group of artists and writers who became known as the Bloomsbury group, most of whom had also been at Cambridge. The group included E. M. Forster, Virginia and Leonard Woolf and Lytton Strachey, and the artists Duncan Grant, Vanessa Bell and Roger Fry. It was among this group that Keynes pursued his passion for the arts in all its forms. The group was sympathetic to the view that there was an 'actual life' and an 'imaginative' life. The former, which must first be satisfied, consisted of supplying the basic needs for sustaining physical existence and the second was, as G. E. Moore had indicated, the enjoyment of beautiful things, which was the ultimate purpose in life. Keynes was optimistic that eventually the physical needs of mankind would be met, so that resources could be devoted for people to be able to enjoy the 'imaginary life'. In his *Essays in Persuasion*, published in 1931, Keynes wrote: 'I draw the conclusion that, assuming no important wars and no important increase in population, the economic problem may be solved, or be at least in sight of solution, within a hundred years. This means that the economic problem is not – if we look to the future – the permanent problem of the human race'. He saw economists as 'the trustees, not of civilisation, but of the possibility of civilisation' (quoted in Goodwin, 2006).

As his financial security became established, Keynes was not only able to explore with the Bloomsbury group the 'imaginary' life of the arts, but also to become an active patron and participant in the task of making the arts more widely available to others and became particularly intimately involved after meeting Lydia Lopokova (1892–1981), whom he married in 1925. She was a ballerina with the Ballet Russes under Diaghilev, with whom she performed throughout the USA and Europe. With her advice, he helped to finance and build the Arts Theatre at Cambridge and to launch its first season when it opened in 1936. In 1941, Keynes became a trustee of the National Gallery and in the following year Chairman of the Council for the Encouragement of Music and the Arts, which was reorganized in 1946 as the Arts Council of Great Britain. He was also Chairman of the Royal Opera House, Covent Garden.

Keynes was appointed a member of the Royal Commission on Indian finance in 1913, the same year as the publication of his book *Indian Currency and Finance*. For the rest of his life, Keynes continued to be closely involved with government economic policies, both as an active participant and as an often acerbic and provocative but constructive critic. He was called upon for advice by governments of every political party through the rest of his life.

In 1915, he joined the British Treasury, following the outbreak of >WORLD WAR I, and was principal representative of the Treasury team at the Peace Conference held at Versailles, but resigned his post in 1919 because of his frustration and despair at the lack of foresight he believed was displayed by the Allies in their treatment of the defeated Axis powers. In the following year he published *The Economic Consequences of the Peace*, in which he set out the reasons for his resignation. In it he decried the distortion of view caused by the passion for revenge and gave trenchant portraits of the

participants in the Conference. The book included economic analyses of the provisions of the Treaty and suggestions for dealing with the current economic problems which all Europeans shared:

'If the European Civil War is to end with France and Italy abusing their momentary victorious power to destroy Germany and Austria-Hungary now prostrate, they invite their own destruction also, being so deeply and inextricably intertwined with their victims by hidden psychic and economic bonds.' (Keynes, 2004) (>WESTERN EUROPE)

The book turned out to be a bestseller and financially rewarding. Thereafter, Keynes continued his policy of publicizing his ideas as widely as possible through papers, pamphlets and journalism generally. Articles were written for British newspapers and journals, both serious and popular, which were syndicated throughout Europe and the USA.

The British government had intimated in 1919 its intention to return to the >GOLD STANDARD at the pre-war parity. Keynes published *A Tract on Monetary Reform* in 1923 in which he proposed that the prime objective of economic policy should be price stability and concluded that the exchange rate should not be set at a fixed rate but free to be adjusted by the Bank of England. However, Winston Churchill, who was the Chancellor of the Exchequer at the time, returned >BRITAIN to the gold standard at the pre-war parity in 1925, and Keynes published *The Economic Consequences of Mr Churchill*. He argued that the consequent overvaluation of sterling would put pressure on export industries and create unemployment. He cited the example of the >COAL industry as needing to reduce costs by 10 per cent to retain competitive prices, which could not be done without reducing wages:

'Like other victims of economic transition in past times, the miners are to be offered the choice between starvation and submission, the fruits of their submission to accrue to the benefit of other classes... to satisfy the impatience of the City fathers to bridge the "moderate gap" between $4.40 and $4.86. They (and others to follow) are the "moderate sacrifice" still necessary to ensure the stability of the gold standard.' (Quoted in Moggridge, 1992)

When Britain left the gold standard in 1931, he said on the radio:

'It is a wonderful thing for our businessmen and our manufacturers and our unemployed to taste hope again. But they must not allow anyone to put them back in the gold cage, where they have been pining their hearts out all these years.'

In 1929, in *Can Lloyd George Do It?*, he argued in favour of the Liberal Party proposals in their election manifesto for public expenditure to reduce unemployment. The Conservative Government accepted the Treasury view that such expenditure would have no such effect because it would 'crowd out' expenditure that would have otherwise occurred in the private sector. Keynes argued that there would be no significant crowding out. There would, however, be an increase in employment and a rise in national income. There would be an increase in employment from the direct hiring of labour to work on the government projects, plus an additional employment by those suppliers of goods and services to the new projects and, finally, a general expansion in economic activity arising both from the increase in incomes of the newly employed and also from improved expectations and a resurgence of the 'animal spirits' of businessmen.

In 1930, the effects of the slump were exercising the members of the government's Economic Advisory Council, which accepted Keynes's suggestion of the setting up of a small committee of professional economists to 'review the present economic condition of Great Britain, to examine the causes which are responsible for it and to indicate the condition for recovery' (quoted in Moggridge, 1992). Unfortunately, the members had extreme difficulty in reaching consensus. Lionel Robbins, the Professor of Economics at the London School of Economics, insisted on writing a minority report (>GREAT DEPRESSION). The differences between the members of the group reflected the fundamental conflict emerging between Keynes and the neo-Classical economists (>CLASSICAL AND NEO-CLASSICAL ECONOMICS). The latter viewed the problem of economic policy as that of easing the stickiness of wages and relative prices, which they saw as the root cause of the unemployment of resources, whereas Keynes saw it as the deficiency of effective demand. Before the end of the year, he published further insights into the monetary factors which generated fluctuations in activity in *Treatise on Money*, which foreshadowed his major work which was to have such a revolutionary impact on economic theory and public policy.

In 1936, he published *The General Theory of Employment, Interest and Money*. In the Classical model of the economy, the National Income was determined by the level of employment, which in turn depended on the level of real wages. The economy had an inherent long-run tendency to full employment, given flexibility in wages and relative prices (>BUSINESS CYCLES). The quantity of money determined the price level (>FRIEDMAN). Savings were brought into balance with investment through changes in the rate if interest. An excess of savings relative to the demand for funds for investment would be reduced by a fall in the rate of interest and vice versa. In the *General Theory*, savings and investment were brought into balance by changes in the level of National Income. For instance, an increase in investment would raise income and therefore savings. These relationships worked through Keynes's concept of the propensity to consume and the multiplier. Only a proportion of additional income is saved and the rest is spent. Moreover, the recipient of this expenditure also spends a proportion and so on, with the result that the effect of the initial expenditure is multiplied throughout the economy. For Keynes, the rate of interest was determined by the quantity of money in the economy compared with the willingness of people to hold it in their liquid balances. Therefore, in Keynes's system, if you increased the propensity to consume or invest you increased effective demand and therefore total National Income and did not simply raise the rate of interest. Keynes disagreed with the Classical economists' belief that there could be no involuntary unemployment when the economy is in equilibrium. He showed that it could stick at a point at which there was an unemployment of resources and that there was no in-built tendency to recovery. Although expectations were not an explicit part of the model in the *General Theory*, they played an important part in Keynes's

thinking. Expenditure on public projects would be desirable if only because they assisted in generating a more optimistic outlook among businessmen and therefore encouraged them to look for new investment opportunities.

Although Keynes's theory had its ancestry in Classical economics, its great contribution was to revive and re-establish macro-economics, which had been neglected and lain moribund to the point that Keynes felt that it had been a great pity that >MALTHUS's criticism of the acceptance of Say's Law, which held that there could not be a persistent lack of demand in the economy overall, had been neglected. As a result, a great stimulus was given to the collection and compilation of national account statistics and the application of mathematics in economic model building, analysis and prediction. Finally, after Keynes, governments could no longer avoid their responsibility for the level of unemployment (>SCHUMPETER).

From 1942, Keynes took a leading role in the discussions leading up to the conference at Bretton Woods, New Hampshire, USA, in July 1944, which led to the establishment of the International Monetary Fund and the International Bank for Reconstruction and Development. Keynes had proposed an International Clearing Union (ICU) through which international debts would be cleared between its members on a multilateral basis. Each member would have a quota that determined the limits of its credit facilities with the ICU. There would be a set of safeguards and penalties to encourage the elimination not only of deficits but also of surpluses. The USA submitted their own scheme which dealt differently with countries in surplus, which was eventually accepted by the British delegation, and a joint proposal was put to the conference which was close to what was finally accepted by the conference delegates. The first meeting to inaugurate the new institutions was held at Savannah, in Georgia, in March 1946, which Keynes attended with his wife. Keynes's health had been deteriorating through the years of the war but he thought that the trip to the USA would be not be too stressful. In practice, there were decisions, such as the location of the institutions in Washington, which Keynes fought against. As a result, he returned from the USA in March 1946 a very sick man and died in April at his home in Sussex.

## References

Backhouse, Roger E. and Bateman, Bradley W. (eds), *The Cambridge Companion to Keynes*, Cambridge University Press, 2006.

Goodwin, Craufurd D., 'The Art of an Ethical Life: Keynes and Bloomsbury', in Roger E. Backhouse and Bradley W. Bateman, (eds), *The Cambridge Companion to Keynes*, Cambridge University Press, 2006.

Keynes, John Maynard, *The Economic Consequences of the Peace*, Macmillan, 1920, reprinted by Dover Publications, 2004.

Moggridge, D. E., *Maynard Keynes: An Economist's Biography*, Routledge, 1992.

Skidelsky, Robert, *John Maynard Keynes, Volume I: Hopes Betrayed, 1883–1920*, Macmillan, 1983.

Skidelsky, Robert, *John Maynard Keynes, Volume II: The Economist as Saviour, 1920–1937*, Macmillan, 1992.

Skidelsky, Robert, *John Maynard Keynes, Volume III: Fighting for Britain, 1937–1946*, Macmillan, 2000.

Skidelsky, Robert, *John Maynard Keynes, 1883–1946: Economist, Philosopher, Statesman*, Macmillan, 2003.

# L

## Luddism

A term given to the destruction of plant and buildings by workers in >BRITAIN in an attempt to protect their livelihood, caused by replacement of their employment and the lowering of the prices of their product from the use of machinery and unskilled labour. Such attacks had taken place from time to time throughout the 18th century but the term is generally understood to refer specifically to the period from 1811–16 in the Midlands and the northern counties. The general economic background was one of rising food prices and falling money and real incomes. Wheat (>GRAIN) prices, which had been 56 shillings per quarter in 1790, reached a peak of 176 shillings in 1812. In contrast, weavers' wages had peaked at 23 shillings in 1805 and fell to 13 shillings and sixpence in 1815 (Burnett, 1994). At the same time, the political philosophy of 'laissez-faire' had become fashionable, by which state intervention in the economy was kept at a minimum. The weavers lobbied parliament for a minimum wage in 1807 but a Select Committee rejected it on the grounds that: 'Fixing a minimum for the price of labour in the cotton manufacture is wholly inadmissible in principle, incapable of being reduced to practice by any means which can possibly be devised and, if practicable, would be productive of the most fatal consequences' (quoted in Burnett, 1994). In 1813, part of the Elizabethan Statute of Artificers, which gave magistrates the authority to set wages, was repealed and, in the following year, its restrictions relating to the employment of apprentices in craft trades.

The government took the riots very seriously and the breaking of machinery was made a capital offence. At one time, as many as 12,000 troops were deployed to maintain order. Recurrent riots persisted well into the 19th century, such as the 'Swing' riots in southern England in 1830 and 1831 against the use of threshing machines. Again the government reacted strongly. Over 1,000 people were found guilty and almost a half were executed or transported.

Luddism was not simply some inherent distaste or fear of machinery or technical change as such. The destruction of plant or buildings was used as a lever, often effectively, to persuade employers to negotiate. For instance, miners destroyed winding gear to prevent mine owners from employing blackleg labour. There has been and continues to be debate among historians as to the nature of Luddism and its relationship to the development of the labour movement (>TRADE UNIONS). Luddism has been viewed as an early primitive version of labour cooperation and the seed-bed out of which grew trade unionism and sophisticated collective bargaining, possessing a measure of revolutionary idealism. Others have refuted this. Although Luddism was often well organized, it was not really national. Each Luddite activity was grounded in and drew support from its community and was defined by the culture of that local community. It was a part of a spectrum of the means of protest from the petitioning of authority from the local magistrate to parliament to strikes and rioting. It had direct and limited industrial objectives.

## References

Archer, John E., *Social Unrest and Popular Protest in England, 1780–1840*, New Studies in Economic and Social History series, Cambridge University Press, 2000.

Burnett, John, *Idle Hands, The Experience of Unemployment, 1790 to 1990*, Routledge, 1994.

Rule, J., 'Labour in a Changing Economy, 1700–1850' in Anne Digby, Charles Feinstein and David Jenkins (eds), *New Directions in Economic and Social History*, II, Macmillan, 1992.

# M

## Machine Tools

Machine tools have been, and remain, essential for industrialization. We define them here as powered equipment for cutting and shaping metal, including such operations as drilling, threading, tapping (threading inside holes), turning, milling, sawing and finishing surfaces by grinding and honing. Machine tools are needed to make other machines and their manufacture is part of the engineering industry, which of course also produces machines to work other materials, such as wood and plastics. Many of the pioneers of machine tools, as we define them, also designed and made printing, textile machinery and other types of capital goods. Once it got underway in the 19th century, the development of modern types of machine tools was rapid. Rolt, in his short history, quotes the President of the British Association as saying, as early as 1861, that 'there is no operation of the human hand that it [the machine tool] does not imitate' (1965). The displacement of large numbers of skilled workers by machines has allowed enormous increases in >PRODUCTIVITY and standards of living for the mass of the population, though it has created social and economic stresses and strains (>LUDDISM). Rolt mentions that an Etruscan wooden bowl dating from 700 BC was found with features, such as a centre-mark, which suggests that it was turned on a lathe. By the second century BC, the use of lathes for turning such things as wooden spokes and hubs was known throughout Europe and the Near East. These simple machines at first required two operators, one to drive the lathe by winding and unwinding cords on a drum or later by turning a crank. Later still, in an early case of technological redundancy, the development of the treadle allowed a single operator to drive the lathe. As early as the 15th century, German clock makers were able to produce screw threads in metal.

Machine tools thus have a long history which led, through the use of hand power, to water power, >STEAM POWER and belt drives, to individual machines, to electric motors built into the machine. Modern types of machine tools were fully developed first in the >INDUSTRIAL REVOLUTION IN BRITAIN in the 18th and 19th centuries, though there were some important advances made elsewhere and especially in France, Holland and Switzerland. For example, in 1755 a Dutchman, Jan Verbruggen, constructed a horizontal boring mill for cannon in which the casting (workpiece) revolved against a cutting tool. In >BRITAIN, John Wilkinson (1728–1808), patented a cannon lathe with a screw feed to advance the cutting tool at the rate of 0.046 inches per revolution. Watt's lathe was devised in 1774 and was used to produce cylinders for James Watt's steam engines. The production of armaments has played an important part in the development of machine tools because of perceived urgency and the relatively minor importance of cost. Another example of the role of armaments is the achievement of parts interchangeability for small arms components in the >USA to which we come later. In the late 1830s in Britain, David Napier (1788–1873) invented a hand-driven machine to press bullets from strips of lead, instead of by the old and slower way of casting them. Napier's machine could produce 25,000 bullets a day for the government's Woolwich Arsenal. Napier also produced steam-powered gun-finishing machinery for the Board of Ordinance.

David Napier was one of the many distinguished engineers trained between 1814 and 1831 in the London workshops of Henry Maudslay (1771–1831). Maudslay himself started at the Woolwich Arsenal and later worked for Joseph Bramah (1748–1814) who had patented the hydraulic press. Bramah, who has been described as the father of metropolitan engineering, employed Maudslay for eight years until he rose to works foreman and left to start his own business in 1797 in the Oxford Street area of London. In 1802, Maudslay was contracted to build 45 machine tools to produce pulley blocks for the Admiralty in collaboration with Sir Marc Isambard Brunel at the Portsmouth naval dockyard. Maudslay, among other innovations, developed the first advanced screw-cutting machine. Like other leading engineers of his time he had learned his skills on the job but he was greatly to influence others. Among the engineers, in addition to Napier, who worked at one time or another in Maudslay's workshops were: Richard Roberts who built gear-cutting and planing machines; Joseph Clement (drawing office technology and machine tools) and Joseph Whitworth, one of whose many achievements was to get the engineering industry to adopt his standards for screw threads. Two other famous engineers who joined Maudslay's firm soon after his death in 1831 were James Nasmyth, best known for his steam hammer, and William Muir who patented a double grindstone machine, treadles and lathes and other things. Muir was an especially versatile engineer who developed machinery for winding cotton balls and bobbins and invented a letter-copying and embossing press. Richard Roberts became famous for railway locomotives. An illustration of the way standards of accuracy rose during the period is given by Rolt (1965). James Watt spoke of accuracy to the thickness of a thin sixpence (about 0.05 of an inch); Clement, in the context of printing machinery said that it had to be accurate to the thickness of paper. By the 1880s mechanics were working to a thousand part of an inch. Cantrell and Cookson (2002) describe the Maudslay 'family' of engineers in detail and show that they were crucial to the development of 'self-acting' or semi-automatic machines, such as the slide-rest lathe, planers, slotters and shapers, as well as precision instruments such as standard gauges and micrometers.

Many innovations were made in the USA, quite early on. For example, in 1819 Thomas Blanchard (1788–1864) of Millbury, Massachusetts, patented a profile lathe for the manufacture of irregular shapes, such as gun stocks. Early American leading engineers were, in most ways similar to their earlier British equivalents in that they were mostly self-employed, learned on the job and set up their own general engineering businesses, some of which were to grow to significant size. The well-known firm of Brown and Sharpe in Providence, Rhode Island, produced sewing machines in large numbers as well as woodworking machines and progressively shifted to metal working tools. The firm patented a file-cutting machine in 1864 and employed 7,500 in 1918. From the 1850s, the lead in machine tool design passed from Britain to the USA. There were differences in production methods between the two countries. British manufacturers were using flexible production methods (>INDUSTRIAL DISTRICTS) to produce a wide range of products, a large proportion made to order. American firms by this time were more specialized and their products more standardized and often built for stock. These differences had implications for the workforce and for costs. By the end of the 19th century, 50–60 per cent of British engineering workers were classified as skilled, whereas the Americans made more use of semi-skilled labour and were able to bring their prices down considerably (see Jonathan Zeitlin's contribution on the British engineering industries in Sabel and Zeitlin, 1997). American methods had been influenced by Federal government policies to stimulate the use of interchangeable parts in the small arms industry. Large numbers of small arms were needed in the conquest of the western USA (>AMERICAN WESTWARD EXPANSION), where there was a shortage of gunsmiths to effect repairs. As early as 1798, Eli Whitney (1765–1825) was awarded a government contract for muskets using the interchangeable system. Although, according to Rolt (1965), it took Whitney eight years to fulfil the contract for 12,000 weapons, instead of an expected two years, he finally overcame the problems and was awarded a further contract for 30,000 guns in 1812. From 1815 onwards, Federal government contracts specified that parts should be interchangeable, not only for the contract but

for all weapons of the same design made for national armouries. Samuel Colt, who invented the repeating revolver, got Whitney to make them, but Whitney also had competitors; among them was Smith and Wesson founded by a former employee of Whitney's, Horace Smith.

Between the 1850s and the 1860s, the system of standardized products with interchangeable parts was adopted by US manufacturers of light consumer goods such as sewing machines, bicycles, typewriters and agricultural implements and by the machine-tool builders that served these industries. In this period it was much debated in Britain whether or not British industry should adopt what came to be called the 'American System of Manufactures'. There were arguments on both sides, one of them being that British customers wanted tailored products for their more varied markets, including those overseas, while the costs of adapting machines for special requirements in America were left with the users. Floud (1976) concludes that for machine-tool production, the US system was not necessarily superior and that the British industry did not fail its customers, even though the performance of the economy as a whole may have been deficient. In any event, imports of machine tools from the USA increased considerably, if only because of quicker deliveries, and the American system did come into use to some extent in Britain. Alfred Herbert, which was to become a well-known British machine-manufacturing firm, started by importing machines and in the 1890s began manufacturing American-type machine tools, such as turret lathes, with some success. (Turret lathes are fitted with multiple chucks and tools and the turret is moved round to allow successive operations on a given workpiece.) The turret lathe was one American innovation but there were many others. Precision grinding was a particularly important development. Grinding was often necessary to correct distortions to machined components which occurred during the later hardening process. The Carborundum Company was founded in Pennsylvania in the 1890s to make synthetic grinding stones patented by F. B. Norton in 1877 to replace natural stone. At about the same time, the use of electric motors, pneumatic hammers and scientifically determined cutting speeds emerged. Frederick W. >TAYLOR was prominent in the last of these developments and patented designs for high-speed tools.

The Americans are said to have initially imported the concept of interchangeable parts from military circles in France where it had been invented, though not pursued. It is also true that Maudslay's pulley block factory in Portsmouth worked on the principle of interchangeable parts so that the American System of Manufactures could be said to have arisen in Europe, though it was undoubtedly first fully worked out in the USA. Despite the debate about the American system, German exports of machine tools exceeded those of both Britain and the USA in 1913, when British exports of mechanical engineering products overall were greater than those of the USA, though smaller than Germany's. Zeitlin (Sabel and Zeitlin, 1997) points to the irony that, in fact, German flexible production methods were of the same type as Britain's and later also those of Japan, in contrast to the ultimately less successful American model.

Pressures for innovation in machine tools in the producing countries, and especially in America, came from the rapidly expanding >AUTOMOBILE INDUSTRY. The motor industry was to be the largest user of machine tools in the early 20th century and influenced the development of high-speed tool steels incorporating tungsten, nickel and vanadium, and transfer lines which allowed for components, such as engine blocks, to be shunted automatically from one machine to another for successive operations (automation). In the 1950s and 1960s, numerically controlled machine tools were first developed in Britain thanks to their early adoption by the >AVIATION industry, though that lead was lost to Germany in the early 1970s. At that time the median machine tool manufacturing plant size in Germany was two and a half times that in Britain, which had a greater number of plants than either Germany or the USA (about 3,000 compared with 2,300). As distinct from many of the industries they supply, economies of scale in the production of machine tools are limited. On average, German machines were some 50 per cent more expensive than those of Britain and more expensive than American machines, which was an indicator of the German technological superiority (Jones, 1979). The German share of world machine-tool production surpassed that of the USA in the early 1980s and the US industry, like that of Britain earlier, went into steep decline from which it has not recovered. Japan has vied with Germany as the world's leading machine-tool producer since the early 1980s. By the early 1990s, the USA, according to a study by the Rand Corporation, was only third or fourth in the world rankings, along with Italy, the only other significant producer (although China and India have developed stronger machine industries in their rapid industrialization). Both Germany and Japan had the advantage of modern equipment to replace machines lost during the war, concentrating on machine tools for civilian purposes and, of course, in each case, strong and expanding motor and other industries as major customers.

## References

Cantrell, John and Cookson, Gillian (eds), *Henry Maudslay and the Pioneers of the Machine Age*, Tempus, 2002.

Floud, Roderick , *The British Machine Tool Industry, 1850–1914*, Cambridge University Press, 1976.

Jones, D. T., 'Plant Size and Efficiency in the Production of Metalworking Machine Tools', Discussion Paper No 19 (mimeo), National Institute for Social and Economic Research, 1979.

Rolt, L. T. C., *Tools for the Job: A Short History of Machine Tools*, Batsford, 1965.

Sabel, Charles F. and Jonathan Zeitlin (eds), *World of Possibilities: Flexibility and Mass Production in Western Industrialisation*, Cambridge University Press, 1997.

Scranton, Philip, *Endless Novelty: Specialty Production and American Industrialisation, 1865–1925*, Princeton University Press, 1997.

Wagoner, Harless D., *The US Machine Tool Industry, 1900–1950*, MIT Press, 1966.

# Malthus, Thomas Robert

Robert Malthus, who lived from 1766 to 1834, was born in Surrey, England, to Daniel Malthus, a country gentleman with a lively enquiring mind who was a keen supporter of the radical ideas of Jean-Jacques Rousseau (1712–1728), the Marquis de Condorcet (1743–1794) and William Godwin (1756–1836). Malthus was educated by a private tutor, until he was 16 when he was sent to the Dissenting Academy at Warrington, where he was taught by a Unitarian. In 1784, he went up to Jesus College, Cambridge, where he studied mathematics and philosophy. After graduation in 1788, he was ordained and became a country parson, living with his parents in the family home. In 1799 and 1802, he travelled in France, Russia, Scandinavia and Switzerland and in 1803 he obtained a post of rector in Lincolnshire, enabling him to marry Harriet Eckersall the following year at the age of 38, with whom he had three children. In 1805, he became the first Professor of History and Political Economy at Haileybury College, which had been established by the >ENGLISH EAST INDIA COMPANY to educate boys applying for posts in the Company. He died in 1834 near Bath, Somerset, England.

Malthus's *An Essay on the Principle of Population, as it Affects the Future Improvement of Society* was first published anonymously in 1798. A second enlarged edition was published in 1803 and further editions in 1806, 1807, 1817 and 1826. Among his other publications were *An Enquiry into the Nature and Progress of Rent* and *The Grounds for an Opinion on the Policy of Restricting the Importation of Foreign Corn*, both in 1815, and the *Principles of Political Economy*, which appeared in 1820, followed by a second edition published posthumously in 1836.

Malthus disagreed with his friend >RICARDO on the validity of Say's Law, which postulated that there could be no continuing deficiency of aggregate demand in the economy because the supply of goods and services generated the means to acquire them. Malthus argued that the wages of workers must be less than the prices charged for their output because the latter must also include rents and profits. If landlords and capitalists saved more that meant that more was invested (Malthus believed savings was identical to investment), which led to an increase in production at the same time as expenditure was reduced because of the diversion of income into savings. The maintenance of demand depended on the expenditure of unproductive consumers, particularly landlords. He concluded that it was possible for an economy to suffer from a persistent deficiency of effective demand and a general unsaleable glut of products. It was this opinion, which was against that generally held at the time, which endeared him to >KEYNES. Malthus worried about the persistence of the recession following the end of the war with France in 1815 (>BUSINESS CYCLES: >GREAT DEPRESSION).

'Is it not contrary to the general principles of political economy, is it not a vain and fruitless opposition to that first, greatest and most universal of all its principles, the principle of supply and demand, to recommend saving, and the conversion of more revenue into capital? Is it not just the same sort of thing as to recommend marriage when people are starving and emigrating? ... It is generally said that there has not been a time to transfer capital from the employments where it is redundant to those where it is deficient, and thus to restore its proper equilibrium. But I cannot bring myself to believe that this transfer can require so much time as has now elapsed since the war.' (Section X, *Principles of Political Economy*, 1820)

Although Keynes was sympathetic, the problem with Malthus's views was that they had little theoretical or logical foundation. As Robert Torrens, a contemporary of his put it: 'As presented by Mr Ricardo, Political Economy possesses a regularity and

simplicity beyond what exists in nature: as exhibited by Mr Malthus, it is a chaos of original and unconnected elements' (quoted in Blaug, 1978). Consistent with his conclusions regarding the importance of the income and expenditure of landlords in avoiding gluts, he disagreed with Ricardo and opposed the repeal of the Corn Laws (>BRITAIN) because the consequential fall in the price of corn would lower agricultural rents, lead to a fall in expenditure and an increase in unemployment.

However, it is in the context of the growth of >POPULATION that Malthus's name has reverberated through to the 21st century and captured the rare distinction of his name being added to dictionaries of the English language. This solid achievement and the continuing recurrent references to his work arise from the publication of his views on the stresses arising from the growth of population, a subject which continues to generate anxiety.

Malthus's *An Essay on the Principle of Population* arose out of discussions and disagreements with his father regarding the views expressed by William Godwin in a publication of 1793 and that of the Marquis de Condorcet in 1795. At the time, it was a widely accepted belief that the growth of population in relation to the production of sufficient means of subsistence posed potentially serious problems. Godwin and Condorcet were on the side of the optimists. They believed that mankind was capable of improvement through the application of reason and within appropriate egalitarian social institutions. The purpose of Malthus's *Essay* was to refute their arguments and to denounce the optimists' picture of a utopian future as dangerous as a guide to policy.

His argument was founded on the basis of two laws. The first was that food was necessary to human existence and the second that the passion between the sexes was necessary, and would remain nearly in its present state. He postulated that the means of subsistence increased at the rate of an arithmetical progression. Quite arbitrarily, as an example, he set this at a rate of increase equivalent to that of simple interest of 4 per cent per annum. Population, on the other hand, he argued, grew at an exponential rate which he set at a compound rate of growth of 2.8 per cent per annum. His baseline for this calculation was the estimated population of Britain in 1798 of 7 million and the estimated current growth rate of the population of the >USA. After 25 years, population would double and pass beyond the ability of agricultural production to provide the required level of subsistence because it inevitably lagged behind. In the first edition, he argued that there were positive and preventive checks to population growth and these controls were fraught with vice and misery. The positive checks were those that increased mortality, especially infant mortality, such as the misery of >FAMINE and disease and the vice of war. The preventive checks lowered the birth rate but were also tainted with vice through abortion, infanticide, prostitution and contraception. The second edition of the *Essay* added a more hopeful note for the avoidance of misery and vice by the introduction of moral restraint, such as the practice of celibacy, the postponement of marriage and sexual restraint in marriage. He concluded that no society could exist in which all its members would 'feel no anxiety about providing the means of subsistence for themselves and families' (Chapter 1, 1st edn, *Essay*). He and his fellow pessimists were given a powerful boost from the results of the first population census in 1801 which discovered that the population was not 7 million but 10 million and had, therefore, not been virtually stationary throughout the 18th century as was generally supposed.

Although Malthus was a pessimist in relation to the material human condition in contrast to the views of the optimists such as Condorcet and Godwin, he did not see his inexorable laws as without benefit. 'The exertions that men find it necessary to make, in order to support themselves or families, frequently awaken faculties that might otherwise have lain for ever dormant' (Chapter XVIII, 1st edn, *Essay*). Expenditure in Britain on support for the poor had led to a threefold increase in money raised from the rates between 1780 and 1812 and there was a growing belief in the need for some restraint. Malthus was a leading critic of the >POOR LAWS and played an important role in their reform. He was strongly opposed to the Poor Laws for two main reasons. First, they encouraged a growth in population without increasing the food supply so that there was less available per head and therefore they increased the number that needed support. Second, support for the inhabitants of the workhouses diverted provisions from the more industrious members of society. 'Dependent poverty ought to be held disgraceful ... I feel no doubt whatever that the parish laws of England have contributed to raise the price of provisions and to lower the real price of labour' (Chapter V, 1st edn, *Essay*).

Malthus was against a proposal to build cottages for workers on the grounds that it would encourage early marriages. The strict criticism of the Poor Laws to which his arguments led him were, however, mitigated by his recommendation that their reform should be implemented gradually over time. Under the influence of the his ideas, the Poor Law Commission concluded that the assistance being given to the poor made matters worse by subsidizing early marriages and larger families and so added to the numbers of unemployed. The Commission, therefore, condemned all outdoor relief on principle. Consequently, the Poor Law Amendment Act was passed in 1834. This marked the end of the 'old' Poor Law and the introduction of the 'new' Poor Law. The share of national income devoted to assistance for the poor, thereafter, declined from 2 per cent to 1 per cent through the rest of the century. The Act discouraged outdoor relief to the able-bodied in favour of indoor relief within harshly managed workhouses.

Apart from the criticism that his views lacked coherence and a consistent internal logic, Malthus has also been criticized for his lack of recognition of the possibilities for improvement in agricultural productivity in spite of the fact that Britain had enjoyed an >AGRICULTURAL REVOLUTION. Nevertheless, Malthus's name persists because of the continuing anxiety that population growth must hit some constraint because of diminishing opportunities for increasing agricultural yields and the loss of land to urbanization (>RICE).

### References

Blaug, Mark, *Economic Theory in Retrospect*, Cambridge University Press, 1978.

Gilbert, Geoffrey (ed.), *Thomas Malthus: An Essay on the Principle of Population*, Oxford University Press, 2004.

Lindahl-Kiessling, Kerstin and Landberg, Hans (eds), *Population, Economic Development and the Environment*, Oxford University Press, 1994.

Malthus, T. R., *Parallel Chapters from the First and Second Editions of An Essay on the Principle of Population*, Macmillan, 1909.

Schumpeter, Joseph A., *History of Economic Analysis*, Oxford University Press, 1954.

Winch, David, *Malthus*, Oxford University Press, 1987.

# Marshall Plan

The 'Marshall Plan' is the popular name for the European Recovery Programme (ERP), which provided >USA aid for Europe following >WORLD WAR II. The programme ran from April 1948 to June 1951 and amounted to some $12 billion, a large sum but considerably less than the $17 billion that the Administration originally intended (Milward, 1984). In 1947, Europe was suffering not only from the physical war damage to homes, factories and transport systems, but also political instability and shortages of fuel, food and raw materials. To make matters worse, the 1946/7 winter was exceptionally severe and disrupted food production and transport. Economic recovery was proceeding slower than expected and there was a chronic shortage of dollars to pay for imports. In 1947, the USA had already provided a great deal of aid though UNRRA, the Export–Import Bank, and by other means, but it became clear to the Truman Administration that a more sustained aid programme was urgently needed (>WESTERN EUROPE).

The origins of the European Recovery Programme can be traced to a May 1947 speech given by Dean Acheson in Cleveland, Mississippi. Acheson was standing in for the Secretary of State, General George C. Marshall, who was in Moscow at the conference of foreign ministers. The conference had underlined the desperation of the European situation and the difficulties that the 'big four' (the USA, France, >BRITAIN and the >RUSSIA) were having in resolving the war settlement and the future of the continent. Acheson said: 'The devastation of war has brought us back to elementals, to the point where we can see clearly how short is the distance from food and fuel either to peace or anarchy' (quoted by Kenney, 1955). Acheson outlined a programme for a comprehensive approach to European recovery and Marshall himself was somewhat more specific in a speech at Harvard University on 5 June. However, at this stage, the idea was still undeveloped and, moreover, had yet to receive broad support within the Republican Party. Kenney shows that the timing of both speeches was more or less by chance since Acheson was standing in not only for the Secretary of State, but also for the President himself, who had a commitment to speak in Cleveland that had become politically awkward for him. Marshall, returning from Moscow and deeply concerned about the situation in Europe, found that he had no suitable speaking engagements in his diary so offered himself to Harvard at short notice on the excuse that they had awarded him an honorary degree in absentia, which he had yet to collect. Both speeches were trial balloons and enormous efforts had to be made by the US Administration to get the electorate and the legislature to support the idea of a European Recovery Programme. Although the President and his advisers were committed, both for humanitarian reasons and because of the increasingly apparent need to check the spread of communism, there were large elements against it, not merely isolationists but also those who saw foreign aid as a threat to the curtailment of post-war government spending.

There were also difficulties at the European end. The American Administration wanted the formation of a pan-European organization to plan and administer ERP, a body that would pave the way for the economic and political integration of Europe. The USA did not wish to be seen to be excluding Russia and its Eastern European associates from the ERP but at an early meeting called on Anglo-French initiative to discuss the offer of aid; the Soviet Foreign Minister Molotov walked out and compelled the Eastern bloc to do the same. They were to set up a rival organization, Cominform, shortly afterwards. There was no appetite to use the Economic Commission for Europe (ECE), the regional UN body set up earlier in 1947 to administer the aid, but 16 nations, not associated with the Soviet bloc, did meet in Paris in June of that year and established the Committee for European Economic Cooperation (CEEC), the forerunner of the Organization for Economic Cooperation (OEEC) in 1948, which later became the Organization for Economic Cooperation and Development (OECD). The CEEC did produce the requested report to the American legislature in September on its aid requirements, but with great difficulty. There were many varied and sometimes conflicting interests: the French did not want aid planning to be engaged until there were binding commitments on a German peace settlement to cover the internationalization of the Ruhr; the Italians, who had a chronic unemployment problem, wanted commitments on immigration policy and full employment; Belgium wanted aid dollars to be used mainly to facilitate trade and payments rather than industrial recovery in which they were doing well and they and the other smaller countries feared that the organization would be dominated by the British and the French; and so on.

Despite the difficulties, the Economic Cooperation Act, putting the Marshall Plan into effect, was approved by the Senate and the House of Representatives on 2 April 1948, only a year after Acheson and Marshall had floated the idea. There were some changes from the Administration's intentions. The Act authorized the programme for only a single year, not for the four and a half years proposed, further years having to be reviewed separately. The plan was to be administered by an independent agency, the Economic Cooperation Agency (ECA), instead of the State Department. There were other restrictive provisions, for example, to protect the interests of US agriculture. In an ironic echo of earlier British policy towards its colonies in the Navigation Acts (>AMERICAN WAR OF INDEPENDENCE), 50 per cent of the goods shipped under the plan had to be carried in US ships.

The way the Marshall Plan worked appears to have been as follows. The OEEC (initially the CEEC) formulated recommendations for the allocation of aid based on their dollar deficit requirements, not their GDP or import volumes. Milward (1984) says that plenary agreement among the members, at least initially, was elusive so that the allocations were actually made by a small sub-committee and tacitly, though not formally, approved by the member states. There were bilateral agreements between the recipient countries and the USA covering such things as trade policy and exchange rates. These agreements were another tool of US policy and amounted to conditionality agreements. The ECA

agreed, or negotiated, changes to the allocations, and ordered and paid for the goods requested, about 75 per cent of them from US suppliers. Each participant had to deposit the equivalent of the aid received in national currency in a special account. These counterpart funds could be used as the recipient country wished, subject to the approval of the ECA. This might have been another element of conditionality, but the various countries had varied patterns of use of the counterpart funds, for debt retirement, investment in infrastructure, for example.

An important element in US policy was to achieve convertibility of currencies and to remove tariff and other barriers to trade. Bretton Woods institutions at this stage were not adequate for the scale of the problem. Convertibility was difficult to achieve and Britain's attempt to remove controls on capital flows in 1947 was premature and had to be reversed after a run on the reserves. There was some progress in bilateral and multilateral settlement with the Agreement on Multilateral Monetary Compensation in 1947. This arrangement was replaced by the Intra-West European Payments Agreement in 1948 and was to lead to the European Payments Union (EPU) in 1950. Later the OEEC was to achieve considerable reductions in tariff and non-tariff barriers, as mentioned, another American policy requirement.

As Milward (1984) shows, the funds employed in the ERP were significant, but not unprecedented (annual US grants and loans on a worldwide basis and outside ERP from 1945–6 were actually larger than those of the Marshall Plan in subsequent years). The outflow of dollars under ERP was equivalent to 2.1 per cent of the US GDP in 1948 and peaked at 2.4 per cent in 1949. Over the whole period of ERP, 1948–51, the $12 billion of aid provided was composed of 77.4 per cent in grants, 9.6 per cent in loans and 13 per cent in support of the Intra-European Payments agreements. ERP funds varied as a percentage of National Income and, according to Milward, were 14.0 per cent for Austria, 10.8 for the Netherlands, 6.5 for France, 2.9 for the German Tri-Zone and 2.4 for Britain in 1947–8. About half the aid was spent on imports of food and fuel and only 14 per cent on machinery and vehicles (the rest was spent mainly on raw materials). The analysis of the effects of these imports is, of course, complicated by the fact that some of them would have been made anyway, while the uses of counterpart funds also has to be considered.

There have been several reassessments over the years of the impact of Marshall aid. At the beginning it was seen as having played a major part in triggering European recovery. That view has changed and Milward (1984) shows that the resources of the ERP were quite small in relation to Western Europe's foreign trade and investment and that American exports to Europe did not increase but actually fell during the ERP period. Moreover, the Marshall Plan did not get underway until 1948 by which time industrial production in Europe had already regained pre-war levels. The Plan was certainly not successful in achieving American political objectives as they perceived them. Milward argues that the European nations worked out their own path to the integration America wanted and the way they did it was not in line with American expectations. The European Coal and Steel Community (ECSC), which came into being with the Treaty of Paris in 1951, marked a tangible step towards the Treaty of Rome establishing the

EEC (>WESTERN EUROPE) six years later but it was not an American or even an OEEC initiative, it was a French initiative to resolve her long-standing concerns about German heavy industry.

Contemporary economic historians no longer give the Marshall Plan a significant role in European recovery. Eichengreen and Uzan (1992) found no correlation across countries between the magnitude of ERP allotments and the pace of economic growth (see also, for example, the country studies in Crafts and Toniolo, 1996). It is difficult to deny, however, that from an institutional point of view, that is to say indirectly, it had influence. For example, the first steps towards a European payments system (the Multilateral Monetary Compensation Agreement of 1947) were largely the work of the CEEC, which came into being to administer the European end of the Plan. The ERP may also have helped to improve labour relations through its sponsorship of the Economic Recovery Trade Union Advisory Committee and the Anglo-American Council on Productivity (AACP). Vickers (2000) and Eichengreen and Uzan (1992) also argue that the Marshall Plan operated by means other than altering the rate of investment and the current account or government spending. They point out that markets were not functioning properly after the war: there was both open and repressed inflation and price controls were discouraging producers from bringing goods to the market. The Marshall Plan, in their view, helped markets to work by promoting financial stability and the liberalization of production and prices. Perhaps even more important, the success of the Marshall Plan, to quote Van der Wee, came from creating Europe's, 'own pattern of institutionalised economic inter-dependence' (1986).

## References

Crafts, Nicholas and Toniolo, Gianni (eds), *Economic Growth in Europe since 1945*, Cambridge University Press, 1996.

Eichengreen, B. and Uzan, M., 'The Marshall Plan: Economic Effects and Implication for Eastern Europe and the Former USSR', *Economic Policy*, 14, 1992.

Kenney, Elinor M., *The Origin of the Marshall Plan*, Bookman Press, 1955.

Milward, Alan S., *The Reconstruction of Western Europe, 1945–51*, Routledge, 1984.

Vickers, Rhianon, *Manipulating Hegemony: State Power, Labour and the Marshall Plan in Britain*, St Martin's Press, 2000.

Wee, Herman Van der, *Prosperity and Upheaval: The World Economy 1945–1980*, Viking, 1986.

# Marx, Karl

Karl Heinrich Marx, who lived from 1818 to 1883, was born in Trier, Prussia, the eldest son of Heinrich and Henrietta Marx. His father was a gentle man who was to be frequently beset with anxiety over the consequences of his son's radical views. He was born Herschel Levi, of a family of Jewish rabbis, but changed his name to Marx and became established as a lawyer until his business became untenable because of laws enacted against the Jews. He was received into the Christian Church in 1817 and accordingly changed his name to Heinrich. Karl's subsequent detestation of religion probably sprang from such early exposure to its influences on family life. From the age of 12 years he was educated at school in Trier until, at 17, he went up to the university at Bonn but stayed there only a year. In 1836, he transferred to the University of Berlin to study Philosophy and Law. At Berlin, the philosophical ideas of Hegel were dominant at that time and they had a fundamental influence on Marx's intellectual development. A radical group of 'Young Hegelians' emerged which encouraged the criticism of existing institutions of society by drawing on Hegelian ideas of dia-lectical progress. The recurrence of wars and destruction was viewed as a necessary inevitability. At any par-ticular stage in evolutionary progress, contrary forces emerged which gener-ated a tension which eventually built to breaking point and into a violent resolution. Hegel taught that this dia-lectic was a law of nature. It applied not only to the institutional struc-tures of civil society but also to the arts and sciences. It is only through this process of conflict and resolution that progress through history could be achieved by the World Spirit, or the sum of human understanding. The Prussian government became alarmed at the perceived threat to social order from the Young Hegelians and accordingly tightened its grip on the university. The hope for a more liberal regime on the accession to the throne of Frederick William IV in 1840 proved unfounded.

In 1842, Marx accepted an invi-tation to submit articles to the *Rheinische Zeitung*, a liberal newspaper newly established at Cologne, and he was so successful that before the end of the year he was made editor. The paper became increasingly critical of the government and eventually went too far in lambasting >RUSSIA, an ally of Prussia at the time, as the most oppressive authoritarian regime in Europe. The *Rheinische Zeitung* was closed down in 1843 but not before it had given Marx a productive train-ing in provocative journalism and a liking for it. In the same year, he married Jenny von Westphalen, the daughter of Ludwig von Westphalen. Ludwig was a friend of Marx's father and a Prussian civil servant who was a highly educated man from whom Marx had learned a great deal. Ludwig had approved of his marriage to his daughter in 1837, against the opposition of members of his family and even the doubts of Marx's own father, who feared for Jenny's happiness. Later in 1843, the couple moved to Paris, following Marx's acceptance of the offer to edit a new publication which had been launched there, the *Deutsch-Französische Jahrbücher*, and so began a period which had a profound influence on Marx's life both through the development of his ideas and in his practical affairs.

Following the dethronement of Charles X by the revolution of 1830 and the appointment of Louis-Philippe as the King of the French, which opened France to more liberal ideas at least initially, Paris had become a city which attracted artists and reformists of all kinds from every corner of Europe (>WESTERN EUROPE). It was here that Marx began to search for the answer to such a question as why the >FRENCH REVOLUTION of 1789 failed, against his dissatisfaction of the Hegelian dialectic as offering a solution. He read widely and particularly the economists such as François Quesnay (>PHYSIOCRACY), Adam >SMITH and David >RICARDO and was attracted to them by their application of logical analyses devoid of emotion and flights of utopian fancy. Their fault, as he saw it, was their lack of an historical perspective and their apparent assumption that their model was universally applicable. Engels was to remark, 'the economists of the day speak as if Richard Coeur de Lion, had he only known

a little economics, might have saved six centuries of bungling, by setting up free trade, instead of wasting his time on the crusades' (quoted in Berlin, 1996). Marx believed that the analysis of economic relationships could not but be sterile unless it embodied within it the structures and forms of the civil society existing at the time and also the evolving historical forces by which change was constrained and determined.

In 1844 he met Friedrich Engels, who had submitted an article to the *Deutsch-Französische Jahrbücher*, and thus begun a long and fruitful friendship without which Marx would have found great difficulty in continuing his work. Friedrich Engels was born in 1820 at Barmen in Prussia. His father owned a textile business there and was also a partner in Ermen and Engels, which owned another in Manchester, in >BRITAIN. From 1842–4, Engels worked in Manchester, where he gained practical knowledge about the condition of the working people which Marx greatly appreciated. In spite of his revolutionary views and atheism, Engels continued to have the support of his family and was a successful businessman.

In Paris, Marx was attracted to a loose grouping of men, most of whom were simple workers, who called themselves 'communists'. Their aim was the abolition of private property and the overthrow of the privileged classes. In the *Deutsch-Französische Jahrbücher* he published an article 'Zur Kritik der Hegelschen Rechtsphilosophie' ('Critique of Hegel's Philosophy of Right'). In this he postulated that the proletariat must be the instrument by which change could be precipitated. It was in this article that he agreed with the view that religion was a fantasy by which men escaped the harsh realities of their lives and it was but the opium of the people.

In 1845, Marx was forced to leave Paris on representations to the French government being made by the Prussians and went with his wife and young daughter to Brussels, where he was joined by Engels. In 1846, he and Engels wrote the *Die Deutsche Ideologie* (*German Ideology*), which was not, however, published until after their deaths. In this publication Marx gave the fullest account of the development of his conception of historical materialism. He retained the Hegelian idea of progress through history by which each stage was determined by previous stages though being unique and that there were laws which governed this progress which could be determined. However, he rejected, as being uselessly metaphysical, Hegel's belief that it was the progressive development of the 'World Spirit' or human culture from which was defined the characteristics of a society at any particular stage. Marx argued that this was the wrong way round. It was the material foundations of society that determined its 'spiritual' or cultural superstructure and that the understanding of the laws governing this historical progress could only be determined by the application of scientific analysis to real world data. This he made clear some time later:

'I was led to the conclusion that legal relations, as well as forms of state, could neither be understood by themselves, nor explained by the so called general progress of the human mind, but that they are rooted in the material conditions of life which Hegel calls…civil society. The anatomy of civil society is to be sought in political economy.' (Quoted in Berlin, 1996)

In 1847, the Communist League was formed and they invited Marx and Engels to write a programme of action for them. It was published in the following year as the *Manifesto of the Communist Party*. It starts off with a touch of terror: 'A spectre is wandering over Europe today – the spectre of communism', and ends, 'The workers have nothing to lose but their chains. They have a world to win. Workers of all lands, unite' (Berlin, 1996).

The year 1848 proved to be the year of revolutions in Continental Europe (>WESTERN EUROPE). In particular, violent demonstrations broke out in Austria, France, Italy and Prussia. After initial successes, the attempted revolutions failed in Austria, Italy and Prussia. In France, the Second Republic was established based on universal suffrage but internal dissension led to another revolt in 1848 and the return to the Empire under Napoleon III in 1852. The initial success enabled Marx to return to Prussia and contribute articles to the *Neue Rheinische Zeitung*, which had been launched in 1849. However, the restoration of authority by the King led to the closure of the journal, which printed its last edition in red. Marx was expelled from Prussia in 1849 and went with his family to London, where he made his last home.

There followed for Marx, his wife Jenny and their four children years of miserable poverty. On one occasion he wrote to Engels: 'I could not and cannot fetch the doctor because I have no money for the medicine. For the last eight days or ten days, I have fed my family on bread and potatoes, and today it is still doubtful whether I shall be able to obtain even these' (quoted in Berlin, 1996). He survived through the financial generosity of Engels, who became in 1864 a partner in the Manchester business. His finances were also helped by his being made the European Correspondent of *The New York Tribune*, to which he contributed several hundred articles, many of which were written by Engels for him on those subjects he was unqualified to cover. His main activity, however, was in the Reading Room of the British Museum with the voracious reading of a wide range of social, economic and historical works in the preparation of his major treatise, *Das Kapital*, the first volume of which was published in 1867, though the second and third volumes did not appear, edited by Engels, until 1885 and 1894, after his death. However, in 1859, he published *Zur Kritik der Politischen Ökonomie* (*A Contribution to the Critique of Political Economy*).

The cultural attitudes that inform civil society were reflections of its class structure, and that structure was determined by the processes of production. As the economic base developed, it brought new forms of production and with it new institutions, ideas and beliefs. The early societies were replaced by the mediaeval, slavery by feudalism and feudalism by bourgeois industrialism and the capitalist society. The class to which a man belonged was determined by his place in the production process. Under capitalism, there were essentially two classes: the bourgeoisie who owned the means of production and the proletariat which did not. It was in this dichotomy that the Hegelian tension existed because of the antagonistic contradiction of the conflicting self-interest of the two classes which built up until class war erupted. It was this class war which then triggered into reality the potential inherent in the historical inevitability of the next stage in evolutionary progress in which class and the ownership of private property were eliminated (>CAPITALISM).

It was through economic development that progress was achieved in other spheres of activity and Marx set out in *Das Kapital* to show how the capitalist economy was inherently unstable and its decay arose from its own internal logic inevitably leading to the classless society.

Marx's economic theory was derived from that of the early Classical economists, particularly Adam Smith and David Ricardo (>CLASSICAL AND NEO-CLASSICAL ECONOMICS). He inherited from them a labour theory of value which held a central place in his argument. For Marx, however, the quantity of labour used up in the manufacture of a product determined value, and this value was fundamental and immutable. Labour used in production determined exchange value, which differed from use value. The distinction between the two in the case of labour, regarded in itself as a commodity, was a vital one in Marx's analysis. The capitalist paid wages which were determined by the exchange value of workers. This exchange value was, in turn, determined by the socially necessary labour time required to 'produce' the worker, that is, the labour inputs required to rear, feed, clothe and educate him. However, in return the capitalist received the labourer's use value. The value of the labourer to the capitalist who used him was greater than the value the capitalist paid in exchange for his services. This difference Marx called 'surplus value' ($s$). Only labour yielded surplus value. Other production inputs, such as plant and machinery and raw materials, reproduced only themselves in the productive process. The amount of capital required to pay wages Marx called variable ($v$), and the remainder he called constant ($c$). Gross national product in the Marxian system therefore was given by $c + v + s$. The ratio of constant capital in total capital $c/(c + v)$ he called the organic composition of capital. The *exploitation rate* was $s/v$. The rate of profit was $s/(c + v)$. The desire for further wealth, coupled with competition and technical change, induced capitalists to invest from the surplus (which they expropriated from the workers) and in labour-saving machinery. The organic composition of capital, therefore, rose over time as more was spent on plant and machinery ($c$) compared with wages ($v$), with the result that, as only variable capital produced a surplus (and assuming that the exploitation rate remained constant), the rate of profit tended downwards. Diminishing profits and stronger competition led to monopoly and the concentration of wealth to a few. At the same time, there was an increasing squeeze on the real incomes of workers by the capitalists in their attempt to maintain profits. There also emerged a large 'reserve army of unemployed' arising from mechanization. The class conflict became increasingly acute until the environment was such that the change inherent in the economic structure was made manifest in the overthrow of capitalism.

In 1864 an international meeting took place in London of trade union representatives and their sympathizers at which it was agreed to establish an international federation of working men and Marx was appointed to its executive and became instrumental in the drafting of its constitution. Its purpose was as stated in its opening declaration:

'That the economic emancipation of the working class is therefore the great end to which every political movement ought to be subordinate as a means. That all efforts aiming at this great end have hitherto failed from want of solidarity between the manifold divisions of labour in each country, and from the absence of fraternal bond of union between the working classes of different countries...the undersigned...have taken the steps necessary for founding the International Working Men's Association.' (Quoted in Berlin, 1996)

In July 1870, the Franco-Prussian war broke out and the French were decisively defeated at Sedan in the following month. Napoleon III was deposed and the Third Republic was proclaimed in France. However, the socialists were uneasy about the intentions of the new National Assembly because they had little representation there. There was an insurrection by a group of working men in Paris who took over the government and became known as the 'Commune'. There followed a reign of terror which was matched by the army when it suppressed the insurgents in May 1871. Marx published a pamphlet, 'The Civil War in France', in which he took the opportunity of proclaiming that the Commune demonstrated that the only way for the classless society to be achieved was by the destruction completely of the bourgeois regime; he only criticized the Commune for not being ruthless enough. This support for what many regarded as appallingly bestial activity by the Commune created conflict in the International Working Men's Association and the beginning of its end. It shifted its base from London to New York and eventually closed down in Philadelphia in 1876.

Marx, in his last years, was encouraged by the spread of his form of socialism through Europe but despaired at the indifference to his views in Britain. He wrote that 'In England prolonged prosperity has demoralised the workers...the ultimate aim of this most bourgeois of lands would seem to be the establishment of a bourgeois aristocracy and a bourgeois proletariat side by side' (quoted in Berlin, 1996). He continued his work on *Das Kapital* but with diminishing application and it was left to Engels to edit the unfinished work and publish the last two volumes after his death in 1883.

There is no doubt that Marx has had a major political impact, though through its germination in the relatively backward society of early 20th-century >RUSSIA rather than in the advanced capitalist bourgeois society of 19th-century Britain, which might have been expected by the Marxian/Hegelian dialectic view of progress. The economic theory upon which he constructed his argument, although derived from his reading of Classical economics, did not form part of its development and was weakened by gaps in the structure of his theoretical model which he failed to fill or resolve. Nevertheless, his interrelation of economic systems within a social and historic context has had a significant influence (>ECONOMIC IMPERIALISM).

### References

Berlin, Isaiah, *Karl Marx, His Life and Environment*, with a foreword by Alan Ryan, Oxford University Press (4th edn), 1996.
Desai, Meghnad, *Marxian Economic Theory*, Gray-Mills, 1974.
Marx, Karl and Engels, Fredrich, *Collected Works* (50 volumes), Lawrence and Wishart, 2007.

## Mercantilism

During the 16th century and into the 18th century, ideas were expressed which became common currency through a number of books and pamphlets concerning the appropriate policies for governments to pursue in order to ensure a strong state. Because of their identification with the merchant class, Adam >SMITH referred to the body of thought as Mercantilism and devoted some time in setting out its ideas and criticizing them in Book IV of his *An Inquiry into the Nature and Causes of the Wealth of Nations* ([1776] 1812).

The central axiom of the Mercantilist philosophy was that the accumulation of treasure, such as bullion or specie in the form of gold and silver, was required to ensure that the state had power and international influence. In the earlier period, governments were recommended to prohibit the export of bullion but this was abandoned later in favour of the government intervening in the economy in order to promote a surplus on the balance of trade. If exports of commodities exceeded imports of commodities, it would follow that there would be a net inflow of gold and silver to pay for the excess and the stock of money in the economy would rise. Some Mercantilists suggested that a surplus should be sought in the trade of each individual country, although this was later abandoned in favour of an overall surplus in international trade in its entirety. They advised that exports should be encouraged by subsidy and restrictions imposed to discourage imports of high-value manufactures and domestic industries appropriate to this policy should be supported by the government (>INTERNATIONAL TRADE).

Gerald de Malynes (1586–1641) was an English merchant who published *A Treatise of the Canker of England's Commonwealth* and *St George for England, Allegorically Described* in 1601, *England's View in the Unmasking of Two Paradoxes* in 1603, *The Maintenance of Free Trade* in 1622 and *The Centre of the Circle of Commerce* in 1623. Malynes argued that the rate of exchange should be at mint par because if it falls below that level, it pays merchants to export bullion and this leads to a fall in prices on the domestic market and a rise in prices in the foreign market. He recommended some form of foreign exchange control to improve the terms of trade which he regarded as practicable on the grounds that the prices of English exports were inelastic in that a given percentage increase in prices would not lead to a commensurate fall in demand for English goods. He was in favour of the imposition of high import duties and the banning of the export of bullion. He condemned usury but believed it arose from the outflow of specie from the country which reduced the availability of funds. >SCHUMPETER praised his analysis of the effect on prices of changes in the quantity of money in the economy as an important contribution to economic analysis (>BRITAIN).

Sir Thomas Mun (1571–1641), a director of the >ENGLISH EAST INDIA COMPANY, disagreed with Malynes' advocacy of the banning of the export of bullion. He published *Discourse of Trade from England unto the East Indies* in 1621 and, a collection of papers, *England's Treasure of Forraign Trade: Or The Balance of our Forraign Trade is the Rule of our Treasure* (posthumously) in 1664. His central position was that government should seek to obtain a surplus on the balance of trade; the reference to 'treasure' in the title of his book is pertinent. In spite of this he did worry, in a touch of the quantity theory of money, as with Malynes, that the inflow of specie would make domestic commodities dear and therefore threaten the balance of foreign trade through a rise in the price of English exports He disagreed with Malynes concerning the export of bullion and was wary of restrictions on trade in so far as they could attract retaliation. Nevertheless, a surplus on the balance of trade was to be sought because export surpluses were the only source of gain to a country.

These two examples from the Mercantilist literature, illustrate the central tenet of Mercantilist thought. The purpose of government policy should be to seek a balance of trade surplus. This was because the Mercantilists viewed such a surplus as *the* indicator of a country's prosperity.

Adam Smith was very critical of these policy recommendations. In the chapter in Book IV of the *Wealth of Nations* entitled 'Of the Principle of the Commercial or Mercantile System' he wrote:

'The attention of government was turned away from guarding against the exportation of gold and silver, to watch over the balance of trade, as the only cause which could occasion any augmentation or diminution of those metals. From one fruitless care it was turned away to another care much more intricate, much more embarrassing, and just as fruitless...The inland or home trade, the most important of all...was considered as subsidiary only to foreign trade.' (Smith, 1812)

Adam Smith, as also the >PHYSIOCRATS, believed that governments should avoid interfering in the free interchanges of the economic processes. As to gold and silver, these were commodities like any other and could be bought and sold like any other and a country would be able to obtain the quantity of specie it required without a government's assistance.

Government intervention, however, was a central tenet of Mercantilism. The ideas of Mercantilism reflected the practical realities of its time. The countries of >WESTERN EUROPE in the 16th and 17th centuries were still in the pre-industrial age and agriculture the dominant activity. It has been estimated, for instance, that about 73 per cent of the population of France, the largest Western European country by population, was engaged in agriculture and this percentage was still as high at about 63 per cent in 1700 (Allen, 2000). Population growth was slow and uncertain and warfare endemic. International relations were of continuing and paramount importance and were viewed as a zero-sum game. There was no net benefit to be enjoyed by the international community from international trade, what was one country's gain was another country's loss. Beggar-my-neighbour was policy and protectionism, therefore, was a feature of the Mercantilist doctrine. State intervention was specifically directed towards individual sectors in such a way as to benefit the attainment of a surplus on international trade. Bernard de Mandeville (1670–1733), a Dutchman with an MD from Leyden, who established himself in London as a general practitioner, published in 1705 a poem entitled 'The Grumbling Hive', reissued in 1714 and 1729 as 'The Fable of the Bees or Private Vices, Public Benefits', which displeased Adam Smith by pointing out that the motives of individuals may very well achieve social benefits but they nevertheless were likely to be morally dubious. One edition of 'The Fable' added an essay entitled 'A Search into the Nature of Society' in which he wrote 'Private Vices by the dextrous Management of a Skilful Politician may be turned into Public Benefits' (quoted in Deane).

The policies pursued by Jean-Baptiste Colbert (1619–1683) were heavily influenced by Mercantilist ideas. Colbert was the Minister of Finance to Louis XIV of France from 1665 and introduced measures to encourage a favourable balance of trade by granting aid to private sector industries, establishing state manufactures and imposing import tariffs. In particular, he encouraged the expansion of the French merchant fleet. Emigration was controlled and sailors were banned from serving on foreign vessels. These policies were pursued in the 18th century in France in the establishment of the *manufactures royales* and the *manufactures privilégiées*, with their subsidies and monopoly rights. In Prussia, similar policies were pursued in a number of industries, including coal mines, and in >RUSSIA by setting up enterprises wholly or partly state owned (Supple, 1973). In Britain, direct government intervention of the kind which was pursued on the Continent was not implemented but the manipulation of foreign trade was. The regulation of trade in agricultural products had existed in England since the 14th century. In the latter half of the 17th century exports were encouraged through subsidy and imports were controlled. For instance, there was a number of Acts of Parliament, referred to as the Corn Laws, controlling the trade in corn, which were not repealed until 1846. Through the Navigation Acts from 1651 not only were tariffs imposed on foreign imports but also the shipping which transported British trade was controlled. British-made goods could only be transported in British-owned vessels and other goods by the vessels of the country producing them. Cross-trading was prohibited. The Navigation Acts were repealed in 1849. While the influence of mercantilist doctrine can be seen in the exercise of government policy, nevertheless England did not embrace the relatively heavy state interventionism which prevailed in the rest of Europe. Britain was in the happy position of benefiting from an >AGRICULTURAL REVOLUTION and an >INDUSTRIAL REVOLUTION (>INDUSTRIAL REVOLUTION IN BRITAIN) and a rapidly growing population. It was in the ascendant industrially and commercially in the 18th century and had not the same needs and anxieties of the other countries of Europe.

Adam Smith's *Wealth of Nations*, which promulgated powerful arguments in favour of free markets, undermined Mercantilism. This is not to say that Mercantilism did not make any useful contributions to the development of economic thought. Although they were so very much exercised over foreign trade, nevertheless, they had a theory of interest based on the interaction between the yield on investment and the availability of loans in the market and the interrelation between prices and demand. Their consideration of the labour force and the size of markets was not incompatible with the views of Adam Smith. >KEYNES had a good word to say in support of the Mercantilists. In Chapter 23 of his *The General Theory of Employment, Interest and Money*, which was published in 1936, under the title 'Notes on Mercantilism' he wrote:

'As a contribution to statecraft, which is concerned with the economic system as a whole and with securing the optimum employment of the system's entire resources, the methods of the early pioneers of economic thinking in the 16th and 17th centuries have attained to fragments of practical wisdom which the unrealistic abstractions of Ricardo (>RICARDO) first forgot and then obliterated.' (Keynes, 1996)

The Mercantilist advocacy of an inflow of precious metals, Keynes argued, reflected an understanding of the connection between the generous availability of money, low interest rates and profitably high prices, which encouraged investment and growth. Schumpeter is kindly but rather scathing about this. 'Lord Keynes is not only generous but over generous in his recognition of the Mercantilist contribution' (1954). However, there was a flavour of Keynesianism about some of the Mercantilists' proposals, such as the advantage of the rich spending their money on luxuries and investment in public works programmes. Keynes's view was criticized by Heckscher, in *Mercantilism* (1955), who pointed out that Keynes had overlooked the fact that unemployment in the predominantly rural societies of the 16th and 17th centuries was due to poor harvests and the seasonal nature of agricultural work. This was quite different from the structural and demand deficient, cyclical unemployment typical of the industrialized countries. The unemployment that concerned the Mercantilists was more likely to do with what they perceived as idleness and the preference for leisure over work.

The fatal flaw, of course, in their work, in so far as economic analysis was concerned, was their consideration of the balance of payments surplus as the indicator of economic strength.

## References

Allen, Robert C., 'Economic Structure and Agricultural Productivity in Europe, 1300–1800', *European Review of Economic History*, 4(1), 2000.

Blaug, Mark, *Economic Theory in Retrospect*, Cambridge University Press, 1978.

Deane, Phyllis, *The Evolution of Economic Ideas*, Cambridge University Press, 1978.

Heckscher, Eli F., *Mercantilism*, rev. edn ed. E. F. Söderlund, George Allen & Unwin, 1955.

Schumpeter, Joseph A., *History of Economic Analysis*, Oxford University Press, 1954.

Smith, Adam, *An Inquiry into the Nature and Causes of the Wealth of Nations* (1776), Ward Lock, 1812.

Supple, Barry, 'The State and the Industrial Revolution, 1700–1914, in Carlo M. Cipolla (ed.), *The Fontana Economic History of Europe*, Fontana, 1973.

Winch, Donald, 'The Emergence of Economics as a Science, 1750–1870', in Carlo M. Cipolla (ed.), *The Fontana Economic History of Europe*, Fontana, 1973.

# Migration

Between 1815 and 1930, over 50 million people emigrated from Europe to North and South America and Australia (Baines, 1991). About 3 million also emigrated from >RUSSIA overseas but these numbers were insignificant when compared to the 10 million people who moved from there into Siberia. There were also migrations from >INDIA, >CHINA and Japan. Between 1871 and 1915 about 16 million people left India to work in Ceylon, Malaya, Africa and elsewhere but about three-quarters returned (Foreman-Peck, 1995). Overseas emigration fell during the >GREAT DEPRESSION in the 1930s.

The voluntary emigration of people from Europe in the 19th and early 20th centuries was unprecedented and unsurpassed in numbers and distances travelled. The only comparable movement from an earlier period was the forced shipment of about 8 million black people from Africa to America prior to 1820 (>SLAVERY). >BRITAIN also shipped 160,000 convicts to Australia between 1787 and 1868. The destination countries for these European emigrants were in the under-developed new world of North and South America and Australia. The >USA was the country of choice, absorbing over 60 per cent of all European emigrants. The other major destination countries were Argentina, Australia, Brazil and Canada. Within Europe, Britain, Ireland and Italy together accounted for 55 per cent of total emigration, followed by Austria/Hungary, Germany and Spain, which together accounted for a further 27 per cent. However, these broad percentages conceal changes during the period. Early in the 19th century most emigrants originated from Britain and Ireland; in the mid-19th century, Germany and Scandinavia became more important and in the early 20th century, Southern and Eastern Europe and Italy were dominant. The levels of emigration also conceal substantial variations in the rate of emigration per thousand of population. For instance, at one extreme, Ireland persistently had the highest rate in the 19th century reaching a top average rate of 14.6 per thousand during 1861–70, being replaced in top position throughout the early 20th century by Italy, which reached a high of 16.3 per thousand in 1913. At the other extreme, France throughout the whole period persistently had the lowest average rate of emigration per thousand population, not rising above an average of 0.3. There were also variations in the rate of emigration between different regions of the same country. For instance, emigration was relatively much higher from Sicily than from Sardinia although economic conditions were similar.

Another variable characteristic was the percentage of emigrants that returned home. The rate tended to increase generally through the 19th century but more always returned home who emigrated from Southern and Eastern Europe than from North and West Europe. Overall, about 25 per cent of emigrants from Europe returned home. In the early period, migrants were mainly young families and the number of males was roughly equal to the number of females. These were the settlers who went into >AGRICULTURE in their adopted country. Later emigrants were mainly young single adults and there were twice as many males as females. These later emigrants went into urban, industrial employment. The Irish were unusual in that there was always a high proportion of females among their emigrants.

The forces driving and regulating these large emigrant flows from Europe to the Americas and Australia were economic and informational. The economic conditions in the home countries interacted with those in the destination countries to induce a propensity in the home labour force to move. However, this propensity could only be realized if the prospective migrant had the financial means to travel, the necessary information about conditions in the new country and assessed the risks to be acceptable.

The >POPULATION of >WESTERN EUROPE doubled between 1800 and 1900 and increased a further 38 per cent between 1900 and 1950. In 1800, the country with the largest population in Western Europe was France, with 28 million; by 1950 the population had increased by only 48 per cent. The population of Germany doubled by 1890, the population of Italy doubled by 1913 and Spain by 1910. In contrast, the population of Britain doubled by 1850. The inference may be drawn that France's low emigration rate was due to its low population growth. This rapid increase in the labour supply in European economies lowered the real wage rate compared with the Americas and Australia, where there was a shortage of labour relative to capital and land available. The population growth increased the number of young adult males who had less invested in their home country and more time over which to realize gains from their move. With industrialization (>INDUSTRIAL REVOLUTIONS) and improved agricultural productivity (>AGRICULTURAL REVOLUTION) there was an increase in internal migration to the cities and through this a psychological acceptance of migration. For instance, it has been estimated that, between 1861 and 1900, about 67 per cent of emigrants from Britain (England and Wales) came from urban areas, of which 33 per cent had been born in the countryside.

Specific economic events triggered particular spurts of migration. For instance, there was severe famine in southern Germany and Ireland in the 1840s. The famine in Ireland (>IRISH FAMINE) between 1846 and 1848 caused a revolution in Irish agriculture that led to surplus labour. There was little alternative employment. On the other hand, migration was also accelerated or retarded depending on the economic conditions in the overseas countries. For instance, there was little net immigration into Australia between 1893 and 1903, when the economy suffered a recession.

As emigration developed so did information links between the home and destination countries. Letters were sent back to home villages with news about conditions met with by emigrants. Later, returning emigrants themselves would add to the pool of information in their home districts. Financial support to meet travel costs was often arranged by established emigrants to help relatives and friends to follow them. A US Congressional Inquiry, the 'Dillingham Commission' (1907–10), reported that, between 1908 and 1914, one-third of all immigrants into the USA had had their passage paid by earlier immigrants. The links with home were reinforced by a tendency of emigrants to settle among their compatriots. It is estimated, for instance, that in 1914, about one-third of the 1 million Italian emigrants to Argentina lived in Buenos Aires and one quarter of the 1.5 million in the USA lived in New York. The Australian and New Zealand governments subsidized the passage of 45 per cent of immigrants prior to 1939 and under the Empire Settlement Act of 1922 Britain also subsidized passages to these countries and Canada.

A great stimulus to increased immigration was the revolution in transport. The steamship (>SHIPPING) was introduced on the North Atlantic in the 1860s and shipping lines were established which offered scheduled services. By sail, the crossing from Liverpool to New York in 1850 not only cost a labourer the equivalent of two months' wages in fare but took from three to ten weeks, during which time he was not earning. With the steamship, although there was little change in the fare itself, ranging from £3.10s to £5, there was a dramatic drop in the time taken for the Atlantic crossing; from 14 days in 1867, to nine days 16 hours in 1875 and to seven days 15 hours in 1890 (Foreman-Peck, 1995) Added to this was the development of the >RAILWAYS, both in the home as

well as in the receiving countries. In the second half of the century, therefore, improved transportation made it considerably less expensive to travel in terms of the cost of wages forgone and more attractive to return home.

In the early 20th century, governments began to impose restrictions. The USA introduced a literacy test under the Immigration Act 1917 and passed the Immigration Quota Act 1921 and the Immigration Act 1924. In 1924, only 160,000 immigrants from outside North and South America were allowed entry, Britain and Germany being allocated 73 per cent of these. After >WORLD WAR I, Russia, Hungary and later Germany and Italy also restricted emigration. The USA Immigration and Nationality Act 1952 imposed a quota of 155,000 of which 69 per cent were allocated to Britain and Germany. In 1965 Amendments were passed to the Immigration Act, which abolished country quotas, and the 1990 Immigration Act favoured skilled immigrants under a global quota. Similarly, in Canada quotas in favour of immigrants from Britain, France and the USA were abolished in 1962 and a points test introduced in 1967 reflecting specific attributes such as education and language. Eventually, the level of control depended on labour requirements. Similar points schemes were introduced in Australia and New Zealand.

Emigration had substantial effects on the economies of the receiving countries. Not only did it accelerate the growth in the population and the labour force but also reduced the share of the dependent population. Moreover, these countries enjoyed the windfall proceeds from the investment in the skills of the emigrants, the cost of which were paid for by their home countries. Emigration also had the benefit of narrowing the gap between the real wages of the home and receiving countries. There was also an opposing capital (>CAPITAL MARKETS) effect partially offsetting these labour effects on real wages. The growth in population and markets diverted capital into the immigrant countries and thereby raised the marginal product of labour in these countries and lowered it in the home countries. The net effect was a closing in the international gap between real wages. Between 1870 and 1913 the real wage gap between Europe and North America fell from 136 per cent to 87 per cent (Chiswick and Hatton, 2005; Hatton and Williamson, 1994a).

After >WORLD WAR II, there was a fall in the numbers and a shift in the direction of migration. There was less emigration from India, China and Japan. Latin America, particularly Mexico and the Caribbean, became net suppliers of migrants particularly to the USA. Net emigration from Europe was about 3 million in the period between 1950 and 1960 but fell to about 400,000 in the period between 1960 and 1970. During the latter period, however, there was a net immigration of 2.2 million into France and 2.1 million into West Germany, mainly from other European countries, Turkey and North Africa. By the mid-1970s, there were about 11 million foreign workers in Western Europe. Between 1945 and 1975 about 3 million people emigrated to Australia. About half of these were from Britain but there was an increasing proportion from Asia. The last quarter of the 20th century, however, saw an increase in the pace of migration. According to the United Nations, the rate of growth in world migration, which had averaged about 1.2 per cent per annum in the decade 1965–75, rose to 2.6 per cent per annum by the 1990s. In 1965 the world total of the number of migrants (defined as the number of people not born in their country of residence) was 75 million and this had risen to 175 million by 2000. The forces generating these emigration flows had similar characteristics to those of the 19th century. The movement was from the developing countries to the more advanced countries, attracted by the prospect of work, higher real wages and assisted by the revolution in the flow of information internationally       (>ELECTRONICS: >GLOBALIZATION).

## References

Baines, Dudley, *Emigration from Europe, 1815–1930*, Studies in Economic and Social History series, Macmillan, 1991.

Baines, Dudley, 'European Emigration, 1815–1930: Looking at the Emigration Decision Again', *Economic History Review*, XLVII(3), 1994.

Chiswick, Barry R. and Hatton, Timothy J., 'International Migration and the Integration of Labour Markets', in Michael D. Bordo, Alan M. Taylor and Jeffrey G. Williamson (eds), *Globalisation in Historical Perspective*, University of Chicago Press, 2005.

Foreman-Peck, James, *A History of the World Economy: International Economic Relations Since 1850*, Wheatsheaf Books, 1983.

Grubb, Farley, 'The End of European Immigrant Servitude in the United States: An Economic Analysis of Market Collapse, 1772–1835', *Journal of Economic History*, 54(4), 1994.

Hatton, Timothy J., 'Emigration from the U.K., 1870–1913', *European Review of Economic History*, 8(2), 2004.

Hatton, Timothy J. and Williamson, Jeffrey G. (eds), *Migration and the International Labour Market, 1850–1939*, Routledge, 1994a.

Hatton, T. J. and Williamson, J. G., 'What drove the mass migrations from Europe in the late 19th Century?',

*Population and Development Review*, 20, 1994b.

Hatton, Timothy J. and Williamson, Jeffrey G., *The Age of Mass Migration: Causes and Economic Impact*, Oxford University Press, 1998.

Taylor, Alan M. and Williamson, Jeffrey G., 'Convergence in the Age of Mass Migration', *European Review of Economic History*, 1(I) April, 1997.

# Money and Banking

The development of money as a medium of exchange, a standard of value (or unit of account) and as a means of holding wealth (its three functions), was essential for the progression from subsistence production to specialization and the division of labour. Inflation (persistent depreciation in the value of money) threatens all the functions (>PRICES AND INFLATION). The need for some means of anchoring monetary values to achieve stability, originally by using >GOLD or silver in coinage or as backing for paper money and more recently by the use of monetary policy (control of interest rates) is a motif throughout the history of money. Governments have always been tempted to solve economic problems by debasing currency and in recent years central banks charged with responsibility for monetary control have increasingly been given independence (>CENTRAL BANKING). As financial intermediaries, banks usually offer a range of financial services, including insurance, credit cards and foreign exchange, which may also be available from 'non-banks'. What distinguishes banks from other financial institutions is their role in the money supply (the quantity of money in circulation in the economy (>FRIEDMAN)). When a bank makes a loan it incurs a book debt to a customer in return for a promise to repay the loan, which may or may not involve the pledging of some asset as security (collateral). That loan (as a right to draw on the bank) is money and the extent to which banks can create money in this way is limited only by the need to ensure that enough cash is available in the bank at any time to meet customer demand. It is also limited by regulatory requirements to hold a certain proportion of liquid assets.

Money pre-dates written history and there were national or regional coinage systems in both China and the West in antiquity. Vestiges of early, more primitive, systems for example, using cowrie shells or animals, such as goats or horses, as units of account for such purposes as dowries or for barter could still be observed until quite recently in many developing countries. Coinage was the first step in the evolution of organized money and Chown (1994) puts that in Europe at about 800 BC. The development of modern money has passed successively through coinage (usually a function of governments), bank notes and bank deposits, though payments at distance were being achieved by exchange letters, resembling later bills of exchange, as early as the end of the 12th century (Weber, 2003). By the end of the >COMMERCIAL REVOLUTION, and certainly by the late 18th century, most of the issues which confront monetary historians had already emerged. Coinage was being increasingly supplanted by banks, paper money and credit instruments. The attitude of most religious authorities to >USURY (the charging of interest on borrowed money) was giving way to the imperatives of economic development. Confidence was secured by giving paper money holders the right to exchange notes for precious metals at a predetermined price. The sterling price of gold was fixed in 1717 by Sir Isaac Newton, who, besides his other achievements in mathematics and physics, was also the Master of the Mint in England and that price (£3.17s.10 ½d per standard ounce) remained fixed for almost 200 years, although occasionally, in periods of crisis such as wars, convertibility had to be suspended, as it was in Britain during the Napoleonic Wars. In the 18th century, the French and American revolutions (>WESTERN EUROPE: >AMERICAN WAR OF INDEPENDENCE) and later the >AMERICAN CIVIL WAR were largely financed by paper money, which was eventually to become worthless (both France and America went back to gold after these experiments with paper money). This was the way fiat, or non-convertible money, generally began. However, it seems that unconvertible paper money was actually invented in China and at the time of Marco Polo's travels there in the 13th century it had been in use for a very long time. The use of unbacked paper money and credit gave rise to great scandals in Europe in the early 18th century, for example John Law's activities in France and the South Sea Bubble, to which the development of credit and paper money gave rise and which put earlier problems of debased coinage (by clipping or false attribution of metal content) in the shade (>COMPANIES).

Although the >GOLD STANDARD was abandoned in the 20th century, under the Bretton Woods system established after World War II, >GOLD still played a role in underpinning currency stability; the US dollar remained linked to gold at a fixed price and the paper money of industrial countries was linked indirectly to gold through a system of exchange rates based on the US dollar. Only when this system broke down with the US suspension of convertibility in 1971 did government face the challenge of securing confidence in paper money without any link to gold or other precious metal. The episode of very rapid inflation experienced in the 1970s illustrated the dangers of government control of the money supply. The longer-term solution was for governments to hand over the task of maintaining a degree of price stability to independent >CENTRAL BANKING and since then most people have become persuaded to have confidence in unconvertible money. Nonetheless, at dates as far apart as 1923 and 2008 (in Germany and in Zimbabwe respectively), hyper-inflation has reduced the value of paper money to the point where commodities such as cigarettes or the use of foreign currencies as a medium of exchange have appeared.

Banking – the taking of deposits or making loans or both – is of quite ancient origin. Weber (2003) says that banking existed in Babylon and included the circulation of depository receipts. The Bank of Amsterdam, founded in 1609, is generally considered to be the first modern bank. Initially it acted as a mint, receiving worn and clipped coins and issuing new ones. It accepted deposits but made a charge for them and the bank money which resulted (in the sense that debts could be paid by transfers to other account holders) was 100 per cent backed by specie and, according to Chown (1994), actually commanded a premium over coinage. Initially, the bank made no loans. Similar banks were opened in Hamburg (1619) and Sweden (1656). The Swedish bank was the first to issue bank notes and, in 1688, was taken over by the state to become the world's first central bank (>CENTRAL BANKING). The Bank of Amsterdam foundered in 1819, having started making loans to the Dutch East India Company with which it had overlapping directors (>ENGLISH EAST INDIA COMPANY). Much earlier than all this, Italian merchants (not commercial banks in the modern sense, but merchants who made loans and investments) dominated throughout the Middle Ages. Until the 1340s, Bardi & Peruzzi, a firm of merchants, was the largest European business with branches all over the Continent. It was forced into bankruptcy by a defaulting monarch. South German banks then took over the lead, but were later, in the 18th century, eclipsed by the Dutch, who led a new era of international banking. This was the classic age of the merchant banks. The British merchant bank Barings, with Hopes & Co. of Amsterdam, helped to finance Thomas Jefferson's purchase of Louisiana from France (>AMERICAN WESTWARD EXPANSION). Although there were many small private banks throughout Europe, the merchant banks were the largest banking institutions until the strong emergence of joint stock banks in the second half of the 19th century (Cameron and Bovykin, 1991).

In >BRITAIN, commercial banking had its origins in scrivenors (who wrote contracts and acted as agents in managing estates) and gold merchants, who kept gold in safe deposit and whose certificates of deposit began to be used in the settlement of debt. By the 18th century, private commercial banks were accepting deposits and making loans and also issuing bank notes. These bank notes were backed by gold. The Bank of England, founded in 1694, was given a monopoly of joint stock banking in England and Wales (arrangements in Scotland, which invented limited liability banking, were different) and

rival private (i.e., unincorporated) banks were limited to six partners. In 1750 there were only 12 banks outside London, but expanding use of bills of exchange led local business people to establish approaching 700 country banks by 1825. These country banks had close links with the accepting houses in London and funded not only trade credit but also made long-term loans for fixed investment. In 1826, the availability of joint stock status was extended to all banks, which began a second phase in the growth of banking. By 1875 there were still 236 private banks alongside 122 joint stock banks. The banks were allowed to issue bank notes but these had to be fully backed by specie.

Early in the 19th century, there was a famous debate about the convertibility of bank notes at a time when the government had suspended convertibility (from 1797–1821) because of the Napoleonic Wars. In this controversy, the Bullionists, who included >RICARDO, argued for convertibility on the grounds that non-convertibility was inflationary. The anti-Bullionists argued against convertibility on grounds of facilitating bank note issues and trade. This debate resurfaced in the 1840s in the debate between the Currency and Banking schools, prior to the 1844 Banking Act, over the need to regulate note issues, particularly those of the country banks. The Currency School prevailed and the right of the private banks to issue notes was gradually extinguished. Britain was to maintain convertibility to gold until 1914. Meanwhile, France and the USA used gold and silver interchangeably, this created problems because the market values of the two metals were not always aligned (>BIMETALLIC SYSTEM).

The third phase of banking development in England and Wales was characterized by the absorption of the provincial banks by the London houses. Between 1888 and 1894 there were 67 bank mergers. Branch networks expanded so that by 1913 there was an average of 156 branches per bank compared with only five in 1850. The merger movement created a small number of major banks with Barclays, Lloyds and Midland as the largest. By this time the merchant banks were concentrating on overseas securities and the mixed industrial banks of the kind which existed in Continental Europe did not emerge in Britain, though there were large numbers of smaller banks also in Europe. The capital needs of local business were partly met by provincial stock exchanges but most relied on self-financing, especially since business owners did not wish to dilute their control. The trend towards >CONCENTRATION in banking continued into the inter-war period. In 1875, the top ten London banks accounted for 56 per cent of total deposits but by 1920 the 'big five' accounted for almost 66 per cent (Wilson, 1995).

Although domestic security issues were increasing in the inter-war period, they still accounted for only 10 per cent of the issues quoted on the British stock exchanges, most of which were overseas issues. At this time the banks were turning to financing industrial and commercial activities and there was an increasing demand for bank finance, especially for mergers. These tendencies were reinforced by the introduction of controls on capital exports which followed Britain's abandonment of the gold standard in 1931. That year, the Macmillan Committee, whose members included >KEYNES, published its report which adopted the Treasury view that expenditure on public works was not the answer to

the >GREAT DEPRESSION. The report also identified a gap in the availability of long-term finance for smaller firms (>SMALL AND MEDIUM ENTERPRISES). Post->WORLD WAR II this gap was closed by the creation of the Industrial and Commercial Finance Corporation (subsequently 3i), the development of unlisted securities markets and venture capital and by increased funding from the commercial banks. These developments were partly the result of increased competition between the large commercial banks which followed the Bank of England's initiative, 'Competition, Credit and Control', in 1971. Under the new regime, constraints on the banks and other financial institutions were removed and the Treasury reduced its use of credit control as a weapon against inflation and balance of payments problems.

There have been considerable changes in British banking since 1971. More overseas banks have been attracted by the success of the City to set up in London. Most British merchant banks and security houses have been taken over by foreign firms following the removal of restrictions on foreign ownership in 1986 (>CAPITAL MARKETS). Other changes include the conversion of some building societies to banks and the growth of mortgage lending for residential property by the commercial banks, credit card lending and a general breakdown of the distinctions between banks, insurance companies and other financial institutions. There have also been regulatory changes. The Financial Services Authority (FSA), created under legislation in 1986, has taken over the functions of a host of sectoral regulators and is now responsible for virtually the whole of the financial services industry, including the banks, though the Bank of England, which had previously supervised the banks, remains responsible for ensuring 'systemic stability' of the financial system as a whole. A tripartite division of responsibility between the Bank, the FSA and the Treasury for banking may have contributed to the failure of the regulators to prevent the collapse and subsequent nationalization of Northern Rock, which in 2007 experienced the first major bank run in Britain since the 19th century. This failure was followed by government action to shore up other banks in what proved to be a global banking crises. Depositors with banks are, to some extent, protected in most countries by some sort of depositor insurance but only up to a limit.

The evolution of the banking system in the USA has followed a very different path from that in Britain. In Colonial America, private banks were not permitted by the British authorities. After independence, the various states developed their own banking laws. By 1860 there were 1,600 state-chartered banks and some 1,100 private (unchartered) banks. Two attempts to set up Federal National Banks proved to be short-lived because the states feared that a central bank would result that would restrict their freedoms. During the American Civil War (1861–5), the National Currency and National Banking Acts were enacted. There were two objectives of these acts. One was to achieve a national currency and this was badly needed since the contemporary situation was chaotic with some 7,000 different types of bank notes in issue. This objective was quickly achieved because the Federal government imposed a prohibitive tax on state bank note issues which made them unprofitable and drove them out. The second objective was to create a system

of Federally chartered banks which might eventually supplant the state-chartered banks. This second aim, however, was never achieved. This was because, through pressure from the states, the national banks were hampered by various restrictions, such as being barred from accepting bills of exchange. At first, most state-chartered banks were driven into the national system so that by 1870 there were only 261 state chartered banks and 1,612 national banks. Private banks, unaffected by the restrictions, flourished and there were 1,903. The states subsequently liberalized their banking laws to favour state-chartered banks so that by 1890 the number of state-chartered banks grew to 2,830, though the number of national and private banks also grew considerably. The result was a dual system of national and state banks which persists today (see contribution by Carosso and Sylla in Cameron and Bovykin, 1991).

The Federal Reserve Act of 1913 created a central bank system for the first time and also permitted national banks to discount bills of exchange and open branches abroad. Later, in 1933, the Glass–Steagal Act prohibited commercial bankers from acting as investment banks, that is issuing securities or owning a firm dealing in securities, encouraging the further development of the great private banks such as J. P. Morgan. The inter-war depression exposed the weaknesses of the fragmented US banking system and between 1931 and 1932 about a fifth of all US banks went out of business. The provisions regulating branch banking have been greatly relaxed in the post-World War II period. Over the period 1990–6, the number of banks in the USA fell by a third but the number of branches increased by 50 per cent. Despite these changes, the US banking system remains more fragmented than in most other countries. In the 1980s there was a savings and loan (S&L) crisis. The S&Ls, or thrifts, are savings banks, very roughly comparable to the British building societies. Large numbers, well over 1,300, failed in the 1980s following the impact of inflation and regulatory changes which unintentionally encouraged risky diversification. The result was the greatest rate of insolvencies since the 1930s, costing the US taxpayers enormous sums in compensation from the Federal Savings and Loan Insurance Corporation.

The role of banks in >ECONOMIC DEVELOPMENT has long fascinated economic historians. Rudolf Hilferding, a Marxist, in *Finance Capital* (1910), argued that banks were the driving force in >CONCENTRATION. Joseph >SCHUMPETER, at about the same time, identified banks and >ENTREPRENEURSHIP as the key agents in economic development. It was Alexander >GERSCHENKRON, another Austro-Hungarian, who made the greatest impact on thinking about banks and development. He argued that the >INDUSTRIAL REVOLUTION IN BRITAIN largely involved small-scale units of production that could grow by reinvesting earnings and did not need banks for fixed investment. The finance requirements of German and other late-comer industries in Europe, by contrast, were on a larger scale. This was why the large 'mixed' or Universal Banks evolved in Germany and elsewhere to make long-term loans and arrange public securities issues, whereas in the British and American systems these functions were carried out by different institutions. Gerschenkron did not see the universal banks as an instrument of finance capitalism, like Hilferding, but as essentially transitory institutions

that would diminish in importance as the leading enterprises expanded to the point where they could become self-financing. It was certainly true that banking did develop differently in much of Continental Europe (and in Japan) from that in the USA and Britain. It also turned out to be correct that the importance of universal banks would diminish later on. Gerschenkron's thesis was clear and appealing, but later work was unable to verify it empirically. This seems to be the fate of most of the great generalizations in economic history, for example, those of >CHANDLER and >ROSTOW; the value of these generalizations lies in the debates that they stimulate. There have always been differences in the evolution of banking systems and countries have industrialized early and late with and without universal banks, as the examples of the Netherlands and Norway, which did not have universal banks, illustrate.

Universal banking might be said to have been pioneered in France with the Credit Mobilier, founded in the mid-19th century, though it did not develop there to the extent that it did in Germany. Universal banking was taken up by Austria, Hungary, Sweden and other countries. The nature of the US banking system was shaped by regulation driven by political motives, but the absence of large mixed banks did not prevent the adoption of capital-intensive industry. For infrastructure, including the railways and in particular for canals, where 70 per cent of construction was financed by state and municipal government between the 1850s and 1880s, government assistance in America was important. For infrastructure, therefore, the Gerschenkron thesis does get some support since it was not until later on in the 19th century that investment finance was easily available from investment banks. The scale of Federal government help for >RAILWAYS was considerable and consisted not so much in financing but in the provision of land and the granting of monopolies. For industry, however, there seems to have been relatively little help from government, even though banking was still primitive in the early 19th century. As Licht (1995) demonstrates, industrialization in the USA, as in Britain, was financed primarily from retained earnings and by the pooling of funds from partners who had previously made money in commerce.

Gerschenkron did exaggerate the merits of universal banks and indeed described them as 'a powerful invention, comparable in economic effect to that of the steam engine' (quoted by Collins, 1998). Gerschenkron and his followers have also drawn attention to the role of universal banks as members of supervisory boards (>GOVERNANCE) in holding and exercising voting proxies of the equity shares deposited with them and even in making up for deficiencies in entrepreneurship by guiding enterprises strategically. Today, the importance of most of this is downplayed (Edwards and Ogilvie, 1996). The large literature attributing the slowing down of British growth after 1870, the insufficiency of restructuring of British industry in the interwar period and weaknesses in the British economy in the early post->WORLD WAR II era as also partly the fault of the banking system now looks rather dated. In any event, the German banking system is much less concentrated than the British and the universal banks have never been really dominant. Britain has about 700 banks, of which a large number are effectively London branches of overseas banks. According to Edwards

and Fischer (1994), at the end of 1987, the share of the five largest German banks in the consolidated balance sheet total for the largest 25 banks, was 44.6 per cent, while a roughly comparable figure for Britain was 73.7 per cent. There were some 4,000 banks in Germany, including 163 regional and other commercial banks and thousands of savings and cooperative credit banks, which compete with them. The US system is even more fragmented than the German one, though it is concentrating rapidly with the relaxation of regulatory restraints. The number of 'main bank offices' in the USA, which was about 12,000 in 1990, fell by about one-third between 1990 and 2006, while the number of branches increased by some 50 per cent.

The development of modern banking in Japan started with the Meiji Restoration (1868). It was decided to establish a national banking system along the lines adopted earlier in the USA. The national banks were permitted to issue bank notes which had to be redeemable in gold. Since unconvertible government currency was also circulating and the interest on the government bonds which had to be deposited with the government as backing for the note issue was insufficient for any profit to be made, however, the banks were soon drained of their gold reserves. The regulations were revised in 1876 and bank notes ceased to be convertible. The result was that there was an inflationary boom, especially since the government continued to print money. From 1882, when the central Bank of Japan was founded, the new bank was allowed to issue notes only against specie, there was a fiduciary issue but this was limited by taxation. A deflationary policy was pursued and the gold standard was adopted in 1897. A number of special banks were formed as instruments of government policy and partly financed by it. The special banks made long-term loans to industry and agriculture and a Foreign Exchange Bank was also established. A system of commercial banks, including some of the reformed national banks, developed. In 1901 there were 2,359 separate banking concerns in Japan, including private savings banks. A Treasury Deposits Bureau with the savings banks, collected savings from the less well off (Allen, 1972; contribution by Kanji Ishii to Cameron and Bovykin, 1991).

With the encouragement and assistance of the government, long-established wealthy merchant families, which had helped to achieve the Meiji Restoration, together with recruits from the *samurai*, became agents of government and concentrated a major proportion of economic power in *zaibatsu*. These conglomerates were dominated by a bank holding a controlling interest in other members of the group of companies. The *zaibatsu* did not have a monopoly of big business, but were huge groups. During World War II, the government had enforced amalgamation among the commercial banks to facilitate control. After the war, however, the occupying authorities separated the *zaibatsu* banks from the other firms in each group so as to break down the integration of finance and industry; it also converted the special banks into commercial banks. Over time, however, and as Japan achieved full sovereignty, many of the previous arrangements were re-established. The *zaibatsu* reappeared in the different form of *keiretsu*, with companies in interlocking shareholdings. The *keiretsu* included a bank but it was not the vehicle for control since legislation reduced a bank's permitted

shareholding in a company to 5 per cent. In 1954 the Bank of Tokyo was founded as a successor to the original Foreign Exchange Bank, an Industrial Bank (now independent) and an Export–Import Bank. The commercial banks effectively operated as universal banks and stock market finance for industry was fairly limited. The Japanese financial system, therefore, had elements of both the Anglo-American system and a universal banking system linking business and the state on German lines. Japan's phenomenal growth rate from the 1960s to the early 1970s drove the country into the top flight of world economies (>ASIAN MIRACLE). By the early 1990s, however, growth stopped and the banking system was in severe distress because of the bursting of a real estate and equity bubble which brought down collateral values to a fraction of their previous levels. Japan's share in world trade fell and with it productivity growth, revealing the deep-seated distortions and weaknesses in the financial system. Reforms were embarked upon but political difficulties limited progress. Nevertheless there was considerable bank restructuring and Japanese banks seem to have had much less exposure to the problems which beset banks in other countries in 2008.

Perhaps the most striking feature of money and banking in the post-World War II era has been the extent to which it has been affected by >GLOBALIZATION. From being largely a matter for nation states, the management of national currencies is passing into the international sphere. The number of currencies in Europe has fallen sharply with European Monetary Union (>WESTERN EUROPE). Of 181 currencies in use in the world in 1997, 21 were pegged to the US dollar, 47 had managed floats and 51 were independently floating (Cohen, 1998). International capital flows, freed from most regulatory restraints, have increased enormously and monetary policies have to take as much account of this, if not more, than domestic considerations. The semi-fixed exchange rates under the Bretton Woods system now lie in the distant past. One of the results of these changes has been the increasingly rapid transmission of financial problems between countries, as illustrated by the 1997 Asian Banking Crisis and the sub-prime credit crisis in the USA in 2007–8. By curtailing the supply of credit and inter-bank lending, this crisis brought down two major investment banks (BearSterns and Lehman Brothers) and forced others to engage in mergers or seek financial support from government. Banks have always been prone to failure, not only through over- or imprudent lending but also because their liabilities (such as bank deposits and borrowing from other banks) tend to be much more liquid than their assets (loans and investments); this feature makes even sound banks potentially vulnerable to rumours and 'contagious mistrust' at times of bank panics. This vulnerability has recently been increased by the securitization of loans and the use of other credit derivatives.

The failure of the Bank of Amsterdam, the collapse of the Credit Anstalt (a large Austrian universal bank) in 1931 and widespread bank failures in the USA during the 1930s, as well as a series of bank failures in Scandinavia in the early 1990s and many others, illustrate bank vulnerability. Regulatory authorities have done their best to limit failures and their consequences, by surveillance, minimum capital adequacy ratios, prudential limits and other means, including deposit insurance, but not always with success. The latest banking troubles, which have triggered a stock market crash, have called into question the relaxation of regulation that has taken place since the 1970s and re-regulation is likely. The reaction of governments around the world has confirmed that it is unlikely that any government would allow a really major bank to fail, though there is a risk that this expectation of a rescue, in itself ,will only encourage banks to continue to take undue risks (moral hazard).

## References

Allen, G. C., *A Short Economic History of Modern Japan* (1946), George Allen & Unwin (rev. edn), 1972.

Cameron, Rondo and Bovykin, V. I. (eds), *International Banking 1870–1914*, Oxford University Press, 1991.

Chown, John, *A History of Money from AD 800*, Routledge, 1994.

Cohen, Benjamin J., *The Geography of Money*, Cornell University Press, 1998.

Collins, Michael, 'English Bank Development within a European Context, 1870–1939', *Economic History Review*, February, 1998.

Cottrell, P, L., Lindgren, Hakan and Teichova, Alice (eds), *European Industry and Banking between the Wars*, Leicester University Press, 1992.

Edwards, Jeremy and Fischer, Klaus, *Banks, Finance and Investment in Germany*, Cambridge University Press, 1994.

Edwards, Jeremy and Ogilvie, Sheilagh, 'Universal Banks and German Industrialisation: A Reappraisal', *Economic History Review*, August, 1996.

Licht, W., *Industrialising America: The Nineteenth Century*, Johns Hopkins University Press, 1995.

Morgan, E. Victor, *History of Money*, Penguin, 1965.

Weber, Max, *General Economic History* (1927), Transaction Publishers (new edn), 2003.

Wilson, John F., *British Business History, 1720–1994*, Manchester University Press, 1995.

# Multinational Enterprises

Multinational enterprises (MNEs) are also variously known as global corporations, multinational corporations (MNCs) and transnational corporations (TNCs). Multinationals are companies which own value added-producing assets outside their country of origin, in other words they engage in foreign direct investment (FDI) (>INTERNATIONAL TRADE). The growth of MNEs has paralleled the rise of big business (>CONCENTRATION) and is an aspect of >GLOBALIZATION. However, not all MNEs are very large and not all large businesses are MNEs, although most are. UNCTAD, which maintains a database on FDI, identified 35,000 MNEs in 1990, of which 20,000 employed fewer than 500 persons (>SMALL AND MEDIUM ENTERPRISES). UNCTAD demonstrated the growth of MNEs by identifying 60,000 in 2000 with some 820,000 foreign affiliates. Some large 19th-century corporations, including railway companies, had no assets abroad and did not count as MNEs, although these firms did provide a test bed for the management techniques and modes of organization used by MNEs (> CHANDLER).

Economic historians have traced the existence of MNEs back to the earliest times, to the Phonecians, to the international Italian bankers of the Middle Ages (>MONEY AND BANKING) and to the state-sponsored trading companies of the 17th and 18th centuries (>ENGLISH EAST INDIA COMPANIES). However, the modern form of MNEs, which are characterized not so much by trading but by the production of goods and services abroad, really began only following the >INDUSTRIAL REVOLUTIONS and the ensuing growth of international trade

(>COMMERCIAL REVOLUTION). From 1500 to 1800 world trade grew by only about 1 per cent per annum but in the 19th century this quickened to 3.5 per cent. Other factors promoting the emergence of MNEs were >MIGRATION, >ECONOMIC IMPERIALISM and the emergence of international >CAPITAL MARKETS. Others were dramatic improvements in >SHIPPING, >TELECOMMUNICATIONS and information technology (>ELECTRONICS). These improvements, for example, the completion of the first trans-Atlantic cable in 1866, resulted not only in greater speed but also laid the basis for a long-term decline in communications and transport costs.

In the 1850s and 1860s, modern MNEs established plants abroad, for example Siemens, the German electrical engineering company, and the Singer Sewing Machine Company of the >USA. By 1914, there were many multinationals manufacturing chemicals, pharmaceuticals, branded foods and other goods, including motor vehicles. In the period 1870–1914 there were also British, Dutch and French free-standing companies that did not produce at home but engaged in mining and plantations and other activities abroad, for example, rubber in Malaya (see the contribution by Mira Wilkins in Chandler and Mazlish, 2005). In this early period (and still today) there were several types of MNEs. Some, like Singer, were extending successful domestic operations abroad and were growing mainly from internal sources; this was the early American model. Others, especially European enterprises, were more in the nature of conglomerates, or were to become conglomerates, such as Lever Brothers, which evolved into Unilever, which today has some 200 principal companies in

90 countries. Many of the early MNEs were resource-specific, for example, in mining (Metallgesellschaft), oil (Shell), rubber (US Rubber), tropical fruit (United Fruit) and tobacco (British American Tobacco). The companies mentioned were formed mostly from the late 19th century to the 1930s, though their origins were often much earlier, for example, the London merchant company which was to evolve into Shell started in the 1830s. Some companies grew by acquisition as much or more than by internal expansion. There have been successive international waves of merger activity (for example, in the 1890s, around 1919, the late 1920s and the 1960s) which led to progressive >CONCENTRATION in some sectors. Following the two world wars, many industries, including those where MNEs were prominent, were essentially oligopolistic in nature (a small number of producers often characterized by product differentiation and the heavy use of advertising and other marketing techniques).

Some of the MNEs which appear in the lists of the world's largest, focus on a limited range of branded products, such as Coca-Cola, McDonalds and American Express; others, like General Electric and Mitsubishi, are more varied in the scope of their activities. There are, therefore, quite a few different types of MNE and generalizations are difficult to make, for example, some, such as most of those just mentioned and the big motor company groups, have been in the lists since well before >WORLD WAR II; others, such as Vodafone using new technologies, are of relatively recent origin. The growth of MNEs slackened but did not stop during the >GREAT DEPRESSION and after World War II the pace of MNE expansion and extension quickened again up to the early 1970s, when it began to change in character.

Much of the earlier implantation of multinationals outside Europe was based either on natural resources or on import substitution. From 1970, more MNEs moved into, or sourced from, developing countries (>ECONOMIC DEVELOPMENT) in search of lower labour costs, in part made possible by the de-skilling of production which technological developments had permitted. Continuing falls in shipping and communication costs were also a factor. Ocean freight costs and port charges fell by half between the late 1940s and the early 1990s and the cost of a London–New York telephone call fell tenfold; airline costs also fell sharply (>AVIATION). The new mode of MNE expansion was based on exports of manufactures and later services such as software development and call centres back to the developed countries. The emerging countries of East Asia and, successively, China and India were favoured by these developments.

The most recent phase in the history of MNEs, as already mentioned, has been a shift to services, though the origins of this also go back a long way not only in banking but also in communications: MNE were prominent, for example, in the development of telegraph and telecommunications and even in the early movie industry. Mira Wilkins mentions that the French company, Pathé, a pioneer in silent films, had, by 1914, outlets in more than 40 major cities, worldwide. The switch to services, however, has been quite dramatic since 1970, when only one-quarter of the stock of FDI was invested in services, whereas by 2002 it had risen to 67 per cent, with the primary sector accounting for only 4 per cent and manufacturing 29 per cent.

Since 1960, new FDI has grown faster than both world trade and output but the early years of the millennium have seen a decline in FDI even though world trade has continued to expand. The originators of FDI have changed over the years. In 1914, >BRITAIN accounted for 45.5 per cent of the world stock of FDI; by 1960 Britain had been largely displaced by theUSA but the two countries together accounted for well over 50 per cent of the world total up to 1978. Since then their share has fallen, while that of Japan, Germany and France rose sharply, only to fall in turn as investment by the rest of the world grew, including that from other European countries, Australasia, the newly industrialized countries and, increasingly, among the developing countries (LDCs) themselves. FDI, like trade, has now become a pervasive international phenomenon.

About one-third of FDI is invested in developing countries, though investment in LDCs has been increasing faster in recent decades. From the 1960s there has been concern that MNEs would exploit the lower labour costs and environmental standards of the Third World. However, there is now a broad consensus among economists that MNEs have benefited host countries in most cases; this is particularly evident in the Middle East (oil) and in East Asia (>ASIAN MIRACLE), through transfers of technology and the local sourcing of inputs (backward linkages). Indeed, as labour costs in the emerging countries have risen, the MNEs' local sub-contractors have in turn sub-contracted to other countries further down in the development scale, as in footwear in Indonesia and textiles in Southern Africa. Nike, which in 1993 had world sales in excess of $4 billion, is a good example of these trends: it employs a core staff of designers, technicians and administrators of only 9,000 in the USA but 75,000 in independent sub-contractors in East Asia (Cypher and Dietz, 2004).

The growth of MNEs has aroused enormous interest from governments from the developmental, >TAXATION and >ANTI-TRUST viewpoints and from various lobby groups and the general public. One of several myths about MNEs is that they no longer have national identities. In fact, most MNEs do reflect their national origins in many ways, for example, in their systems of governance, their patterns of investment, in exhibiting a home bias in the location of Research and Development (R&D), in membership of Boards of Directors and in other ways (Doremus, 1998). It was feared in the 1960s and later that a small number of MNEs, and particularly American enterprises, would come to dominate world trade and production. A famous book, Servan-Schreiber's *The American Challenge* (1968), eloquently voiced these fears and attributed the success of the American corporations to their great size and to superior technology and management practices. The fears have not been borne out; Japanese and European MNEs were able to make major encroachments into the USA domestic market, for example in the >AUTOMOBILE INDUSTRY and consumer >ELECTRONICS. In fact, it was soon the turn of the Americans to proclaim the need to emulate the superior management techniques of the Japanese. European fears persist, even though, as we have seen, the American share of world FDI has fallen back sharply. More recently, with the rejuvenation of American enterprise, European concerns have turned to cultural as much as economic domination from the USA. It is true that all MNEs and their affiliates account for about one-third of exports of goods and services and a similar proportion of output and that the 100 largest MNEs account for two-thirds of new FDI; however, there is a long way to go before these MNEs, whatever their national origins, can be said to dominate the world economic system, important though as they are.

## References

Amatori, Franco and Jones, Geoffrey (eds), *Business History Around the World*, Cambridge University Press, 2003.

Chandler, Alfred D. and Mazlish, Bruce (eds), *Leviathans, Multinational Corporations and the New Global History*, Cambridge University Press, 2005.

Cypher, James M. and Dietz, James L., *The Process of Economic Development*, Routledge, 2004.

Doremus, Paul N., Keller, William W., Pauly, Louis W. and Reich, Simon, *The Myth of The Global Corporation*, Princeton University Press, 1998.

Jones, Geoffrey, *Multinationals and Global Capitalism from the Nineteenth to the Twenty-First Century*, Oxford University Press, 2005.

Schmitz, Christopher J., *The Growth of Big Business in the United States and Western Europe, 1850–1939*, Macmillan, 1993.

Servan-Schreiber, J.-J., *The American Challenge*, Hamish Hamilton, 1968.

United Nations Conference on Trade and Development, *World Investment Report*, 2004.

# N

## New Deal

The social and economic reforms introduced by the government of newly elected President Franklin Delano Roosevelt (FDR) from March 1933 were the 'New Deal' promised in his acceptance speech. The >USA at that time was in the depths of the >GREAT DEPRESSION. Farm prices fell by 55 per cent between 1929 and 1932, industrial production had fallen by almost half and a quarter of the labour force was unemployed. The banking system was in crisis: no less than 1,400 banks had failed in 1932 (>BANKING). Following the closure of leading banks by state government in Michigan on 14 February, other states were also declaring bank moratoria. Distress was being experienced by all levels of society: the stock market crash (>CAPITAL MARKETS) ruined many financiers and speculators, hundreds of thousands of farm families lost their farms and literally millions of people lived by begging and itinerant labour. The urban black population was particularly badly hit. On the whole it is remarkable that some form of social order was maintained. As Himmelberg (2001) explains, the American people were, for the most part passive, though the famous march of unemployed war veterans to Washington (the Bonus Expeditionary Force) had been put down by General Douglas McArthur by force in the summer of 1932. Paradoxically, it was not until a recovery had begun in 1934 and the Democrats were in power that labour militancy increased significantly. It was also only then that irresponsible demagogic figures, such as Huey Long, assassinated in November 1935, emerged to call for a radical redistribution of income and wealth.

Roosevelt was inaugurated on 4 March 1933. During his campaign, though promising immediate action, he had been vague about what he would actually do and apparently had no detailed plans. However, early in 1932 FDR, as New York's governor, had appointed a 'Brains Trust' of professors at Columbia University to advise him. The advisory group included: Professor Adolf A. Berle, a lawyer who had co-authored a book on >CONCENTRATION published that year; Rexford Tugwell, a young left-leaning economist; and Raymond Moley. The central figure of the Panel was Moley, another lawyer who coined the term 'New Deal'; later, in 1936, he was to become a critic of FDR. All three wanted social as well as economic reform and the latter two in particular were in favour of much more planning and regulation. Some preparatory work must have been done because FDR acted with remarkable speed. On 4 March 1933, in his inaugural address, he memorably said 'the only thing we have to fear is fear itself' and went on 'This Nation asks for action and action now.' The next day, under the doubtful authority of the World War I Trading with the Enemy Act, he ordered that all banks should be closed, and prohibited the export of >GOLD, effectively taking the USA off the >GOLD STANDARD. He called Congress into special session for 9 March at which the Emergency Banking Relief Act was passed. Banks judged sound (about two-thirds of the total) reopened on 13 March and currency and gold flowed back into the banking system.

Three months of intense legislative activity (dubbed the First 100 Days) followed 9 March. Under the influence of FDR's speeches and self-confidence, public sentiment improved greatly. In fact, the contraction, which began in 1929, was brought to a halt and recovery, albeit slow, continued in the four years from 1933 so that, by 1937, national product just exceeded 1929 levels. Unemployment, however, remained high and, with the onset of a recession within the depression, actually rose again from 1937–8, accompanied by a decline in GNP. This was probably the result of policy errors by the Federal Reserve (>CENTRAL BANKING). There was no decisive and sustained recovery until after 1941, with spending on war production rising to unprecedented levels (>WORLD WAR II). This is central to the assessment of the economic impact of the New Deal. The adoption of Keynesian policies (>KEYNES) in the USA was not really to come until the 1960s. In the 1930s, FDR adhered to the orthodoxy of the day, which prescribed balanced budgets; indeed, in his election campaign he had criticized Herbert Hoover his predecessor for his modest budget deficits and one of his first actions in the Economy Act of 1933 was to cut the government budget by 10 per cent.

There were at least two phases of the New Deal. The first began in 1933 with FDR's election and the 100 days, though it continued until 1935–6, when he was elected for a second time. The second phase began with a Second 100 days and continued until 1940, when he was elected for a third term and became preoccupied with

>WORLD WAR II. (Some writers have distinguished a third phase within the second, that is, between 1937 and 1940.) Although there were common elements, a search for social balance and measures for planning and regulation, the emphasis of the New Deal varied somewhat between the different phases. The initial objective was to deal with the depression by structural reform and by promoting reflation, not by the later Keynesian approach of public expenditure but by planning, to restrict farm output and industrial policy to raise prices and profitability in cooperation with private enterprise. In the second phase, the emphasis shifted towards improving the purchasing power of less-favoured groups and to restoring the balance between agriculture, industry and the consumer. In this second period, emphasis switched to breaking up cartels and monopolies. At no point was the objective to adopt socialism, as many of the bitter opponents of the New Deal maintained; on the contrary FDR wanted to save >CAPITALISM.

The New Deal covered a vast range of measures. In addition to banking, capital markets and currency, the New Deal also dealt with: agriculture (attempts to push up prices by restricting output); the maintenance of soil resources; industry regulation (at first to increase prices as in farming, later to improve efficiency and competition); transportation and utilities (regulation mainly to reduce prices); civil works to increase employment; unemployment relief; social security; and measures to improve the rights of labour and working conditions. Few corners of the economy and society escaped attention; the New Deal even subsidized theatre to give employment to actors, for example. It is worth noting that some of the elements of the programme were actually a continuation of initiatives taken under the discredited previous President, Herbert Hoover. Hoover's administration, for example, bought in agricultural surpluses, built the Boulder (later, Hoover) Dam and instituted the Reconstruction Finance Corporation. The previous administration did make errors, however; it failed to appreciate the gravity of the economic situation and, for example, introduced the Smoot–Hawley Tariff, which brought about retaliation by other countries and the collapse of world trade.

Many of the New Deal measures were successful, and many were not. In agriculture, where planning was most comprehensive, farmers benefited, especially in relief from the pressures arising from indebtedness. However, the whole concept of curtailing farm production to push up farm incomes when millions of people were on the verge of starvation was obviously subject to criticism. As Faulkner (1960) points out, the benefits to farmers were at the expense of consumers and taxpayers. He also shows that, by 1937, government agencies held about half of long-term agricultural debt, which drove out commercial financing of the sector. In any event, the first Agricultural Adjustment Act was declared unconstitutional in January 1936 and had to be replaced by a second Act in 1938.

The reorganization of industry under the National Industrial Recovery Act (NIRA) involved the setting of codes for labour conditions in return for self-regulated controls on prices and production (in other words cartelization) and failed on several counts, not least in the eyes of both business and labour. NIRA was also declared unconstitutional by the Supreme Court in May 1935, which led to its liquidation. The loss of two of his most important measures led FDR in 1937 to unveil a bill for the enlargement and reform of the Federal Court system. This was perceived as a means for packing the Supreme Court with New Deal Justices ('court packing') and putting too much power into FDR's hands. The measures were roundly rejected by a new coalition of Democrats (his own party) and Republicans, a coalition which achieved some permanence and made it more difficult for the President to get other legislation through in the future.

The various measures to promote public works began with the Civilian Conservation Corps in March 1933 and the Civil Works Administration (CWA) in November, which employed many hundreds of thousands in road and airport construction and other public works. (The CWA was, in the following year, merged into the Works Progress Administration, WPA.) These initiatives certainly absorbed many unemployed but were not, as already noted, sufficient to lift the country out of the depression. The New Deal made important changes to the system of government, permanently increasing the level of government intervention in the economy (not only Federal but also state). It began the process of providing better labour conditions and a safety net of social insurance. It also left much better-regulated commercial >BANKING and >CAPITAL MARKETS. Many of the institutions established during the New Deal have endured to this day, for example, the Federal Deposit Insurance Corporation (FDIC) and the Securities and Exchange Commission (SEC). Himmelberg also points out that 'the New Deal conferred upon "ethnics", mainly Catholics and Jews, a new, more powerful, position in American politics' (2001). Wallis (1998) demonstrates that responding to economic distress was good politics and ensured that FDR was returned to office regularly. As a programme to get the USA out of the depression, however, it failed. That objective was to be realized only in wartime. But the Great Depression and the New Deal were a turning point in American political and economic history.

## References

Atack, Jeremy and Passell, Peter, *A New Economic View of American History from Colonial Times to 1940*, W. W. Norton, 1994.

Faulkner, Harold Underwood, *American Economic History*, Harper & Row, 1960.

Himmelberg, Robert F., *The Great Depression and the New Deal*, Greenwood Press, 2001.

Wallis, John Joseph, 'The Political Economy of New Deal Spending Revisited Again: With and Without Nevada', *Explorations in Economic History*, 35, April, 1998.

# O

## Oil

In 1855, a group of entrepreneurs (>ENTREPRENEURSHIP) in the >USA received a report which they had commissioned that confirmed that an analysis of a substance called 'rock oil' showed that it could be distilled into products suitable as lubricants or for use in lanterns for lighting and the Pennsylvania Rock Oil Company was formed to exploit the discovery. There was no doubt that there was a need for a cheap material for illumination which would improve on the animal and vegetable fats widely used at the time but which would also competitively match the coal-derived >GAS which was becoming available in towns. To achieve this, it was necessary to find rock oil in sufficient quantities to generate the necessary economies of scale. In 1859, near Titusville, Pennsylvania, the Company struck rock oil by drilling for the first time in America. Its storage and transport problems were solved by the use of locally available whiskey and other barrels and so the barrel, standardized to 42 (US) gallons, became the unit of measurement of the oil industry. Rock oil, refined into kerosene, found its market as an effective lighting medium. Oil production in the USA increased rapidly from about 450,000 barrels in 1860 to 3.6 million barrels in 1866; the first pipelines were built to transport the oil to the nearest railhead and refineries proliferated to process the crude oil. One of those refineries was owned by John D. Rockefeller.

The rapid expansion of production led to a fall in prices which affected the profitability of both the oil producers and the refiners. In 1870, the Standard Oil Company of Ohio was established of which Rockefeller owned 25 per cent and which covered 10 per cent of the refinery capacity of the USA. By 1879, Standard Oil's share of this market had risen to 90 per cent. Standard Oil itself did not own the spread of refineries which it controlled, but its shareholders, the shares of the dependent companies being held for them in trust. In the 1880s, a new oilfield was discovered in Ohio which was developed rapidly to account for a major proportion of the total production of the USA and, by 1891, Standard Oil had grasped the control of a quarter of it. Standard Oil eventually controlled 85 per cent of the US oil market and became the first vertically integrated petroleum company, with assets ranging from production at the wellhead, through refining to distribution of the final product. Standard Oil's aggressive capture of the oil market led to a political backlash and its eventual demise as a single entity. In 1911, it was found to be in contravention of the Sherman Anti-Trust Act of 1890 and Standard Oil was split into its constituent parts, of which the biggest was Standard Oil of New Jersey (>ANTI-TRUST). All this high achievement from the technology of drilling for crude oil and its refining, the building of pipelines and the distribution to the final consumer was generated by the success of kerosene as a fuel for illumination. Its success was international. As much as 50 per cent of US output was exported, principally to Europe (Yergin, 1992).

Drilling had also commenced in Baku, >RUSSIA (Azerbaijan), on the Caspian Sea in the early 1870s. Refinery products were shipped out by >RAILWAY to the ports of Batum and Poti on the Black Sea. Later, in the early 1900s, a pipeline was completed from Baku to Batum. In 1892, the first purpose-built tanker, built in >BRITAIN, picked up a cargo of kerosene at Batum and, sailing via the Suez Canal, delivered it to Singapore and Bangkok (>SHIPPING). Russia, therefore, developed as a serious competitor to Standard Oil of the USA in the international market. By the mid-1890s, Russia was producing about 46 million barrels of crude oil, compared with about 52 million barrels in the USA.

The only significant producer in Europe was at Ploesti in Romania, which began refining its crude oil in 1856 and produced about 600,000 barrels in the mid-1890s (American Petroleum Institute, 1959). Oil was also coming on stream in the Dutch East Indies (Indonesia), where the first successful drilling was made in 1885. The Royal Dutch Company was established in 1890 and began marketing its kerosene in 1892, soon reaching an output of over 1 million barrels per year.

The profitable success of all this investment and technical ingenuity rested on the demand for kerosene as a lamp oil but it could be foreseen that the market for that had a doubtful future. In 1878, Thomas Alva Edison established the Edison Electric Light Company and, in 1880, the Edison Electric Illuminating Company built a generating station in Pearl Street in New York City, which began operating in 1882 (>ELECTRICITY), marking the beginning of the end of oil lamps for illumination in favour of electric light. But three years later came the first four-wheeled vehicle powered by petroleum, which is credited to Gottlieb Daimler (1834–1900), but Karl Benz (1844–1929) ran the first effective motor vehicle driven by the internal combustion engine. In 1903, the Ford Motor Company, founded by Henry >FORD, produced its first motor car and, in 1908, the highly successful Model T. Demand grew rapidly and by 1914 there were a 1 million cars registered in the USA (>AUTOMOBILE INDUSTRY). In addition to gasoline for automobiles, a new market was also emerging for fuel oil in railway locomotives and ships.

These new demands were met with increased output. In 1901, at Spindletop, Texas, a major oilfield was discovered, to be soon followed by others in Louisiana and particularly Oklahoma. The rapid increase in production led to a dramatic drop in prices, down to 3 cents per barrel (Yergin, 1992) and encouraged the switch to oil as a heating fuel. The railways began converting from >COAL to oil and both the USA and Britain decided to replace >COAL with fuel oil in their navies in 1911 (>SHIPPING).

In the 25 years, from 1875 to the end of the century, world oil production grew from about 13 million barrels to about 160 million barrels. The major producers were the USA, which accounted for 51 per cent of the total, and Russia, which produced 45 per cent. Production increased further to about 388 million barrels by the eve of >WORLD WAR I (Yates, 1959). However, a combination of political disturbances and inadequate investment undermined the development of Baku and Russia's share dropped to 17 per cent, while that of the USA rose to 64 per cent.

The perceived vulnerability of Britain to the monopolistic dangers of the existence of only two dominant oil combines, Standard Oil and Royal Dutch/Shell, persuaded the British government to take a controlling interest in Anglo-Persian in 1914. Anglo-Persian took over a company called British Petroleum, which operated a distribution network in Britain and also invested in a tankers to become a vertically integrated company (Anglo-Persian eventually changed its name to British Petroleum in 1954).

In the immediate post-war period, fears were expressed in the USA that its output would not match the growing demand for oil and its reserves would be depleted. The British government favoured American participation in the development of oil in Mesopatamia (Iraq). A major field was found in Iraq in 1927. An agreement was reached that the participating companies, British, French and American, would cooperate in developing the discovery and also any other in the Middle East region (excluding Iran and Kuwait).

In spite of new discoveries in California such that, in 1923, that state alone accounted for about 25 per cent of world output, there was still nervousness about the adequacy of supply and the depletion of US reserves and yet in 1926 and in 1927 more major discoveries were made in Oklahoma, New Mexico and, finally, the largest, in East Texas. Prices fell from $1.85 per barrel in 1926 to 15 cents per barrel in 1931. In spite of attempts to control production in Texas and Oklahoma, prices continued to remain low. The Federal government and the states cooperated in a system to restrict domestic production to maintain prices. In addition, tariffs were imposed on crude oil, gasoline and fuel oil imports. Prices were underpinned by these actions and they stayed in the USA above $1 per barrel until >WORLD WAR II.

Oil production was growing rapidly throughout the world in the inter-war years, on the eve of World War II total production being four times higher than in 1918 (American Petroleum Institute, 1959). Oil had been discovered in Venezuela and by 1929 the country was producing 137 million barrels and became the dominant exporter of crude oil. In 1931, oil was also discovered in Bahrain, and, in 1938, in Kuwait and in Saudi Arabia.

After World War II, there was a resurgence in oil production in Russia, with the result that by 1960 it had replaced Venezuela as the second largest producer after the USA and had become an important exporter. World production doubled between 1950 and 1960 and there was downward pressure on prices. The USA imposed quota restrictions in 1959 to keep imports within 9 per cent of consumption (Yergin, 1992) to support domestic producers. The fall in revenues accruing to the producing countries consequent to the drop in prices induced them to reconsider their contracted relationships with the oil companies. In 1960, Iran, Iraq, Kuwait, Saudi Arabia and Venezuela established the Organization of Petroleum Exporting Countries (OPEC), a consortium which covered 80 per cent of crude oil exports.

In the century between 1850 and 1950, 91 giant fields, each with initial reserves of between 0.5 and 5 billion barrels, were discovered and ten super-giant fields, each with initial reserves of over 5 billion barrels. In the following 30 years to 1980, 144 giant fields were discovered and 25 super-giant fields. The overwhelming majority of these discoveries were in the Middle East so that, by 1980, this region accounted for about 56 per cent of world reserves. In the 1950s, world crude oil production grew at an average rate of 7.2 per cent per annum and in the 1960s at an average rate of 8.3 per cent per annum (International Energy Agency, 1982). The expansion in available oil reserves was matched by the rapid growth in demand, generated by the expansion of the world economy. World gross domestic product rose at an average rate of 4.6 per cent between 1950 and 1960, expanded further to an average growth rate of 5 per cent per annum in the following decade, before falling back to an average growth of 3.7 per cent per annum between 1970 and 1980 (Maddison, 1995). In 1973, OPEC introduced production constraints and raised the posted price of crude oil, the price of which rose to $11.65 by the end of 1973, compared with a posted price of $1.80 per barrel in 1970. The oil-producing countries justified their actions in terms of controlling the rate at which their reserves would be depleted and their need for finance for investment. It was also argued that it was necessary for both consuming and producing countries to be cognizant of the need in the long run to develop other sources of energy (Mahmoud Abdel-Fadil, 1979). The policy had a dramatic effect. The average rate of growth of the world economy dropped to 2.8 per cent per annum between 1973 and 1983, compared with an average per annum growth rate of 5.3 per cent in the previous decade. In addition, consumer prices rose rapidly. For instance, inflation in the USA increased to 8.2 per cent per annum, in France to 11.2 per cent per annum, in Italy to 16.7 per cent per annum and Japan to 7.6 per cent per annum between 1973 and 1983 (Maddison, 1995) (>PRICES AND INFLATION). The

share taken by oil in total primary energy demand rose from 36 per cent in 1960 to a peak of 53 per cent in 1973, subsequently falling to 40 per cent in 2000 (International Energy Agency, 1982, 2000).

Recurrent fears that perceived oil resources as a finite asset and therefore subject to inevitable early decline in the face of rapidly expanding world demand have proved unfounded. The US Geological Survey estimated that the world reserves of crude oil (including natural gas liquids) were 960 million barrels in 2000, larger than in the 1970s, thanks to improvements in technological and geological expertise and the emergence of markets for associated natural gas, which improved the economic benefits from particular fields (International Energy Agency, 1982, 2000). The concern is not for the possible immediate absolute world shortfall in the supply of oil in relation to worldwide demand but the risk of supply interruptions arising from the distribution of reserves. In the last decades of the 20th century, the countries of the Middle East and the members of OPEC in particular dominated the distribution of oil reserves. By 2000, the OPEC countries of the Middle East possessed 53 per cent of world reserves of crude oil and the other members of OPEC a further 10 per cent (Odell, 2005). After 2000, oil prices began to climb and reached a peak of $147 in July 2008, after which they weakened as the world economy began to fall into recession.

## References

American Petroleum Institute, *Petroleum Facts and Figures, Centennial Edition*, American Petroleum Institute, 1959.
Ashworth, William, *A Short History of the International Economy Since 1850*, Longman, 1994.

Chisholm, George G., *Handbook of Commercial Geography*, Longmans, Green, 1922.

International Energy Agency, *World Energy Outlook*, OECD, 1982, 2000.

Maddison, Angus, *Monitoring the World Economy 1820–1992*, OECD, 1995.

Mahmoud Abdel-Fadil, *Papers on the Economics of Oil*, Oxford University Press, 1979.

Odell, Peter R., *Why Carbon Fuels Will Dominate the 21st Century's Global Energy Economy*, Multi-Science Publishing, 2005.

United Nations, *Energy Statistics Yearbook*, 1998.

Yates, P. Lamartine, *Forty Years of Foreign Trade*, George Allen & Unwin, 1959.

Yergin, Daniel, *The Prize: The Epic Quest for Oil, Money and Power*, Simon & Schuster, 1992.

# P

## Peasantry and Serfdom

The peasantry are social-economic groups of farmers managing small plots of land for their own subsistence and for a residual surplus for exchange at market. Their distinctive characteristic is that their enterprises are family-based under a family head, although the family may include, for instance, servants who are not kin or occasional hired help. They may own or rent their land. As a group, because of the heavy family dependency and the inherent fluctuations of the product of their labour, they tend to be risk-averse and reluctant to accept innovations until their benefits are fully established. The group contrasts with that of farmers with sufficiently large plots to warrant the employment of labour and who have capital to pay their wages and invest in buildings and machinery. On the other hand, they are also distinguished from landless wage-labourers. Their income may not be derived exclusively from farming. Family members would do off-farm work where possible. This supplementary work changed over the centuries from the skilled traditional crafts, such as that of the wainwright and blacksmith, through the piecework of the cottage industries of >PROTO-INDUSTRIALIZATION to the earning of wages in the post-industrialization factories.

The Feudal System in the Middle Ages had developed a structure of authority in which the King exercised power through a hierarchy of vassals, each level of which held defined rights and responsibilities. At the bottom of the structure were serfs. They were obliged to work for a given number of days in the year for their lord and could not marry or leave his domain without his permission. Serfs could not own land. They were an integral part of the lord's assets and could be bought and sold with the estate. In England (>BRITAIN), they did have some rights. They could take a grievance to the Manor Court and the lord could not treat him arbitrarily against what was established in local custom. Magna Carta, in 1215 (which, of course, had nothing whatever to do with serfs directly but, only at the time, the relationship between the barons and the king), did embody the important principles, that the king was not above the law and 'no extraordinary scutage or aid shall be imposed on our kingdom unless by common council of our kingdom'. These principles percolated over time throughout the political and social mores of Britain. As early as the 13th century, cracks had begun to appear in England in the feudal structure. Landlords were happy to take money for rent rather than product and to hire labour for wages. In 1348/9, the Black Death reduced the population of England from 4 million to 2.5 million, labour was scarce and wages rose. The serfs found that they could leave and be accepted as free labourers in the towns and elsewhere. The emancipation of the serfs in England was virtually completed in the 15th century, and, finally, all traces legally swept away in the 17th century.

Serfdom was much more harsh and persisted longer, the further east across the countries of Continental Europe. In France, serfdom was overthrown by the Montagnard Convention of 1793, which abolished all remaining traces of feudalism, without compensation (>PHYSIOCRATS; Sutherland, 2002). The emancipation of the serfs followed the Revolutionary Wars, as French achieved hegemony over other European countries in Naples (1806), Spain (1808), Prussia (1807/1811) and Austria-Hungary (1848) (>WESTERN EUROPE).

The path to complete emancipation in practice, however, was not short. In Prussia, for instance, all feudal traces were not eliminated until 1865. In parts of Italy, traces of feudalism lingered on until the end of the 19th century. In >RUSSIA, serfdom was legally enforced in 1649. Under a law of 1721, serfs could be allocated to factories and became a part of the factory's assets to be sold or bought with the business. Serfdom was legally abolished in 1861 but the peasant was tied to his village in so far as it was the village that allocated to him the land for him to farm and had the power to redistribute it. This power was not repealed until 1905. Following the Meiji Restoration in Japan in 1868, the feudal structure was eased and land given to the peasants. There persisted for a while, however, a type of feudal bondage in which a person could be given to a creditor as collateral for a debt. He would never be free as long as the debt remained unpaid.

The decline of the peasant in Western Europe was evolutionary, rather than dramatic, with the development, on the one hand, of >AGRICULTURE, with its emphasis on large acreages and capital investment making the smallholding uncompetitive, and, on the other, the growth of factory production, which changed the nature of and opportunities for off-farm work. In Britain, the decline was more rapid than elsewhere in Europe and the peasant was virtually extinct in Britain by the mid-19th century. It has been argued that the persistence of the peasantry in Europe and the associated feudal attitudes was one factor contributing to the delayed appearance of the >INDUSTRIAL REVOLUTION there compared with Britain. The early emancipation of the serfs opened up the prospective landscape for individual enterprise and this gave Britain the social structure and attitudes to exploit the opportunities when they arose.

By the end of the 20th century, the peasantry, as a group, was confined mainly to the developing countries, though they were more open to the influence of local and international markets on their output decisions than the peasantry of Europe had been accustomed to (>CHINA: >INDIA: >POOR LAWS: >SLAVERY: >WESTERN EUROPE).

### References

Landes, David, *The Wealth and Poverty of Nations*, Little, Brown, 1998.

Rösener, Werner, *The Peasantry of Europe*, Blackwell, 1994.

Sutherland, D. M. G., 'Peasants, Lords, and Leviathan: Winners and Losers from the abolition of French Feudalism, 1780–1820', *Journal of Economic History*, 62, March, 2002.

Trevelyan, G. M., *The History of England*, 1952.

## Pedlars

Itinerant merchants selling from door to door or at trade fairs were to be seen in Europe and other areas from the Middle Ages until the late 19th century and later. The great variety of pedlars (also spelled peddlers) is evidenced by the names given to them: tinkers, hawkers, petty traders, chapmen (after cheapmen). They dealt in plants, seeds, eggs and other commodities and in artisanal (and later) small manufactured goods, for example, toys, metal items, such as cooking utensils and tools, as well as crockery, spectacles, jewellery, medicines and books. Some pedlars were specialized; perhaps most carried a range of things. Better-off merchants travelled on horses and supplied shops, some had push-carts and many simply walked, carrying their goods on their backs (hence packmen in English, *porteballe, colporteur* in French).

Fontaine (1996), whose book seems to be the first modern full-length treatment of a somewhat neglected subject, shows that most pedlars were not rootless vagrants – though the poorer ones operated on the borders of income and charity – but had roots in their home villages and in a town for supplies, as well as fairly well-defined sales campaign areas, and were sustained by credit and trading networks. Credit and trading relationships were important because supplies were obtained on credit and pedlars often extended credit to their customers. Customer credit increased the size of the trader's market and gave rise to regular visits and further sales opportunities. Many, especially in Continental Europe, originated in mountainous areas where they had family farms. There were even ocean-going merchant pedlars who brought back exotic goods and plants from as far away as the Americas, Bombay and Hanoi.

Pedlars were not necessarily operating solely on their own account, some worked for sedentary merchants or as travelling salesmen for producers, though mostly they seem to have been self-employed and this, together with itineracy, seems to be a defining characteristic. At its fringes the profession seems to have had affinities with travelling players and entertainers and also with knife grinders and others offering door-to-door repair services.

It is not known how many pedlars there were. There were attempts to regulate them (>REGULATION) from early days, both in response to complaints from shopkeepers and from the desire of the authorities to curtail their activities in distributing banned books and publications. At some points in time pedlars have been seen to be associated with thieving and other petty crime. In England there was, according to Brown (2000), some local regulation from 1552 and in 1697 a national system of licensing was introduced, administered by excise officers. In 1843 there were 5,762 licensed hawkers and pedlars in England and Wales, but Brown says that this understated the actual number by at least 50 per cent. According to Fontaine (1996), regulation of pedlars began later and was relaxed earlier in England than in Continental Europe.

By the 19th century, economic fluctuations and improved transport, making it easier for consumers to get to shops, led to the decline of pedlars. Fontaine (1996) shows that this decline began in Britain in the 18th century, though not until the mid-19th century in France and later still in Spain and Germany. Clapham (1930) wrote that in Germany, less urbanized than France at the time, there were few shops except those of artisans even in the 1840s so that pedlars played an important role in distribution. This and the spreading of knowledge through the books they sold meant that pedlars were an important element in early industrialization. They provided an outlet for products and helped to stimulate consumer tastes (>CONSUMER REVOLUTION). Brown quotes Matthew Boulton (>STEAM POWER) as having written to his London agent: 'hawkers, pedlars and those who supply petty shops do more towards supporting a great manufactory than all the Lords in the nation' (2000).

Itinerant salesmen still operate in rural areas today in Europe, offering credit services, selling fish and other commodities and even providing the ancient services of knife grinding, window cleaning and chimney sweeping, albeit in motorized form. Mirroring earlier European history and despite complaints from sedentary shopkeepers and the efforts of the authorities to confine them to market areas, large numbers of street traders and hawkers throng the cities of the developing countries (>ECONOMIC DEVELOPMENT), though most of these countries do not support large numbers of itinerant traders in rural areas as they existed in early Europe.

### References

Brown, David, 'Importance of Pedlars', *Textile History*, 31(1), 2000.

Clapham, J. H., *An Economic History of Modern Britain: The Early Railway Age, 1820–1850* (2nd edn), Cambridge University Press, 1930.

Fontaine, Laurence, *History of Pedlars in Europe*, Duke University Press, 1996.

# Physiocrats

In the 17th century, France had become the dominant country in Europe but its position was weakened through a series of costly wars during the reign of the 'Sun King' Louis XIV (1638–1715). The resulting pressure on the country's resources continued under Louis XV (1710–1774), as France became enmeshed in the War of the Spanish Succession (1701–1714) and the Seven Years' War (1756–1763). The country not only had to endure the dislocation caused by continuing warfare, but also, in the late 17th century, the effect on agricultural output also of the so called 'Little Ice Age', which afflicted Europe with exceptionally low temperatures. There was a serious >FAMINE in 1693. It has been shown, for instance, that not only was there a check to population growth but the consequent loss of adequate nutrition shortened the height of the average adult French male to 1.617 metres (5ft 4in). There was an improvement in the beginning of the 18th century, such that average height increased to 1.655 metres (5ft 5in), such an extraordinary change being indicative of how severe conditions had been in the earlier period (Komlos, 2003) (>ANTHROPOMETRIC HISTORY).

As in other countries of >WESTERN EUROPE at the time, agriculture was the leading economic activity. At the beginning of the 17th century, about 68 per cent of the population of France was engaged in agriculture and by the beginning of the 19th century it was still as high as about 59 per cent. Across these two centuries, the total population had increased about 50 per cent from 19 million to 28.3 million. In England, meanwhile, an >AGRICULTURAL REVOLUTION had been taking place. In 1600, about 69 per cent of the population of England, a percentage similar to France at that time, was engaged in agriculture but by 1800 the ratio had fallen to 35 per cent and the population had more than doubled to 9.1 million. During the same two centuries, labour productivity in agriculture had increased in England by 88 per cent and in France by only 15 per cent (Allen, 2000).

In the 17th and early 18th centuries, >MERCANTILISM had the greatest influence on economic policy. Although it may not be regarded as a coherent body of thought, its major tenet was that government policy should be directed to the manipulation of foreign trade with the aim of maximizing the inflow of specie, such as gold and silver. It was nationalist and interventionist in its policy proposals. French agriculture was neglected and the country was in thrall to a complexity of restrictions and injustices. Corn could not be transported freely from one part of the country to another. The *'taille'*, a direct tax, was not borne by the nobility or the clergy and varied from place to place. The collection of taxes was contracted out at the beginning of each financial year at a fixed price which entitled the collector to keep whatever he succeeded in extracting. The *'corvée'* under which the peasantry had to supply their labour without payment for such tasks as the repairing of the roadways, applied throughout France from 1737 (>PEASANTRY AND SERFDOM). The government did not encourage criticism.

There was a sign of change in 1754 when an edict was issued which permitted the free movement of corn within France and in 1755 with the publication of Richard Cantillon's (1680–1734) *Essai sur la nature du commerce en général*. In this work, Cantillon emphasized the importance of land as the source of wealth and he gave one of the first significantly comprehensive analyses of the economic process. In the following year, Victor Riqueti, Marquis de Mirabeau (1715–1789) published his *Ami des Hommes, ou Traité de la Population*, which also laid emphasis on land as the source of wealth. The book was a tremendous success and Mirabeau was honoured as the 'Ami des Hommes' until his death. It was the vigorous style of writing that enchanted its readers. François Quesnay (1694–1774) read the book and the birth of 'Les Economistes', subsequently called the Physiocrats, may be dated from their meeting in 1757. They made an effective combination. Mirabeau was scatterbrained but a persuasive and popular writer and publicist. Quesnay was the very able, constructive and serious thinker. Quesnay was certainly quite aware of Mirabeau's shortcomings. 'The child', he wrote, ' has been nursed on bad milk. The strength of his constitution often sets him right in the end, but he has no knowledge of principles' (quoted in Higgs, 1897).

An example of Mirabeau's flamboyance can be found from his quoted opinion of Quesnay's *Tableau Économique*:

'There have been, since the world began, three great inventions which have principally given stability to political societies, independent of many other inventions which have enriched and adorned them. The first, is the invention of writing, which alone gives human nature the power of transmitting, without alteration, its laws, its contracts, its annals, and its discoveries. The second is the invention of money, which binds together all the relations between civilised societies. The third, is the Economical Table, the result of the other two, which completes them both by perfecting their object; the great discovery of our age, but of which our posterity will reap the benefit.' (Quoted in Smith, *Wealth of Nations*, Book IV, Chapter IX, 1812)

François Quesnay was a doctor by profession who became physician to Louis XV in 1752, having been physician to his mistress, Madame de Pompadour (1721–1764) since 1749. In her, he found an intelligent and influential ally, which J. A. Schumpeter claimed 'should assure to the lady the lasting gratitude of economists' (1954). Quesnay's major economic works were *Fermiers*, *Grains* and *Hommes*, published in the *Encyclopédie* between 1756 and 1757, the *Tableau Économique*, first published in 1758, and *Maximes*, a commentary on the *Tableau* published in 1758. Mirabeau published *Explication du Tableau Économique*, a commentary on Quesnay's *Tableau* in 1759. A collection of Quesnay's writing, *La Physiocratie, ou Constitution Naturelle de Gouvernment le plus Avantageaux ou Genre Humaine*, was published by Du Pont de Nemours (1739–1817) in 1767. Other Physiocrat works published by Mirabeau were *Théorie de L'Impôt*, in 1760, and *Philosophie rurale*, in 1763. Another member of 'Les Economistes' was Pierre-Paul Mercier de la Rivière, who published *L'Ordre Naturel et Essentiel des Sociétés Politiques* in 1767. These authors and others, however, revolved around and were, in effect, students of Quesnay and were dominated by him. To put it into the words of Schumpeter, 'the group reduces to one man, Quesnay, to whom all economists look up as one of the greatest figures of their science' (1954).

The economic principles of Quesnay's Physiocrats were developed within the concept of the Natural Law and Natural Justice by which man should be guided and which should not be contradicted. The proper action in conformity to these laws may be discovered by reason so that people may achieve their full potential. Fundamentally, people were the same everywhere but their achievements varied greatly from place to place and from time to time, the application of reason should uncover what it was in different societies that caused these differences. As outlined above, France had suffered terrible economic hardship and international humiliation, compounded by the emergence of a flourishing England. Physiocracy emerged to try to find the solutions to these problems (Meek, 2003).

Quesnay believed that the key to economic success was economic liberty. Natural justice meant the right to economic liberty and, therefore, the protection of private property was vital. Security was the prime purpose and responsibility of the state. The function of the state was to ensure security and, indeed, it had little other function. Quesnay believed in 'enlightened despotism', a single philosopher king in which all authority should rest. The Dauphin asked Quesnay, 'What would you do if you were king?' 'Nothing,' Quesnay replied. 'Then who would govern?' 'The Law' (quoted in Higgs, 1897).

Quesnay believed that the maximum benefit to society would only be attained if individuals were allowed to pursue their own self-interest within a framework of perfect competition, a proposition which foreshadowed Adam >SMITH's assertion that we do not get our bread because of the goodwill of the baker but because it is in his own interest to provide it. The different classes in society were economically interconnected and each individual should spend his net income and not attempt to accumulate money because it would deprive others of income and lead to recession. Agriculture was the sole source of real wealth. It is only agriculture that produces a surplus, the *produit net*; all other activities were sterile, only covering their costs. Nevertheless, the sterile classes were essential to the stability of the economy in so far as they were sources of demand for agricultural output. The *Tableau Économique* traced how the *produit net* circulated between the different classes of society. The farmers made available three types of capital: (1) *Avances Annuelles*, or working capital, which was required to pay agricultural wages, seeds, etc.; (2) *Avances Primitives*, capital for the purchase of livestock and farm equipment; and (3) *Avances Foncières*, capital for land improvements such as fencing, drainage and building. A fourth was also added called *Avances Souveraines*, which was capital invested in infrastructure such as roads, canals and ports which was derived from the government's share of the *produit net*.

As a simplified illustration of the process of circulation, at the beginning of the period there is available a gross product valued at, say, 5 million livres. The farmers keep 2 million livres for *Avances Annuelles*. The *net produit* of 3 million livres is the value of the farmers' product. This is assumed to be made up of food to the value of 2 million livres and raw materials (such as wool) to the value of 1 million livres. The farmers also hold from the previous period currency to the value of 2 million livres. The landlords have nothing except a claim for rent and the sterile class have a stock of goods which they produced in the previous period to the value of 2 million livres. The farmers pay to the landowners their rent of 2 million livres. The landowners use this to buy 1 million livres of food from the farmers and spend the other 1 million livres to buy manufactured goods from the sterile class, who spend the income thus received on buying food from the farmers.

The farmers also buy manufactured goods to the value of 1 million livres from the sterile class, who in turn use it to buy raw materials from the farmers. The cycle is completed.

Because only agriculture produced a surplus, taxes applied to any other class would finally settle on the agricultural sector in the course of the inter-sectoral transactions as a natural consequence and, therefore, the Physiocrats recommended *l'impôt Unique*, a tax imposed solely on agriculture to minimize collection costs. Government economic policy should be solely aimed at maximizing agricultural output. This meant free internal and foreign trade in agricultural products, as this would ensure a proper return to agricultural investment. The Physiocrats believed that government restrictions which inhibited this should be abolished and, as a consequence 'laissez-faire, laissez-passer' emerged as a byproduct of their policy.

Quesnay and his fellow 'Economistes' were attempting to find solutions to the problems of the time, which particularly beset agriculture. The farmsteads, divided and sub-divided under the inheritance customs, were too small; serfdom and feudalism persisted and a complexity of regulations and restrictions inhibited domestic and foreign trade. Some progress was made in putting their recommendations into action, particularly when Anne-Robert-Jacques Turgot (1727–1781) was appointed by Louis XVI Contrôleur Général des Finances in 1774. In that year, Turgot had enacted an edict enabling free international and domestic trade, which had the following preamble:

'to animate and extend the cultivation of land, whose produce is the most real and certain wealth of a state, to maintain abundance by granaries and the entry of foreign corn, to prevent corn from falling to a price which would discourage the producer; to remove monopoly by shutting out private licence in favour of free and full competition and by maintaining among different countries that communication of exchange of superfluities for necessaries which is so conformable to the order established by Divine Providence.' (Quoted in Higgs, 1897)

However, attempts by Turgot to pursue reform further through the promulgation of six edicts in 1776, including the reform of guilds and the abolition of the *corvée*, roused powerful vested interests which the King was unwilling to confront and he was dismissed. While Turgot was not a member as such of the Physiocrats, being essentially an objective civil servant, his fall marked the end of their influence. The ideas of the Physiocrats did achieve international recognition but their influence rapidly faded. Quesnay had died in 1774 and, while many of the ideas of the subsequent Revolution were coincident with those of the Physiocrats, the revolutionaries were hardly likely to be sympathetic to a school of thought which supported despotism, even if enlightened. The final straw was another event in 1776: the publication of the *Wealth of Nations* by Adam Smith.

Nevertheless, many of the ideas of the Physiocrats foreshadowed subsequent developments in economic thought. The *Tableau Économique* was a primitive quantitative demonstration of the interconnections between the different activities in a macro-economic framework, which was to see its full flowering in a Leontif input–output model (Phillips, 1955). The principles relating to the benefits of free competition and free trade would become a recurring theme in >CLASSICAL AND NEO-CLASSICAL ECONOMICS. Quesnay's concern was that if any sectors of society failed to spend all their income, the consequent failure of demand would cause a drop in total output in the economy, a feature of macro-economic behaviour that was the central concern of Keynesian (>KEYNES).

There is no doubt that Quesnay and his economic ideas were highly regarded by Adam Smith, although he disagreed on certain points, particularly on the dominant role of agriculture. Considering the stage of development reached in the second half of the 18th century by England, compared with France, this is not surprising.

'This system, however, with all its imperfections is, perhaps, the nearest approximation to the truth that has yet been published upon the subject of political economy, and is upon that account well worth the consideration of every man who wishes to examine with attention the principles of that very important science.' (Smith, 1812)

It could be argued that the study of economics as a rational, scientific discipline was born in the work of the Physiocrats and, particularly, in that of François Quesnay, although they did not, of course, envision this.

## References

Allen, Robert C., 'Economic Structure and Agricultural Productivity in Europe, 1300–1800', *European Review of Economic History*, 4(1), 2000.

Blaug, Mark, *Economic Theory in Retrospect*, Cambridge University Press, 1978.

Deane, Phyllis, *The Evolution of Economic Ideas*, Cambridge University Press, 1978.

Higgs, Henry, *Six Lectures on the French 'Économistes' of the 18th Century*, Macmillan, 1897.

Komlos, John, 'An Anthropometric History of Early-Modern France', *European Review of Economic History*, 7(2), August, 2003.

Meek, Ronald L., *Economics of Physiocracy*, Routledge, 2003.

Phillips, A. W. H., 'The Tableau d'Écommuniqué as a Simple Leontief Model', *Quarterly Journal of Economics*, 1955.

Schumpeter, Joseph A., *History of Economic Analysis*, Oxford University Press, 1954.

Smith, Adam, *An Inquiry into the Nature and Causes of the Wealth of Nations* (1776), Ward Lock, 1812.

Winch, Donald, 'The Emergence of Economics as a Science, 1750–1870', in Carlo M. Cipolla (ed.), *The Fontana Economic History of Europe*, Fontana, 1973.

# Poor Laws

A system of support for the poor in times of unemployment, sickness and old age that was established in England (>BRITAIN) in the 16th century and persisted until the welfare legislation of the 20th century.

Poor Law Acts of 1597 and 1601 consolidated previous statutes that went back to 1536. Parishes were made responsible for their poor and were empowered to raise local taxes on property to finance their support. In 1723, parishes were given authority to build workhouses if they so wished. The workhouses were built with the intention of putting to work in them the voluntary unemployed. (The early legislators perceived a difference between voluntary and involuntary idleness.) The Gilbert Act of 1782 enabled parishes to find outside work for able-bodied unemployed men and pay them a subsistence. From that year, also, parishes could form unions with other parishes for the administration of the Poor Law. Outdoor relief grew in importance, so that by the end of the 18th century it accounted for about 90 per cent of the total. In 1795, the Speenhamland System, named after a village in Berkshire, was adopted by many parishes. In times of need, income support was granted on a scale related to the price of bread and the size of the recipient's family. The support given to the needy in the late 18th century and early 19th century (until the 'old' Poor Law was replaced by the 'new' Poor Law), in England was on the whole higher than other countries in Europe, although there is some debate about this (Lindert, 1994, 1998; King, 1997; Solar, 1994, 1997). There is, however, a consensus that the actual effective assistance given to the poor did vary widely from parish to parish, particularly as to the differences pertaining in the Northern parishes of England compared with those in the South. This variability did, however, also occur on the European Continent. The percentage of national income distributed to the poor in England rose to 2 per cent in the first quarter of the 19th century. In England at that time as much as 80 per cent of the income from local authority rates was distributed to support the poor. The income raised from the Poor Law rates trebled between 1780 and 1812. Per capita expenditure on poor relief in England was as much as seven times that of France, five times that of Belgium and over twice that of the Netherlands about this time. The USA did not offer any such support of any significance until the 20th century (Lindert, 1994, 1998).

Attitudes towards the English Poor Law assistance hardened in the early 19th century. There was a complete change of attitude which was encapsulated in the *Poor Law Commissioners' Report of 1834*, which condemned the old system as an encouragement to idleness, an unacceptable expansion of the population and to depression in the level of wages and rental incomes. The *Commissioners' Report* asserted that the old system was inherently contradictory in that its effect in the long run was to increase rather than reduce poverty. This report reinforced the belief that aid to the needy was suspect and the Commission, therefore, condemned all outdoor relief on principle. Consequently, the Poor Law Amendment Act was passed in 1834. This marked the end of the 'old' Poor Law and the introduction of the 'new' Poor Law. The share of national income devoted to assistance for the poor, thereafter, declined to 1 per cent through the rest of the century. The Act discouraged outdoor relief to the able-bodied in favour of indoor relief within workhouses. These workhouses were designed as though they were prisons and were run harshly to discourage the poor from seeking assistance. The workhouses tended to be institutions for orphaned children, the disabled, the sick and the old, without family support. The percentage of the population getting outdoor relief declined from 3.5 per cent in last quarter of the 19th century to under 2 per cent by 1914 (Lindert, 1998).

The Poor Law system began to wither away in the early 20th century, as social welfare legislation replaced it: the Old Age Pensions Act, 1908; Labour Exchanges Act, 1909; National Insurance Acts of 1911 and 1946; the National Health Services Act, 1946; and the National Assistance Act, 1948. The latter stated explicitly that the existing Poor Law should cease to have any effect. The shift had finally been completed which moved the financial burden of social welfare from local to central funding.

There have been, therefore, in England several centuries of tradition of the acceptance of general responsibility for the needy. The 'old' Poor Law was exceptional in its time in so far as it had the force of statute, the benefits were clear to everybody and they were disbursed locally from locally raised property taxes. The Guardians of the Poor and the Justices of the Peace were local people who knew the local demands for and supply of labour. The local unit of management, the parish, was small; 80 per cent of the parishes in England in the 1830s had a population of less than 800. The benefits were relatively generous. Continental European countries had to rely on charities, private donations and special government subsidies to too great an extent to form a base for reliable and stable financial support to the poor. In England, social welfare was regarded as a right, not only by its recipients but also by the governing elite. It helped to create social stability at a time of political upheaval elsewhere. It has also been argued that it encouraged the growth of a mobile class of wage earner and the growth in farm size. A worker on the Continent, because of uncertain income support, had a greater incentive to own a plot of land, however small, as an insurance against unemployment than his counterpart in England.

With the growth in population, urbanization and the structural and political changes concomitant with the >INDUSTRIAL REVOLUTION IN BRITAIN, it was inevitable that the 'old' Poor Law gave way to the 'new' and some constraint had to be imposed on the growth of the financial burden. During the course of the 19th century and the early 20th century, the cyclical occurrence of periods of high persistent unemployment put great strain on the system. The unemployed faced great hardship with the prospect of being forced into a workhouse and being separated from his or her family. The legislation of the early 20th century finally modernized the 'new' Poor Law (>POVERTY).

### References

Coleman, D. C., *The Economy of England, 1450–1750*, Oxford University Press, 1977.

King, Steve, 'Poor Relief and English Economic Development Reappraised', *Economic History Review*, L(2), 1997.

Lindert, Peter H., 'Unequal Living Standards' in Roderick Floud and Donald McCloskey (eds), *The Economic History of Britain Since 1700*, vol.1 Cambridge University Press, 1994.

Lindert, Peter H., 'Poor Relief Before the Welfare State: Britain Versus the Continent, 1780–1880', *European Review of Economic History*, 2(2), 1998.

Solar, Peter M., 'Poor Relief and English Economic Development before the Industrial Revolution', *Economic History Review*, XLVIII(1), 1995.

Solar, Peter M., 'Poor Relief and English Economic Development: A Renewed Plea for Comparative History', *Economic History Review*, L(2), 1997.

Webb, Sidney and Webb, Beatrice, *English Poor Law History, Part I and Part II*, 1927/1929, reprint Frank Crass, 1963.

# Population

The population of the world increased from about 612 million in 1700 to about 906 million in 1800, an average rate of growth per year of about 0.4 per cent. In the following century, the growth rate rose to an average of 0.6 per cent per year. In the 20th century, it increased further to an average of 1.3 per cent per year, with the second half of the century experiencing a more rapid rise than the first half, averaging 1.8 per cent per year. The 20th century opened with a world population of 1.6 billion; by 2007 it had reached 6.6 billion, although the rate of growth had dropped to about 1.2 per cent per annum.

The growth in the population of Europe matched that of the rest of the world in the period up to 1800, then grew somewhat faster at an average rate of 0.6 per cent per year. Since 1900, however, the population growth of the rest of the world has considerably outpaced that of Europe, which grew at an average of only 0.5 per cent per year up to 2000. In Western Europe, there were differences in population change experienced by the various countries. In particular, >BRITAIN, which had a population of only 40 per cent of that of France in 1700, had overtaken it by 1900.

The population of the >USA accelerated rapidly between the first census in 1790 of about 4 million to 76 million in 1900 stimulated by immigration (>MIGRATION) from Europe. Migration again reinforced population growth in the USA in the second half of the 20th century but there was a change in source from Europe to other countries, particularly Latin America. By 2007, the population of the USA was about 300 million and the OECD estimated that about 10 per cent of the population of the USA was foreign-born, compared with a world average of 7 per cent.

During the 18th century and the 19th century the population of Asia grew more slowly than that of the rest of the world. It has been estimated that in 1700, with a population of about 415 million, Asia accounted for about 68 per cent of the world total. This share fell to about 57 per cent in 1900. The fall in share continued into the first half of the 20th century and in 1950, with a population of 1.4 billion, the share had dropped to about 55 per cent. In the second half of the 20th century, however, there was a turn round. Between 1950 and 2000, the population of Asia expanded at an average annual rate of 2 per cent per year. In particular, by 2007 the population of >CHINA had reached 1.3 billion and >INDIA had reached 1.2 billion, the two countries together accounting for about 37 per cent of the world total.

There was much economic debate towards the end of the 18th century and into the 19th century concerning the possible collision between population growth and the diminishing marginal productivity of land. When >MALTHUS published, in 1798, his *Essay on the Principle of Population as it Affects the Future Improvement of Society* these worries were muted by the belief that the population of England was stable. The first population census of 1801 showed otherwise. In fact, the population of England grew by 50 per cent in the last half of the century. The resulting pessimism was reflected in Malthus's second edition of his essay, expanded into a book, in 1803 and the problem of population growth exercised economists throughout the first half of the 19th century. The view was 'that the population of the world…is limited only by moral or physical evil, or the fear of the deficiency of those articles of wealth which the habits of individuals of each class of its inhabitants lead them to require' (Senior, 1836). Against this, the natural resources of the earth were limited. Famine, war, disease and poverty have all contributed at particular times and in particular places to the restraint

of population growth in the past but the effect of these has been counterbalanced by the benefits of world economic growth (>ECONOMIC DEVELOPMENT) and the associated improvements in >AGRICULTURE and in health care. After the middle of the 19th century, Western Europe was no longer assailed by famine. Serious famines have, however, occurred in other areas of the world (>FAMINE).

Wars have also taken their toll. In the Napoleonic War, France lost 1.3 million men. In the 20th century, 8.5 million lives were lost on military service in Europe in >WORLD WAR I. In >WORLD WAR II, the European countries lost 22.6 million people, Japan 2 million and the USA 300,000. In addition, it has been estimated that up to 20 million lives were lost in the concentration camps and extermination centres established in Germany from 1933.

In spite of these man-made losses and others arising from forces of nature, the growth of the population of the world has accelerated over the past 200 years. Apart from >MIGRATION, the increase in a country's population is determined by the balance between birth and death rates. There are a number of measures that are used to analyze this balance. The 'crude birth rate (cbr)' is the number of live births occurring in a year per 1,000 population. The 'fertility rate (fr)' is the number of live births per 1,000 women between the ages of 15 and 44. The 'birth rate specific (brs) for age of mother' is the number of live births per 1,000 of different age groups of mother. The 'gross reproduction rate (grr)' is the number of female babies an average woman, surviving to 44, would have at the given fertility rate. The 'crude death rate (cdr)' is the number of deaths occurring in a year per

1,000 population; similar rates are used for each sex and age group. The 'expectation of life at birth (elb)' is the number of years a new-born baby may expect to live at given mortality rates.

The early censuses carried out, in the USA in 1790, England (>BRITAIN) in 1801 and in France in the same year, were very rough. Germany did not have a census until 1852. The state registration of vital statistics was not begun in England until 1837. Statistics of population before the taking of modern rigorous censuses can only be estimates but a number of techniques have been developed to refine them. Data may be collected tracing the history of the births, marriages and deaths of particular families, 'family reconstitution', from which generalizations may be inferred. Another approach is to extract data from a specific and complete registers over a period of time and generalize from that ('aggregative analysis'). Finally, another method is to start with a reliable census and project the population backwards from the age structure (back projection) (Anderson, 1988).

Between 1751 and 1821, during which the population of England doubled, the 'gross reproduction rate' increased from 2.3 to 3.0 and the 'expectation of life at birth' rose from 36.6 years to 39.2 years. It has been estimated that the increase in fertility was twice as important to population growth as the lowering of the mortality rate. This increase was due to the reduction in the age at which women first married and in the reduction in the number of women who never married. The 'crude birth rate' rose from 34 to 40 in the period. In contrast, the 'cbr' in France fell from 40 to 30. After the 1820s, the 'cbr' in England fell to 32 towards the end of the 19th century and to 12 by 2000.

Through the late 18th century and early 19th century, there was a general decline in mortality throughout >WESTERN EUROPE and Scandinavia. For instance, in France infant mortality declined from about 280 per 1,000 births in 1790s to 155 in the 1840s. The crude death rate declined in England from 26 in the late 18th century to 19 in the late 19th century and to 11 by the end of the 20th century.

Population changes, excluding migration, derive from the balance between births and deaths. In the 19th century, in France the decline in mortality was offset by a decline in fertility. In England the decline in mortality reinforced the high fertility rate. A number of explanations have been proposed for the widespread drop in mortality in Western Europe in the 18th and 19th centuries. The expansion of economic activity, improvements in >AGRICULTURE and the growth in >INTERNATIONAL TRADE led to a rise in the standard of living above basic nutritional needs. There was an improvement in the resistance to disease, assisted towards the end of the 19th century by improvements in public healthcare. There was a decline in infant deaths due to smallpox, even before the introduction of vaccination in the early 19th century.

Towards the end of the 20th century, the effect of the decline in the birth rate, coupled with an increase in life expectancy began to lower population growth, even to the prospect of a decline in population or at least stability, particularly in the advanced countries. According to the United Nations, the prospect is that there will be a fall in the population of Japan and Russia and significant growth will be confined to the developing countries. The USA will be exceptional because of its high immigration rate (OECD, 2007). The implications of falling birth rates and death rates are the increase in the average age of the population and the increase in the dependency ratio due to the fall in the numbers of working age in the population.

## References

Anderson, Michael, 'Population Change in North-Western Europe, 1750–1850', in Anne Digby and Charles Feinstein (eds), *New Directions in Economic and Social History*, Macmillan, 1989.

Cipolla, M. (ed.), *The Economic History of World Population*, Harvester, 1978.

Dewhurst, Frederic J., Coppock O. John and Yates, Lamartine P., *Europe's Needs and Resources: Trends and Prospects in Eighteen Countries*, Macmillan, 1961.

Foreman-Peck, James, *A History of the World Economy*, Harvester Wheatsheaf, 1995.

Komlos, John, 'Further Thoughts on the Nutritional Status of the British Population', *Economic History Review*, XLVI(2), 1993.

Komlos, John, 'On the Nature of the Malthusian Threat in the Eighteenth Century', *Economic History Review*, LII(4), 1999.

Kenwood, A. G. and Lougheed, A. L., *The Growth of the International Economy, 1820–1990*, Routledge, 1992.

OECD, *World Economic Outlook*, 82, December, 2007.

Senior, Nassau William, *An Outline of the Science of Political Economy* (1836), reprint, Augustus Kelly, 1951.

Wrigley, E. A., 'Population Growth: England, 1680–1820', in Anne Digby and Charles Feinstein (eds), *New Directions in Economic and Social History*, Macmillan, 1989.

# Poverty

Poverty has long been the concern of the compassionate in civilized societies and charitable giving a means to ameliorate manifestations of it. As nation states developed, their governments, some early some more belatedly, began to accept responsibility not only for the granting of assistance for the easing of the symptoms of poverty among their people but also for the development of policies for its eradication. From the 16th century, statutes were promulgated in a number of countries in Western Europe for the support of the poor and from these beginnings was to emerge in the 20th century the Welfare State, the culmination of the recognition that it was the state's responsibility to care for the poor and underprivileged. Optimism grew that the route to the eradication of poverty was through the unprecedented economic growth that was achieved as countries reaped the rewards of the >INDUSTRIAL REVOLUTIONS. In the 20th century, concern for the poor became international as some countries failed to gain sufficient economic growth to lift their people out of poverty and needed assistance from international charitable institutions and international organizations. Even at the end of the 20th century, however, poverty could be found not only in the least developed countries (>ECONOMIC DEVELOPMENT), but still yet in the most advanced countries such as in North America and Western Europe. Poverty is a paradox. We all recognize the manifestation of poverty in the plight of people in Africa emaciated by lack of nutrition but may find it hard to apply the same term to the underprivileged of New York, Paris or London. There are both qualitative and quantitative distinctions behind this paradox. There is the concept of the deserving as opposed to the undeserving poor, which has always influenced the giving of alms and aid, and there is the difficulty of objectively defining poverty and, having defined it, to measure it statistically.

In >BRITAIN under the >POOR LAWS from the 16th century, parishes were made responsible for the support of their poor from revenue raised by taxes on property. In 1782, Gilbert's Act approved the giving of outdoor relief to able-bodied men rather than it being limited to indoor relief in a workhouse. In 1795, a number of parishes had a system of income support for their poor which was determined according to the price of bread and family size. Outdoor relief accounted for about 90 per cent of the total of official relief by the end of the 18th century and about 2 per cent of the British National Income was devoted to the support of the poor. The government of Britain was considerably more generous in supporting the poor at this time than any of the other countries of Europe. Countries in Western Europe also had institutions similar to the English workhouse, such as the *Ateliers* in France. In the Netherlands and Belgium work camps were established which put the poor to outside work but in which they were locked up at night-time. In 1834, British policy towards the poor changed fundamentally with the passing of the Poor Law Amendment Act which reflected a complete reversal of opinion in Britain. The new system was designed to discourage applications for relief by the threat of being sent to workhouses, which were built and run more like prisons than institutions of care. The complete change in attitude was encapsulated in the *Poor Law Commissioners' Report of 1834*, which condemned the old system as an encouragement to idleness, an unacceptable expansion of the population and to depression in the level of wages and rental incomes.

The *Commissioners' Report* asserted that the old system was inherently contradictory in that its effect in the long run was to increase rather than reduce poverty. This report reinforced the belief that aid to the needy was suspect. The Malthusian (>MALTHUS) argument that assistance would do nothing but lower wages prevailed at the time and tenaciously clung on throughout the 19th century. An exasperated Alfred Marshall (>CLASSICAL AND NEO-CLASSICAL ECONOMICS), before *the Royal Commission on the Aged Poor* in 1893, attempted to correct this:

'It seems that whenever I read Poor Law literature of today I am taken back to the beginning of the century... Suppose you could conceive a mad Emperor of China to give to every English working man half-a-crown for nothing: according to current notions... that would lower wages, because it would enable people to work for less. I think that nine economists out of ten at the beginning of the century would have said that that would lower wages. Well, of course, it might increase population and that would bring down wages; but unless it did increase population, the effect according to the modern school would be to raise wages because the increased wealth of the working classes would lead to better living, more vigorous and better educated people with greater earning power, so wages would rise. This is the centre of the difference.' (Quoted in Blaug, 1963)

There was no serious attempt by the Commissioners to base their assertions on historical quantitative facts. Blaug quotes Sidney and Beatrice Webb: 'This ignoring of statistics led, in the diagnosis, to disastrous errors in proportion; and made the suggested remedial action lopsided and seriously imperfect' (1963). (The Commissioners, for instance, stated that the able-bodied who were given support amounted to a million. Sidney and Beatrice Webb calculated that there were, in fact, at the most 300,000. Most of the people given relief were the old and sick.)

The suspicion that the poor could not be trusted to use the aid they received wisely was reflected in the assertion that it was preferable to keep assistance in the form of cash to a minimum, relying more on grants in kind. For instance, statistics quoted in Lindert (2004) show that in 1860 relief from the *bureau de bienfaisance*, first established in France in 1797, was distributed as 55 per cent food and only 21 per cent cash, the rest being such items as clothing, fuel and medical care. Implicit in a policy of this kind is the attempt to avoid the risk of 'moral hazard'. For instance, simple cash grants to the unemployed do not create an incentive to him or her to look for work but rather the contrary.

Solar (1995) argues that, compared with other countries of Europe, the 'old' Poor Law in England had the advantage of being on a uniform national scale and financially supported by a tax on rateable values. It was also considerably more generous. In 1780, per capita expenditure was seven times higher than in France. By the 1820s, it was two and a half times higher than in the Netherlands and about five times higher than in Belgium. In England, as a consequence, there was less economic pressure leading to the fragmentation of farmland which occurred on the Continent because poor relief was a sufficiently robust alternative compared to the risky support of a small holding. On the Continent, relief had to be sought more from one's own friends and family and this discouraged internal migration. The settlement laws in England, by which a migrant could be sent back to his home parish, were not necessarily applied in practice to the able-bodied for whom there was work. Solar (1995) concludes that the 'old' Poor Law was a force for the genuine reduction of poverty because it encouraged capital investment in agriculture, the development of a mobile wage-earning labour force and the expansion of industry. On the other hand, others have argued that the English Poor Law system was not consistent throughout the parishes of England and the poor had to search elsewhere for support in what has been termed the 'economy of makeshifts' (Hufton, 1974; King and Tomkins, 2003). The poor had to look to charities, family members, the pawnshop and even crime in times of trouble. Ultimately, if it was feasible and opportunities existed for their improvement sufficient to make the risks worthwhile, the poor could resort to emigration (>MIGRATION).

Following the Poor Law Amendment Act in 1834, the proportion of the National Income devoted to relief in England fell to about 1 per cent, converging with the share of other West European countries in the 19th century. In the >USA, by contrast, government help given to the poor had always been much less. Poor relief financed from taxation throughout the 19th century was only about a quarter of 1 per cent of National Income and the USA continued to allocate through taxation considerable less for poor relief than countries in Western Europe throughout the 20th century (Lindert, 2004).

The 'old' Poor Law system in England had to be reformulated because of the relative decline of agriculture. However, there is no support for the

Poor Law Commissioners' argument that the help given to the needy was counter-productive, leading to idleness and falling wages (Blaug, 1963). Nevertheless, and in spite of Alfred Marshall's positive assessment of the effect of the giving of assistance to the poor (>POOR LAWS), the 19th century suspicion that it encouraged idleness persisted. Even in 1977, a survey conducted by the European Commission of the European Union (>WESTERN EUROPE) found that, in Britain, 43 per cent of respondents believed that people in poverty were there because of laziness and lack of will power, compared with an average of 25 per cent in the European Union as a whole (Rose, 1992).

A definition of poverty and the measurement of its incidence objectively might be expected to contribute to a better understanding of the reasons for poverty and lessen the readiness to believe that it must be due to irresponsibility and idleness. At the turn of the 19th century, the first comprehensive studies of the poor were undertaken in England. Charles Booth published his research in *The Life and Labour of the People of London*, in several volumes from 1889 to 1902, in which he introduced a definition of poverty, which became known as the 'poverty line', as an income of 18 shillings (90p) to 21 shillings (105p) for a family with three children and found that 30.7 per cent of the population was below this level and 8.4 per cent in distress. Seebohm Rowntree conducted a somewhat more scientifically based study of the poor of York which was published in 1901 as *Poverty: A Study of Town Life*. His 'poverty line' was set at 21s 8d (108p), based on the advice of doctors and other professionals concerning a minimum diet. Rowntree found that about 27 per cent of the population was in poverty, of which 13 per cent

were in distress. This concept of the 'poverty line' has remained as a basis from which to measure poverty and to fix state assistance through 'means tests' and for judging the appropriate level for state benefits and statutory minimum wages.

In spite of the development of the Welfare State in Britain after >WORLD WAR II, surveys showed that poverty persisted, particularly in families with children and among pensioners. The number of people attracting government support because their incomes fell below the 'means-tested' poverty line, increased from 1 million in 1948 to over 4 million in the 1980s (Floud and McCloskey, 1994). This poverty line was based on subsistence levels fixed in 1948, including additions for rent, clothing and fuel. Although the level was subsequently raised, the increase was considerably below the growth in real incomes in the 1960s. In the USA, the poverty line was based on the cost of food for different family sizes and composition derived from the Department of Agriculture economy food plan, adjusted by the average proportion of incomes spent on food and for changes in the cost of living over time. It was officially introduced in 1969. On this measure, the total poverty rate in the USA fell from 22 per cent in 1959 to 12 per cent in the 1970s, increased to 14 per cent in the 1980s and fell back to 13 per cent in the 1990s. On this measure, therefore, the incidence of poverty in the USA appears to have been virtually unaffected by the growth in the economy. However, it was particularly noteworthy that the poverty rate for the elderly, which was 1.75 per cent higher than that for the population as a whole in 1959, fell to 20 per cent below this level by the end of the 20th century, thanks to social security benefits (Hoynes *et al.*, 2005). The poverty rate is calculated in the USA in absolute rather than in relative terms, that is, for instance, as some fraction of average incomes, which is a more commonly used measure in Europe.

Measures of the poverty line were derived from the costing of a shopping list of articles deemed necessities. It has long been recognized that what constitutes a necessity is not limited to that required in a diet adequate to maintain health. In the *The Nature and Causes of the Wealth of Nations*, Adam >SMITH widened the definition of necessaries:

'By necessaries I understand, not only the commodities which are indispensably necessary for the support of life, but whatever the custom of the country renders it indecent for creditable people, even of the lowest order, to be without. A linen shirt, for example, is strictly speaking not a necessary of life. The Greeks and Romans lived, I suppose, very comfortably though they had no linen. But in present times, through the greater part of Europe, a creditable day-labourer would be ashamed to appear in public without a linen shirt.' (Book V, Chapter II, Part II, Article IV)

The 'linen shirt effect' means that it is hazardous to make inter-temporal and inter-country comparisons of poverty. The poverty rate in the USA increased according to the statistics from 12.6 per cent of the total in 1970 to 13.3 per cent of the total in 1997. This does not mean that the poor have got poorer or even that there has been no improvement in their standard of living. For instance, the penetration of household appliances among poor households in 1994 was comparable to that of the rich in 1971. The 18th-century linen shirt of Adam Smith was the personal computer in the 20th century. A computer was found in poor households in 1994 but not in rich households in 1971 (Cox and Alm, 1999). The composition of items in the construction of a poverty line should, therefore, shift accordingly over time and place to reflect the society to which the poor belong. The relative measure based on some percentage below average incomes accommodates these changes in the composition of budgets automatically. By this measure, the poor will not only always exist but also increase when changes in the distribution of incomes lead to greater >INEQUALITY, even though their material condition remains the same (Townsend, 1980).

There has been much debate, therefore, as to the proper measurement of poverty and the best way of achieving a reduction in the number of people in poverty. This debate has been especially pertinent in the context of the developing countries (>ECONOMIC DEVELOPMENT) and the appropriate means by which such countries can achieve levels of real incomes comparable to those of the more advanced countries. Bhagwati (2004) argues that the key is economic growth. It is not necessarily sufficient but it is certainly a necessary condition by which poverty might be reduced. In this he is at one with the view of Adam Smith:

'It deserves to be remarked, perhaps, that it is in the progressive state, while the society is advancing to the further acquisition, rather than when it has acquired its full compliment of riches, that the condition of the labouring poor, of the great body of the people, seems to be happiest and the most comfortable. It is hard in the stationary, and miserable in the declining state. The progressive state is in reality the cheerful and the hearty state to all the different orders of the society. The stationary state is dull; the declining melancholy.' (*Wealth of Nations*, Book I, Chapter VIII)

Following an article by Simon Kuznets in 1955, many economists argued that any economic growth in a developing country would be absorbed by a growth in income inequality and that the poor would not only not benefit from the growth in incomes but could be made worse. However, the research was based on the limited statistical information available at the time and studies were reformulated with the commencement of a flow of improved statistical information from the 1970s, financed by the World Bank. According to Deaton (2003), there is no evidence that growth leaves the poor behind.

The statistical problem of the measurement of the number of poor and the incidence of poverty has meant that there have been a range of estimates made to attempt to determined the progress made in the second half of the 20th century towards reducing world poverty.

Sala-i-Martin (2002) has estimated that the world total of the number of people earning less than $1 per day declined by 235 million between 1976 and 1998 and the number earning less than $2 per day fell by 450 million. However, this success was not evenly distributed. The countries in Asia did particularly well and also, at least early in the period, those in Latin America. Poverty in Africa, however, deteriorated. The number of people earning less than $1 per day in Africa increased by 175 million between 1970 and 1998 and the number earning less than $2 per day increased by 27.7 million.

However, these estimates must be viewed with some caution. As explained by Aisbet (2005), different results are obtained according to the methodology adopted. For instance, results would be influenced as to whether data had been derived from household surveys or national accounts or by which particular method of deriving *purchasing power parity* measures had been applied by which to accumulate data across countries and whether the $1 per day or the $2 per day minimum employed by the World Bank was used. Aisbet quotes four estimates (Chen and Ravallion, 2000; Sala-i-Martin, 2002; Bhalla, 2003) of the total number of people living in poverty based on $1 per day, which range from 350 million to 1,200 million. If the cut-off of $2 per day is applied, the two estimates quoted are more than doubled compared to the $1 per day estimates by the same scholars to 970 million and to 2,800 million. In the 11 years from 1987 to 1998, two of the estimates show that the number of people in poverty increased and four of the estimates showed a decline. The estimates of the percentage of the world population living in poverty vary correspondingly, ranging from a high of 56 per cent to a low of 6.7 per cent in 1998.

There is a general consensus, nevertheless, that considerable progress was made in the second half of the 20th century towards the reduction of poverty through economic growth, particularly in the countries of Asia. Warr (2000) estimates that the average incidence of poverty in >INDIA fell by 0.7 per cent per annum between 1957 and 1992, that in >CHINA by 1.6 per cent per annum and that in South East Asia by 1.4 per cent per annum (>ASIAN MIRACLE). According to the Asian Development Bank (2005), the proportion of the population of China in poverty, based on the $1 per day criterion, was 16.6 per cent in 2001, in

India it stood at 35 per cent in 1999. By contrast, the lack of economic growth in Sub-Saharan Africa in the second half of the 20th century led to increasing poverty in the region. In 1960, 11 per cent of the world's poor lived in Africa, but in 1998, 66 per cent did so (Sala-i-Martin, 2002;).

## References

Aisbet, Emma, *Why are the Critics so Convinced that Globalisation is Bad for the Poor?*, National Bureau of Economic Research, 2005.

Asian Development Bank, *Poverty, Inequality, and Human Development*, Key Indicators, 2005.

Bhagwati, Jagdish, *In Defense of Globalization*, Oxford University Press, 2004.

Bhalla, S., *Crying Wolf on Poverty: Or How the Millennium Development Goal for Poverty has Already Been Reached*, Institute for International Economics, 2003.

Blaug, Mark, 'The Myth of the Old Poor Law and the Making of the New', *Journal of Economic History*, XXIII, June, 1963.

Chen, S. and Ravallion, M., 'How Did the World's Poorest Fare in the 1990s?', World Bank Development Research Group Working Paper w2409, 2000.

Cox, Michael and Alm, Richard, *Myths of Rich and Poor*, Basic Books, 1999.

Deaton, Angus, 'Measuring Poverty in a Growing World (or Measuring Growth in a Poor World)', The Review of Economics and Statistics Lecture, presented at Harvard University, April, 2003.

Floud, Roderick and McCloskey, Donald, *The Economic History of Britain Since 1700*, III, Cambridge University Press, 1994.

Hoynes, Hilary, Page, Marianne and Stevens, Ann, 'Poverty in America: Trends and Explanations', National Bureau of Economic Research, Working Paper 11681, October 2005.

Hufton, Olwen, *The Poor of Eighteenth-Century France, 1750–1789*, Clarendon Press, 1974.

King, Steve, 'Poor Relief and English Economic Development Reappraised', *Economic History Review*, L(2), 1997.

King, Stephen and Tomkins, Alannah (eds), *The Poor in England 1700–1850: An Economy of Makeshifts*, Manchester University Press, 2003.

Kuznets, Simon, 'Economic Growth and Income Equality', *American Economic Review*, 45(1), 1955.

Lindert, Peter H., *Growing Public: Social Spending and Economic Growth Since the Eighteenth Century*, Cambridge University Press, 2004.

Rose, M. E., "Poverty and Self-Help: Britain in the Nineteenth and Twentieth Centuries", in Anne Digby, Charles Feinstein and David Jenkins (eds), *New Directions in Economic and Social History*, Macmillan, 1992.

Sala-i-Martin, X., 'The World Distribution of Income (estimated from individual country distributions)', NBER Working Paper No. 8933, 2002.

Smith, Adam, *An Inquiry into the Nature and Causes of the Wealth of Nations* (1776), with an Introduction by Dugald Stuart, Ward Lock, 1812.

Solar, Peter M., 'Poor Relief and English Economic Development before the Industrial Revolution', *Economic History Review*, XLVIII(1), 1995.

Solar, Peter M., 'Poor Relief and English Economic Development: A Renewed Plea for Comparative History', *Economic History Review*, L(2), 1997.

Townsend, P., 'The Development of the Research on Poverty', reprinted in A. B. Atkinson (ed.), *Wealth, Income and Inequality*, Oxford University Press, 1980.

Warr, Peter, 'Poverty Reduction and Economic Growth: The Asian Experience', *Asian Development Review*, 2000.

## Prices and Inflation

The early Classical economists (>CLASSICAL AND NEO-CLASSICAL ECONOMICS) were circumspect about the concept of a general level of prices. They carried out their monetary analyses either by reference to specific prices which were assumed to be representative or, as >RICARDO did in support of his argument for reasons for the depreciation of bank notes during the Napoleonic War, by reference to the exchange rate between notes and gold bullion. The multitude of prices in an economy even if they may all rise or all fall, do not do so in unison either absolutely or proportionately but in response to different forces depending on their sector. The benefits or costs that arise from these price movements accordingly vary between the different sections of society. Rises and falls, therefore, in the general price level can affect the distribution of real income (>INEQUALITY) and it became recognized that it was an important subject for measurement, record and study. It was not until the second half of the 19th century that progress was made by both statisticians and economists towards the construction of index numbers which gave a means of measuring the average movements in a group of prices sufficiently robust to be meaningful and to guide policy. In 1864, E. Laspeyres (1834–1913) published an index which was a weighted arithmetic average of changes in prices with the weights derived from the relevant quantities in the base year from which the price changes were calculated. In 1887 and 1889, F. Y. Edgeworth (1845–1926), as Secretary to the British Association for the Advancement of Science, wrote two reports on the construction and meaning of index numbers and in 1922 Irving Fisher (1867–1947) published *The Making of Index Numbers* in which he set out the attributes which an index number should possess. With the development of both the statistical and economic framework

of index number construction in the late 19th and early 20th centuries, the use of price indexes as measures of movements in the general level of prices became established and, at least in principle, a target at which economic policy could be directed. However, before >WORLD WAR I, inflation as such was not an economic issue. Indeed, according to Knut Borchardt (1991), the word 'inflation' was hardly known in Germany before the war, even in academic work. When it did arrive, governments were ill prepared for it.

This does not mean that there were not periods in the past during which there was a general rise in prices. In 1928, Sir William (later Lord) >BEVERIDGE and Edwin F. Gay, the Professor of Economic History at Harvard University, launched a project to compile time series of prices and wages for several countries which bore fruit in the 'International Scientific Committee on Price History'. As a result, data was collected covering the period from the 12th century through to the 20th century relating to prices and wages for a number of European cities (Beveridge, 1965; Cole and Crandall, 1964; Phelps Brown and Hopkins, 1958). These studies threw light on four periods during which prices were on a rising trend for long periods, interrupted by times of relative stability. Beveridge coined the phrase 'price revolution' for these periods because the inflation was such as to give rise eventually to social repercussions.

The different causes of such increases may be briefly be summarized as: (1) the rise in the quantity of money in circulation, which might be viewed either as the prime cause or as accommodating the inflation generated by other factors (>CLASSICAL AND NEO-CLASSICAL

ECONOMICS: >FRIEDMAN); (2) cost-push inflation due to the rise in the costs of production of goods and services – this could occur, for instance, from the rise in the price of imported commodities (such as >OIL) or through the exercise of monopoly power over prices by domestic firms or by labour attempting to maintain their real wages in the face of the rising cost of living; (3) demand-pull in which, for instance, particularly in pre-industrial societies, a harvest failure leads to a shortage of basic necessities, the destruction and disruption of supplies by war or the excess of aggregate demand in the economy over aggregate supply which has reached its full employment level.

Towards the end of the 12th century, after a period of stability in Europe, prices began to increase which, although only at about 0.5 per cent per annum, lasted through the 13th century and into the first half of the 14th century. Although the rate of growth varied from one country to another, nevertheless it was general throughout Europe. The probable fundamental cause of the increase was the excess aggregate demand generated by the steadily growing population. For instance, the population of England rose from about 1.5 million at the end of the 11th century to about 4 million when the growth was brought to a halt by the Black Death in 1349. There was also a growth in the circulation of the precious metals from increased output from European mines and from imports from West Africa and their supply was augmented by the debasement of the coinage to meet the demand for money in exchange. Towards the end of the period, there is evidence that the prices of basic necessities such as food and fuel rose the fastest. There was accordingly an increase in >INEQUALITY,

as incomes from rents and interest on loans maintained their value. In the early decades of the 14th century, there was also a series of poor harvests in Europe due to dreadful weather. The European economy deteriorated to the point of serious famine, culminating in the appearance of the Black Death in Sicily in 1347. It is estimated that as a consequence the population of Europe fell by 20 million. There followed an economic depression which lasted until the end of the 14th century during which real wages increased because of the relative shortage of labour as prices in general fell until they levelled out early in the 15th century.

Towards the end of the 15th century, prices began to rise again and initiate the second revolution, which lasted until about 1650 during which time prices rose on average at a rate of about 1 per cent per annum. Again, these price increases were against the background of rising population. For instance, the population of England rose from about 2.2 million from the end of the 15th century to about 3.7 million at the end of the 16th century to about 4.3 million by the mid-17th century (Coleman, 1977). The price of food rose relatively to other prices and there was a fall in real wages. In England rents increased by a factor of nine times from 1510 to 1640, grain by a factor of four times but money wages rose only twice. This demand pull on prices began before their was an influx of imported >SILVER sufficient to have an added monetary effect on prices. The inflow of silver into Spain from her mines in America began in the 1530s, reached a peak towards the end of the 16th century and then slowly declined through the 17th century. The amount of precious metals imported through Spain into monetary circulation in Europe increased threefold. Other influences on prices were the debasement of coinage by governments and by individuals through clipping and the increase in the velocity of circulation of the precious metals. At the same time Europe was ravaged by wars which disrupted production and there was an increase in government deficit financing. The last decade of the 16th century, with static output and rising prices, led into the crises of the 17th century. Early in the century saw a drop in the population of Europe occasioned by wars and inadequate harvests until stability was reached in the second half of the century which lasted until into the early 18th century (Fischer, 1997).

According to Fischer (1997), the third price revolution began in the 1720/30s and persisted until early in the 19th century. Prices rose not only in Europe but also in America, Asia and the Middle East. The driving force leading to the long rise in prices again appeared to be the rise in population, encouraged and accommodated by the increase in the supply of money in circulation, the precious metals being supplemented by commercial notes and bills. The period was also punctuated regularly by wars in Europe. Real wages declined. The 1780s were a period of worldwide recession. The end of the 18th century and the beginning of the 19th century was a time of revolutions and wars in Europe which culminated in the end of the Napoleonic War in 1815. There then followed a period of relative price stability. On average prices had risen through about 90 years at an average rate of about 1.7 per cent per annum. The new period of relative stability was interrupted by the agricultural depression of 1873 in which prices fell. Real wages rose, rent and interest rates fell. From 1873 to their lowest

point in 1896, prices in Britain fell by 18 per cent, from which point they increased steadily to reach a peak in 1920, having averaged about 4.5 per cent per annum (O'Donoghue 2004.) (>AGRICULTURE: >BUSINESS CYCLES).

The outbreak of >WORLD WAR I led governments into deficit financing. Between 1914 and 1919, prices in the >USA and Britain increased by about twice, in France by about five times and in Germany by about 15 times. In Germany, the demands of reparation (>KEYNES) induced the government into more inflationary financing. In mid-1921, the value of the mark fell to 7 per cent of its 1913 value, by mid-1922 to 1 per cent and by 1923 to less than .0004 per cent. In January 1923, a US dollar exchanged for 7,260 marks but by December the value of the mark had dropped to the point at which a dollar exchanged for 4,210 billion marks; a total collapse of the currency. Similar post-war periods of hyper-inflation occurred in Austria, >RUSSIA, Poland and Hungary. Between 1929 and 1931, wholesale prices in Britain fell by 28 per cent, in France by 24 per cent, in Germany by 17 per cent and in the USA by 24 per cent. The price of primary products of countries in Latin America declined by over 50 per cent (>GREAT DEPRESSION).

The recovery from the Great Depression marked the beginning of a further period of inflation, with higher sustained growth rates in prices than in previous periods, exemplified by the behaviour of prices in Britain. Consumer prices in Britain reached their inter-war low point in 1933. From that date there has not been a year in which consumer prices in Britain have not increased. With a few exceptions, notably Japan, the second half of the 20th century was a period of continuous worldwide inflation with a peak average growth rate of prices following 1973. In that year, the >OIL producers raised the price of crude oil to $11.65 compared with a price in 1970 of $1.8. As a result, inflation rose to an average per annum growth rate of 16.7 per cent in Italy, 13.5 per cent in the Britain, 11.2 per cent in France, 8.2 per cent in the USA and 7.6 per cent in Japan between 1973 and 1983 (Maddison, 1995). A recession led to a decline in the prices of food and raw materials in the 1980s to their lowest level since pre-World War II, the price of oil also fell to $8 from $40 per barrel but consumer prices continued to rise. However, in the last decade of the 20th century, the average annual rate of growth in consumer prices began to decline. The median inflation rate of the advanced countries between 1991 and 2000 was 2.4 per cent compared with 6.3 per cent between 1981 and 1990; that of developing countries 7.9 per cent compared with 9.4 per cent, and of countries in transition 1.9 per cent per annum. However, the median inflation rate of countries in transition rose to 165.5 per cent per annum between 1991 and 2000, a period which saw very high rates of growth in price levels in a number of these countries. For instance, the rate of inflation in >RUSSIA was recorded at 1,353 per cent in 1992 and 895.9 per cent in 1993. The average per annum rate of increase in the countries in transition dropped steadily from 1992 to reach 6.1 per cent in 2000 (IMF, 2007).

The post-World War II period was characterized by rising population growth and the pursuance of full employment policies by governments creating demand in excess of available resources. One line of argument for the relative exceptional growth in prices was the lack of the constraints of previous revolutions, such as a silver- or gold-based money supply or, in particular, the >GOLD STANDARD (Mundell, 1997). However, the drop in the inflation rate towards the end of the century may be found in the growth of international competition through the development of newly industrializing countries such as >CHINA and >INDIA, coupled with the containment of inflation expectations by central banks through inflation targeting. (>CENTRAL BANKING)

## References

Beveridge, William (Lord), *Prices and Wages in England: From the Twelfth to the Nineteenth Century*, Frank Cass (2nd edn), 1965.

Borchardt, Knut, *Perspectives on Modern German Economic History and Policy*, Cambridge University Press, 1991.

Cole, Arthur and Crandall, Ruth, 'The International Scientific Committee on Price History', *Journal of Economic History*, 24, September, 1964.

Coleman, D. C., *The Economy of England, 1450–1750*, Oxford University Press, 1977.

Fischer, David Hackett, *The Great Wave: Price Revolutions and the Rhythm of History*, Oxford University Press, 1997.

IMF, *World Economic Outlook*, May, 1999, October, 2007.

Maddison, Angus, *Monitoring the World Economy 1820–1992*, OECD, 1995.

Mundell, Robert A., 'The International Monetary System in the 21st Century: Could Gold Make a Comeback?', St Vincent College, Letrobe, Pennsylvania, 1997.

O' Donoghue, Jim, Goulding, Louise and Allen, Grahame, 'Consumer Price Inflation Since 1750', Economic Trends 604, Office for National Statistics, March, 2004.

Phelps Brown, E. H. and Hopkins, Sheila V., 'Seven Centuries of the Prices of Consumables Compared with Builders' Wage Rates', *Economica*, 23, 1958.

# Productivity

Productivity enhances the efficiency with which inputs of the factors of production produce outputs and is the main contributor to living standards. A distinguishing feature of modern times has been the long-term increase in income per head which results from these productivity changes. It was not always so: according to Maddison (2001), world average per capita incomes in real terms probably fell from 0 to 1000 AD. Between then and 1820 these average incomes rose by about 50 per cent, but since 1820 they have risen eight-fold with a fourfold increase in population. Some countries, the advanced nations, have done much better than this. The 12 largest economies in Western Europe have seen increases in average GDP per capita from $1,232 in 1820 to almost $18,000 in 1998 and the USA from $1,257 to $27,331 over the same period (figures at purchasing power parities, 1990). These increases in income (and output) per head have resulted from increases in investment in new technology and improved working methods. Labour has shared in this increased output so that earnings have risen. The much greater scope that exists for investment in manufacturing means that the prices of manufactures have in most cases actually fallen in real terms. For some services, however, such as hairdressing, there is little scope for productivity improvement, and prices have risen; this depresses the share of manufacturing in the national accounts and is a partial cause of 'de-industrialization' (the 'Baumol effect').

Changes in productivity are measured by changes in the ratio of inputs to output. The most common measure is to divide an index of output by an index of employment, preferably adjusted for hours worked. Increases in this measure of labour productivity underlie the observed increases in GDP per capita. Labour productivity is only a partial indicator since the use of other factors of production (land and capital) also contribute and labour productivity includes these other contributions. The calculation of total factor productivity (TFP) uses a weighted index of all inputs and is the residual of productivity change, ideally after accounting for changes in the quantity of all factor inputs. TFP is generally taken to reflect improvements in the efficiency with which factors are used and resulting from technical progress and improvements resulting from 'learning by doing' and in organization and administration. TFP is affected by changes in the quality of inputs, for example, a more educated labour force, and sometimes efforts are made to refine the measures of inputs to take account of these improvements in quality. The TFP residual change can be negative, reflecting less efficiency in the use of resources. In fact, since the early investigations in growth accounting, which identified the contributions to changes in output made by Robert Solow and others, it has been known that a large proportion of productivity growth resulted from the technical progress in a broad sense, which is reflected in TFP (>ECONOMIC DEVELOPMENT). A defect of TFP calculations is that they normally have to use fixed weights – for example, the remunerative shares of the factors of production in the national accounts. Often, perhaps almost always, economic advance in the medium term results from changes in the proportions of factors used and in changes in organization so that there is the risk that TFP partly assumes away one of the things which it is necessary to explain – how is growth being achieved? As crude measures of technical progress, however, TFP calculations are of value since they help to determine the extent to which growth is being achieved simply by mobilizing more resources and the extent to which innovation and technical progress are involved. It is only when the latter is true that sustained growth in living standards are likely to be achieved (>ASIAN MIRACLE).

All productivity calculations encounter a host of measurement problems of various kinds and these difficulties are intensified in international comparisons where concepts and definitions of aggregates may differ between countries and comparisons are complicated by the use of fluctuating exchange rates (>POVERTY). Measured productivity is affected by various things. Productivity tends to vary with capacity utilization. At low points in the cycle, labour tends to be hoarded rather than laid-off and this depresses output per person. Productivity may also be affected by the degree of competition, which applies pressures on managements to employ best practice, by >REGULATION, by intersectoral shifts from low to high productivity sectors, for example, from agriculture into manufacturing, as well as by numerous other factors.

Following the downward revisions to the trajectory of output growth during the >INDUSTRIAL REVOLUTION IN BRITAIN, traditional growth accounting attributed all of the 0.6 average annual growth in output from 1760–80 to increased inputs of the factors of production. In 1780–1831, these inputs accounted for over 80 per cent of the increased growth rate of 1.7 per cent per annum. With the acceleration of growth to 2.4 per cent in 1831–73, total factor productivity increased

further but then levelled off and finally fell to negligible levels as output growth declined in 1899–1913 to 1.4 per cent per annum. Thus, it is estimated that neither output growth nor TFP growth were high by modern standards, as we shall see shortly. Slow TFP growth was consistent with the fact that factor prices did not change much in the period. Incorporating a rough adjustment for changes in human capital, though reducing the TFP residual did not eliminate it, nor did it greatly modify the pattern of acceleration followed by deceleration. These estimates confirm the view that technological advance in the whole economy was of limited importance during the industrial revolution which, like similar conclusions about limited improvements in living standards in the period, remain controversial (>CONSUMER REVOLUTION: >INDUSTRIAL REVOLUTION IN BRITAIN) but seem to be consistent with what is known from the imperfect data (Crafts, 1995).

The article by Crafts (1995) to which we refer assesses whether the new endogenous growth theories associated with Paul M. Romer (1986) offer a superior explanation of growth to the traditional models which treat technological advance as the result of exogenous technological shocks which cannot be explained. Endogenous growth theory puts technical advance into its models and associates it with investments in human and physical capital rather than as exogenous developments. Crafts concludes that the endogenous model could help to explain why TFP seems to have grown so slowly during the industrial revolution, but not why it was accelerating. He prefers to explain the macro-inventions of the period, such as >STEAM POWER, as the result of 'flashes of human genius' and thus unpredictable. The relevance of this apparently esoteric debate, which is explained well by Mokyr (1999), is that it has important implications for public policy: endogenous growth theory supports the view that governments can and should do more to develop the institutions and incentives for education and research and innovation. It is important to note that we have here been discussing overall output and productivity change. In the fast-growing sectors of the economy during the industrial revolution, such as >COTTON AND TEXTILES, technological advance was rapid but these sectors accounted for only a small proportion of total output, another fact that is consistent with the Crafts views about the relatively slow overall growth in output and productivity.

The long view on productivity growth in the advanced countries is that it was fairly slow from 1870, accelerated between 1950 and 1973, then slowed again, though to higher rates than before >WORLD WAR II. Upward movement in productivity was resumed in the USA from 1990, an acceleration not yet followed in most other countries. In terms of GDP per hour worked there was little difference between the rate of productivity growth in Western Europe between 1870 and 1913 and in the inter-war period: the average was about 1.5 per cent per annum. US performance, however, was better and increased significantly from 1.9 per cent in 1870–1913 to 2.5 per cent from 1913–50. In Europe the really big change came between 1950 and 1973, when productivity increased at an average rate of 4.8 per cent annually. There was also an increase in productivity in the USA in the postwar period, but much less, to 2.8 per cent. Between 1973 and 1998 productivity growth slowed sharply to

2.3 per cent in Europe and to 1.5 per cent in the USA. Within these two decades or so US and European experience diverged and was to diverge further after 1990. From 1990–8 labour productivity growth continued to fall slightly to 2.2 per cent per annum, while in the USA it recovered somewhat to 1.7 per cent (Maddison, 2001). In 1991–2004 the productivity rate fell further in Europe to 1.4 per cent but continued to rise in the USA to 2.8 per cent. While the level of labour productivity is much higher in the USA than in Europe, and has been since the19th century, growth has accelerated in the USA but decelerated in most other industrialized countries (some of the Nordic states are exceptions). The US acceleration has reflected faster TFP growth from 0.7 per cent in 1966–75 to 1.9 per cent per annum in 1996–2004 (Skoczlas and Tissot, 2005).

Skoczlas and Tissot conclude that the recent improvement in US productivity is not solely the result of the greater use of information technology (IT) (>ELECTRONICS), since the bulk of IT investment started after TFP began to accelerate. All countries, including those in >WESTERN EUROPE, have also been investing heavily in IT but the results, as yet, do not seem to be appearing in their productivity performance. Robert Solow was quoted as saying that 'we see computers everywhere except in the productivity statistics'. This is the 'IT Paradox' (Barrell, 2000) and part of the reason may well be, as suggested by Z. Griliches, that productivity in the >SERVICE SECTOR, which now constitutes about 70 per cent of most advanced economies, is underestimated. Paul A. David and Gavin Wright, in David and Thomas (2003), argue that it was to be expected that there would be delays in the productivity benefits of IT investment. The full benefits of IT require changes in the organization of business, which takes time. They point to the fact that in the period 1889–1919 there was a long pause in TFP growth in US manufacturing followed by a surge in the 1920s. They attribute the pause to the delayed impact of electrification technologies (electric motors and dynamos) introduced around the turn of the 19th century. Some of this delay resulted from reluctance on the part of producers to scrap obsolescent but serviceable equipment and also from an increase in labour costs associated with the cessation of mass European immigration after 1914 (>MIGRATION).

An important aspect of the relative productivity performance between countries is the question of whether or not there is a tendency for living standards to converge. Convergence can be interpreted to mean a narrowing of the productivity gap (homogenization) or of catch-up of countries on the leader or leaders (Baumol, 1994). In fact, convergence seemed to be taking place in both senses from 1950 but the position has become less clear since the 1970s. In the first half of the 19th century, >BRITAIN was the leader, but was soon overtaken by the USA and these two countries and some other European states widened the gap between their productivity and that of others. The leaders seemed to be converging but none caught up with the USA. After World War II, convergence continued and more countries joined the convergence 'club' (effectively OECD member countries, >ECONOMIC DEVELOPMENT) with some reduction in the US lead. Since 1970, new members, including some newly industrialized countries, have joined the club, though the USA has retained, and more recently widened, its lead. All this refers only to the advanced

countries; if the analysis is widened to include all countries then there has been negative convergence, for example, the gap between the OECD countries and, say, Africa, has continued to widen. Where convergence has taken place it has been taken to result from the transfer of technology from the leaders to the rest. Not least of the reasons for taking an interest in convergence are its implications for policy. Those who assume it is taking place are more likely to advocate measures to ensure the free transfer and application of knowledge and technology, for example, by promoting competition, while those who resist the hypothesis of convergence will favour government action to promote indigenous innovation capability and absorptive capacity, including education and research and development. This brings us back to the controversy over endogenous growth theory discussed above.

There has been a great deal of interest in the reasons for the relatively poor and deteriorating productivity performance in post-World War II Britain compared with other European countries (though in fact, British productivity growth was superior to that of the USA until the 1990s). Between 1950 and 1979, Britain's growth rate in real GDP per capita compared very unfavourably with that of other European countries – it was at the bottom of the league of 16 countries. Broadberry and Crafts (2003) explain that British productivity levels were relatively high in this period and therefore it lacked scope for catch-up and also had less scope for transferring resources out of agriculture and into higher productivity uses. In 1871, only 22 per cent of British employment was in agriculture compared with 50 per cent in the USA and Germany. Even so, the authors estimate that the

British growth rate could have been 0.75–1.0 per cent per annum higher than it was and it ended the 1970s with significantly lower GDP per capita than its peer group. A major part of the explanation, the authors argue, lies in incentive structures and institutional arrangements. For example, they find that weak domestic competition and multiple trade unionism and plant bargaining across manufacturing provide empirical justification for their views. Other European countries, including Germany, had more successful arrangements for achieving moderate wage settlements in return for high investment. Training facilities were also superior in Germany, while in Britain the apprenticeship systems, which had helped to provide it with the most skilled workforce in the world in 1914, was declining rapidly. So-called 'de-industrialization' in which manufacturing employment in Britain fell by half from 1964–89, was, partly at least, inherent in addressing weak manufacturing productivity performance.

The conventional view has been that Britain's relatively poor performance was largely attributable to weaknesses in the manufacturing sector. However, Broadberry (1998) demonstrated that comparative labour productivity levels in manufacturing between Britain, the USA and Germany have remained relatively stable over a long period. For the whole economy, aggregate labour productivity in the USA, with Britain = 100, was about 90 around 1870, while for Germany it was about 60. By 1890, the USA overtook Britain and although there was some catch-up by Britain on the USA from the 1950s, the USA was still 30 per cent ahead in 1990. Germany, though its labour productivity reached 80 per cent of British levels by the late 1930s, did not overtake Britain until the mid-1960s. Both Germany and, earlier, the USA overtook Britain by shifting labour out of agriculture and improving their relative productivity performance in services rather than industry. With British levels at 100, US industry rose only from 154 to 163 (a 6 per cent improvement) between about 1871 and 1990. The German improvement was much greater in this period – from 86 to 117 (36 per cent). In both the USA and Germany, and this is the point, the improvement was very much greater in services – from 86 to 130 (51 per cent) for the USA and from 66 to 130 (97 per cent) for Germany. Broadberry, in his contribution to David and Thomas (2003), summarizes his earlier work and demonstrates the role of human capital in the German overtaking of Britain. He makes the point that the role of human capital in the superior performance of the USA is less clear and difficult to reconcile with the de-skilling nature of American mass-production technology. Scale economies can be an important contributor to productivity and Broadberry and Crafts (2003) speculate that British plant sizes were smaller than optimal in some sectors and agree with S. J. Prais's view that this could be the result of companies trying to keep factories small in the interest of avoiding labour problems (>CONCENTRATION). Broadberry and Crafts also raise the issue of the greater use of flexible production in Europe as a partial explanation of the persistent USA–European productivity gap (>INDUSTRIAL DISTRICTS).

## References

Barrell, Ray, Mason, Geoff and O'Mahony, Mary (eds), *Productivity, Innovation and Economic Performance*, Cambridge University Press, 2000.

Baumol, William J., Nelson, Richard R. and Wolff, Edward N. (eds), *Convergence of Productivity: Cross National Studies and Historical Evidence*, Oxford University Press, 1994.

Broadberry, Stephen N., 'How Did the United States and Germany Overtake Britain? A Sectoral Analysis of Comparative Productivity Levels', *Journal of Economic History*, 58, June, 1998.

Broadberry, Stephen and Crafts, Nicholas, 'UK Productivity Performance from 1950 to 1979: A Restatement of the Broadberry–Crafts View', *Economic History Review*, LVI(4), November, 2003.

Crafts, N. F. R., 'Exogenous or Endogenous Growth? The Industrial Revolution Reconsidered', *Journal of Economic History*, 55, December, 1995.

David, Paul A. and Thomas, Mark (eds), *The Economic Future in Historical Perspective*, Oxford University Press, 2003.

Maddison, Angus, *The World Economy: A Millennial Perspective*, OECD, 2001.

Mokyr, Joel (ed.), *The British Industrial Revolution: An Economic Perspective* (2nd edn), Westview Press, 1999.

Romer, P. M., 'Increasing Returns and Long-Run Growth', *Journal of Political Economy*, 94, 1986.

Skoczlas, Les and Tissot, Bruno, 'Revisiting Recent Productivity Developments Across OECD Countries', Working Paper 82, Bank for International Settlements, 2005.

# Proto-Industrialization

Household-based manufacture for the market, predominantly in rural areas. Franklin F. Mendels (1972) was the first to coin the term, although he notes the earlier use of the term 'protofactory', in the sense of early centralized workshops, by Freudenburger and Redlich in 1964. For long, prior to 1700, in Europe the town guilds were losing their monopoly of the market for artisanal (or craft) production to workers in rural areas and, of course, before that farm households had made their own clothes and simple tools. The distinctive feature of proto-industry, according to Mendels, was that production was systematic and oriented for sale to merchants, who supplied cottagers with raw materials and sometimes equipment and collected the finished or semi-finished products (that is the *domestic system* or the *putting-out system*). Mendels conceived of proto-industry as providing under-employed farm workers with profitable occupations at certain seasons of the year and as a first step to industrialization (>INDUSTRIAL REVOLUTIONS).

Merchants played a crucial role in the early industrialization process. Beginning with straightforward trading, importing and exporting raw materials, for example, merchants accumulated capital which they invested in the domestic system and in their own workshops to supplement the goods they had to sell. In putting out, they were effectively providing workers with working capital but these household workers had little independence. The domestic system allowed merchants access to cheaper labour in the rural areas and a greater volume of production, although there were higher coordination costs than using their own workshops and it was more difficult to control quality. Not all stages of manufacture were necessarily put out. In the textile trades, combing and sorting wool and cotton and finishing might be done in the merchant's own premises, with spinning, weaving and dyeing, for example, sub-contracted either to households or to independent artisans. The activities of proto-industry therefore created pressures for the integration of work into centralized workshops and Mendel points out that a large fraction of the first English textile mills were built by former merchants. Proto-industry seems to have be a regional phenomenon (Pollard, 1981): there were obvious advantages for the merchants in being served by suppliers concentrated in a particular locality, especially one near sources of supply, such as wool – hence there were clusters of proto-industry in the sheep country near the Devon/Somerset border in England. However, there was proto- industrialization in places where growing population and high or infertile ground or seasonal factors led to manufacturing, as in Switzerland. In >CHINA, home-based manufacture has apparently always been important and is still so today.

There were proto-industrial developments in Flanders, France and Germany, and also outside Europe in the Middle East at various times in history. The idea of the putting-out system, and therefore proto-industry, certainly travelled to North America with the early colonizers, although contemporary American economic historians do not dwell on it. Walter Licht (1995) says that in New England putting-out did not precede the rise of the factory but developed with it and actually increased in importance by 1840 when large numbers of women worked at home making hats, shoes and buttons. The putting-out system predominated in Japan in the late Tokugawa period. Noting this and many other instances, Miyohei Shinohara, in Hoselitz (1968), hypothesized that all market-based industrialized countries had passed through successive stages in which cottage industry gave way to >SMALL AND MEDIUM ENTERPRISES and, finally, large

firms although each of these types of firm continued to exist, even at the final stages of industrialization. In manufacturing, the putting-out system has largely disappeared in the advanced countries (>ECONOMIC DEVELOPMENT), although, to the author's knowledge, it was still used in the glove trade in England as late as the 1950s. In the Yeovil area of Somerset at that time manufacturers distributed blanks for gloves and linings to home workers by lorry for sewing up and collected the finished product. Putting-out still survives, indeed thrives, in some trades, such as bespoke curtain making and in the business service sector, for example, in copy-editing books for publishers and in certain forms of computer-aided design.

As these example show, proto-industrialization was not a once-and-for-all and clear-cut stage in >ECONOMIC DEVELOPMENT. Even before 1830, Maxine Berg, in Floud and McCloskey (1994) and in Berg and Hudson (1992), shows that there were a large variety of organizational forms in small-scale industry. Cooperative, artisanal and putting-out systems co-existed, as did various forms of sub-contracting. Putting-out is, in fact, just one type of sub-contracting and all these types of productive organization might and did sell to one another (as sub-contractors) or to the final consumer, as well as to merchant wholesalers.

Proto-industrialization is perhaps best seen as one of those short-hand concepts, like that of the >INDUSTRIOUS REVOLUTION to which it is related, and for which complete empirical justification has yet to be found. For that reason it has been challenged, for example, by Coleman (1983). He argues that the concept had little relevance to the >INDUSTRIAL REVOLUTION IN

BRITAIN, which began with coal and steel and in areas which had little proto-industry. Some proto-industrial regions did not industrialize; it is not clear where a boundary line, if any, should be drawn between the various forms of early manufacturing. The evolution of present industrial organization has been a complex process and although in retrospect it may be seen to have passed through a number of fairly well-defined stages in most countries, the path taken was not immutable or pre-determined (>INDUSTRIAL DISTRICTS).

## References

Berg, Maxine and Hudson, Pat, 'Rehabilitating the Industrial Revolution', *Economic History Review*, 45, 1992.

Coleman, D. C., 'Proto-industrialisation: A Concept Too Many?', *Economic History Review*, 36, 1983.

Floud, Roderick and McCloskey, Donald, *The Economic History of Britain Since 1700*, I, 1700–1860 (2nd edn), Cambridge University Press, 1994.

Hoselitz, B. F. (ed.), *The Role of Small Business in Economic Growth*, Mouton, 1968.

Hudson, Pat, *The Industrial Revolution*, Edward Arnold, 1992.

King, Steven and Timmins, Geoffrey, *Making Sense of the Industrial Revolution*, Manchester University Press, 2001.

Licht, W., *Industrialising America: The Nineteenth Century*, Johns Hopkins University Press, 1995.

Mendels, Franklin F., 'Proto-industrialisation: The First Phase of the Industrialisation Process', *Journal of Economic History*, 32, March, 1972.

Pollard, Sydney, *Peaceful Conquest: Industrialisation of Europe, 1760–1970*, Oxford University Press, 1981.

# R

## Railways

The rolling of wagons along tracks had been a long-established technique for the movement of material but the principle could not reach its full practical potential until the >INDUSTRIAL REVOLUTIONS. In the 18th century, for instance, wagons pulled by horses along rails were employed for the movement of coal from the mines to the staithes on the River Tyne in North East England for tran-shipment. Industrial development enabled rails to be designed using cast and wrought iron and later steel (>IRON AND STEEL) and the application of >STEAM POWER to traction. >BRITAIN was the lead country in the development of modern industry (>INDUSTRIAL REVOLUTION IN BRITAIN), so it was also in the development of the railways. The first railway was opened in 1825 along a 12.9km (8-mile) route from Stockton-on-Tees to Darlington in North East England. It had been originally planned primarily for the carriage of coal and for horses to be used for traction. The first truly comprehensive public railway was the 48km (30-mile) long Liverpool to Manchester line, which was opened in 1830. It was a common carrier for both passengers and freight. It was established to compete with the canal link (>CANALS).

So the railway era began in Britain and developed rapidly, absorbing an unprecedented proportion of the country's resources. In 1847, for instance, it has been estimated that about 4 per cent of the male working population was engaged in railway construction and, at its peak, railway investment accounted for 7 per cent of national income (Pollard, 1981). Richard Trevithick (1771–1833) is credited with being the first to build a steam locomotive. His first, in 1801, was designed to run on roadways and his second, in 1804, on rails. However, the weight of the engine was too heavy for both. In 1812, a steam locomotive designed by John Blenkinsop (1783–1831) ran on the the Leeds–Middleton Colliery Line. This not only inspired George Stephenson (1781–1848) but also the Grand Duke Nicholas I of >RUSSIA, who visited the line in 1816, although the first railway in Russia was not authorized until 1836. It was George Stephenson who designed the first practical steam locomotive, which ran on the Stockton to Darlington railway. He was accustomed to the tracks used to shift coal to the Tyne. These had a gauge of 4ft 8½in (1.4351 metres) and so this was the gauge he used. This gauge become the standard, with the major exception of the Great Western Railway, the first phase of development of which was finished in 1841 and which was built to a gauge of 7ft ¼in (21.40cm). After a series of gauge conflicts, the last stretch of this wide gauge was switched to the standard gauge in 1892. Eventually, over one half of the world's railways were built to this 'standard' gauge. There is an assumption that this success would be an indicator of the technical superiority of the 'standard' gauge over others. In fact, it is more of a reflection of the early entry into overseas markets of British railway expertise and the path dependency of subsequent expansion of the railway networks.

George Stephenson's success was confirmed by the employment of his steam locomotives on the Liverpool and Manchester. From that time onwards the railway network in Britain expanded rapidly. The Bubble Act of 1720 (>COMPANIES), which had restricted the growth of joint stock companies with limited liability, was repealed in 1825, easing the way for the railway companies to have the means by which they could raise the necessary capital (>CAPITAL MARKETS). By 1840, Britain had built 2,390km (1,485 miles), compared with 1,421km (883 miles) in the whole of the Continent of Europe. By 1850, the network covered 9,797km (6,087 miles), compared with a total then for the whole of the Continent of Europe of 13,227km (8,219 miles) (Ville, 1994). Britain's speed of take-off was matched only by that of the >USA, which had constructed 4,510km (2,802 miles) by 1840 (Cameron, 1993). The major expansion of the British network was achieved by 1870, reaching about 24,944km (15,500 miles). By 1914, the network had been virtually completed at 37,659km (23,400 miles).

Railways were the pre-eminent industry in Britain during the 19th century, being a major market for the coal, iron and steel and metalworking industries. Demand for British railway construction and engineering created new export opportunities in overseas markets, including the USA during the initial phases of its own railway expansion. Later, British capital would flow overseas to finance railway construction in developing countries. By 1914, 40 per cent of British investments overseas were in railway enterprises (Ashworth,

1987) (>INDIA). The influence of the railways permeated the economy through not only the direct reduction in transport costs but particularly through the reduction in travel times. The stagecoach took about 70 hours to travel from London to Edinburgh. The railways were soon able to do the journey in ten hours. Local markets became national markets. Towns extended their reach into dormitory suburbs supported by commuter transport and new towns were created to service the new industry. Government regulations specified maximum third-class fares to encourage the movement of labour. The railways opened up the opportunity for the expansion of the new business of tourism and gave concomitant benefits to seaside resorts. The railways also incurred not insignificant social costs through the disruption caused by the construction of lines and termini. It is estimated, for instance, that between 1850 and 1900, 100,000 people in inner London were made homeless by railway development (Porter, 1994). In the 20th century, the railways reached maturity. Competitive pressure led to amalgamations. In the second half of the 20th century the railways met increasingly effective competition from >ROAD TRANSPORT in the carriage of both freight and passengers. The railways in Britain were taken into public ownership in 1948 and, between 1953 and 1975, the network was cut from 28,000km (17,500 miles) to 17,700km (11,000 miles ). In 1994, the railways were returned to the private sector, although, as common with railways in >WESTERN EUROPE, the USA and elsewhere, they continued to need financial support from the government. The last significant railway investment in Britain was the construction of the 49.93km (31.03-mile) long Anglo-French tunnel under the English Channel which was opened in 1994 and linked by 2008 with a high-speed rail link from the Tunnel to London (>SEAPORTS).

Railway construction in the countries of Continental Europe followed Britain, with development coming later further east. In Britain, railways had arrived after the industrial revolution whereas on the Continent railway expansion occurred at the same time in some countries and later in others. A general implication of this timing was that whereas Britain did not have too much of a problem in raising private capital, other European countries had to look for foreign investment, often supported by government guarantees or loans. Belgium had early decided to create a railway network. The country had seceded from the Netherlands in 1830 and was anxious to assert its independence. It was recognized that for seaports, such as Antwerp, to flourish every opportunity should be given to access and widen their potential hinterlands. Railways were seen as a cheap, fast and efficient means of transport which could achieve this. A network was constructed running north/south and east/west by 1844 which opened up trading opportunities in Germany and France. Finance was found by the government raising loans. Private companies also played a part, though they were subsequently taken over by the state. The very first significant line to be built in France was in the iron and coal region of the Upper Loire Valley in 1833. It was horse-drawn for 17.7km (11 miles) from Saint-Étienne to Rhône et Andrézieux. However, the first railway employing a locomotive ran for 57.9km (36 miles) from Saint-Étienne to Lyons. In 1842, a national plan, drawn up by a director of the long-established government organization, the *Ponts et Chaussées*, was enacted which envisaged six major railway routes terminating in Paris. As in other countries in Continental Europe, the expansion and the location of the railways was influenced not only by commercial demand but also by considerations of military strategy. The government was to supply the basic infrastructure and private companies the rail track, rolling stock and other equipment. This first phase was completed by 1857, a second by 1870 and in 1878 a third development was planned. Private companies were assisted by the provision of government subsidies and the payment of interest on capital employed. The network expanded rapidly to 23,089km in 1880 and to over 40,000km just before >WORLD WAR I, by which time the state railway, the SNCF, employed 56,500 people (Schmitz, 1993; Ville, 1994). In 1938, all private railway companies were taken over by the SNCF. After >WORLD WAR II, the major development, in addition to the Anglo-French construction of the Channel Tunnel, was a high-speed rail link (TGV), which was completed in 1983, linking Paris to Lyons. The TGV service was subsequently extended to Le Mans, Tours and the Channel Tunnel (Meunier, 2002).

A short line was first completed in Germany (Bavaria) in 1835, running between Nuremberg and Fürth, and the main building phase began in the 1840s; the first Prussian state railway was laid through the Saar for the transport of coal in 1847. The Prussian government encouraged the railways by the provision of subsidies to support the civil engineering costs and also to underpin a line's finances if there was insufficient demand. By 1875, about 57 per cent of the railways where in private hands, a further 17 per cent were private but under government control and the rest were government-owned (by World War I, however, most of the German railways were in government ownership) (Pollard, 1981). After 1875, the railway network grew rapidly. In 1860, 11,089km of track had been laid, this rose to 33,838km in 1880, to 51,678km in 1900 and to 61,209km by 1910 (Ville, 1994). This expansion had important implications for the growth of the German economy. Building the railways required 178,500 people in 1846 and as many as 541,000 in 1875. It has been estimated that about three-quarters of the share capital raised between 1850 and 1870 was for railway construction (Schmitz, 1993). Between the turn of the 1850s and 1913 the rate of growth of traffic averaged about 6.5 per cent per annum. The German economy appeared to generate sufficient savings to support these demands and did not have recourse to external finance as, for instance, France. Domestic manufacturing of railway equipment proceeded apace. Initially, in 1841, of the 51 locomotives in operation only one had been made in Germany; in the years 1842–5 during which 124 were installed, 40 per cent were German made and by 1850–3, of the 270 commissioned, 93 per cent were German (Pollard, 1981). The railways played a vital role in the opening up of the coal, iron and steel and the metal-working industries and were an integral part of the industrialization of Germany. They were also appreciated by the government for their strategic value. It has also been suggested that the railways facilitated and encouraged Prussian expansionism (Brophy, 1998). Following the unification of Germany, the West German state railway, the Bundesbahn, and the GDR Reichsbahn were amalgamated into the Deutsche Bahn under government ownership.

The vastness of Russia's territory and the severity of its climate offered the ideal country for the successful operation of an extensive railway network. In spite of Nicholas's interest in the Blenkinsop locomotive, the first railway was not approved until 1836. Even then only 1,626km (1,533 miles) had been constructed by 1860. Thereafter, through the rest of the 19th century, railway construction expanded rapidly, surpassing Britain by 1890 and Germany by 1900, by which time 53,234km (33,078 miles) had been laid. Russia then had the largest network in Europe. Even so, it had still one of the smallest relative to its population and land area. The railways became a major employer with the workforce of 32,000 in 1865 increasing to 252,000 in 1890 (Falkus, 1972). Although the private sector played an important role initially in the financing of construction, the government increasingly began to exert its influence. Projects were supported by government guarantees and subsidies and many new lines were built and operated by the state. By World War I, the Russian government owned nearly 70 per cent of the railway network. The government, also, encouraged the domestic railway industry by granting subsidies to the production of rails, locomotives and rolling stock. Railways penetrated the major grain-producing areas, linked the coal and metallurgical industries and opened up markets to the ports. At the turn of the century, the Trans-Siberian Railway was built which made possible the movement of labour as well as freight to Russia's under-developed 'frontier'. The policy of the Tsar's government had reflected the recognition of the railway as not solely a passive carrier of other industries' freight but as a dynamic activity which generated economic growth through its own interrelated demands on other industries. The railways were encouraged. In 1918, the railways were nationalized by the new revolutionary government and they entered into a period when there tended to be a persistent lack of capital investment. The Soviet planners, when considering the priorities for the allocation of resources, gave railways a relatively low rating compared with other sectors. The Economic Plans favoured the establishment of large industrial complexes in geographically dispersed areas but there seemed to be a lack of appreciation of the extent that such a policy in itself generated a vast expansion in transport demand which could be only met by the railways. Moreover, even the investments planned often did not materialize. For instance, in the First Five-Year Plan for 1927–32, 16,000km of new track was scheduled but only 5,500km actually completed. In the period of the Second Plan from 1932–7, improvements were made and freight and passenger traffic was over 90 per cent higher in 1939 compared with 1932. The economy had been severely disrupted during and after 1914–18 and freight and passenger traffic taken together did not return to the 1913 level until 1926. In spite of recurring crises, traffic did expand through the 1930s. The share of freight increased from 57 per cent in 1913 to 78 per cent in 1928 and further to 85 per cent in 1940, in contrast to the change in the USA where the share of the railways in the movement of freight fell from 75 per cent in 1929 to 62 per cent in 1939, reflecting growing competition from road transport (>ROAD TRANSPORT: Westwood, 1994). After the recovery following World War II, the railways, as in other countries

worldwide, began to meet increasing competition from road transport. By the 1990s, the railway's share of the freight market had dropped to about 10 per cent.

The construction of the first railway in the USA closely followed Britain in 1828 with the start of the Baltimore and Ohio Railroad. Construction developed rapidly surpassing Britain by 1840 with 4,510km (2,800 miles) of line in operation. The total length reached 84,700km (52,600 miles) by 1870, by the end of the century about 322,000km (200,000 miles) were in operation and, by 1914, 410,000km (255,000 miles). The railways grew initially as local networks along the eastern seaboard connecting up centres of traffic potential, such as ports opening up their hinterlands for the attraction of agricultural products for shipment. Later, the railways moved westwards ahead of development. This was characterized by the completion of the transcontinental line by the Union Pacific and the Central Pacific in 1869 (>AMERICAN WESTWARD EXPANSION). The railways rapidly became an effective competitor for the >CANALS and turnpikes (>ROAD TRANSPORT). In the 1840s, 640km (400 miles) of canals were built compared with 9,700km (6,000 miles) of rail track. In the following decade, when there was a fall in the number of canals in operation, about 33,800km (21,000 miles) of rail track were laid (Chandler, 1995). The effect on freight rates was dramatic. The average rate per ton/mile fell from 12/22 cents by road in the 1830s to 4 cents by rail in 1850 and 2 cents by rail in 1880 (Schmitz, 1993). But the railways also had other advantages over the other modes. They could offer shippers faster delivery times and specified, reliable timetables that were less likely to be affected by weather. From the beginning, because of the lack of private capital and the financial risks, public support was forthcoming from municipalities, counties, states and the federal government in the form of subsidies and land grants. Between 1850 and 1880, about 180 million acres of federal and state land was given to the railway companies.

The scale of the railways, as they developed, both geographically and financially, was unprecedented and led to fundamental innovations in business structure and in financial markets. Ownership was divorced from control. The distances over which a railway operated led to the development of hierarchal management structures, the application of sophisticated management accounting techniques and their need for finance influenced the capital markets. In response to the emergence of cartels in the industry, the US Interstate Commerce Act was passed in 1887 (>USA), which set up the Interstate Commerce Commission (ICC) to regulate the railways. The ICC was strengthened in subsequent Acts in 1906 and 1910, which gave it the authority to set maximum tariffs and to delay proposed tariff increases. The railways were taken over by the government during World War I. They were returned to the private sector in 1920 but, by then, the competition from the other transport modes was seriously beginning to encroach on their business. Government control became looser. The Transport Act 1958 allowed the railway companies to close uneconomic lines. In 1971, the National Railroad Passenger Corporation (AMTRAK) was established, supported by government subsidy, and, in 1980, the Staggers Rail Act ended the control of the ICC over the setting of maximum and minimum tariffs. The ICC was abolished in 1996.

The railways reduced transport costs and opened up market opportunities not only domestically but also internationally and not only geographically but also innovatively by realizing new demands, such as tourism. They facilitated the spread of economic development. Economists have argued that the arrival of the railways played a vital role in the promotion of economic growth. Rostow (1960) believed that they were responsible for the 'take-off' of the US economy into self-sustained growth. Others have argued that the case for railways has been exaggerated. Robert Fogel (1964) agreed with this view and reiterated his point in his *Notes on the Social Savings Controversy* in the following year (Fogel, 1995). He carried out in effect a cost-benefit analysis of railway investment. He calculated what would have been the cost of transport between two points with and without the railways. The resultant estimate of the social savings of investing in the railways indicated a relatively small gain. In other words, although there was a gain, the US economy, without the railways, would not have failed to launch itself into sustained growth.

## References

Ashworth, William, *A Short History of the International Economy Since 1850*, Longman, 1987.

Brophy, James M., *Capitalism, Politics and Railroads in Prussia, 1830–1870*, Ohio State University, 1998.

Cameron, Rondo, *A Concise Economic History of the World*, Oxford University Press, 1993.

Chandler, Alfred D. Jr, 'The Railroads: The First Modern Business Enterprise, in Robert Whaples and Dianne C. Betts (eds), *Historical Perspectives on the American Economy*, Cambridge University Press, 1995.

Falkus, M. E., *The Industrialisation of Russia, 1700–1914*, Macmillan, 1972.

Fogel, Robert W., *Railroads and American Economic Growth: Essays in Econometric History*, Johns Hopkins University Press, 1964.

Fogel, Robert W., 'Notes on the Social Saving Controversy', in Robert Whaples and Dianne C. Betts (eds), *Historical Perspectives on the American Economy*, Cambridge University Press, 1995.

Meunier, Jacob, *On the Fast Track: French Railway Modernisation and the Origins of the TGV, 1944–1983*, Praeger, 2002.

Pollard, Sydney, *Peaceful Conquest: Industrialisation of Europe, 1760–1970*, Oxford University Press, 1981.

Porter, Roy, *London, A Social History*, Penguin, 1994.

Rostow, W. W., *The Stages of Economic Growth: A Non-Communist Manifesto*, Cambridge University Press, 1960.

Schmitz, Christopher J., *The Growth of Big Business in the United States and Western Europe 1850–1939*, Macmillan, 1993.

Ville, Simon P., 'Transport and Communications', in Derek H. Aldcroft and Simon P. Ville (eds), *The European Economy, 1750–1914*, Manchester University Press, 1994.

Westwood, J. N., 'Transport', in R. W. Davies, Mark Harrison and S. G. Wheatcroft (eds), *The Economic Transformation of the Soviet Union, 1913–1945*, Cambridge University Press, 1994.

# Regulation

The rise of the state (>STATE, RISE OF THE) has been associated with a major extension in the control of individual and business activity over a long period. In this entry we focus mainly upon the supervision and control of private enterprise in the interests of economic efficiency, health, safety and the environment. In medieval times in Britain, in the towns, economic activity was regulated by the Guilds, commonly acting under Royal Charter. In rural areas, wages and some prices were controlled by local justices. Later, these responsibilities were taken on by local authorities in both urban and rural areas, though a full-going reorganization of local authorities did not begin until after the Municipal Reform Act of 1835. As the administrative capability of government improved, it played a growing role. As new activities emerged, broader and more elaborate regulatory systems were devised. For example in the 18th and 19th centuries, Parliamentary Charters, effectively licenses and governing statutes, were awarded to the new enterprises in utilities and transport such as the turnpikes (>ROAD TRANSPORT), while local authorities assumed direct responsibility for water and gas undertakings. A defect of charters was that Parliament was rarely able or willing to keep them up to date and independent boards and government departments became involved in industrial regulation. Arrangements for regulation have rarely proved of very long duration because administrative and political difficulties, the 'capture' of the regulators by special interests, as well as technological change, have required frequent reorganization. As an example, the Railway Commission, set up by Statute in 1873 and which had the authority of a High Court to set fares and freight rates, was soon replaced in 1888 by the Railways and Canal Commission, and this in turn, in 1921, was succeeded by the Transport Tribunal. Later, the railways were taken into public ownership and, later still, returned to become regulated private monopolies (Baldwin and Cave, 1999). >RAILWAYS: >GAS and electricity and later >TELECOMMUNICATIONS were all classic cases of natural monopolies, nationalized and closely regulated in various ways. By 1912–15, 80 per cent of authorized water undertakings were municipal-owned, in gas 40 per cent, and 60 per cent of employees in the electricity industry were accounted for by publicly owned enterprises. In the railways, as their share of traffic was reduced by competition from road transport, amalgamation was encouraged by government from 1921 and railways and electricity, as well as coal and >IRON AND STEEL (which were not natural monopolies), were nationalized after 1945.

As in the emergence of road transport at the expense of railways and canals, technological development can influence the mode of regulation. This has been a feature of telecommunications, which proved possible to return to private enterprise later in the 20th century without undue risk of lack of competition, though it took some years for satisfactory arrangements to be developed. The early post-war period proved to be the high point of public ownership, not so much for regulatory reasons, but out of a socialist ideological desire to control 'the commanding heights of the economy'. The 1950s and 1960s were also a period when it was believed that governments, not only in Britain, should encourage mergers and amalgamations and promote industrial policy in the interests of improving efficiency and growth. The Conservatives formed the National Economic Development Council (NEDC) in 1962 and the Labour Government, which continued that body, also promoted a National Plan (1965) and created the Industrial Reorganization Corporation (IRC) in 1966. Ideas, however, were to change and from 1979, the Thatcher Government dismantled the planning bodies and embarked on a massive programme of privatization. Between 1979 and 1992 the proportion of total employment accounted for by state-owned enterprises fell from 8 to 3 per cent, that of output from 10 to 3 per cent.

Privatization meant that new regulatory arrangements had to be devised for the natural monopolies. Unlike the USA, the British chose price control within the limit of changes in the Retail Price Index (RPI) minus X, an assumed figure for attainable productivity improvement. It also chose individual regulators supported by staff as the form of regulatory body. The USA tended to rely on control not of prices but of the rate of return earned (an approach introduced earlier by Britain for railways in 1844), and on multi-person boards. Irwin Stelzer (2001) argues that British (and perhaps European) traditions in public interventions have provided less transparency than those of the USA, so that the detail of regulatory activity has not always been exposed to sufficient public scrutiny.

During the 19th century and following growing concern about the social consequences of the >INDUSTRIAL REVOLUTION IN BRITAIN, much new regulation was introduced affecting labour and working conditions. This trend began with the Health and Morals of Apprentices Act 1802. Early industrial regulation was very mild by present-day standards. For example, the Factory Act of 1809 excluded children under the age of nine from working in cotton mills and restricted those over that age to 12 hours (reduced in 1833 to six and a half hours). The 1833 Act for the first time introduced a Factory Inspectorate, which ensured that the social legislation was properly enforced. Other countries followed, but in the USA it was not until the 1930s that all states had child labour legislation. It is noteworthy that, prior to the inter-war period and the

>NEW DEAL, it was the states and not the Federal government that took the initiative in regulation, except in the field of interstate commerce and transportation. For example, trucking regulation began in the states in the 1910s and 20 states had passed >ANTI-TRUST legislation before the Sherman Anti-Trust Act passed by Congress in 1890. The regulation of the learned professions spread quickly among the states in the late 1800s. Texas began regulating medical doctors in 1873 and by 1925 all states had licensing regimes for doctors (Teske, 2004). While pressure for regulation often came not only from the general public, but also from practitioners in the interests of reducing competition, this was not the case in the licensing of professionals where public interest was the main motive. Law and Kim (2005) found that the main motive for the licensing of professionals was not to raise barriers to entry but the desire of the authorities to improve markets as growing specialization and advances in knowledge made it increasingly difficult for consumers to judge the quality of professional services. This was the problem of asymmetric information, which is, for instance, still the main rationale for the regulation of retail financial services.

Regulation spread further after >WORLD WAR I, and this continued through the inter-war period. The trend steepened from the 1960s, particularly in the field of social legislation, including employment law, health and safety, privacy and, more recently, environmental issues. >COMPANIES have been more and more tightly regulated while there have been a host of other interventions in the planning and construction of real estate, temporary labour placement agencies, general minimum wages, pensions, food and drugs and other matters. In some areas there has been self-regulation as in the professions, the media and advertising. >TAXATION in the interests of fairness and the minimization of evasion has generated a very large and complex body of regulatory law.

From about 1980 (earlier in the USA), there were signs of a reaction to the apparently inexorable growth of regulation (Bannock, 2005). This sea-change reflected broader political changes with the coming to power of the Reagan Administration in the USA and the Thatcher Government in Britain. Developments in the economics of public choice, associated with James Buchanan and Gordon Tullock around 1960, had provided an enhanced intellectual basis for the new thinking on regulation. Buchanan was to be awarded the Nobel Prize in Economics in 1986. It was argued that market failure – the usual justification for intervention – did not in itself imply that regulation would improve matters. It became recognized that regulators might have their own agendas, while they were often influenced or even 'captured' by special-interest groups. There might be a choice between imperfect free markets and imperfect regulated markets in which intervention inhibited competition and market discovery of new products, services and ways of doing things.

The USA deregulated trucking and air transportation (>AVIATION) and took measures to simplify the tax system (Tax Reform Act 1986). Fixed commissions on the New York Stock Exchange were abandoned in 1975 to be followed by the Big Bang on the London Stock Exchange in 1986 marking a worldwide trend to the deregulation of >CAPITAL MARKETS. Britain privatized much of its state-owned industries, it also simplified taxes and, for example, removed the remaining elements of exchange control which had been in place since 1939. Prior to 1980 there had been attempts at regulating incomes and prices in the interests of controlling inflation but these attempts were discontinued. (Price controls were widely used in >WORLD WAR II.) There were other developments in the way of freeing markets around this time, such as the deregulation of >BANKING. The sea-change in ideas, however, was not to result in any slowing down in the growth of regulation overall. Paradoxically, the European Union (>WESTERN EUROPE), in its measures to achieve a single European market for goods and services, also introduced many new regulations, partly in the interests of harmonization. In the Financial Services Acts of 1986 and 2000 in Britain there was a major extension of regulation in this important sector. Many of the initiatives, for example, in tax reform, were eroded in time, a phenomenon known as 'regulatory creep'. In the 1990s and into the millennium there were new regulations affecting personal behaviour, such as laws on smoking and alcohol consumption (previously deregulated), as well as laws providing for maternity leave for employees.

Administrative compliance costs bear particularly heavily upon >SMALL AND MEDIUM ENTERPRISES. Bannock (2005) cites a 1978 study by Professsor Cedric Sandford, which found that compliance costs for Value Added Tax as a percentage of turnover were 1.17 per cent for firms with taxable turnover under £50,000, compared with only 0.04 per cent for firms with a turnover of £1 million or more. Subsequent reforms have probably reduced this differential somewhat, but it remains true that large firms enjoy considerable economies of scale in dealing with regulation.

Regulation incurs considerable costs as well as benefits. The first and most readily measurable of these costs are *administrative compliance costs* which, for business, include the staff time spent in dealing with regulation and the paid-out costs of professional advisers such as accountants and consultants. In the 1980s European governments began to set up machinery to control the growth of regulatory compliance costs. This machinery, in Britain, included, from 1998, a requirement for all proposed new legislation imposing significant costs on business to be accompanied by a Regulatory Impact Assessment (RIA). These instruments are based on similar ones used earlier in the USA and are, in effect, cost-benefit statements. Partly because of the implementation of new EU directives, the RIA system had no effect on the levels of compliance costs, the growth of which actually accelerated. Accordingly, in 2005 the British Cabinet Office instigated a measurement exercise in which compliance costs imposed on business by some 20 government departments, the tax authorities and the Financial Services Authority were assessed. These costs, clearly for many reasons considerable underestimates, amounted to over £20 billion or 1.6 per cent of GDP. Taxation and company and other laws administered by the Department of Trade and Industry accounted for half of the total estimated costs. Targets have been set to reduce compliance costs by 25 per cent by 2010. Similar, though less radical, systems have been in place in the USA for many years and are paralleled in the Netherlands, Denmark and Germany. It remains to be seen if these systems will curtail the growth of compliance costs, but their existence is evidence of widespread concern about the issue.

More important than administrative compliance costs are the *efficiency costs* or *excess burdens* that result from the market distortions created by regulation. Some idea of these costs can be gained by the beneficial results of the deregulation of airlines by the US and European governments. These measures have led to increased competition, lower prices and more choice for consumers. Another example is the effect of excessive regulation of labour markets in Europe. There is ample evidence that lack of labour market flexibility has been a major cause of slower economic growth and higher unemployment in Europe than in the USA (Galli and Pelkmans, 2000). Excessive and inefficient regulation, either inherited from former European colonists or put in place through emulation of the advanced countries, has also been identified by the World Bank and academic researchers as being a major impediment to >ECONOMIC DEVELOPMENT in the poorer countries.

There are other costs of regulation over and above efficiency losses and compliance costs. There are costs to government itself of administering the regulation system, while some additional compliance costs are also borne by consumers, as in compiling tax returns. Businesses probably pass on the whole of compliance costs to the end consumer. Karl Polyani (2001) argued that the economy has always been regulated, even in the days of the manorial system and also under >MERCANTILISM. It is clear, given the tensions between social interests and >CAPITALISM, as Polanyi argued, that the economy could not survive without some regulation, but the challenge now, is to manage the costs of the system. Given the difficulties of measurement, regulatory compliance costs may well be of a similar order of magnitude in all the advanced countries. Competition from emerging countries with lower levels of regulatory costs, however, may help to achieve a better balance of costs and benefits, just as tax competition in Europe has reversed the growth in business taxation.

Just as the >NEW DEAL during the >GREAT DEPRESSION gave rise to a surge of regulatory activity, corporate scandals and the credit crisis of 2007–8 (>CORPORATE GOVERNANCE) are likely to lead to a further surge, particularly in financial services.

### References

Baldwin, Robert and Cave, Martin, *Understanding Regulation: Theory, Strategy and Practice*, Oxford University Press, 1999.

Bannock, Graham, *The Economics and Management of Small Business: An International Perspective*, Routledge, 2005.

Galli, Giampaolo and Pelkmans, Jacques (eds), *Regulatory Reform and Competitiveness in Europe*, Edward Elgar, 2000.

Law, Marc T. and Kim, Sukkoo, 'Specialisation and Regulation: The Rise of Professionals and the Emergence of Occupational Licensing Regulation', *Journal of Economic History*, 65, September, 2005.

Polanyi, Karl, *The Great Transformation: The Political and Economic Origins of Our Time* (1944), Beacon Press (new edn), 2001.

Stelzer, Irwin M., *Lectures on Regulation and Competition Policy*, Institute of Economic Affairs, 2001.

Teske, Paul, *Regulation in the States*, Brookings Institution, 2004.

## Ricardo, David

David Ricardo, who lived from 1772 to 1823, was born, the son of Abraham Ricardo, of a Jewish family that had established itself in Amsterdam from Italy at the beginning of the 18th century. With the relative decline of the Netherlands, there was a transfer from there of financial and trading services to >BRITAIN and Abraham had joined members of his family in London in the 1760s. He quickly succeeded in developing his own business in the City and was highly regarded in the Jewish community in which he adhered to the Sephardic tradition. David Ricardo was brought up within this close community; from the earliest days his education was directed at following his father into a career in finance and he was sent to Amsterdam for two years to work and learn within his uncle's business. At the age of 14, he left formal schooling to work in his father's firm in London in which he gained experience trading in government securities and bills of exchange. David, however, could not accept the strictures of orthodox religion and the patriarchal constraints imposed by his father. The final, irrevocable, demonstration of his independence came with his affection for a Quaker girl, whom he married in 1793, as soon as he was free to do so. As a result, he was cut off by his father from his family and was left to make his own living from scratch. This he succeeded to do and by his late 20s he was financially secure. He took advantage of this security by investing time out from work to widen his education. He had a scientific bend of mind and studied geology, chemistry and mathematics. He became a member of the Geological Society in 1808 soon after its formation.

Ricardo's interest in economics in practical terms was stimulated by the questions of the day. Ricardo lived through a tumultuous time. The manifest effects of the >INDUSTRIAL REVOLUTION IN BRITAIN created the tensions inevitable in the unprecedented transition of an agricultural society into an industrial one. The wars with France raised problems of government finance and questions about the optimum way in which government obligations should be met. His discovery of economics as a subject for study, however, was remarkably casual. During a stay in Bath, a spa town in the West of England, where he was staying for his wife's health, he borrowed a book from a circulating library called *An Enquiry into the Nature and Causes of the Wealth of Nations* by Adam >SMITH (1776) which launched him into the development of his own ideas in economics. In working to establish the principles and conclusions of his economic thought, Ricardo was able, of course, to draw upon his considerable understanding of and experience in practical business affairs. He drew heavily on the *Wealth of Nations*, but he was also by all accounts a very amiable, likeable and honest man and enjoyed the benefit of numerous able friends, such as Thomas >MALTHUS and James Mill, with whom he could debate and test his ideas.

Ricardo's early works were primarily concerned with money and banking. In 1810, he published a short piece on *The High Price of Bullion, Proof of the Depreciation of Bank Notes*, in 1811, the *Reply to Mr Bosanquet's Practical Observations on the Report of the Bullion Committee* and, in 1816, *Proposals for an Economical and Secure Currency*.

The Bank of England (>CENTRAL BANKING) had suspended the convertibility of sterling bank notes into gold in 1797 and the following years the market price of gold rose from the mint parity of £3 17s 10½d (£3.89375) per ounce to £4 6s (£4.3) in 1801 and to £4 12s 10½d (£4.64375) in 1809 (>GOLD STANDARD). A debate arose as to the reasons for this decline in the currency. David Ricardo was on the side of the bullionists and argued that the currency had depreciated because of the excessive issue of bank notes by the Bank of England and not by the disruption of trade or poor harvests.

What would become the essence of the Classical (>CLASSICAL AND NEO-CLASSICAL ECONOMICS) quantity theory of money (>FRIEDMAN: >KEYNES) through the 19th century was adumbrated by David Ricardo in *The High Price of Bullion*:

'However abundant may be the quantity of money or of bank-notes; though it may increase the nominal prices of commodities; though it may distribute the productive capital in different proportions; though the Bank (of England), by increasing the quantity of their notes, may enable A to carry on part of the business formerly engrossed by B and C, nothing will be added to the real revenue and wealth of the country... There will be a violent and an unjust transfer of property, but no benefit whatever will be gained by the community.' (Ricardo, 1810)

In 1815, he published an *Essay on the Influence of the Low Price of Corn on the Profits of Stock* in refutation of the argument of Thomas Malthus in favour of protection (>INTERNATIONAL TRADE) during the debate on the Corn Laws (>BRITAIN) and he was encouraged by his friends to develop his ideas further in a major work. Accordingly, in 1817, he published his most important contribution to economics in *The Principles of Political Economy and Taxation*.

In contrast to Adam Smith's *Wealth of Nations*, the study and criticism of which formed the foundation of his own work, Ricardo saw the distribution of National Income between labour, land and capital rather than its total level as the major concern of his analysis. In a letter to Malthus, he said that political economy, 'should rather be called an inquiry into the laws which determine the division of the produce of industry amongst the classes who concur in its formation' (quoted in Deane, 1978). His method was to construct a theoretical model of the economy on simplified assumptions based on the production of corn in order to reveal those laws.

As population increased, less and less fertile land was available to be brought into cultivation and the cost of producing a bushel of corn increased. The price of corn rose to the level to cover the cost at the margin but this price would prevail over the whole market. Profits must be the same everywhere, otherwise capital would be attracted into the location earning higher profits until they fell. Therefore, income was generated on intra-marginal land which was surplus to profits and the cost of labour. This surplus accrued to landlords as rent. Rent, therefore, was not a cost of production.

The growth of >POPULATION was determined by the balance between the desire to have children and the level of material subsistence. In *The Principles*, Ricardo states that the natural price of labour was that 'necessary to enable the labourers, one with another, to subsist and to perpetuate their race'. Given that the share of National Income accruing to labour had of necessity to be no less than that required to maintain subsistence, which Ricardo conceded could be influenced by custom, the share of profits would fall with rising population as more and more marginal land was brought into production, real wages remained constant and rents increased. Profits would, therefore, tend to zero and herald the stationary state.

'Supposing corn and manufactured goods always sell at the same price, profits would be high or low in proportion as wages were low or high. But suppose corn to rise in price because more labour is necessary to produce it; that cause would not raise the price of manufactured goods in the production of which no additional quantity of labour is required. If, then, wages continue the same, the profits of manufacturers would remain the same; but if, as it is absolutely certain, wages should rise with the price of corn, then these profits would necessarily fall.' (*Principles*, quoted in Roll, 1973)

The interests of capital and labour were, therefore, closely related. It was the interest of the landlord which was adverse. 'The interest of the landlord is always opposed to that of the consumer and manufacturer... All classes, therefore, except the landlord will be injured by the increase in the price of corn' (*Principles*, quoted in Roll).

Following Adam Smith, Ricardo held a labour theory of value but, unlike Smith, he argued that it was as relevant to a developed society as to a primitive one. The value of a commodity was determined by the amount of labour which was embodied in its production. It was possible, therefore, to conceive of a commodity which was always produced by the same number of units of labour and could be used as a *numéraire* against which to measure the value of all other commodities. In long-run equilibrium and perfect competition, the relative exchange values of different commodities were equal to the relative quantities of labour embodied in their production. In the case of an advanced economy in which labour was mixed with invested capital in production, the value of the capital element was the amount of labour which in the past was used to produce the investment. The value of a commodity is determined, therefore, by the sum of the current labour used in its production and the past labour embodied in the capital equipment used along with labour in its production. The value of the product gained by the capitalist is divided between the payment of wages and profit required in order to cover the time required to bring the product to fruition and to market. (Ricardo's theory of value was interpreted by Karl >MARX as the exploitation of labour. The exchange value of the commodities which the wages the capitalist-paid labour could buy was less than the value of labour embodied in the commodities the capitalist bought from labour. The capitalist, therefore, gained a surplus which belonged to labour.)

Ricardo postulated that following a rise in wages the relative prices of those commodities which required a relatively high input of fixed capital or of fixed capital with a long life would fall, and the relative prices of those commodities with relatively high labour input and less fixed capital or of fixed capital with a short life would rise. This has come to be referred to as the 'Ricardo Effect'. For instance, in an economy with falling real wages and rising commodity prices, firms would tend to cut investment in industry with a long production cycle in favour of those in which the product can be brought to market in a shorter time.

Although in general he assumed the validity of Say's Law, that labour and capital must always be fully employed, Ricardo did acknowledge in a chapter which was added to the third edition of *Principles*, that labour could be displaced by its substitution by 'machinery'.

The stationary state was a possibility because of the limitation of a country's resources as exemplified by the increasing costs of production on the falling fertility of progressively more marginal land. This constraint on growth imposed by the limitation on a country's resources could be eased by technical progress, which raised productivity, and by >INTERNATIONAL TRADE. Ricardo believed in free trade and opposed the Corn Laws because they led to the need for domestic production of corn to move to high-cost marginal land.

In the chapter on 'International Trade' in *Principles*, by the Law of Comparative Costs, he showed that a country could advantageously import a commodity from another country even when it could produce it cheaper at home.

Consider two countries, Portugal and England producing cloth and wine. There are three possibilities. In the first, the relative costs of producing cloth and wine are the same in both countries. In this case no trade would take place because there would be no gains from trade. In the second, if a country has an absolute cost advantage in, say, wine and the other country an absolute advantage in, say, cloth, the former will export wine to and import cloth from the latter. Ricardo showed that trade could take place even when one country could produce both wine and cloth more cheaply than the other. This is illustrated in the Table below:

Man-hours required per unit of output

| Country | Wine | Cloth |
|---------|------|-------|
| A | 120 | 100 |
| B | 80 | 90 |

If Country B exports one unit of wine to country A, it can import 120/100 units of cloth. If Country B had devoted the 80 man-hours needed to produce a unit of wine for export to the production instead of cloth, it would have only 80/90 units of cloth. If country A exports a unit of cloth to country B, it could exchange it for 90/80 units of wine. If country A had devoted the 100 man-hours needed to produce a unit of cloth, to the production of wine instead, it would have only 100/120 units of wine. Country B, therefore, gains from trade are given by 120/100–80/90 and country A gains from trade are given as 90/80–100/120. Therefore, both countries gain from trade and both would do so provided the rates of exchange of between cloth and wine fall within the range 120/100–80/90.

Ricardo advocated taxation rather than borrowing as a means of financing government debt, although he did not believe that there was any real difference between them as far as the economy was concerned. This idea has been developed in recent times as the 'Ricardian Equivalence Hypothesis' by Barro (1974). Government borrowing has no real economic effect because the private sector anticipates that the debt will need to be paid sometime and increases its savings correspondingly.

Along with Adam Smith, David Ricardo is regarded as a founder of what became known as Classical economics. David Ricardo is seen by many as the inspiration for the study of economics along the same principles as any scientific subject. According to Schumpeter:

'Though others did the same, his advocacy was more brilliant, more arresting, than was theirs; there is no superfluous sentences in his pages, no qualification, however necessary, weakens his argument; and there is just enough genuine analysis about it to convince practically and, at the same time, to satisfy high intellectual standards but not enough to deter. ... It is neither his advocacy of winning policies per se, nor his theory per se, that, to this day, makes of him, in the eyes of some, the first economist of all times, but a felicitous combination of both.' (Schumpeter, 1954)

## References

Barro, Robert J., 'Are Government Bonds Net Worth?', *Journal of Political Economy*, 1974.

Blaug, Mark, *Economic Theory in Retrospect*, Cambridge University Press, 1978.

Deane, Phyllis, *The Evolution of Economic Ideas*, Cambridge University Press, 1978.

Hollander, Jacob H., *David Ricardo, A Centenary Estimate* (1910), University Press of the Pacific, 2002.

Roll, Eric, *A History of Economic Thought*, Faber and Faber, 1973.

Schumpeter, Joseph A., *History of Economic Analysis*, Oxford University Press, 1954.

Sraffa, Piero (ed.), *The Collected Works and Correspondence of David Ricardo*, Cambridge University Press 1951–5.

## Rice

Rice, *Oryza saliva*, is a member of the grass family, *Gramineae*; its grain grows on spikes from a stem which can reach up to 5 metres long in deep water. There are two major groups, the *indica*, which is suitable for growing in tropical or semitropical climates, and the *japonica*, which is more suited to temperate climatic conditions; there is a smaller Indonesian group, *javanica*, but there are thousands of varieties in total.

Within each of these groups, some varieties are grown on 'wet' irrigated areas, either upright or floating in deep water, and some on 'dry', rain-fed land. 'Wet', irrigated rice accounts for most of world production. A great attribute of rice is that it is capable of achieving more than one harvest a year and can be grown repeatedly on the same plot of land.

Rice is comparable to wheat as the world's major cereal crop. Total world production of rice was 608 million tonnes in 2004, compared with 630 million tonnes of wheat (Food and Agricultural Organization, 1998). However, production of rice is not as widely distributed as that of wheat, about 90 per cent of the production of rice being located in Asia. >CHINA and >INDIA are the largest producers, accounting for 30 per cent and 21 per cent respectively in 2004. The cultivation of rice in Asia is in the area stretching from Pakistan to Japan and from Northern China to Indonesia. Rice yields a higher tonnage per hectare with greater calorific value than does wheat, although its protein content is about half. In 1980, the world average yield for rice was about 2.75 tonnes per hectare, 41 per cent higher than the 1.95 tonnes per hectare for wheat. By the end of the 20th century, while both the average rice yield and the average wheat yield had increased to 3.75 tonnes per hectare and 2.68 tonnes per hectare respectively, there remained a 40 per cent margin in rice's favour (Food and Agricultural Organization, 1998; Bray, 1994). Rice, also has the advantage, particularly important for a small farmer, in that it reproduces at a high yield to seed ratio so that the proportion of seed from a harvest that a farmer has to retain for his future crop could be only about 1 per cent, much lower than other cereals such as wheat. At the end of the

20th century, rice accounted for 60 per cent of the amount which poor families in Asia spent on food.

Bray (1994) records evidence of the cultivation of rice in the Chinese province of Zhejiang (Chekiang) in the Yangzi Delta as far back as 5000 BC. Similar early sites have also been found in North Thailand, in India in about 1800 BC and much later in about 300 BC in Japan, followed later still in Indonesia (Java). It also spread to Europe and, from the 15th century, it was grown in Italy and in the Balkans and in the 17th century in North America, but Asia remained by far the major production area. Rice became the cornerstone of economic prosperity in the rice-producing areas and so enabled powerful civilizations to develop and flourish in Asia, particularly so in China. There was a rapid increase in the population of China from about 60 million to 120 million between the 10th and 13th centuries and the production of food was recognized by the government of China at that time as vital not only to meet the demand of the growing numbers but even also to encourage the expansion in population as a defence against invaders. Rice yielded more calories than the traditional barley, millet and sorghum. As the Han moved south, they introduced the cultivation of rice in paddies and succeeded in being able to harvest up to three crops a year by the selection of quick-growing varieties, the use of natural fertilizers and by the raising of rice plants in seedbeds before planting out into the paddy fields.

The cultivation of rice was a labour-intensive operation but in harmony with the reality of the availability of a large labour force compared with the relative shortage of suitable land. Land was the comparative scarce factor of production. There were few animals apart from buffalo, which were used generally only for preparing the soil in this agricultural system; horses and mules were mainly employed in North China. In Japan, in the 17th century, the increase in population to 30 million was made possible by an increase in the production of rice through the construction of irrigation systems, the use of fertilizers and improved rice varieties.

The relative scarcity of land to population and the paddy field system in which irrigated water was channelled into and flowed through small bunded fields, led to an agricultural system quite different from that of Europe, particularly in the absence of animal husbandry for meat and dairy products and the limited use of draught animals. The small size of the paddy fields restricted the use of machinery and the considerable skill required in rice cultivation in the paddies limited the scope for its substitution by machinery because of the difficulty of replicating such operations mechanically. The increase in the productivity of the land was achieved not only by the selective cultivation of new varieties and the correct choice of varieties for particular conditions but also by the application of organic and later chemical fertilizers and pesticides. The major capital input was in the construction of the irrigation systems.

By the beginning of the 20th century, only Japan had moved ahead in rice cultivation thanks to planned research projects and the industrial back-up capable of producing chemical fertilizers. The country also had a viable communication structure in support of its farming community. Research into the development of machinery suitable for work in the paddies was pursued after >WORLD WAR I but without success until the rotary tiller was launched by Japan in the 1950s and transplanters and small reaper-binders in the 1960s and combine-harvesters in the 1970s. The prime objective was to improve the productivity of the land, which was the scarce resource, compared with that of the agriculture of Europe and North America, in which the balance of the factors of production was the reverse and investment was directed at the improvement of the productivity of labour (Bray, 1994).

Even at the end of the 20th century, rice in Asia was grown on small farms of less than half a hectare in China, Java (Indonesia) and the Red River Delta in Vietnam, and over two hectares only in Thailand, Myanmar, Cambodia and India (Punjab). Because the surplus available after meeting the requirements of the farmer and his family was small, considerable fluctuations appeared in the quantity available on the market, with a consequential affect on prices. Many governments, therefore, set up systems for controlling the price. Support was given to rice farmers in order to maintain domestic self-sufficiency on the argument that the irrigation system would not be maintained if the farms were abandoned and could not quickly be brought into operation in times of need. The international trade in rice was low, therefore, and remained so (Hossain and Narciso, 2005).

In 1962, the International Rice Research Institute was established in Los Banos, in the Philippines, to pursue a programme for the development of improved strains of rice to raise yields.The Institute achieved its first success with IR8 in 1966 and continued this with further strains up to IR72 in 1994. China also began research in 1956 and achieved the same result with a similar strain. The IR8 variety had a potential production of 10 metric tonnes per hectare for one harvest in ideal conditions and this was not improved upon until the 1980s. (Subsequently developed new varieties were theoretically capable of yielding 20 tonnes per hectare.) These successes launched the 'Green Revolution', which enabled a considerable increase in the production of rice through the improvements in yield. Between 1967 and 1985, world production of rice grew at an average growth rate of about 3 per cent per annum, a growth entirely due to yield improvement, as the area devoted to production declined (Food and Agricultural Organization, 1998). One result of the improvement in productivity was the major decline in the real price of rice. This lowered the cost of living of poor families in Asia but the improvement in yield also benefited the small rice farmers themselves by raising their incomes. In the last quarter of the 20th century, the price of rice declined by about 50 per cent, measured in Asian currencies. Moreover, this decline was greater than the fall in the prices of other cereals such as maize and wheat. Improved production techniques also reduced the fluctuations in production which had been previously experienced so that price volatility was reduced. All these factors also contributed to the growth in the international market for rice. International trade was further encouraged when agricultural trade restrictions were eased through the GATT Uruguay Round of Trade Negotiations, which were concluded in 1994.

Myanmar, Thailand and Vietnam were the top rice exporters from the second half of the 19th century and until >WORLD WAR II, after which Thailand became the dominant exporter. Asian countries accounted for about 93 per cent of total world exports in 1935 but this had fallen to

70 per cent in the 1960s. Similarly, Asian imports fell from 75 per cent in 1935 to 65 per cent in 1975 and to 39 per cent in 1980. Asian imports of milled rice remained at around 4–5 million tonnes between 1950 and 1980, while total world trade increased from 8 million tonnes in the 1970s to 12 million tonnes in the 1980s (Barker *et al.*, 1985). World trade in milled rice further increased from an average of 13.5 million tonnes per annum in the period from 1984–93 to an average of 23.9 million tonnes between 1994 and 2003, an average growth rate of just under 6 per cent per annum. In addition to this substantial increase in trade there also occurred a reorientation, in that the share of world imports of rice into Asian countries halved, as the Middle East and African countries increased their share (Dawe, 2005). The statistics of production measures the tonnage of 'unhusked' rice, but trade is measured 'milled' as it is marketed internationally in that form (apart from rice exports from the USA to South America). Milled or white rice has the bran layer and the rice germ removed, as well as the husk.

World rice production increased from an average of 145 million tonnes per annum in the period from 1931–40 to an average of 351 million tonnes in the period from 1971–80, an average increase in the 40 years of 2.2 per cent per annum, which was slightly higher than the 2.1 per cent per annum that was recorded by the Asian countries alone, so that their share of total production fell from 96 per cent to 92 per cent. This fall in share continued in the following decade to 88 per cent, when world output accelerated to 3.7 per cent per annum, compared with 3.3 per cent per annum for the Asian countries.

In the last decade of the 20th century, both world and Asian output rate growth fell to 1.1 per cent per annum, following a drop in the rate of improvement in yield. This decline applied throughout Asia, with the exception of India which recorded continued improvements in yield from the application of new varieties and investment in irrigation systems. There were indications towards the end of the 20th century that the application of additional inputs aimed at improving yield were meeting diminishing returns (Barker *et al.*, 1985; Brookes and Barfoot, 2003; IRRI, 1998).

## References

Barker, Randolph, Herdt, Robert W. and Rose, Beth *The Rice Economy of Asia*, Resources for the Future, 1985.

Bray, Francesca, *The Rice Economies. Technology & Development in Asian Societies*, University of California Press, 1994.

Brookes, Graham and Barfoot, Peter, *GM Rice: Will This Lead the Way For Global Acceptance of GM Crop Technology?*, PG Economics, ISAAA, 2003.

Dawe, David, 'Changing Structure, Conduct and Performance of the World Rice Market', in *Proceedings of the FAO Rice Conference, 2004*, Food and Agricultural Organization, 2005.

Food and Agricultural Organization (FAO) *Statistical Yearbook*, FAO, 1998.

Hossain, Mahabub and Narciso, Josephine, 'Global Rice Economy: Long -Term Perspectives', in *Proceedings of the FAO Rice Conference, 2004*, Food and Agricultural Organization, 2005.

IRRI, *Report of the Fifth External Programme and Management Review of International Rice Research Institute (IRRI)*, Food and Agricultural Organization, 1998.

Landes, David, *The Wealth and Poverty of Nations*, Little, Brown, 1998.

# Road Transport

All modes of transport contribute to the economy and economic development. There are several alternatives: air (>AVIATION); water (>CANALS: SHIPPING) and >RAILWAYS. In the field of transport and >ECONOMIC DEVELOPMENT there are many apparent contradictions of experience. >BRITAIN industrialized before the railway, in the American West, railways often preceded settlement (>AMERICAN WESTWARD EXPANSION) and development was heavily dependent upon them, as it was in some other countries, notably Germany where railways promoted heavy industrialization (>WESTERN EUROPE). Swiss development has apparently not been hampered by the country being landlocked, but early development in the USA clustered around the coasts and waterways. Robert Fogel, in a 1964 study (>RAILWAYS), argued that America could have achieved sustainable growth without rail by using other transport modes. The point which emerges is that the role of particular modes of transport varies according to geographical circumstances and technological development. One thing is clear and that is that road transport, the earliest form, is always essential because it is needed for connections to the other modes. There is plenty of evidence of the positive role of transport in development. For example, in Britain, pottery and iron making remote from navigable rivers grew enormously when canals were built in the 18th century. New roads or railways increase land values and stimulate activity. Improved transport contributes to the economy by linking markets, helping labour mobility, stimulating the exploitation of natural resources and in many other ways, including its effects on the demand for and production of transport equipment.

As Barker and Gerhold (1993) point out, because road transport has always been there and there is little early documentation on the volume of road traffic, it has tended to be neglected by economic historians. The Romans had built a large network of straight, paved roads on which the legions marched and used horse-drawn wagons and chariots, but these roads were neglected for 1,000 years. Roads were poor in the 17th century and mainly little more than dirt tracks. Travel was predominantly by foot for the poor and horseback for the well-to-do. There were pack-horse or mule trains for higher-value freight and push-carts and wagons, but long-distance traffic was generally seasonal because many roads were impassable in winter. Yet there was a surprising amount of wheeled road traffic, even in 15th-century Britain. For example, Barker and Gerhold cite research by Olive Coleman on the considerable cart traffic between London and Southampton in the mid-1400s and by D. F. Harrison on the number and quality of road bridges existing in 1530. They also show that, by the late 17th century, almost all English counties had direct carrier services (wagon or pack animal) to and from London with transfer points at such centres as Exeter and York for on-shipping to remoter places. The first scheduled passenger coach service began in 1637. At the end of the 17th century, half of the carrier services were by pack-horse and half by wagons, which travelled about 20–5 miles a day; pack-horses were faster (up to 30 miles a day). Numbers and capacity of wheeled traffic increased threefold and ton miles fivefold between 1690 and 1838 as roads improved. In the early part of this period particularly, the goods carried were mainly textiles but also some light manufactures and high-value agricultural products, such as butter. In the reverse direction, shop goods, groceries and draperies came from London. From the 1770s there was a huge increase in coach passenger traffic, which increased fourfold between 1773 and 1796. Turnpikes (tollways) improved roads and made possible large reductions in journey times. In 1754, it took four days to travel from London to York by the fastest coach, three days by 1761 and by 1836 it was down to 20 hours. Mail coaches, which also carried passengers, averaged 7¼ miles an hour and at the sound of their horns turnpike gates were opened.

Wheeled transport is very old indeed; it is thought that the wheel was invented somewhere between 3000 and 4000 BC, though rollers and dragged sleds were used before that. At first wheels were solid sections of tree trunks, later they were made up of planks and had fixed axles rotating between pegs. Spoked wheels came in about 2000 BC, then reinforced hubs and separate axles. The fuller development of wheeled transport awaited further technical improvements, such as the use of iron and steel rims for strengthening. There were a series of improvements to the suspension of vehicles, necessary because of the jolting of passengers and cargo on bad roads. Notable among these was the invention and patenting of the steel elliptical spring in London, in 1804, by Obadiah Elliot. With the axle suspended in this way, the ride became smoother and carriages more stable because a lower centre of gravity became possible. There was also a series of innovations in motive power from oxes, mules and donkeys and horses, bred respectively for strength and speed according to application. >STEAM POWER, electric and eventually reciprocating oil and petrol engines were developed

>AUTOMOBILE INDUSTRY. These technological advances both required and stimulated better road-building techniques and the construction of more roads. Originally, the impetus for these came from military requirements, as it had for the Romans but also in other countries, including France in the 18th century. Roman road building required heavy paving stones but without enforced labour this became prohibitively expensive. There were important early developments in France, but best documented is the work of three British pioneers in road-building technique. John Metcalfe (1717–1810) was a Yorkshireman, blinded by smallpox as a child, who emphasized drainage, with ditches each side of the road and a convex surface. He supervised the construction of 180 miles of turnpike and, incredibly, surveyed the route himself, tapping his way across country with a staff. Thomas Telford (1717–1834), a Scotsman, originally a stonemason, built bridges and docks, surveyed the Glasgow–Carlisle Road and was the engineer for the great coaching road between Holyhead and London begun in 1815. His emphasis was on strong foundations, gentle curvature and width of surface (Hill, 1985). Greatest of all was John Loudon Macadam (1756–1836), another Scotsman, who reduced the cost of road building. Macadam discovered that a foundation of large, heavy stones was unnecessary. He used closely packed angular stones (which would pass through a 2in ring) and packed 6–10in deep. Rolled by traffic (and eventually steamrollers) this material solidified into a compact, waterproof mass. Later roads were surfaced by a mixture of bitumen and gravel to lay dust and prevent stones from lifting, techniques still in use today. Macadam's ideas were controversial because, like

Metcalfe, who used packed heather underneath small stones and gravel to found roads across bogs, he believed in resilient, elastic, roads that, he argued, would last longer than very hard surfaces. His methods were eventually well proven and he was called the 'Colossus of Roads' by the coaching fraternity (Devereux, 1936).

Financing roads has never been easy and the earliest system was for them to be built and maintained by the communities through which they passed. From the 16th century in England, under the Acts of 1555 and 1563, local residents had to provide six days' labour a year and bigger landowners carts and horses. This system was also used in France, where it was called the *corvée* and has been used in many places, including Japan; it was adopted in the USA for a while. Obviously, the *corvée* was not popular because people did not want to leave their business and farms to do unpaid and arduous work which would benefit passing strangers. As traffic increased, turnpike trusts emerged to build or improve roads with borrowing powers secured on toll revenues. Individual legislation was necessary to authorize the imposition of tolls, the first being the Turnpike Act of 1663 for part of the Great North Road. The second Act did not come until 1695, but, in the 1750s and 1760s, 300 trusts were established along 10,000 miles of road. By 1830 the trusts covered 20,000 miles of road or 17 per cent of the main road network. There has been some controversy about the extent to which turnpikes increased road expenditure, since local parish activity would also have increased. Bogart (2005) concludes that turnpikes accounted for most of the fourfold increase in total road spending between 1730 and 1800 and that

road improvements contributed materially to the >INDUSTRIAL REVOLUTION IN BRITAIN. By 1840, the turnpike trusts faced calamity through competition from the railways (to the delight of the coaching trade and local residents, who always resented gates on their roads), but, as Clapham (1930) says, the trusts problems were also the result of incompetence, financial mismanagement and occasional corruption. Many of the trusts were also ignorant of modern road-building techniques, as Macadam's son explained to a committee of inquiry at the time, and there was no central authority to set standards. From 1871, as turnpike trust terms expired they were not renewed. The last trust ceased to exist in 1895, at Anglesey. On the eve of the Industrial Revolution, roads in Britain were recognized by foreign visitors as being much superior to those of other European countries, even France. Clapham, however, points out that this applied only to the main roads, the rest were mostly poor. Knowles (1932) contrasts the British road system at the time with that of France as being good in places, but 'piecemeal and patchy' as a direct result of the minimal role of the state in planning and building roads.

Within towns and cities there was a great deal of freight traffic because of the density of population. Much of this was carried by street porters and coster girls, the latter according to Barker and Gerhold (1993) bearing baskets of produce on their heads for distances of up to ten miles and loads of up to 200 pounds.In rural areas, in addition to horse and mule traffic, there were >PEDLARS carrying goods for sale from place to place. The movement of livestock from country to town was also very important. Barker and Gerhold say that much droving was off road in the pre->ENCLOSURE days, since cross-country droving avoided tolls and was kinder to animals' feet, while grazing was available. The numbers must have been very large: in 1771, 300,000 calves and cattle, 700,000 sheep and lambs and 240,000 pigs were slaughtered in London. The railways were eventually to capture much of this traffic for longer journeys, since droving was labour-intensive and there was costly weight loss on the hoof. However, there was a big increase in horse traffic serving the stations. By 1855 there were 800 horse-drawn buses running in London and also large numbers of hackneys and cabs, including the famous two-wheelers with the driver sitting high up at the back. The well-to-do had their own carriages. The last horse-drawn buses and trams disappeared from London in 1914 and 1915. At peak, there were 11,500 public horse-drawn cabs and carriers, creating considerable environmental problems with horse droppings. Barker and Gerhold cite >THOMPSON's estimate that the total number of horses not on farms was 487,000 in 1811 and 1.8 million in 1901, indicating that road traffic continued to grow vigorously well into the railway age. Bicycle usage expanded once the 'Penny-Farthing' gave way to the safety bicycle with a smaller front wheel and a diamond frame in the mid-1980s. Steam engines were used from 1850 for heavy haulage and for steam trams. Trolley buses introduced in Richmond, Virginia, in 1888 spread to Britain.

From 1900, motor cars and motor cycles rapidly took over road passenger traffic (>AUTOMOBILE INDUSTRY). By 1913, only 6 per cent of passengers in London travelled in horse-drawn vehicles. The substitution of motors for horses was much slower for freight because of capital costs and because sufficiently powerful engines took time to emerge, but commercial vehicle design and production was greatly stimulated by >WORLD WAR I. From the 1920s, trucks began to take over longer-distance freight. By 1938 motor vehicles had deprived railways of much of merchandise freight for distances up to 60 miles. This began the long process of the erosion of the railways and of public road transport in favour of trucks and private cars. In terms of total British domestic passenger miles, the share of rail was down to 17.4 per cent in 1952 and was only 5.6 per cent by 1992. Air traffic increased rapidly in this period, from 0.2–4.8 per cent. By 1992, therefore, road accounted for 93.7 per cent of passenger traffic and within that total, bus and coach travel fell sharply: the car and to a small extent taxis and motor cycles had taken over. For freight traffic, the shrinkage of the rail share was slower. In 1953, the share of road in total domestic freight transport was 36.0 per cent and by 1993, 64 per cent. There were also increases in the share of water traffic and pipelines for gas and bulk liquids.

>REGULATION of road transport began early. In order to protect road surfaces, there were restrictions on the size of teams and wheel dimensions from 1663. Public coaches were regulated in terms of the number of passengers travelling on top. Commercial vehicle drivers' working hours were regulated in the Road and Rail Traffic Act of 1933. There was a series of important changes in road administration. The Local Government Act of 1878 made County Councils responsible for maintaining main roads and Rural District Councils for rural roads. A Road Board was established in 1910 to supervise local authorities and act

in their place if necessary. This body became the Ministry of Transport in 1919. The Road Act of 1920 provided for the creation of the Road Fund with revenue from vehicle licences, new vehicle excise duties and drivers licences. This system of dedicated revenue did not last and raids on the substantial funds by other departments began in 1926. To the fury of the road lobby, the Finance Act of 1936 provided for money for the Road Fund to be voted by Parliament on an annual basis. The Ministry of Transport classified roads and made grants for improvements and in 1936 the Ministry became responsible for designated trunk roads and eventually motorways. An Act of 1930 had introduced a more comprehensive vehicle licensing system. The Transport Act of 1947, which nationalized the four railway companies, also took ownership of public road freight carriers, though these were partly denationalized between 1954 and 1956; much later the railways were to be privatized. Increasingly, after 1950, Traffic Commissioners controlled fares for buses and coaches. This and other provisions of the Act encouraged concentration of the industry into larger units.

The advent of motorways in Britain from the late 1950s gave a further boost to road transport. The first substantial length of motorway was the London to Birmingham M1, which was not fully completed until 1977 because of construction delays in the urban areas. By 1981 there were 1,447 miles of motorways in Britain and by 2000 this had been increased to 2,100 miles or 7 per cent of the total trunk-road network. In densely populated Britain, the progress of motorways was somewhat less than in other European countries. Charlesworth (1984), interestingly, establishes that much of the motorway network in

Britain followed the pattern of the Roman road system.

British road building after 1750, as we have seen, was largely a local affair and largely the result of private enterprise. In France, the state was firmly in charge. The 'ancien régime' had planned a national system and L'École des Ponts et Chaussées (the School of Roads and Bridges) was set up in 1767 and there were comprehensive improvements. Labour was provided by corvée, under which local inhabitants had to provide 30 days labour a year (five times more than in Britain). This system, which started in 1720–50, was abolished shortly before the 1789 Revolution, after which roads fell into disrepair again. With the accession of Napoleon, large amounts were spent on routes impériales (1807–12), straight, paved roads from Paris to Italy, Germany, Switzerland, Holland and Spain. Costs for these roads were borne by the state and the routes départementales were paid for by the local authorities (départements). The Restoration Kings and Louis Phillippe kept these roads in good repair and, according to Knowles (1932), by the 1830s France had the finest road system in the world. The development of the French road system after >WORLD WAR II has much in common with that of Britain. For example, the construction of a system of motorways began at about the same time. In 1961 there were only 255km of motorways in France but by 1986 this had expanded to 5,000km, though unlike Britain, France and Belgium, made extensive use of toll motorways to finance them. Despite substantial public investment in the rail system, the share of rail in total traffic has continued to fall in France, as elsewhere. As a percentage of freight ton/km, the rail share fell from 66 per cent in 1954 to 34 per cent in 1982, while that of road rose from 2–46 per cent.

Road transport in Germany was retarded before the railway age and afterwards by customs barriers, though some (Prussian) roads were built for military purposes. Between the world wars, however, there were spectacular developments. Although they were begun earlier, in 1933 the Nazi government set ambitious plans for a system of motorways or *auto-bahn*. By the outbreak of World War II, 3,200km of *autobahn* were in use, 2,000km were under construction and a further 3,200km planned. The share of road traffic in total traffic in Germany again followed a similar pattern to Britain and France. From 1954–83, for example, the share of road in inland freight rose from 18 to 43 per cent. Italy began a system of motorways (*autostrada*) long before Britain and France. The 80km of *autostrada* between Milan and Varese opened as early as 1925 and was followed by others. These roads were constructed by state-subsidized companies, with ownership reverting to the state after the financing period (>WESTERN EUROPE).

In the eastern >USA, road conditions in the 18th and early 19th centuries were similar to those in Britain earlier. In 1800, according to Atack and Passell (1994), a wagon from New York to Washington took four days (a 2½ hour journey by train today), while New York–Ohio was a two-week trek. These journey times led to high costs, restricted commerce and favoured water traffic, including trading with Europe in preference to domestic trade. In 1815, road freight cost 3 cents per ton/mile, boat (upstream) 6 cents and ocean only 1 cent. Turnpikes appeared following the >AMERICAN WAR OF INDEPENDENCE; these cut the costs of moving heavy freight

by half. In New England there were 2,800 miles of turnpikes by 1810 and by 1820, 10,000 miles. In the West it was a different matter, there were no alternatives but to travel by horseback, mule trains or wagons across trails (>AMERICAN WESTWARD EXPANSION). Inland waterways were very important (and still today account for about 15 per cent of freight traffic in the USA), but there were no rivers that allowed a cross-continental journey. Most of the great rivers in the USA flow north–south. Goods had to travel by water down the river and between rivers on roads or trails between the headwaters. There was a sea route from the East via the Gulf of Mexico but Mexico took advantage of it by imposing stiff customs duties. From the 1820s, it turned out to be cheaper to bring goods to St Louis and Independence on the Mississippi and Missouri rivers and then along the Arkansas River by pack and wagon trains to Santa Fe, a 700-mile five- to six-week trek. This was long before the immigrants developed the covered wagon trail to California in the 1840s, a hazardous journey which took five to six months. The transcontinental railway to San Francisco was not completed until 1869. Prior to this railways were limited to the region east of the Mississippi. It was the railway, not roads, which opened up the West, although there was a stage coach service from Independence to Santa Fe in 1849 followed by other services, including Pony Express (1860). The Federal government built the Cumberland Road, 830 miles between Williamsport in the East to Jefferson City in Missouri. It was begun in 1811 but did not reach Vandalia in Illinois until 1852, where it was terminated and interest lost in the project because of the coming of the railways. The National Pike, as it was called, was based on a famous report on internal transport improvements by Senator Albert Gallatin, but his nationwide Federal road project was not fully realized until the enormous 42,500-mile Interstate Highways programme began in the 1950s (Faulkner, 1960). However in 1916, the Federal government did begin assisting the states to build primary and secondary roads. The coming of the automobile age in the 1920s and 1930s had further stimulated local and state road-building activity throughout the country.

There were continuing technological developments. In the 1920s, the solid rubber tyres of motor vehicles were replaced with balloon tyres, which cushioned loads and reduced road damage. The 'fifth-wheel coupling', allowing a semi-trailer, was another important innovation permitting a better weight distribution and a doubling or tripling of cargo loads. It also allowed the more efficient use of costly tractor units, since the trailer could be left behind for loading and unloading while the tractor got on with other work. Inter-city roads, which covered 387,000 miles in 1921, were extended to 1.3 million miles by 1940. The interwar period also saw the building of famous highway tunnels and bridges such as the Holland Tunnel between New York and Jersey City and the Golden Gate Bridge connecting San Francisco with Marin County, California (John C. Spychalski's contribution, 'Transportation', in Bulliet, 1998). From the 1920s, with road developments and the continuing expansion of the automobile industry, there was tremendous growth in road transport. By 1970, the private automobile accounted for 86.9 per cent of inter-city domestic passenger traffic. Passenger air traffic in the USA grew much faster than in

Europe and by 1997 accounted for 17 per cent of the total, with a reduction in the automobile share to 81.3 per cent. Rail freight held up better than in Europe, with its share falling only from 39.8 per cent in 1970 to 38.1 per cent in 1997. Trucks increased their share of total inter-city freight from 21.3–27.8 per cent between 1970 and 1997. The total volume of freight rose by 87 per cent in the period and that of passenger traffic by 110 per cent. The share of water freight transport fell from 16.5 to 14.7 per cent and air freight's doubled to 0.4 per cent ('Transport Statistics of the United States').

In Japan, road transport was highly developed before industrialization. The feudal governments of the Shogun and Daimyo constructed a system of five roads radiating out from present-day Tokyo. Every 10km or so there were post stations under the control of a government official with horse, bearers and inns ready to meet the travel needs of the *samurai*, which had preference, or the public (Yamamoto, 1993). Effectively, these roads were turnpikes because charges were made but they were maintained by *corvée* labour. When the Meiji government came into power in 1868 transport standards were far behind those of the West at the time, where canals, railways and improved roads already existed. Government railway construction began in 1870 and in 1875 the system of messengers and freight companies that had developed was controlled by their association, the *Rikuun MotoKaisha*, and granted a government monopoly. In 1863 transport of goods by ox-driven freight wagons and rickshaw passenger traffic were allowed on the main roads. In 1869 horse-drawn vehicles were permitted (previously only horseback riders, or ox-driven carts were allowed). The number of freight wagons went from only 45 in 1875 to over 29,000 in 1890. There was a large road development programme and vehicle taxes were introduced to cover the greater part of the cost. Japan did not have a great age of horse-driven traffic as the West did. In 1910 there were 167,000 horse-drawn public service vehicles but 1.8 million carts and rickshaws and 240,000 bicycles. By 1892 there were 3,000km of railways (two-thirds government-owned). The technology of road construction and the amount of road building lagged behind the West until the 1920s and thereafter there was a large increase in motor traffic and a decline in the older forms of transport. By 1930, private motor vehicles had 41 per cent of the freight traffic and 12 per cent of passenger traffic over distances of 50km or less. Motor vehicles were imported or locally assembled but in May 1936 the government moved to stimulate domestic automobile construction. It was in this period that the Toyota and Nissan companies were founded. Private road freight and passenger operations were controlled and consolidated and these controls were not relaxed until after World War II. In the post-war period the decline of rail freight and passenger traffic in competition with road transportation seen elsewhere took place, though for freight, domestic shipping actually increased its share from 35.5–50.6 per cent between 1955 and 1980 at the expense of rail.

## References

Atack, Jeremy and Passell, Peter, *A New Economic View of American History from Colonial Times to 1940*, W. W. Norton, 1994.

Barker, Theo and Gerhold, Dorian, *The Rise and Rise of Road Transport 1700–1990*, Macmillan, 1993.

Bogart, Dan, 'Did Turnpike Trusts Increase Transportation Investment in Eighteenth Century England?', *Journal of Economic History*, 65, June, 2005.

Bulliet, Richard W. (ed.), *The Columbia History of the 20th Century*, Columbia University Press, 1998.

Charlesworth, George, *A History of British Motorways*, Thomas Telford, 1984.

Clapham, J. H., *An Economic History of Modern Britain: The Early Railway Age, 1820–1850*, Cambridge University Press (2nd edn), 1930.

Devereux, Roy, *John Loudon McAdam*, Oxford University Press, 1936.

Faulkner, Harold Underwood, *American Economic History*, Harper & Row, 1960.

Hill, C. P., *British Social and Economic History, 1700–1982* (1957), Hodder & Stoughton (5th edn), 1985.

Knowles, L. C. A., *Economic Development in the Nineteenth Century: France, Germany, Russia and the United States*, Routledge, 1932.

Yamamoto, Hirofumi (ed.), *Technological Innovation and the Development of Transportation in Japan*, United Nations University Press, 1993.

# Rostow, Walt Whitman

Economic historian and adviser to the US government, Rostow, who lived from 1916 to 2003, was born in New York City and educated at Yale and at Balliol College, Oxford, as a Rhodes scholar. He held academic posts at Cambridge (1949–50), Massachusetts Institute of Technology (1950–65) and, until his death, the University of Texas. During >WORLD WAR II, he served in the Office of Strategic Services. He was a foreign policy and economic adviser to presidents Johnson, Eisenhower and Kennedy. Rostow wrote about his career as an adviser in his posthumous book (Rostow, 2003).

In terms of economic history, Rostow was primarily interested in long-term economic change and is best known for his 'stages of growth' theory, though he also wrote on Kondratiev cycles (>BUSINESS CYCLES) and other matters, including contemporary political affairs such as the Cold War. *The Stages of Economic Growth* (Rostow, 1960) postulates that all societies lie within one of five categories:

(1) *The traditional society*: low income, predominately agricultural and characterized by lack of change in thought and modes of production.

(2) *Preconditions for take-off*: at this stage the idea spreads that economic progress is possible, perhaps from expanding commerce or other endogenous influences or from external colonization; entrepreneurs emerge. Some countries, Rostow argues, such as Australia, are 'born free' with few traditions to hold them back.

(3) *Take-off*: the interval when restrictions are finally removed and growth becomes a normal condition. Political groups dedicated to growth emerge and technological development in industry or agriculture leads to a doubling in the rate of investment from about 5–10 per cent. A few manufacturing sectors develop with high rates of growth.

(4) *The drive to maturity*: when the economy continues to become more sophisticated, export industries develop and the economy demonstrates a capacity to develop new industries on a continuous basis.

(5) *The age of high mass consumption*: when incomes have risen to the point where much of the population can command consumer durables and services.

Several writers anticipated stage theory, including those of the German Historical School and Colin Clark (1940), as well as >MARX. In his book, Rostow sharply distinguishes his theory from that of Marx. The difference, he says, is that, in his account, human motivation is not solely a consequence of a drive for power and property but 'an act of balancing alternative and often conflicting human objectives in the face of the range of choices men perceive to be open to them' (Rostow, 1960). In this respect he has more in common with Joseph >SCHUMPETER and later economists such as Douglass North (>INSTITUTIONS).

Both Rostow and his contemporary critic, >GERSCHENKRON, believed that there were a succession of take-offs in Europe and North America in the 19th century (Britain slightly earlier), but they differed in that Gerschenkron did not find that countries necessarily followed similar patterns of growth nor had the same 'preconditions' for doing so. Crafts and others have, in fact, successfully demolished the notion of take-off in the sense of a spurt of growth and shown empirically that there were no clear discontinuities in growth rates in the European >INDUSTRIAL REVOLUTIONS and that in England, in 1780–1830, there was no sign of a massive increase in investment. Rostow's theory is also difficult to apply to the developing world and now looks dated in that respect; for example, he put take-off dates at 1952 for both >CHINA and >INDIA, whereas it now appears that industrial acceleration came later in both cases. Latin America has for the most part not followed the paths described by Rostow.

Cypher and Dietz , in a recent reassessment of Rostow's stages of growth theory, say that, 'it has been his fate to serve as a lightning rod for criticisms of virtually all schools of thought in development economics' (2004) (>ECONOMIC DEVELOPMENT). Rostow did, however, stimulate thought beyond the narrow bands of macro-economic growth theory to embrace the modern political economy approach in which institutions are seen as a key factor in change. In the movement typified by Douglass North and Mancur Olson (1982), which began in the 1970s, Rostow's influence is clearly discernable and the notion of take-off does seem applicable to the cases of Japan and later to elsewhere in East Asia (>ASIAN MIRACLE). Rostow also opened up the debate on the impact of colonialism: was it a means for jolting countries out of traditional ways of thought, as he argued and was certainly the case for Japan, or did it lead to the entrenchment of backward notions and, after independence was regained, to the dominance of exploitative indigenous elites with few incentives for change, as it did in parts of Africa? It should be pointed out that Rostow recognized the limitations of his influential generalizations on the sweep of modern history and even referred to them himself in the book as 'limited and arbitrary'.

In *How it All Began*, Rostow (1975) develops some of the material in his earlier *Stages of Economic Growth* book and fills it out with examples of historical change around the world. The theme of the book is that the failure of traditional societies to grow lay not in lack of innovation or technological progress as such (as the example of early >CHINA with its development of gunpowder, printing and much else shows), but the lack of widespread application of these things and, above all, in a lack of

the conception that regular growth was possible. Traditional societies were subject to cycles of Malthusian pressures (>MALTHUS), wars and over-extension resulting from wars and fiscal crises. Widespread technological change was needed to escape from these cycles and this required political change, >COMMERCIAL REVOLUTION, >SCIENTIFIC REVOLUTION and an >AGRICULTURAL REVOLUTION.

In addition to the publications referred to here, Rostow also wrote many journal articles and a number of other books, including: *Essays on the British Economy in the Nineteenth Century* (1948), *The Processes of Economic Growth* (1952) and *The World Economy: History and Prospect* (1948).

## References

Clark, Colin, *Conditions of Economic Progress*, Macmillan, 1940.

Cypher, James M. and Dietz, James L., *The Process of Economic Development*, Routledge, 2004.

Olson, Mancur, *The Rise and Decline of Nations: Economic Growth, Stagflation and Social Rigidities*, Yale University Press, 1982.

Rostow, W. W., *The Stages of Economic Growth: A Non-Communist Manifesto*, Cambridge University Press, 1960.

Rostow, W. W., *How it All Began: Origins of the Modern Economy*, Methuen, 1975.

Rostow, W. W., *Concept and Controversy: Sixty Years of Taking Ideas to Market*, University of Texas Press, 2003.

# Russia

Russian society under the tsars was strictly hierarchical, with the nobility, the clergy and merchants at the top and the peasantry at the bottom, with membership of each class generally allotted by heredity. Those at the bottom bore a heavy weight from this social structure. The peasantry was sub-divided into seigniorial peasants (serfs), who worked on the land of the nobility, state peasants, church peasants and *appanage* peasants who worked on land owned by the tsar's family. Serfs made up about a half of the total peasant population and were bound to the land and to the landowner and subject to his jurisdiction. The landowner could shift his serfs about among his holdings and buy and sell them. The serfs were obligated to give service to the landowner either through labour time (*barshchina*) or through the payment of dues in money or goods (*obrok*). In the first half of the 19th century, *barshchina* peasants gave about one-third of their labour to their landlord and *obrok* peasants about one-third of their income. Serfs could also be deployed to work in factories. After 1724, peasants were also liable to a Poll Tax, which applied to all males other than members of the nobility and clergy and, from 1775, merchants. The peasantry was also subject to other taxes such as that on vodka, which alone extracted from their income double that of the Poll Tax. Peasants were, from the early 18th century through until the 1860s, also subject to conscription into the military, initially to serve for life and later for 20 years. Noblemen were exempted from conscription from 1762. Between 1720 and 1867, about 4.8 million peasants were drafted into the military such as to lead to a fall in the proportion of the peasantry in the total population from 90 per cent to 83 per cent. From the 1860s a number of reforms were introduced. In 1861, serfdom was abolished, conscription was extended to the nobility and made less arduous in 1874. The Poll Tax was replaced by indirect taxes between 1883 and 1887. Internal passports, which had been imposed in 1719, were not finally abolished entirely until 1906 (>PEASANTRY AND SERFDOM: Moon, 1999).

Russia was predominantly an agricultural nation and through the 18th and 19th centuries most of the arable land was used for the production of grain. The village commune (*mir*) held common possession of the land. Even if a peasant left the *mir*, he remained liable to his share of his *mir*'s tax payments. Each peasant household worked on strips of land allocated to it by the *mir* according to the number of people and workers in the household. The size and the locations of the strips were not fixed and periodical reallocation took place from every three to 12 years. Crops were planted through three fields in rotation, one for winter crop, one for summer crop and the third left fallow, extended to a four-field cycle with clover late in the 19th century. Subsistence farming was prevalent, with commercial farming developing only slowly from the 18th century, when about 10 per cent of the grain harvest was sold commercially, until the end of the 19th century, when it reached about 25 per cent. Growth in output was achieved not so much by improvements in productivity but predominantly by the extension of the land under cultivation, which doubled between the 18th and the 19th century, as also did the peasant population. In addition to farming, the peasants also worked in handicraft trades such as pottery and metalwork, as well as processing agricultural and timber products.

Following the emancipation of the serfs in 1861, the peasants were granted land but were obliged to pay compensation in return and this compensation amounted in effect to a tax in that it was based upon a valuation of the land which was at the time excessive. The redemption payments arising from this were eventually written off in 1905. In 1906, Stolypin, the prime minister, issued a decree that introduced reforms which enabled peasants to own the freehold of their land, have their strips collected into one plot and made it possible to leave the *mir* without its approval. The decree was confirmed by laws in 1910 and 1911 (Rösener, 1994).

Many historians have argued that there was a serious agrarian crisis in Russia from 1870 to the early 20th century and Alexander >GERSCHENKRON in particular supported this view. Gerschenkron believed that the crisis stemmed from the 1861 reforms which gave the land to the *mir* and not to individual peasants and made the *mir* responsible for paying the redemption payments on the mortgaged value of the land. The *mir* was made in effect a tax collection service. A peasant had to settle his share of the debt before he could leave the *mir* and this, coupled with the initial excessive valuation of the land, resulted in a lack-lustre land market. The periodic reallocation of a peasant's land holding was also a disincentive to him to improve it and farming in multiple strips was wasteful and inefficient. >FAMINES in the 1890s and in 1901 were indicative of the precarious nature of the peasants' subsistence farming. As a result of the constraints on the rural economy there was little movement of labour into industry and no domestic consumer market was able to develop which would have supported a vigorous industrial expansion. What Gerschenkron called the 'Asian Model', in which industrialization was forced by government intervention, induced lower rural standards

of living by the consequent diversion of resources.

From a re-evaluation of national statistics of the period, Gregory (1982, 1994) concluded differently. There was no doubt that there were areas in rural Russia in which the peasants suffered from severe poverty but in other areas progress was such that in aggregate the agricultural economy did make significant progress after 1861. In the period 1883/97 to 1909/13, the total real national product of Russia grew by 3.2 per cent per annum with an increase in population of 1.6 per cent per annum yielding a growth in per capita income of 1.6 per cent which can be compared favourably with other countries at the time. Between 1860 and 1913, the population of Russia grew from 74 million to 170 million. Given that agriculture engaged about 75 per cent of Russia's labour force and contributed to about 57 per cent of the National Income, there is small likelihood that agriculture was in a serious nationwide crisis during this time as this would not be consistent with such growth. Moreover, real agricultural wages and the amount of grain consumed on the farms per capita were also increasing during the period, both of which were indicators of rising living standards. Furthermore, Russia became a major international supplier of >GRAIN and in 1909/13 was the top world exporter of wheat, accounting for 24 per cent of the total, compared with the >USA at 15 per cent. The rural economy was also helped by the fact that from 1900–13 the prices of agricultural goods rose by 41 per cent but the general price level by only 29 per cent. The *mir* regulations were not strictly applied in practice and after 1861 there was a significant migration of labour from the land into industry. Nevertheless, the commune system, as Gerschenkron said, did stifle incentives to improve agricultural productivity.

Another area of debate has been whether and to what degree Russia experienced an >INDUSTRIAL REVOLUTION before 1913; whether the test applied was that of 'take-off', in the manner of >ROSTOW, or signs of spurts of accelerated industrial output, as postulated by Gerschenkron.

Through the first half of the 19th century, the development of industry in Russia was slow and hesitant. Industrialization was handicapped by the employment of a labour force that was not free and less than enthusiastic. About 54 per cent of industrial workers were *obrok* serfs and in cotton textile enterprises this proportion was as high as 95 per cent. Cotton textiles emerged as the major industrial growth area but did not reach its full potential because of low productivity and a reluctance to invest in labour-saving machinery. Similarly, the iron and >COAL industry failed to modernize and output languished, with enterprise not helped by stifling government bureaucratic controls. By the 1860s, Russia was still relying on imports for its requirements for manufactures and there was little sign that industry had yet spurted ahead or taken off.

The emancipation of the serfs in 1861 did initiate the easing of significant constraints on industry but it was the expansion of the >RAILWAYS that was the real spur to and a necessary condition for the industrialization of Russia. Earlier industrial development was severely constrained by the vast distances across which resources such as iron ore and coal had to be transported and over which communication between markets had to be made. The means to overcome such obstacles had to await the development of the railways, as the waterways and the road network

were inadequate to the task. In 1874 the rail network reached 18,220km, 30,596km had been built by 1890 and 38,984km by 1913. The railways were initially developed by private industry but with government assistance, but by 1913 two-thirds were state-run and it was the largest railway network in Europe. The construction of the railways gave the communications network for freight and people which was essential for the Russian economy but it also generated a spin-off demand for plant and materials that stimulated domestic producers and, by 1890, gave employment to 252,000 workers (Falkus, 1972).

From 1877, the government switched its policy from the previous free trade stance to a protectionist one and increased import tariffs through the 1880s and the 1890s, raising the revenue from duties as a percentage of the value of imports from 12.8 per cent in 1869/76 in stages to 33 per cent in the 1890s in order to assist the establishment of domestic industry (>INTERNATIONAL TRADE). The government encouraged foreign investment and, consistent with this policy, adopted the >GOLD STANDARD in 1897. The >COAL, >IRON AND STEEL industries and >OIL all expanded with the assistance of foreign finance and expertise. Development was predominantly in heavy industry but there was an upturn in the progress of the consumer goods industries in the five years to >WORLD WAR I as consumers began to replace the government in creating the market for domestic industrial production, so shifting industrial development from the 'Asian' forced variety of Gerschenkron to an at least incipient self-sustaining growth economy. There is no doubt that there was a change of pace. It has been estimated that industrial production increased by about 5 per cent per annum from 1860–1913, compared with the growth in population of 1.5 per cent per annum (Falkus, 1972). By 1913, Russia had progressed industrially and begun to close the gap with the leading industrialized countries of Europe and had achieved notable successes. The cotton textile industry was comparable to that of Germany and in 1900 Russia produced 45 per cent of the world output of oil, second to the USA, which produced 51 per cent of the total. Less relative progress had been made, however, in coal and iron and steel production by 1913. Moreover, in 1913 the primary sector still accounted for 58.6 per cent of total employment, compared with, for instance, Germany with 36.8 per cent and Russia was the poorest of the major countries in Europe, having an income per capita which was 70 per cent below that of Britain. By 1913, Russia was possibly about to 'take off'. But its industrial development started too late to reach maturity before it was overwhelmed by conflict.

From August 1914, Russia was at war with Austria–Hungary, Germany and the Ottoman Empire; in spite of some successes, the Russian army suffered from considerable losses in its campaign against the Axis invasion and the economy was subject to severe disruption (>WORLD WAR I). A revolution in February/ March 1917 deposed the Tsar and, in October 1917, the Bolsheviks under Lenin took control of government and signed an armistice with Germany in December 1917. A civil war ensued which lasted until 1920, during which the Bolshevik Government's priority was to mobilize its available resources for its survival. War Communism emerged as an economic policy which was driven by necessity though interrelated

with Marxist ideology (>MARX). Various institutions were set up to control the economy, designed to diminish and eventually abolish the part played by the private sector. In 1917, a Supreme Council of National Economy (VSNKh) was formed which was responsible for the 'organization of the national economy and state finance' and had 'the right of confiscation, requisition, sequestration, compulsory syndication of the various branches of industry, trade and other measures of production, distribution and state finance' (Nove, 1992). The Council worked through Regional Councils for local control. In 1920, the Council of Labour and Defence (STO) was established as a supreme body over the VSNKh which began to draw up national plans, such as the GOELRO for the electrification of the USSR (>ELECTRICITY). In 1922, four Socialist Republics were united into the Union of Soviet Socialist Republics which subsequently also absorbed others until by 1990 there were 20 autonomous republics in the Union (Nove, 1992).

The state took over the ownership of the land with each peasant allocated only the amount which he could cultivate himself. The conscription of labour services and the direction of labour were introduced. All banks, the railways and the merchant navy were nationalized and the government reneged on foreign debts. In 1918, a decree nationalized factories, although initially it did not apply to complete industries but only to specific plants, which were nationalized by local decision. Surplus grain was confiscated from the peasants by force in order to feed the army and the urban population, with the result that agricultural output fell and serious shortages emerged. The rouble collapsed in hyper-inflation as the government had printed money excessively to finance the war, so that by 1921 prices were 16,800 times higher than in 1914 and barter became common. Transactions between state enterprises were made as book entries and not in cash and workers were paid in goods not money. This 'naturalization' or demonetization of the economy, although not an intentional part of economic policy, was nevertheless seen by some as an inevitable step towards the destruction of capitalism and the creation of a Marxist society. However, the combination of the vicissitudes of civil war, demanding immediate practical solutions, mixed with the displacement of management expertise by assorted inept government organizations and workers' councils, led to an economy on the brink of collapse. The population of Russia had suffered serious losses and in 1922 had dropped to a low of 152 million, compared with the population of 156 million in 1913 (Maddison, 1995). In 1920, industrial production was only 20 per cent of the level of output in 1913, agriculture only 64 per cent and foreign trade was virtually non-existent (Gregory, 1994). There was a drought and the grain harvest fell to 43 per cent below the 1909/13 average in 1921; there was a severe famine and millions died. Peasant discontent led to riots and, finally, the mutiny of sailors at Kronstadt in 1921, which convinced Lenin to change tack and initiate the New Economic Policy.

The government introduced measures to appease the peasants. The compulsory acquisition of grain was replaced by a tax, initially paid in kind for each product and later by money, which was set low enough to leave the peasants a surplus which they were not obliged to sell to the government agencies. The peasants were also allowed to take on labour

and lease land. While the large banks and heavy industry remained nationalized and foreign trade remained under government control, other smaller enterprises were privatized and were free to hire labour. The private sector grew and, by 1922, retail enterprises accounted for about 75 per cent of retail turnover. The New Economic Policy (or NEP) enabled the rise of the profit-seeking market dealer or 'Nepman' but was accompanied by a ban on all political parties except the Bolsheviks.

A new currency based on gold, the 'chervonets', was issued which eventually replaced the rouble in 1924 (the rouble was restored in 1947) and the state budget brought into surplus in 1924/5. By 1927/8 the economy had shown strong recovery, although there is some dispute as to whether it had yet surpassed the pre-war levels of National Income (Davies, 1998). Compared with Russia under the tsars, there were also improvements in welfare such as an eight-hour day, equal pay for women and greater income equality. However, this equality, which had been achieved in the countryside by the removal of the landowner and the reduction in the holdings of the kulaks (a derogatory term for rich peasants), led to a conflict with the government's policy aims. The share of output coming from the peasant holdings on to the market fell to about 16 per cent compared with about 22 per cent or so in 1913 and foreign trade remained depressed because of the lack of agricultural commodities for export. The pre-war surplus coming to market had been proportionately more from the landowners and kulaks because of their greater and therefore more productive size of holdings. In effect, the land reform had reduced agricultural efficiency by extending subsistence farming and such agriculture could not support the government's ambitions to develop industry.

Moreover, the price of manufactures rose relative to that of agricultural commodities in what became known as the 'Scissors Crisis', because the increasing gap between the two price indexes looked like the opening of the blades of a pair of scissors. It was believed that this would induce the peasants to cut further their supplies because of the turn against them in their terms of trade but agricultural output had to be maintained to feed the army and the towns and to support the Bolshevik policy of industrialization, for which agricultural raw material inputs were needed as well as export revenues to finance imports of manufactures. The government reacted by setting price caps on industrial goods which led to shortages so that the peasants had to buy from the *Nepmen*, whose prices were as much as 30 per cent higher than those of the government-controlled retailers. It was not surprising, therefore, that the *Nepmen* were regarded as enemies of the state. Speculation became a crime in 1926, followed by private trade in 1930. In 1926/7 the government lowered grain procurement prices to the point where the peasants stopped selling to state agencies, so that in 1929 the government restored compulsory quotas. Therefore, in spite of the fact that by 1928 the NEP had succeeded in delivering a strong industrial and agricultural recovery, it was abandoned and eventually replaced by government control through central planning (Gregory, 1994). The share of the private sector in National Income had reached about 54 per cent in 1925/6 but this had fallen to 39 per cent in 1929 and to about 9 per cent in 1932 (Nove, 1992).

The NEP was regarded by the Party as a necessary but temporary policy to appease the peasants at a particular time, but the rise of peasant prosperity and the flourishing *Nepmen*, nurtured within a free market, conflicted with the Party's Marxist ideology. The Scissors Crisis demonstrated the painful fact that the free market peasantry could sabotage the state-controlled industrial sector. It was through the state encouragement of industry that economic and social development was to be achieved but this could not be done under NEP without creating an agricultural crisis and a dangerous confrontation with the peasants. Preparations for the first Five-Year Plan began in 1927. Central to economic policy was industrialization through the development of heavy industry in conformity with Marxist ideology, but also the perceived vulnerability of the only Bolshevik state to attack from the more advanced capitalist countries. Stalin had become General Secretary of the Party in 1922 and he eventually succeeded in transforming the authority of the Party into an invulnerable personal dictatorship. Stalin made the economic objectives clear in 1931: 'We are fifty or a hundred years behind the advanced countries. We must make good this distance in ten years. Either we do so, or we shall go under' (Nove, 1992). (A prescient statement as the Soviet Union was invaded by Germany in 1941.)

It was necessary to find the means of transferring resources to meet the investment needed to meet the planned objectives of industrialization and it was the surplus obtainable from agriculture from which it was sought. Compulsory acquisition of the peasants' surplus backed up by the threat of fines, imprisonment and confiscation of property and the collectivization of holdings into state farms (*kolkhozy*) was launched in 1929. The deportation of *kulaks* began and reached a peak in 1930/1, amounting to about 300,000 households or 1.5 million people. The purpose of this treatment of the *kulaks* was to encourage peasants into the collectives by the threat of being deported by being accused of being *kulaks* and by reducing the incentive to remain outside by abolishing the existence of a once relatively wealthy class to which they could aspire. It did have the effect, however, of depriving agriculture of valuable expertise. By 1936, 90 per cent of all peasant households were in collectives. Collectivization was an agricultural disaster, compounded by the excessive procurement quotas, which in 1931 and 1932 left insufficient food for the peasants and their livestock to survive. The result was a devastating famine in which about 7 million people perished (>CHINA). The standard of living of all workers, both in agriculture and in industry, slumped following a rapid rise in prices between 1928 and 1933. The prime objective of Soviet policy, however, was achieved in that a sound base for the further development of industry was established, paid for by the forced savings of the peasants. Recovery got underway after 1933 and it has been estimated that National Income per capita grew by about 55 per cent between 1932 and 1937 and there were improvements in labour productivity both in agriculture and industry. Some aspects of a market economy were allowed; crops, surplus to government procurement, could be sold in a 'collective farm market' and income could be spent in state shops. Workers could change employment but there was growing resort to forced labour, which is estimated to have reached 3 million by 1939 (Davies, 1994). Priority was given to defence expenditure and the

number in the military increase from 1.5 million to 5 million between 1937 and 1941, when Germany invaded. Russia suffered the most severely in the war with a loss of as many as 27 million lives, with 25 per cent of its assets destroyed (>WORLD WAR II).

After the war, there were 25 million people homeless, agricultural output and non-military industrial production were each down by a third compared with pre-war and in 1946 the agricultural harvest failed because of poor weather – the ensuing famine led to 1 million deaths. The fourth Five-Year Plan (1946–50) period saw a substantial recovery in industry to levels in excess of the pre-war period as the plan targets were surpassed with, again, the capital goods industries given priority in the allocation of resources. The administration of planning was reorganized so that there were 33 ministries responsible for industry and construction, 12 more than in 1939, in addition to those for agriculture and other sectors, all of which reported to the Kremlin.

Agriculture, however, suffered from Stalin's determination to force the peasantry to finance industrial development. There was no increase in procurement prices for agricultural products in spite of the escalation of inflation. For instance, the price the peasants were paid for potatoes was less than the cost of delivery, which they were obliged to undertake to meet their quota obligations. They had to supply their milk quota even if they had no cow. Agriculture was planned by direct edict from the centre to the finest detail. The collectives were told what to plant in defiance of local conditions (Nove, 1992). Agriculture was also bedevilled by Stalin's total acceptance and approval of the unscientific work of Lysenko, who was the director of the Institute of Genetics of the Academy of Sciences of the USSR from 1940–65. Lysenko believed in the theory of the inheritance of acquired characteristics postulated by the French biologist Lamarck. For instance, he believed that if you chilled wheat it would grow in winter, which was a very attractive idea for Siberia. On top of this, the taxes levied on the collectives were increased in 1948. In 1952, the production of grain was 4 million tonnes less than in 1940 and there were 3 million fewer cows (Nove, 1992).

Major changes in the allocation of planned resources were delayed until Khrushchev came to power on Stalin's death in 1953. The procurement prices for agricultural products were substantially increased, transport costs were borne by the state, the debts of the collectives were written off, taxes reduced and direction from the centre eased. Between 1953 and 1956, the area of cultivated land was increased by 36 million hectares through the extension to fallow and virgin land, which required the migration of 300,000 people. By 1960, 8.6 million people were employed in agriculture. In the following plan, which was for the seven years, 1959–65, the emphasis was on the development of the chemical industry, which had been neglected and in realigning the fuel industry towards oil and natural gas.

In the 1970s, there was a further stimulus to agriculture with an increase in its share of investment to 26 per cent compared with 20 per cent in 1961/5, and there was an increase in output. There was, however, still a shortage of labour on the farms and up to 15 million people had to be drafted in for the harvests. There was a shortfall compared with target for the outcomes of the 1971–5 plan period because of failures in agriculture and construction. The gap between plan and actuality widened in the period 1976–80. In the plan period 1981–5, the plan again failed to meet reality. From 1988, the economy was in decline and in 1990 National Income fell by 4 per cent, industrial production by 1.2 per cent and agriculture by 2.3 per cent. In the first half of 1991, National Income fell by 10 per cent compared with the first half of 1990, industrial production by 6 per cent and agricultural production by 11 per cent. Oil output in 1991 was half that of two years earlier (Nove, 1992). Attempts were made by Gorbachev to introduce reforms through *perestroika* (restructuring) and *glasnost* (openness), but he was met by opposition from entrenched, privileged officials. As the authority of the central government weakened, the crisis deepened until the Republics declared their independent sovereignty and the USSR disintegrated.

The Marx/Lenin vision of the inevitability of evolution through economic development to a classless communist society proved, in practice, to be unachievable, essentially because it had to be purged of all traces of free markets. As the economy progressed it increased in complexity and, consequently, the necessary physical planning of the command system simply could not match the signalling efficiency of prices in a free market in the allocation of resources. Further, the central direction of the planning system destroyed local and personal initiative and was fraught with errors of internal consistency so that input directives often did not match those for outputs. The result was subservience to the Plan directives, which led to inertia in the introduction of new procedures and technical innovation. Finally, the discouragement of open discussion and criticism led to the perpetuation of errors.

From 1992, Russia became the Russian Federation and the government under Yeltsin pursued a policy of privatization of state enterprises and the abolition of restraints on free enterprise, but there was a financial crisis in 1998 and the government defaulted on foreign debt. However, there was then a rebound and GDP grew at an average of 6.7 per cent per annum between 1999 and 2005, assisted by substantial gains in its terms of trade because of rises in the price of >OIL and gas which accounted for 62 per cent of total exports in 2005 (OECD, 2006).

## References

Davies, R. W., *Soviet Economic Development from Lenin to Khrushchev*, Cambridge University Press, 1998.

Davies, R.W., Harrison, Mark and Wheatcroft, S.G. (eds), *The Economic Transformation of the Soviet Union, 1913–1945*, Cambridge University Press, 1994.

Falkus, M. E., *The Industrialisation of Russia, 1700–1914*, Macmillan, 1972.

Gerschenkron, Alexander, *Economic Backwardness in Historical Perspective*, Harvard University Press, 1962.

Gerschenkron, Alexander, 'Agrarian Policies and Industrialisation: Russia, 1861–1917', *Cambridge Economic History of Europe*, 6, Cambridge University Press, 1965.

Gregory, Paul R., *Russian National Income, 1885–1913*, Cambridge University Press, 1982.

Gregory, Paul R., *Before Command. An Economic History of Russia from Emancipation to the First Five-Year Plan*, Princeton University Press, 1994.

Maddison, Angus, *Monitoring the World Economy 1820–1992*, OECD, 1995.

Moon, David, *The Russian Peasantry 1600–1930: The World the Peasants Made*, Longman, 1999.

Nove, Alec, *An Economic History of the USSR, 1917–1991*, Penguin, 1992.

OECD Economic Surveys, *Russian Federation*, Volume 2006/17, November, 2006.

Rösener, Werner, *The Peasantry of Europe*, Blackwell, 1994.

# S

## Schumpeter, Joseph Aloisius

Schumpeter, who lived from 1883 to 1950, was an Austrian/American economic theorist and historian whose provocative writings still figure frequently in academic discussions of >ENTREPRENEURSHIP, innovation, monopoly (>ANTI-TRUST) and the nature of >CAPITALISM. Schumpeter is probably more widely appreciated now than he was during his lifetime since, as his two excellent biographers, Swedberg (1991) and McCraw (2007) point out, he was concerned with many of the preoccupations of our own time and, in particular was dismissive of crude Keynesianism (>KEYNES). Schumpeter's basic and seminal ideas on the role of entrepreneurship in economic development appeared originally in *The Theory of Economic Development'* (hereafter TED) in 1911, but this book was not translated into English until it was in its second edition in 1934 and did not achieve wide currency until the publication of *Capitalism, Socialism and Democracy* (hereafter CSD) (Schumpeter, 1942), the book which introduced the term 'creative destruction'.

TED was not Schumpeter's first significant work (though it is the best known of his technical works); it was preceded by *The Nature and Essence of Theoretical Economics* (1908) and followed by *Economic Doctrine and Method: An Historical Sketch* (1914) and *Business Cycles* (1939). The long delays in the appearance of English translations of these books shows how long it took for Schumpeter's genius to be recognized; TED was not available in English until 1954, by which time Schumpeter was living in the USA and writing in English. CSD, his most popular book, ran into three editions. His monumental *History of Economic Analysis* appeared posthumously in 1954 and was completed by his third wife, Elizabeth Boody Schumpeter, who was also an economist. In addition to these books, Schumpeter also wrote a number of important articles, most of them conveniently collected in *Essays* by Clemence (1951) and in *Ten Great Economists* (Schumpeter, 1952).

TED addressed 'the question how the economic system generates the force that incessantly transforms it' (Schumpeter's introduction to the 1937 Japanese edition). He believed that crises (cycles) were an essential part of the capitalist process of development, not the result of exogenous shocks as most economists believed. In Schumpeter's view, the capitalist system in equilibrium had no tendency to cyclical movement, though, in this sense of Walrasian equilibrium, it could still grow as the consequence of population expansion and capital accumulation. Cycles came about, as he was to elaborate later, as a result of 'swarms of innovations', which led businessmen to need expanded bank credit and which as a result of competition and falling prices as innovations were emulated, set in train forces which led to the downturn. It was this 'creative destruction' which allowed the capitalist system to advance to higher stages of development, or, as Schumpeter put it, to superior states of equilibrium. All this sounds very abstract and theoretical and it was. Schumpeter was not concerned with short-term cycles but only with longer-term movements and his theory offered little of immediate practical value to policy-makers. Schumpeter was never much interested in remedies, only with 'science' (see Peter Hammon, 'Schumpeter and the Economic Problems of Today', in Seidl, 1984) and he admitted that the process he described could be and was disrupted or aggravated by institutional factors (>INSTITUTIONS). This was the case with the 1930s depression which, he wrote, 'would have been due anyhow' through the need to adapt to 'changes in the method of production in the widest sense' following World War I, but was intensified and prolonged by an agrarian recession on top of an industrial one, price rigidities, war reparations, monetary policy and other factors ('The Present World Depression, A Tentative Diagnosis', in Clemence, 1951). In fact, an assumption of his enormous book, *Business Cycles*, which elaborated his cyclical theory, was that there would be no change in such institutional factors. Schumpeter intended to follow this book with another on the influence of institutions, but never wrote it.

In Schumpeter's theory, the entrepreneur, someone whose function is 'the carrying out of new combinations' is the key figure. Entrepreneurs were of several kinds, of which the purest was the business founder, though others could play the same role, including, as his views on >ENTREPRENEURSHIP developed later on, salaried managers. Qua entrepreneurs, these people were never risk-takers as such, they were leaders driven to change things

rather than pursuing profit and typically using other people's (capitalists') money. The entrepreneur was not an inventor, though he could combine that role as with that of capitalist; he was essentially someone who got things moving. In CSD Schumpeter was to launch the notion that in the modern economy innovation and change were to become routine in the monopolistic large corporation and carried out by salaried managers and staff in substitution for the traditional entrepreneur-founder (>USA). These views were to be very influential (for example, in the work of John Kenneth Galbraith), though attempts to verify the innovative superiority of monopolies empirically have not been very successful, because of the continuing role in innovation by >SMALL AND MEDIUM ENTERPRISES run by owner-managers. Nevertheless, Schumpeter's later characterization of entrepreneurship is now widely accepted as being true of at least a large part of the economy (see Baumol, 2002, who also accepts that radical innovations are often made outside large corporations). The other well-known theme of CSD, of course, was that capitalism would gradually evolve into socialism, not as a result of violent revolution as Marx had predicted, but through a weakening of the entrepreneurial spirit and internal criticism of the basis of capitalism. This prediction has not been borne out. The emergence of the highly regulated mixed economy in all advanced countries has given some credence to Schumpeter's thesis, but the entrepreneurial spirit shows little signs of weakening (see Arnold Heertje, 'Schumpeter's Model of the Decay of Capitalism', in Frisch, 1981).

Schumpeter wrote much else of importance, indeed everything he wrote is studded with original ideas, the force of which is enhanced by his vivid and assertive writing style. An example of his far-sighted minor work is *Die Krise des Steuerstaates* (1918) (translated as 'The Crisis of the Tax State' in Swedberg, 1991). This article traces the origin of the modern state to the needs of kings and princes for funds for war and other purposes and anticipated the impact which, under the ever-expanding demands of the public for more services from the state, excessive taxation could have upon the functioning of the capitalist system and indeed upon the survival of the state itself. It can be seen, as pointed out at the beginning of this entry, that Schumpeter, long ago, was wrestling with most of the economic and political issues – growth, innovation, the role of the state – which concern us today. He was not content to limit himself to narrow economic issues (he did not consider that the state was an economic phenomenon). Influenced by Max >WEBER, Schumpeter was concerned to widen economics to *sozialokonomik* – including economic sociology. His *History of Economic Analysis* tried to be a history of *sozialokonomik*, and he wrote there that: 'Scientific economics, or political economy as it used to be called has four fundamental fields: economic history, statistics, economic theory and economic sociology'. He considered economic history to be the most important of these and commented that 'most of the fundamental errors currently committed in economic analysis are due to lack of historical experience'.

Schumpeter's whole approach put him in opposition to >KEYNES. In his obituary of Keynes, Schumpeter assessed *The General Theory* as a short-run theory of depression containing many 'inadmissible' simplifications, including the assumption that methods of production and the capital stock do not change and 'All the phenomena incident to creation and change, that is to say, the phenomena that dominate the capitalist process, are thus excluded from consideration' ('John Maynard Keynes (1883–1946)', in Schumpeter, 1952). >MARX on the other hand, whose model *was* one of long-term change, wrongly implied that the economy determined social structure, whereas the one interacted with the other, while his theory of labour value was 'dead and buried' (Swedberg, 1991).

Schumpeter's vivid and assertive writing, if sometimes long-winded and obscure, is quite unique and his position as one of the great economists is secure. His life was quite eventful. He was born in Triesch, then part of the Austro-Hungarian Empire, and educated in Vienna, graduating in 1906 with a degree in law. He briefly practiced law in Cairo then lectured at Czernowitz (now in the Ukraine), where he produced TED. In 1911 he moved to the University of Graz as a full professor. In 1913 he was an Austrian exchange professor at Columbia University. After the collapse of the Austro-Hungarian Empire he was briefly Minister of Finance for the newly founded Austrian Republic in 1919, only to become the chairman of a bank and to lose his own money (largely borrowed) in some speculative business ventures. In 1925 he became a professor at Bonn University and, in 1927–8, a visiting professor at Harvard. He returned permanently to Harvard in 1932 as Professor of Economics, became an American citizen and remained there until his death in 1950.

### References

Baumol, William J., 'The Free Market Innovation Machine: Analysing the

*Growth Miracle of Capitalism'*, Princeton University Press, 2002.

Clemence, Richard V. (ed.), *Essays of J. A. Schumpeter*, Addison-Wesley, 1951.

Frisch, Helmut (ed.), *Schumpetarian Economics*, Praeger, 1981.

McCraw, Thomas K., *Prophet of Innovation: Joseph Schumpeter and Creative Destruction*, Harvard University Press, 2007.

Schumpeter, Joseph A., *The Theory of Economic Development: An Enquiry into Profits, Capital, Credit, Interest and the Business Cycle* (1911), in English, Harvard University Press, 1934.

Schumpeter, Joseph A., *Business Cycles: A Theoretical, Historical and Statistical Analysis of the Capitalist Process*, McGraw Hill, 1939.

Schumpeter, Joseph A., *Capitalism, Socialism and Democracy* (1942), Harper Brothers (3rd edn), 1950.

Schumpeter, Joseph A., *Ten Great Economists: From Marx to Keynes*, George Allen & Unwin, 1952.

Schumpeter, Joseph A., *History of Economic Analysis*, Oxford University Press, 1954.

Seidl, Christian (ed.), *Lectures on Schumpeterian Economics*, Springer-Verlag, 1984.

Swedberg, Richard, *Joseph A. Schumpeter: His Life and Work*, Polity Press, 1991.

# Seaports

The world's seas and inland waterways have provided the natural network for the transport of goods since societies began to trade. Ports have been established to make access to these networks possible and to provide the accommodation and services appropriate and necessary for the ships (>SHIPPING) carrying the trade. The history of ports is one of their continual adjustment to the shifting balance of pressures impinging on them from the changes in the size and configuration of vessels, the volumes and direction of trade and their location and spread of their hinterland.

As international trade grew in the 17th and 18th centuries, port cities grew also. Before the impact of the >INDUSTRIAL REVOLUTION on urbanization, major centres of population growth were around those cities in which a port was located and so had access to international, ocean-going and national, coastwise, transport systems. By the mid-19th century, about 40 per cent of the world's major cities were seaports (Lee and Lawton, 2002) and this close association of ports and their urban environment continued into the 20th century, as could be seen in ports such as London, Liverpool, Bordeaux, Marseilles, Amsterdam, Rotterdam, Calcutta, Mumbai (Bombay), Shanghai, Hong Kong, Singapore, Tokyo, Osaka, New York and Los Angeles. In their early development, ports were an important focal point for the reception and dissemination of information but were also corresponding receptors and transmitters of disease. They were prone to overcrowding with a continual inflow of migrants from the surrounding country looking for work. It was common practice to employ workers casually. This meant that accommodation had to be sought close to the quayside to ensure early arrival each day to stand a chance of being picked for work and there was a consequential persistent inadequate supply of housing to meet the demand.

In the 18th century, through the 19th century and into the 20th century London was the world's pre-eminent city port, benefiting from the leading position that >BRITAIN had in international trade but also from the expansion of its coastal trade, particularly >COAL. In the mid-18th century, about 650,000 tons of coal were arriving coastwise into the Thames every year from the North East of England and by 1830 this traffic had reached about 20 million tons. At the beginning of the 18th century, somewhere between 70 per cent and 80 per cent of the total British foreign trade was loaded or discharged in London and, in addition, nearly 90 per cent of its re-export business. As British trade with North America grew, the ports on the west coast of Britain such as Liverpool and Bristol captured a higher proportion of traffic. By the beginning of the 20th century London's share of trade had fallen to about 30 per cent to 35 per cent but nevertheless it remained the leading British port and port city worldwide. This drop in the percentage of British trade passing through London was in the context of a rapid expansion in British foreign trade. Between 1820 and 1913, British exports at constant 1990 prices grew by about 3.8 per cent per annum (Maddison, 1995). By the 1790s, congestion in the London docks became acute and the average vessel size was increasing. A development programme was begun. Between 1802 and 1807, new docks were built: West India, London, East India and Surrey. Development continued into the 20th century with the construction of the Royal Albert, Royal Victoria, King George V and, about 30 miles downstream, at Tilbury Docks. By >WORLD WAR I, London's docks had a water area of 750 acres and extended over 2,200 acres on land. London achieved its highest level of traffic in the 1950s with a throughput of 70 million tons but the second half of the 20th century saw a transformation in the ports industry by the new container-ship technology, ship specialization and the growth in the size of vessels.

In the early stages of the development of domestic and international trade, the sea lanes and waterways were often the only viable means of transport and, therefore, they were utilized to their full extent by the loading and discharging of vessels as close to the origin and destination of the cargo as physically possible. Port cities expanded because they had access to these economical means of transport. This encouraged the processing of imported raw materials close to the point of discharge, raw sugar was refined, tobacco cured, ships repaired and built but also services were established such as banking, insurance, warehousing and commodity exchanges. Specific ports benefited by having a thriving hinterland to which it had access through extensive waterway networks. The prosperity of a particular port could be influenced by shifts in the direction of international trade. During the 19th century, this was particularly evident in Europe as the deep-sea trade with North America increased its share of traffic compared with the old established colonial trades in the East. This effect was evident in the expansion of Liverpool on the west coast of England, reflecting, particularly, the growth of the British >COTTON AND COTTON TEXTILES industry. It is axiomatic that port traffic would tend to gravitate to that through transport route, from origin to destination of the goods carried, which has the lowest costs of the alternative routes available. This cost of carriage is proportionately greater in the total cost of a commodity the heavier it is. Low-value bulk commodities, such as coal, salt and clay, benefit from a minimum of overland movement compared with that by sea, river or >CANAL. The reduction in inland transport costs in the 19th and 20th centuries with the expansion of the railway and the road networks widened port hinterlands by increasing the overland distances which even low-value high-tonnage goods could be economically transported. There was, therefore, an increase in competitive pressure between ports as their local monopoly was constrained by the ability of other ports to pick up business within what had been an exclusive hinterland. Ports diversified, taking on different characteristics depending on their trade, and many became specialized to a particular type of business. An example of this was the large industrial port which imported bulk commodities for processing in the immediate vicinity of the port. A number of ports expanded in the 20th century within the context of maritime industrial development areas in which major industries such as >OIL refining and petro-chemicals were located. A prime example of this was Rotterdam. The Mainz Convention in 1831 and the Mannheim Treaty in 1868 had established that shipping along the Rhine should be free and this freedom from dues offered a great opportunity for Rotterdam. In 1872, the Nieuwe Waterweg (New Waterway) was completed, which gave Rotterdam the direct access from the North Sea for large vessels. This enabled the port to exploit its position on the Maas to access its vast hinterland into Germany through the Rhine and it became that country's main port for its foreign trade. Since that time, the port continued to grow. Prior to World War II, it constructed Waalhaven and Merwehaven to accept the newly growing trade in >OIL. After a period of reconstruction following the war, it built Europoort to accept oil tankers up to a draft of 20 metres, and in 1973 it further extended its port facilities on reclaimed land at Maasvlakte. By the end of the 20th century, four refineries were located at Rotterdam,

importing over 1 million barrels of oil per day (including refineries at Vlissingen and Antwerp, the area was home to about 12 per cent of Europe's refinery capacity) and Rotterdam had become a leading port of the world in terms of total freight-tonnes, with a throughput of 322 million metric tonnes, of which 98 million metric tonnes were crude oil.

In the second half of the 20th century, there was a major revolution in the transportation of general cargo with the switch from conventional break-bulk to purpose-built container vessels, the specialization of vessels into a wide variety of different types catering to particular trades and the inexorable growth in the size of ships (>SHIPPING). These developments had two major impacts on the ports industry worldwide, on labour and on location.

Containerization virtually automated the loading and discharge of vessels and port operation became a capital-intensive rather than a labour-intensive activity. The effect on productivity was dramatic. A deep-sea container berth had the capacity of ten conventional berths and two container cranes did the work of 40 conventional cranes. A conventional cargo-liner spent ten to 15 days in port to discharge and load, whereas a large container ship only required two days. For a ship, time in port is idle time and containerization effected a dramatic improvement in ship productivity. Seaports had to adjust quickly to the provision of the technology required to match the expectations of the shipping lines to meet the potential of their vessels. At the same time there was a corresponding development to challenge the port authorities. Because of the vastly improved cargo handling rates in the port, it became feasible to increase the size of vessels without any bottleneck appearing at the port to prevent the larger and more expensive ship from earning its keep. This meant not only longer quay faces and larger operational areas behind the berths but also deeper water to accommodate the deeper draft of vessels. The size of specialized container ships grew threefold between the 1960s and the end of the 20th century.

Not only did the ports have to invest substantially in new facilities to remain in business but they had also to confront the reality of a complete change, not only in the demand for labour but also in the skills required in their labour force. On a conventional berth, every 10,000 tonnes of cargo a year required ten men; on a container berth it required only one man. The new labour force had to be skilled in the operation of the new cargo handling equipment and computer systems. Between 1966 and 1976, the number of employees in the British ports industry fell from 124,000 to 74,000, during which period total British non-fuel foreign port traffic grew by nearly 25 per cent (National Ports Council, 1976).

The increase in the size of vessels meant that port authorities had often to relocate their facilities by moving to deep water in order to accommodate the deeper-draft vessels. If they could not, they lost their deep-sea container business to those ports which were able to do so or already had access to the depth required. The post-war developments at Rotterdam were towards the sea from Waalhaven and Merwehaven, to Europoort and Maasvlakte. The upper Thames facilities at London gave way to Tilbury and to other ports such as Felixstowe and Southampton. In their search for the economies of scale inherent in the employment of larger ship sizes,

the shipping lines began to employ the concept of the hub port in their through transport networks. These ports were able to service the largest container ships and their loads were then distributed by smaller feeder vessels to lesser ports located in the network area. By such activities grew the major hub ports such as Hong Kong and Singapore, which in 2000 were the two top world container ports with throughputs of 18 million teus (20ft equivalent units of a standard length of 20 feet) and 17 million teus respectively; these throughputs compare with a throughput at Rotterdam of 6 million teus, which nevertheless ranked in that year as the world's number seven. World container traffic grew rapidly in the last decades of the 20th century, increasing from 36 million teus in 1980 to 266 million teus in 2002 (Notteboom, 2004).

The variety of types of domestic and international traffic, the economies of port hinterlands, the size and nature of vessels in the various trades all resulted in a world population of ports with a correspondingly wide spectrum of various sizes from the large industrial and container hub ports to the small ports serving a local market. In addition, because of their strategic place in local, regional and national economies, there had evolved different administrative and legal frameworks under which they were governed. There has been a general presumption that there were aspects of a public utility in port operations and, therefore, they should be subject to some government control or support and they should not be left entirely to compete in a free market.

In the 1960s, the British ports industry was in disarray and on the recommendation of a government committee of inquiry, a National Ports Council was established in 1964 to which all major port investments, government grants and loans had to be submitted for appraisal. The British industry comprised a wide range of types of organization; a number of ports were nationalized, a number were owned by their municipalities, others were non-profit trusts and some were private sector companies. The governance, therefore, of the ports, on which was superimposed some form of government control, differed widely and were influenced by different objectives. The Council found it difficult in these circumstances to formulate a coherent system of economic appraisal (Baxter, 1977). In 1981, policy was reversed, the Council was abolished and close government control over the ports was abandoned. The nationalized sector was privatized and the trusts given powers to do so also. Few countries went so far with the loosening of government control as Britain did, although arguments persisted into the 21st century as to the nature of any national ports policy and whether central government should play any part except through the process of planning applications and enquiries. In Europe, most ports continued to be operated by a local authority or an autonomous body (such as the *ports autonomes* in France) over which, however, the central governments have a very strong influence (Commission of the European Communities, 1986). In the USA most ports continued to be operated by boards appointed by the municipality or the state and capital and maintenance dredging (except at the quay face) was done by the US Army Corps of Engineers. There was no Federal ports strategy but, as in many other countries, considerable government financial assistance in some form. In the last decade or two of the 20th century, increasing consideration was given to port governance questions in the context of governments moving towards policies favourable to privatization in the last 20 years of the 20th century and the World Bank published a *Port Reform Toolkit* (2005) to assist in the decision-making and implementation of the appropriate structure of governance for a country's ports (Brooks, 2004).

## References

Baxter, R. E., 'The Political Economy of Port Development', *National Ports Council Bulletin*,10, Spring, 1977.

Brooks, Mary R., 'The Governance Structure of Ports', *Review of Network Economics*, 3(2), June, 2004.

Commission of the European Communities, *Report of an Enquiry into the Current Situation in the Major Community Sea-Ports*, 1986.

Lee, Robert and Lawton, Richard, 'Port Development and the Demographic Dynamics of European Urbanization', in Richard Lawton and Robert Lee (eds), *Population and Society in Western European Port Cities, c. 1650–1939*, Liverpool University Press, 2002.

Levinson, Marc, *The Box: How the Shipping Container made the World Smaller and the World Economy Bigger*, Princeton University Press, 2006.

Maddison, Angus, *Monitoring the World Economy 1820–1992*, OECD, 1995.

National Ports Council, 'Port Perspectives, 1976', *National Ports Council Bulletin*, 9, 1976.

Notteboom, Theo E., 'Container Shipping and Ports', *Review of Network Economics*, 3(2), June, 2004.

Porter, Roy, *London, A Social History*, Penguin, 2000.

World Bank, *Port Reform Toolkit; Overview; The Evolution of Ports in a Competitive World*, 2005.

## Service Sector

One definition of services is that they are marketed commodities (or government services) that do not have a tangible form. This was in essence Adam >SMITH's definition. He wrote that 'services generally perish at the very instant of their performance' (1776). He felt that, unlike manufacturing, services do not add much, if anything, to the value of the materials used. This view is no longer acceptable today since services clearly provide value for consumers and therefore create value. Many economists are nonetheless far less interested in services than in manufacturing and for some this amounts to an aversion, if only because many services, like hairdressing, cannot be traded internationally. In the past, the views of a few economists about services in Britain have verged on what would now be regarded as the fantastic. In the 1960s, Nicholas Kaldor argued that an over-large service sector was the cause of the (then perceived) poor performance of the British economy. Government was persuaded by Kaldor's arguments to impose a Selective Employment Tax (SET) on service sector employment to encourage the transfer of labour from services to the 'more productive' manufacturing sector. The tax was not maintained for long but, soon after, William Baumol did argue more defensibly that because >PRODUCTIVITY in capital-intensive manufacturing was likely to rise faster than in services, rising wages would stimulate more demand for the latter and the resulting transfer of labour to services could reduce overall productivity. In his contribution, 'The Service Industries', to Floud and McCloskey , Clive Lee concludes that both the Kaldor and Baumol models have been falsified by events and that 'the view that services are optional, unproductive, stagnant and low-wage needs historical revision' (1994). Nonetheless, Baumol's insights do explain why it is that

manufactured products get cheaper and cheaper, while services become more expensive and why the share of manufacturing in GDP has declined so fast ('Baumol effect').

There has been some debate about what should be included in the service sector. It has been argued that transport and communications should be included since they do not involve the production or modification of physical objects. Certainly transport services, once provided, leave nothing tangible behind. Utilities are a more difficult case, but it is usual not to include them with services, along with construction. Services are, therefore a residual after the primary sector (agriculture, forestry and fishing), the extractive, construction and manufacturing industries and the utilities (gas, water and electricity). Government is included with services and is part of the explanation for their increase (>STATE, RISE OF).

According to Maddison (2007), the share of total employment in services (defined as above) has increased from 22 per cent in >BRITAIN in 1700 to 75 per cent in 2003, while that of the primary sector has fallen from 56 per cent to 1 per cent. Industry (mining, construction, manufacturing and the utilities) rose from 22 per cent in 1700, to 43 per cent in 1890, then declined to 24 per cent by 2003. The successive shifts of employment from agriculture to industry and then to services has been a common feature of >ECONOMIC DEVELOPMENT. The >USA was the first of the major countries to have more than half of its total employment in services and is still slightly ahead of Britain in that respect, while Germany has a relatively larger manufacturing sector than either Britain or the USA.

The internal structure of the service sector and the composition of its labour force have also changed.

In Britain, the number of 'indoor' domestic servants was over 800,000 in 1851 and grew rapidly over the following 20 years, to be curtailed eventually by changes in income distribution, by >WORLD WAR I, as women took over men's jobs, and later by the diffusion of domestic appliances. By 1871, a third of working women had been in domestic service, which had long been the largest sector in personal services. By 1861, the service sector as a whole in Britain accounted for a larger share of employment than agriculture. Distribution was of growing importance as the national market developed and the City of London and other >SEAPORTS, such as Liverpool, were already generating more and more employment in finance, banking and professional services which account for a large proportion of invisible trade. In fact, the share of total British exports accounted for by services has been on an upward trend since the middle 1980s and after the millennium has been about 30 per cent. Recent years have also seen a major growth in business services such as computer support, consultancy and market research. One of the consequences of the post->WORLD WAR II service sector has been the greatly increased role of women. There has been a corresponding decline in the demand for unskilled male labour. The female labour force participation rate in Britain, at 65.2 per cent (2000), is below those of the Scandinavian countries and somewhat below that of the USA but well ahead of Southern European countries. For example, the female participation rate in Italy is only 39.7 per cent. These differences reflect differences in the size of the service sector, which in Italy accounts for only 61 per cent of total employment compared with almost 73 per cent in Britain, though cultural factors are also at work (Crafts, 1993: >EMPLOYMENT OF WOMEN AND CHILDREN).

The long-standing concern about the relative decline in Britain's economic performance, compared with most other advanced countries from the 1870s onwards after World War II, became coupled with a fear of continuing 'de-industrialization'. Between the middle 1960s and the late 1980s, employment in British manufacturing fell by almost 4 million or 40 per cent. These fears, also shared in the USA and elsewhere, were greatly increased in Britain by the impact of the discovery of North Sea Oil and the strengthening of the Sterling exchange rate in the 1980s. Many observers (for example, Correlli Barnet in *The Audit of War* (1986) and M. J. Wiener in *English Culture and the Decline of the Industrial Spirit, 1850–1980* (1981)) gave predominantly cultural explanations for Britain's relative decline. These cultural explanations encouraged calls for renewed industrial policies (already tried and failed), but the vogue for them has recently given way to a more balanced assessment. The earlier notion that services do not contribute significantly to economic growth has also been largely abandoned in the face of the fact that their role has increased in all the advanced countries, as well as by a resurgence of growth in the British and US economies from the early 1990s. The cultural explanations for the relative decline have been directly refuted by many historians and economic historians, Crafts (1993), Thompson (2001) and Booth (2001) among others, who have also pointed out that the evils of de-industrialization have been exaggerated. It is now increasingly accepted that the balance of trade in manufactures is less important for some countries, including Britain, than was once thought. Britain, it seems, though the first to industrialize has developed a comparative advantage in certain internationally traded services in contrast to Germany and Japan and other Asian economies (>ASIAN MIRACLE), though, as noted below, relative efficiency in the service sector in Britain has not been a constant.

Productivity is difficult to measure in services because of the frequent lack of physical measures of output. A doctor may spend less time with patients so that he can deal with say, 30 a day, instead of seven, but has his or her output increased? The quality of the doctor's services may well have declined. Although net output in services can be measured, there are almost always difficulties in finding appropriate measures of price changes with which to deflate output into volume terms. Despite these difficulties, important conclusions have been drawn about trends in service productivity. It used to be assumed, for example, that the USA and Germany overtook Britain from the end of the 19th century largely through higher productivity growth in manufacturing. However, Broadberry (1998) has demonstrated that although absolute levels of manufacturing productivity were much higher in the USA than in Britain, and remain so to this day, relative levels of manufacturing productivity have actually not changed much over the longer period, while those in services have changed. The USA and Germany overtook Britain largely because Britain's lead in productivity in services, which was well ahead of the other two countries in 1870, fell behind them by 1900. Broadberry (1998) attributes the decline in the British relative position to its comparative advantage in customized services and networks still manifested today in its success

in banking, finance and professional services, which account for a large proportion of its strong position in invisible trade. As persuasively argued by Broadberry, Britain found it difficult to adjust to the emergence of standardized transactions in large, hierarchical organizations in the second half of the 19th century (>CHANDLER). Since the 1970s technology and other factors have tended to shift to in favour of >SMALL AND MEDIUM ENTERPRISES, though this has not been fully reflected in improved productivity in the service sector because of under-investment in human capital (>EDUCATION) and perhaps also in a delayed impact of investment in information technology (>PRODUCTIVITY). Nonetheless, Britain started to reduce some of the US lead in both service and manufacturing productivity in this period (see Robert Millward's contribution, 'The Rise of the Service Economy', in Floud and Johnson, 2004b) (>ACCOUNTING: >MONEY AND BANKING: >CAPITAL MARKETS: >COMMERCIAL REVOLUTION: >CONSUMER REVOLUTION: >RAILWAYS: >SHIPPING: >TELE-COMMUNICATIONS).

## References

Booth, Alan, *The British Economy in the Twentieth Century*, Palgrave, 2001.

Broadberry, Stephen N., 'How Did the United States and Germany Overtake Britain? A Sectoral Analysis of Comparative Productivity Levels', *Journal of Economic History*, 58, June, 1998.

Crafts, N. F. R., *Can De-Industrialisation Seriously Damage Your Wealth?*, Institute of Economic Affairs, 1993.

Crafts, N. F. R., Gazeley, Ian and Newell, Andrew (eds), *Work and Pay in Twentieth-Century Britain*, Oxford University Press, 2007.

Floud, Roderick and Johnson, Paul (eds), *The Cambridge Economic History of*

*Modern Britain*, II, *Economic Maturity, 1860–1939*, Cambridge University Press, 2004a.

Floud, Roderick and Johnson, Paul (eds), *The Cambridge Economic History of Modern Britain*, III, *Structural Change and Growth 1939–2000*, Cambridge University Press, 2004b.

Floud, Roderick and McCloskey, Donald, *The Economic History of Britain Since 1700*, II, *1860–1939* (2nd edn), Cambridge University Press, 1994.

Fuchs, Victor R., *The Service Economy*, Columbia University Press, 1968.

Gershuny, J. I. and Miles, A. D., *The New Service Economy: The Transformation of Employment in Industrial Societies*, Francis Pinter, 1983.

Maddison, Angus, *Contours of the World Economy, 1–2030 AD: Essays in Macro-Economic History*, Oxford University Press, 2007.

Thompson, F. M. L., *Gentrification and the Enterprise Culture, Britain 1780–1980*, Oxford University Press, 2001.

# Shipping

Xenophon, the classical Greek historian and soldier who lived between about 430 BC and 354 BC wrote in the *Oeconomicus* the following about a Phoenician merchant ship he came across:

'A ship is brought to anchor, and again got under way, by a vast number of wooden implements and of ropes, and sails the sea by means of a quantity of rigging, and is armed with a number of contrivances against hostile vessels, and carries about with it a large supply of weapons for the crew, and, besides, has all the utensils that a man keeps in his dwelling house, for each of the messes. In addition it is loaded with a quantity of merchandise, which the owner carries with him for his own profit. Now, all the things I have mentioned, lay in a space not much bigger than a room that would conveniently hold ten beds; and I remarked that they severally lay in such a way that they did not obstruct one another, and did not require any to look for them, and they were neither placed at random, nor entangled with another, so as to consume time when they were suddenly wanted for use. Also I found the captain's assistant so well acquainted with the position of the articles, and with the number of them, that even when at a distance he would tell where everything lay, and how many there were of each sort.' (Thomas, 1968)

In this extract, Xenophon mentions three characteristics of merchant shipping: the motive power of sail, the need for some defence as a protection against pirates and the skill of economical and safe stowage of the commodities being carried for profit, all of which remained unchanged for 2,000 years. If the Phoenician captain had been able to view the merchant ships around his Mediterranean at the end of the 18th century, he may have marvelled at their size and the complexity of their rigging, but he would have understood the principles by which they operated. Indeed, when Captain Thomas published the sixth edition of the manual on the stowage of vessels in 1968, in which the above extract from Xenophon is quoted, our Phoenician captain may have been bewildered by the huge variety of commodities traded but would have appreciated the labour and skills still being applied in the stowage of that cargo.

There had, of course, been important developments in the sailing ship such as the invention of the stern rudder, the introduction of the ship's wheel and in navigation aids such as the marine compass and the marine chronometer. Further, in the second half of the 18th century, there began a transformation in the size of vessels. For instance, the ships on the deep-sea routes of the >ENGLISH EAST INDIA COMPANY increased in size from about 600 tons to about 900 tons and increases in vessel size were also recorded in the short-sea trades such as the Baltic. Before the mid-18th century, the largest vessels on the Atlantic were about 200 tons but by the turn of the century the size had risen to about 325 tons. Piracy in the 17th and 18th centuries continued to impose a cost burden on vessels, particularly in times of war, but the need for merchant vessels to carry weapons began to be reduced. There were exceptions such as the Far East so that the ships of the East India Company carried armament of up to 28 guns and the West Indies too was prone to piracy so that merchant vessels had to be armed. The British passed the Convoy Act in 1798, requiring merchant ships to travel in convoy with an armed escort. Piracy became less of a problem as the 19th century progressed but was never entirely eliminated. (Indeed, the International Maritime Bureau reported that pirates boarded 311 ships in 2003.)

While redesign of the vessels, sails and rigging achieved improvements in speed, it was the technology and products of the >INDUSTRIAL REVOLUTION in the 19th century that began the complete transformation of the merchant ship. The introduction of iron and, later, steel in shipbuilding, although it was taken advantage of also in the design of sailing vessels in addition to wood, enabled steamships and their engines to be constructed with the strength, stability and size suitable to their cost-effective operation. Investigation into the application of

steam to vessel propulsion began just before the end of the 18th century but the first patent for a steamboat was taken out by William Symington (1763–1831) in 1801 and it operated on the Forth and Clyde Canal in Scotland for a while but failed commercially. The first successful enterprise was a steamboat built in 1807 by Robert Fulton (1765–1815), which operated on the Hudson River from New York to Albany. Initially, steam-driven vessels were restricted to tugs and steamboats on rivers and lakes (>STEAM POWER).

The early engines were handicapped because sea-going vessels had to use sea water in their boilers, which caused salt scale to form, and they had to be cleaned frequently. In 1838, Samuel Hall (1781–1863), a British engineer, invented a surface condenser which meant that ships could fill their boilers with fresh water which was replenished through a cycle in which the exhaust steam was condensed and returned to the boilers. A paddle steamer called the *Sirius* had a surface condenser when it operated on the Atlantic in 1838 but condensers did not become really effective until the development of lubricants from 'rock oil', the possibility of which was discovered in the >USA in 1855 (>OIL). The lubricants previously used were based on animal or vegetable fats, which were unstable.

The drive of the early steam-powered (>STEAM POWER) ships was through paddle wheels but these were very unsatisfactory. For efficient operation each wheel should be submersed to the same optimum depth but in practice this was difficult to achieve. Ocean-going ships pitched, rolled and heaved and a ship's draught varied according to the cargo it was carrying. Nevertheless, successes were recorded. For instance, the

British ship *Great Western*, designed by I. K. Brunel (1806–1859), was a steam-powered paddle steamer built of wood which, from April 1838, ran a successful operation on the trans-Atlantic from Bristol to New York. The construction of paddle steamers, first in wood and then in iron, continued through the first half of the 19th century until the 1860s.

For their full potential to be realized, however, steamships had to await improvements in their drive mechanism and in the efficiency of their engines. The first requirement was met in the invention and application of the screw propeller. The theory of the properties of a ship propeller has a long ancestry, going back as far as the Archimedes screw. The earliest successful application to a vessel was in 1801, when Robert Fulton demonstrated to the French his submarine the *Nautilus* in which the screw propeller was turned by the crew manually. However, the breakthrough did not come until 1836 when Sir Francis Pettit Smith (1808–1874), a British farmer, was granted a patent. Successful sea trials of his propeller were made in a small boat which travelled around the coast of England from London to Folkestone and back. Smith's boat was able to tow the *Great Western* into dock in London. Smith's screw propeller was adopted in the wooden-built *Archimedes*, which was launched in 1838 and which made the first sea crossing by a ship driven by propeller in a voyage to Portugal from Plymouth. Brunel's *Great Britain*, a ship of 3,270 tons, was the first constructed of iron and incorporating a screw propeller, having drawn on experience with the *Archimedes*.

The second requirement for efficient steamship operation did not begin to be made until 1854. Patents for triple and quadruple expansion

engines were taken out by John Elder (1824–1869), a British engineer, and, in that year, he introduced the first practical compound steam engine. However, the further development of the engine had to wait until the end of the 1870s before steel of reliable quality became available at an economic price so that the necessary high steam pressures could be achieved. This led to significant reductions in coal consumption, which was a critical element in the costs of running steamships particularly on long ocean voyages. In 1881, the steamship *Aberdeen*, of 30,616grt, powered by a triple expansion engine, sailed from Plymouth to Melbourne in 42 days and only needed one coaling stop. Its fuel consumption was some 40 per cent less than a similar size steamer of a decade earlier (Gardiner, 1993). Steel had the advantage that lighter gauges of plate could be used in ship construction so that by 1885 about 50 per cent of all new construction of steamships was of steel and by the end of the century about 95 per cent (>IRON AND STEEL).

Steamship design and technology had now reached the point at which the steamship would be able to compete directly with the sailing ship in their last remaining markets, but it was not until 1880 that steamships had captured up to a half of the main trade routes. Although steamships accounted for only a quarter of the total tonnage of the world fleets, they could carry about double that because of their greater speed compared with the sailing ship. For instance, in 1838, the *Great Western* crossed the Atlantic in 15 days whereas sailing ships could take up to 40 days. The progressive improvements in steamship technology was being achieved during a period when >INTERNATIONAL TRADE in commodities carried by sea grew from about 10 million tons in 1830 to about 150 million tons in 1890 (Lilley, 1973). This growth in trade helped to reassure potential investors anxious about the risks involved in supporting the new technology incorporated in the construction and operation of steamships.

A major handicap which the steamship had to bear in competition with the sailing ship was the need to carry its own coal fuel. The longer the voyage the more otherwise revenue-earning cargo space had to be lost in a steamship to accommodate its fuel. Coaling stations had to be established along the longest ocean routes and they had to be replenished with coal, which was progressively more expensive the further away from >BRITAIN, as the latter was the major world supplier (>COAL). Through the course of the 19th century, therefore, world seaborne trade became polarized between the steamship and the sailer. The former was attracted first into the short- and near-sea trades and the latter into the deep-sea trades. Steamships looked to high-value and perishable cargoes and sailing ships to low-value bulks.

The trades in high-value and perishable cargo became attracted to the steamships because of their speed, whereas the sailing ships were able to capture the markets for low-value bulk commodities for which speed was less important compared with a low tariff. In keeping journey times short, compared with the sailing ship, the steamship had the advantage of being able to follow the shortest grand circle route and not be constrained by the prevailing winds and currents. Findlay and O'Rourke (2003) quote trading figures on the route from Calcutta to Britain which show that in 1874, whereas steamships carried 90 per cent of the traffic in commodities such as ginger, poppy seed and tea, they only carried between 30 and 40 per cent of jute and rice. Improvements in the efficiency of sailing ships continued in the first half of the 19th century, up to the development by the USA of the clipper ships in the 1850s, which were designed principally for speed.

The Far East routes were completely altered in 1869. The opening of the Suez Canal in 1869 reduced the distance by sea from Britain to Bombay from about 11,500 miles to just over 6,200 miles and to Calcutta to about 8,200 miles. Moreover, the canal was not suitable for the sailing ship. The percentage steamship tonnage of all vessels arriving in Britain from Bombay rose from hardly any to 28 per cent in 1870 and to 65 per cent in 1873 and virtually all in 1890 (Harley, 1971). Kerosene continued for a while to be shipped by sail around Africa until Marcus Samuel obtained permission to ship his tankers from Batum on the Black Sea to the Far East through the Canal in 1892 (>OIL). Sailing ships remained on the routes to Burma and Bengal and the tea clippers began shipping Australian wool. By 1900, a quarter of the total world tonnage was still accounted for by sailing vessels. They were able to compete against steam in their remaining markets of the longest voyages, such as round-the-world trades, until >WORLD WAR I.

Through the second half of the 19th century and the early years of the 20th century until World War I, Britain dominated the world merchant fleet. Between 1850 and 1911, the tonnage of the world merchant fleet grew from about 9 million net tons to about 35 million tons and Britain accounted for about 30 per cent of this. (The income from shipping produced a third of Britain's total invisible earnings (Palmer, 1985).) In 1911, its nearest competitor was Germany, with only 9 per cent of the world fleet. The share in the total of the USA had fallen from 17 per cent to 2.5 per cent. British ship-owners had the important advantage over their rivals in the dominance of Britain in international trade, which was growing rapidly. It has been estimated that 40 per cent of world seaborne trade passed through British >SEAPORTS in 1914. British shipping was also helped by the pre-dominance of coal, which accounted for as much as 50 per cent of world exports in 1914. This not only served to supply their coaling stations but gave ships an assured load for the outward voyage to balance against the costs of their inward voyage. The British ship-owners also took better advantage compared with their rivals of the opportunities afforded by the increasing efficiency of the steam-ship. In 1913, about 50 per cent of the total world steamship tonnage was on the British Registry. In 1918, the British Departmental Committee on Shipping and Shipbuilding reported that, 'at the outbreak of war, the British Mercantile Marine was the largest, the most up to date and the most efficient of all the mer-chant navies of the world' (quoted in Palmer, 1985).

The improvements in ship tech-nology described above and in the increased size of vessels put down-ward pressure on freight rates in a competitive market. Freight rates for wheat from New York to Liverpool fell from 14.3 cents per bushel in 1852/6 to 5.7 cents per bushel in 1895/99 and down to 4.9 cents per bushel in 1910/13 (Harley, 1980).

The tramp charter rate for rice from Rangoon to Europe fell from 73.8 per cent of the Rangoon price to 18.1 per cent between 1822 and 1914. The freight rate for coal shipped between Shanghai and Nagasaki compared to its export price fell by 76 per cent between 1880 and 1910 (O'Rourke and Williamson, 2002). British tramp freight rates fell in real terms between 1869/71 and 1911/13 by 22 per cent (Findlay and O'Rourke, 2003).

Harley (1988) disputes previous claims that the decline in freight rates in the 19th century was more a consequence of improved organ-ization than of technical change. There had been some decline in rates before 1850 but Harley argues that these were biased by the US freight index, which was influenced by US cotton (>COTTON AND COTTON TEXTILES) exports and the improved methods of packing cotton bales dur-ing the period. Harley constructed new indices of freight rates in real terms for the years from the middle of the 18th century until the early 20th century. This index indicates that freight rates were, in real terms, more or less constant until the middle of the 19th century except for peaks in times of war. Thereafter, the index falls during the rest of the period. In the early 20th century, freight rates on this measure were about one-third of what they had been in the first half of the 19th century. Harley estimates that between the 1850s and the early 1900s the productivity of steam ship-ping increased by about 1.3 per cent per annum. This was about twice the rate he estimates was achieved by sail-ing ship in the first half of the 18th century. He concludes that lower fac-tor costs and competition led to the fall in freight rates.

This 19th-century decline in freight rates encouraged the growth and diversity of international trade and, it may be argued, even initiated the process of >GLOBALIZATION. The Heckscher–Ohlin Principle shows how the free flow of >INTERNATIONAL TRADE may act in the same way as the international migration of factors of production through the effect of the convergence of the traded commodity prices between countries. Whereas imports of wheat (>GRAIN) into countries of Western and Central Europe in the first half of the 19th century were negligible, by 1914 over 30 per cent of their consumption was imported and three-quarters of British consumption (Harley, 1980). Harley shows that, in the period from 1850 to 1914, the prices of wheat in Chicago and in Britain converged, prices rising in Chicago and falling in Britain. O'Rourke and Williamson (2002) calculate that the difference in the US and the British price of wheat fell from 54 per cent in 1870 to zero in 1913, the barley gap from 46 per cent to 11 per cent and that for oats from 138 per cent to 28 per cent. These changes implied a reduction in rents in Britain, France and Germany of between 10 and 20 per cent; in effect a surplus factor of production (land) in the USA had been exported to Western Europe (>GLOBALIZATION: >INTERNATIONAL TRADE).

Since >OIL had been discovered in the USA in 1859, production had grown rapidly and by early in the 20th century, its assured availability and fall in price brought it into the market as a viable alternative fuel to coal. Although Britain lacked domestic supplies of oil, the British government decided to switch the Royal Navy to oil in 1911. The US Navy opted for oil in its ships at the same time. The US Emergency Shipbuilding Programme established by the Shipping Act of 1916 also chose oil for all the new merchant ships it commissioned. Oil had major advantages over coal. It was less labour-intensive, which yielded a 50 per cent reduction in the size of crews; it took up less space and less time for refuelling; and did not have

to rely on coaling stations dominated by Britain. The internal combustion engine had also arrived and with progressive improvements the diesel engine came to dominate the world merchant fleet in the 20th century.

In 1882, the French began building the Panama Canal under the management of Ferdinand de Lesseps. In 1904 the project was taken over by the USA and eventually opened in 1914. It cut a 51-mile link through Panama between the Caribbean and the Pacific with a minimum width of 110ft in the locks and a minimum depth of 41ft. It did not have the dramatic effect that the opening of the Suez Canal had had but it lowered costs to shippers by their being able to avoid the need to tran-ship cargo at east and west coast ports on the overland route.

Although millions of tons of the world's merchant fleet had been destroyed in World War I, a major expansion of shipbuilding took place after, so that by 1939 the world merchant fleet was about 50 per cent larger than in 1914. The British fleet, by contrast, fell in the period by 40 per cent. The share of the US fleet rose from about 6 per cent to about 15 per cent of the total in the period (Gibson and Donovan, 2001). During World War II, millions of tons of merchant shipping were again destroyed, including 50 per cent of the British fleet. After the war, there was again a vigorous growth in shipbuilding tonnage so that the world merchant fleet was able to grow to 80 million tons by 1948 and to 268 million tons by the early 1970s. This expansion was supported by the continued use of subsidies.

The protection and support of a state's shipping industry has a long history. The English Navigation Acts, embodied in a series of acts of parliament, were passed between 1651 and 1733. They were finally repealed in 1849. In general, the Acts laid down rules which were designed to divert trade into English ships. For instance, imports from the European Continent had to be carried either in English ships or in the country of origin of the goods. Similarly, all imports from the colonies had to be conveyed in British or Colonial ships and imports into the colonies had to be tran-shipped through an English port and carried from there in an English ship. Similar shipping restrictions were applied in France, the Netherlands, Portugal and Spain. Restrictions which excluded foreign-owned vessels from a country's domestic coastal trade (cabotage) were and continued to be common. For instance, the USA passed such legislation in 1789 and 1817. The US Merchant Marine Act of 1920 (referred to as the Jones Act) included overseas possessions into its cabotage rules. The member countries of the European Union (>WESTERN EUROPE) did not abolish cabotage restrictions between member countries until between 1999 and 2004. Although Britain abolished its Navigation Laws in 1849, it had introduced a policy of granting subsidies to shipping lines by means of very favourable terms for the transport of the Royal Mail, which was particularly favourable to the new steamships. The US Ocean Mail Act of 1891 granted subsidies on a scale depending on the size and speed of the vessel. The system was further expanded in the Merchant Marine Act of 1928 and further reorganized in the Merchant Marine Act of 1936. This Act, which set up the Maritime Commission, tightened up the granting of mail subsidies. A policy of subsidized support and protection was pursued by the USA throughout the 20th century but a heavy regulatory

regime was also placed on US shipping lines in an attempt to support US shipbuilders and to employ US crews. The protection of the shipping industry and its regulation in some form was government policy, pursued worldwide. Baldwin (1971) states that 41 countries supported their own shipping by limiting the freedom of foreign shipping trading through their ports.

The laws and regulations pertinent within the operation of a merchant ship are those of the country in which it is registered and which flag it flies. There are two types of registries, open and closed. A closed registry is one in which the vessels must be owned and crewed by citizens of the country of registry. An open registry is one in which other nationals may own the vessel. Open registries are of two broad groups; those of countries with a tradition of merchant shipping such as the USA, France, Britain and Japan and the International Open registries of such countries as Panama and Liberia. These latter, often referred to as flags of convenience, are set up by countries solely for the purpose of raising revenue. They are generally characterized as not being subjected to any government regulations, the ships do not attract any tax burden, non-nationals are able to own the ships and transfer ownership at will and they impose no restrictions on the employment of crews. The use of flags of convenience, in response to the competitive pressures on the operations of merchant fleets, the rise in costs associated with the employment of national crews and the introduction of stricter standards of health and safety in the closed and traditional registries, grew substantially in the second half of the 20th century from about 2 per cent to about

50 per cent of the total by 2000 (UNCTAD, 2000).

The specialization of vessels to the transport of particular commodities began to emerge in the 19th century with examples such as exemplified by Marcus Samuels' oil tankers in 1892 (>OIL) and the refrigerated ship at the turn of the century, with the first temperature-controlled bananas from Jamaica in 1901, following the first ocean transport of refrigerated meat from Argentina. Through the 20th century, hundreds of vessel types were developed specialized to a particular purpose or to carry a particular cargo. Merchant ships were able to exploit economies of scale by increasing size. In particular, for instance, oil tankers such as the very large crude carriers (VLCCs) reached about 250,000dwt. The ultra large crude carriers (ULCCs) went even further and reached 564,000dwt in the *Seawise Giant* in 1980, although the ULCCs proved to have taken a step too far commercially.

In 1956, Malcolm McLean, the owner of a US road haulage company, recognized that it would be cheaper to shift his road trailers on board a ship from one location with a port to another also with a port rather than to route them overland. His trailers could be driven off and on to the ship. The concept of containerization was thus launched and cargo handling was translated from 'bits to boxes'. The port operation became a capital-intensive activity rather than a very labour-intensive one and the break-bulk general cargo ship was replaced by container and roll-on roll-off vessels and the port became part of a through intermodal transport system. The conventional break-bulk cargo handling rate had been such as to limit the size of vessel that it was economic to run because too much vessel capacity was tied up in the time taken in discharging and loading. The container operation released the ship from this port restraint and the size of vessel grew considerably. In the late 1960s, containers ships on the Atlantic trade could carry up to 1,500 20ft equivalent containers (TEUs). In 2006, the Maersk Line of Denmark operated the *Emma Maersk* of 156,907dwt, capable of carrying 11,000 TEUs (>SEAPORTS).

It was not until the second half of the 20th century that beak-bulk cargo handling, the last of the characteristics of the operation of a merchant ship noted by Xenophon in the Phoenician harbour, was finally rendered obsolescent by modern technology. After 2,000 years during which the merchant ship remained still recognizable to the Phoenician captain, the >INDUSTRIAL REVOLUTIONS effected complete change in 200.

## References

Baldwin, Robert E., *Non-Tariff Distortions of International Trade*, George, Allen & Unwin, 1971.

Clark, Gregory and Feenstra, Robert C., 'Technology in the Great Divergence', in Michael D. Bordo, Alan M. Taylor and Jeffrey G. Williamson (eds), *Globalisation in Historical Perspective*, University of Chicago Press, 2003.

Findlay, Ronald and O'Rourke, Kevin H., 'Commodity Market Integration, 1500–2000', in Michael D. Bordo, Alan M. Taylor and Jeffrey G. Williamson (eds), *Globalisation in Historical Perspective*, University of Chicago Press, 2003.

Gardiner, Robert (ed.), Conway's History of the Ship. *The Heyday of Sail*, 1995, *The Advent of Steam*, 1993, *The Shipping Revolution*, 1992, Conway Maritime Press.

Gibson, Andrew and Donovan, Arthur, *The Abandoned Ocean: A History of United States Maritime Policy*, University of South Carolina Press, 2001.

Harley, Charles K., 'The Shift from Sailing Ships to Steamships, 1850–1890; A Study in Technological Change and its Diffusion', in Donald N. McCloskey, 'Essays on a Mature Economy: Britain after 1840, Princeton University Press, 1971.

Harley, C. Knick, 'Transportation, The World Wheat Trade, and the Kuznets Cycle, 1850–1913', Explorations in Economic History, 17, 1980.

Harley, C. Knick, 'Ocean Freight Rates and Productivity, 1740–1913: The Primacy of Mechanical Invention Reaffirmed', Journal of Economic History, XLVIII, December, 1988.

Levinson, Marc, The Box: How the Shipping Container made the World Smaller and the World Economy Bigger, Princeton University Press, 2006.

Lilley, S., 'Technological Progress and the Industrial Revolution 1700–1914', in Carlo M. Cipolla (ed.), The Fontana Economic History of Europe, Fontana, 1973.

O'Rourke, Kevin H. and Williamson, Jeffrey G., 'When did Globalisation Begin?', European Review of Economic History, 6(I), April, 2002.

Palmer, Sarah, 'The British Shipping Industry, 1850–1914', in L. R. Fischer (ed.), Change and Adaptation in Maritime History, 1985.

Persson, Karl Gunnar, 'Mind the Gap! Transport Costs and Price Convergence in the Nineteenth Century Atlantic Economy', European Review of Economic History, 8(2), 2004.

Thomas, O. O., Stowage, The Properties and Stowage of Cargo, Brown, Son and Ferguson, 1968.

UNCTAD, Review of Maritime Transport, 2000.

Ville, Simon P. 'Transport and Communications', in Derek H. Aldcroft and Simon P. Ville (eds), The European Economy, 1750–1914, Manchester University Press, 1994.

# Silk

The ancient industry of silk production began in >CHINA and was supposedly instigated by the Empress Hsi Ling Shi in 2640 BC. It may have started there because in China the white mulberry and the moth silkworm, for which the tree provides food, co-exist naturally. It is said that the Empress discovered silk by accident when a silkworm cocoon dropped from a tree into a cup of hot tea and began to unravel its thread. This story illustrates the process by which silk is still obtained today, though now silkworm eggs are hatched in controlled conditions, though the caterpillars are still fed with white (or black) mulberry leaves. The caterpillars grow a silk cocoon to provide a safe place in which to turn into a chrysalis and a moth. The production process arrests this by placing the cocoons in hot water to kill the moth and soften the gum which binds the silk so that the fibre can be pulled out (reeling). The average length of silk filaments is some 700 metres and they are about one micron (a thousandth of a millimetre) thick. The final stages of the production process require 'throwing' the strands of silk by twisting them on reels, dyeing and weaving the cloth.

Silk has very desirable properties since it has high tensile strength, low combustibility, is light and elastic and refracts light. Mainly used for clothing, it has also had a number of other, minor, uses including parachutes, in musical instruments and, in ancient times, body armour. Chinese emperors took extreme measures to preserve the secrets of silk production, including a ban on the export of silkworm eggs, and enjoyed a monopoly for hundreds, perhaps thousands, of years. Legend has it that, in the 6th century, Persian monks smuggled silkworm eggs out of China to Constantinople in hollow canes and even before this there is evidence that Korea and Japan acquired the necessary knowledge for silk production. This knowledge soon spread to >INDIA, probably Bengal. There was early production in the Middle East and Spain and sericulture (the breeding of silkworms) was also established in Italy, which, by the 13th century became pre-eminent in the industry in Europe, a position it held until the early 18th century. High-quality silk is still produced in Italy today at Como.

Product and information travelled from China to Europe along the 'Silk Road', a route which has fired the imagination of travellers and writers from the time of Marco Polo (1256–1323). The Silk Road was given its name by a German geographer long after it ceased to be of importance. The 'Road' was not, in fact, a single route but rather a network of overland routes. As Feltwell (1990) points out, sea routes, which became of increasing importance, also have to be taken into account. These seaways over time brought silk to the coasts of North and South America. Very few people walked or rode the length of the Silk Road, goods travelled between relay trading points on camels or mules and horses covering a distance of 5,000–7,000 miles from North West China through Central Asia, Iran and Turkey to Rome. Silk was only one of the goods which travelled the route and which had a two-way traffic, including plants, spices, ceramics, jewels and other goods. Religious missionaries also travelled west to east.

In France, Louis XI established silk production at Tours in 1480, bringing in skilled workers from Genoa, Venice and Florence and curbing the import of silk products. The trade finally became concentrated in particular in Lyon where, by the late 18th century, there were 18,000 silk looms in operation. The >FRENCH REVOLUTION promised to destroy the French silk industry (silk was banned as a symbol of the aristocracy) but it was to recover. Lyon out-competed the younger English industry, which had benefited from large numbers of Huguenot (Protestant) silk workers that fled France and became established in Spitalfields, London, and elsewhere. James I had earlier tried to promote a silk industry in England in the 17th century and, although his initial efforts were not successful, an industry did become established. By 1815, London had 12,000 silk looms. It was thought that silk production would develop along the same lines as >COTTON AND COTTON TEXTILES, that is, with big companies and big mills. However, the Lyon model of small producers proved superior at dealing with the 'relentless variation' of the fashion trades in silk. In the 19th century, unlike its cotton equivalent, the industry in Britain went into steep decline. Though Britain did capture much of the European entrepôt trade in raw silk, there were only 900 silk mills left in Britain by 1901 at a time when there were still over 11,000 in Lyon (see Alain Cottereau's contribution to Sabel and Zeitlin, 1977). Widespread silkworm disease ruined sericulture in France and Italy in the mid-19th century. French silk production fell from 21,000 tons in 1853 to 600 tons in 1855. Italian output was smaller but fell by about 80 per cent in the same period. By 1870, the disease had been largely eradicated but, meanwhile, imports from Asia, mostly via Britain, filled the gap in the supply of raw silk. Chinese exports of silk to Britain quadrupled between 1850 and 1860, though with the opening of the Suez Canal in 1869 France and Italy began importing directly (Ma, 1966).

It had not been until the opening of the Treaty Ports, following the Treaty of Nanking in 1842, that China became a large-scale exporter. By 1900, silk exceeded tea as China's leading export and silk continued to be important until the 1930s, by which time Japan had long overtaken her as the world's leading silk exporter. Japan had begun to develop its silk industry in the Meiji period (1868–1911). In the 1920s, the Chinese government and merchants belatedly tried to modernize the industry but it was too late. World trade in silk, stimulated by rising incomes and demand in all the industrialized countries, grew rapidly. By 1938 Japan accounted for 76 per cent of world production of raw silk and China less than 9 per cent. Thereafter, Chinese production recovered and by 1980 accounted for about half of world silk production and 80 per cent of raw silk. Japan's output fell rapidly from 1970 as its rapid industrialization raised wages and rendered labour-intensive raw silk production uneconomic (Sinha, 1990; Feltwell, 1990). The aggregate value of world silk trade in 1927–30 reached 65 per cent of the value of the wool and 30 per cent of cotton. Silk exports were very important for the economic development of Italy, China and Japan. Raw silk as a percentage of total exports accounted for 40 per cent for Japan, 30 per cent for China and 20–5 per cent for Italy before >WORLD WAR I.

Technology transfers were important in influencing these developments. Mechanized reeling, using >STEAM POWER, was developed in Italy and France. By 1870 mechanization was in use throughout Europe and was beginning to be adopted in China. The Japanese were more independent technologically and actually led the world in technical development in the silk industry in the late 1930s. Japan could not match the quality of European output however, and focused on exporting raw silk to the USA. Japan accounted for more than 50 per cent of US raw silk imports in 1909 and over 70 per cent after 1916. These US imports were maintained at high levels until World War II, after which a decline set in and synthetic substitutes for silk and other textile fibres (rayon, for example) appeared. There are reports that, as with other innovations, >CHINA was first with loom pre-patterning systems. Min-Hsiung (1976) refers to the use of a Jacquard-type draw loom as long ago as the Han Dynasty (206 BC–AD 220). Be that as it may, nothing seems to have come of it and it was not until 1804 that Joseph Marie Jacquard, the son of a weaver in Lyon, building on earlier inventions, built a punched-card machine to allow accurate weaving of complex patterns. This important innovation, which was also a forerunner of the computer (>ELECTRONICS), reduced labour costs because it allowed relatively unskilled labour to produce high-quality woven products. The adoption of the power loom for silk weaving came more slowly than with other textile fibres, except in the USA, where producers were more interested in consistency and volume than in complex patterns. Today, some of the earlier aspects of silk production have been automated, including silkworm feeding.

In the 18th and early 19th centuries in Japan, silk weaving was carried out in rural households and located near sources of power and raw silk. From about 1850 weaving began to be concentrated in towns (Francks, 1999). The expansion of exports was helped by the development of new silkworm varieties capable of producing crops of cocoons over the summer and autumn, when farmers had more labour to spare than in the spring, which is the time the traditional varieties spin their cocoons (>PROTO-INDUSTRIALIZATION). The growth of cocoon output put pressure on the reeling stage, which became a separate activity. At first water power, and later steam power, speeded up output and improved quality. Competition from India and China encouraged change and loom production shifted to town mills. To increase the labour catchment area and reduce labour turnover, dormitories were built for young female workers. As in other countries undergoing >INDUSTRIAL REVOLUTIONS, conditions were grim, with 12-hour days to allow 24-hour working. Gradually conditions were improved as it became understood that it paid to encourage a core skilled workforce, although unionization did not happened extensively until the 1920s.

Though never an important exporter and always dependent upon imported raw silk, the rise of the silk industry in the >USA was, after initial failure, eventually quite spectacular. In the early colonial period and after there were repeated attempts to raise silkworms on an economic basis. The earliest attempts were, it is said, motivated by the desire of James I to avoid dependence on the raising of tobacco, to which he was strongly averse. According to Faulkner (1960), sericulture failed not because of the climate but because high American labour costs would not allow such a labour-intensive activity. The first silk mill was in Massachusetts in 1810. John Ryle commenced silk production at Paterson, New Jersey, in 1840. Paterson had water power and water of the right quality and was to become pre-eminent in the American trade before World War I. By 1860, there were 42 silk mills

in the north east of the USA. Up to 1860, the American mills used European technology, but they then evolved a technology of their own, especially in the adoption of power mills, which by 1905 had wiped out the hand looms which were still widespread in Europe. Total US silk production by value rose from $10 million in 1870 to $172 million in 1910, and the number of silk mills rose from 67 in 1850, to 483 in 1900. Silk mills spread from New England to the Middle and Atlantic states. By the early 1910s, the US industry had overtaken the French to become the world's largest, though Lyon in France and Como in Italy continue to have leadership in pattern design and sophisticated weaving (Ma, 1966).

In >INDIA, silk was imported from China from the earliest days of that trade but mulberry culture was first introduced in the 15th century, probably in Bengal. By the second half of the 17th century, Bengal had replaced China as a supplier of raw silk to Indian looms, while the English started the export of raw silk from India to Continental Europe. The >ENGLISH EAST INDIA COMPANY promoted the export of raw silk to Britain after the Battle of Plassey in 1757 and also mulberry cultivation (Sinha, 1990). By the mid-1980s, India was ahead of Japan in the production of mulberry silk, pushing Japan into third place after China. India has a monopoly of 'wild silk', which is tougher than the conventional product.

After World War II, exports of silk from Korea, once ahead of those of Japan declined. The Soviet Union became the fourth largest producer of raw silk but Brazil and other countries have become significant producers. According to Feltwell (1990), there are over 30 countries producing silk today, including Thailand and Indonesia, while production in Europe is reviving.

## References

Faulkner, Harold Underwood, *American Economic History*, Harper & Row, 1960.

Feltwell, John, *The Story of Silk*, Alan Sutton, 1990.

Francks, Penelope, *Japanese Economic Development*, 1999.

Li, Lillian M., *China's Silk Trade: Traditional Industry in the Modern World, 1842–1937*, Harvard University Press, 1981.

Ma, Debin, 'The Modern Silk Road: The Global Silk Market 1850–1930', *Journal of Economic History*, 56, June, 1966.

Min-Hsiung, Shi, *The Silk Industry in Ching China*, University of Michigan, 1976.

Sabel, Charles F. and Jonathan Zeitlin (eds), *World of Possibilities: Flexibility and Mass Production in Western Industrialisation*, Cambridge University Press, 1997.

Sinha, Sanjay, *The Development of Indian Silk: A Wealth of Opportunities*, Intermediate Technology Publications, 1990.

# Silver

Silver has been mined from the earliest days of economic activity, not only as a useful workable commodity with attractive and marketable attributes but also as a universally acceptable medium of exchange and medium of account facilitating commercial transactions. Techniques for the extraction of silver from ores in Anatolia were discovered and records have demonstrated the use of silver for financial transactions as early as the 18th century BC. Darius, who was King of Persia between 521 BC and 486 BC, issued coins of silver and >GOLD which circulated throughout his Empire from the Mediterranean to >INDIA. Silver eventually became the dominant precious metal as the supply of gold was limited at the time because an Egyptian monopoly controlled the gold mines located in Nubia. As the Greek city-state of Athens grew more powerful, it exploited the development of its highly productive silver mines at Laureion, which proved to be very profitable. These mines were the largest producer of silver worldwide until the first century AD. The silver coins which Athens issued were accepted throughout the trade routes of the Mediterranean as a medium of exchange as they were respected for their standards of quality, which the Athens authorities were careful to maintain. Athens was able for a number of years to impose in effect a silver standard on the city-states which it controlled.

As Laureion passed its peak of production, the extraction of silver shifted to mines in Spain, which were developed by the Romans after they had defeated Carthage, and these mines became the major source of silver until the 8th-century invasion of Spain by the Moors. Thereafter, silver was discovered and developed in Germany, Austria-Hungary and Eastern Europe. The Romans produced a silver coin, the denarius, and a bronze coin, the as, later augmented by a gold aureus worth 25 denarii. The denarius, or silver penny, became the coin of Europe until the 12th century and the basis of a unit of account of 12 pennies to a shilling, a structure that formed the basis of the monetary regime of >BRITAIN with 12 pennies in a shilling and 20 shillings in a pound until the decimalization of its currency in 1971. The development of new techniques and processes for the extraction of silver from lead ore enabled a rapid expansion in silver production in Europe in the late 15th and early

16th centuries until they lost profitability with the fall in silver prices following the importation of silver from the New World, as the Spanish began in the 16th century to develop the silver-bearing ores of South America.

The two major areas of silver production exploited by the Spanish were in Mexico at Zacatecas, discovered in 1546, and Guanajuato, discovered in 1550, and in Upper Peru in what is now Bolivia. These areas presented quite different sets of problems. In Mexico there were few people and the Spanish imported Indians and slaves from other places to work the mines; in due course a labour force became established which worked for wages. In contrast, Upper Peru was well populated and the manpower problem was met by an annual recruitment drive and transportation to the mines of workers and families who remained under the direct control of the Spanish government. In 1545, silver was discovered at Potosí, which proved to be the most productive site in the region. The Spanish invented a refining process which exploited the property that silver was soluble in mercury and which was applied from the 1550s to improve greatly the recovery of silver from ore. The mercury required for this process was mined only in Almaden in Spain and at Huancavelica in Peru and was under the control of the Spanish state. As a result, silver production increased in the 1570s and reached peak levels between 1610 and 1645. After a period of decline, silver production recovered and reached new peaks towards the end of the 18th century (Williamson, 1992). During the 300 years after 1500, the region produced over 80 per cent of world supplies of silver.

It has been estimated that it took 600 years to produce about 45,000 tonnes of silver from the mines of the countries around the Mediterranean. Spain's American mines took only 200 years to produce about the same (Stein, 2000). As a consequence, the quantity of precious metals entering through Spain into monetary circulation in Europe increased threefold. The inflow began in the 1530s, reached a peak towards the end of the 16th century and then declined slowly through the 17th century. Flows of silver radiated out from Seville to Italy, France and North Western and Eastern Europe and eventually through the Middle East to >INDIA and >CHINA. The increase in the quantity of money reinforced a growth in the general level of prices. By the end of the 16th century they were about 300 per cent higher than at the beginning of the century (>PRICES AND INFLATION). During this period, the purpose of government policy was generally considered to be for the accumulation of treasure in the form of gold and silver because treasure was the indicator of wealth and enabled the state to finance the defence of its overseas interests. Spain, for instance, for a short period, even attempted to ban the export of gold and silver (>MERCANTILISM).

Silver also became an established monetary medium in China, although there were periods when the government issued paper money, such as during the Song Dynasty (900–1200 AD), the Mongols (1276 and 1367) and the Ming Dynasty (1360–1644). Initially, during the Ming Dynasty, precious metals were not permitted as a medium of exchange, the function being carried out by paper notes and bronze coins. However, the use of paper did not survive and in the 15th and 16th centuries silver was accepted for the payment of taxes and a >BIMETALLIC SYSTEM emerged in which silver was used for large payments and for long-distant trade and bronze coins for small cash payments. In the 16th century, the rising demand for silver in China was met primarily from west Japan, where silver deposits were discovered in the 1530s and supplemented from American silver shipped through Manila from 1571, as well as through Europe. International arbitrage businesses flourished by exploiting the differential between the gold/silver ratio that existed between Europe, India and China. In spite of the inflow of silver into China, the gold/silver ratio in China stayed below the international level except for a brief period in the 1640s. 'Silver wanders throughout all the world in its peregrinations before flocking to China, where it remains as of its natural centre' (quoted in Glahn, 1996). By the end of the 17th century, little silver was available from Japan, and China met its demand mainly from silver imported across the Pacific from America.

Latin America dominated world silver production until improved mining and refining techniques together with new discoveries, particularly in the >USA, Australia and in Europe, led to a growth in other sources which led to the level of world output increasing by four times in the course of the 19th century. In 1850s, world production of silver averaged about 886 metric tonnes per annum and of this the USA accounted for less than 1 per cent, but by the beginning of the 1870s world production had increased to 1969 tonnes per annum of which the USA accounted for nearly 30 per cent.

As with other countries in Europe, Britain had long been on a silver standard. However, in the 17th century, the currency became seriously debased through the clipping of the silver coinage, a temptation that coins were prone to when they emerged from the manufactory irregularly shaped because of the old method of manufacture by hammering them out. With the invention of the press, better accuracy and regularity was obtained in the coinage and the problem of clipping was averted. When France began to use the new manufacturing techniques, it recalled its old coinage to replace them with the new. Britain did not do so. It has been estimated that by 1695, the silver content of the coins left circulating in Britain was on average less than a half of its original weight. Eventually, a major re-coinage was completed in 1696 and technically Britain was on a bimetallic standard. However, the silver/gold ratio was set higher than that in France and, although the value of the gold guinea which had been 21½ silver shillings was reduced to 21 shillings in 1717, it was still too high to prevent silver from tending to leave circulation and Britain from becoming de facto on the gold rather than the bimetallic or silver standard (Quinn, 1996). After suspending convertibility during the Napoleonic War, Britain officially began to move on to the gold standard by the Coinage Act of 1817 and completed the process in 1821 (<GOLD STANDARD).

At the beginning of the 19th century, only Britain was on a gold standard, other countries were either on a bimetallic standard, using gold and silver, or on a silver standard. During the course of the century, however, changes in the gold/silver ratio began to impose strains on these monetary systems. In the first two decades or so after the end of the Napoleonic Wars, the price of silver relative to gold was stable. By the mid-century, the price of silver began slowly to appreciate. The major effect of this appreciation arose from the French bimetallic standard, which had fixed its gold/silver ratio at 15.5 to 1 which became out of line with the market. As a consequence, gold was exported to France and profitably exchanged there for silver, which was in turn sent to India and China. As a result, the French monetary system became deficient in silver and the French franc became, in effect, solely based on gold. In spite of this, the Latin Monetary Union, a currency union formed in 1865 between France, Belgium, Italy and Switzerland, was based on a bimetallic system. In 1867, Greece and the Papal States adopted compatible currencies, Romania joined in 1868 and in 1871 Austria also concluded an agreement with the Union (Cottrell, 1992).

The price of silver reached a peak in 1860 of 62.1 pence (£0.25875) per ounce and from that date began a decline. By 1880, it had fallen to 52.2 pence (£0.2175) per ounce by 1890 to 47.7 pence (£0.19875) per ounce and by 1914 it hit a low of 24.1 pence (£0.10042) per ounce. This long collapse in the price was a result of the combination of many factors. World silver production in the second half of the 19th century grew rapidly as a result of new discoveries particularly in the USA, with such major finds as the Comstock Lode in Nevada and in Leadville in Colorado, as well as in Australia and elsewhere. Production rose from about 2,000 tonnes per annum in the early 1870s to reach 5,400 tonnes by 1900 and 7,000 tonnes by 1913. At the same time, encouraged by this fall in the value of silver, countries eventually abandoned silver and followed Britain on to the gold standard.

In the 19th century, the USA was legally on a bimetallic system. The Coinage Act of 1792 had set the silver/gold ratio at 15 to 1, which priced gold too low. An increase in production of silver in Russia, Mexico and Latin America caused the market price to fall. The Coinage Act of 1834 changed the official silver/gold ratio to 16 to 1 to bring it more in line with the market rate. However, the discovery of major new gold deposits, in the USA in 1848 and in Australia in 1851, led to a fall in the relative price of gold. The silver dollar became worth 104 cents on the market and as a consequence there was a loss of silver from circulation. With the beginning of the Civil War, the rise in the price of silver led to silver coinage leaving circulation, much of it being exported to Canada and Latin America. In 1873, the US government passed the Coinage Act which, by omitting the silver dollar from a re-coinage of the currency, in effect shifted the country on to a de facto gold standard. In 1878, the Bland–Allison Act authorized the coinage of between $2 million and $4 million of silver per month and by 1890, when the Act was repealed, $380 of silver coins had been minted. An attempt was made to underpin the price of silver by the Silver Purchase Acts of 1880 and 1890.

From the 1870s, the increase in the supply of gold reaching monetary circulation in the developed economies fell behind economic growth and with the additional demand for gold from countries adopting the gold standard, the resulting monetary shortage led to a fall in prices. In the USA, from 1870–80, there was a fall in the general level of prices of 16 per cent and a fall in the same period in farm prices of 28 per cent. In the following decade the general level of prices fell a further 11 per cent and farm prices fell 13 per cent (Rockoff, 1995). Agriculture, therefore, suffered particularly during this period and the farming communities strongly supported the 'free silver' political movement to expand the money supply through the re-establishment of a true bimetallic standard with the return of silver. The general view has been that the advocates of silver were appreciative of the quantity theory of money and envisaged a consequential inflation which would float agriculture off its burden of debt. However, after the Civil War there was a shortage of small denomination currency and the Act of 1873 aggravated the problem. Further, the Coin Act of 1876 placed a limit of $50 million on subsidiary silver coin and fractional currency, in effect committing the economy to a level of such currency below that which existed before the Civil War. This restriction was not legally raised until 1900. Allowing for the change in the value of a dollar, it is as if in today's USA the smallest denomination coin or currency was $50. A typical farmer had had to accumulate debts with his supplier until they reached an exchangeable amount (Gramm, 2004). In 1896, the Democratic Presidential candidate, William Jennings Bryan, campaigned on his refusal to suffer mankind 'to be crucified on a cross of gold'. The recession, however, was coming to an end and prices were beginning to rise and unemployment to fall. Gold supplies were on the rise following new discoveries in Canada and South Africa, augmented by improved technology for the refining of low-grade ore. In a way, the quantity theory of money argument of the free silver movement was vindicated. The struggle between the opposing forces supporting silver, gold or bimetallism swirling around the free silver movement was finally encapsulated in the allegory of a literary classic in Dorothy's silver shoes and the yellow brick road of L. Frank Baum's 1900 book *The Wonderful Wizard of Oz* (the production company MGM changed the silver shoes to ruby in the 1939 film of the book) (Dighe, 2002; Rockoff, 1995). The USA went officially on to the gold standard on the passing of the Gold Standard Act in 1900.

## References

Cottrell, P. L., 'Silver, Gold and the International Monetary Order, 1851–1896', in S. N. Broadberry and N. F. R. Crafts (eds), *Britain in the International Economy, 1870–1939*, Cambridge University Press, 1992.

Dighe, Ranjit S. (ed.), *The Historian's Wizard of Oz: Reading L. Frank Baum's Classic as a Political and Monetary Allegory*, Praeger, 2002.

Glahn, Richard von, 'Myth and Reality of China's Seventeenth-Century Monetary Crisis', *Journal of Economic History*, 56(2), June, 1996.

Gramm, Marshall and Gramm, Phil, 'The Free Silver Movement in America: A Re-interpretation', *Journal of Economic History*, 64(4), December, 2004.

Quinn, Stephen, 'Gold, Silver, and the Glorious Revolution: Arbitrage between Bills of Exchange and Bullion', *Economic History Review*, XLIX(3), August, 1996.

Rockoff, Hugh, 'The "Wizard of Oz" as a Monetary Allegory', in Robert Whaples and Dianne C. Betts, *Historical Perspectives on the American Economy*, Cambridge University Press, 1995.

Stein, Stanley J. and Stein, Barbara H., *Silver, Trade, and War*, Johns Hopkins University Press, 2000.

Williamson, Edwin, *The Penguin History of Latin America*, Penguin, 1992.

## Slavery

Slaves from Sub-Saharan Africa were shipped to East and North Africa and the Middle East from the 7th century and this trade still persisted at the end of the 20th century. It has been estimated that about 8.5 million people were transported along these routes between 1500 and 1890, about 60 per cent of the total for the whole period. The first modern European country to enter the slave trade was Portugal in the15th century. The European interest did not become significant, however, until they began to develop their colonies in the Americas. This trans-Atlantic traffic began early in the 16th century and lasted until the 1870s. About 11 million slaves from Africa were shipped to the Americas on these routes. In total, therefore, it has been estimated that over 25 million Africans were enslaved and transported. The conditions in which these people were transported were appalling and their treatment cruel in the extreme from the time at which they were captured and incarcerated in West Africa to their arrival in chains in America and the Caribbean. In Britain their treatment was concealed behind euphemisms and silence but once this was broken and the realization of the truth began to emerge among the general population the movement for its abolition gathered pace. An important figure influencing this was Thomas Clarkson (1760–1846), who helped to form the Society for Effecting the Abolition of Slavery in 1787. In 1789, he published a diagram showing the method of loading 482 slaves into a slave ship, which showed in an unambiguous undeniable image the cruel treatment of the slaves as inanimate parcels of freight cargo. He organized a boycott of sugar consumption and gained the support of William Wilberforce (1759–1833), who eventually got a bill passed in Parliament for abolishing the slave trade in 1807. Britain had made slavery illegal in Britain in 1772 but did not abolish slavery throughout its Empire until 1833. Classical economists were supportive of the evangelical anti-slavery movement and came

into conflict with the ideas of literati such as Thomas Carlyle (1795–1881), who accused them of being in a coalition against white planters. A riot by impoverished ex-slaves in Jamaica in 1865 was so brutally suppressed by the Governor John Eyre (1815–1901) that J. S. Mill (1806–1873), together with Herbert Spencer (1820–1903) and Thomas Huxley (1825–1895), recommended his trial for murder but were opposed successfully by Thomas Carlyle and John Ruskin (1819–1900) (>CLASSICAL AND NEO-CLASSICAL ECONOMICS).

All the states in the north eastern >USA had abolished slavery by the end of the 18th century, having followed the lead given by Pennsylvania and Massachusetts in 1780. By 1821 slavery was illegal north of the Mason–Dixon Line. Britain's naval blockade from 1808 is estimated to have had some effect on the North Atlantic trade, although 1.5 million slaves did reach Cuba and Brazil between 1821 and 1865 and about 250,000 were shipped to the Southern states of the USA. The Emperor, Don Pedro II, freed the slaves in Brazil in 1889. Slavery was finally abolished in the USA in 1865 on the conclusion of the >AMERICAN CIVIL WAR. Three Amendments to the American Constitution were passed; Article XIII abolished slavery; Article XIV established the Rights of Citizens under the law; and Article XV established the rights of citizens whatever their race, colour or previous condition of servitude.

An important initiator of the Atlantic slave trade was the >SUGAR business. The cultivation of sugar in Europe had spread from the Eastern Mediterranean to the Portuguese islands of Madeira and Sao Tome in the Atlantic and the experience gained had been applied to Brazil, which by 1700 had become the world's largest sugar producer. Sugar plantations were also established by a number of other European countries throughout the Caribbean. The colonists found, however, that the supply of land could not be productively matched with a corresponding supply of labour because diseases introduced by Europeans had severely reduced the indigenous populations. The importation of slaves from Africa began in order to correct this labour deficiency.

The first African slave to reach the mainland of North America was landed by the Dutch at Jamestown in 1619. By the end of the 17th century African slaves were working on the tobacco plantations of Virginia and Maryland. The plantation system, specializing in crops such as tobacco and cotton as well as sugar, proved an ideal structure for the employment of slave labour and the demand for these crops in the European markets grew rapidly with the fall in their prices. Early in the 18th century, >BRITAIN became a leading player in this trade. Of the 6 million Africans shipped across the Atlantic in the 18th century, 40 per cent were in British ships.

Slavery generated economic activity in three locations, each at the corner of a triangular trade. In Europe, particularly Britain because of her early industrial development (>INDUSTRIAL REVOLUTION IN BRITAIN), manufactures, such as textiles, weaponry, alcohol and metal goods, were exported to West Africa in exchange for slaves. From West Africa, the slaves were transported to North and South America and the Caribbean islands and exchanged for the primary products of the plantations for shipment to Europe. Some of the slaves were refugees from famine, debt or the law but the majority was taken in war or captured specifically

for trade. The capture of people into slavery, their transport to the coast, their buying and selling became institutionalized in Africa into, in some places, a major economic activity. The activities of the slavers caused population loss and, because of their preference for young males, population imbalances in the immediate hinterlands of the ports of shipment and their boundaries continued to be pushed further inland. In the course of time, individual state governments played an increasingly interventionist role in the business in order to get access to its profits. The surpluses from slavery were narrowly distributed among the powerful in politics and business in Africa and led to damaging military conflict. The debilitating effect on population growth and structure and the loss of economic potential due to dysfunctional institutions suggest that the countries of Africa affected by the slave trade could hardly have derived any benefit in spite of the profits that may have been made by individuals.

There has been some debate as to whether the Atlantic slave trade was a significant factor in the industrialization of Europe (>INDUSTRIAL REVOLUTIONS) in so far as the excess profits generated could have assisted in supporting investment in the new technology. However, the rate of return earned in the business has been estimated to have hardly differed from that of the alternative investments available and could have played only a minor role, if any. However, the trade did bring down the prices of the products of the plantations such as sugar, tobacco and >COFFEE in the European markets and established these products to the benefit of consumers (Eltis and Engerman, 1993).

There had been a long debate among economic historians with

arguments for and against the efficiency of the slave plantation system in the American South, the spiritual and physical impoverishment of the slave workers and their families and the motivation of the planters, whether paternalistic or harshly profit-seeking (Phillips, 2006; Stampp, 1956; Conrad and Meyer, 1958; Elkins, 1959; Blassingame, 1972). In 1974, Fogel and Engerman published *Time on the Cross*, which, on the basis of the analyses of an extensive data set, concluded that the plantation system was profitable and the slave labour force was generally treated with consideration and not abused. They argued that the slaves were fed even better than free workers, were as well accommodated and cared for when sick. The plantation system was estimated to be more productive than equivalent free farms and was still flourishing at the time of the Civil War. Fogel and Engerman concluded that the planters earned a healthy rate of return of 10 per cent on their investment. A very high proportion of a planter's capital was invested in his slaves and so it was in his own interest to look after them. Fogel and Ederman estimated that slaves retained 90 per cent of what they produced; others argued that it was much lower. Fogel and Enderman recognized that the slaves were subject more to the law of the plantation than the state, they had little or no prospect for advancement, no matter how talented, and their families were at risk of separation when sold. Fogel and Engerman's study attracted considerable criticism, beginning with a review article by David and Temin in 1974 (followed, in 1976, by David *et al.* and in 1989 by further work by Fogel), which disputed their interpretation of the data but also argued that there was a conceptual fault line throughout their argument. Their perspective was biased towards those of the planters and the consumers in the markets for their products. The economic analysis was inconsistent with the propositions of welfare economics. There was, however, a logical flaw implicit in the economic analyses applied to slavery. Welfare economics and the theory of social cost benefit analysis rest on the premise that consumers, producers and workers are free, within the law, to make choices. The slave has been deprived of the ability to choose between alternatives. A menu may be drawn up of the meat, fruit and vegetables consumed by a typical slave and its quantities of calories, protein and vitamins shown to be comparable with a free worker. But, the free worker chooses his menu, the plantation owner the slave's. The loss of freedom is an immeasurable loss to the slave in itself but is also to be compounded over and over throughout life in the continuous loss of choice between alternatives that a free person makes every day. Fogel and Enderman, in 1977, emphasized that 'It should, of course, be emphasised that greater efficiency does not mean greater good'.

The plantations may have benefited from economies of scale but they also benefited from the disciplined regulation of slave labour on production-line working methods and the avoidance of costs associated with the employment of free labour. The slave plantation system established a feudal structure (>SERFDOM) inimitable to the growth and development of a modern capitalist society. In 1978, Wright argued that taking the long run, the plantation system was inefficient because it was embedded in a structure that inhibited change. The rate of growth of the South was comparable with that of the North in the antebellum period, but it was distorted by the excessive proportion of capital invested in the plantations to the detriment of commerce and infrastructure investment.

Slavery in some form persisted into the 21st century world wide. In 1998, the International Labour Organization (ILO) issued a *Declaration on Fundamental Principles and Rights at Work* and in 2005 published a study which estimated that about 10 million people were subjected to forced labour in the private sector, 2.4 million of whom had to endure the degrading practice of human trafficking. The ILO calculated that the trafficking of women, children and men yielded profits amounting to US$ 32 billion per annum.

### References

Blackburn, Robin, *The Making of New World Slavery: From Baroque to the Modern 1492–1800*, Verso, 1997.

Blassingame, J. W., *The Slave Community; Plantation Life in the Antebellum South*, University of Chicago Press, 1972.

Conrad, Alfred and Meyer, John, 'The Economics of Slavery in the Antebellum South', *Journal of Political Economy*, April, 1958.

David, Paul, Gutman, Herbert, Sutch, Richard, Temin, Peter and Wright, Gavin, *Reckoning with Slavery: A Critical Study in the Quantitative History of American Negro Slavery*, Oxford University Press, 1976.

David, Paul A. and Temin, Peter, 'Slavery: The Progressive Institution?', *Journal of Economic History*, September, 1974.

Elkins, Stanley, *Slavery: A Problem in American Institutional and Intellectual Life*, University of Chicago Press, 1959.

Eltis, David and Engerman, Stanley L., 'Fluctuations in Sex and Age Ratios in the Trans-Atlantic Slave Trade, 1663–1864', *Economic History Review*, XLVI(2), 1993.

Eltis, David and Engerman, Stanley L., 'The Importance of Slavery and the Slave Trade to Industrializing Britain', *Journal of Economic History*, 60(1), 2000.

Evans, E. W. and Richardson, David, 'Hunting for Rents: the Economics of Slaving in pre-Colonial Africa', *Economic History Review*, XLVIII(4), 1995.

Fogel, Robert William, *Without Consent or Contract*, Norton, 1989.

Fogel, Robert William and Engerman, Stanley L., *Time on the Cross: The Economics of American Negro Slavery*, W. W. Norton & Company, 1974.

Fogel, Robert W. and Engerman, Stanley L., 'Explaining the Relative Efficiency of Slave Agriculture in the Antebellum South', *American Economic Review*, June, 1977.

Hanes, Christopher, 'Turnover Cost and the Distribution of Slave Labor in Anglo-America', *Journal of Economic History*, 56(2), 1996.

Inikori, Joseph E., 'Market Structure and the Profits of the British African Trade in the Late 18th Century', *Journal of Economic History*, 41, 1981.

International Labour Organization, *A Global Alliance Against Forced Labour*, Geneva, 2005.

Phillips, Ulrich Bonnel, *American Negro Slavery: A Survey of the Supply, Employment and Control of Negro Labor as Determined in the Plantation Regime* (1918), Echo Library, reprinted 2006.

Ransom, Roger L. and Sutch, Richard, 'Capitalists Without Capital: The Burden of Slavery and the Impact of Emancipation', *Agricultural History*, 62(3), 1988.

Stampp, Kenneth M., *The Peculiar Institution: Slavery in the Ante-Bellum South*, Alfred A. Knopf, 1956.

Wright, Gavin, *The Political Economy of the Cotton South: Households, Markets, and Wealth in the Nineteenth Century*, Norton, 1978.

# Small and Medium Enterprises

Business enterprises obviously vary in scale and this has always been so; some trades require more people and resources than others, while some firms are more successful than others. Before the 18th century, however, there were very few really large enterprises and these were mostly engaged in construction, finance or trading. There were quite large enterprises in banking and trade at least as long ago as those of Bardi and Peruzzi in 13th-century Florence and whose activities spanned several countries (>MONEY AND BANKING). The later great government-chartered trading companies such as the >ENGLISH EAST INDIA COMPANY were also international in scope. Markets were small and local for the most part, however. Communications were slow and technology had yet to develop sufficiently to require scale, with a few exceptions, such as shipbuilding, and for these state involvement was usual. Another important limitation on scale was the constraint on raising capital under the prevailing sole proprietor or partnership legal forms (>COMPANIES). In the 18th and 19th centuries, all these limitations on enterprise scale were progressively reduced or removed as production and communications technology developed and as markets expanded following the continuing >COMMERCIAL REVOLUTION, the >CONSUMER REVOLUTIONS and the >INDUSTRIAL REVOLUTIONS. The emergence of the corporate form of business enterprise which did not require government charter, together with developing >CAPITAL MARKETS in the second half of the 19th century, were more important than anything else in allowing the growth of very large commercial enterprises.

The economic history of the business population is one of long-term increases in the average size of enterprises, though in terms of numbers the majority of enterprises have remained small (the size distribution is heavily skewed to the left). Reliable and comparable data on these size distributions did not become generally available until the inter-war period and even then mostly for manufacturing. In >BRITAIN it was not thought necessary to collect census data for retailing, for example, until 1950. All the indications are, however, that the share of smaller enterprises in output and employment was on a downward trend from the 19th century until the 1960s when this well-established trend reversed (Segenberger, 1990). There were temporary reversals before this, for example, in the 1930s when there was an increase in new firm formations as founders started businesses because of a lack of employment opportunities in the >GREAT DEPRESSION. Formation rates have also varied regionally: it seems that small firms in close proximity breed other small firms by sub-contracting and the transfer of experience among employees working closely with owner-managers (Foreman-Peck, 1985). The reasons for the interruption of the overall long-term trend, however, are not fully understood. It does not seem to be the result of the growing importance of the service sector in the economy, since the change has also taken place in manufacturing. On balance, technological development seems to be favouring smaller organizations, but this hardly seems an adequate explanation; nor can the changes be explained by politics. Policy changes in the Reagan–Thatcher era led to some improvement in the environment for smaller firms but the change of trend in the 1960s preceded these political developments by two decades. The international and enduring character of the shift to smaller firms suggests that more fundamental factors are at work. Increased competition from the resurging economies in Asia and the developing world, a reduction in protectionism (>INTERNATIONAL TRADE) and, later, the unwinding of the inflationary pressures (which tend to affect SMEs adversely because of their weaker market positions) have put pressure on larger firms. These firms have sought greater efficiency by shedding labour, refocusing on core activities and increasing sub-contracting to smaller firms.

It is interesting to note that the number of businesses in relation to the human population seems to differ considerably between countries. These differences seem to be attributable in part to differences in tastes and culture (see, for example the case of retailing in Italy in >CONSUMER REVOLUTIONS). Some of the apparent differences reflect lack of comparability in the data but in particular there do appear to be more small firms in Southern European countries than elsewhere. Japan, contrary to common opinion, has somewhat fewer firms in relation to the human population than the >USA, which in turn has about the same number as the Britain (Bannock, 2005).

The emergence of large capital-intensive enterprises under managerial, rather than proprietorial, direction, from the end of the 19th century led economists to emphasize the importance of large firms and economies of scale and scope and to underplay the complementary roles of SMEs. Although SMEs have always accounted for a majority of employment (though not of net output) their importance has tended to be neglected since the Second Industrial Revolution (>INDUSTRIAL REVOLUTIONS), which many accounts imply was solely the result of large-firm activity. Notable in this tradition has been Alfred Chandler,

who explained the lagging performance of Britain in that period compared with Germany and the USA in terms of slowness in adopting managerial capitalism. This thesis has attracted much criticism (>CHANDLER). Earlier economists such as Alfred Marshall were well aware of the importance of small firms (>CLASSICAL AND NEO-CLASSICAL ECONOMICS). Piore and Sabel (1984) were to resurrect Marshall's analysis of the *external economies* of scale, which could be enjoyed by small firms in >INDUSTRIAL DISTRICTS, as distinct from the *internal economies* of scale emphasized later. Scranton (1997) has attempted to recast the conventional description of the history of the Second Industrial Revolution in the USA from the Civil War to the 1920s in terms of the role of speciality manufacturers, that is, smaller firms. Others have argued that crude comparisons of labour >PRODUCTIVITY between small and large firms are an oversimplification since SMEs are perforce relatively efficient users of capital. Even in the field of science and innovation, it has been demonstrated that small firms, some of which like Microsoft have grown into large firms, account for a disproportionate share of technical developments (for an early study of this, see Jewkes, 1969).

These are some of the issues relating to SMEs which have interested economic historians. Another is the extent to which imperfections in capital markets have constrained their ability to raise finance for expansion (>MONEY AND BANKING). Yet another is the role of family businesses. It was an over-attachment to family ownership to which Chandler pointed as one of the causes of Britain's under-performance. Others have stressed, however, that family businesses remained important in all Chandler's comparative countries and also in Japan and other Asian countries (Kirby and Rose, 1994). There are difficulties in defining family ownership. Since the vast majority of businesses are small, often employ members of the family and, where successful, tend to be passed on to other family members, then in one sense a major part of business is family-owned. The persistence of large family firms (industrial dynasties) can be explained by a number of factors. They have the advantage of reduced transaction costs, which are particularly important in rapidly changing environments. Also, in principle, they can take decisions quickly and normally have a strong commitment to long-term planning and prudent financing in the interests of succession (Colli, 2003). These advantages are not restricted to the older industries nor to particular sectors. Quantitative studies of performance relative to other forms of ownership have produced inconclusive results. Certainly strong family interests are to be found in many very large corporations such as FIAT, Michelin, Ford, Benetton, in Greek ship-owning and Japanese 'high technology'. Of course, family firms may decline over time or even break up over problems of succession, but transitional problems are common to all types of business.

The continuing importance of small firms, not least in terms of employment and innovation, has led virtually all governments to promote them as a matter of policy. This is not a recent development; the Netherlands introduced a consultancy service for SMEs in 1910 and Japan has had comprehensive policies for small-business support from the 1930s. Government activity in small business promotion increased after World War II when fears about the effects of continuing >CONCENTRATION on competition intensified. These concerns existed even though at the same time European governments were encouraging mergers of larger enterprises to compete against what then seemed to be a risk of domination by US-owned >MULTINATIONAL ENTERPRISES. There was special legislation, such as the US Small Business Act 1953, and legal frameworks for small-firm policies in Germany (at regional level, 1960) and in Japan (1963), as well as later in many other countries, including the newly independent states of Eastern Europe. Britain has never found it necessary to introduce comprehensive legislation on small firms but nonetheless has had extensive support systems since 1971. Policies in Britain and elsewhere have covered support for the various perceived disadvantages suffered by SMEs, including >TAXATION, >REGULATION, technical assistance and finance. It is not clear that these policies in practice have had much impact, according to Bannock (2005), except possibly in the field of science and innovation, but their existence confirms the strong social interest in the subject. It is argued that we cannot rely on large firms to maintain competition or innovation and in some countries, notably the USA, it is believed that small enterprise offers important scope for individual self-expression and, through the dispersal of economic power, support for democratic values. The fact is that small as well as large firms are characteristic of all capitalist economies and small firms have been the driving force in the recent economic resurgence of >CHINA (>ENTREPRENEURSHIP).

## References

Bannock, Graham, *The Economics and Management of Small Business: An*

*International Perspective*, Routledge, 2005.

Blackford, Mansel G. *The Rise of Modern Business in Great Britain, the United States and Japan*, University of North Carolina Press, 1998.

Colli, Andrea, *The History of Family Business, 1850–2000*, Cambridge University Press, 2003.

Foreman-Peck, J. S., 'Seedcorn or Chaff? New Firms and Industrial Performance in the Inter-War Economy', *Economic History Review*, 38, August, 1985.

Jewkes, John, Sawers, David and Stillerman, R., *The Sources of Invention*, Macmillan, 1969.

Kirby, Maurice W. and Rose, Mary B. (eds), *Business Enterprise in Modern Britain from the Eighteenth to the Twentieth Century*, Routledge, 1994.

Piore, Michel J. and Sabel, Charles F., *The Second Industrial Divide: Possibilities for Prosperity*, Basic Books, 1984.

Scranton, Philip, *Endless Novelty: Specialty Production and American Industrialisation, 1865–1925*, Princeton University Press, 1997.

Segenberger, W., Loveman, G. W. and Piore, M. J., *The Re-emergence of Small Enterprise: Restructuring in Industrialised Countries*, International Institute for Labour Studies, 1990.

# Smith, Adam

Adam Smith, who lived from 1723 to 1790, was born in Kirkaldy, Scotland. At the age of 14, he became a student at Glasgow University, where he studied mathematics, natural philosophy and history. In 1740, he went on to Balliol College, Oxford, having won a scholarship to help finance his studies. He stayed at Oxford for seven years before returning to Kirkaldy for two years, then moving to Edinburgh. Here, with the support of a patron, he delivered lectures on rhetoric. He was appointed to the post of Professor of Logic at Glasgow University in 1751 and, in the following year, to that of Professor of Moral Philosophy. His lectures were very popular and his reputation spread beyond the University. In 1759, he published *The Theory of Moral Sentiments*. From 1764, he travelled to France as tutor to the Duke of Buccleuch, until returning in 1766 to live with his mother at Kirkaldy until her death in 1784. In 1776, he published *An Inquiry into the Nature and Causes of the Wealth of Nations*. In 1778, he accepted the post of Commissioner of Customs in Scotland. He died in Edinburgh in 1790, regretting to a friend that he had done so little. In 1795, was published *Essays on Philosophical Subjects by the late Adam Smith*.

Adam Smith's *Wealth of Nations* provided the stimulus for the subsequent study of Economics to develop into a structured system of thought with the intellectual, logical discipline comparable to other sciences. The extraordinary impact of Adam Smith's influence is revealed at one point in >SCHUMPETER's extensive history of economic analysis, in which he wrote that he viewed the *Wealth of Nations* as not only the most successful book on economics but, of books on science, second only to Darwin's *Origin of Species* (Schumpeter, 1954).

Adam Smith was by temperament and training a moral philosopher and he viewed political economy, as economics was called at the time, as a part of moral philosophy and subject to its teaching. He propounded a concept of a natural order towards which the activities of men and women aspire (>PHYSIOCRATS). He conceived the economic system as similar to a machine which, if free to act, would yield the optimum of benefits for mankind. The machine was self-functioning, it may require to be maintained and serviced but it did not require to be controlled. In the

*Theory of Moral Sentiments* (1759), he argued from the premise that there existed a divine structure the purpose of which was beneficent: 'The happiness of mankind as well as of all other rational creatures, seems to have been the original purpose intended by the Author of nature when he brought them into existence'. Provided people act within the precepts of the natural law, human motivations will lead towards the best outcomes. Although individuals may be selfish as well as altruistic, on the whole they are, at heart, social and reluctant to antagonize others. The arguments, propositions and conclusions expounded in the development of his explanation of the structure of the economic system in *The Wealth of Nations* imply this natural order set out in *Theory of Moral Sentiments*. Within such a system, the interplay of the various activities, if allowed to function without interference, would lead to the optimum outcome. Economics would supply the tools necessary for the statesman to minimize such interference and so maximize the benefits. He gave a definition of the purpose of economics:

'First, to provide a plentiful revenue or subsistence for the people, or, more properly, to enable them to provide such a revenue or subsistence for themselves; and secondly, to supply the state or commonwealth with a revenue sufficient for the public services. It proposes to enrich both the people and the sovereign.' (*Wealth of Nations*, Book IV, Introduction)

The key word in this definition is revenue.

The 'Wealth' in *The Wealth of Nations* is not a stock of assets, whether of goods or money (>MERCANTILISM), but a flow, which would be called in today's terminology Gross National Income. Adam Smith was concerned with the growth in, not just the level of, the Gross National Income because he believed such growth to be vital for a harmonious and happy society. There are non-pecuniary, social benefits of economic growth as well as, non-pecuniary social costs:

'It deserves to be remarked, perhaps, that it is in the progressive state, while the society is advancing to the further acquisition, rather than when it has acquired its full compliment of riches, seems to be the happiest and the most comfortable. It is hard in the stationary, and miserable in the declining state. The progressive state is in reality the cheerful and the hearty state to all the different orders of the society. The stationary state is dull; the declining melancholy.' (*Wealth of Nations*, Book I, Chapter VIII)

Adam Smith set out his arguments on the nature of the economic system in five sections of the *The Wealth of Nations*, concerned with (1) Labour, (2) Stock, (3) Growth, (4) Systems (which include critiques of >MERCANTILISM and >PHYSIOCRATS) and (5) Public Finance.

Labour, he argued, is the fundamental measure of value and a variable in the determination of the price of a commodity:

'If in a nation of hunters, for example, it usually costs twice the labour to kill a beaver which it does to kill a deer, one beaver should naturally exchange for, or be worth two deer. It is natural that what is usually the produce of two days' or two hours' labour, should be worth double of what is usually the produce of one day's or one hour's labour.' (*Wealth of Nations*, Book I, Chapter VI)

The true value of any commodity is the amount of labour which it can command in the market:

'The value of any commodity, therefore, to the person who possesses it, and means not to use or consume it himself, but to exchange it for other commodities, is equal to the quantity of labour which it enables him to purchase or command. Labour, therefore, is the real measure of the exchangeable value of all commodities.' (*Wealth of Nations*, Book I, Chapter V)

Labour is a more reliable and truer measure of real value than money or even corn because of their market variabilities.

Nevertheless, he also acknowledged the part played by the influence of the level of demand and the availability of supply in determining the actual price of a commodity in the market. There are, therefore, two aspects to his approach to value: an apparent cost-of-production determinant and a market determinant. He had a concept of a natural price towards which the market price was always tending:

'When the market price of any commodity is neither more nor less than what is sufficient to pay the rent of the land, the wages of the labour, and the profits of the stock employed in raising, preparing, and bringing it to market, according to their natural rates, the commodity is then sold for what may be called its natural price.' (*Wealth of Nations*, Book I, Chapter VII)

The market price is determined by the short-run interplay of supply and demand. The natural price is the long-run equilibrium price.

Labour is the source of all wealth and the growth of a country's National Income comes from the increase in the labour supply and improvements in labour productivity. The supply of labour is determined by the same forces as those applying to commodities. In the long run, the wages of labour will determine their number. Although low wages do not appear to lower the birth rate, wages falling close to the subsistence level do increase severely the death rate of infants and high wages improve their survival rate. He noted that wealthy women had fewer children than the poor (>POPULATION). Improvements in productivity depend on the division of labour. As an example, Adam Smith quotes what he refers to as a very trifling manufacture, the trade of the pin maker. One workman could, he argues, scarcely make one pin a day. But when the business is organized such that pin manufacture is divided up into about 18 different tasks, a greatly increased output per man employed is achieved. In outlining this example, he indicates that improvements in labour productivity can come not only from the division of a particular operation into separate tasks but also from the specialization of an enterprise to the production of a particular output and the specialization of machinery to enable the different tasks to be carried out. The degree to which the division of labour can be pursued depends, he pointed out, crucially on the size of the market for the products being produced.

The underlying driving force of the economic system is the motivation of people to pursue their own interests and to improve their own condition:

'It is not from the benevolence of the butcher, or the brewer, or the baker, that we expect our dinner, but from their regard to their own interest. We address ourselves, not to their humanity, but to their self-love; and never talk to them of our necessities, but of their advantages.' (*Wealth of Nations*, Book I, Chapter II)

'As every individual, therefore, endeavours as much as he can both to employ his capital in the support of domestic industry, and so to direct that industry that its produce may be of the greatest value, every individual necessarily labours to render the annual revenue of society as great as he can. He generally, indeed, neither intends to promote the public interest, nor knows how much he is promoting it. By preferring the support of domestic to that of foreign industry in such a manner as its produce may be of the greatest value, he intends only his own gain, and he is in this, as in many other cases, led by an invisible hand to promote an end which was no part of his intention.' (*Wealth of Nations*, Book IV, Chapter II)

The structure and components of the system, the machine as it were, are such not only to drive it forward in terms of Gross National Income but also to allocate its available resources in a manner compatible with the wishes of society. The implication is that it is better not to interfere with the working of the mechanism and to ensure that the machine is allowed to run without impediment:

'The statesman, who should attempt to direct private people in what manner they ought to employ their capitals, would not only load himself with a most unnecessary attention, but assume an authority which could safely be trusted, not only to no single person, but to no council or senate whatever, and which would nowhere be so dangerous as in the hands of a man who had folly and presumption

enough to fancy himself fit to exercise it.' (*Wealth of Nations*, Book IV, Chapter II)

It was not only government that had to be discouraged but there were also imperfections in the system which ought to be attended to. Markets should be free and competitive but there was a tendency towards collusion and monopoly. He argued against long apprenticeships which serve only to restrict entry into their trades to inflate wages and profits to the detriment of society and the poor man who would otherwise have employment:

'The property which every man has in his own labour, as it is the original foundation of all other property, so it is the most sacred and inviolable. The patrimony of a poor man lies in the strength and dexterity of his hands; and to hinder him from employing this strength and dexterity in what manner he thinks proper without injury to his neighbour, is a plain violation of this most sacred property.' (*Wealth of Nations*, Book I, Chapter X, Part II)

He was particularly concerned with the behaviour of employers and merchants. There is, he argued, an inherent conflict between workers and their masters, given the former seek higher wages and the latter lower wages. But, the conflict is one sided:

'It is not, however, difficult to see which of the two parties must, upon ordinary occasions, have the advantage in the dispute, and force the other into a compliance with their terms. The masters, being fewer in number, can combine much more easily; and the law, besides, authorises or at least does not prohibit their combinations, while it prohibits those of the workmen…In all such disputes the masters can hold out much longer.' (*Wealth of Nations*, Book I, Chapter XIII)

'People of the same trade seldom meet together even for merriment and diversion, but the conversation ends in a conspiracy against the public, or some contrivance to raise prices.' (*Wealth of Nations*, Book I, Chapter X, Part I)

Society is divided into three producer groups, landlords, labourers and capitalists, and revenue was, thus, divided into rent, wages and profits, corresponding to these groups. The level of rent, unlike wages and profits, is determined by the level of prices. Rent, therefore:

'enters into the composition of the price of commodities in a different way from wages and profit. High or low wages and profit are the causes of high or low price; high or low rent is the effect of it. It is because high or low wages and profits must be paid, in order to bring a particular commodity to market, that the price is high or low; but it is because its price is high or low, a great deal more, or very little more, or no more, than what is sufficient to pay those wages and profit, that it affords a high rent, a low rent, or no rent at all.' (*Wealth of Nations*, Book I, Introduction Chapter XI)

The self-interest of landowners, therefore, is coincident with the interests of society as a whole and, consequently, policy advice offered by this group should be considered to be beneficial to society in so far as it should be objective. However, Adam Smith was a little sceptical:

'the proprietors of land never can mislead it, with a view to promote the interest of their own particular order; at least, if they have any tolerable knowledge of that interest. They are, indeed, too often defective in this tolerable knowledge. They are the only one of the three orders whose revenue costs them neither labour nor care, but comes to them, as it were, of its own accord, and independent of any plan or project of their own. This indolence…renders them too often, not only ignorant, but incapable of that application of mind which is necessary in order to foresee and understand the consequences of any public regulation.' (*Wealth of Nations*, Book I, Conclusion Chapter XI)

The interests of wage earners are also identical to those of society as a whole in so far as they flourish more in a growing economy. The interests of merchants and manufacturers, on the other hand, not only often do not coincide with those of society as a whole but because of the nature of their business they are constantly mentally active and, as a consequence,

'they have frequently more astuteness of understanding than the greater part of country gentlemen. …The proposal of any new law or regulation of commerce which comes from this order, ought always to be listened to with great precaution, and ought never to be adopted till after having been long and carefully examined, not only with the most scrupulous, but with the most suspicious attention.' (*Wealth of Nations*, Book I, Conclusion Chapter XI)

This contrast between the effects on intellectual ability of different lifestyles reflects Adam Smith's belief that people were born with more or less the same level of intelligence and it was their varying education, application and opportunities which led to such observed differences in maturity:

'The difference of natural talents in different men is, in reality, much less than we are aware of; and the very different genius which appears to distinguish men of different professions, when grown up to maturity, is not upon many occasions as much the cause, as the effect of the division of labour. The difference between the most dissimilar characters, between a philosopher and a common street porter, for example, seems to arise not so much from nature, as from habit, custom, and education.' (*Wealth of Nations*, Book I, Chapter II)

In addition to the specialization of labour, the accumulation of capital was necessary to generate economic growth. Capital made available the sums necessary for the employment of labour and arises from the savings generated from the profits earned on the capital employed. Its accumulation encourages an increase in population and the specialization of labour as the market increases. This accumulation is generated by savings which are assumed to be spent and not hoarded. The commercial and manufacturing sectors are important in this process in that there is in them more scope for improvements in productivity through the specialization of labour and more scope for increasing the size of the market. This continued accumulation of capital, however, would lead to a fall in the rate of profit as the economy approached a limit governed by its natural resources, real wages rose and competition between capitalists increased. Nevertheless, profits would continue to exist and incentives remain for the accumulation of capital, and, therefore, economic growth.

Adam Smith believed that interference in the free movement of international trade was to be condemned as much as in domestic trade:

'To give the monopoly of the home market to the produce of domestic industry, in any particular art or manufacture, is in some measure to direct private people in what manner they ought to employ their capitals, and must, in almost all cases, be either a useless or a hurtful regulation. ... The tailor does not attempt to make his own shoes, but he buys them of the shoemaker.' (*Wealth of Nations*, Book IV, Chapter II)

'To prohibit by a perpetual law the importation of foreign corn and cattle, is in reality to enact, that the population and industry of the country shall at no time exceed what the rude produce of its own soil can maintain.' (*Wealth of Nations*, Book IV, Chapter II)

However, he did allow that there were cases when intervention in international trade was justified. The first was for the protection of that domestic industry which might be important for the defence of the country, such as shipping. For this reason he supported the Navigation Acts (>SHIPPING) in spite of the fact that such controls were detrimental to foreign trade. 'As defence, however, is of much more importance than opulence, the act of navigation is, perhaps, the wisest of all the commercial regulations of England' (*Wealth of Nations*, Book IV, Chapter II). A second constraint which was justifiable was the application of a tax on the import of a foreign commodity to countervail that of a tax at a similar level applied to the commodity on the home market so that it 'would leave the competition between foreign and domestic industry, after the tax, as nearly as possible upon the same footing as before it' (*Wealth of Nations*, Book IV, Chapter II). Adam Smith also considered that there could be a case for the implementation of import duties as a retaliation against those countries which discouraged foreign imports from competing in their domestic market. He also argued for a phasing in of imports which had been previously restricted to protect the domestic industry from too sudden a market shock. Foreign trade was important to Adam Smith in so far as it gave opportunities for the augmentation of the extent of the market which contributed to the specialization of labour and therefore growth in the economy. Nevertheless, domestic industry was of prime importance. He criticized >MERCANTILISM for its emphasis on the balance of trade (>INTERNATIONAL TRADE).

Although throughout his work he emphasized the benefits of allowing the markets to act freely without government interference, nevertheless government action was vital in many areas. Government regulation was necessary to offset the actions of interest groups which would otherwise run counter to the interests of society as a whole. In addition, government must ensure the security of the country, the maintenance of justice and the development of education. Finally, government should be responsible for the infrastructure of the country:

'[The] duty of the sovereign or commonwealth is that of erecting and maintaining those public institutions and those public works, which though they may be in the highest degree advantageous to a great society, are, however, of such a nature, that the profit could never repay the expense to any individual or small number of individuals, and which it therefore cannot be expected that any individual or small number of individuals should erect or maintain.' (*Wealth of Nations*, Book V, Chapter I, Part III, Article I

He emphasizes the importance of transport infrastructure in particular:

'Good roads, canals and navigable rivers, by diminishing the expense of carriage, put the remote parts of the country more nearly upon the level with those in the neighbourhood of the town. They are upon that account the greatest of all improvements.' (*Wealth of Nations*, Book I, Chapter XI)

They bring competition into the towns and so destroy local monopolies and bring into use land and labour in remote places which would otherwise remain idle.

Taxation being necessary to finance government, Adam Smith laid down a number of maxims relating to it:

'I. The subjects of every state ought to contribute towards the support of the government, as nearly as possible in proportion to their respective abilities; that is, in proportion to the revenue which they respectively enjoy.

II. The tax which each individual is bound to pay, ought to be certain and not arbitrary.

III. Every tax ought to be levied at the time, or in the manner, in which it is most likely to be convenient for the contributor to pay it.

IV. Every tax ought to be so contrived as both to take out and to keep out of the pockets of the people as little as possible over and above what it brings into the public treasury of the state.' (*Wealth of Nations*, Book V, Chapter II, Part II)

The publication of *The Wealth of Nations* proved to be a huge success and it was translated into many languages. Leading economists such as >MALTHUS and >RICARDO responded to the challenges explored by Adam Smith and through their work and others grew the tradition of what came to be called >CLASSICAL AND NEO-CLASSICAL ECONOMICS which continued to influence economic thought and policy throughout the 20th century (>FRIEDMAN: >KEYNES: >MARX).

### References

Deane, Phyllis, *The Evolution of Economic Ideas*, Cambridge University Press, 1978.
O'Brien, D. P. O., *The Classical Economists*, Clarendon Press, 1975.
Roll, Eric, *A History of Economic Thought*, Faber and Faber, 1973.
Schumpeter, Joseph A., *History of Economic Analysis*, Oxford University Press, 1954.
Smith, Adam, *An Inquiry into the Nature and Causes of the Wealth of Nations* (1776), with an Introduction by Dugald Stuart, Ward Lock, 1812.
Winch, Donald, 'The Emergence of Economics as a Science, 1750–1870', in Carlo M. Cipolla (ed.), *The Fontana Economic History of Europe*, Fontana, 1973.

## South Africa

The beginnings of what is now the Republic of South Africa were in the establishment of a provisioning post at the Cape of Good Hope in 1652 by the Dutch East India Company (DEIC). It was Portugal, not Holland, that first opened up the sea route to the Indian Ocean. Da Gama had first circumnavigated the Cape and sailed up to East Africa in a series of voyages from 1497. The Portuguese did not find the Cape suitable for a trading post because the hinterland did not, at the time, provide a basis for exports; instead they decided to move on to Mozambique, which offered greater opportunities. The Dutch, after a failed attempt to dislodge the Portuguese from Mozambique, therefore established their position in the Cape Town area. That settlement was intended to supply fresh water, fruit, vegetables and meat for vessels engaged in the long-distance trade. It was not intended to form the basis of an independent colony and, indeed, the DEIC initially banned the small number of early immigrants from occupying the land to the north of the outpost. In the late 1680s further immigrants from Holland were permitted, as were some 200 Huguenots from France who provided wine-making skills. As the post's need for labour increased, the DEIC, chose to bring in slaves from other parts of Africa and from their territories in the East Indies rather than to encourage European immigration. By 1700 the European population was only about 1,300, though by the 18th century it had grown to 22,000.

The indigenous Khoi-san Bushmen were nomadic herdsmen and were able to supply the settlement with sheep and cattle but the quantities they were willing to sell were insufficient and they were not much interested in European goods. The Dutch established horticulture and their own herds. As the range of European settlement expanded in the decades after 1652, the settlers came into contact with groups of indigenous Africans who, unlike the Khoi-san, regularly practised settled agriculture, employed an iron-age technology and had long been accustomed to trade as a result of contacts with the Arab, Indian and Portuguese trade networks along Africa's East Coast. The Khoi-san population was greatly diminished by violence and by exposure to unfamiliar diseases during the 18th century, but the iron-using peoples had much greater resistance than their predecessors both to disease and to settler attempts to expand their lands (Austen, 1987; Feinstein, 2005).

After Napoleon invaded Holland, Britain occupied the Cape in 1795 at the invitation of the Dutch government in exile. Later, in 1806, and after a brief reversion to Dutch rule, the Cape was occupied permanently by Britain. Immigration was encouraged and British immigrants in numbers began to arrive from the 1820s. The British, who had never enslaved the local population, abolished slavery in 1834, thus emancipating the 'imported' slaves. The emancipation, the British policy of granting limited land rights to indigenous people and their enthusiasm for missionary efforts to extend education beyond the 'white' community, were strongly disapproved of by many Afrikaners. A group of particularly displeased 'Boers' therefore embarked on the 'Great Trek' away from direct British control. In 1838, the Boers established a republic in Natal, with its valuable Port Natal (now Durban). This created further friction and the British annexed Natal in 1843, from where many Boers moved further north and east, leading to the establishment of the republics of the Transvaal and the Orange Free State. These states were recognized by Britain in 1852. Britain encouraged foreign trade and the development of a financial system. A branch of the government-owned Lombard Bank was established in 1808, followed by a series of private banks in the 1830s. Further immigration from Britain was encouraged after 1837 and wool exports from Spanish Merino flocks became South Africa's first export staple. Wool exports grew from 20,000 pounds in 1822 to 26 million pounds in 1862. The immigrants also brought with them experience of the >INDUSTRIAL REVOLUTION IN BRITAIN and institutions favourable to economic development were reinforced. The system of Imperial Preference (>INTERNATIONAL TRADE) benefited the colonies, for example, by allowing imports of wine into Britain at rates below those for French exports.

In this period, there were continuing conflicts between Africans and Europeans. With their greater firepower, Boers and British were gradually able to destroy the independence of the indigenous African societies, although the process of bringing the African population under direct colonial rule was not completed until very near the end of the 19th century. There were continuing conflicts also between the Boers and the British. South Africa did not assume its current shape until the final defeat of the Boers in the Boer War (1899–1902) and the formation of the Union of South Africa in 1910. According to Austen (1987), there is no real evidence that the British instigated the war to capture the mineral rights; the ostensible reason was that the Boer government and the British could not agree on rights for the non-Boers who moved into the Transvaal following the discovery of gold there (see below). The British protectorates of Basutoland (now independent Lesotho), Bechuanaland and Swaziland, as well as areas of British influence to the North, did not become part of the Union. In the discussions preceding the Union of 1910, the British accepted the Boer position that only the white population should have the vote.

The pivotal events in early South African economic history were the discovery of diamonds on the Cape Colony frontier in 1867 and deep but extremely large and consistent seams of gold in the Transvaal from 1886. The exploitation of these mineral resources, which was eventually on a very large scale, required large amounts of both labour and capital. Indigenous Africans had been carrying out alluvial mining for at least a millennium but, by the mid-1870s, surface diamond deposits had been exhausted. In the Witwatersrand goldfields little of the precious metal was near the surface, but the deep seams were rich and steady, so deep mining was both necessary and reliably profitable from the beginning. The depth and scale of the mines required sophisticated technological investment and mining was to become dominated by large foreign corporations. De Beers ultimately established a monopoly of the international marketing of diamonds. The Anglo-American Corporation (actually British and South African-controlled) came to dominate gold mining and took over de Beers.

Cecil Rhodes (1853–1902), an Englishman, who made an early fortune in diamonds, was the main entrepreneur behind de Beers. He also formed the British South Africa Company (BSAC), which was initially given control of Southern and Northern Rhodesia (now Zimbabwe and Zambia). BSAC was not able to make money from either gold or copper in these territories, though by the 1920s changes in technology and market demand allowed other investors to make Northern Rhodesia one of the world's largest producers of copper. Rhodes was an important political figure and backed the Jameson Raid in 1896, which was an abortive attempt (probably without the knowledge and certainly without the consent of the British government) to overthrow the government of the Transvaal.

Labour in large number was required in the mines and initially this consisted of Europeans, and unskilled African migrants under short-term contracts. A system of highly regimented closed compounds was developed to house and feed a stable workforce that could be trained for higher-level skills and substitute for the more expensive European workers. Africans, without their families, came from as far off as Mozambique and Malawi, but also from neighbouring areas with poor agricultural prospects, such as present-day Lesotho. Enormous damage was done to the health and dignity of workers and to family life. The compounds facilitated the control of labour and provided economies of scale in mass housing and feeding, as well providing access to distant labour sources. From the 1890s, to avoid the competition for labour, which pushed up wages, central recruitment organizations were established and from about the same time regulations began to be introduced restricting certain skilled trades and occupations to 'European' workers. There were costs for both sides of the compound system since the circulation of workers by 12–18 month contracts necessitated frequent induction and training.

In the early 1920s and before, the mine-owners' policy of employing skilled African workers at lower wages to replace whites provoked strikes by white workers. These strikes were defeated with the support of the pro-British, pro-business

Smuts Government, but that government was replaced with an Afrikaner nationalist/white labour 'Pact' Government in 1924. The 'Pact' sought to defend the interests of the 'civilized' against the pressures generated by 'big capital', and intensified the policy of restricting the rights and freedom of movement of indigenous Africans. It is important to emphasize, however, that this was not entirely new but an intensification of earlier trends in the Boer republics and the British colonies. Much of the white politics of the inter-war period can be seen as a squabble over African labour: how much was to be directed to the mines, and how much kept available for use on white-owned farms? Both sides of the debate agreed, however, that legislated restrictions on the Africans' freedom of movement and on their ability to purchase land were essential tools in keeping up the supply of labour while keeping wages down. By 1936, according to Feinstein (2005), average annual income per head for whites was £130, for Africans in towns and mines, £31, on white-owned farms it was £7 and in the generally poor areas officially reserved for African occupation, £3. Infant mortality in the reserves was high, with 50 per cent failing to survive to the age of five.

The development of mining and urbanization and the early manufacturing associated with them required a major expansion in commercial agriculture. This expansion was mainly carried out by white farmers. The white farmers had the best land and as we have shown it was government policy to discourage indigenous production, both for the market and for subsistence, so as to provide commercial farm labour and workers for the mines. The government also denied Africans the support it

provided on a large scale to white farmers in terms of loans, technical assistance, help with irrigation and other improvements. White farmers received export subsidies, rebates on railway rates, grants for drought relief and other benefits.

Generally, progress in South African agriculture was slow. Using official statistics, Feinstein (2005) shows that in 1936 although 33 per cent of the total working population, excluding casual labour and Africans in reserves, was occupied in farming, this sector produced less than 12 per cent of the National Income. Because of deficient rainfall, only about 8 per cent of the white-owned land area could be used for arable farming before World War II, after which irrigation was greatly extended. Irrigated agriculture accounted for over half of the total value of agricultural production. After the war, yields were still low by international standards – less than 40 per cent of those in the USA and 30 per cent of Argentine levels.

Industry, that is manufacturing, construction and utilities, was boosted by the rapid development of mining, with its need for machinery, electrical equipment, wire cable, cement, explosives and other products. The backward linkages were promoted by the mining companies themselves. In 1925 protective tariffs were adopted to promote manufacturing which, despite low wages, was uncompetitive with imports. From that time the government pursued a more active policy towards industry because it was recognized that mining was a wasting asset. There was extensive government ownership in transport and utilities and a state Iron and Steel Industrial Corporation. Growth in industry continued until 1929, but suffered in the >GREAT DEPRESSION. The increased price of >GOLD from 1933, however, benefited the economy, as did >WORLD WAR I. In 1911, mining accounted for 27.3 per cent of GDP, agriculture 21.5 per cent and industry only 5.9 per cent (Feinstein, 2005). By the time of >WORLD WAR II, these proportions were more nearly equal and by 1970 industry accounted for twice the share of agriculture and mining combined. Although productivity in commercial farming remained poor by international standards, it did improve from the mid-1960s: between then and 1980, employment in agriculture fell by 20 per cent and real output increased by 80 per cent.

In the late 1970s and into the 1980s the South African economy ran into serious problems. There was a structural break in economic performance around 1973 – as indeed there was in much of the rest of the world, but South Africa was worse hit. Mining output fell and consumer price inflation, which had averaged 3.6 per cent per annum from 1948–73 rose to 14.5 per cent from 1981–94. Unemployment rose to record levels. At first these problems reflected the international situation following the oil price hikes. In 1971, the USA abolished the fixed price of gold and the market price rose. The South African mining companies found it economic to extract gold from lower grades of ore but the quantity of gold produced fell by 30 per cent between 1970 and 1977. Costs rose, despite considerable technological advances, because of the greater throughput of ore and because wages rose following a shift to reduce dependency upon labour from neighbouring countries hostile to the apartheid system. Increased platinum production by contrast was a very favourable development; indeed, by the year 2000, this metal had surpassed gold as the country's leading mineral. Coal

production also increased. There was an increase in South Africa's real exchange rate and real output in manufacturing failed to grow at all between 1981 and 1994. There were successive balance of payments crises following a decline in export earnings. Parallel with these, mostly unfavourable, developments was a growing international campaign against apartheid. Sanctions were tightened, especially from the mid-1980s, and inward investment was seriously affected. Before the democratic transition in 1994, total real GDP growth rates were in long-term decline from the 1960s, when they averaged 4.9 per cent, to 4.6 per cent 1964–73, 3.5 per cent in 1973–81 and only 0.8 per cent in 1981–94.

As shown earlier, the forced separation of races that characterized 20th-century South Africa had its origins in the laws and customs of the 18th- and 19th-century colonies and the republics. Segregation and racial repression were tightened considerably after Union and especially after 1948 when the National Party was elected with a mandate from the by now almost exclusively white electorate to implement its 'apartheid' policy. Apartheid was distinctive for the systematic ruthlessness of its bureaucracy and police rather than for any genuinely new policies. Especially after the 1963 Sharpeville shootings by police at unarmed demonstrators against the Pass Laws that controlled the movement of Africans and the killing of 70 people, international sanctions, which had first been introduced by the United Nations on arms, were tightened and internal agitation increased. In 1961, South Africa became a Republic and withdrew from the Commonwealth. Repression was intensified and opponents of the regime were put in jail. Repression was largely successful until the mid-1970s, when apartheid began to break down under a combination of internal and external pressures, the former being the more important. The government had begun reforms by 1986. The Pass Laws were abolished, there was more expenditure on education and all racial restrictions on trade unions were removed but it was too late. In 1991, Nelson Mandela, the icon of the struggle against apartheid, was released from jail and in 1994 universal suffrage was introduced.

Apartheid fell under the weight of its own contradictions; the white minority could not enforce such a system indefinitely and economic forces were against it. The logic of apartheid required that black people should be dispersed and isolated in reserves, and kept out of skilled occupations when in the cities, whereas industrialization required them to be in towns to provide the necessary and increasingly skilled labour for continuing economic development. Contrary to Marxist analysis (>MARX), which argued that exploitation of the proletariat was essential for >CAPITALISM, many South African capitalists knew that apartheid had enormous costs. The lack of training and education for blacks not only impaired industrialization directly; it prevented the emergence of mass markets for consumer goods and the enjoyment of economies of scale for an internationally uncompetitive manufacturing sector (Lipton, 1985).

Thanks to the statesmanship of Mandela and others, South Africa has achieved, against all odds, a largely peaceful transition to a democratic society. But apartheid has left a legacy of very high unemployment, exceptional inequality, very high levels of violent crime and the enormous task of integrating a poorly educated and untrained black majority into a modern capital-intensive economy, the first of its kind in Africa.

The post-1994 democracy has been grappling with these issues with a considerable degree of success. Stephen Gelb, in Daniel *et al.* (2005), describes an implicit bargain in which white-owned big business has agreed to participate in the modification of the racial structure of asset ownership, while the ANC government has committed to macro-economic stability and international openness. Unlike most of the other former colonial territories in Sub-Saharan Africa, which achieved independence from the 1960s (>ECONOMIC IMPERIALISM), South Africa has avoided the extreme socialist policies under which much valuable time and development opportunities were lost. The ANC governments of Mandela (1994–9) and Mbeki (2000–8) embraced neo-liberal orthodoxy in the form of tight monetary and fiscal policies. Socio-economic problems are being tackled by Growth, Employment and Redistribution (GEAR) and Black Economic Empowerment (BEE) strategies.

Macro-economic stability has been broadly achieved since 1994. The inherited fiscal deficit has been virtually eliminated and economic growth has improved to some 2.8 per cent per annum, though after a population growth rate of 2 per cent the annual improvement in GDP per capita has only been about 0.8 per cent. There seems to have been an upward trend in incomes for all population groups but unemployment and inequality remain high. African per capita incomes are still approximately 7.7 times lower than those for whites (Benjamin Roberts, in Daniel *et al.*, 2005). The state still owns 20–5 per cent of all land and there has not been much privatization of state-owned enterprises. The South African economy remains highly concentrated (>CONCENTRATION) and foreign ownership has gradually increased, even though foreign direct investment performance has been disappointing. There are fears that South Africa is increasingly dominated by 'crony capitalists' with redistributed assets being captured by a small and politically well-connected (black) elite. Despite these enormous problems, political stability has so far been maintained and South Africa seems to be achieving a transition which is quite unique in Africa.

### References

Austen, Ralph A., *African Economic History, International Development and External Dependency*, James Currey/Heinemann, 1987.

Daniel, J., Southall, R. and Lutchman, J. (eds), *State of the Nation: South Africa 2004–5*, HSRC Press, 2005.

Feinstein, Charles H., *An Economic History of South Africa, Conquest, Discrimination and Development*, Cambridge University Press, 2005.

Houghton, D. Hobart, *The South African Economy*, Oxford University Press, 1967.

Lipton, Merle, *Capitalism and Apartheid, South Africa, 1910–1986*, Gower Publishing, 1985.

## State, Rise of the

Today, with fairly (though not unprecedented) high levels of taxation during lifetimes and, in many cases on death, and when governments touch virtually all aspects of life, including education, health, welfare and the economy, it is difficult to imagine that this was not always so. The rise of state activity in the past 200 years or so in the now-developed countries is very striking. There are various ways of measuring the importance of government (central and local) statistically. According to Tanzi and Schuknecht (2000), expenditure by governments as a percentage of GDP in a large sample of developed countries rose from just under 11 per cent in 1870 to 45 per cent in 1996. Over the same period, the proportion of all employment accounted for by government rose from 2.4–18.4 per cent. Most government employees are in various branches of administration and in social services and the armed services but there have also been state enterprise sectors of varying importance – quite large in some European countries, especially France, but very small in the >USA. In the socialist countries, of course, virtually all enterprise at times has been state enterprise but we are writing here of the developed market economies. Tax revenues have risen proportionately with expenditure. In the 18th century, government revenue was mainly from customs duties and excise taxes. Income taxes were not introduced permanently until the 19th century or later (1842 in >BRITAIN and 1913 in the USA (>TAXATION)). While local and provincial governments have their own sources of tax revenue, these do not finance all of their expenditure because central governments redistribute some national revenue to them, especially in the poorer regions.

Well over half of present-day government taxation and expenditure and much of the increase since the 19th century is accounted for by social spending (poor relief, health, education, unemployment compensation and housing subsidies). Lindert (2004) shows that the median percentage of social transfers (the above elements less education), negligible in the late 18th century, rose rapidly from 1880 until 1980, then slowed down or even reversed. By 1980, all OECD countries spent more than 10 per cent of GDP on these transfers, which, by 1995, accounted on average for about 23 per cent of GDP. There are quite large differences between countries in the recent levels of social transfers. For example, they were over 30 per cent of GDP in most of Scandinavia and less than 14 per cent in the USA and Japan, but the upward movement was common to all countries. Taxes and government activity have risen sharply during wartimes, during the inter-war depression and especially after both world wars. Peace has normally brought a reduction in government expenditure but typically it has remained higher than pre-war levels, giving rise to a ratchet effect. Lindert brings out the contrast between social spending now and in the late 18th century:

'In 1776, when Adam >SMITH's classic 'Inquiry into the Nature and Causes of the Wealth of Nations' was published and the American colonies declared their independence from Britain, the modern age of social spending had not yet dawned. People paid hardly any taxes for the social programs that take such a large tax bite from pay checks today. Most people received negligible help from anybody. The elderly received no public pensions, mainly because few people survived to be elderly and average working incomes were too low to support many dependents. Most children did not go to school, and parents had to pay for those who did.' (Lindert, 2004).

The impact of the growth of government spending on economic growth is controversial. Richer countries spend a larger proportion of GDP on government services than poor countries. For example, in the low- and middle-income countries (incomes below $9,386) in the World Bank's *World Economic Indicators* (2005), government revenue as a percentage of GDP is about 12 per cent and social spending 32 per cent, while in the high-income countries (over $9,386 per capita), the corresponding figures are 26 per cent and 60 per cent (2003). The relationship between average incomes and government spending is not uniform and seems to level off at higher levels. This relationship is not necessarily a causal one and many factors affect the levels and rates of growth of GDP (>ECONOMIC    DEVELOPMENT). Maddison looked at the role of government from a long-term dynamic perspective and concluded:

'Over the long run there seems little doubt that state action has strengthened the forces making for economic growth and stability. It has also made capitalistic property relations and the operation of market forces more legitimate by removing most of the grievances which motivated proponents of a socialist alternative.' (Maddison, 1991)

The increase in state spending has, of course had costs in terms of efficiency. In some areas the generosity of social transfers reduces incentives and lowers labour force participation, the downward flexibility of prices has disappeared, government 'economic services' are often a euphemism for subsidies to inefficient enterprise, and there is some bureaucratic waste involved in the 'churning' process of high social levies and benefits. However, these costs are modest in comparison with those involved in communist countries, where the level of state intervention has been very much higher.

Initially, of course, by introducing law and order and stable >INSTITUTIONS, laying down infrastructure and improving health and education, government activity is clearly beneficial to economic development. No country seems to have developed without strong government. >WEBER wrote in 1927 that capitalism can only flourish in the 'rational state', by which he meant a government with sound laws and expert officials. Socialist countries have been able to speed up development by removing controls on private enterprise – this has clearly been the case with the recent surge of growth in >CHINA and >INDIA. Except in the early state-controlled economies of, for example, >RUSSIA, government economic planning has not led to growth and then only to unbalanced growth at a heavy human cost. The Russian experience influenced the adoption of planning techniques in several developing countries without success and there was a belief in the use of 'indicative planning' in some European countries, including France and Britain, after World War II but again without any demonstrable impact.

The experience of government intervention at industry level (that is the exercise of industrial policy) is more mixed. It is possible to think of examples where government objectives in particular sectors have been realized (for example, in the French >SILK industry), though how much government action influenced the final outcome is arguable. Japan used to be cited as an example of successful government intervention in industry and its general protectionist policies probably did have a favourable effect in re-establishing Japan as a major industrial power after World War II. There is, however, ample evidence that, at the micro-industrial level, success in Japan was often achieved in spite of bureaucratic interference, not because of it (Friedman, 1988). The legacy of excessive government interference in markets, including financial markets, has been a major contributory factor to the stagnation of growth in Japan since 1980. In >CHINA too, while the communist regime has been successful in unleashing capitalist forces for growth more recently, this did not go according to plan at the micro-economic level and the authorities have struggled to keep up with events on the ground (Studwell, 2005). Paradoxically, it is possible to argue that industrial policy in the newer industries in the USA, purportedly the least interventionist of countries, have had considerable impact. Britain had made considerable advances in various technical fields during >WORLD WAR II, for example radar, the >JET ENGINE and computing, but was not able to continue to pour government funding into innovation when peace came; in fact, much of its technology was transferred to America. The USA emerged from the war with its economy stronger than ever and government spending played a major role in giving the USA a post-war lead in >ELECTRONICS and later the internet.

Lindert (2004) argues that the lack of a correlation between the level or rate of growth of GDP in the advanced countries and spending on social transfers means, paradoxically, that these transfers are costless. While it must be true that rising subsidies and the taxes to pay for them have the potential to create distortions and weaken incentives, these costs are held down in richer countries for two reasons. The first reason is that the high budget democracies show much more care in choosing the design of taxes and transfers so as to avoid compromising growth. This is because at higher levels of affluence trade-offs in favour of enterprise become easier and this may be why consumption taxes, which are less harmful for growth have increasingly taken over from taxes on income and wealth (>TAXATION). The second reason is that the administrative costs of taxation as a percentage of revenue tend to fall as tax bases are widened and more taxes are collected. Also poorer countries tend to use costly means testing for social benefits which richer countries tend to make universal.

Explaining the growth of government is less difficult than assessing its impact on economic growth. The prime force for higher social transfers has been the extension of democracy. Maddison (1991) cites data showing that for 11 now-advanced countries, the electorate as a percentage of persons aged 20 and over averaged only 17.8 per cent in 1869–73, but by 1972–5 it had risen to 96.2 per cent. In 1820, the franchise was limited to property owners and the state was mainly concerned with looking after their interests. >SCHUMPETER's fears that >CAPITALISM would inexorably evolve into socialism have not materialized for the very reason that democracy has curbed some of its potential evils for the mass of the electorate but without suppressing its ability to foster economic prosperity.

There are many views about the role of government in modern economies. The Public Choice School in economics, associated particularly with James Buchanan and R. A. Musgrave in the USA, recognizes that government officials, politicians and special-interest groups (industry and trade unions, for example) have their own agendas to pursue, leading to higher budgets and more government activity. Offer (2001) labels this the 'Leviathan' School, after the book of that title by the political philosopher, Thomas Hobbes (1588–1679), who called the all-powerful state the 'Leviathan'. Offer also refers to the argument in the 1976 book, *Britain's Economic Problem: Too Few Producers*, by R. W. Bacon and Walter Eltis. The thesis of this book was that a bloated public sector was crowding out the market sector of the economy. Offer however, also argues that consumers tend to be myopic, preferring immediate gratification rather than collective goods, such as improved infrastructure, that take a long time and considerable investment to provide. In Victorian times public goods were to a large extent initially provided by profit-making or voluntary organizations but this gave way to state activity. Once satiated by collective state investment in the century after 1870, the demand for consumer expenditure increased again. This is happening now with 'prudential' crises in pensions, education, health and transport which may herald another shift in the cycle, or at least provide dilemmas which need to be resolved.

Creveld (1999) in a sweeping and powerful survey of the rise of the state, charts the growth of state activity from its beginnings in 16th- and 17th-century Europe. He describes the transition of power from nobles and kings to bureaucracies via wars and >MERCANTILISM. The state has become separate from both its members and its rulers in a similar way to the modern corporation, which has an identity separate from that of its shareholders (>CORPORATE GOVERNANCE). A notable development in the formation of professional bureaucracies was the introduction of a system of civil service examinations by Frederick II of Prussia in 1770 and in the reforms of Sir Charles Trevelyn in Britain. These reforms instituted not only entrance exams but promotion ladders and retirement pensions modelled, incidentally, on the systems of the >ENGLISH EAST INDIA COMPANY. In 1773, the Regulating Act prohibited tax collectors and those in the administration of justice from taking part in trade or accepting presents.

Creveld (1999) asserts convincingly that, since about 1975, the power of the state has waned. The end of interstate wars from 1945, decolonization (>ECONOMIC IMPERIALISM), the demise of communism in Europe, the impotence of modern armies in local conflicts in Vietnam and Iraq, as well as the growth of global communications and trade all have something to do with this. In purely economic terms, governments have also surrendered earlier policies to control exchange rates and even monetary policy (>CENTRAL BANKING). Undertakings to provide secure pensions for all as well as nationalized industries (via privatization) have also been abandoned. Socialism, in short, has become unaffordable. Creveld adds that possibly, by way of compensating for their growing impotence, governments are increasingly meddling in people's lives, intruding into their privacy and even determining what they should eat, drink and smoke.

### References

Creveld, Martin van, *The Rise and Decline of the State*, Cambridge University Press, 1999.

Friedman, David, *The Misunderstood Miracle: Industrial Development and Political Change in Japan*, Cornell University Press, 1988.

Lindert, Peter H., *Growing Public: Social Spending and Economic Growth Since the Eighteenth Century*, Cambridge University Press, 2004.

Maddison, Angus, *Dynamic Forces in Capitalist Development: A Long-Run Comparative View*, Oxford University Press, 1991.

Offer, Avner, *Why Has the Public Sector Grown So Large in Market Economies: The Political Economy of Prudence in the UK c. 1870–2000*, Oxford University Press, 2001.

Studwell, Joe, *The China Dream: The Elusive Quest for the Greatest Untapped Market on Earth*, Profile Books, 2005.

Tanzi, V. and Schuknecht, L., *Public Spending in the 20th Century: A Global Perspective*, Cambridge University Press, 2000.

World Bank, *World Economic Indicators*, 2005.

## Steam Power

Steam, when condensed by cooling, creates a vacuum which can be used to drive a piston in a steam engine to produce power or, in one variant, used directly to suck up liquids, that is, as a steam pump. The advent of steam power of these types in the 18th century was a major element in the >INDUSTRIAL REVOLUTION IN BRITAIN and in the development of >RAILWAYS and steamships (>SHIPPING). Eventually, after further innovations, steam-powered turbines were used to drive ships and in electric power generation. (Steam turbines work by directing steam through nozzles onto a rotor with radial vanes to produce.) The history of the development of steam power is a very long one. Hero of Alexandria in the first century BC left writings showing that he understood the principles of steam power, cylinders and pistons. The Marquis of Worcester (1601–1667) invented a steam pump for raising water, though nothing came of it at the time. Otto von Guericke (1602–1686) carried out experiments using cylinders and pistons and the principles of atmospheric pressure and vacuums (Matschoss, 1939). At about the same time French engineers experimented with engines using the explosive power of gunpowder, an abortive attempt which was nonetheless to find fruition in internal combustion or gas engines many years later (>AUTOMOBILE INDUSTRY). There were also developments in the use of steam in China in the 17th century. In 1671 a Jesuit missionary demonstrated working models of a steam turbine carriage and a steamboat but little is known about them (Pomeranz, 2000).

Dr Denis Papin (1647–1712) is usually credited with the invention, in 1690, of the use of the condensation of steam to operate a steam engine, though his working model found no application. Thomas Savery (c. 1650–1715) patented a steam pump in 1698 which used a vacuum to raise water and which came into use in mines. A very urgent and practical problem in mining was that as mines went deeper they became subject to flooding. The first reciprocating operational steam engine was built for this same purpose by Thomas Newcomen in 1712. Newcomen was a blacksmith and ironmonger from Dartmouth and his beam engine, developed in collaboration with Savery, was also used in mines. According to Ashton's (1948) succinct account of the early development of steam power there were about 100 Newcomen engines in use in collieries around Tyne and Wear by 1765 and soon in all the large mines in the country. All the steam engines mentioned so far had very low thermal efficiencies. According to Landes (1969), the Newcomen engine had a

thermal efficiency of only 5–6 million foot-pounds per bushel of coal, equivalent to about 1 per cent. This was just about acceptable for pumping water out of mines, but rendered steam power uneconomic for wider use.

The crucial breakthrough in steam engine design was made by James Watt (1739–1819), a Scottish mathematical instrument maker. He was called upon to repair a model of the Newcomen engine in use at the University of Glasgow. He saw that the chief defect of this engine was that the heat was wasted in heating the cylinder and then cooling it again to condense the steam. Famously, in 1765 in the course of a Sunday walk on Glasgow Green, he realized that the solution was a separate condenser which would allow the cylinder to be kept permanently hot. He was able to make a working model quite quickly to test the idea but had a family to support and little time or money to spend on further experiments. By now he had diversified from instrument making to surveying and civil engineering to earn his living. Dr John Roebuck, a mine owner with a pressing need for pumping technology, financed the initial development work in return for a share in a patent granted to Watt in 1769, but Roebuck, too, ran out of money and transferred his share in the patent to Matthew Boulton and Watt moved to Birmingham. Boulton, who had a factory there, could see the potential of Watt's invention and encouraged Watt to apply for an extension of the life of his patent to 1800 to give more time for its development. Boulton engaged William Murdock, like Watt a Scotsman and an inventor, and he made a major contribution, particularly in the development of Watt's invention of a sun and planet gear to convert the output of the engine to rotary motion (the use of a crank was prevented by the existence of other patents). At Boulton's Soho works were the craftsmen needed to make precision parts for the engine and nearby was the Coalbrookdale Ironworks for castings (>IRON AND STEEL). John Wilkinson, who was able to use his patented techniques for boring canon, and also nearby, was able to make accurate cylinders (accurate to within 0.05 of an inch). After many difficulties, Watt and Boulton started manufacture of the improved engine (which had thermal efficiencies four times greater than the Newcomen machine and was capable of considerable further development). The first commercial installation was in 1776 at a colliery near Tipton. Initially engines were supplied on royalties based on the energy savings gained compared with the Newcomen engines they replaced. This arrangement created financial difficulties for Boulton, who was laying out lumps of capital for a return admittedly large but spread over many years. In 1781 commercial rotating engines were built to drive machinery in factories and mills. Further patented improvements followed, including a double-action system in which steam was both compressing and pushing the piston (1782) and, in 1788, the addition of a centrifugal governor to maintain the smooth running speed needed for textile mills. Later improvements included steam jacketing to help thermal efficiency.

By 1800 there were some 1000 steam engines in use in >BRITAIN. Thereafter, according to Landes, diffusion was rapid with over 20,000 in use by 1815 and 120,000 by 1850 when only about one third of power for cotton mills came from water (>COTTON AND COTTON TEXTILES). The use of steam power allowed factory production to develop outside areas with sources of water power and for factories to locate near coalfields, which minimized transport costs. Steam power was also used to drive iron rolling mills and for puddling (>IRON AND STEEL) and stimulated developments in >MACHINE TOOLS. Watt's patents had probably slowed other improvements, but after their expiry in 1800 there was much further development, including that of Richard Trevithick (1771–1833), the pioneer of the high-pressure engine and steam locomotion. In 1807, the American engineer Robert Fulton (1765–1815) who, among other things, invented a human-powered submarine while in France, developed a steam-powered paddle boat. In 1807, Fulton's first commercial paddle steamboat, the *Clermont*, travelled from New York to Albany, a distance of 150 miles in 32 hours, an astonishing performance for the time. Steamships were to prove very important in opening up the lands of the Mississippi and the Missouri rivers, where good roads were absent. Much later, in 1884, the versatile inventor Sir Charles Parsons (1854–1931) patented his designs for the first practicable steam turbine, which were initially applied by him for electrical generation and later for marine propulsion. The steam turbine made possible the generation of power at many multiples of that of the reciprocating piston engine and with much less vibration and wear. The steam turbine was the forerunner of the gas turbine and the >JET ENGINE.

After numerous experiments in several countries, steam power was used in the first automobiles (>AUTOMOBILE INDUSTRY) and began to be applied in >AGRICULTURE from about 1850. Steam engines were too heavy for extensive use as tractors on farms (though they were excellent for road-rolling), but were used for stationary purposes, such as threshing machines and belt-driven crushing plants and grinding machines. Steam ploughing, where ground conditions were appropriate, made some progress in North America and for a while there was some use of cable-driven ploughs in which the steam engine could remain stationary. Steam power never had the same impact in agriculture as the internal combustion engine, however, which overtook it to transform farming in the late 19th and early 20th centuries.

The use of steam power in Continental Europe followed the same evolution as in England, with initial use in mining and ironworks and later in the cotton industry with Belgium and France leading the process (>WESTERN EUROPE). In the early stages, most of the Continental steam engines were imported from Britain. By 1820, machines were being built on the Continent, often to British designs and using British personnel. In 1840, the capacity of steam engine horsepower (a unit of measurement, incidentally, devised by Watt) was about 620,000hp in Britain with 90,000hp in France and 40,000 in Germany. This capacity grew rapidly on the Continent as it did in Britain. By 1896, Britain had 137,000hp, about the same as in France and Germany combined. In the USA growth was faster still and by 1850 substantially exceeded that in Britain (Landes, 1969). Steam power continued to spread around the world, for example, a steam-powered spinning mill was established in Japan at Osaka in 1882.

The impetus that steam power gave to Britain's economic development continued into the 20th century. There are many people alive today who can remember steam engines in use on farms. It was argued at one time that the extension of steam power exhausted its scope in Britain in advance of the big developments in the new industries of electricity, the internal combustion engine and chemicals which emerged after >WORLD WAR I. This was held to explain the check to the growth of real incomes in the 1890s (a climacteric). However Crafts and Mills (2004) were able to show that the contribution of steam to industrial output and labour productivity growth was actually higher after 1870 than before.

It took 86 years between Dr Papin's first working model in 1690 and Watt and Boulton's first commercial installation in 1776. Fortunes were not made by these early pioneers, although Boulton and Watt died in comfort and the former's sons continued the business. Boulton had taken heavy risks, raising some £40,000, an enormous sum at the time, to develop Watt's ideas and came near to financial failure once or twice. Papin went bankrupt and Roebuck, Watt's first funder, as well as Trevithick, the developer of the high-pressure engine and its use in railways, died penniless.

## References

Ashton, T. S., *The Industrial Revolution, 1760–1830*, Oxford University Press, 1948.

Crafts, Nicholas and Mills, Terence C., 'Was 19th Century British Growth Steam Powered? The Climacteric Revisited', *Explorations in Economic History*, 41, April, 2004.

Landes, David S., *The Unbound Prometheus: Technological Change and Industrial Development in Western Europe from 1750 to the Present*, Cambridge University Press, 1969.

Matschoss, C., *Great Engineers*, Bell & Sons, 1939.

Pomeranz, Kenneth, *The Great Divergence: China, Europe and the Making of the*

*Modern Economy*, Princeton University Press, 2000.

Tunzelmann, G. N. von, *Steam Power and British Industrialisation to 1860*, Oxford University Press, 1978.

# Sugar

The development of sugar has had such profound influences throughout the world economy over the past 400 years that economic historians have referred to its effects as tantamount to a revolution, the only single commodity to be accorded such a distinction. In agriculture, sugar encouraged the introduction of the cultivation of single crops on large plantations, as compared with multi-crop cultivation on small farms. Sugar caused large shifts in population both in numbers and ethnic mix through its encouragement of the Atlantic slave trade and the emigration of indentured labour. It even caused radical changes in the European diet. Furthermore, there is debate among historians concerning the significance of sugar in the progress of the >INDUSTRIAL REVOLUTION IN BRITAIN (Higman, 2000: >SLAVERY).

Sugar may be extracted economically from two plants: the sugar cane (*Saccharum officinarum*) and sugar beet (*Beta vulgaris*). The former is a semi-tropical and tropical grass that can grow up to a height of seven metres and the latter is a root crop suitable for temperate climates. One or other of these crops, therefore, may flourish throughout the world and, by the end of the 20th century, 130 countries harvested them to produce sugar.

The cultivation of sugar cane spread from the East, through the Mediterranean, to reach the Portuguese islands of Madeira and Sao Tome in the 15th century and other islands off the coast of Africa. From this base, the Portuguese established cane sugar production in north-eastern Brazil in the late 16th century and, by the following century, Brazil had become the world's largest producer. The growing, harvesting and processing of the sugar cane was centred around the mill. A large enterprise or *engenho* consisted of various buildings to house the plant and workers and employed about 200 slaves, together with skilled workers, to operate and maintain the machinery and for managerial supervision. There were also small enterprises that only farmed the sugar cane and sold their output to the mills for processing. Some of these did not own their land. In the second half of the 17th century competition from the newly established plantations in the Caribbean led to a fall in sugar prices. There was a drop in prices of about one-third from about mid-century to the 1680s (Williamson, 1992). >BRITAIN and France established sugar plantations in the Caribbean islands throughout the 17th century: the British in Barbados in 1643, followed by Antigua, St Kitts, Nevis, Montserrat and Jamaica (captured from Spain in 1655); the French in Guadeloupe and Martinique and, by the turn of the century, Saint Domingue (Haiti), ceded to France by Spain in 1697.

Throughout the 18th century, sugar production expanded rapidly based on the plantation system. Large estates required capital investment in the mills, for crushing the cane, which had to be presented to the mills soon after harvesting, and also in plant for boiling and storing the cane. In addition, there was a need to obtain, house and support plantation workers. The work was arduous and dangerous and no free labour could be induced to submit to it. Moreover, the local indigenous populations had been reduced so much by disease and warfare that they could not supply the labour needed. Accordingly, the plantation owners turned to Africa for slaves (>SLAVERY) and continued to do so because the slave population could not reproduce itself. Saint Domingue (Haiti) became the dominant producer of cane sugar, accounting for as much as 40 per cent of world production until the slave revolt there at the end of the century brought its plantations to an end.

After the abolition of the slave trade by Britain in 1807 and slavery itself in 1833, production in the West Indies was maintained by the import of indentured workers from >INDIA and >CHINA. About 536,000 arrived in the West Indies between 1834 and 1918 (Kenwood and Lougheed, 1992). Dominant player status in the Caribbean shifted to the Spanish colony of Cuba which had begun to develop sugar plantations in the 1760s. Cuba's sugar industry was transformed in the late 19th century by the replacement of small producers by large centralized establishments and the introduction of new technology made possible by an inflow of American capital. Cane sugar production also flourished in Java (Indonesia) under the control of the Dutch East India Company. A cultivation system was operated there under which a proportion of each village's land had to be devoted to crops for export. The prices paid to the farmers was set by the Company, which sold the output at a profit. This system was eased in the middle of the century and finally replaced by private enterprise in the 1870s. With a shift out of the production of indigo and more investment in

land and plant, sugar production in Java increased from about 46,000 tonnes in 1840 to 130,244 tonnes in 1869 (Chandra and Vogelsang, 1999). Output from cane sugar plantations also expanded in Fiji and Hawaii in the late 19th century, supported by indentured labour. About 250,000 arrived in Hawaii from Japan and China between 1860 and 1900 and over 60,000 in Fiji from India between 1879 and 1916. Prior to >WORLD WAR I, the major sugar exporters were Cuba, which exported 1.8 million tones a year in 1909/13, and Indonesia, which exported 1.3 million tonnes. The major importers were the >USA with 2.0 million tonnes and Britain with 1.8 million tonnes (Yates, 1959).

The first plant for the extraction of sugar from beet was constructed in Poland (Silesia) in 1802. The British blockade of the European ports during the Napoleonic wars induced the French government to encourage the production of beet sugar so that by the end of the war small factories were operating in Austria, Belgium, France and Germany. With the support of export subsidies and import tariffs, beet sugar production increased rapidly through the 19th century. By 1880, world beet sugar output had reached 1.8 million tonnes, comparable to cane sugar production of 1.9 million tonnes. By the turn of the century, beet sugar output passed 6 million tonnes, compared with 3.8 million tonnes for cane sugar (Bairoch, 1993). The countries of >WESTERN EUROPE, with the exception of Britain, became virtually self-sufficient in sugar by World War I. Beet sugar production did not attract specific government support in Britain until subsidies were introduced in 1925.

During the first half of the 20th century, world production of sugar continued to grow. Exports reached 12.8 million tonnes in 1953/4 compared with 7.1 million tonnes in 1903/13, although there had taken place a change in the country profile. In particular, Cuba, which accounted for 26 per cent of the world export total in 1903/13, increased its share to 37 per cent. Indonesia, which had had 19 per cent of the market, was no longer a significant exporter (Yates, 1959). In the second half of the 20th century, the tonnage of exports doubled between the beginning of the 1960s and the turn of the century, reaching 40 million tonnes in 2000; of this total between 65 and 70 per cent was produced from cane. However, in the last two decades of the 20th century, although the tonnage increased by about 45 per cent, the total value measured in US dollars decreased by about 40 per cent. According to the Food and Agricultural Organization (FAO), the world price of sugar fell from about 65 US cents per kilo in the 1980s to 20 US cents per kilo in 2000. In this period, exports from Cuba, which had achieved about $5 billion in 1985 fell to less than $0.5 billion, but Brazil, which emerged as the most cost-efficient producer, grew from $0.4 million to $1.2 billion against the trend, comparable to the $1.3 billion exported by the European Union (>WESTERN EUROPE), the lead exporter in that year. Developing countries in total accounted for 53 per cent of total world exports in 2000, down from 67 per cent in 1980 and 73 per cent in the 1960s.

The growth in production of sugar both from cane and beet, together with technological investment in production and improved strains, which lowered unit costs, led to increased competition for market share. As a consequence there has been throughout its history a persistent downward pressure on prices. Sugar – which was a luxury good in the 15th century when, in Western Europe, it cost about two months' income to buy 1kg – became a commodity which cost only a few minutes of income. This drop in the real price stimulated an explosion in demand as sugar became effectively a basic necessity, demand growth easing only in some countries as sugar consumption approached saturation. For instance, consumption per head per year in Britain rose from 3kg in the 1750s to 11kg in 1850s (Minchinton, 1973) to 35kg in the 1900s (Yates, 1959) and to about 40kg in the 1990s.

Attempts to underpin prices by international trade agreements and to protect domestic markets through government subsidies and import restrictions have long been a characteristic of the sugar regime. Domestic prices were kept high in most of the European sugar beet-producing countries through the 19th century by the imposition of high import duties and the encouragement of exports by subsidies. An agreement was signed in Brussels in 1902 to cease granting the latter. By the mid-20th century, there were two major preferential trading areas. Britain had a preferential trading area with the Commonwealth. The >USA, which was the world's largest importer, gave special tariff and quota treatment to Porto Rico, Hawaii, the Virgin Islands, the Philippines and Cuba. From 1934 until 1974, quota restrictions regulated the US market. From 1977 quotas were replaced by a price support system until they were reinstituted in 1982. Quotas were placed on domestic producers as well as importers. In the 1950s, Cuba's quota was reduced from 40 per cent to 35 per cent and it has been argued that this had a detrimental influence on Cuba's economy as it could not find alternative markets (Dye and Sicotte, 2004). With the formation of the European Union in 1957, sugar became a product supported within the framework of the Common Agricultural Policy of the European Union (>INTERNATIONAL TRADE).

Control schemes were established for sugar in the 1920s and, in 1931, an International Sugar Agreement was concluded in an attempt to bring production in line with demand to counter the weakness in prices. After World War II, International Sugar Agreements were concluded and renewed in 1953, 1958, 1968, 1977, 1984 and 1987, which again attempted to support prices. However, a further attempt to renew the latter agreement in 1992 failed to include provisions for regulating prices but continued as a forum for the collecting and dissemination of information and intergovernmental consultation.

## References

Bairoch, Paul, *Economics and World History*, Harvester Wheatsheaf, 1993.

Chandra, Siddharth and Vogelsang, Timothy J., 'Change and Involution in Sugar Production in Cultivation-System Java, 1840–1870', *Journal of Economic History*, 59, December, 1999.

Dewhurst, Frederic J., Coppock O. John and Yates, Lamartine P., *Europe's Needs and Resources: Trends and Prospects in Eighteen Countries*, Macmillan, 1961.

Dye, Alan, *Cuban Sugar in the Age of Mass Production: Technology and the Economies of the Sugar Central, 1899–1929*, Stanford University Press, 1998.

Dye, Alan and Sicotte, Richard, 'The US Sugar Program and the Cuban Revolution', *Journal of Economic History*, 64, September, 2004.

Higman, B.W., 'The Sugar Revolution', *Economic History Review*, LIII(2), May, 2000.

Kenwood, A. G. and Lougheed, A. L., *The Growth of the International Economy, 1820–1990*, Routledge, 1992.

Minchinton, W., 'Patterns of Demand, 1750–1914', in Carlo M. Cipolla (ed.), *The Fontana Economic History of Europe*, Fontana, 1973.

Williamson, Edwin, *The Penguin History of Latin America*, Penguin, 1992.

Yates, Lamartine P., 'Forty Years of Foreign Trade' George Allen & Unwin, 1959.

# T

## Taxation

The compulsory transfer of resources from individuals and enterprises to rulers has a long history. In modern times this history has been marked by a secular increase in the economic role of the state, including the financial demands of wars, and by the development of more efficient means of raising revenue (>STATE, RISE OF THE). There are some alternative methods for governments to raise revenue, including outright seizure, lotteries, the operation of, or sale of, state monopolies and, of course, printing money (seignorage, >MONEY AND BANKING) and borrowing. All of these alternatives have been and are still used but the advanced states rely mainly on borrowing and the taxation of income, property and expenditure. To some extent, user charges, for example, parking or licensing, are used to pay for public services, especially by local government.

The beginnings of the modern tax system in Britain can be traced to the Glorious Revolution of 1688–9 after which the control of tax revenue shifted from the monarchy to Parliament. The ancient and wasteful system of tax farming in which 'tax farmers' paid the government a sum of money for the right to collect specific taxes was phased out in >BRITAIN by 1700. Commissioners of Revenue were appointed and a bureaucracy developed to administer taxes. According to Ron Harris's contribution to Floud and Johnson (2004a), tax collection staff numbered just a few hundred in 1690 but this figure had increased to over 8,000 by 1782/3. From 1715 to the end of the 18th century, tax revenues rose tenfold at current prices and fourfold in real terms, equivalent to an increase from 10–18 per cent of GDP. New taxes had recently been introduced: the infamous Window Tax began in 1689 and the Land Tax in 1698, but most tax revenue came from customs duties on imports and excises levied on goods produced for home consumption. Excises were levied on beer, soap and candles, for example, but, in 1723, excise taxes were extended to imported tea, coffee and chocolate, which required a system of bonded warehouses. In 1733 excises were further extended to wine and tobacco (where they remain to this day). Unlike the Land Tax, excises bore upon the less well off (were regressive) and there were mass demonstrations in the streets against any extension of the system. At the beginning of the 18th century, indirect taxes accounted for 26 per cent of total tax revenue, rising to 50 per cent by mid- century, while direct taxes, in which Harris includes taxes on land, houses servants and carriages, fell from 36 to 15–20 per cent.

The wars with France which began in 1793 greatly escalated the need for government revenues. At first the wars were financed by increasing existing taxes and by borrowing. In 1799, William Pitt, who had been improving the management of the national finances, for example, by creating the Consolidated Fund into which all taxes were paid, imposed an income tax for the first time. The new tax was initially levied at the rate of 10 per cent on incomes above £60 and had several features in common with more modern forms of income tax, for example, deductions for children and insurance premiums. Income tax was abolished in 1816 after the end of the Napoleonic Wars, only to be reintroduced permanently from 1842 (Hill, 1985). The National Debt also grew rapidly from £1 million in 1688 to £15 million in 1698 and £244 million by 1790. The British system of public finance was greatly superior to those of other European countries and enabled it to finance its powerful armed forces. It may be that the development of Britain's >CAPITAL MARKETS was stimulated by the burgeoning National Debt and therefore contributed to the finance of the canals, railways and industry (>INDUSTRIAL REVOLUTION IN BRITAIN). However, it has also been argued that the demands of public finance crowded out private provision. Most of the revenue raised was spent on war. By modern standards, government expenditure on health, education and infrastructure was relatively low and did not increase much until the middle of the 19th century, when the social evils of rapid urban growth had become apparent to all. Expenditure on the >POOR LAWS, which was mostly a local government responsibility, did increase, however.

At one time it was argued that the crushing burden of taxation on the poor was a major contributory cause of the 1789 >FRENCH REVOLUTION. It has been established, however, that in fact at the time taxation in Britain was much higher than in France. Mathias and O'Brien (1976) demonstrated that total British tax revenue (in terms of wheat equivalents and per head of the population) was twice as high as that in France in both 1750 and 1800. Also, potentially regressive indirect taxation in Britain represented 76 per cent of tax revenue as against 45 per cent in France in 1755 and it was also much higher in 1800. This does not necessarily dispose of the matter because perceptions about the burden of taxation and the means of collecting it were very different. The behaviour of tax farmers, for example, which no longer operated in Britain, was much resented in France; in fact the tax farmers fell to the guillotine. Also the nobility had been exempt from some taxes (White, 2004).

In the 19th century, rising national wealth and increasing tax yields as well as a long period of peace after 1815 eased the fiscal situation. Free trade doctrine (>INTERNATIONAL TRADE) led to a reduction in import duties in the 1820s and 1840s, while W. E. Gladstone, Chancellor of the Exchequer 1852–5 and 1859–65, attempted to reduce income tax and reform indirect taxation. However, the Crimean War (1854–6) and the continuing growth of public expenditure on armaments, health and education led to new pressures on public finance. Death duties were introduced in 1894 and from 1908 income tax was increased and a super-tax on high incomes (over £3,000) imposed, as well as increases in indirect taxes. Public sector receipts as a percentage of GDP, which had fallen from 11.0 per cent in 1860 to 9.7 per cent in 1900, thereafter rose to 12.4 per cent in 1913 and grew to 20.9 per cent in 1920 and 24.9 per cent in 1939. There was a particularly large jump in the yield of income tax as a percentage of GDP, from 1.8 per cent in 1913 to 10.2 per cent in 1920 though it declined again up to 1939. The yield of income tax after >WORLD WAR I had fallen but it remained above pre-war levels. It has been a common experience in the 20th century that major wars lead to a ratcheting-up of the share of government in National Income, the same thing happened after >WORLD WAR II, not only in Britain but in the USA and elsewhere. Indirect tax yields also increased and continued to rise in the inter-war period, unlike those of income tax. By 1939, taxes on income amounted to only 7.4 per cent of GDP but taxes on expenditure were 11.5 per cent (Roger Middleton in Floud and Johnson, 2004b).

World War II was followed by new commitments to social welfare in Europe and consequently, after the initial decline in taxation, a renewed upward trend. From the 1950s, governments were also committed to 'fiscal activism' – the Keynesian-type policies which had not been used before the war – and which amounted to attempts to manage the macro-economy by fiscal means (>KEYNES). By the 1970s, with the oil price hikes and inflationary pressures, there was a reaction followed by a revolution in economic policy and a shift to rule-based monetary management (>CENTRAL BANKING). In Britain, government revenue as a percentage of GDP was 37.6 per cent in 1943 and, after an initial fall after the war, tended upwards until the mid-1970s, then declined and started rising again; in 2000 it was 40.2 per cent. There were many changes in the tax system in the post-World War II period, many new taxes were devised, some have endured and some have gone (among those removed were Purchase Tax, introduced in 1961, and Selective Employment Tax, introduced in 1966 (>SERVICE SECTOR)). Two things stand out: income tax, together with National Insurance contributions, has become a mass tax and Value Added Tax (VAT), which

replaced Purchase Tax in 1973, has become a major source of revenue. Income tax was originally conceived of as a tax on the better off and in 1938–9 it was paid by 3.8 million families; by 1988–9 it was paid by 21.5 million families (25 million individuals) (Tom Clark and Andrew Dilnot in Floud and Johnson, 2004c). The change to a mass tax occurred during World War II and, in recognition of this, in 1943, Pay-As-You-Earn (PAYE) was brought in, a system in which employers were given tax codes for wage and salary earners so that the right amount of tax could be deducted over the year. Under PAYE there is no need for employees with relatively simple affairs to make detailed annual tax returns.

Value Added Tax (VAT) was introduced in Britain following full membership of the European Economic Community (>WESTERN EUROPE). VAT in its modern form is of post-war origin and in Europe was first introduced in France; it has subsequently been adopted in many countries around the world. Virtually all OECD member countries have adopted VAT, the notable exception being the USA. Surprisingly, given its bookkeeping requirements and heavy compliance costs, VAT is also used in many developing countries. Since 1990, over 50 countries have adopted VAT and the total number exceeds now 100. Most developed countries have used the European multi-stage system in which enterprises deduct, or are refunded, VAT paid on their inputs so that in theory the whole of the final burden of the tax is borne by the end consumer. This means that a very large number of enterprises above a turnover threshold are involved in the system (1.7 million are registered for VAT in Britain). Japan, which introduced a VAT in 1989, uses a simpler single-stage system in which value added is calculated from books of account. This system is obviously better from a compliance point of view but is not practicable with the multiple tax rates used in Europe, which discriminate against non-essential expenditure. The widespread adoption of VAT is due to its appeal as an efficient revenue raiser and because, in its multi-stage form, it is partly self-policing as well as imposing relatively few distortions on economic structure compared with the turnover or cascade taxes which preceded it in some countries. Also, VAT does not significantly enter into export prices. VAT is not necessarily economically superior to the sales tax used in the USA but it is believed to facilitate higher rates of tax (Bannock, 1990).

Tax evasion can be a problem with all taxes. With income tax there can be evasion by under-reporting of income by self-employed persons, but today as much tax as possible is deducted at source; this is simple for wages and salaries and also for such items as bank interest and dividends where responsibility for collection of at least basic rates of tax can be shifted to enterprises. There are particular problems with direct taxes where there are interest payments between tax jurisdictions. The European Commission and the OECD have tried to get international agreement on the use of withholding taxes but off-shore centres that benefit from foreign investment resist this, as do many other countries with important earnings from financial transactions. The League of Nations tried unsuccessfully to get support for double taxation agreements between the world wars and in the post-World War II period this task has been taken up more successfully by the OECD. The growing use of the internet for selling goods and

services has created new problems for the enforcement of national indirect taxes. With conventional taxation, compliance is probably quite high in most advanced countries, though not, perhaps, in Southern Europe. Indeed, it has been observed that with audit rates at no more than 2 per cent, what needs to be explained is not the extent of tax evasion but the lack of it.

Little mention has been made so far of local taxation. Before the rise of the nation state, most taxation was local, although tributes often had to be made to some higher authority, king or emperor. In the manorial system, for example, the peasants had to provide a proportion of their produce to the lord of the manor and also to provide labour. The lord, in turn, was often required to pay tributes to the higher authority and to provide armed men at times of war. As towns grew and provincial governments became stronger, more sophisticated systems emerged, mostly employing customs and excise duties but also user fees and property taxes. According to Weber (1981), in medieval Europe cities sold annuities and also used the Guilds to levy taxes. In Britain it was the king that instigated this and, of course, almost everywhere use was made of tax farmers. The essential difficulty with local taxation is that individuals and enterprises can move to more favourable regimes and also people may live and work in different jurisdictions. For these reasons and because governments are reluctant to give local jurisdictions complete tax freedom, central governments employ 'fiscal federalism', that is, central government tax revenues are shared with local government. In most countries immobile property taxes are a major source of local government revenue but a variety of sources are used including user fees and taxes on expenditure. In Britain, a highly centralized state, local taxes are only a small proportion of total tax revenue and a large proportion of local revenue comes from property. Until 1990 *domestic rates* were proportional to the estimated rentable value of business and domestic properties (farms were exempt). In 1990 rates for households were replaced with the *Community Charge*. This was a flat rate per capita charge on all adults and aroused such hostility that in 1993 the government reverted to a property tax similar to the previous one and called *Council Tax*. In general, there is probably more variety in the types of local taxation than in the systems used by central government. In the USA, where a far greater proportion of total tax revenue is raised locally than in Britain, property taxes are no longer as important as they once were. In Germany, small business are mostly exempt from local taxation and it is usual in most countries, especially since the 1960s, for some elements in their tax systems to favour >SMALL AND MEDIUM ENTERPRISES.

In Britain, as already shown, the 1688 Revolution, the Napoleonic Wars, the two world wars and membership of the European Economic Community all triggered major changes in the tax system. Brownlee (2004), on whose work we draw heavily in what follows, makes it his thesis that decisive changes in taxation in the USA have always been associated with crisis or emergency and points to the constitutional crisis of the 1780s, the >AMERICAN CIVIL WAR, the Great Depression (>NEW DEAL) and the two world wars, though others have pointed to exceptions to his thesis. The modern tax system in the USA began with the ratification of the Constitution of 1788, which gave the Federal government

powers to impose indirect taxes. Taxation had been relatively light in the colonial period, though attempts by the British to raise taxes gave rise to the cry 'no taxation without representation' (>AMERICAN WAR OF INDEPENDENCE: >HAMILTON). By the time of the American Civil War, most states had a general property tax which was the dominant source of state revenue. The property tax did not apply only to real estate but also to financial assets (although the Supreme Court ruled in 1819 that state taxes on Federal bonds were unlawful). The heavy costs of the civil war necessitated increases in taxation and import and excise duties were raised. In 1862, the Office of the Commissioners of Internal Revenue was created. Consumption taxes applied to most consumer goods. Income tax was applied in 1861 at the rate of 3 per cent on incomes over $800 but this was of doubtful legality and it was removed in 1872 after the end of the Civil War. Changes to the Constitution allowed the introduction of Federal Income Tax from 1913. The Revenue Act of 1916 doubled the corporate income tax introduced earlier and taxed both corporate earnings and dividends for the first time (the *Classical corporation tax system*; many European countries, including Britain give tax credits for dividends – the *imputation system*). In contrast to the Civil War period, import duties were of little importance during World War I but excise taxes were again increased. Income tax was not yet the mass tax it would become during World War II and, in 1918, only 15 per cent of American families paid it.

It was the 1942 Revenue Act which broadened the base of the US income tax and added a surtax on incomes over $200,000. In 1943, withholding taxes, through monthly payroll deductions or quarterly payments, were reintroduced (they had been employed both during the Civil War and World War I). The number of individual taxpayers rose from 3.9 million in 1939 to 42 million in 1945. Payroll taxes for social security had been in place since the 1930s. In 1944, individual income taxes accounted for 40 per cent of Federal tax revenue and corporate income taxes for about one-third. World War II was much more costly than World War I and extensive borrowing was necessary, debt accounting for over 55 per cent of the total cost. Home mortgage interest deductions had been in the US Tax Code since 1913, but in the 1960s the number of deductions grew considerably. Under President Reagan there were significant changes to the tax system. The 1986 Tax Reform Act reduced tax rates while widening the tax base. Over the period 1986–2000, however, many of the previous reliefs and complications were reintroduced, reflecting another common pattern in tax reforms: once simplification is achieved, complications soon creep back in. As an example, capital gains taxes were reduced (in the 1986 reform capital gains had been taxed at the same rates as income) on the argument that this would promote entrepreneurial activity and financing. George W. Bush, elected President in 2001, made tax reductions but his promised reforms, which included relief of double taxation of corporate dividends, were not realized.

Most states in the USA have income taxes, but general sales taxes, which emerged in the 1930s, have become the largest single source of revenue. Sales taxes accounted in 1979 for 32 per cent of state tax revenues, with personal income tax at 26 per cent and corporate income tax at 10 per cent of the total. Sales taxes are broadly based, covering most goods and some services with exemptions for food and clothing and other things. The states also derive considerable revenue from user charges and taxes on motoring, such as fuel, operator licensing and parking. Property taxes, which in 1902 accounted for over 68 per cent of state tax revenue, had fallen to 26 per cent by 1989. The Federal government relies to a much greater extent than the states on direct taxation, and income tax, corporate tax and social security charges amounted to 91 per cent of revenues in 1979 (Netzer and Drennon, 1977).

In the OECD countries as a whole, 90 per cent of revenue comes from income taxes, social security contributions and consumption taxes, though there are differences between countries in their relative importance. Tax revenue as a percentage of GDP has risen persistently over the 20th century. According to OECD 'Revenue Statistics', the unweighted average in OECD countries rose from 25.8 per cent of GDP to 37.4 per cent between 1965 and 2000, though recently there are some signs that the tax ratio might plateau. Taxes remain somewhat lower in Japan (27.1 per cent) and the USA (29.6 per cent) but are much higher in the European Union (41.6 per cent). The European Union relies slightly more than the average on consumption taxes (VAT and excise) and social security contributions and less on personal income tax than the OECD average.

Global competition in product markets and growing international capital flows (>GLOBALIZATION: >INTERNATIONAL TRADE) have been associated with some shift in the burden of taxation from capital, which is mobile, to labour, which is less mobile. Evidence for this is that personal tax rates on interest income are now well below the top marginal rates applicable to wage and salary income in the majority of European Union countries. Corporate tax rates in the European Union fell by more than 13 percentage points between 1980 and 1999, though revenue actually increased as a result of broadening of tax bases and high levels of company profitability (Haufler, 2001).

The Reagan (and, in Britain, Thatcher) tax reforms were part of a global wave of tax reforms and discussions about reform in the 1980s. The inflation of the 1970s led to increased tax rates and international competition encouraged countries to respond to tax reforms elsewhere. The focus of the reforms was to make taxation more economically neutral with lower marginal rates of tax reflecting broader tax bases as tax expenditures (allowable deductions) were reduced. These concerns, as well as others about tax shelters, avoidance and evasion, have continued to preoccupy governments. This is not new. Adam >SMITH postulated four maxims that should govern taxes – they should be: proportionate to the means of the taxpayer (equality), certain, convenient to pay and economical to collect. Unfortunately, in modern democratic societies these requirements to some extent conflict, particularly in so far as equality of treatment entails complexity, which in turn undermines certainty and is unfair to the poor who cannot afford tax advice. The compliance costs (>REGULATION) and distortions of tax systems have stubbornly resisted reforms and the realization of Smith's maxims remains elusive.

### References

Aaron, Henry J. and Slemrod, Joel (eds), *The Crisis in Tax Administration*, The Brookings Institution, 2004.

Bannock, Graham, 'VAT and Small Business', NFIB Foundation, 1990.

Brownlee, W. Elliot, *Federal Taxation in America: A Short History*, Cambridge University Press, 2004.

Floud, Roderick and Johnson, Paul (eds), *The Cambridge Economic History of Modern Britain*, I, *Industrialisation, 1700–1860*, Cambridge University Press, 2004a.

Floud, Roderick and Johnson, Paul (eds), *The Cambridge Economic History of Modern Britain*, II, *Economic Maturity, 1860–1939*, Cambridge University Press, 2004b.

Floud, Roderick and Johnson, Paul, *The Cambridge Economic History of Modern Britain*, III, *Structural Change and Growth 1939–2000*, Cambridge University Press, 2004c.

Hill, C. P., *British Social and Economic History, 1700–1982* (1957), Hodder & Stoughton (5th edn), 1985.Haufleur, Andreas, *Taxation in the Global Economy*, Cambridge University Press, 2001.

Mathias, Peter and O'Brien, Patrick, 'Taxation in Britain and France, 1715–1810: A Comparison of the Social and Economic Incidence of Taxes Collected for the Central Governments', *Journal of European Economic History*, Winter, 1976.

Netzer, Dick and Drennon, Matthew P. (eds), *Readings in State and Local Public Finance*, Blackwell, 1977.

Weber, Max, *General Economic History* (1923, trans. Frank 1927), Transaction Publishers (new edn), 1981.

White, Eugene N., 'From Privatised to Government-Administered Tax Collection: Tax Farming in Eighteenth Century France', *Economic History Review*, November, 2004.

## Taylor, Frederick W.

Taylor, who lived from 1856 to 1915, was the father of scientific management who wrote a book of that title (1912) and indeed has the phrase on his tombstone, according to his biographer (Kanigel, 1997). Peter Drucker wrote:

'Frederick W. Taylor was the first man in recorded history who deemed work deserving of systematic observation and study. On Taylor's 'scientific management' rests, above all, the tremendous surge of affluence in the last seventy-five years which has lifted the working masses in the developed countries well above any level recorded before.' (Drucker, 1973)

In a later book, *Post-Capitalist Society* (1994), Drucker elevated Taylor to the level of Freud and Darwin as one of the three makers of the modern world. He pointed out that using Taylor's principles, US industry was able to train unskilled workers to produce large numbers of ships in a matter of months and so contributed to the defeat of Hitler in >WORLD WAR II. (Kanigel tell us that, in fact, one of these 'liberty ships' launched in 1942 was the SS *Frederick Taylor*.)

Taylor was born in Philadelphia. His father came from a landed family and his mother from prosperous whaling ship-owners in Maine. His background was a well-to-do one and Taylor spent three and a half years with his parents on a European tour that equipped him with fluent French and German. With this background, he was destined for an education at Harvard, but although he passed the entrance examinations with distinction he never studied there. Instead, he left school at 18 and took a four-year apprenticeship at a factory making steam pumps, an experience he was to draw upon for the rest of his life. He learned there that workers on piece rates never produced as much as they could for fear that higher output would lead to lower rates, and he identified many ways in which their work could become more productive.

In 1879, on completion of his apprenticeship, Taylor joined the Midvale Steel Co., where he was to remain for many years. Starting as a machinist, he soon became a foreman and, eight years later, chief engineer. He worked on improving material flows, reducing the need for inspections by standardization and introducing templates, jigs and gauges, carried out experiments to replace the rules of thumb traditionally used to determine cutting speeds and lubrication in metal machining; he also started time study. He investigated the materials used in the belting, which transmitted power to machines, and speeds at which they were driven. Taylor encouraged more specialization, for example, by taking away responsibility for tool sharpening and machine oiling from machinists and making these functions separate jobs. Many of these innovations laid the ground for Ford's assembly line and much later for the quality control movement.

Taylor was largely self-taught. He was awarded a degree in Mechnical Engineering at the Stevens Institute of Technology in New Jersey (without apparently spending much time there) and he also enrolled in a course in metallurgy at the University of Pennsylvania while working at Midvale, but again this was a part-time and not continuous affair. In addition to holding down his job, Taylor found time to win the US Open Doubles Tennis Championship in 1881 and to patent many inventions, some connected with his tennis-playing activities. A person of prodigious energy, he jogged to work and back (before that term came into use) and Kanigel describes how Taylor once cleared a blocked drain at the factory by crawling along it underground for 100 yards. He contributed many papers on various aspects of his work and researches to the American Society of Mechnical Engineers (ASME); his only book was not published until near the end of his life, in 1912. His work and principles were followed by a group of contemporaries, including H. L. Gant ,who developed his own famous process network charts, and Frank Gilbreth.

Taylor left Midvale in 1890 to work on paper mills for William Collins Whitney in Maine, but, after three years at that, embarked on a new career as a management consultant, where he branched out into developing accounting and bookkeeping systems. Long well known in engineering circles, Taylor was not to achieve wider fame until around 1911. Two events took place at that time. Taylor's methods and findings were cited by a lawyer, Louis Brandeis (six years later appointed to the Supreme Court by Woodrow Wilson), in a court case between the railroads and freight users. The Mann–Elkins Act of 1910 had required railroads and other carriers to prove that they needed higher freight rates and in this case Brandeis had cited Taylor's work to show that there was ample scope for efficiency savings. The other event was a strike at the government arsenal at Waterton, near Boston, where it was said that Taylor's methods were being used to reduce costs. The House of Representatives set up a Special Committee to Investigate the Taylor and other Systems of Shop Management. Although Taylor himself was not involved in the changes being introduced at Waterton he was called before the Committee to defend his system. The proceedings were often acrimonious and Taylor was accused by trade union representatives as treating human beings as if they were machines. Taylor had few person skills, had a temper and

lacked tact but there is little evidence that he had a disregard for workers' feelings and indeed always insisted that they should share in the savings made by the adoption of his methods. Nonetheless 'Taylorism' remains associated with inhuman working conditions to this day. Taylor died from complications following a bronchial condition contracted after a cold night on a train from Cleveland, returning from a speaking engagement.

## References

Drucker, Peter F., *Management: Tasks, Responsibilities, Practices*, Harper & Row, 1973.
Drucker, Peter F., *Post-Capitalist Society*, HarperBusiness, 1994.
Kanigel, Robert, *The One Best Way: Frederick Winslow Taylor and the Enigma of Efficiency*, Little, Brown, 1997.
Taylor, Frederick W., *Scientific Management*, Harper's, 1912.

## Telecommunications

Both the telegraph, which sends signals by wire, and the telephone, which carries speech, were mainly invented and initially most fully developed in the >USA. The inventions depended upon a series of advances in electricity and magnetism in Europe which date back to the Middle Ages. Before the telegraph, there were optical systems for long-distance communication; these systems depended upon lines of sight between high points, though similar results were also achieved by primitive peoples with drums. At the end of the 17th century, France had a successful system devised by Claude Chappe using semaphore arms, telescopes and a code book which, subject to weather conditions, permitted communication between Paris and Marseilles in a matter of hours. Since then, various technologies have been developed using wires, fibre-optic cables, radio waves and satellites in space. These means of transmission have more recently become fused with computers (>ELECTRONICS) to create global communications networks capable of transmitting not only voice and messages but also data and video. Initially, telegraphy and telephony diffused more rapidly in the USA than elsewhere. More recently, however, wireless communications in the form of mobile phones have achieved higher densities in some European countries than in America, while Europe has also been a leading centre for the development of the necessary technologies.

Edward Cooke and Charles Wheatstone, in Britain, filed for a telegraph patent in 1837, four months before Samuel Morse registered his in the USA. The British system was analogue, in which electrical current moved an arrow pointing to a letter of the alphabet. Construction of telegraph lines began earlier in Britain than in America and the first commercial telegraph line opened in 1839 along a portion of the Great Western Railway near London. Initially there were difficulties in obtaining rights of way for lines. The 1846 and 1863 Electric Telegraph Acts allowed telegraphs to be built over public land and highways. An 1899 Act permitted the establishment of telecommunications networks by local authorities. Of these, only the one in Hull, granted a monopoly in the area in 1912, has survived to today (as Kingston Communications). The telegraph was strategically important during wartime and for communication across the British Empire, and in 1902 a line was laid by the British across the Pacific Ocean. In 1869, the

telegraph companies were nationalized and placed as a monopoly in the Post Office. The courts later ruled that the nationalization act of 1869 also covered the telephone (Noam, 1992). The telegraph, like the postal system before it and the telephone subsequently, was pioneered by private firms but later taken over by the state. This was to be a common experience in Europe, though in America regulated private companies held on to telecommunications, though not postal services, from the beginning.

The first commercial telephone services began in the late 1870s in both Britain and America. The Post Office in Britain was initially not keen on taking on telephones, having recently acquired responsibility for telegraphy. There were patent disputes with Bell, who invented telephony, and Edison, who improved it, and they were also in dispute with each other. In 1880 the United Telephone Company, in which the Americans were shareholders, was given a concession by the Post Office to operate services and merged with several competitors to form the National Telephone Company (NTC). In 1911, the government bought NTC at the expiry of its licence. Telephony developed slowly in Britain, dogged by outdated technology and resistance from the Union of Postal Workers. Even so, progress was faster than in France, where the Société Générale de Téléphone (SGT) was nationalized in 1889. As late as 1974 the French telephone system was notoriously inefficient and had half as many lines as Britain. In 1969, the Post Office in Britain became more autonomous and split into two divisions, post and telecommunications, but retaining its monopoly in both.

After years of complaints about services and debate, the new Thatcher Government introduced, in the

1981 British Telecommunications Act, competition into the industry by licensing two joint ventures, Cable & Wireless and Mercury. In time, the former took over the latter and other telephone licenses were granted. In 1982, 51 per cent of the former national monopoly, now called British Telecom (BT), was sold in the first flotation of a public utility. Further tranches of BT were sold in 1984 and 1991. In 1982, BT introduced electronic mail and in 1995 BT Cellnet launched a mobile telephone service in a joint venture with Securicor (at the time it was not allowed to become a mobile network operator directly). In 1993, its remaining shares were sold and BT created an alliance, Concert, with MCI the long-distance carrier in the USA, but it was overreaching. In 1997, the MCI stake was disposed of, as was Cellnet in 2002. Cellnet, later renamed O2, was acquired by Telefonica, a Spanish company.

On privatization, new regulatory arrangements had to be devised. The first director general of OFTEL was appointed in 1984. The approach common in regulating US utilities, of a multi-member commission instead of an individual and of controlling rates of return, was rejected. Instead, BT was allowed to raise prices by the change in the Retail Price Index (RPI), minus an arbitrary 3 per cent for productivity growth (raised to 4.5 per cent in 1989). BT has had its vicissitudes but it retains a dominant position in the British market and, despite enforced agreements to allow its local lines to be used by competitors, has promoted broadband. Its global ambitions frustrated, it is focusing on Europe and on specialized services for international corporations. Overall, privatization has been greatly to the benefit of British consumers. Call prices have fallen in real

terms and service levels improved. The number of British lines rose from 17.5 million in 1980–1 to a recent peak of 29.6 million. Employment has fallen from 241,000 in 1984 to 106,000 in 2007, much of this, though not all, presumably reflecting increased productivity.

In the USA, Samuel Morse who invented the telegraph as an early version of a digital transmission system, patented it in 1837. Morse code is still used today. Morse obtained a grant from Congress a few years later to build a line between Baltimore and Washington. There were some competing technologies, but eventually the Morse system prevailed. Morse determined to exploit his invention but was forced, through lack of a single powerful backer, to split his patent rights among four partners for use on a geographical basis. By 1850 there were many competing telegraph companies but Western Union (WU) led the apparently inevitable consolidation. In 1861 WU completed the first transcontinental telegraph line, eight years before the completion of the railway link between the East and the Pacific coast. By 1866 a successful trans-Atlantic cable had been laid and the USA had a vast network of lines covering the whole country. WU had some 90 per cent of the market in all the US regions. This was the first case in the USA where a single company achieved a national monopoly, to be followed by steel and oil. The telegraph proved to be a boon for the railways, which could use it for scheduling and avoiding collisions, especially on single-track lines. The telegraph was also invaluable for stock control in retailing and had great military worth during the >AMERICAN CIVIL WAR. It helped in the development of newspapers. According to Salehi and Bulliet's contribution, 'Communications' in

Bulliet (1998), Associated Press (AP), founded in 1848 to share telegraph costs, fed the whole of Lincoln's 1862 inaugural address exclusively to two Californian newspapers, which paid WU the then considerable sum of $600 for the transmission.

In the 1870s, Alexander Bell discovered how to transmit speech electrically and patented the invention of the telephone in 1876. (Bell was born in Scotland and the young assistant to whom he spoke in the next room during his early experiment was Thomas A. Watson, later of IBM fame (>ELECTRONICS).) Again, there were several competing technologies, notably by Elisha Gray whose patent was lodged a few hours later on the same day. Gray, who made many inventions, had founded his company, Western Electric, in 1872. Western Electric entered the fiercely competitive telephone market and was sued by the Bell Company for patent infringement in 1878, a case which Bell won; Bell took over Western Electric in 1881. Western Union, who did not initially appreciate the importance of telephony, later launched a competing telephone service but in 1879 Bell and WU agreed to carve up the market, in particular leaving WU with the telegraph while Bell focused on long-distance telephony. In 1889, American Telephone and Telegraph (AT&T) consolidated all the various Bell companies. AT&T franchised local operations and concentrated on the cities and long-distance traffic. The company came to dominate telephony as WU had dominated telegraphy but after 1900 the growth of telegraph traffic slowed down and, from 1930, declined in the face of competition from telephones. In 1908 AT&T gained control of Western Union but divested it in 1913 under the threat of >ANTI-TRUST action.

WU subsequently declined in importance, though in 1958 it launched the Telex – direct-dialled communication between teletype terminals – and today concentrates on money transmission services. The telephone industry was regulated from its early days but state regulation proved largely fruitless because of interstate traffic; in 1934 the Federal Communications Commission was established.

AT&T's domination of the US telephone market lasted until 1984, when it was the world's largest company. Under an anti-trust suit 'Ma Bell' was splintered into seven regional holding companies ('Baby Bells') for local and regional services, while AT&T was confined to long-distance services and had to provide access to its lines to competitors. Bell Laboratories was spun off in the 1990s to a new company, Lucent Technologies (now Alcatel-Lucent). Bell Labs, formed in 1925 and jointly owned with Western Electric, made major contributions to various technologies, including the 1947 invention of the transistor, fundamental to the subsequent development of >ELECTRONICS. In 1994, AT&T merged with McCaw Cellular Communications, giving it a powerful position in the mobile telephone market which had emerged in the early 1980s. The Telecommunications Act 1996 deregulated the industry and allowed more competition between its various segments, which led to a wave of mergers between the Baby Bells, long-distance companies and cable television providers. The industry thrived and experiments in the 1960s led to the use of satellite communications, which greatly extended the range of microwave communications between towers and along cables, a cheaper alternative to wire communications.

Although a portable 'wireless telephone' was demonstrated by Nathan Stubblefield, an American melon farmer-inventor in Kentucky in 1908, the origins of the modern cellular telephone are very complex and dependent upon a large number of developments in various countries. Radio telephony was in its infancy in the inter-war period. AT&T established a regular service between New York and London in 1927 and, by 1936, according to Bulliet (1998), all of the company's 34 million telephones could be interconnected by wire or radio. Somewhat earlier, radio telephony was coming into use in Europe on trains and ships and had already begun in aircraft, 'walkie-talkies' or bulky two-way radio handsets designed in World War II. Mobile technology for direct-dialled calls using cellular radio was developed in Europe, especially by Scandinavian producers (notably Ericsson), as well as by Bell, Motorola and others in the USA. The technology was available for use early in the 1980s. A second generation of mobile telephones (GSM) emerged in the 1990s and later generations have made internet access available from these handsets.

The organization of the telephone industry in Europe was very different from that in America. Early in the 20th century, although telecommunications were more advanced in America than in Europe, London was still the principal centre for long-distance communications. The Cable and Wireless Company, with government support, had created a communications system encircling the globe. The USA did not have such a network and it was shared with them during and after World War II. Typically, in Continental Europe, as in Britain, state PTTs (post, telephone and telegraph companies) assumed monopolistic responsibility for telecommunications after early periods of fierce, and often ruinous, private competition. The PTTs were major sources of government revenue and, in addition to the government itself, the supporters of the monopolies included the private equipment suppliers (which invariably received some protection from foreign competition), newspaper publishers (whose postal and telegraph rates were subsidized), >TRADE UNIONS and the political left. Arguments included the belief that electric telecommunications were a 'natural' monopoly and the importance of providing a universal service, with prices in rural areas subsidized by business and long-distance users. The PTT lobbies easily prevailed in most countries and these state organizations lasted from the 1920s or earlier until the 1980s, when the vogue for regulated privatization began. The inefficiencies of the monopolies were concealed to some extent by the downward trend in the cost of electronic technology (though, as Noam (1992) points out, this was the result of the efforts of the equipment industry rather than the PTTs). Davies (1994) argues that the alternative of decentralized structures for telecommunications lost out not to economics but to politics. In the Netherlands, Finland and Denmark, as in the municipal system in Hull, private competition worked perfectly well. Britain and other member states had to struggle to get agreement on liberalizing the European telecommunications market and this was not achieved until 1998.

As part of the movement towards the so-called information society, world telecommunications have continued to develop rapidly. At present, we are embarked upon a second technological divide as telecommunication becomes fully digitized, bringing it into line with other media, including computers and television. In some ways, the divide is as important as the one in the 19th century (though surely not as revolutionary). In the early stages of the telephone age, the driving force was the needs of business; now it is ordinary consumers who want entertainment, including music and video, and information as well as communication and such add-ons as digital photographic capability. The business-user share of Post Office/BT exchange connections fell from 59 per cent in 1931 to 38 per cent in 1961 and 24 per cent in 1995 (Wheatley, 1999). The growth of telecommunications in the 20th century has been very rapid and seems to be accelerating. In the USA, from 7.6 (fixed line) telephones per 100 inhabitants in 1900, the number had risen to 58.3 in 1970. Mobile telephony has spread faster: in 1985 it was negligible but by the year 2000 the number of mobile subscribers in the USA was 110 million and only three years later was 159 million, or 55 per cent of the population. On a world basis, the number of cellular mobile subscribers per 100 inhabitants was 91 in the developed world and even in developing countries it was 32. The density of both fixed and mobile telephone ownership is now higher in some European countries than in the USA and Japan. In Britain and Germany there are about 118 mobile subscribers per 100 inhabitants (many people have more than one mobile telephone) (figures from the International Telecommunications Union).

### References

Bulliet, Richard W. (ed.), *The Columbia History of the 20th Century*, Columbia University Press, 1998.

Chandler, Alfred D., *The Visible Hand: The Managerial Revolution in American Business*, Harvard University Press, 1977.

Davies, Andrew, *Telecommunications and Politics: The Decentralised Alternative*, Pinter, 1994.

Noam, Eli, *Telecommunications in Europe*, Oxford University Press, 1992.

Sterling, Christopher H., Berut, Phyllis W. and Weiss, Martin B., *Shaping American Telecommunications*, Lawrence Erlbaum Associates, 2006.

Thompson, Robert Luther, *Wiring a Continent: The History of the Telegraph Industry in the United States, 1832–1866*, Princeton University Press, 1947.

Wheatley, Jefferey J., *World Telecommunications Economics*, Institution of Electrical Engineers, 1999.

# Thompson, Edward Palmer

Thompson was a social historian and political activist, who lived from 1924 to 1993; Thompson was not an economic historian. However, he left his mark on the subject as did other social reformers such as Arnold Toynbee, who really did found the economic history of the >INDUSTRIAL REVOLUTION IN BRITAIN, and J. L. and Barbara Hammond, in whose steps Thompson trod. Thompson's written output, which included books, journal articles, pamphlets and journalism, was prodigious but only a small part of it covered social history as such; most is about politics in one way or another (Palmer, 1994). E. P. Thompson's reputation, at least among economic historians, is based upon *The Making of the English Working Class* (1980), which deals with the condition of working people, their origins as a class, the influence of methodism and the politics of the industrial revolutionary period. The book argues that the working class emerged for the first time in the period 1790–1830, essentially as a consequence of the changes brought about by the industrial revolution. It suggests that the causes were not solely economic but the result of shared experience of political alienation, as well as economic exploitation. He traces, by the end of the period, an array of self-conscious working-class institutions, including >TRADE UNIONS, friendly societies and educational bodies, and asserts that the self-identification of class was made by themselves and not imposed from outside. For Thompson, the industrial revolution was truly catastrophic and the many documents and contemporary testimonies he reviews in his 'history from below' leave no doubt that very many contemporaries saw it as such. On the standard of living debate, he accepts that there may have been a slight improvement in average standards between 1790 and 1840, but points out that conditions were bad at the beginning of this period and bad at the end of it with an indeterminate group of the population at the point of subsistence. He quotes J. H. Clapham as saying that 'some 50% of the figures averaged will be below the average line' (Thompson, 1980). Like the >HAMMONDS, he also recognizes that deprivation is not necessarily quantifiable and may be a subjective condition affecting family ties and human dignity as much as pounds, shillings and pence.

Thompson was born near Oxford and his father, early on 'in the service of methodism', spent much of his working career in India and the Far East and later became an academic. His son took a degree in history at Cambridge University but did not go on to take a higher degree. Thompson spend two decades in adult education, he was an extra-mural lecturer at Leeds University. In 1965 he became

director of the Centre for the Study of Social History at Warwick. His time there was short and he preferred to think of himself as a writer rather than as an academic. Long a Marxist, he nonetheless took an independent approach and was critical of some of the doctrines of >MARX. He was a member of the Communist Party in the 1940s, but left in 1956 after the Soviet Union invaded Hungary. He became a thinker and polemicist for the New Left (and a founder of the European Campaign for Nuclear Disarmament, which catapulted him to national and international fame).

## References

Currie, R. and Hartwell, R. M., 'The Making of the English Working Class', *Economic History Review*, 2nd series(3), 1965.

Palmer, Bryan D., *E. P. Thompson: Objections and Oppositions*, Verso, 1994.

Thompson, E. P., *The Making of the English Working Class* (1963), Penguin (rev. edn), 1980.

## Trade Unions

Although trade unions, which emerged first in >BRITAIN in the 19th century, were not direct descendants of the earlier craft guilds, there was some affinity at least in regard to the aims and purposes for which they were formed, which in essence was the protection of the interests of their members – something they would have difficulty in achieving as individuals. The need to form protective or aggressive groups is a characteristic of business as much as unionism. Combinations of workers were certainly not unknown in 18th-century Britain in addition to the craft associations, although they were often very local and set up solely to resolve only a particular dispute, and were dissolved on its resolution. The history of trade unionism is the history of their fight to get established, to grow and to be recognized and to be accepted by the state. It is also of the maturing of the relationship between the conflicting parties in business, from the open warfare characterized by >LUDDISM, lock-outs and strikes to collective bargaining and reconciliation by discussion.

Trade union density in Britain by 1895 had reached 10 per cent, measured as the percentage of the total workforce available for work. In 1901, out of a possible population of workers of 14.7 million, 1.9 million were in trade unions, a density of 13 per cent overall. By 1910, trade union density had increased to 16 per cent. (This ratio did not reach 50 per cent until 1974.) Unionization, however, was not spread evenly across industries. In 1910, union density in >COAL mining was as high as 69 per cent, in glass making 33 per cent and in printing 32 per cent. By 1914, membership of British trade unions reached 4.1 million, 23 per cent of people in employment, it rose to 8.3 million in 1920, 45 per cent of the labour force, and then fell back to 4.4 million in the >GREAT DEPRESSION. In 1931, unionization was 51 per cent of coal miners, 53 per cent of those employed in the cotton, flax and man-made fibres industry, 27 per cent in the metals and engineering industries and only 15 per cent in the food and drink industries.

Wrigley (1992) shows that in Britain, prior to >WORLD WAR II, there were four periods of growth in the numbers recruited to trade union memberships and these periods coincided with growth in the economy.

From 1888–90, from 750,000 to 1.5 million members.

From 1910–13, from 2.6 million to 4.1 million members.
From 1915–20, from 4.3 million to 8.3 million members.
From 1935–9, from 4.8 million to 6.2 million members.

With the development of the economy and the consequential changes in its structure, the proportion of manual workers in employment fell from 64 per cent in 1951 to 48 per cent by 1981 with a consequential dampening effect on union membership as union penetration of white-collar workers was much less successful, partly due to the failure of the unions in the recruitment of women. In 1911, women accounted for about 30 per cent of non-manual workers but this percentage had risen to 43 per cent by 1981. This rise traced the increase in women doing office work. In 1911, there were only 179,000 women doing clerical work, just 3 per cent of all female workers, but, by 1981, there were 2.9 million, about 29 per cent of all females in employment (Williams, 1995).

British trade unions reached their maximum size in 1979 with 13.2 million members, having risen by 4 million since 1950, and then fell by the turn of the century to 7.5 million, of which 5.4 million union members were party to collective bargaining. By this time about 29 per cent of people in employment were in a union, with a much higher proportion of those employed in the public sector (60 per cent) than in the private sector (20 per cent) (Fernie and Metcalf, 2005).

In France, about 100,000 workers were in trade unions in 1886, rising to 500,000 in 1900. Restrictions against strike action were lifted in 1864 but it was not until 1901 that trade unions were free from legal restraint. In Germany, in 1869, the free trade unions had 47,192 members and there were, in addition, 30,000 in the Hirsch–Duncker Trade Associations. Max Hirsch and Frank Duncker supported the view that unions should have a conciliatory tone in the settlement of disputes, should behave lawfully, have systems of benefits for their members and look to the improvement of working conditions. Trade associations were formed based on these precepts. These conciliatory ideas suffered from the failure of strikes in 1869 and 1870 and, following the Franco-Prussian War in 1870/1, membership fell. In 1878, the free trade unions had a membership of 56,275 compared with 16,525 in the Hirsch–Duncker Trade Associations. Thereafter, trade union membership grew rapidly to reach, in 1890, a total of 357,194, of which 62,643 were in Hirsch–Duncker Trade Associations. In 1894, the Christian trade union movement was founded, which had a similar conciliatory approach as the Hirsch–Duncker Trade Associations, and they surpassed the latter in membership by 1905, when total union membership reached 1,733,552, of which 188,106 were in Christian trade unions and 116,143 in Hirsch–Duncker Trade Associations. In 1913, total union membership in Germany was 2,973,395 (a density of about 16 per cent), of which 314,735 were in Christian trade unions and 106,618 were in Hirsch–Duncker Trade Associations (Schneider, 1991).

This growth in union membership in the first two decades of the 20th century was similar in other countries of >WESTERN EUROPE. There was also growth in union membership in the USA. In 1913, membership reached 2.6 million, a density of 10 per cent, up from 7.5 per cent in 1900. Growth was generally resumed after >WORLD WAR I. In Germany, membership peaked at 9.4 million in 1920, a density of 46 per cent, compared with Britain at 8.3 million, a density of 48 per cent. The free trade unions were banned by the National Socialist government in Germany and the other fascist dictatorships in Austria, Italy and Spain from the 1930s and the trade unions did not recover until after >WORLD WAR II.

After the war, there was a general expansion in trade union membership in Western Europe from the 1950s until the 1970s and then, with the exception of Sweden and Denmark, membership declined during the rest of the century. In the USA, trade union density peaked earlier after the war. In 1970, trade union density in Britain was 48 per cent, in France, 21 per cent, in Germany, 33 per cent, in the USA, 27 per cent, and in Sweden it was 80 per cent.

Excluding Greece, Portugal and Spain, who gained or regained in the period the right to join free unions, total membership in OECD countries increased by 14 million between 1970 and 1980 but in the 1980s the unions lost 5 million. All OECD countries experienced losses or at least a drop in growth, although the most severe falls were in Britain, France and the USA. The average density rate for 18 OECD countries fell from 35 per cent in 1970 to 28 per cent in 1988. In the USA, in particular, trade union density fell from its peak reached in 1945 of about 33 per cent of all non-agricultural workers to 16 per cent at the close of the 1990s. By this time, only France and Spain had lower union penetration rates. These low figures contrast with the high levels of membership in Sweden, Finland and Denmark, which reached between 70 per cent and 85 per cent (Visser, 1996). The decline in trade union membership in the last two decades of the 20th century was widespread throughout the member countries of the OECD and for common reasons. By 2000, the density in Britain had fallen to 29 per cent, France to 10 per cent, Germany to 25 per cent and the USA to 13 per cent, with Sweden, in contrast, was virtually unchanged at 80 per cent (Wrigley, 2007).

In Britain, at the end of the 18th century, there existed legal constraints on the activities of workers which had survived for centuries, such as the Elizabethan Statute of Artificers of 1563 and the law governing the relationship between masters and servants, which had its origins in the 14th century. The Combination Act of 1799 and the Combination Act of 1800, which somewhat ameliorated the bias in favour of employers in the earlier Act, were the first to impose a general ban on all combinations. This ban technically applied to employers as well as workers. In effect these statutes simply re-emphasized the existing legal constraints on workers and, in particular, the master and servant laws under which the workers could be prosecuted for breach of contract. The Combination Acts were repealed in 1824, although it was not until 1875 that the Employers and Workman Act repealed laws relating to master and servant. Workers were then put on an equal footing with employers in contracts of employment subject to the civil law, as opposed to the criminal law as had previously been the case. In the USA, in the 19th century, the law was able to be used against trade unions for acts of coercion or conspiracy and in constraint of trade. The Sherman Act of 1890 was used against a strike in 1894 (>ANTI-TRUST).

Unlike unions in Western Europe, the British trade unions never took a revolutionary stance. Karl >MARX was frustrated by the indifference with which his views were received in Britain. He wrote that, 'In England prolonged prosperity has demoralised the workers... the ultimate aim of this most bourgeois of lands would seem to be the establishment of a bourgeois aristocracy and a bourgeois proletariat side by side' (quoted in Berlin, 1996). This attitude on the part of the British trade unions was indeed partly due to the fact of increasing prosperity but also the progressive easing of the laws which had inhibited the growth of trade unions until they were completely free of them after 1875.

In the 1890s, a political party was formed which, in 1906, took the title of the Labour Party, which gave the trade union members constitutional access to a platform from which to influence government in favour of socialist policies, a process that persisted through the 20th century until the rise of 'New' Labour, which sought to reduce the influence of the trade unions in its policy decisions.

In France, the legal right to strike is embodied in the Constitution and strikes could be launched against government policy, for instance, government proposals for the reform of the health service. Under French law, contracts are suspended during a strike, not terminated, and, therefore, strikers must be reinstated on the resolution of the industrial action. Although, there was a commensurate growth in trade unionism in Germany after 1895, the environment for the unions was more difficult than in Britain. For instance, employers generally succeeded in sidestepping collective bargains. In 1913, 82 miners were covered by collective bargains compared with 900,000 in Britain, and in metalworking, 1,376 compared with 230,000. In Britain, in 1889, there was only one national agreement (in cotton) along with regional agreements, but, by 1910, national collective agreements had been made in a range of industries. Collective bargaining was further encouraged in Britain during World War I (Wrigley, 1992) and given support by the government. The Railways Act of 1921, for instance, enforced national collective bargaining on the railway companies. By the end of the 20th century, collective agreements in most European countries were legal contracts, the exception being Britain, and negotiated union settlements were extended to non-members, a practice not generally accepted in the USA. Further, in many West European countries, the trade unions had close links directly with firms through the legal requirement for worker representatives. No such legal requirement existed in Britain or the USA (OECD, 1996).

As shown above, the growth of British trade unions in the late 19th century and until the last two decades of the 20th century was correlated with periods of growth in the economy, punctuated by setbacks in times of recession and during the two world wars. However, in addition, there were more long-run influences. During wartime, the British trade unions established themselves as an accepted voice, in addition to business interests, to be heard in the formulation of government policies. Through this influence, and eventually directly on the gaining of power in government by the Labour Party, they found themselves in sympathy with the promulgation of a welfare state after World War II. During this time, however, there were fundamental changes taking place in the structure of the economy and in employment which proved to have a debilitating effect on membership numbers. In the 1980s, the Conservative Government passed legislation which constrained trade union activity in industrial disputes but the unions were already in decline in Britain as elsewhere.

The reasons for the worldwide decline in union membership were universal. The industries and the blue-collar workers in which the trade unions were dominant were giving way to the service industries and white-collar workers and a rising number of women in employment. There was a long-standing prejudice against women in work. There was a belief that women were part-time workers, being expected to marry and to be supported by their husbands, and it was thought 'reasonable' for them to have lower wages than men. Trade unions were not sympathetic to women. Moreover, both the craft and professional male unions were also prejudiced against female members (>EMPLOYMENT OF WOMEN AND CHILDREN). (European Trade Union Confederation, 2001)

The decline in union membership occurred through the slowness of the unions to adapt to the change in the industrial and employment structure of economies in the 20th century; not only the rising proportion of the service industries in the GDP but also the emergence of flexible working, part-time work, the increase in the number of women and immigrants in employment. By the end of the 20th century, only in Sweden did unions have a representative in more than a half of the places of work; in Germany it was only 6 per cent. Moreover, in Germany, for example, one-third of union members were retired or out of work. Nevertheless, in Western Europe the trade unions continued to be regarded as part of the government policy-making process, although in Britain this role had diminished in importance. In Sweden and Denmark, state functions, such as the distribution of unemployment benefit, were sub-contracted to the trade unions.

It has been argued that trade unions obtain wage increases for their members which they would not otherwise gain. Attempts have been made to measure this effect, with generally a distinction being made between the craft unions and others, with the former exercising constraint on entry and the closed shop to maintain their position. In a study on the influence of collective bargaining in 1978, it was found that manual workers could benefit by up to a 25 per cent premium on wage levels as a result of this collective approach but for skilled workers there was no benefit (Layard *et al.*, 1980). However, such increases in wages could increase unemployment because the firms granting their demands lost their competitive ability. Moreover, by the nature of the entrenched interests of their existing members trade unions could be biased in favour of the status quo and would obstruct change. There was an increasing sentiment in support of this view, particularly in Britain in the 1970s, which gave the government the political authority to constrain the trade unions, seen to be damaging economic growth through the excessive power they exercised in their individual satrapies. On the other hand, the trade unions had been a force for the improvement in the working conditions of labour and offered their members welfare benefits, such as for unemployment and sickness relief, which were the harbinger of and inspiration for the welfare state.

## References

Berg, Maxine, 'Factories, Workshops and Industrial Organisation', in Roderick Floud and Donald McCloskey (eds), *The Economic History of Britain Since 1700*, I, 1700–1860, Cambridge University Press, 1994.

Berlin, Isaiah, *Karl Marx, His Life and Environment*, with a foreword by Alan Ryan (4th edn), Oxford University Press, 1996.

European Trade Union Confederation, *Trade Unions in Europe*, Brussels, 2001.

Fernie, Sue and Metcalf, David (eds), *Trade Unions: Resurgence or Demise?*, Routledge, 2005.

Layard, R., Metcalf, D. and Nickell, S., 'The Effect of Collective Bargaining on Wages', in A.B. Atkinson (ed.), *Wealth, Income and Inequality*, Oxford University Press, 1980.

OECD, 'Trends in Trade Union Membership', in *Employment Outlook*, OECD, 1996.

Rule, J., 'Labour in a Changing Economy, 1700–1850', in Anne Digby, Charles Feinstein and David Jenkins (eds), *New Directions in Economic and Social History*, II, Macmillan, 1992.

Schneider, Michael, *A Brief History of the German Trade Unions*, Dietz, 1991.

Snyder, Francis G. and Hay, Douglas (eds), *Labour, Law and Crime*, Routledge, 1987.

Visser, Jelle, 'Trends in Trade Union Membership', in *Employment Outlook*, OECD, 1996.

Williams, Chris, 'Britain', in Stefan Berger and David Broughton (eds), *The Force of Labour: The Western European Labour Movement and the Working Class in the Twentieth Century*, Berg, 1995.

Wrigley, C., 'Labour and Trade Unions in Great Britain, 1880–1839', in Anne Digby, Charles Feinstein and David Jenkins (eds), *New Directions in Economic and Social History*, II, Macmillan, 1992.

Wrigley, C., 'Industrial Relations', in Nicholas Crafts, Ian Gazeley and Andrew Newell (eds), *Work and Pay in 20th Century Britain*, Oxford University Press, 2007.

# U

## USA

The rise of the USA is probably the most dramatic of all the major episodes in economic history. In the 250 years between 1700 and 1950, and in what was effectively a developing country in a sparsely populated continent, the economic weight of the American colonies grew from negligible levels to account for 27 per cent of world GDP. The British colonists prevailed over their Dutch, Spanish and French rivals and were, in turn, pushed out by their own settlers (>AMERICAN WAR OF INDEPENDENCE). Had the British, the world superpower of the time, appreciated the potential they might have tried harder to retain their American colonies, but apparently mistakenly thought that preserving the wealth derived from >SUGAR in the Caribbean was worth more serious attention. In the same way, Spain was more interested in its precious metal discoveries in South America, while Britain's enemy, Napoleon, sold the French possessions west of the Mississippi to President Jefferson for a token amount. It was really a catalogue of mischance, because even the discovery of North America by Columbus in 1492, as well as that of the Hudson valley by the Dutch in 1623, were accidental in a search for the North West Passage. In any event, things moved slowly; the first successful British settlement was not made in Virginia until 1607, followed by New England (1620) and Maryland (1632). The British, developing along the eastern seaboard, took over what was to become New York from the Dutch in 1664.

The USA, of course, was built by the energies of its people but what was to become a young republic in 1790 had great advantages in terms of its relative isolation from the European predators, its space, climates and natural resources. There was no question of a Malthusian trap (>MALTHUS). Arthur Schlesinger, in Harris (1961), writes that the early American population was fairly advanced, culturally, politically and morally. The early settlers had a Calvinist work ethic (>WEBER), a rising faith in democracy and were mostly literate and believers in education. No less than eight colleges, later to become universities, were established early on (Harvard 1636, Yale 1701, for example), but only one, William and Mary, in the South. In the northern colonies, only 5 per cent of the population were slaves. Many >INSTITUTIONS favourable to development were inherited from Britain whose mercantilist restrictions were less onerous than those of the Spanish. Although the Navigation Acts (>MERCANTILISM) did force American exports to be routed via England, they also favoured access to other Empire markets and allowed the American colonies to build a large merchant fleet. The British colonies were also decentralized under the Crown, a structure which was to find permanent expression in the Federal system of government.

Substantial industrialization in the East at first consisted of flour and lumber mills, leather tanneries and iron production. Iron output was initially limited by the lack of suitable iron ore and coal, but techniques for using anthracite from Pennsylvania were to emerge by 1850 and, later, ore deposits from Lake Superior (>IRON AND STEEL). Textile production, which grew faster than iron output, was concentrated in New England, where water power was available. A textile mill on Rhode Island using technology developed in Britain opened in 1790 and others were to follow. After the Declaration of Independence in 1776, imports of British manufactures continued but industrialization was later stimulated by President Jefferson's 1807 embargo on trade with both sides of the Revolutionary Wars (>WESTERN EUROPE), which lasted up to the war with Britain, 1812–14. Apart from textiles and to a lesser extent iron and metal products, brewing, meat-packing, boots and shoes, enterprises were typically small, unincorporated businesses engaged in a wide variety of activities. Over time firms grew and, especially after the >AMERICAN CIVIL WAR, specialized, for example in >MACHINE TOOLS. Techniques were developed for making arms and other products using interchangeable parts, a precondition for mass production. In these and other areas of manufacturing the USA was soon to take a leading international position.

The traditional view of American industrialization, which started in the East and later expanded in a manufacturing belt extending up to the Great Lakes, is that as the early settlers moved westward in the region, lower-quality land reduced agricultural yields and encouraged the growth of manufacturing for import substitution. Later on, this view continues, with >AMERICAN WESTWARD EXPANSION, agricultural competition

from the Middle West and the South, leading more Easterners to abandon farming and 'export' manufactured goods to the West and South. It is estimated that, between 1840 and 1860, national manufacturing employment tripled and productivity rose almost fivefold as America went through its industrial revolution. The revisionist view, however, is that agricultural and manufacturing development went hand in hand and were closely integrated. The South and Middle West were actually minor markets for Eastern manufactures in 1840, and even by 1860 these markets accounted for only 10–15 per cent of its output. What happened was that the increase in agricultural productivity released labour for manufacturing while growing and prosperous urban areas provided both markets and capital. By 1860, the East was accounting for 74 per cent of manufacturing value added in the three regions, the Middle West 18 per cent and the South 8 per cent. The Middle West's manufacturing grew by the same process of labour release from agriculture; the East's share of the total fell to 60 per cent and that of the Middle West rose to 32 per cent by 1900. There was some North–South movement of textile production and regional markets on the Pacific Coast, protected by distance, were also expanding. The dominance of the East–Middle West manufacturing belt was largely to continue until major new industries in aerospace and electronics emerged from the 1950s. Agriculture and manufacturing, in the revisionist view, benefited one another just as Alexander >HAMILTON had argued they would in 1760, in contrast to Thomas Jefferson's fear that the interests of industry were contrary to those of agriculture (Meyer, 2003).

The South, both before and after the Civil War, did not benefit much from the growth of manufacturing and join the industrial belt. This has traditionally been explained as a consequence of the institutional structure of >SLAVERY and the ownership of large plantations which did not generate a large demand for manufactures, especially since the Southerners looked mainly to Europe for their needs. However, this view, too, is being increasingly challenged. The new views do not deny that the industrial sector in the South was relatively small compared with the North after 1840, but rather that the plantation owners were rational entrepreneurs (>ENTREPRENEURSHIP) and not 'agrarian patriarchs'. There was some manufacturing (not only food processing), both on and off the estates and many small independent producers. This was concealed in the statistics because plantation-based activities were often included with agriculture. For example, Thomas Jefferson manufactured iron nails on his estate. Stanley Engerman, in Delfino and Gillespie, says that, in fact, the pre-Civil War (antebellum) South, if counted as an independent nation, 'was about fourth in per capita income ahead of all Europe except Britain, ranked high in canal and railroad construction, was sixth in the world in cotton textile production ... and was eighth in pig iron production' (2005). The South also had extensive educational and banking systems (for whites) and a general degree of literacy greater than that in most of Europe at the time.

Income growth per capita in the period 1820–70 in the USA was very much faster than that of Western Europe, 1.34 per cent per annum compared with 0.98 per cent, though growth was far from uniform throughout the period. In 1820 US incomes already exceed those in Europe (by

5 per cent) and by 1870 they were 25 per cent higher (Maddison, 2007). Although the data for the early years are not very robust, it seems that incomes grew at about 1.6 per cent per annum from 1790 with expanding foreign trade but this growth was interrupted by the trade embargo of 1807 and the 1812–14 war. There was a second spurt of growth from the 1820s to the 1830s at a rate of over 2 per cent, slowing and then a pre-Civil War boom from the mid-1840s. Much of this growth was driven by agriculture, although there was the first railway boom around 1830–50, which resumed in a second boom after the Civil War (1860–4) and continued until the 1880s. There was a serious depression starting in 1873 during which the price level dropped by 25 per cent and the rate of business failures doubled, and another worse, but short-lived, recession in 1893. There was a further growth spurt from the late 1890s until about 1903 (Atack and Passell, 1994; Alfred Conrad, in Harris, 1961; Heilbroner and Singer, 1977).

Interrelated changes in land area, population growth and transport facilities were important aspects of the relatively very fast US economic growth path. Between 1800 and 1860, the land area of the USA tripled. The Louisiana Territory was acquired in 1803, Florida in 1819, Texas in 1845, Oregon in 1846 and parts of Mexico including present-day California in 1848–53. All these acquisitions, whether by war or purchase, were bargains. The Louisiana Territory, over 828,000 square miles in the central part of the continent west of the Mississippi and 23 per cent of the present US land area, cost only $23 million, including the write-off of some debts. Alaska, purchased from Russia, was added in 1867 and Hawaii was annexed in 1898.

The population of the USA increased sixfold from 1800–60, due mainly to a marked decrease in the death rate and to immigration (>MIGRATION). In the whole, in period 1820–1955, immigration was very important though never more than half the annual increase in population (Peter B. Kenen, in Harris, 1961). There were also large movements in population westwards (>AMERICAN WESTWARD EXPANSION). The share of the West in the total population rose from negligible levels in 1800 to 1.9 per cent in 1860 and 13 per cent in 1950. The population in the eastern states did not decline but grew more slowly. There was growing urbanization: the percentage of the population in urban areas increased from 5.6 per cent in 1800 to 39.7 per cent in 1900, according to Kenen. The native American population, however, was decimated. When British settlement began in the 17th century it is estimated, according to Atack and Passell (1994), that there may have been 300,000 Indians in the eastern half of the country (with very many more in the West). By the time of the Revolution, the indigenous population had shrunk to 100,000 as a result of European diseases brought by the settlers and to which the native population had no resistance.

From 1815–60 there were major innovations in transport, including >CANALS and an early boom in >RAILWAYS. Opened in 1823, the Erie Canal was constructed by the State of New York. It was funded by bond issues and recouped its costs after only a few years. The canal connected the Great Lakes with New York City, made Ohio, Indiana and Michigan an integral part of the world market in wheat and turned New York into the largest seaport (>SEAPORTS) on the East Coast. The Mississippi, with its barges and steamboats, became the main source of transport between the South and the Middle West. In the 1840s, the port of New Orleans near the mouth of that great river carried nearly as much traffic as New York. According to Merton J. Peck (in Harris, 1961), transport innovation halved the cost of land transport from 1820–60 and halved it again from 1860–1900, stimulating big shifts in population and industry and creating a national economy. Railway mileage tripled between 1860 and 1880 and doubled between 1860 and 1900. Refrigerated rail cars were introduced in the 1870s, giving a further boost to the food processing industries of the West. The second railway boom between the 1860s and 1900 included the linking of the Union Pacific and Central Pacific railways, which spanned the continent by 1869. These lines were built ahead of the traffic and the railway companies actively promoted western migration. From 1867–73, railway investment amounted to 10 per cent of GDP, enormously stimulating the production of >IRON & STEEL.

Having more than doubled between 1700 and 1820, US GDP per capita on Maddison's (2001) numbers almost doubled again by 1913 leaving it 50 per cent higher than Europe's, a gap which has more or less persisted up to the present. On other measures, however, the gap is very much less (>POVERTY, for the qualifications attaching to international income comparisons). The USA not only became the world's leading industrial nation but also had a commanding position in commodities. It was the world leader in the production of grain, livestock and cotton. The acceleration of growth in the USA from 1820 was accompanied by faster technical progress as well as an ever-expanding workforce and physical capital stock. In most of the period before 1900 the USA was a net importer of capital and especially in the 1880s. As a result it was a major international debtor, though this position reversed by >WORLD WAR I. (The USA was to become a creditor nation also after >WORLD WAR II.) More recently, of course, the USA has been able to finance enormous payments deficits by capital imports. Immigration, of great importance before World War I, declined sharply between 1931 and 1940 (>MIGRATION). In the period up to 1913, US tariffs were quite high and an important source of income for the Federal government. Tariffs on dutiable goods averaged about 20 per cent in the pre-Civil War period but increased to double that level afterwards. There was a downward trend in tariffs from 1913 but they rose again in the 1920s and in the 1930s notably in the Hawley–Smoot Bill of 1930 (Douglass North, in Harris, 1961).

As elsewhere, the industrial revolution in the USA was accompanied by social problems (>INDUSTRIAL REVOLUTIONS). Tenements and ghettos for blacks moving up from the South and immigrants arose in the big cities and especially in New York and Chicago. In 1869, for example, New York had over 15,000 tenements containing almost half a million people and by 1890 there were over 37,000, housing one and a quarter million people. Conditions in these places were very bad; how bad can be seen from the 1867 New York Act for the Regulation of Tenement and Lodging Houses. Among the provisions of this Act were that cellars could not be used as dwellings unless the ceilings were at least one foot above street level, while there should be at least one toilet for every 21 inhabitants (Heilbroner and Singer,

1977). >TRADE UNIONS were slow to develop, partly through legal impediments and partly because, despite immigration, labour was scarce and wages were moving upwards. In 1870, union membership was only 300,000 and did not pass 1 million until after 1900. The greatest growth of unions took place after the >NEW DEAL and peaked at 25 per cent of the non-farm labour force in 1955 (Lloyd Ulman, in Harris, 1961).

World War I marked the end of the 19th-century globalized economy until it reappeared again after World War II (>GLOBALIZATION). World trade was much smaller than it had been in 1913 and the USA was severely hit by the inter-war depression. Between 1929 and 1933, real output fell by 29 per cent and did not recover pre-depression levels until 1938. The proportion of the labour force which was unemployed rose from 3.2 per cent in 1929 to 21–5 per cent in 1933 (the latter figure including government work programmes). The Federal Reserve Index of Industrial Production had already turned downwards in the summer of 1929, while the stock market peak was not reached until mid-September. No single or simple explanation for the 1929–33 slump, its severity, or for that matter the recovery which subsequently took place, is generally accepted (>GREAT DEPRESSION).

Over the inter-war period as a whole, technical progress continued, including, for example, in >ELECTRICITY, domestic appliances, the >AUTOMOBILE INDUSTRY, >AVIATION and the chemical industry, in all of which the USA played a leading role. The Hollywood film industry, which was beginning to achieve international dominance, was a source of distraction from bad economic conditions. Film-making and distribution was one of the most profitable industries of the period with a domestic weekly cinema attendance of 55 million people and the release of 300–400 new motion pictures a year. There was also progress in the equally important matter of industrial and commercial organization, for example in large corporations (>CHANDLER). As an indication of technical advance, Maddison (2001) calculates total factor >PRODUCTIVITY (TFP) for the period 1913–50. He estimates that TFP in the USA grew by 1.6 per cent per annum, four times as much as in 1870–1913.

From the 19th century onwards, it has been widely asserted that technological innovation was becoming an organized activity (>SCHUMPETER). Alfred North Whitehead has often been quoted as writing, in *Science and the Modern World* (1925), that 'The greatest invention of the 19th Century was the invention of the method of invention'. The view that innovation is a rational, ordered, plannable process emerged because increasing corporate scale and the expanding opportunities for intensive research in such industries as chemicals and telephony (>TELECOMMUNICATIONS) led many large companies to set up their own laboratories. The first in-house laboratories were established in the German chemicals industry during the 1870s. The Sherman Act (1890) in the USA (>ANTI-TRUST) stimulated horizontal mergers and diversification, which encouraged the establishment of laboratories to identify technical developments for acquisition and exploitation, according to Mowery and Rosenberg in Engerman and Gallman (2000). This trend continued; the employment of scientists and engineers in laboratories of large manufacturing companies increased

from 2,775 in 1921 to 45,941 in 1946. Large expenditures on Research and Development (R&D) have been characteristic of the US economy. Between half and two-thirds of R&D has been financed by the Federal government, though 70 per cent of it has been performed in private industry. In 1969, according to Mowery and Rosenberg, the combined R&D expenditure of France, Germany, Japan and >BRITAIN was less than half that of the $25.6 billion spent in the USA in that year. By 2003, this gap had narrowed, but R&D expenditure as a percentage of GDP was only 1.9 per cent in the European economic area (>WESTERN EUROPE) compared with 2.6 per cent in the USA. Research for military purposes has dominated the US Federal R&D budget, falling below 50 per cent in only three of the years between 1949 and 1993. In industry, chemicals and pharmaceuticals, rubber, petroleum and branches of the electrical industry have been particularly important for R&D spending. Mowery and Rosenberg give some examples of the results of this industrial research. Shortly before World War II, polythene, the most versatile of plastics, was invented by ICI in Britain, though, thanks to US defence requirements, DuPont became by far the largest producer. Nylon was discovered by DuPont in 1935 (women's nylons first appeared on the market in 1939) but nylon output was largely absorbed by the military. Synthetic rubber was actually invented in the DuPont laboratories in 1931 but because of its high cost was not exploited until Japanese troops overran the plantation sources of natural rubber in South East Asia. The US government sponsored a large synthetic rubber research programme, which in scale came second only to the Manhattan (Atom Bomb) project. In 1940, synthetics accounted for only 0.4 per cent of the rubber market, but by 1945, under the pressure of war needs, this had risen to 85 per cent. Among the most important of the results of industrial laboratory research were those of Bell Labs (spun out from AT&T in 1925). The >ELECTRONICS industry, which arose from Bell Labs' invention of solid-state devices, along with the pharmaceutical and biotechnology industries, are now among the heaviest practitioners of industrial research.

Economic historians and economists no longer accept simplified views on the sources of innovation, though organized research may be responsible for much of the incremental innovation now routinely carried out by large companies (Baumol, 2002). Industrial laboratories, therefore, do play a major role, but there are many other players in national innovation systems and these systems are no longer, if they ever were, isolated from one another (Nelson, 1993). The US innovation system (though it is not really a system but a complex process), involves entrepreneurs, corporations, universities and government. Venture capital in early-stage investment has an important role and informal investors (business angels) are also much more prominent than in Europe. Advances are still being made by lone inventors and in >SMALL AND MEDIUM ENTERPRISES. It does not seem entirely true that invention is exogenous to the economic system in which bolts from the blue transform existing affairs, as was once assumed, though basic inventions undoubtedly are sometimes random events. The so-called linear model of innovation (which may never have been more than a straw man) and which depicts fundamental academic research feeding directly into industry, which applies it to new products and services, is now regarded as obsolete as a depiction of reality (Grandin et al., 2004).

World War II again saw the economic supremacy of the USA over the rest of the world re-emphasized. With its recovery from wartime devastation and the opportunity to absorb American technology (and with some help from the >MARSHALL PLAN), Europe grew much faster than the USA. In the 'Golden Age', 1950–73, GDP per capita in Western Europe grew at the rate of 4.05 per cent per annum compared with 2.45 per cent in the USA. After the first oil shock in 1973, growth rates in Europe and the USA were very similar until 1995, when the USA pulled ahead. After 1988, however, the US net foreign asset position moved into deficit as the rest of the world financed its huge payment deficits (Maddison, 2001, 2007).

The American population has traditionally had a fear of excessive industrial and financial >CONCENTRATION. This distrust can be traced back to the early days of the Republic when the Federal structure emerged with power decentralized among independent states, to the resistance of President Andrew Jackson to the Second Bank of the United States (>CENTRAL BANKING) and indeed to Jefferson's fear of the impact of the growth of manufacturing on independent farming which was mentioned earlier. Distrust was reinforced by the merger boom at the end of the 19th century and by the great wealth and power accumulated by the 'Robber Barons': John D. Rockefeller (Standard Oil), Cornelius Vanderbilt (railways), Andrew Carnegie (steel) and J. P. Morgan (US Steel, General Electric, International Harvester). Small businesses and farmers and the Populist movement pressed for >ANTI-TRUST Acts. The distinctively fragmented nature of American >BANKING and the separation of deposit from investment banking is also attributable to a public mistrust of large private accumulations of wealth and power which was very evident in the >NEW DEAL. Mark Roe (1994) argues that the 'distinctive' form of the US corporation, with its scattered shareholders and managers in control, results from laws which have prevented financial intermediaries from exercising some coordination and control over corporations, which can also be explained by the same political forces. In fact, the US corporation is not so distinctive and much the same can be said about the largest British and Continental European corporations. However the laws ensuring fragmentation of the banking system in the USA are different from those obtaining elsewhere. German and Japanese financing structures are somewhat different again, though arguably not necessarily superior to the Anglo-Saxon, at least in terms of serving economic growth (>CORPORATE GOVERNANCE).

In the post-World War II period, the rate of growth of the US population rose again to that reached in 1870–1913, recovering from the relatively depressed levels of the inter-war period. By 2003, the total population exceeded 290 million, getting on for twice as much as in 1950 and having grown twice as fast as in Western Europe. Between 1945 and 1964, the rate of population growth was boosted with the arrival of the post-war 'Baby Boom' generation. Immigration also increased again over pre-war levels after 1970 and its composition changed, with fewer coming from Europe and more from low-income areas in Asia, Central and South America, and especially Mexico. There was also a large,

but unknown, number of illegal arrivals (French, 1997). Urbanization continued, and also suburbanization, especially in the first two post-war decades, to reach 75 per cent of the population in urban areas. Employment patterns also changed. In 1820, 70 per cent of the labour force were in agriculture, forestry and fishing but by 2003, only 2 per cent. As in other advanced countries, but faster, employment in services (>SERVICE SECTOR) grew to over half of the labour force in 1950 and 78 per cent in 2003 (Maddison, 2007). The number of people living on farms fell from 24.4 million in 1945 to 4.6 million in 1990, while the number of farms fell from 5.8 to 2.1 million. Female participation in the labour force also increased. This was a long-term trend, although it was checked in the 1930s and again immediately after the war. In 1900, only 19 per cent of all women were at work, in the inter-war period it was a quarter or less but rose from 26 per cent in 1940 to 58 per cent in 1987 (68 per cent for single women but 58 per cent for married women). Women were (and are) paid less than men – about 64 per cent in terms of median annual income in 1955 (Heilbroner and Singer, 1977) – though this figure partly reflected differences in occupational distribution (>EMPLOYMENT OF WOMEN AND CHILDREN).

Racial minorities also tended to be paid less than the average. The median income of black families as a percentage of white median family incomes edged up but did not change very much between the early 1950s and the 1990s, remaining in the range of 51–64 per cent (51 per cent in 1947 and 57 per cent in 1991). Hispanics were somewhat better off at 71 per cent of white family incomes but with a tendency to decline as immigration increased. These trends occurred despite the successful result of the 1945–60 civil rights movement, which greatly improved the legal rights of minorities but did not remove discrimination as such, especially in the South. Poor education has been a barrier to the upward mobility of working-class African-Americans. Minorities remained concentrated in lower-paid activities (French, 1997), though this has recently begun to change.

As in other advanced market economies, the role of the state ratcheted up with the war (>STATE, RISE OF THE). US government expenditure as a percentage of GDP rose from 20.9–33.7 between 1940 and 1999, almost entirely through higher Federal rather than state spending. It became accepted that it was the responsibility of government to maintain high levels of employment and economic activity. Successive presidents, including Truman, Eisenhower and Johnson (though not Reagan), enhanced expenditures on social welfare. With the ending of the second long post-war boom (1955–2007) and a series of bank failures unprecedented since the 1930s, it remains to be seen what is going to happen to state activism and economic policy in the second decade after the millennium (>FORD: >GOLD: >GOLD STANDARD: >ROAD TRANSPORT: >TAXATION).

### References

Atack, Jeremy and Passell, Peter, *A New Economic View of American History from Colonial Times to 1940*, W. W. Norton, 1994.

Baumol, William J., 'The Free Market Innovation Machine: Analysing the Growth Miracle of Capitalism', Princeton University Press, 2002.

Delfino, Susanna and Gillespie, Michele (eds), *Global Perspectives on Industrial Transformation in the American South*, University of Missouri Press, 2005.

Engerman, Stanley L. and Gallman, Robert E. (eds), *The Cambridge Economic History of the United States*, Cambridge University Press, 2000.

French, Michael, *US Economic History Since 1945*, Manchester University Press, 1997.

Grandin, Karl, Wormbs, Nina and Widmalm, Sven (eds), *The Science-Industry Nexus: History, Policy, Implications*, Science History, 2004.

Harris, Seymour E. (ed.), *American Economic History*, McGraw-Hill, 1961.

Heilbroner, Robert and Singer, Aaron, *The Economic Transformation of America: 1600 to the Present*, Harcourt Brace, 1977.

Maddison, Angus, *The World Economy: A Millennial Perspective*, OECD, 2001.

Maddison, Angus, *Contours of the World Economy, 1–2030 AD: Essays in Macro-Economic History*, Oxford University Press, 2007.

Meyer, David R., *The Roots of American Industrialisation*, Johns Hopkins University Press, 2003.

Nelson, Richard R. (ed.), *National Innovation Systems: A Comparative Analysis*, Oxford University Press, 1993.

Roe, Mark J., *Strong Managers, Weak Owners*, Princeton University Press, 1994.

# Usury

Usury originally meant any lending that involved a charge (interest) or profit. Today it means charging excessive interest on loans. The origin of prohibitions on usury was concern that it would result in the exploitation of the poor. The detestation of informal money lenders ('loan sharks') is the modern residual of this belief. By charging very high rates of interest, loan sharks can trap poor borrowers in a vicious circle in which more borrowing is necessary to pay accumulated interest, a situation some credit card holders find themselves in today. In the earliest pre-capitalist communities of tribal villages and clans, charges for transfers of value were unknown and neighbourly help would be given for emergencies or to build a house, as Weber (2003) pointed out, without compensation, as indeed it may still be among families or friends and neighbours today. As societies developed and became more dispersed, however, the question of whether it was morally right to charge interest arose (Nelson, 1949). In general, the church took the view that interest was not legitimate because it involved exploitation of the poor by the rich.

The history of thinking on usury is long and tortuous. Usury has been prohibited by most religions, including Christianity (in both its Catholic and Anglican guises) and by Islam and other religions such as Brahminism. There are several references to usury in the Old Testament of the Bible, for example, in Deuteronomy 23: 'Thou shalt not lend upon usury to thy brother'. Among Jewish people this was interpreted to mean that they could charge interest to a Gentile but not among themselves, a source of discrimination against them as illustrated by Shakespeare's portrayal of Shylock in *The Merchant of Venice*. The references to usury in the Bible (and in other religious texts) are brief and ambiguous and have left plenty of scope for avoidance and, especially among the Scholastics of the Middle Ages, finely spun argument. Controversy goes back further than the Middle Ages, however. Aristotle argued that money was sterile and simply a medium of exchange and that therefore interest was unnatural. The Romans allowed interest to be charged but regulated the rates. In the Middle Ages, although there was a presumption that interest was illegal under Canon law it was recognized that where the borrower shared a risk with the lender, for example, in financing a merchant's sea voyage, then a passive lender could legitimately share in the profits of the voyage.

Shariah law of Islam seems to always have interpreted the interdiction of interest (*riba*) in the Qur'an, and in the sayings of Mohammed, quite severely and continues to do so (though not without ambiguity). Today, Islamic banks have developed products for both deposits and loans which effectively allow interest to be paid and received by the use of mechanisms to permit lenders and borrowers to share risks. For example, deposit account holders may not receive interest but it seems permissible for depositors to share in the overall profits of the bank.

The Classical and neo-Classical economists (>CLASSICAL AND NEO-CLASSICAL ECONOMICS) were still discussing usury in the 18th and 19th centuries. Adam >SMITH believed that the prohibition of interest was wrong: 'As something can everywhere be made by the use of money, something ought everywhere to be paid for the use of it' (1776). He went on to say that where a maximum rate was fixed, this should be somewhat above the market rate on good security but not much above. Higher rates would put borrowed money into the hands of 'prodigals and projectors'. John Stuart Mill, writing later when Britain's usury laws had already been softened somewhat, disagreed with Smith and argued against any regulation of interest rates. Mill wrote: 'no law can prevent a prodigal from ruining himself...The only effect of usury laws upon a prodigal is to make his ruin more expeditious, by driving him to a disreputable class of money-dealers' (1990). Mill believed that regulated rates could prevent a businessman in difficulty, but on the verge of success, from raising money at high market rates and generally obstruct high-risk projects, which were potentially capable of servicing high rates of interest.

There have always been get-outs from prohibitions against charging interest, which incidentally never seem to have applied to insurance or the sale of annuities, presumably because of the assumption of risk. Chown says that:

'The story of how the business community adapted by inventing 'loopholes' which the canon lawyers then tried to close will sound familiar to anyone whose role it has been to guide business through the maze of tax, regulatory control and other laws imposed by twentieth century interventionist states.' (Chown, 1994)

In the West, after the Reformation, sanctions against interest began to be eased and by the 17th century; with the rise of >CAPITALISM, religious and secular authorities were gradually removing restrictions on the payment of interest. This took time. The old usury laws in Britain were not abolished until 1854 and even then statutes relating to pawnbrokers were preserved. The Catholic Church did not completely abandon the notion that charging interest could lead to eternal damnation until about 1900. Many countries today regulate money lenders and there are laws to deal with the charging of excessive interest rates for personal,

as distinct from business, lending. The Consumer Credit Acts of 1974 in Britain require the registration of anyone making loans to individuals on a commercial basis and set out such provisions as rules for calculating and quoting interest rates charged and the granting of a pause in which the borrower can change his mind about proceeding with the loan. As amended in 2006, the Act covers unincorporated businesses, which now receive similar protection to personal borrowers.

In Western circles, disputes about the morality of charging interest at all (the original sense of the term usury), though not about the evils of excessive rates for personal borrowers, have faded into history. Kindleberger wrote: 'Usury, whether charging interest at all, or setting a limit above which it is illegal to charge it, belongs less to economic history than to the history of ideas, since neither stopped usurers nor shackled economic advance' (1984) (>MONEY AND BANKING).

## References

Chown, John, *A History of Money from AD 800*, Routledge, 1994.

Kindleberger, Charles P., *A Financial History of Western Europe*, George Allen & Unwin, 1984.

Mill, John Stuart, *Principles of Political Economy* (1840), Longmans, Green, 1900.

Nelson, B. N., *The Idea of Usury from Tribal Brotherhood to Universal Otherhood*, Princeton University Press, 1949.

Weber, Max, *General Economic History* (1923, trans. Frank 1927), Transaction Publishers (new edn), 2003.

# V

## Veblen, Thorstein Bunde

Veblen, who lived from 1857 to 1929, coined the phrases: 'conspicuous consumption' and 'conspicuous leisure'. Criticizing the mores of his time, he argued that distinction in society was not conferred by productive work but by leisure and property. To gain esteem, the rich had to abstain from productive work and impress others by a display of wealth and consumption. Wealthy women, for example, wore jewels, long hair and inconvenient clothing, such as corsets and bustles, to emphasize that they did not work. Businessmen were not interested in production as such but only in money-making. These businessmen depended upon engineers and scientists for the productive process, a different class of people whose values contrasted with their own. These attitudes, argued Veblen, had emerged as society developed from the primitive state. At the earliest stage of 'primitive savagery' there was neither ownership nor leisure. Later, in the 'predatory stage', wealth was acquired by seizing the property of other communities by force so that ownership of property conferred honour. The arts of war were practised by a warrior class who did not work: women did the work. Later still, the 'industry stage' was an extension of women's work and direct participation in industry brought no esteem. An unequal distribution of income and wealth opened up between those who worked productively and the rich who did not.

This analysis, the core of Veblen's thought, is all to be found in his first and most successful book, *The Theory of the Leisure Class* (1953). This book also has much to say about the distinction between 'higher' and 'lower' learning. The former is distinguished from the latter by a lesser degree of vocational practicability. Higher learning, which included, for example, the teaching of dead tongues, also shows the remnants of its origins in priestly rituals (the cap and gown, for example). Veblen argues that the exclusion of women from establishments of higher learning and the learned professions reflect(ed) their original subservient position, though he acknowledged that this was changing. The position of women was also changing in relation to consumption: 'the wife who was at the outset the drudge and chattel of the man, both in fact and in theory – the producer of goods for him to consume – has become the ceremonial consumer of goods which he produces' (Veblen, 1953).

Needless to say, Veblen's views on academia did not endear him to his scholarly colleagues; this was apparently compounded by his unconventional domestic arrangements and general eccentricity. Born into a largely Norwegian farming community in Wisconsin, and later brought up in Minnesota, he studied economics at Carleton College, from which he graduated in 1880. He studied at Johns Hopkins and Cornell, gaining a PhD in philosophy at Yale. He was unable to get an academic post until 1892, in Chicago. This lasted only four years, after which he was asked to resign. He subsequently lectured at Stanford and Missouri universities and in New York at the New School for Social Research. He left New York in 1926, dying three years later in a shack in the woods near Stanford. He never rose higher than the rank of assistant professor. In his introduction to the 1953 edition of Veblen's 1899 book, C. Wright Mills says that there is no failure in American academic history quite so great as Veblen's. But his failure was in academic status only. His books were widely read in his time and today he is regarded as one of the founders of the American School of Institutional Economics (>INSTITUTIONS). Veblen's books are still read and indeed most if not all of them are still in print.

Veblin's work amounted to a devastating criticism of American society of the 1890s and, by implication, of the whole methodology of >CLASSICAL AND NEO-CLASSICAL ECONOMICS, which assumed that unchanging rational economic calculation is the sole basis of economic activity. Veblen, from his Darwinist perspective, saw that 'the life of man in society, just like the life of any other species is a struggle for existence, and therefore it is a process of selective adaptation' (1953). As is clear from Veblen's views summarized above, he saw the characteristics and roles of institutions as changing, not fixed and reflecting the interaction of man's instincts and cultural and institutional development. While human nature in terms of these instincts may be immutable, institutions do change and no science based on fixed, anti-historical axioms can retain its explanatory power. For Hodgson (2001) this was Veblen's major contribution to >ECONOMIC HISTORY. Hodgson also points out that Veblen, in his conception of the role of engineers and scientists, was one of the first to recognize the fundamental importance of knowledge in the economic system. In this, and other respects, Veblen influenced many other economists.

Like >MARX, with whom he had some things in common, it is Veblen's method and approach that have assumed enduring significance. Like Marx, Veblen expected that the internal contradictions of capitalism would lead to its overthrow, although he did not expect a violent transition to socialism as Marx did (>SCHUMPETER). Veblen foresaw the possibility that it would be the engineers and scientists upon whom the productive system vitally depended, not the workers who would change the system. Backhouse quotes Veblen as saying that a strike by the Technocracy: 'no more than a minute fraction of one per cent of the population; yet it would swiftly bring a collapse of the old order and sweep the timeworn fabric of finance and absentee sabotage into the discard for good and all' (2002). (This passage comes from one of Veblen's later ten or so books: *The Engineers and the Price System 1921*).

Influenced by Veblen, not only by his method but also by his use of irony and satire, J. K. Galbraith was also to write about the 'Technostructure' in his *The New Industrial State*(1967). Of course, Galbraith did not expect his Technostructure to bring down the system, its members were doing too well out of it. In his history of economics, Galbraith (1987) gave a lively account of Veblen's life and works, to which he attributed major importance. Veblen, like Marx, did not foresee that rising wealth would spread to the working population and thus dampen criticism of >CAPITALISM and render some of his strictures obsolete. Nonetheless, much of his contribution remains and the appreciation of the importance of institutions seems to be gradually gaining ground over the conventional economic stereotypes which he satirized.

## References

Backhouse, Roger E., *The Penguin History of Economics*, Penguin, 2002.

Galbraith, John Kenneth, *The New Industrial State*, Houghton Mifflin, 1967.

Galbraith, John Kenneth, *A History of Economics*, Hamish Hamilton, 1987.

Hodgson, Geoffrey M., *How Economics Forgot History*, Routledge, 2001.

Veblen, Thorstein, *The Theory of the Leisure Class* (1899), Macmillan (new edn), 1953.

# W

## Weber, Max

Weber, who lived from 1864 to 1920, was an eminent and seminal German political economist, economic historian and sociologist who worked also in general history, philosophy and theology. He is best known for his book, *The Protestant Ethic and the Spirit of Capitalism*, which first appeared in 1904–5 , though not in English until 1930 (Weber, 1930). Although regarded as the founder of modern sociology, Weber did not actually consider himself to be a sociologist until the end of his life. His influence on economic history was perhaps more in his methodology than in substance. Weber pioneered the use of systematic historical international comparisons. He influenced >GERSCHENKRON in these and >SCHUMPETER in the importance of combining social and economic studies. Weber's theory of bureaucracy is, to give another example, recognizable in the work of >CHANDLER (all three of these writers were at Harvard in the 1920s with Talcott Parsons, a business sociologist and Weber's translator).

Weber's wide interests were reflected in his career. Born at Erfurt in 1864 and completing school in 1882, he studied at the universities of Berlin, Heidelberg and Goettingen, where he graduated in law and economics. He came from a well-to-do family, his father was a jurist and an active politician. After teaching law in Berlin, he was appointed Professor of Economics at the University of Friedburg in 1894, where he replaced Karl Knies (1821–1898),

one of the heads of the German Historical School, at the University of Heidelberg. The invitation from Friedburg had been the direct result of a study Weber carried out on the condition of agricultural workers east of the Elbe. The study had demonstrated to Weber that in choosing between quasi-servile annual labour contracts and free or 'day' labour in increasing numbers, workers were showing that economic considerations were not paramount since in the long run they were more secure and better off in the former role but preferred the status of the latter. Swedberg (1991) has carried out an interesting analysis of Weber's economics and its relationship to his other interests. Weber's reading lists for students attending his lectures at Friedburg suggest that, as well as the German Historical School, he was familiar with Carl Menger and colleagues' work of the Austrian School as well as with that of Alfred Marshall and the English neo-Classicists (>CLASSICAL AND NEO-CLASSICAL ECONOMICS). Swedberg surmises that Weber did not share all the values of the Historical School since he did clearly recognize the value of abstract economic theory and the deductive method (>ECONOMIC HISTORY).

Weber's early academic career was truncated by ill health and depression after the death of his father in 1897 and, apart from a brief sojourn in Vienna, he was not to return to a full-time academic post until he accepted a Chair in Munich in 1919, only to die the following year at the age of 56. For most of his professional career he was a private scholar. He did intermittent military service and in 1918 was a consultant to the German Armistice Commission and to the commission that drafted the Weimar constitution (>WESTERN EUROPE). At that time he was nominated for election to the National Assembly but did not pursue it. Deeply interested and committed to politics (he was a founding member of the German Democratic Party), having grown up in the age of Bismarck's *Realpolitik*, Weber believed in the necessity for a strong state. He was critical of the agrarian *Junker* class and deplored the absence of a politically educated middle class, which meant that after the death of Bismarck (1898) power rested with the *Junkers* whose interests were incompatible with economic modernization. He was torn between his liberal beliefs in the importance of individual freedom and the need for authoritarian modernization of the German state and the fulfilment of German destiny (which he perceived to be a bulwark against Soviet Russian influence). He famously defined the state as an entity which has a monopoly of violence.

Many of Weber's writings were scattered and only collected and published in English after his death. These writings, rich in original ideas, are not an easy read. For him, as Bendix put it, 'every generalisation was a precarious victory over the infinite complexity of facts' (1960). The translators of Weber's *Essays* characterize his writings as of the German gothic school, which uses 'parentheses, qualifying clauses, inversions... [that] at their best erect a grammatical artifice in which mental balconies and watch towers, as well as bridges and recesses, decorate the main structure' (Gerth and Mills, 1920). Given the breadth, volume and complexity of these writings we can in this entry only provide a brief and selective account of some of Weber's ideas and methodology.

A prominent aspect of Weber's method was the use of the paradigm, the *ideal type*. This corresponded to the abstractions in economics such as perfect competition, and for Weber had no evaluative connotations, good or bad. His idea was that sociological phenomena are varied and changing and can only be analyzed in terms of an abstract state in which their characteristics are projected to an extreme or ideal form. Weber's approach was neither solely inductive nor deductive. Thus, *economic man* was not seen by him as a literal or comprehensive description of human motivation but as an analytical device. He was to criticize economics as being split into two schools, economics and historical economics: 'one that was abstract and non-historical and one that was overly historical and non-theoretical' (Swedberg, 1991). He proposed a synthesis of the two, *Soczialokonomic*, an idea that was to inspire >SCHUMPETER. Another aspect of Weber's methodology was his belief in *causal pluralism*, a conception he shared with the Italian economist and engineer Vilfredo Pareto (1848–1923). Cause and effect, he thought, were interchangeable because one affected the other. Something aimed at, once achieved, can lead to a new activity which was not originally foreseen. Everything can be seen to lead to something else so that causes are lost in an eternal chain affected by rational and non-rational motivations as well as by tradition.

In his analysis of the spirit of >CAPITALISM, which he defined as the ideas and habits that favoured the rational pursuit of economic gain, Weber perceived a scale of types with particular features (>INSTITUTIONS). There was *political capitalism* often related to *fiscal capitalism*, for example, as in tax farming (>TAXATION), and modern *industrial capitalism*, which was based on production establishments and the joint stock company. These different forms of capitalism in the sense of the pursuit of profit have existed at different historical stages, for example, those of the Roman and British empires, but were only superficially similar to modern capitalism which is highly 'rational', indeed, in Weber's view, the highest form of rationalism. In the same way, Weber's conception of *bureaucracy* – an organization, centrally controlled through hierarchies which coordinates the work of many individuals engaged in large-scale administrative tasks – is not new and is to be found in all civilizations, including ancient ones, though only in its pure form in modern capitalism. The early bureaucracies were linked to powerful leaders. Bureaucracies of this early kind were unstable because there was a tendency for individual officials to pursue their own independent interests. In the modern bureaucracy, impersonality and the dependence of its members is accepted. For Weber, though, nothing is ever simple and durable social authority requires legitimacy as in democratic regimes. Despite this, the individuals in society may cede authority to charismatic leaders because they admire and believe in them. Charisma can be a balancing factor but it too, over time, may become routinized into traditionalism and bureaucracy.

There are two unifying threads in Weber's view of history: one is his belief in the importance of individuals as the atoms which make up society; the other is in the principle of *rationalism* defined as calculation and systematic arrangement which is ultimately prevailing in modern society. These two streams of thought clearly can conflict. Weber regretted the trend to rationalism which, though inevitable in large-scale organization, leads not only to the suppression of individual will and aspiration but to a loss of magic and poetry; Weber often quoted Friedrich Schiller's phrase, 'disenchantment of the world'. Weber detected a pervasive historical trend towards rationality, even, for example, in the music of various civilizations, such as those of Asia, pre-literate Indian tribes, the Middle East and the West, culminating in the standardization of the use of certain instruments in the symphony orchestra. This was typical of Weber's eclecticism and his use of the history of various civilizations to arrive at generalizations by induction.

The inductive method was again apparent in Weber's work on comparative religion where the same trend of rationalization could be seen. His essay, 'The Protestant Ethic and the Spirit of Capitalism', first brought him to fame when it appeared in 1904–5 in a journal he helped to promote, *Archiv fur Sozialwissenschaft und Sozialpolitik*, though it was not available in English until much later (Weber, 1930). In the 'Protestant Ethic', Weber noted that religious devotion was usually associated with the rejection of materialist values. However, the ideas of the Reformation, including Calvinism, gave a positive spiritual and moral meaning to denial and orderly planning of affairs as a means of salvation. Although in its original conception Calvinism laid down that Man was dammed, men had to be given hope and it came to be accepted that salvation could be achieved by individualism (not falling prey to the temptations and ideas of others), the avoidance of extravagance and ostentation and a doctrine of thrift and hard work which favoured capital accumulation. Thus, religious beliefs adapt to worldly reality in this way as in the disappearance of the prohibition of >USURY in the Protestant faith as obstructive to the development of capitalism. Weber did not mean to imply that Protestantism was the cause of capitalism, this would have been inconsistent with his belief in causal pluralism and other forces were at work, but it was an important contributory cause and one not common to the then non-industrializing parts of the world, notably Asia. Weber was to go on to make intensive studies of the sociology of other religions, including Confucianism and Taoism of China and Hinduism and Buddhism of India. These religions required asceticism but also spiritual values and contemplation that were quite different from the values of Protestantism and were unfavourable to capitalism. For example, in >CHINA, technical innovation, or at least the implementation of it, was opposed as going against the spirit of accepting the world as it was instead of trying to change it. Notions of kinship in China, a bureaucratic 'literati' and an absence of state pressure for economic development and, in India, the castes, also mitigated against the emergence of a middle class and the legal reforms which Weber saw as fundamental to the development of capitalism. Finally, in his study of Judaism, which fathered Protestantism, Weber perceived various features such as freedom from mysticism and an emphasis on law which helped to create the rationalism of the West. Weber's contemporary member of the Historical School, Werner Sombart (1863–1941), perhaps influenced by Weber, who wrote *The Jews and Economic Life* (1911), attributed considerable significance to Judaism in the rise of capitalism, overturning an earlier view of his that religion was not very important. Sombart had placed the beginnings of capitalism in medieval Italy and later reverted to this view. The difference between Weber and Sombart, of course, was that Weber thought that modern capitalism was very different from earlier versions. Many criticisms have been heaped upon the 'Weber thesis', as it has come to be called. Catholics and Protestants alike have found the thesis offensive, though it was not part of Weber's intention to criticize religion or to devalue the importance of the spiritual as against the material. In fact, Weber specifically criticized >MARX for over-emphasizing economic determinism. Another criticism has been that capitalism existed before the Reformation, but as we have shown, this is a misinterpretation of Weber's position.

Weber's wife, Marianne Weber, whom he married in 1893, wrote what is generally regarded as the authoritative life: *Max Weber: A Biography* (1950, in English 1975). In addition to the *Protestant Ethic*, his essays and his three major books on religion, numerous other books by Weber are now extant in English. Weber's last and posthumously published work was *General Economic History* (Weber, 1981). This book is a reconstruction of his final lectures. It is basically a text about the historical evolution of Capitalism; it includes material from China, India and other early civilizations, as well as from Europe from early times to the 19th century.

## References

Bendix, Reinhard, *Max Weber: An Intellectual Portrait*, Heineman, 1960.

Bottomore, Tom and Nisbet, Robert (eds), *A History of Sociological Analysis*, Heineman, 1979.

Gerth, H. H. and Mills, C. Wright (eds), *From Max Weber: Essays in Sociology*, Heineman, 1920.

Swedberg, Richard, 'Max Weber as an Economist and as a Sociologist', *American Journal of Economics and Sociology*, October, 1991.

Weber, Max, *The Protestant Ethic and the Spirit of Capitalism* (1904), trans. Talcott Parsons, George Allen & Unwin, 1930.

Weber, Max, *General Economic History* (1923, trans. Frank 1927), Transaction Publishers (new edn), 1981.

# Wedgwood, Josiah

Wedgwood is one of the most famous entrepreneurs of the >INDUSTRIAL REVOLUTION IN BRITAIN. He built a thriving business in domestic pottery and china and the firm he founded still has a prominent position in the industry today. Wedgwood, who lived from 1730 to 1795, grew up and spent most of his life in the >INDUSTRIAL DISTRICT of The Potteries in Staffordshire. He was born into a family of potters in Burslem, one of the Five Towns written about by Arnold Bennett (1867–1931) in his *Clayhanger* series of novels. The district had both coal and clay and also, nearby, lead ore for glazing. In the 17th century, pottery was produced in primitive conditions: each piece fashioned by hand on a wheel by large numbers of small producers; ovens were surrounded by earthen clods and, in the earliest times, the wares were sold by travelling packmen on horseback (>PEDLARS). Raw materials and product came in and out by sea and river and thence by horses and donkeys through narrow lanes until proper roads and canals were built. Even in Wedgwood's time, and according to a letter he wrote, there were 500 separate potteries for stoneware and earthenware in Burslem alone. Prior to Wedgwood, considerable advances were made, for example, in the use of a salt glaze, crushed flint was used to whiten the local clay and later whiter clay was brought up from Devon and Cornwall. Imported domestic ware from China and other countries was much coveted by the wealthy. Techniques were more advanced in Continental Europe, especially in Holland and Germany. From about 1730, however, the pace of innovation in Britain quickened. Moulds were adopted to make the bodies of pots and replaced throwing on a wheel for all but the most expensive pieces. Various new methods of glazing and double-firing came into use. Some of the innovations in glazing were said to have been brought in by two brothers named Elers who came over from Holland with William of Orange in the Glorious Revolution of 1688. Between 1671 and 1818, 48 patents were taken out for ceramic processes. The recipe for bone china was taken out in 1749, though it was not taken up in The Potteries until the 1790s (Berg, 2005). From 1755, a Liverpool firm, Saddler & Green, developed transfer printing. Wedgwood did not make the innovations mentioned, but he was an early user of them and made his own. It was Wedgwood who was instrumental in improving transport by agitation and active participation in road and canal development and it was he who put the industry onto a more efficient and capitalist basis (>HAMMONDS, THE).

Josiah was forced to leave school at the age of nine and go out to work when his potter-father died. When he was 11 he caught smallpox, which left a bad abscess on his knee that prevented him from using a foot-operated wheel. For many years he worked with others but in 1759 started his own business. Several commentators have speculated that his physical impairment helped him to broaden his horizons and think creatively about the whole process of pottery making. Anyway, in a couple of years he introduced cream-coloured earthenware, which was a great success. An accident with a bolting horse further damaged his knee but incidentally led to an introduction to Thomas Bentley, a local businessman with whom he later went into partnership. Undaunted by his disability, he worked hard to build his business and in 1765 he welcomed an order from Queen Charlotte (wife of King George III) for a tea set, which other potters had refused. A few years later he perfected a new line of pottery, Black Basalt, which was made from a dark clay found near coal seams. He took the decision in 1768 to have his leg amputated, a courageous thing to do because in those days there was still no proper anaesthetic. In 1769, he opened a new factory at Etruria, next to a canal and in between Hanley and Newcastle. The demand for pottery and china was growing as a result of the new fashions for drinking tea and displaying fine china in homes, as well as due to an expanding >POPULATION. His reputation was growing and in 1773 he received an order from the Empress Catherine of Russia for a dinner and dessert service of 952 pieces. In 1783 he was elected a fellow of the Royal Society, partly in recognition of his invention of a pyrometer to measure oven temperature.

In 1790 Wedgwood brought his two sons, John and Josiah II (Jos), into the partnership, just five years before his death. Up to that point Wedgwood had been in sole control of production and marketing following the death of his partner,

Bentley, in 1780. Reilly (1992) argues that Bentley's contribution to the development of the business has been underrated by historians and that the partnership was 'more complex and complete' than has generally been acknowledged. This may be partly the result of the fact that although Wedgwood's copious correspondence with Bentley has been well studied, few of Bentley's letters to his partner have survived. There is evidence, however, that Bentley influenced innovation in production and design as well as in the marketing with which he is normally only credited. Bentley was better educated than Wedgwood and had an easy entry into London society, which was important for the understanding of vital trends in fashion. Bentley's death at the early age of 50, probably from a heart attack, was a serious loss to Josiah for they were friends as well as business partners. Wedgwood's sons were not as committed to the business as he or Bentley had been. After their father's death, the brothers bought country estates in Surrey and Wiltshire and by 1799 the firm was foundering, despite the efforts of a loyal manager. It was not until 1806 that Jos returned with his family to take control of the firm.

Wedgwood's industrial enterprise did not depend upon the use of mechanical power (though he used >STEAM POWER for mixing materials), but the division of labour in his factories was very extensive. Like other entrepreneurs of the time he struggled with the problems of getting workers accustomed to cottage industry or farming to adapt to factory disciplines. Like others he tried to achieve this by both sticks and carrots. He built a village to accommodate workers at the new factory at Etruria, adopted payment by piecework and imposed fines or dismissal for infractions of the rules. He also, like others, employed women and children, who were thought to be less difficult to manage. Hammond and Hammond (1926) draw attention to the generally bad working conditions in The Potteries: the diseases caused by the use of crushed flint and lead and harsh policies such as refusal to pay piece rates for pottery damaged in the ovens. They describe the bitter strikes which took place in the district in the 1830s and point out that the Factory Acts did not apply to the pottery industry until the 1860s (>REGULATION).

Josiah was a pioneer in many of the modern techniques of management and marketing. He devised a system of clocking-in, with cards deposited at a lodge by the factory gates. In 1772, a period of low demand, he investigated his costs thoroughly, using what would be described today as spread sheets. His analysis enabled him to reduce prices for some lines and push up demand to reap economies of scale. Josiah had not previously been aware of what a large proportion of his costs were fixed. He was thus a pioneer of cost accounting (McKendrik, 1960, 1970) (>ACCOUNTING). The price reductions were only temporary because Wedgwood's policy was to go for quality and fashionable appeal. He employed painters and sculptors to develop new designs and consciously aimed at gaining the approval of monarchies, the nobility and connoisseurs by gifts of fine pieces, flattery and asking for advice in the belief that fashion spread downwards. He enlisted the help of ambassadors to gain access to foreign courts and nobility. Josiah also had showrooms designed to attract the fashionable gentry in London, Bath and elsewhere and experimented with the use of travelling salesmen,

as well as producing catalogues. By 1784, Wedgwood was exporting 80 per cent of output (Berg, 2005). As he wrote to Bentley in 1769, the partnership was engaged in the pursuit of 'Fortune, Fame and the Public good', aims that seem to have been achieved.

## References

Berg, Maxine, *Luxury and Pleasure in Eighteenth Century Britain*, Oxford University Press, 2005.

Hammond, J. L. and Hammond, Barbara, *The Rise of Modern Industry* (1925), Methuen (2nd edn), 1926.

McKendrik, Neil, 'Josiah Wedgwood and Cost Accounting in the Industrial Revolution', *Economic History Review*, 23(1), 1970.

Reilly, Robin, *Josiah Wedgwood 1730–1795*, Macmillan, 1992.

# Western Europe

The notion of a European identity is relatively modern and its geographical and cultural boundaries are still disputed. Europe has been defined in terms of its shared religious and Graeco-Roman heritage rather than geography. Whether or not >RUSSIA is part of Europe has long been questioned. In any event, for reasons of space and clarity, in this entry, Western Europe is limited to the larger members of the European Economic Area (EEA), effectively EU-15 (including >BRITAIN) plus Norway and Switzerland, as it existed before the enlargement of the EU to 25 countries in 2004 and 27 in 2007. Even limiting coverage in this way, however, leaves difficult problems of exposition. Economic historians have approached these problems in different ways. There are, of course, a number of modern textbooks which cover the history of individual countries, such as, on Italy, Zamagni (1993) and, on Germany, Ogilvie and Overy (2003), while there are a number of books on Europe as a whole for selected periods. The latter mostly adopt a chronological structure, for example, Aldcroft (1995), Crouzet (2001) and Vittorio (2006). Finally, there are a large number of studies of particular periods and events, some of which are included in the list of references below. In this entry, our review is roughly in chronological order but is highly selective and gives weight to a few episodes not covered in other entries in the encyclopedia.

The second half of the long 18th century (to 1815) was dominated by political and industrial revolutions (>INDUSTRIAL REVOLUTION IN BRITAIN: >INDUSTRIAL REVOLUTIONS) and the later effects of the >COMMERCIAL REVOLUTION. There were also major changes in transport by road and water (>CANALS: >SEAPORTS: >SHIPPING: >ROAD TRANSPORT). >RAILWAYS did not develop until the next century. The two main political revolutions were the >AMERICAN WAR OF INDEPENDANCE (1775–83) and the >FRENCH REVOLUTION (1789 onwards).

The Revolutionary Wars, which continued until 1815, started before Napoleon assumed power, first as Consul in 1799 and then as Emperor in 1804. The wars, ostensibly motivated by the need to defeat the enemies of the Revolution, were also aimed at raising funds by plunder for the Treasury and at spreading the new values. Invasions were followed by the imposition of the Revolutionary changes in the conquered countries, including Napoleon's standardized taxation and codified laws. France occupied the Low Countries in 1796 and in the following year defeated

Austria to take Italy. Britain became embroiled on strategic, not political, grounds. She was concerned about the balance of power on the Continent. Along with Spain, France lost its Atlantic colonies and this, John A. Davis, in Vittorio (2006), says, encouraged Napoleon to create a Continental system and to exclude British commerce from its territories. The idea was that the conquered, now satellite, countries would become subordinate to the needs of the French economy by guaranteeing supplies of materials and providing markets for French producers. This system failed, both through resistance from the satellites and from an enormous increase in smuggling. The Napoleonic Wars certainly dislocated trade, especially for Holland, though the reforms that followed the armies – better education, infrastructure and tax systems – were beneficial. The Wars were, however, very costly. Prussia, for example, according to Davis, spent 70–80 per cent of state revenues for military purposes. Britain was better placed because it had the capacity to borrow and raise taxes so avoiding the crises which occurred in the other monarchies (>TAXATION). All in all, the Napoleonic Wars led to a widening of the development gap between Britain and Continental Europe. There were some benefits; the Blockade did encourage import substitution, while industry in Northern France gained from integration with Belgium.

In 1800, the vast majority of people in Continental Europe worked in >AGRICULTURE. British improvements in farming were being brought to the Continent; there was some shift to larger farms by >ENCLOSURE as well as to new crops, including maize and potatoes. In the second half of the 18th century, the price of grain, which had fallen in the first half, rose and this stimulated production. Perhaps the most striking feature of the period was the increase in >POPULATION, which rose from 132 million in 1700 to 204 million in 1800. This widespread increase is still not fully explained. It was not, at this stage, the result of improved hygiene or medical services, but apparently there was a tendency towards younger marriage, which pushed up birth rates. Internal trade was expanding as a result of urbanization. International trade was also expanding but this was a result rather than a cause of industrialization. It was industrialization which brought new, cheaper products to the markets, such as >COTTON AND COTTON TEXTILES.

There was a spread of >PROTO-INDUSTRIALIZATION in rural areas on the Continent, but industrialization was not unique to Britain. The Southern Netherlands (which included present-day Belgium) had been part of the Habsburg Monarchy until invaded by the France in 1797 and was in some respects in advance of Britain. As late as 1850, the Belgian network of canals and roads was three times greater than that of Britain. In the 18th century this region already had advanced ironworks, coal mines and textile production. There were also pockets of industrialization elsewhere in Western Europe, for example, in Catalonia and the Rhineland. France developed differently from Britain, with labour-intensive consumption goods, while in Switzerland there was clock manufacturing and high-quality fabric production, using, according to Crouzet (2001), flexible specialization (>INDUSTRIAL DISTRICTS: >INDUSTRIAL REVOLUTIONS). Some of the more backward areas, for example, the present day Czech Republic (then in Bohemia), also had fairly advanced industrial areas. For these

and other reasons, Sidney >POLLARD, in *Peaceful Conquest* (1981), argued for regional rather than national units of analysis in economic history. This view has gained ground, although analysis is often difficult because some statistics are frequently not available on an appropriately regional basis.

The 19th century as a whole, after 1815, was relatively peaceful and it was characterized by accelerating industrialization. There was continuing economc growth, at least up to 1870. Per capita incomes on Maddison's figures rose by almost 1 per cent per annum, with Britain enjoying a much faster rate and Italy the slowest among the major countries (Maddison, 2001). From 1870–1913, growth in Britain slowed down, while the European average rose from 0.98 per cent to 1.33 per cent per annum, still slow by modern standards but an enormous improvement on earlier periods. In 1820, GDP per capita was $1,707 at 1990 international dollars in Britain, compared with $1,230 in France and $1,117 in Italy which was, at that time, ahead of Germany, the >USA per capita income being $1,257. By 1913, US GDP per capita exceeded that in all these countries, even though Germany had gained ground on Britain. Italy continued to lag behind the others and was to industrialize relatively late. Industrialization brought big structural changes, especially in Britain where the percentage of GDP accounted for by the primary sectors, fell from 40 to 6 per cent between 1788 and 1907. Agriculture remained much more important in France (32 per cent of GDP in 1911) and Germany (25 per cent in 1907) (Luigi Fontana, in Vittorio, 2006).

From 1840, growth in Germany accelerated, thanks especially to the

Zollverein Customs area and to railway construction. Unified in 1871, Germany built the largest steel, engineering and chemical industries in Europe and from the 1880s became a large-scale exporter. German exports grew much faster than Britain's (4.1 per cent per annum compared with 2.8 per cent between 1870 and 1913), though Britain's were still somewhat larger in total. Germany was rapidly doing what Napoleon had failed to do: it was making satellites out of its neighbours. Crouzet writes that: 'in 1913, out of eighteen European countries, ten had Germany as their largest supplier and seven as their best customer' (2001). France grew more slowly than the Western European average in the 19th century, partly because of slower population growth, and remained behind Britain in incomes. Germany became the dominant industrial power in Continental Europe. Italy, although it had ample water power, lacked coal and suffered from acute regional imbalances. Italy also had poor transport and communications, though it joined the industrial nations in a spurt of growth at the end of the century, which continued to 1914. In the 19th century, Europe had avoided the Malthusian trap (>MALTHUS) as agricultural output grew and there were improvements in diet and hygiene (sanitation and modernization of towns), which, with advances in medical care, reduced mortality. The population of Britain overtook that of France and urbanization everywhere increased. Between 1800 and 1910, according to Fontana (see Vittorio, 2006), the population of London grew from 1.1 to 7.3 million, Paris from 0.6 to 2.9 million and Berlin from 0.2 to 2.1 million. There was a high level of emigration to the Americas (>MIGRATION).

The 1850s saw a boom in Europe and especially in France and Germany, but it was punctured by a stock market crash in 1873, the exchange in Vienna was particularly hit. Until the late 1890s, aggregate growth slowed to about 1 per cent per annum and per capita growth was halted. Mostly agriculture was affected but a fall in food prices improved standards of living. According to Crouzet (2001), gross agricultural product fell by 20 per cent in value between 1869–73 and 1884–8 and did not return to its 1869 level until 1907. This period used to be called the Great Depression, which is misleading because it was mild compared with that in the 1930s (>GREAT DEPRESSION) and did not affect some countries at all, especially those at the European periphery.

The long 19th century (1815–1914) was a period of relative monetary stability and international trade grew faster than output as Europe became more integrated. There was an effective exchange rate mechanism and London dominated credit markets (>GOLD STANDARD). The prosperous British invented fashionable sea bathing and mountaineering and discovered the French and Italian rivieras as tourist destinations. The years between 1900 and the summer of 1914 have been called the Belle Epoque. It was also a period of relative prosperity for many of the developing countries and the gap in incomes between them and Europe was very much less than it is today. Albert Carreras, in Vittorio (2006), points out that it is only fairly recently, that is, in the period of the 1970s to the 1990s, that the extent of commercial and financial integration of the Belle Epoque has been surpassed (>GLOBALIZATION). The Belle Epoque, of course, was brought to a brutal end with >WORLD WAR I.

The 20th century divides fairly clearly into three periods. The first, 1913–50, included >WORLD WAR II as well as World War I. It was a period of depression and recovery. The second period, 1950–73, was the 'Golden Age' of economic expansion in the West. On Maddison's figures, the annual growth rate in GDP per capita for Western Europe fell from 1.33 in 1870–1913 to 0.76 per cent between 1913 and 1950 and shot up again to 4.05 per cent in 1950–73. The third period of the 20th century, from 1973–2003, was marked by another fall in per capita growth to 1.87 per cent per annum (Maddison, 2007). In the first period (1913–50), there was a slowing down in population growth compared with the 19th century, but population growth speeded up in the 'Golden Age', only to fall sharply again in the third period, despite increasing longevity as birth rates fell with approaching economic maturity.

The inter-war period was not uniformly bleak. The first few years, 1919–24 were very bad after a brief post-war boom, particularly in Germany, where the Weimar Republic could not, and would not, cope with the heavy demands for reparations demanded by the Allies, especially France and Belgium. This problem was dramatized by >KEYNES in his book, *The Economic Consequences of the Peace* (1919). The Europeans were heavily in debt to the USA and wanted to link repayments to the receipt of reparations, but this link was denied by the Americans, apparently on the grounds that the European Allies were less likely to default than the Germans. The amount of the reparations demanded was totally unrealistic and amounted, initially, to three times Germany's 1913 GNP. The amount was not fixed in the Treaty of Versailles (which established the

ill-fated League of Nations and various boundary changes) after the war, but preliminary payments were due immediately. Germany lost most of its merchant fleet, gold reserves and a great deal of moveable equipment (Feinstein *et al.*, 1997). The amounts of reparations were not 'finally' reduced and fixed until 1924 under the Dawes Plan. There were further easements under the Young Plan (1929) and later at Lausanne in 1932, when the European Allies agreed to end reparations and 'more or less defaulted on their war debts to the USA' (Balderston, 2002). In the meantime, France and Belgium had tried, without success, to enforce reparations by occupying the Ruhr in 1923.

World War I had resulted in inflation in all European countries and in the period 1914–18 prices roughly doubled. Many countries were able to get inflation under control after the short, post-war boom ended in depression (>PRICES AND INFLATION). In Germany and Austria, however, inflation gave way to hyper-inflation. This was not only the result of the reparations but also of large post-war economic and social programmes. The Weimar Government, unable to agree on adequate tax reforms, adopted the same solution to its budgetary problems as had earlier the revolutionary government in France and resorted to printing money. In 1924, however, Germany was able to pursue a deflationary policy and restored a form of the gold standard with the Reichsmark. It has been argued that the unnecessarily severe deflationary policies adopted by the German Chancellor Heinrich Bruning, from 1930–2, precipitated the slump in 1928–31 and paved the way for the assumption of power by the Nazis. The German economic historian, Karl Borchardt, argued, however, that the German government had little alternative to deflation. The German economy had chronic structural problems and could not borrow for reflation, for which there was no political support at the time anyway. Borchardt (1991) also argued that no one at the time could have foreseen the severity of the depression which took place in Germany a year earlier than the 1929 crash in the USA. There is an extensive literature on this debate which, according to Balderston (2002), has never been resolved. It is, in any event, a purely hypothetical issue, because there is no way of knowing what would have happened had the Weimar pursued different policies. Despite the developments in Germany, France was able to return to the gold standard at one-fifth of its pre-war parity under a new government and there was a reasonably stable situation in Europe from 1925–9. Britain returned to gold in 1925 at its pre-war parity but had to leave the gold standard again in 1931 as general depression overtook the world. From 1929–32, according to Crouzet (2001), industrial output in Western Europe fell by 27 per cent (41 per cent in Germany and 45 per cent in the USA) and was back to its 1913 level.

The 1930s depression did not mean that there was no economic progress in the inter-war period. New technology, mostly developed before the war, permitted expansion in some industries, including electricity and electrical equipment, artificial textiles, the >AUTOMOBILE and >AVIATION industries, and >PRODUCTIVITY was on an upward trend. Recovery came at different rates and times and many countries in 1938 had higher GDP per capita than in 1929. Germany was the first major Continental European country to achieve a full recovery from the depression. This recovery was based on large-scale public works and, especially from 1936, military expenditure which accounted for 3 per cent of GNP in 1933 and 28 per cent in 1938 (Crouzet, 2001). These developments in Germany were not inspired by Keynes, who had little influence at the time, or by the >NEW DEAL in the USA, but by the abhorrent political and ideological purposes of the Nazi regime (Overy, 1996).

After World War II, the economy of Western Europe, particularly Continental Europe, was devastated, with food and energy shortages, a large-scale refugee problem and, especially in Germany, damage to the housing stock. In many cases, monetary arrangements had broken down, the use of barter was widespread and cigarettes were being used as currency. Politically, Europe was dwarfed by Russia (which imposed communist regimes over much of Eastern Europe, including East Germany) and, politically and economically, by the USA. Britain was still accepted as one of the Big Three but had been impoverished by the war. There were demands from democratic electorates for a reorientation of society and the war was the occasion for a permanent extension of the role of the state (>STATE, ROLE OF THE). The mistakes that were made after World War I were not repeated after World War II. Instead of squeezing the losers, the whole of Western Europe was helped to recover and a new era of international economic cooperation opened up (>MARSHALL PLAN). Growth after 1950 was at rates which have never been exceeded before or since. The 'Golden Age' was a global phenomenon. Not only Western but Eastern Europe, >RUSSIA, Latin America and the Continent of Africa grew faster than before. Growth in GDP per capita in Britain and the

USA also speeded up, though the rates were well below those of the rest of Western Europe. The performances of Germany and Italy stand out with per capita rates of about 5 per cent between 1950 and 1973, rates exceeded only by Japan. (Italy also performed well during World War I. In 1918, its GDP was a third higher than in 1919.) Expansion in Britain was only half the rate in Germany and Italy and this has generated a large literature on its relative decline, even though its performance was better than ever before. Some of the peripheral European countries (notably Ireland, Portugal, Spain and Greece) also did well by their historical standards, though Ireland's 'miracle' was to be reserved for the last quarter of the 20th century.

Various explanations have been put forward to account for the 'Golden Age', which saw the emergence of Europe as a world economic power with a 46 per cent share in world exports in 1973. Some of these explanations are indigenous to the countries concerned, for example, Germany had exceptionally good economic policies under Economics Minister, Ludwig Erhard, and recent research has shown that its industrial plants were modernized during the war and much of its equipment survived intact, despite reparations. The favourable performance of countries on the European periphery, which were the poorest in 1950, can be explained as a catch-up or convergence story. Europe as a whole was also catching up (though it did not catch) the USA and there was a massive transfer of technology, for example, in automobile production. However, Europe was unable to capture a strong indigenous position in the new industries based on >ELECTRONICS, which became dominated by the USA and Japan

(mobile telephony is an exception). The continued removal of trade barriers over the period, as well as the scope that existed outside Britain for the continued transfer of labour from agriculture to higher productivity industries, also contributed to 'Golden Age' growth. Some countries, notably Germany, benefited from immigration from Turkey and elsewhere. Vonyo (2008) concludes that explaining *differences* between national performances of the core countries can mostly be attributed to structural modernization (investment in material and human capital) and labour force expansion.

As mentioned earlier, the 'Golden Age' came abruptly to an end from 1973. European growth had already slowed from 1958 and there were warning signs of 'Eurosclerosis' (rising inflation, institutional rigidities, social conflicts) well before 1973, as well as from the collapse of the Bretton Woods exchange rate mechanism in 1971, which replaced more or less fixed exchange rates by floating rates. The end was precipitated by the first oil shock in which OPEC raised oil prices by a factor of four, and this was compounded by a second oil shock in 1979. The impact of these shocks on balances of payments was mitigated because the world financial system was able to recycle the surplus petro-dollars for which there was insufficient reinvestment scope in the oil-exporting (mainly Middle Eastern) states. Nonetheless, Europe was heavily dependent on imported oil and consumption and investment had to fall. Unemployment rose and there was a combination of inflation and stagnation (stagflation). Competition in manufactured goods from East Asia increased in the 1980s but helped to curb inflation in the West. From the mid-1990s there was a resurgence in economic growth in the USA. Since 1973, the relative orders of growth rates between the USA and Europe were reversed compared with 1950–73, though only by a little; from 1995, however, the margin was much wider. Recently, further large increases in the price of oil, and, in 2007–8, a credit crisis following excessive property asset inflation, have cast a cloud over the West's growth prospects. Moreover, demand from the expanding emerging countries, particularly >CHINA, for grains, iron ore, oil and other commodities have introduced further price pressures.

Individual countries fared differently in the slowdown from 1973. Following the Thatcher Government reforms from 1979, Britain's position improved to better than the European average. German growth in per capita incomes fell from 4.04 per cent per annum in 1950–73 to only 1.72 per cent as it coped with the difficulties of unification with East Germany. Switzerland's rate of expansion fell from 3.08 to 0.67 per cent per annum but Norway's only from 3.25 to 2.8 per cent, thanks to its oil resources. Ireland was the only country where growth actually increased and in general, and with this exception, the process of convergence seemed to have come to a halt. In 1987, GNP per head in Ireland had been 59 per cent of the EU-15 average, about the same as in 1960, but by 1997 it had risen to 88 per cent. Ireland's success can be partly attributed to inward foreign direct investment (>INTERNATIONAL TRADE), through appropriate fiscal policy and incentives and its membership of the EU (along with Britain and Denmark in 1973). Ireland also benefited from increased education levels and favourable labour market policies in this period, as well as access to EU structural funds (Barry, 1999).

The emergence of an enlarged and increasingly integrated European Community, since it was formed by the Treaty of Rome in 1958, has been a major feature of the post-war history of Western Europe. The progressive removal of tariff barriers between the original six members of the EEC and the adoption of a common external tariff was followed by the addition of three new members in 1973, as mentioned, and in 1990 further members were added (Greece, 1981, Portugal and Spain, 1986, and Austria, Finland and Sweden, 1995). Ten further states in Central and Eastern Europe, the Baltic and Mediterranean became members in 2004 and two more in 2007. The European Economic Area (EEA) was formed in 1994 comprising former members of the European Free Trade Area (EFTA) that had not joined the EU. The EEA includes Iceland, Liechtenstein and Norway. Switzerland has bilateral agreements with the EU. Among the members of EU-15, the removal of internal import duties, although it did stimulate a great deal of trade, did not create a true single market because of many non-tariff barriers (NTBs), for example, technical standards, exchange controls and various regulations, affecting financial services. These NTBs were reduced, though not entirely eliminated, under the Single European Act of 1986 with a target for completion of 1992. Under the Maastricht Treaty of that year, it was decided to adopt a single European currency, the euro, which became fully effective in 2002. Britain, Denmark and Sweden did not participate in the euro zone. The path to the adoption of the euro was a long one from the basic decision to go that route in 1970. On the way there were considerable difficulties following the end of the Bretton Woods era in 1971. The EU finally set up its own

European Monetary System (EMS) with an Exchange Rate Mechanism (ERM), which allowed for realignments, in 1979. Britain initially opted out though it joined in 1990 only to drop out in 1992 (Neal, 2007).

Compared with the USA, Western Europe has a larger population (36 per cent larger), but a smaller GDP so that US GDP per capita is considerably greater. The EU has also had a slightly slower rate of growth than the USA since 1973 and particularly so since 1995. Rates of inflation have been similar. The Americans work longer hours but unemployment is much higher in Europe, no doubt, largely because of more restrictive labour market regulation (Galli and Pelkmans, 2000). The original motivation for the formation of the EU was political: to prevent the recurrence of the warfare, which occurred twice in the 20th century. In this the EU has been successful. Despite the prediction of many, if not most, economists, the euro has also, so far at least, been a great success, thanks partly to good work by the independent European Central Bank (>CENTRAL BANKING). It was argued that a single monetary system and accompanying limits on budget deficits would create intolerable strains for the management of public finances for some countries. However, the euro has made much lower interest rates possible and this has reduced the cost of debt service. There are strains in some countries, particularly in the South, and it is easy to see that problems in the future may increase, particularly as the European population is ageing and the cost of state pensions increasing. Predicted benefits of the euro in terms of lower transaction costs and increased trade, competition and economic growth have, moreover, been elusive.

In fact, the Western European economy has never fully been able to close the gap which opened up between it and the USA in the 19th century. There are aspirations that it should do so. In March 2000, the EU Council of Ministers meeting in Lisbon, set a goal of making Europe 'the most competitive and dynamic knowledge-based economy in the world by 2010', an objective which even at the time seemed to many to be out of reach. Of course, quality of life is not adequately measured by GDP statistics. The USA has greater inequality, longer working hours, a larger prison population and less social protection than Europe and average earnings have risen more slowly, reflecting lower unemployment.

## References

Aldcroft, Derek H., *The European Economy, 1914–2000*, Routledge, 1995.

Balderston, Theo, *Economics and Politics in the Weimar Republic*, Cambridge University Press, 2002.

Barry, Frank (ed.), *Understanding Ireland's Economic Growth*, Macmillan, 1999.

Borchardt, Knut, *Perspectives on Modern German Economic History and Policy*, Cambridge University Press, 1991.

Crouzet, François, *A History of the European Economy, 1000–2000*, University Press of Virginia, 2001.

Davies, Norman, *Europe: A History*, Oxford University Press, 1996.

Feinstein, Charles H., Temin, Peter and Toniolo, Gianni, *The European Economy Between the Wars*, Oxford University Press, 1997.

Galli, Giampaolo and Pelkmans, Jacques (eds), *Regulatory Reform and Competitiveness in Europe*, I, Edward Elgar, 2000.

Maddison, Angus, *The World Economy: A Millennial Perspective*, OECD, 2001.

Maddison, Angus, *Contours of the World Economy, 1–2030 AD: Essays in Macro-Economic History*, Oxford University Press, 2007.

Neal, Larry, *The Economics of Europe and the European Union*, Cambridge University Press, 2007.

Ogilvie, Sheilagh and Overy, Richard, *Germany: A New Social and Economic History, Volume 3: Since 1800*, Arnold, 2003.

Overy, R. J., *The Nazi Economic Recovery 1932–1938*, Cambridge University Press, 1996.

Pollard, Sydney, *Peaceful Conquest: Industrialisation of Europe, 1760–1970*, Oxford University Press, 1981.

Vittorio, Antonio Di (ed.), *An Economic History of Europe: From Expansion to Development*, Routledge, 2006.

Vonyo, Tamas, 'Post-War Reconstruction and the Golden Age of Economic Growth', *European Review of Economic History*, August, 2008.

Zamagni, Vera, *The Economic History of Italy, 1860–1990*, Clarendon Press, 1993.

# Wool and Wool Textiles

The farming of sheep for wool has been widespread throughout Europe for centuries. Spain had been long known for the quality of its fleeces, giving way in the 18th century to Saxony, Silesia and Bohemia. These wools were produced by the merino sheep, which had a short staple in contrast to the also highly regarded British breeds, which had a long staple. The short-staple merino wool was manufactured into 'woollens'. The process involved carding, spinning, weaving and the fulling of the cloth. The long staple wools were manufactured into 'worsteds'. The fibres were combed before spinning and no further treatment was given to the cloth after weaving. The woollen cloths were heavier and more expensive than the worsteds.

Wool textiles had for several centuries been a leading British export and accounted for as much as 85 per cent of all manufactures exported at the end of the 17th century. The share fell to 62 per cent in the middle of the 18th century and to 22 per cent by its close, although exports did grow in absolute terms. In contrast, the share of cotton textiles increased from 1 per cent in the middle of the 18th century to 35 per cent at its close (>BRITAIN: >COTTON AND COTTON TEXTILES).

In the late 18th century, there was a flowering of industrial invention which had a profound affect on the textile industries, such as James Hargreaves' (1720–1778) spinning jenny of 1764, Richard Arkwright's (1732–1792) water frame of 1769 (a spinning frame powered by water) and Samuel Crompton's (1753–1827) spinning mule of 1779 (called a mule because it contained features of both the jenny and the water frame). (>INDUSTRIAL REVOLUTION IN BRITAIN). The pace of technical development in the wool industry was, however, slower than in cotton. The mule was not successfully applied to the spinning of woollen fibres until 1816. For worsteds, although the automated loom invented by Joseph-Marie Jacquard (1752–1834) in 1801 replaced the labour-intensive draw loom, the combing of wool was not mechanized until the middle of the 19th century.

In the 18th century, Yorkshire became the dominant location for the production of wool textiles in Britain and by the end of the 18th century accounted for 60 per cent of British production. In Continental Europe, there had been a movement away from the towns into the countryside to exploit lower labour costs there. Output of wool textiles increased generally throughout Europe in the 17th and 18th centuries, with worsteds gaining ground in the total. This expansion of wool textiles in Europe continued through the following century. In the early 19th century, there was a diffusion of technology from Britain throughout Europe, although Britain kept its lead. By the middle of the 19th century, the mechanization of production within a factory system had been completed for worsteds, as it had already for cotton. In France and Germany, the transformation to a mechanized factory system took longer. It was not until towards the end of the century that the gap was closed. The consumption of wool in France, Germany and Britain increased by five or six times from the early 19th century to reach an average of about 200,000 tonnes each by 1913. This growth spurred the demand for new sources of wool (>WESTERN EUROPE).

Europe had always been self-sufficient in wool and in the early 19th century accounted for over 90 per cent of world production. From the middle of the 19th century, Europe was able to meet its growing requirements from more distant sources as international transport costs fell (>SHIPPING). At the end of the 18th century, the merino sheep had been introduced into Australia and cross-bred to give a longer staple. In the 1830s, there was a rapid growth in sheep farming there and wool became an established industry, reaching over 40 per cent of total exports by value. Australia and New Zealand became major world suppliers along with Argentina and Uruguay. By the beginning of the 20th century, Australia had surpassed total European production of wool and captured 25 per cent of the world export market.

British production of wool textiles doubled from the 1870s to the outbreak of World War I, although the domestic wool shear fell by about 20 per cent. Britain imported most of its wool from Australia. The French, Belgian and German industries relied on imports from Argentina and Uruguay. In the great agricultural depression from 1873–96 (>AGRICULTURE) there was a world over-production of wool and a decline in trade in wool textiles. Protection became more entrenched (>INTERNATIONAL TRADE). Increased tariffs particularly damaged British wool textiles exports to Europe and the USA, which were its main markets. There was a recovery after 1905 and Britain substantially increased its share of the export markets in wool textiles in the period up to >WORLD WAR I. Europe maintained its lead in world production of wool textiles, thereafter, until the 1950s, by which time Japan and the USA had become more significant producers.

According to the Food and Agricultural Organization (FAO), in 1970 the major importers of wool were 12 member states of the European Union (of which Italy predominated), which accounted for about 53 per cent of the total, and Japan, which accounted for 22 per cent. By 2000, the European share in a diminishing market had fallen to 43 per cent and Japan's place had been replaced by >CHINA, which accounted for 27 per cent of the total. Throughout this period the major suppliers of wool for export remained Australia and New Zealand, which maintained a share of the around 70 per cent. Wool production from the 1960s faced continuing competition from cotton and synthetic fibres and by 2000 accounted for less than 5 per cent of total world consumption of textile fibres. Production in the high-wage economies of the advanced countries was also put under pressure from the low costs of the developing countries. In 1974, the Multi-Fibre Arrangement (MFA) was agreed, which allowed quotas to be established to protect home production from cheap imports and was not phased out until 2005 (>COTTON AND COTTON TEXTILES).

### References

Floud, Roderick and McCloskey, Donald, *The Economic History of Britain Since 1700* (2nd edn), Cambridge University Press, 1994.

Goodman, Jordan and Honeyman, Katrina, *Gainful Pursuits, The Making of Industrial Europe, 1600–1914*, Edward Arnold, 1988.

Jenkins, David (ed.), *Cambridge History of Western Textiles*, Cambridge University Press, 2001.

Yates, P. Lamartine, *Forty Years of Foreign Trade*, George Allen & Unwin, 1959.

# World War I

On 28 June 1914, Archduke Francis Ferdinand the heir to the Austria-Hungarian throne was assassinated by a Serbian nationalist at Sarajevo, in Bosnia. Serbia had been a part of the Ottoman Empire since the battle of Kosovo in 1389 but had finally achieved its independence from the Turks in 1878 and became ambitious to free its ethnic cousins in the Austria-Hungary empire, which had annexed Bosnia-Hercegovina in 1908. The assassination prompted Austria-Hungary to insist on guarantees from the Serbian government that there would be no further agitation and they issued an ultimatum attached to which were conditions such that Serbia could not accept. Austria-Hungary's action was supported by Germany and it prompted >RUSSIA to mobilize to prevent the loss of Serbia's independence. Germany, having sent ultimatums to Russia and to France, which had formed an alliance with Russia, attacked France through Belgium and, on 4 August 1914, >BRITAIN entered the war in support of its obligation to protect Belgium neutrality. The immediate locus of the war was the instability in the Balkans that followed the declining power of the Ottoman Empire but at its heart was the growing assertiveness of the Germans since they had defeated France in the war of 1870–1 from which they had captured Alsace-Lorraine (>WESTERN EUROPE).

At the outbreak of the war, the major combatants on the side of the Allies were Britain, France and Russia, including their dependences, colonies and the British dominions. In addition there were the Balkan states of Bosnia-Hercegovina, Montenegro and Serbia and Japan. The Allies were joined in the following years by Italy, Portugal and Romania and, in the last two years of the war, by Brazil, >CHINA, Greece, Siam and the >USA. The Central Powers comprised Germany and its dependences, Austria-Hungary, the Ottoman Empire, which included Syria, Palestine and Iraq, and, in 1915, Bulgaria. However, the major powers who were critical to the outcome of the war were, for the Allies, Britain, France, Italy, Russia and the USA and, for the Central Powers, Germany, Austria-Hungary and the Ottoman Empire.

The German strategy had been to inflict a rapid defeat of France on its western front through its invasion of northern France through Belgium and then to turn its full forces to its eastern front against Russia. However, their thrust was stopped by the British and French at the Battle of the Marne in September 1914. From that time, the opposing forces fought along lines of trenches, up to several miles in depth and protected by barbed-wire entanglements, that eventually stretched from the Channel Coast near Ostend to the Swiss border, through which no lasting effective breakthrough was achieved in spite of an unprecedented sacrifice of lives and material resources. On the eastern front, after early success, the Russians suffered a defeat in August 1914 at the Battle of Tannenburg. In an attempt to relieve Russia, the Allies launched an attack on Turkey on the Gallipoli Peninsula in 1915, which was a complete failure for the loss of over 200,000 troops. In the three years before the war, Britain had reinforced its navy and had opted for >OIL rather than >COAL as the means of propulsion and in consequence it was anxious to protect its sources of supply. Accordingly, the Allies landed at Abadan in Persia (Iran) in 1914 and, after a lack of success initially, they captured Baghdad and Jerusalem in 1917 and Damascus and Aleppo in the following year.

In 1915, the Germans occupied Poland and captured hundreds of thousands of Russian troops. In the following year, Russia achieved successes in the Ukraine, captured Czernowitz and inflicted heavy losses on the Austrians. However, they failed to exploit their advantage against the arrival of German reinforcements and through their campaign their forces were debilitated by the loss of up to a million men. In March 1917, revolution deposed the Tsar. In July the Germans defeated the Russians in Galacia and by October occupied Latvia. Finally, in November the Bolsheviks under Lenin took control of government and signed an armistice with Germany in December 1917.

In the west, the war reached a stalemate and became one of attrition. Perceiving Britain as being vulnerable because of its relatively small agricultural economy, the Germans deployed their U-Boat fleet for the express aim of destroying any vessels supplying the Allies, of any nationality, neutral or not, and their campaign achieved successes. However, the U-Boats proved in the long run less effective than that of the blockade of German ports maintained by the British fleet. In May 1915, a British passenger liner, the *Lusitania* was sunk by a German U-Boat with the loss of 1,195 lives, including Americans, and this helped to shift sentiment in the USA in favour of the Allies. In January 1917, British intelligence discovered an approach by Germany offering Mexico an alliance and the USA entered the war in April 1917. The German government finally accepted armistice terms and the war ended on 11 November 1918.

World War I occurred at the dawn of the fruition of technological advances which heralded a revolution in the art and conduct of warfare. The war exhibited a rich mixture of the old and the new. Transport, and consequently the continuing conduct of the war, depended crucially on the supply of horses. The British, for instance, by 1918 had employed about a million horses in logistical support for its operations, most of them imported from the USA. At the battle of the Marne in 1914, Allied and German cavalry regiments fought each other with lances but it was at this point that the German advance on Paris was halted with the help of the internal combustion engine. In order to move reinforcements quickly enough to the weakening French resistance in the face of the German attack, the military governor commandeered all the taxi-cabs in Paris and transported several thousand troops in their convoys to the front. The German advance was consequently stopped at the Marne. The machine gun put an end to the cavalry charge and, together with the development of heavy artillery, brought the war to a stalemate in the entrenched defensive positions of the western front. It was the development of the tank, an armoured vehicle on tracks, that eventually was able to bring to an end the effectiveness of the trenched defensive positions. Tanks were designed both by the French and the British and had been used in 1916 but it was in late 1917 at Cambrai that the British first used tanks successfully. The tanks broke through the German lines; supported by cavalry. Warfare also reached the civilian populations from the air for the first time when a German dirigible, the 'Zeppelin', bombed London in 1915 and one was shot down by an aeroplane. In 1914, the British forces had 827 motor cars. By 1918 they had 23,000, together with 56,000 trucks (>AUTOMOBILE INDUSTRY). During the war, France built 68,000 aeroplanes, Britain 55,000, Germany 48,000 and Italy 20,000 (Yergin, 1992).

World War I was the first time in history that war was fought by nationally conscripted civilians and necessitated the mobilization of resources that reached throughout the whole economy. Success or failure in such a total war depended, therefore, not only on the magnitude of the resources available to a combatant but also on its ability to organize those resources effectively.

The Industrial Revolution which had originated in Britain in the 18th century (>INDUSTRIAL REVOLUTION IN BRITAIN) had spread in the 19th and early 20th centuries through firstly North Western Europe and then later into Eastern and Southern Europe. The timing of this progression was reflected in the corresponding diminishing level of development attained by countries in Europe by 1913 the further east and south they were located from the north-west corner of Europe (>WESTERN EUROPE). Although, as a consequence of this progress of industrialization, the dominating lead enjoyed by Britain had been and was being eroded, particularly by the USA and Germany, nevertheless in 1913 it yet retained a pre-eminent world position. Although Germany's Gross Domestic Product (GDP) had reached a comparable level of that of Britain, its GDP per capita was 25 per cent less; its population being 20 million greater. Britain's GDP per capita was about the same level as that of the USA. The degree of development achieved by the countries of the European continent may be measured by their GDP per capita compared with Britain. This data ranged from 20 per cent below in Belgium, 30 per cent in France, about 46 per cent in Austria-Hungary, 48 per cent in Italy, 70 per cent in Russia to 75 per cent in Portugal and 78 per cent in the Ottoman Empire (Broadberry and Harrison, 2005). Moreover, the structure of the British economy was significantly different from that of other countries in Europe. Its early industrialization and its policy of free trade had led to a relatively rapid shift away from >AGRICULTURE to manufacturing and services (>SERVICE SECTOR). During the 19th century, the population of Britain had grown exceptionally quickly (rising by 77 per cent between 1861 and 1911) and had overtaken that of France by 1900. The concomitant expansion in the labour force found employment in the industrial and service sectors, the numbers employed in agriculture falling. As a result, in the years leading up to 1913, the primary sector accounted for only 9 per cent of total employment, compared with 37 per cent in Germany, 41 per cent in France, 55 per cent in Italy, 57 in Austria and 59 per cent in Russia (Aldcroft, 1994). As a consequence of these structural changes, Britain depended relatively more on >INTERNATIONAL TRADE for the supply of food and raw materials and world export markets for its manufactures. This dependence is reflected in the shares Britain still achieved in 1913 in world merchandise trade in spite of the growth in competition, particularly from the USA and Germany. In 1913, Britain still had a leading share of 14 per cent in total world merchandise exports, compared with 13 per cent for Germany and 13 per cent for the USA (Alford, 1996). Britain had also built its trade on the deep-sea rather than the short- and near-sea routes. As a result, whereas about 78 per cent of exports from the Continental European countries were shipped within Europe, 65 per cent of British exports were to the rest of the world (Aldcroft, 1994).

The Allies were significantly superior compared with the Central Powers in terms of their aggregate availability of resources of land, population and National Income. Excluding colonies, dependencies and the British dominions, the Allies had over twice the population of the Central Powers and almost twice the National Income in 1914. By 1918, after Russia had been replaced by the USA, the population advantage of the Allies had fallen to about one and a half times of that of the Central Powers but National Income had risen to two and a half times greater. Moreover, during the course of the war, there were significant differences between countries in the growth rates of their National Incomes. The economies of Russia, France and the Ottoman Empire experienced the most severe falls of the order of about 40 per cent by 1918, compared with 1913. The National Incomes of Germany and Austria-Hungary fell by about 20 per cent and 25 per cent respectively. However, in Britain, National Income rose by about 15 per cent and in the USA by 13 per cent (Broadberry and Harrison, 2005). There had been a view that countries with large agricultural economies would have a long-term advantage because of their ability to feed themselves. In the event, their low labour productivity in agriculture was exacerbated by the loss of young male workers to meet the needs of the military. Germany failed in spite of the initial superiority of its army because it became trapped into a war of attrition, which in the long run it could not win because of the relative lack of resources which it was able to mobilize.

The human and physical destruction of the war was unparalleled in its magnitude. The US War Department recorded that 65 million troops were conscripted by all the belligerents in total and there were 37.5 million casualties (including prisoners and missing). According to figures quoted in Cameron (1993), the total number of deaths of military personnel amounted to about 10 million and another 20 million were severely wounded. In addition, there were about 30 million civilian casualties, including the effects of famine and disease. The relative magnitude of the losses varied between countries. The largest numbers of military fatalities were incurred by Germany, about 2 million, Russia about 1.8 million, France about 1.4 million,

Austria-Hungary about 1.2 million, Britain about 0.7 million (including the dominions about 0.9 million) and also Italy about 0.7 million. On average these military losses amounted to about 8 per cent of the male working population, although for Germany and France the proportion was significantly higher at 12.5 per cent and 13.3 per cent respectively and Russia lower at 4.5 per cent (Gatrell and Harrison, 1993). These casualties, including those of the civilian population and the concomitant drop in the birth rate, led to a check in the growth of the >POPULATION of Europe. The country which suffered most population loss was Russia, which had had to endure also revolution and civil war. In Western Europe, France suffered most from population decline. According to Maddison (1995), France did not regain its 1913 level of population until 1930, during which time the population of Britain increased by 3 million and that of the USA by 26 million.

To be added to the military and civilian casualties were the losses arising from the physical destruction of property. Various estimates have been made of the magnitude of the various categories of losses in monetary terms to arrive at a total cost of the war. At one time, it was believed that war could only be a total comprehensive loss. However, it has been argued that this is not necessarily the case (Milward, 1984). For instance, in Britain, women benefited from the opening up of opportunities for work and many men who had suffered from long-term unemployment enjoyed an improved standard of living because of the shortage of labour. In the particular case of the USA, some estimates suggest that for the country as a whole the war yielded net benefits. Drawing up a balance sheet of costs and benefits, however, is fraught with difficulties of measurement and interpretation. A value has to be put on human life, such as the present value of prospective life-time earnings, but this might be excessive in an environment of unemployment. Benefits could accrue from the destruction of plant and machinery in so far as they were obsolete (Milward, 1984). The prime study of these costs was that of Bogart in 1920, which concluded that the costs of the war totalled $338 billion. These calculations are reviewed and interpreted in Broadberry and Harrison (2005). They estimate that, as a proportion of a country's pre-war national assets, the losses incurred by France and Germany reached about 55 per cent, compared with Britain, whose losses amounted to 15 per cent. The estimate for Germany, however, includes the bill for reparations.

In addition to these short-run costs, there should also be considered any long-term effects of the war. Britain's foreign assets had declined by about 15 per cent with a consequential loss of income and it had become a net debtor, whereas the USA had became a net creditor. Britain's merchant fleet, which had been the world's largest before the war, never recovered and steadily declined in the face of the sinking of vessels during the war and the emergence of the USA as a competitor which had subsidized a shipbuilding programme. The German merchant fleet, which had been the world's second largest, had to be part of the reparations bill. In general, the removal of Europe from the international world economy during the war gave opportunities for other countries to develop alternative competitive supplies and move into the vacuum left in the international market. It has been argued that World War I stimulated technological development in, for instance, transport and communications, encouraged innovative production methods, initiated changes in the acceptable limits of the state in economic life and induced social change, such as in the employment of women (>EMPLOYMENT OF WOMEN AND CHILDREN).

Many of these effects of the war, however, accelerated trends which were already evident. More important were the long-run implications of the reparations which were demanded from Germany. >KEYNES was incensed by the short-sighted mean-spirited attitudes which informed the process by which reparations were determined:

'The future life of Europe was not their concern; its means of livelihood was not their anxiety. Their preoccupations, good and bad alike, related to frontiers and nationalities, to the balance of power, to imperial aggrandisements, to the future enfeeblement of a strong and dangerous enemy, to revenge, and to the shifting by the victors of their unbearable financial burdens on to the shoulders of the defeated.' (Keynes, 2004)

Germany lost over 13 per cent of its territory and 10 per cent of its population. Germany lost its merchant fleet and its armed forces were severely restricted. In Central and Eastern Europe, with the break-up of Austria-Hungary, more independent states were formed, such as Czechoslovakia, Estonia, Finland, Latvia, Lithuania, Poland and Yugoslavia. This political reorganization was imposed on economies which were severely weakened by the war. Moreover, the Allies had to rely on reparations from Germany to pay the debts they owed to the USA. Germany defaulted on its debts in 1921, was granted a moratorium on

them in 1931 and they were eventually written off in 1932. In spite of the clear need for assistance for the economies of Europe to help them to recover, international aid was inadequate. Assistance was provided by the American Relief Administration but little in the form of grant aid; most of it had to be paid on credit or, for the defeated countries, by cash (Aldcroft, 1995).

Germany was caught between the impossible demands for unrealistic levels of reparations and the needs for its reconstruction and renewed economic development. The extensive revision of national boundaries in Europe also imposed added burdens by distorting interregional trade flows. The resulting economic hardship encouraged nationalism and protectionism (>INTERNATIONAL TRADE), the renewal of German imperialism and led into >WORLD WAR II. Lessons were learned and applied in the aftermath of World War II from the >MARSHALL PLAN to the international Bretton Woods Conference and the European Union (>KEYNES).

## References

Aldcroft, Derek H., 'The European Dimension to the Modern World', in Derek H. Aldcroft and Simon P. Ville (eds), *The European Economy, 1750–1914*, Manchester University Press, 1994.

Aldcroft, Derek H., *The European Economy, 1914–2000*, Routledge, 1995.

Alford, W. E., *Britain in the World Economy Since 1880*, Longman, 1996.

Bogart, E. L., *Direct and Indirect Costs of the Great War*, Oxford University Press, 1920.

Broadberry, Stephen and Harrison, Mark, 'The Economics of World War I: An Overview', in Stephen Broadberry and Mark Harrison (eds), *The Economics of World War I*, Cambridge University Press, 2005.

Cameron, Rondo, *A Concise Economic History of the World*, Oxford University Press, 1993.

Gatrell, Peter and Harrison, Mark, 'The Russian and Soviet Economies in Two World Wars: A Comparative View', *Economic History Review*, XLVI(3), August, 1993.

Keynes, John Maynard, *The Economic Consequences of the Peace*, Macmillan, 1920, reprinted by Dover Publications, 2004.

Maddison, Angus, *Monitoring the World Economy 1820–1992*, OECD, 1995.

Milward, Alan S., *The Economic Effects of the Two World Wars on Britain*, Studies in Economic and Social History series, Macmillan, 1984.

Yergin, Daniel, *The Prize: The Epic Quest for Oil, Money and Power*, Simon & Schuster, 1992.

# World War II

The Second World War differed from >WORLD WAR I in important respects. The death toll of perhaps 40 million was larger because, although fewer soldiers were killed, civilian casualties from the ground war and bombing and the terrible mass extermination policies of the Nazis, not to mention other atrocities, starvation and disease were enormous. There was more physical destruction than in the Great War and the conflict covered much of the globe: eight countries fought on the Axis side and 26 for the Allies. Air power and science and invention were much more important and World War II changed economy and society permanently. Whereas World War I was followed by the >GREAT DEPRESSION, the second war was followed by an exceptional and fairly durable period of prosperity (>USA: >WESTERN EUROPE).

The origins of World War II were similar to those of World War I – a struggle for power and aggrandisement resulting from frustrated nationalism – indeed the combatants were the same in both wars except that Japan, Turkey and Italy were on different sides. The causes of the conflict built up slowly over a long period of time, so that, as many people foresaw in the 1930s, the war became inevitable. The roots of this conflict lay in a botched settlement after World War I which left unnatural boundaries and no effective means of curbing the ambitions of the disgruntled losers, particularly Germany. Taylor (1961) argued that none of the combatants actually wanted war, including Germany which tripped into it because Hitler overestimated the reluctance of Britain to engage in another war. Hitler had no master plan but was an opportunist and, but for futile attempts at appeasement and an unnecessary failure to reach a defensive agreement with Russia, Britain and France might have prevented war. Other writers have emphasized economic causes: the three 'have-not' powers, Germany, Japan and Italy, which had no colonies and lacked resources of raw materials and markets. Taylor rejects this view at least for Germany, which in the 1930s suffered from credit inflation and not over-production. The countries which Germany conquered were exploited for resources not markets, although there were ideas for a Nazi commercial and cultural empire in Europe. Hitler did not expect a long war and was not prepared for one. His policy of *Blitzkrieg* (1939–42), which took the form of surprise rapid advances with lightly armed but mobile troops, although initially successful could not continue to be so in the face of the vastly greater economic potential of the Allies, especially following his error in declaring war on both Russia and the USA in 1941. By 1942 defeat of Germany was inevitable. So even if the causes of the war were not economic the outcome was the result of economic factors.

Britain had enormous support from its empire and dominions in terms of food, materials and armed forces. President Roosevelt's 'Arsenal of Democracy', which was expanding long before the >USA entered the war, brought the conflict to an early close after war production peaked in 1944. According to Aldcroft (2001), the USA, Britain and >RUSSIA alone had accounted for about 60 per cent of world manufacturing production in 1936–8 against about 17 per cent for the main Axis powers. By 1944, the general provision of goods and services for war for just >BRITAIN and the USA probably exceeded those available to Germany by 75 per cent, while in munitions output the ratio was two and a half times greater. German resources included the exploitation of the countries occupied. At first this took the form of the seizure of stocks of goods, but later 'occupation costs', which greatly exceeded the cost of maintaining German armies, were levied. These costs were based on a large overvaluation of the Reichsmark used to convert currencies. According to Milward (1977), foreign inputs amounted to about 40 per cent of German income tax revenues, France being the most profitable of the occupied countries. Aldcroft (2001) reckons that the foreign contribution to Germany's wartime GNP was about 14 per cent. There was some attempt later on to organize the foreign economies and to build up their production potential so as to contribute more to Germany's war effort, but these attempts did not come to much because Germany made little effort to encourage voluntary cooperation.

From 1942, the Allies had a significant superiority in armed forces, almost twice as many by 1944. What is surprising is not so much that the Axis was eventually defeated, but how they were able to stave off defeat for so long. Harrison (1998) explains that the German and Japanese strategy relied on quality of armies and armament to compensate for their deficiencies in the quantity of overall resources. They also made strategic innovations, such as the use of U-Boats and flying bombs by Germany, to compensate for the inferiority of their sea and air forces respectively. By 1943, at the peak, annual military outlays by Germany amounted to 70 per cent of National Income, a figure exceeded only by Japan and then only in 1944. Russia was also spending a great deal on the war, amounting to an even greater sacrifice given its lower levels of income. Italy was spending only 21 per cent. Among the Allies, the British percentage was 55 per cent at the peak, up from 15 per cent in 1939 and 44 per cent in 1940. The build-up in the USA was slower, but from very low levels: only 1 per cent in 1939 to reach 42 per cent by 1943. Once the US production machine got going the results were unprecedented. Between 1940 and 1944 aircraft and shipbuilding rose over tenfold, munitions nearly 15-fold. Many innovations in production technique were made. For example, the industrialist Henry J. Kaiser had never built ships before but mass-produced ships like the standardized Liberty ships, using welding in place of the traditional riveting of ships' plates. Ships were a central part of the Allied effort, which required continuous transport across the Atlantic.

Through secrecy and problems of definition, satisfactory data on military expenditure are not available for the inter-war period, which has probably allowed scope for some misapprehensions about the preparedness of Britain for the conflict. It does not seem to be true that Britain disarmed in contrast to other countries in the 1920s and 1930s. Edgerton maintains that, 'in absolute terms Britain spent at least as much as any country on warfare while its expenditure was concentrated on two technological arms, the navy and the airforce, both of which were among the very strongest in the world' (2006). Nevertheless, expenditure on armaments by the Axis (Germany, Japan and Italy) increased much faster in the period 1934–8, perhaps twice as fast as that of Britain, Russia and France. Milward (1977) cites figures from A. J. Brown indicating percentage increases in the real value of expenditure on armaments over this period of 470 for Germany, 455 for Japan and 370 for Russia, compared with 250 for Britain and only 41 per cent for France. US expenditure at this time was very low as mentioned. Aldcroft (2001) says that the three Axis powers accounted for 52 per cent of all war expenditure of 30 nations in 1938, compared with 35 per cent in 1934.

The massive increases in war expenditure had to be paid for from increased output, reduced consumption (in most countries but not the USA) and disinvestment by capital depletion, which Aldcroft (2001) puts at 2 per cent of output. For Britain especially, the disposal of foreign investments was an important element in financing the war. Most countries used physical rationing, even the USA for certain goods, and price controls to contain inflation alongside macro-economic management. Except in the occupied territories, inflation was generally more muted than in World War I. In his *How to Pay for the War* (1939) >KEYNES advocated the use of national accounts to calculate an 'inflationary gap' to be filled by transfers from taxpayers, including forced savings to be repaid after the war. In the event, the British government did raise taxes and introduce post-war credits, but relied heavily on borrowing to finance the budget deficit. By 1943, export volumes had fallen to less than a third of the pre-war level. A heavy external deficit was to a large extent financed by lend-lease from the USA and protected by a battery of import and foreign exchange controls. Manpower planning, including measures to ensure increased female participation and wide powers of labour direction and compulsion, was made necessary by over 5 million in the armed services by 1945 out of a labour force of 22.5 million. Japan and Germany both used forced and foreign labour on a large scale.

Living standards during the war among the combatants fell, except in the USA. By 1945, about half of British consumption was rationed and personal consumption fell by 22 per cent compared with pre-war. According to Hugh Rockoff, in Harrison (1998), consumption levels in the USA were maintained at a high level, especially among the lower income groups. In Russia, living standards by 1943 had fallen to perhaps three-fifths of the already depressed 1940 level. Civilian living standards also fell sharply in Japan. In Germany, although the production of consumer goods did not fall before 1942, direct indicators suggest that real consumption was falling in 1939 and was at least one-fifth below the pre-war level by 1941. Germany would have done worse but for the exploitation of its occupied territories.

Preparations for war brought down unemployment in Britain

and the USA from the early 1930s peaks of 15 per cent in Britain (1932) and almost 25 per cent in the USA (1933). However, by 1938, unemployment was still 9 per cent in Britain and almost 19 per cent in the USA. Germany was different; unemployment had been over 17 per cent in 1932 but was greatly reduced by public expenditure on infrastructure and rearmament to under 5 per cent in 1936 and to 1.3 per cent in 1938 (Maddison, 1982), bearing out Keynes's later prescription. Werner Abelshausser, in his contribution to Harrison's book, cites the Cambridge economist Joan Robinson as saying: 'Hitler had already found how to cure unemployment before Keynes had finished explaining why it occurred' (Harrison, 1998). Abelshausser shows that the share of public expenditure in National Income in 1938 was 35 per cent in Germany, just under 24 per cent in Britain and only 10.7 per cent in the USA.

In the USA, according to Hugh Rockoff's contribution to Harrison (1998), between 1942 and 1945, a period of high public deficits, taxes accounted for 47 per cent of government spending, printing money 26 per cent and borrowing from the public 27 per cent. All authorities agree that war finance was better managed in World War II than in the first war in the USA, even though the funds expended were vastly greater. Runaway inflation was avoided. Consumer prices rose by only 10.5 per cent between 1942 and 1945, partly through the application of wage and price controls. These controls will have led to some deterioration in quality (smaller candy bars) and thus some underestimation of the actual price increases.

Generally, World War II was accompanied by a permanent move to a greater role for government and away from the use of market mechanisms (>STATE, RISE OF THE). A chart of government spending as a percentage of GDP since 1900 for Britain shows a clear ratchet effect in the upward trend, from 12 per cent or so up to World War I, kicking up to 45 per cent during World War I, falling back to around 25 per cent in the 1920s and 1930s, then kicking up again to over 60 per cent in World War II, falling back to 35 per cent and a rising trend up to the mid-1980s and levelling off at about 40 per cent (Tom Clarke and Andrew Dilnot's contribution to Floud and Johnson, 2004) (>TAXATION). In the USA more intervention in the economy had begun before the war with the >NEW DEAL, which prepared the way for the new organization necessary for the war effort. Some of the New Deal bodies, such as the Maritime Commission, established to rejuvenate the depressed shipbuilding industry (>SHIPPING), played a major part in the ensuing conflict.

According to Milward (1977), machinery to control the allocation of raw materials and for planning purposes had been set up in the USA before Pearl Harbor. Later, a Supply Priorities and Allocation Board and later still a War Production Board were established. This machinery relied mainly on exhortation and financial incentives (loans, tax reliefs) and it was not until 1942 that outright direction was resorted to. The USA was thus following Britain where supply ministries, dominated according to Edgerton (2006) by the military and not the Treasury, were responsible for coordinating production. Russia and Germany, even in the 1930s, had relied heavily on physical controls.

Issues of material supply and production were so important during the war that conscious policies were adopted by the Allies to attempt to disrupt enemy war production by naval blockades, bombing and other means, such as 'pre-emption' – buying up scarce supplies of raw materials – and sabotage. This approach was a natural one for the Allies since they had superiority in sea power, while Germany and Japan were vulnerable to shortages of key raw materials. Britain set up a Ministry of Economic Warfare in September 1939, but had been planning its activities as long before as 1936. The USA followed with its Board of Economic Warfare. Research was carried out to establish what imports or domestic sources were crucial to the war effort, such as oil and aviation fuel, industrial diamonds and precision bearings. There is some doubt about the extent to which economic warfare impeded the German war effort since large stocks had been built up, substitutes developed and sources of supply obtained in the occupied territories. Certainly economic warfare must have contributed to defeat of the Axis but it was not decisive. Milward (1977) says, however, that in the case of Japan economic warfare could have crippled the economy if it were not overtaken by other means. Martin Fritz's entry on economic warfare in Dear and Foot (2005) speculates that fear of blockade may have encouraged Hitler in his fatal decision to invade Russia.

With the necessary shifts of the labour force out of agriculture and into the industrial war economy, lack of manpower was a serious problem in farming in Britain. Germany and Japan relied heavily on the occupied territories for the supply of food and also on the use of foreign labour and women and children in domestic agriculture. Germany was not seriously short of food until near the end of the war. Increased mechanization

played only a relatively small part. Russia suffered particularly acute shortages of food after the German invasion since two-thirds of its pre-war food production had come from areas controlled by the Germans. Men had disappeared from the countryside, with four out of five collective farmers being women. Milward explains that in the allocation of shipping space to Russia, food had the same priority as military equipment, so serious was the problem. He also shows that in all combatant countries, the demand for food, if not the supply, actually grew during the war as a result of higher levels of employment, longer hours of work and other factors, including the fact that many members of the armed services were better off than they had been as civilians. International trade in food was disrupted, one of the main reasons why the USA had to introduce rationing.

Britain had the biggest strategic problem. In 1939, 60 per cent of her foodstuffs came from overseas and domestic agriculture had been neglected. The response was impressive. In 1939, County War Agricultural Executive Committees were set up to get as much land as possible immediately ploughed up and planted. The Ministry of Agriculture intensified its efforts to bring the latest techniques and equipment into use. A National Farm Survey was carried out in 1940, the first time since the 11th-century Doomsday Book that this had been done. Between 1939 and 1944, 6.5 million acres had been newly ploughed and the land lost 98,000 skilled men, who were replaced by 117,000 women (the Land Army). By 1944, there were over 175,000 tractors in Britain compared with 55,000 in 1939. Arable land has a much greater yield in terms of food than grassland devoted to animals so there were big changes in crops. Over the period 1934–8 to 1943–4 the number of poultry, sheep and pigs fell, though that of cattle increased. Wheat and potato tonnage increased by well over 100 per cent, oats and fruit production by well over 50 per cent (Ministry of Information, 1945). Increases in output were achieved mainly by additional resources of land and female labour and productivity growth was limited. The government's objective was output of food and not efficiency; probably given the increased use of machinery total factor productivity actually fell during the war. Home dwellers were urged to 'Dig for Victory' in their allotments and gardens.

Estimating the cost of the war for the combatants is very difficult and a distinction has to be made between the short-term and long-term costs. The latter in physical terms were probably of limited significance, though the human and spiritual costs are a different matter. Despite the short-term devastation, Germany emerged from the war with it economic potential largely intact. Japan, too, was much more industrialized at the end of the war than at the beginning and the American occupation can be said to have helped Japan post-war to modernize its institutions. Olson (1982) argues that for both Germany and Japan the strength of their post-war recovery can be explained by the destruction of accumulated institutional barriers to economic change and development (>INSTITUTIONS). Certainly the USA emerged from the war stronger than ever.

What is clear is that, however measured, the costs of the war varied considerably between the combatants. The various contributors to Harrison's book (1998) provide interesting material on war costs. Russia suffered most and Mark Harrison's chapter on that nation is entitled 'The Soviet Union: The Defeated Victor'. It is estimated that Russian 'excess mortality' 1941–5 was of the order of 27 million and that, of these premature deaths, 9 million were accounted for by the military. Some 25 per cent of physical assets and 18.5 per cent of human assets were destroyed in the war. Japan's overall national wealth, not including human capital, on one estimate, was reduced by 35 per cent by the end of the war, back to 1935 levels. Japan suffered 2 million military and 350,000 civilian losses. Italy came off quite lightly with 400,000 military losses; as mentioned, Italian military expenditure was the lowest of all the combatants and losses of civilian human and physical assets were relatively modest. Britain lost about 19 per cent of its physical assets but human losses were small compared with those of the Axis powers and causalities amounted to only 0.75 per cent of the 1938 population. The USA suffered very little physical damage and its military losses of 274,000 were less than Britain's 300,000.

Economic historians have speculated about the long-term economic impact of the war. One consequence already noted was an increase in the role of the state. In Europe in particular there was a major extension of the welfare state presaged in Britain by the appearance during the war of the Beverage Report (>BEVERIDGE), which proposed, among other things, a national minimum income, a National Health Service and guarantees for employment, all of which were to come to pass after the war, though not necessarily in the form proposed by Beveridge. It has been suggested that the example of mass-production in the USA may have promoted the adoption of American manufacturing techniques in other countries after the war. Certainly, post-war >PRODUCTIVITY growth was faster throughout Europe than it had been pre-war. Maddison (1982) attributes this to sustained higher levels of demand and the acceleration in the growth of the capital stock which higher demand stimulated. Also there were major shifts of employment out of agriculture and into manufacturing. European countries did not necessarily speed up technical advance in production processes but did reduce some of the lag behind the technology production frontier of the USA.

The war saw many important innovations. Radar, long-range bombers and the jet engine laid the basis for post-war civil >AVIATION. Developments in synthetic materials, medicine (including penicillin), in nuclear fission and many other fields were stimulated by the war. These developments, however, might well have been made anyway with the advance of science. The war may also have led to the deferral of research and development in non-war-related fields. Peter Howlett's contribution to Floud and Johnson (2004) points out that the long-term post-war impact of the war on female employment, which some historians have argued was important, may only have been transitory and was more the result of labour shortages than sustained changes in attitudes. Hugh Rockoff, on the other hand, says that in the USA, as a result of the war, it became accepted that fiscal policy could be used to maintain full employment and that macro-economic policy in general, including the later use of monetary policy, meant that the policy errors in the USA in the 1930s were not repeated (>CENTRAL BANKING).

The favourable impacts of the war mostly came some time after 1945.

The immediate result was devastation in Continental Europe. Many cities were in ruins, agricultural production was well down, much of manufacturing inoperative, transport and communications had broken down and there were severe shortages of raw materials, fuel and food, intensified by the exceptionally severe winter in 1946-7. Aldcroft (2001) says that by the end of the war there were more than 15 million displaced persons awaiting transfer from one country to another. Governments had large budget deficits and there were chronic shortages of foreign exchange for imports, particularly dollars. It was feared that after a short-lived restocking boom and as infrastructure was repaired, the falls in prices and output that occurred in 1920 after World War I would be repeated. There were also fears of a communist takeover. There was common agreement in Europe and America that the circumstances of the 1920s should be avoided and that the USA should help European governments to achieve this (Milward, 1977). The most lasting legacies of this period were the new European and international economic institutions that were created and the new spirit of international cooperation that would usher in a golden economic age which, after the Cold War, has lasted to this day.

## References

Aldcroft, Derek H., *The European Economy, 1914–2000*, Routledge, 2001.

Dear, I. C. B. and Foot, M. R. D. (eds), *The Oxford Companion to World War II*, Oxford University Press, 2005.

Edgerton, David, *Warfare State, Britain 1920–1970*, Cambridge University Press, 2006.

Floud, Roderick and Johnson, Paul, *The Cambridge Economic History of Modern Britain*, III, *Structural Change* and Growth 1939–2000, Cambridge University Press, 2004.

Harrison, Mark (ed.), *The Economics of World War II: Six Great Powers in International Comparison*, Cambridge University Press, 1998.

Maddison, Angus, *Phases of Capitalist Development*, Oxford University Press, 1982.

Maddison, Angus, *The World Economy: A Millennial Perspective*, OECD, 2001.

Milward, Alan S., *War Economy and Society 1939–1945*, University of California Press, 1977.

Ministry of Information, *Land at War*, HMSO, 1945.

Olson, Mancur, *The Rise and Decline of Nations: Economic Growth, Stagflation and Social Rigidities*, Yale University Press, 1982.

Taylor, A. J. P., *The Origins of the Second World War*, Hamish Hamilton, 1961.

# Author Index

Locators are generally to the first mention of specific works in each entry or otherwise to the list of references for that entry. Where works have multiple authors they are indexed by the first named. Irrespective of the dates of publication indicated in the text, dates in this index generally refer to the date of original publication in the English language. References are also given to authors whose works are not specifically included in the lists of references.

Aaron, Henry J.
  2004  484
Abramovitz, Moses
  1986  151
Abramovitz, Moses
  1996  170
Aftalion, Florin
  1990  204
Aisbet, Emma 2005  366
Aldcroft, Derek H.
  1964  196
Aldcroft, Derek H.
  1990  169
Aldcroft, Derek H.
  1994  532
Aldcroft, Derek H.
  1995  534
Aldcroft, Derek H.
  2001  536
Alford W.E. 1996  64, 532
Allen, G.C 1946  334
Allen, G.C. 1972  35
Allen, G.C. 1979  34
Allen, Robert C. 1999  11
Allen, Robert C. 2000  9,
  320, 352
Altshuler, Alan 1984  44
American Petroleum
  Institute 1959  345
Anderson, Michael
  1989  360
Anderson, Terry L.
  2004  25
Archer, John E.
  2000  301
Aristotle  507
Arrighi, Giovanni
  2003  36, 111
Ashley, James  155
Ashton, T.S. 1924  284
Ashton, T.S. 1948
  256, 471

Ashworth, William
  1987  381
Ashworth, William
  1994  120, 346
Asian Development Bank
  2005  366
Atack, Jeremy 1994  17,
  25, 239, 342, 404, 500
Auerbach, Paul 1988  287
Austen, Ralph A. 1987  461

Baack, Ben 2001  23
Backhouse, Roger E.
  2002  511
Backhouse, Roger E.
  2006  299
Badiane, Ousmane
  2002  146
Baines, D. 1991  322
Baines, D. 1992  234
Bairoch, Paul 1973  10
Bairoch, Paul 1993  10,
  149, 231, 1993
Balderston, Theo
  2002  522
Baldwin, Robert
  1999  386
Baldwin, Robert E.
  1971  435
Bannock, Graham
  1966  38
Bannock, Graham
  1971  41
Bannock, Graham
  1990  481
Bannock, Graham
  2005  37, 93, 130,
  198, 388
Baran, Paul 1957  161
Bardini, Carlo 1997  118
Barker, Randolph
  1985  398

Barker, Theo 1993  399
Barnett, Corelli
  1972  196
Barnett, Correlli
  1986  427
Barrell, Ray 2000  374
Barro, Robert J.
  1974  394
Barry, Frank 1999  526
Baskin, Jonathan Barron
  1997  87, 126
Bauer, Peter 2000  153
Baumol, William J.
  1994  375
Baumol, William J.
  2002  93, 150, 196,
  419, 504
Baxter, R.E. 1977  425
Bayoumi, T. 1996  228
Beard, Charles 1986  23
Bendix, Reinhard
  1960  513
Bennett, Arnold  516
Benson, John 1992  135
Berg, Maxine 1992
  261, 265
Berg, Maxine 1994
  378, 497
Berg, Maxine 2004  132
Berg, Maxine 2005
  133, 516
Berle, A.A. 1932  129
Berlin, Isaiah 1996
  317, 495
Bernanke, Ben S.
  2004  237
Beveridge, William
  1965  368
Beveridge, William H.
  1942  57
Beveridge, William H.
  1944  58

Bhagwati, Jagdish
  2004    220
Bhagwati, Jagdish
  2004    220, 365
Bhalla, S. 2003    366
Billington, Ray Allen
  1959    24
Blackburn, Robin
  1997    449
Blackford, Mansel G.
  453
Blair, John M. 1972    130
Blassinghame, J.W.
  1972    448
Blaug, Mark 1963    362
Blaug, Mark 1978    73,
  116, 235, 309, 395
Bodin, Jean 1576    223
Bogart, Dan 2005    401
Bogart, E.L. 1920    534
Boltho, Andrea 2001
  92, 139
Booth, Charles 1899    364
Borchardt, Knut
  1991    237, 368, 526
Bordo, Michael D.
  2005    215, 229
Boulding, Kenneth    194
Bowers, B. 1973    176
Bray, Francesca 1994    395
Brezis, Elise S. 1995    70
Broadberry, Stephen
  2003    67, 375
Broadberry, Stephen N.
  1998    376, 228
Broadberry, Stephen N.
  2005    531
Brookes, Graham
  2003    398
Brookes, Mary R.
  2004    425
Brown, David 2000    351
Brown, Jonathan
  1993    79, 197
Brown, Richard 1905    4
Brunt, Liam 2002    9
Brunt, Liam 2004    11
Buchanan, James
  388, 469
Buck, Trevor 2000    141
Bulliet, Richard W.
  1998    405
Bulmer-Thomas, Victor
  1994    122, 232
Burdon I. 2000    176

Burnett, John 1994    189
Burns, Arthur, F.
  1946    72
Burt S. 1993    136
Byatt, I.C.R. 1979    173

Cain, P.J. 1993    162
Cairncross, Alexander
  1994    68
Cairnes, J.E. 1874    116
Cameron, Rondo
  1991    330
Cameron, Rondo
  1993    381, 532
Cantillon, Richard
  194, 352
Capie, Forrest 1994    74,
  94, 280
Card, David 2004    69
Carlyle, Thomas
  1849    116
Carlyle, Thomas    446
Carnevali, Francesca
  2004    255
Carreras, Albert
  2006    521
Carrington, C.E.
  1950    160
Casson, Mark 1982    195
Central Banking
  Publications 2005a    94
Central Banking
  Publications
  2005b    102
Chamberlin, E.H.    30
Chandler, Alfred
  1956    102
Chandler, Alfred
  1971    102
Chandler, Alfred D.
  1962    102
Chandler, Alfred D.
  1977    102
Chandler, Alfred D.
  1989    79, 103, 286
Chandler, Alfred D.
  1990    197
Chandler, Alfred D.
  1997    103
Chandler, Alfred D.
  2002    102, 177
Chandler, Alfred D.
  2005    102, 335
Chandra, Siddharth
  1999    475

Charlesworth, George
  1984    403
Chartres, J.    1992    82
Chaudhuri, K.N.
  1978    191
Cheffins, Brian R.
  2001    140
Chen, S. 2000    366
Chernow, Ron 2004    238
Chisholm, George C.
  1922    347
Chiswick, Barry R.
  1994    325
Chown, John 1994
  326, 508
Church, Roy 1990    78,
  103, 197
Church, Roy 1993
  103, 197
Cipolla, Carlo M.
  1973    221
Cipolla, M. 1978    361
Clapham, J.H. 1926    243
Clapham, J.H. 1929    155
Clapham, J.H. 1930    132,
  351, 401
Clarence-Smith, William
  Gervaise 2003    123
Clark, Christine 1998    52
Clark, Colin 1940    408
Clark, Gregory 1998    268
Clark, Gregory 2001    9, 60
Clark, Gregory 2003    436
Clark, J.B.    30
Clark, Tom 2004    480, 538
Clavin, Patricia
  2000    232
Clemence, Richard V.
  1951    419
Clemens, Michael A.
  2001    280
Cliometric Society
  1994    157
Coase, Ronald    156
Cohen, Benjamin J.
  1998    334
Cohen, David J.
  2000    102
Cole, Arthur 1964    368
Coleman, D.C. 1977 189,
  191, 358, 369
Coleman, D.C. 1983    378
Coleman, D.C. 1992    261
Coleman, Olive    399
Colli, Andrea 2003    452

Collins, Michael
  1998  332
Coman, Katharine
  1912  28
Commission of the
  European Communities
  2008  185
Competition Commission
  2000  136
Condorcet, Marquis
  de  306
Congdon, Tim 2004  100
Conrad, Alfred 1958  448
Conrad, Alfred 1961  500
Corey, B. 1980  176
Corley, T.A.B. 1993  194
Cottereau, Alain
  1977  438
Cottrell, P.L. 1992  444
Cournot, Augustine  30
Cox, Michael 1999  365
Crafts, N.F.R. 2000
  262, 263
Crafts, N.F.R. 1977  29
Crafts, N.F.R. 1991
  214, 263
Crafts, N.F.R. 1993  427
Crafts, N.F.R. 1994
  70, 260
Crafts, N.F.R. 1995  373
Crafts, N.F.R. 1996  312
Crafts, N.F.R. 2004
  150, 473
Crafts, N.F.R. 2007  428
Crouzet, François
  1993  51
Crouzet, François
  1996  263
Crouzet, François
  2001  160, 259, 263, 519
Cunningham, Hugh
  2000  186
Cunningham,
  William  155
Currie, R. 1965  492
Cyert, R.M. 1996  288
Cypher, James M.
  2004  337, 408

Daniel, J. 2005  465
Darwin, Charles  273
David, Paul A. 1974  448
David, Paul A. 1976  448
David, Paul A. 2003  374
Davies, Andrew 1994  490

Davies, Norman 1996  204
Davies, R.W. 1994  199,
  231, 386, 413
Davies, R.W. 1998  417
Davis, Dorothy 1966  132
Davis, John A. 2006  519
Davis, L.E. 1986  163
Dawe, David 2005  398
Dawidoff, Nicholas
  2002  214
Dawson, Virginia P.
  1995  292
Deane, Phyllis 1969
  262, 286
Deane, Phyllis 1978  115,
  234, 320, 392, 460
Dear, I.C.B. 2005  541
Deaton, Angus 2003  367
Defoe, Daniel  77
Delfino, Susanna
  2005  506
Deng, Kent G. 2000  108
Denison, Edward F.
  1974  150
Desai, Meghnad
  1994  318
DeSoto, Hernando
  1989  153
DeSoto, Hernando
  2000  153
Devereux, Roy 1936  401
Dewhurst, Frederic J.
  1961  477
Dickens, Charles  266
Digby, Anne 1989  361
Digby, Anne 1992  497
Dimson, Elroy 2002  84
Dixon, Chris 1991  36
Doremus, Paul N.
  1998  337
Dormois, Jean-Pierre
  2004  163
Dow, Christopher 1998  73
Drucker, Peter 1946  38
Drucker, Peter 1973
  75, 486
Drucker, Peter 1994  485
Drucker, Peter  92
Drukker, J.W. 2006  150
Dumett, Raymond E.
  1999  163
Dye, Alan 1998  477
Dye, Alan 2004  477

Ebenstein, Alan 2001  244

Ebenstein, Lanny
  2007  205
Edelstein, Michael
  1994  65, 159
Edgerton, David 1991  49
Edgeworth, F.Y. 1887  368
Edwards, Jeremy
  1996  332
Eichengreen, Barry
  1992  236, 312
Eichengreen, Barry
  1994  227
Eichengreen, Barry
  1985  227
Elkins, Stanley 1959  449
Eltis, David 1993  447
Eltis, David 2000  449
Elvin, Mark 1973  112
Engels, Frederick
  1845  260
Engels, Frederick  314
Engerman, Stanley
  2000  503
Engerman, Stanley
  2005  500
Erhard, Ludwig 1958  35
Estaban, Javier Cuenca
  1997  144, 261
Estaban, Javier Cuenca
  1999  144
European Trade Union
  Confederation
  2001  496
Ewart, Ulf Christian
  2006  29

Falkus, M.E. 1967  210
FAO 1998  395
FAO 2008  14, 395
Faulkner, Harold
  Underwood 1960  17,
  35, 124, 137, 238, 341
Federer, J. Peter
  1994  233
Feinstein, Charles H.
  1997  522
Feinstein, Charles H.
  2005  461
Feltwell, John 1990  438
Fernie, Sue 2005  493
Ferrero, Guglielmo
  1919  215
Ferry,Georgina 2003  182
Findlay, Ronald
  2003  432

Findlay, Ronald
2005   279
Fischer, David Hackett
1997   370
Fisher, Irving 1922   368
Flandreau, Marc 1996
59 226
Flandreau, Marc 2004   59
Floud, Roderick,
1976   304
Floud, Roderick, 1990   29
Floud, Roderick 1994   83,
143, 169, 230, 260, 364,
378, 426, 497, 529, 538
Floud, Roderick 2004
54, 289
Floud, Roderick
2004a   478
Floud Roderick,
2004b   429
Floud, Roderick
2004c   480
Flynn, Dennis O.
2004   215,
Fogel, R.W. 1957   156
Fogel, Robert 1972   25
Fogel, Robert W.
1964   385, 399
Fogel, Robert W. 1977   448
Fogel, Robert W.
1995   82, 385
Fogel, Robert William
1974   448
Fogel, Robert William
1989   448
Fontaine, Laurence
1996   351
Fontana, Luigi 2006   520
Ford, Henry 1923   202
Ford, P. 1936   135
Foreman-Peck J.S.
1985   195
Foreman-Peck, James
1983   162
Foreman-Peck James
1994   275
Foreman-Peck, James
1995   44, 230, 322,
361, 450
Forester, Tom 1981   178
Forster, E.M.   294
Francks, Penelope
1999   439
Frank, Zephyr L.
2001   162

French, Michael
1977   28, 506
Freyer, Tony A. 2006   32
Friedman, David
1988   470
Friedman, Milton,
1946   204
Friedman, Milton
1956   206
Friedman, Milton
1957   206
Friedman, Milton
1959   207
Friedman, Milton
1962   114, 205
Friedman, Milton
1963   207, 235
Frisch, Helmut
1981   421
Fritz, Martin 2005   539
Fuchs, Victor R.
1968   429

Galbraith, J.K. 1967   510
Galbraith, J.K.
1987   510
Galbraith, J.K.   90,
273, 419
Gale, W.K.V. 1967   282
Galli, Giampaolo
2000   33, 390, 526
Gapinski, James M.
1991   38
Gardiner, Robert
1993   431
Gardiner, Robert
1995   191
Garnaut, Ross 2005   110
Gatrell, Peter 1993   535
Geiger, Reed G. 1994   82
Gelb, Stephen 2005
465, 466
Gerschenkron, Alexander
1943   213
Gerschenkron, Alexander
1962   214, 417
Gerschenkron, Alexander
1965   417
Gerschenkron, Alexander
1968   214
Gerschenkron, Alexander
1970   215
Gershuny, J.I. 1983   429
Gibson, Andrew
2001   121, 434

Gilbert, Geoffrey
2004   309
Gimpel, Jean 1976   265
Glahn, Richard von
1996   443
Godwin, William 306
Gold Commision
1982   224
Goldin, Claudia 1973   16
Goldin, Claudia 1975   16
Goldin, Claudia 2001   167
Goldin, Claudia
2007   271
Golley, John 1987   290
Gordon, Jordan
1988   529
Goodall, Francis
1993   211
Goodman, Edward
1989   255
Goodman, Jordan
1988   146, 176
Goodwin, Craufurd D.
2006   295
Gourvish, T.R. 1994   56
Gramm, Marshall
2004   445
Grandin, Karl 2004   506
Gregory, Paul R.
1982   410
Gregory, Paul R.
1994   414
Griliches, Z.   374
Grubb, Farley 1994   325
Guiso, Luigi 2008   186

Hacker, Louis 1940   17
Halley, Mike 2005   182
Hammon, Peter 1984   419
Hammond, J.L. 1926   124
Hammond, J.L.
1917   186, 242
Hammond, J.L. 1919   242
Hammond, J.L. 1925   242
Hanes, Christopher
1996   449
Hannah, Leslie 1976   130
Hannah, Leslie 1977
137, 130
Hannah, Leslie 1991   197
Hannah, Leslie 1994   176
Hannah, Leslie 2007
84, 103
Harley, C. Knick
1980   437

Harley, C. Knick
    1988    437
Harley, C. Knick
    1994    63, 125
Harley, C. Knick
    1998    144
Harley, Charles K.
    1971    437
Harper, Lawrence, A.    19
Harris, Ron 1997    129
Harris, Ron 2004    478
Harris, Seymour E.
    1961    498
Harrison, D.F.    399
Harrison, Mark 1998    536
Hartwell, Ronald Max
    1977    90
Hatton, Timothy, J.
    1994a    325
Hatton, Timothy J.
    1994b    325
Hatton, Timothy, J.
    1998    326
Hatton, Timothy J.
    2004    325
Hawkins, K.H. 1979    56
Hayek, Friedrich
    1972    245
Hayek, Friedrich
    1978    245
Hayward, Keith 1989    49
Heckscher, Eli F.
    1955    321
Heertje, Arnold 1981    419
Heilbroner, Robert
    1977    500
Hejeebu Santhi 2005    193
Herodotus    221
Herrigel, Gary 1996    254
Hicks, J.R. 1950    73
Higgs, Henry 1897    352
Higman, B.W. 2000    477
Hilferding, Rudolf
    1910    331
Hill, C.P. 1957    400, 479
Hilt, Eric 2008    143
Himmelberg, Robert F.
    2001    339
Hirschman, Albert    152
Hirschmeier, Johannes
    1975    128
HMSO 1965    67
Hobsbaum, J.    260
Hobson, J.A.    161

Hodgson, Geoffrey M.
    2001    510
Hollander, Jacob H.
    1910    395
Horn, Jeff 2006    263
Horrell, Sara 1995    184
Hoselitz, B.F. 1968    378
Hossain, Mahabub
    2005    397, 397
Houghton, D. 1967    466
Howlett, Peter 2004    541
Hoynes, Hilary 2005    364
Hudson, Pat 1992    262,
    284, 379
Hughes, Thomas P.
    1993    172
Hurst, James Willard
    1970    128
Huxley, Thomas    446

Inikori, Joseph E.
    1981    449
International Energy
    Agency (IEA)
    1982    174, 212, 346
International Energy
    Agency (IEA)
    2000    118, 174
International Labour
    Organization 1995    449
International Labour
    Organization
    1998    449
International Labour
    Organization (ILO)
    2007    188
International Labour
    Organization (ILO)
    2008    185
International Monetary
    Fund (IMF) 2007    371
International Rice Research
    Institute 1998    398
Irwin, Douglas
    2001    144, 240
Ishii, Kanji 1991    333
Issing, Otmar 2004    102

James, John A. 1994    262
James, Lawrence
    1997    193, 253
Jantti, Markus 2006    268
Jefferys, J.B. 1954    132
Jenkins, David 2001
    146, 529

Jevons, William
    Stanley    155
Jevons, William Stanley
    1871    116
Jewkes, John 1969    451
Johnson, H. Thomas
    1987    6
Johnson, Paul 1994    58
Jones, D.T. 1979    306
Jones, Eric 1993    37, 199
Jones, Eric 2003    272
Jones, Glyn 1989    290
Jones, J. 2003    176
Jones, Richard    273

Kadish, Alon 1989    156
Kadish, Alon 1996    63
Kahn, Haider, A.    38
Kanigel, Robert
    1997    486
Kenney, Elinor M.
    1955    310
Kenwood, A.G. 1992    59,
    274, 361, 475
Keynes, John Maynard
    1913    296
Keynes, John Maynard
    1919    296
Keynes, John Maynard
    1920    296, 534
Keynes, John Maynard
    1921    294
Keynes, John Maynard
    1923    296
Keynes, John Maynard
    1930    297
Keynes, John Maynard
    1931    295
Keynes, John Maynard
    1936    117, 234, 245, 297
Keynes, John Maynard
    1939    537
Keynes, John Neville
    1884    294
Keynes, John Neville
    1891    205, 294
Kindleberger, Charles P.
    1984    86, 127, 508
Kindleberger, Charles P.
    1996    71, 232
King, Stephen 2003    367
King, Steve 1997
    358, 367
King, Steven 2001
    263, 379

Kirby, Maurice 1994    77,
    139, 452
Kirzner, I.M.    195
Kitchen, Joseph 1923    72
Knies, Karl    155, 512
Knight, Frank 1921    195
Knowles, John 1998    29
Knowles, L.C.A.
    1921    158
Knowles, L.C.A.
    1930    124
Knowles, L.C.A.    156
Komlos, John 1993    361
Komlos, John 1998    29
Komlos, John 1999    361
Komlos, John 2003    351
Kondratief, Nikolai D.
    1935    72
Kroos, Herman E.
    1974    128
Krozewski, Gerald
    1993    164
Krugman, Paul 1994    37
Kunz, Andreas 1995    82
Kuznets, Simon
    1955    161, 367
Kuznets, Simon S.
    1961    72

Landes, David 1998    149,
    164, 173, 190, 251,
    349, 398
Landes, David S.
    1969    289, 471
Laspeyres, E. 1864    368
Law, Marc T. 2005    388
Layard, R. 1980    497
Lazonick, William
    1993    104
Lazonick, William
    1997    104
Leary, William M.
    1995    48, 292
Lecuyer, Christopher
    2006    183
Lee, Clive 1994    426
Lee, Robert 2002    421
Leibenstein H.L.    195
Lenin, Vladimir
    1915    161
Leslie, Thomas Edward
    Cliffe    155
Leunig, Timothy
    2003    29

Levinson, Marc
    2006    425, 437
Levitt, Theodore
    1983    215
Levy, David M.
    2002    116
Lewchuk, Wayne
    1987    44
Lewin, Bryan 2004    123
Lewis, Arthur    151–2
Licht, W. 1995    176, 240,
    332, 378
Lilley, S. 1973    176, 432
Lindahl-Kiessling, Kerstin
    1994    309
Lindert, Peter 1982    410
Lindert, Peter H.
    1994    356
Lindert, Peter H.
    1998    357
Lindert, Peter H.
    2004    466
Lipton, Merle 1985    466
List, Friedrich 1841    277
Lopokova, Lydia    296
Luxemburg, Rosa    161

Ma, Debin 2008    110
Macfarlane, Alan
    1978    262
Machlup, Fritz
    1977    245
Maddison, Angus
    1982    538
Maddison, Angus
    1991    467
Maddison, Angus
    1995    147, 121, 232,
    274, 346, 371, 413,
    422, 533
Maddison, Angus
    2001    36, 148, 157, 372,
    501, 520, 542
Maddison, Angus
    2002    38
Maddison, Angus
    2003    62, 168, 252
Maddison, Angus
    2007a    107, 426,
    506, 522
Maddison, Angus
    2008    107
Madsen, Axel 1999    41
Madsen, Jacob B.
    2001    13

Mahmoud, Abdel-
    Fadil    346
Malthus, Thomas Robert
    1798 (1803)    306
Malthus, Thomas Robert
    1820    306
Malthus, Thomas,
    Robert    149, 199
Malynes, Gerald de    318
Mandeville, Bernard de
    1705    320
Marland, E.A. 1973    176
Marshall, Alfred
    1890    116, 135
Marshall, Alfred
    1919    254
Marshall, Alfred    30, 58,
    155, 194, 294,
    364, 512
Marx, Karl 1848    89
Matchschoss, C.
    1939    471
Mathias, Peter 1959    56
Mathias, Peter 1976    479
Mathias, Peter 1983    262
Matthews, Derek 1997    5
Matthews, Derek 2006    6
McCloskey, Donald
    1994    61
McCloskey, Donald M.
    1971    196, 437
McCraw, Thomas K.
    1998    179, 202
McCraw, Thomas K.
    2007    418
Meek, Ronald L.
    2003    356
Mendels, Franklin F.
    1972    377
Menger, Carl    155, 245,
    512
Menger, Carl 1874    116
Meunier, Jacob 2002    386
Meyer, David R.
    2003    499
Mill, John Stuart
    1848    116, 507
Miller, Ronald 1968
    49, 293
Millward, Robert
    1991    210
Millward, Robert
    1997    67
Milward, Alan S.
    1997    536

Milward, Alan, S.
1984  309, 535
Minchinton, W.
1973  476
Mingay, G.E. 1956  8
Mingay, G.E. 1997  189
Min-Hsiung, Shi
1976  439
Ministry of Information
1945  540
Mises, Ludwig von  245
Mitchell, Duncan G.  272
Moehling, Carolyn M.
2005  187
Mofford, Juliet H.
1997  186
Moggridge, D.E. 1992  294
Mokyr, Joel 1985  282
Mokyr, Joel 1990  284
Mokyr, Joel 1993  146
Mokyr, Joel 1994  70
Mokyr, Joel 1999  133,
259, 374
Mokyr, Joel 2002  199
Mokyr, Joel 2005  168
Moon, David 1999  409
Moore, G.E.  294
Morck, Randall K.
2005  140
Morgan, E. Victor 1965  3
Morrell, W.P., 1968  225
Morris, Jonathan,
1999  137
Moselle, Boaz 1995  189
Moses, Leon N. 1989  48
Mowery, David C.  183
Mowery, David C.
1991  181
Mowery, David C.
1998  177
Mowery, David C.
2000  503
Mun, Thomas  319
Mundell, Robert A.
1997  226, 371
Musgrave, A.  469
Myrdal, Gunnar
1974  253
Myrdal, Gunnar  273

Nader, Ralph  43
National Ports Council
1976  424
Neal, Larry 2007  526

Needham, Joseph  106
Nelson, B.N. 1949  508
Nelson, Richard R.
1993  504
Netzer, Dick 1977  483
Nishimura, Kiyohiko G.
2001  138
Noam, Eli 1992  487
North, Douglass C.
1961  502
North, Douglass C.
1990  125, 272
Notteboom, Theo E.
2004  424
Nove, Alec 1992  120,
173, 199, 412
Nurkse, Ragnar  152
Nye, R.B. 1965  82

O'Brien, D.P.O. 1975
118, 460
O'Brien, Patrick K.  163
O'Donoghue, Jim
2004  370
O'Grada, Cormac
1993  281
O'Grada, Cormac
1999  282
O'Rourke, Kevin H.
1994  217
O'Rourke, Kevin H.
1997  168, 221, 230
O'Rourke, Kevin H.
2001  274
O'Rourke, Kevin H.
2002  221
Obstfeld, Maurice
2004  86
Odell, Peter R. 2005  347
Odlyzko, Andrew
2004  81
OECD 1996  496
OECD 2006  417
OECD 2007  361
OECD 2008  70
Offer, Avner 1993  163
Offer, Avner 2001  470
Ogilvie, Sheilagh
2003  519
Ohlin, Bertil 1933  216
Okun, A.M. 1980  268
Oldcastle, Hugh  3
Olmstead, Alan L.
2002  10

Olmstead, Alan L.
2008  146
Olson, Mancur 1982  27,
408, 540
Olson, Mancur  273
Overton, Mark 1996  11
Overy, R.J. 1996  523

Pacioli, Luca  3
Palmer, Bryan D.
1994  491
Palmer, Sarah 1985  432
Pareto, Vilfredo  513
Parker, Randall E.  234
Parker, William N.
1996  264
Parsons, Talcott  512
Pattillo, Donald M.
1998  46
Peck, Merton J. 1961  501
Persson, Karl Gunnar
2004  437
Phelps Brown, E.H.
1958  368
Philips,C.H. 1940  192
Phillips, A.W.H. 1958  206
Phillips, Ulrich Bonnel
1918  448
Pigou A.C. 1913  234
Pinker, Susan 2008  188
Piore, Michael J.
1984  112, 254, 451
Polanyi, Karl 1944  93, 390
Political and Economic
Planning (PEP)
1950  40
Pollard, Sidney 1981  82,
146, 262, 265, 275, 378,
380, 383, 520
Pollard, Sidney 1992  289
Pollard, Sidney 1994  232
Pomeranz, Kenneth
2000  111, 154,
162, 471
Porter, Michael E.
1990  183
Porter, Roy 1994  386
Porter, Roy 2000
122, 425
Powelson, John P.
1994  106, 153
Prais, S.J. 1976  130
Prebisch, Raul  152
Purvis, Martin 1992  134

Quesnay, François  352
Quinn, Stephen
  1996  443

Ransom, Roger L.
  1988  449
Redish, Angela 1995  59
Reilly, Robin 1992  518
Ricardo, David 1817  392
Richardson, Philip
  1999  106
Richmond, Lesley
  1990  52
Rinaldi, Alberto
  2005  256
Ringe, Astrid 2000  68
Ritschl, Albrecht
  1998  233
Robbins, L. 1971  57,
  235, 297
Robbins, Lionel
  1940  161
Robbins, Lionel
  1963  279
Robbins, Lionel  246
Roberts, Benjamin
  2005  465
Robinson, Joan  30
Robinson, Ronald
  1953  160
Rockoff, Hugh 1995  444
Rodrik, Dani 2004  251
Roe, Mark J. 1994  141, 505
Rogers, Thorold  155
Roll, Eric 1973  115, 460
Rolt, L.T.C. 1965  302
Romer, Christina D.
  1994  72
Romer, Paul 1986  373
Romer, Paul 1994  151
Roscher, Wilhelm  155
Rose, M.E. 1992
  364, 367
Rose, Mary B. 1994  78
Rose, Mary B. 1996  146
Roseberry, William
  1995  123
Rosener, Werner
  1994  349, 410
Rostow, W.W. 1960
  386, 407
Rostow, W.W. 1975  408
Rostow, W.W. 2003  406
Rothermund, Dietmar
  1993  250

Rowntree, Seebohm
  1901  364
Roy, Tirhankar 2006  253
Royal Commission
  1980  269
Royle, E. 1989  106
Rubenstein, James M.
  2001  44
Rubenstein, W.D.
  1993  78, 196
Rule, J. 1992  301, 497
Ruskin, John  446

Sabel, Charles F.
  1997  254, 304, 438
Sala-i-Martin, X.
  2002  272, 366
Sampson, Anthony
  1962  196
Samuelson, Paul
  1948  216
Sandberg, L.G. 1982  168
Sarachek, Bernard
  1978  198
Saul, S.B. 1960  251
Sawers, Larry 1992  19
Say, Jean Baptist  194
Schatzberg, Eric 1999  49
Schlesinger, Arthur
  1961  498
Schmitz, Christopher J.
  1993  35, 383
Schmoller, von-,
  Gustav  155
Schnabel, Isabel
  2004  233
Schneider, Michael
  1991  494
Schofield, Roger
  1994  62
Schumpeter, Joseph A.
  1911  418
Schumpeter, Joseph A.
  1919  195
Schumpeter, Joseph A.
  1939  74, 419
Schumpeter, Joseph A.
  1942  418
Schumpeter, Joseph A.
  1943  197
Schumpeter, Joseph A.
  1952  418
Schumpeter, Joseph A.
  1954  71, 118, 309, 353,
  418, 460

Schumpeter, Joseph A.
  88, 130
Scott, John 1986 91
Scranton 1997  254, 451
Seidl, Christian
  1984  419
Seltzer, Lawrence, H.
  1928  39, 202
Sengenberger, W.
  1990  450
Senior, Naussau William
  1951 361
Servan-Schreiber, J.J.
  1968  40, 337
Shakespeare,
  William  507
Shannon, H.A. 1954  129
Shaw, Ronald E. 1990  82
Shinohara, Miyohei
  1968  378
Shorrocks, Anthony
  2006  271
Siegler, Mark 1998  73
Sinha, Sanjay 1990  439
Skidelsky, Robert
  1983  299
Skidelsky, Robert
  1992  299
Skidelsky, Robert
  2000  299
Skidelsky, Robert
  2003  299
Skinner, William
  1985  106
Skoczlas, Les 2005  374
Slade, Margaret 1998  56
Sloan, Alfred P. 1963  42
Smith, Adam 1759  454
Smith, Adam 1776  70,
  80, 113, 149, 167, 205,
  215, 274, 318, 352, 365,
  391, 426, 453, 467, 507
Snooks, Graeme Donald
  1993  149
Snyder, Françis C.
  1987  497
Solar, Peter M. 1997  358
Solomou, Solomos
  1988  71
Solomou, Solomos
  1999  75
Solow, Robert  374
Sombart, Werner  515
Spencer, Herbert  446
Spychalski, John C.  405

Stampp, Kenneth M.
  1956   448
Stearns, Peter N.
  1993   264
Steckel, Richard H.
  1998   29
Stein, Stanley J.
  2000   442
Stelzer, Irwin M.
  2001   387
Sterling, Christopher, H.
  2006   491
Stern,David 1996   169
Storaci, M. 1998   176
Storey, David J. 1994   195
Strachey, Litton   294
Streeck, Wolfgang
  2001   92 141
Studwell, Joe 2005   470
Supple, Barry 1973   320
Supple, Barry 1994   69
Sutherland, D.M.G.
  2002   349
Swedberg, Richard
  1991   418, 512
Sylla, Richard 1991   215
Sylla, Richard 2002   87
Szostak, R. 1991   82
Szreter, Simon 1998   71

Tanzi, V. 2000   466
Taylor, A.J.P. 1961   535
Taylor, Alan M. 1997   326
Taylor, Frederick W.
  1912   486
Teich, Mikulas 1996   263
Temin, Peter 1991   237
Temin, Peter 1997   261
Teske, Paul 2004   33, 388
Thomas, O.O. 1968   429
Thomas, Robert 1965   19
Thompson, E.P.
  1963   492
Thompson, E.P.   260
Thompson, F.M.L.
  2001   196, 427
Thompson, Grahame
  1994   137
Thornton, Henry
  1802   115
Tinbergen, Jan   73
Tomlinson, B.R.
  1996   250
Toms, Steven 2005   143
Torrens, Robert   307

Tortella, Gabriel
  1994   167
Toynbee, Arnold
  1884   263
Toynbee, Arnold   260
Tremblay, Carol Horton
  2005   55
Trevelyn, G.M., 1952   349
Trimble, William F.
  1995   45
Tullock, Gordon 388
Tunzelmann, G.N.
  1978   474
Turner, F.J. 1893   24, 28

Ulman, Lloyd 1961   502
UNCTAD 2000   436
UNCTAD 2004   338
United Nations 2000   10
United Nations 2004   80

Veblin, Thorstein Bunde
  1899   509
Veblin, Thorstein Bunde
  1921   510
Veblin, Thorstein
  Bunde   273
Vernon J.R. 1994   237
Ville, Simon P. 1994   82,
  383, 437
Visser, Jelle 1996   494
Vittorio, Antonio Di
  2006   519
Vonyo, Tamas 2008   524
Voth, Hans Joachim
  1998   268

Wallis, John Joseph
  1998   341
Walras, Leon 1874   116
Walton, Gary M. 1971   19
Wang, Yueping
  2002   111
Warr, Peter 2000   367
Watts, Steven 2005   202
Webb, Beatrice   260
Webb, Sidney   260, 358
Weber, Marianne
  1975   515
Weber, Max 1927   326,
  481, 508
Weber, Max 1930   515
Weber, Max   3, 88
Webster, Anthony
  2006   192

Westwood, J.N.
  1994   386
Whaples, Robert
  1995   385
Wheatcroft, Stephen
  1956   47
Wheatley, Jefferey J.
  1999   491
White, Eugene N.
  2004   479, 484
Whitehead, Alfred North
  1925   503
Whittle, Frank 1953   293
Wiener, Martin J.
  1981   196, 427
Wieser, Friedrich
  von   245
Wilkins, Mira 2005   335
Williams, Chris
  1995   493, 497
Williams, Eric 1944   162
Williamson, Edwin
  1992   122,
  442, 474
Williamson, Jeffrey G.
  1996   218
Williamson, Jeffrey G.
  2002   219
Williamson, Oliver   156
Wilson, John F. 1995   77,
  129, 329
Wilson, Ted 2000   59
Winch, David 1987
  237, 309
Winch, Donald
  1973   322, 460
Winstanley, Michael
  1994   134
Womack, James
  1990   42
Woods, Robert 1992   282
Woolf, Virginia   295
World Bank 1993   36
World Bank 2003
  165, 273
World Bank 2005   276,
  425, 470
World Bank 2006   253
World Bank 2008   253
World Trade Organization
  2001   274
Wright Mills, C.
  1953   510
Wright, Gavin 1978   449
Wrigley, C. 1992   493

Wrigley, C. 2007   495
Wrigley, E.A. 1989   361
Wrigley, E.A. 2006   71
Wrigley, N. 1989   136
Wrigley, N. 1989   136

Xenophon   429

Yamamoto, Hirofumi 1993   51, 405
Yates, Lamartine P., 1959   124, 232, 280,
   344, 475, 529
Yergin, Daniel 1992   212, 345, 535

Zamagni, Vera 1993   519
Zeitlin, Jonathan, 1997   304

# Subject Index

This Index gives selective source locations for topics but excludes references to authors, except those covered in main entries. It excludes references to companies and political figures. Main entry titles are given in bold type.

**Accounting, 3**
double-entry
bookkeeping, 3
exceptional number
of accountants in
Britain, 5
inflation and
standards, 7
Africa *see* **South Africa**
'Scramble for' 159
Zimbabwe, 165
**Agricultural Revolution,
8**, 60–1
**Agriculture, 11**
proportion of the
population in, 11; -in
Europe, 519; -in the
Great Depression,
13; in India, 249; -in
World War II 13, 17,
539
Air Mail, 45
**American War of
Independence, 17**
**American Civil War, 15**
American Revolution, 18
American System of
manufactures *see*
**Machine Tools**
**American Westward
Movement, 23;** *see
also* **United States**
Amsterdam Stock
Exchange, 87
Anti-bellum, 500
**Anthropometric
History, 28**
**Anti-Trust, 29**
brewing industry in, 55
Clayton Act, 32
Glass-Steagal Act, 32, 330
electronics, 180
in retailing, 135–6

Standard Oil case, 343
Robinson-Patman
Act, 136
Sherman Anti-Trust
Act, 31, 33, 503
telecommunications,
in, 489
used against unions, 495
Argentina, 230, 231
Arkwright, Richard,
144, 257
**Asian Miracle, 35** *see also*
**China,** Japan
Asian banking crisis, 334
Australasia
economic
development, 148
industrialization, 264
major world supplier of
wool, 528
automation, 305
**Automobile Industry, 38**
**Aviation, 44**

Backwardness *see*
**Gerschenkron,
Alexander**
Bank for International
Settlements (BIS) 94
Bank of Amsterdam, 327
Bank of England, 94–6,
101, 113–15, 126,
234, 236, 330
Bank of Japan (BoJ) 101
Barber, John, 290
Baumol Effect, 372, 426
**Beer, 52**
Belgium
Industrial Revolution,
264, 520
poor relief, 357
railways, 382
Bell, Alexander, 489

Belle Epoque, 521
Bentley, Thomas, 517
Benz, Karl, 39
Berle, Adolf A., 339
Berners-Lee, Tim, 183
Bessemer, Henry, 285
**Beveridge, William
Henry, 56**
**Bi-metallic System, 58**
Black Death, 348, 369
Blanchard, Thomas, 303
Blenkinson, John, 380
Boston Route 128, 180
Boston Tea Party, 20
Boulton, Matthew, 257,
471–2
Bramah, Joseph, 303
Bretton Woods, 225, 279,
298–9
**Britain, 59;**
**Agricultural Revolution**
in, 8 *et seq;* Aircraft
industry, 44 *et seq;*
Anti-Trust in, 33–4;
banks, 328–30;
banking crisis, 69–70;
British Empire,
64, 65, 159–60 (*see
also* **Economic
Imperialism**);
Consumer credit Act,
508; corn laws, 63;
de-industrialization
debate, 427; domestic
servants in 19th
century, 427;
educational levels,
69; education and
economic growth,
168–9; electrification
of, 173–4; electronics,
British innovation
in, 179;

**Britain, 59** – *continued*
and European Monetary
System, 526; foreign
exchange crises and
'Stop-Go, 67; GDP
per capita surpassed
by France, Germany
and Japan from, 1967,
68; Gold standard,
226; importer of
wheat, largest, 230;
in Great Depression,
233, 234; industrial
revolution, 60–1
(*see also* **Industrial
Revolution in
Britain**); industrial
lead eroded after, 1913
65; labour relations,
69; productivity,
68–9; machine tool
industry, 302–4;
multinational
companies, 337;
nationalization of
coal industry, 120;
National Plan, 387;
North Sea Oil, 427;
nuclear energy,
175; perceived
entrepreneurial
failure, 196;
privatization, 387;
population, 60, 62;
position in world
trade, 63–4, 68;
railways, 380–2;
regulation, 386–7,
389; Selective
Employment Tax,
426; silver coinage,
441, 443; sixteen years
of uninterrupted
growth after, 1991;
slavery, abolition of,
446; steel industry,
282, 284–5, 286,
288; suspension
of convertibility,
1797, 114, 223;
telecommunications,
487–8; trade unions,
493–4
Brunel, I.K. 431
Bubble Act, 126–7

Bullion Controversy
*see* **Money and
Banking**
Bundesbank, 96
**Business Cycles, 71**
Hayek on, 245
Business History, 156
**Business Management, 75**
styles of management, 76
contribution of
railways to
development of, 77
'scientific management'
78; *see also* **Taylor,
Frederick W.**
influence of family
ownership, 78; *see
also* **Chandler;
Alfred**

Callan, Nicholas, 171
Calvinism, 514
Canada, 21–2
as supplier of wheat,
230, 231
industrialization, 264
**Canals, 80,**
'canal mania'80
in Britain, 81
in industrial
revolution, 82
in USA 81
**Capital Markets, 82**
**Capitalism, 88**
accounting as key
to, 3
competitive
managerial –, 197
cooperative
managerial –, 197
definition of, 88
personal –, 197
Weber's view of,
513–4
Cartwright, Edmund, 144
Census of population,
first in, 1790 in
US, 360
**Central Banking, 93**
**Chandler, 102**
Chappe, Claude, 486
Chartered companies *see*
**Companies**
**Chartism, 105**
Chemical industry, 503

children –employment,
60, 62, 105, 243,
260, 267, 387 *see
also* **Employment
of Women and
Children**; and
education, 188; and
poverty, 364, and
slavery, 449
Chernobyl Nuclear Power
Plant, 212
**China, 106**
economic growth,
36–7; cotton
industry, 145–6;
production
distribution led, 112;
proto-industry, 378;
rice production,
395–6, 397; steam,
use of, 471
Treaty Ports, 109, 439
**Classical and
Neo-Classical
Economics, 113,
297, 368**
Clayton Act *see*
**Anti-Trust**
Clement, Joseph, 303
Cliometrics, 156
**Coal, 118**
**Coffee, 122**
Colonization *see*
**Economic
Imperialism**
Combination Acts
Commercial Partnerships
(*commenda*) 125
Commercial vehicles
(CVs) 43
**Commercial Revolution,
124**
Commodity agreements,
international, *see*
international
commodity
agreements
Common Agricultural
Policy (CAP) 231
Common Land *see*
**Enclosure**
**Companies, 125**
limited liability, 125–8
Competition policy, *see*
**Anti-Trust**

Concentration, 129
 aggregate
  concentration, 130
 in automobile
  industry, 39
 in banking, 329
 in brewing, 52,
  54, 56; market
  concentration, 130
 in retailing see
  Consumer
  Revolutions
Consumer Revolutions, 131
Communist League, 313
Convergence
 in GDP per capita,
  150–1
 in productivity growth,
  375
Cooke, Edward, 487
Cooperatives, 134
Corn Laws, 63
Corporate Governance,
 139
 Anglo-Saxon, German
  and Japanese systems
  compared, 140–143
corvée system, 401, 403
Cort, Henry, 284–5
Cottage system see Proto-
  Industrialization
Cotton and Cotton
  Textiles, 143,
 in American Civil
  War, 17;
 early invention in
  manufacture, 257
 English East India
  Company, 191;
 as leader in the
  Industrial Revolution
  in Britain, 143
 in India, 248–9
Credit Anstaldt Bank, 233
Crompton, Samuel,
 144, 527
Cugnot, Joseph, 39
Czech Republic, 520

Daimler, Gottlieb, 39
Darby, Abraham, 284
Davy, Sir Humphry, 171
Decolonization
 see Economic
  Imperialism

De-Industrialization, 372,
 376, 427
Depression see Great
  Depression, Business
  Cycles
Developing Countries
 see Economic
  Development
Development Economics
 see Economic
  Development
Dismal Science, 116
Domestic System
 see Proto-
  Industrialization
Double-entry bookkeeping
 see Accounting
Dutch East India
  Company, 83, 157,
  460, 475
Dutch colonialism, 157, 162

East Asia see Asian
  Miracle
East India Company
 see Dutch, English
  Companies
Economic backwardness,
 213–14
Economic growth
 see Economic
  Development
Economic Development,
 147
 convergence of growth
  rates, 150–1
 dependency theory, 161
 developing countries,
  151
 impact of Napoleonic
  Codes, 160
 impact of education,
  168–9
 less developed
  countries, 151
 measurement of
  economic growth,
  147–8
 multinational
  companies, 337
 theories of economic
  growth, 149–50
 Third World countries,
  151
Economic History, 155

Annales School, 156;
 German Historical
 School, 30, 155,
 273, 512; Chicago
 School, 30;
 cliometrics, 156; New
 Economic History,
 156; -in USA
 Methodenstreit, 155
 Weber, influence of, 512
Economic Imperialism,
 157
 contribution to indus-
  trial revolutions,
  162; cost–benefit of,
  163–4; independence
  of British colonies in
  America, 17;
  decolonisation, 160
Economic planning, 252
Edison, Thomas Alva,
  171–2; 344
Education, 165
 Business education, 8,
  104; in Britain, 67,
  69; in Europe, 166;
  in USA 167; impact
  on economic growth,
  168–9; Impoverished
  Sophisticate 168;
  literacy rates, 167,
  168; cultural bias
  and vocational
  training, 169
Eckert, J. Prosper, 179
Erie Canal, 501
Elder, John, 431
Electricity, 170
Electronics, 176
 Electronic Numerical
  Integrator and
  Computer (ENIAC)
  179; integrated circuits
  (ICs) 177; internet,
  the, 183; mainframe
  computers, 178–9;
  microprocessors, 178;
  minicomputers, 180;
  Moore's Law, 178;
  personal computers
  (PCs) 180; Silicon
  Valley, 180, 254;
  solid state devices,
  transistors, 177 vacuum
  tubes (valves) 177

Elliot, Obadiah, 400
Empire, British *see*
    **Britain**
**Employment of Women
    and Children, 183**
child labour, 186, 187
female participation
    rates, 184, 185, 505
industrialization,
    and, 267
rates of pay in USA, 505
regulation of working
    conditions, 187–8
and **Trade Unions**,
    184, 186
and **World War I**
    and **World War II**
    184, 185
**Enclosure, 188**, 9, 10, 133
endogenous growth
    theory, 151, 373
England, *see* **Britain**
**English East India
    Company** (EIC), **190**
India, 247–8, 251, 280
Trade, 191
Enlightenment, The, 203
**Entrepreneurship, 194**
Britain's perceived
    entrepreneurial
    failure, 196
definition of, 195
Schumpeter on, 419
supply of, 195
EU-15, 518, 525
European Central Bank
    (ECB), 97–8
European Coal and Steel
    Community (ECSC),
    288
European Commission
    and anti-trust, 33
European Community,
    525–6
European Economic Area
    (EEA), 518, 525
European Free Trade Area
    (EFTA), 525
European Monetary
    System (EMS), 526
European Monetary
    Union, 525–6
European Payments
    Union (EPU), *see*
    **Marshall Plan**

European Recovery Plan
    (ERP), *see* **Marshall
    Plan**
Euroscellerosis, 524
Evans, Oliver, 38
External economies, 254

Factory Acts, 105, 187,
    188, 243, 260, 518
    *see* **Regulation**
**Famine, 199**, 249,
    251, 351
in China, 107, 199
in India, 199, 249
Irish Famine, 280
in Russia, 199, 230,
    410, 413, 415
in Africa, 199
Malthus, 308
and Migration, 323
in North Korea, 199
Faraday, Michael, 171
Federal Reserve Board,
    99–101, policy in
    Great Depression, 235
Feudalism, 9 *see also*
    **Peasantry and
    Serfdom**
Fifth Wheel Coupling, 405
First Bank of the United
    States, 94
Flexible Production, 254,
    304, 376
**Ford, Henry**, 39, **200**
Fordism, 200
Foreign direct investment
    (FDI), *see also*
    **International Trade,
    Multinational
    Enterprises**
France
agriculture and
    population in the
    17th and 18th
    centuries, 351–2
aviation, 51
banks, 331
bimetallic system, 58
colonialism, 159, 162
education, 166, 170
electronics, 182
gas, 210, 212
industrial revolution,
    263, 520
in India, 191

gold standard, 227
nuclear energy, 175
poor relief compared
    with Britain, 357;
industrialization cf.
    Britain, 521
population growth, 521;
railways, 382
Revolution 1789, *see*
    **French Revolution**
Revolutionary wars,
    349, 519
road transport, 403–4
serfdom abolished, 349
silk industry, 438, 439
silver coinage, 443–4
telecommunications, 487
trade unions, 493,
    494, 495
free banking, 94
free trade, 277, 278
**French Revolution, 203**
**Friedman, Milton, 204**
Feudal System, *see*
    **Peasantry and
    Serfdom**
Fulton, Robert, 430, 431,
    472

**Gas, 210**
General Agreement on
    Tariffs and Trade
    (GATT), 279
Gentrification of
    entrepreneurs, 196,
    427
German Historical
    School, *see* **Economic
    History**
Germany
anti-trust, 34
aviation, 50
banks, 331, 332
canals, 81
corporate governance,
    140–1
gold standard, 227, 228
hyper-inflation, 522;
    in Great Depression,
    232, 233, 523
electrical industry, 173
Erhard, Ludwig, 524
machine tool industry,
    305–6; productivity
    performance, 376

Germany – *continued*
  railways, 382–3
  road transport, 404
  satellites, 521
  small business
    promotion, 452
  steel industry, 282
  trade unions, 493–4, 495
  unification, 525
  war reparations, 232,
    522, 534
  Zollverein, 278, 521
  Weimar Republic,
    233, 513
  World War I, impact on
    economy, 532
**Gerschenkron,**
  **Alexander, 213**
  on banking, 331
  on Rostow, 407
  on Russia, 410
Gibrat's Law, 130
Gini Coefficient, 270
Glass–Steagal Act, *see*
  **Anti-Trust**
**Globalization, 215**
  benefits of, 220
  convergence of
    commodity prices,
    217–9
  convergence of real
    wages, 219
  definition, 215–217
  voices against, 220
Glorious Revolution
  (1688), 478, 516
**Gold, 221**
  guinea issued in
    Britain, 223
  in California, 24
  influx from South
    America, 222–3
  in South Africa, 225
  qualities of, 222
**Gold Standard, 226**
  defined, 226
  gold exchange
    standard, 227
  theory and practice, 227;
    end of, 229
Golden Age (1950–73),
  148, 522
**Grain, 229**
  influence of shipping
    costs on prices, 230

prices increase in,
  18th century, 229
world output, 230
Gray, Elisha, 489
Great Agricultural
  Depression,12, 521
**Great Depression, 232,**
  *see also* **New Deal**
  automobile industry
    in the, 40; bank
    failures, 233; Britain
    in the, 64, 65, 234;
    brewing industry in
    the, 54, 66; views
    on, 13, 66, 235–6
  Friedman's views
    on causes of, 207; in
    Germany, 232, 233;
    iron and steel, 287;
    and Keynes, 207,
    297; in nineteenth
    century, 74, 232,
    521; and prices, 370;
    technical progress
    during the, 523; in
    USA 232, 233; world
    trade, 232, 275
Growth accounting, 150
Guericke, Otto von, 471
Guilds, 126, 131, 386, 492
Griffith, Alan Arnold, 291

Hall, Samuel, 430
**Hamilton, Alexander,**
  **238**
  Federal coinage,
    239–40;
    manufacturing policy,
    240; national bank,
    239 Public debt, 238;
    taxation, 239;
**Hammonds, The, 241**
Hargreaves, James, 144,
  257, 527
Hawkers, *see* **Pedlars**
**Hayek, Friedrich August,**
  **von, 244**
  on Great Depression, 235;
    on institutions, 273
Heckscher–Ohlin Principle,
  216, 276, 433
Hero of Alexandria, 290,
  470
Homestead Act, 17, 25
Huntsman, Benjamin, 284

Imperial Preference, 278
Income per capita,
  international
    comparisons of,
    147–8, 366
Incorporation, *see*
  **Companies**
Index Numbers, 147, 213,
  214, 368
**India,** 193, 247, 440
**Industrial Districts, 253**
**Industrial Revolution in**
  **Britain, The, 256**
  shifts in population,
    288; science and
    technology, 258;
    regional phenomenon,
    and social cost,
    259–60; transport
    system, 258; why
    Britain first? 258–9
  *see also* **Hammonds,**
  **The Industrial**
  **Revolutions, 262**
  four revolutions, 264;
    process, not event,
    262; regional nature
    of, 264; social
    problems, 502
**Industrious Revolution,**
  **266**
**Inequality, 268**
  in Britain, 69; and
    economic growth,
    161, 162, 366;
    between male and
    female incomes, 185;
    human height as
    an indicator of, *see*
    measurement of, 269;
    and inflation, 368
Inflation, *see* **Prices and**
  **Inflation**
Information Technology,
  *see* **Electronics**
Innovation
  in agriculture, 10;
    macro-inventions, 373;
    simultaneous, 293; *see*
    *also* esp. USA 502–4
  instalment buying (Hire
    Purchase), 135, 136
**Institutions, 259, 272**
  *see* esp. **Veblin,**
  **Thorstein Bunde**

integrated circuits (ICs),
see **Electronics**
internal combustion
   engine, 38, 43, 471
international commodity
   agreements, 14, 476
**International Trade,**
   **273;** see also
   **Globalization**
internet, the, see
   **Electronics**
Interstate Commerce
   Commission (ICC),
   33, 385
Inter-War Depression, see
   **Great Depression**
Itinerant trades, see **Pedlars**
Ireland, Republic of,
   economic growth
   of, 524, 525; see also
   **Irish Famine**
**Irish Famine, 280**
**Iron and Steel, 282,** blast
   furnace, origins, 283;
   blister steel, 284;
   Oxygen Steelmaking,
   286; reverberatory
   furnace, 284;
   Siemens- Martin
   open hearth, 285
Islamic finance, see **Usury**
Italy
   electronics, 182;
   Emilia-Romagna,
   255; female
   participation rate,
   427; industrial
   revolution, 264;
   retailing, 136; road
   transport, 404;
   serfdom lingered
   until end of 19th
   century, 349
itinerant salesmen, see
   **Pedlars**

Jacquard Loom, 178,
   439, 527
Japan
   Anti-Trust, 34–5;
   aviation, 50–1;
   banks, 332–3;
   Commodore Perry,
   159; costs of state
   interventions,

468; corporate
   governance, 141;
   cotton industry,
   145, 473; economic
   growth, 36;
   electronics industry,
   181–2; gold standard,
   227; keiretsu,
   333;machine
   tools, 305–6;
   management
   techniques, 40, 337
Meiji Restoration, 128,
   332, 333; MITI 34;
   retailing, 136–8; rice
   production, 396–7;
   road transport, 405–6;
   serfdom, 349; small
   business, 452; steel
   industry, 287–8;
   share of international
   trade, 219; silk
   industry, 439–40;
   Value Added Tax,
   simpler form of,
   480–1; wool, major
   importer of, 528;
   zaibatsu, 333
**Jet Engine, 472, 290**
Judaism, 515

Kay, John, 144, 257
Keiretsu, 141, 333
Kelly, William, 285
**Keynes, John Maynard,**
   **294**
   and Classical
   Economics, 117; on
   the Gold Standard,
   64; and the Great
   Depression, 66;
   Mercantilism,
   321; and Milton
   Friedman, 205–7;
   and Malthus, 234,
   307; on Ricardo,
   234; on German war
   reparations, 534
Konzern, 141
Korea, 440
Kuznets hypothesis, 161

Lamm, Uno, 172
Latin America economic
   growth in, 148;

dependency (trapped
   into supplying raw
   materials), 152; in
   Great Depression,
   232
Law, John, 126
League of Nations, 159, 278
Lend-Lease, 537
Lenoir, Jean Etienne, 39
Less Developed Countries
   (LDCs), see **Economic**
   **Development**
Limited liability, see
   **Companies**
London Stock Exchange
   (LSE), 103, 273; see
   also **Capital Markets**
**Luddism, 300**

Maastricht Treaty, 525
M' form companies,
   see **Business**
   **Management**
Macadam, John Loudon,
   400–1
**Machine Tools, 302**
   American System of
   Manufactures
   (interchangeable
   parts), 302–5
Macmillan Committee, 87
Magna Carta, 348
Mainz Covention, 423
**Malthus, Thomas**
   **Robert,** 149, 298,
   **306,** 359
Mannheim Treaty, 423
Marconi, Guglielmo,
   176, 177
Marco Polo, 327, 438
**Marshall Plan, 309**
Martin, Pierre Emile, 285
Matsushita, Konosuke, 181
**Marx, Karl, 313**
   on collapse of
   capitalist system,
   89, 150; on
   concentration, 129,
   254; on colonialism,
   161; on economic
   development, 149,
   156, 161, 251, 412;
   on recessions,
   73–4; on workers in
   Britain, 260, 317–18

Mauchly, John W., 179
Maudslay, Henry, 303
**Mercantilism, 318**
  in colonial America,
    19; in developing
    countries, 153; in
    English imperialism,
    157; in relation to
    gold, 223
Merchants, 377
Metcalfe, John, 400–1
Middle East, 345–6
**Migration, 322**
  Changes after World
    War II, 325;
    Dillingham
    Commission, 324;
    emigrants returning
    home, 323; forces
    driving migration,
    323; population
    movements to 1930,
    322; restrictions
    on, 324; impact on
    receiving economies,
    324–5
Missouri Compromise, 15
**Money and Banking,
  326; see also**
  **Bi-Metallic System;**
  **Central Banking;**
  **Friedman; Gold;**
  **Gold Standard;**
  **Prices and Inflation.**
  in colonial America,
    15, 16, 22; banking
    in Great Depression,
    339–40; Bullion
    Controversy, 115,
    328; and control of
    inflation, 96–7; First
    National Bank of
    the US, 239; Federal
    Reserve policy in
    Great Depression,
    340; Keynes on, 297;
    monetarism, 96–7;
    Friedman on, 204–8
Money markets, 82
Monopolistic
    competition,
    *see* imperfect
    competition
Monopoly policy, *see*
  **Anti-Trust**

Moore's Law, *see*
  **Electronics**
Moral hazard, 334
Morse, Samuel, 487, 488
Muir, William, 303
Multiple retailers, 134
Murdock, William, 210, 471
Muscovy Company, 126

Napier, David, 303
Napoleonic Wars, *see* France
National Banking System,
    (US) 99
National Industrial
    Recovery Act (NIRA),
    *see* **New Deal**
Native Americans
    (Indians), 18, 26–7
Navigation Acts, 19, 63,
    158, 277, 320, 434–5,
    458, 498
Naysmith, James, 303
Neo-Austrians, 195
Netherlands
    Bank of Amsterdam,
    327–8; industrial
    revolution, 264;
    natural gas, 212; poor
    relief compared with
    Britain
**New Deal, 339**
New Economic History,
    *see* **Economic**
    **History**
new firm formations, *see*
    **Entrepreneuship**
New Growth Theory, 151
Newcomen,
    Thomas, 471
Newton, Isaac, 327
New York Stock
    Exchange, 83
Nielson, James, 285
Norway, 525
Nuclear energy, 121, 175,
    212

Ohain, Hans, *see* **Jet**
    **Engines**
**Oil, 343,** 121, 212, 225,
    524; electricity
    generation, 170, 175;
    North Sea, 67
Organisation for
    Economic

Cooperation and
    Development
    (OECD) formerly
    Organisation
    for Economic
    Cooperation (OEEC),
    310
Organization of
    Petroleum Exporting
    Countries (OPEC),
    *see* **Oil**
Otto, Nicolaus, 39, 41

Panama Canal, 434
Papin, Dr Dennis, 471
Parsons, Sir
    Charles, 472
Partnerships, *see*
    **Companies**
**Peasantry and Serfdom,
    348**
**Pedlars, 349**
People's Bank of China
    (PBC), 98–99
**Physiocrats, 351**
Political Economy, 155
**Poor Laws, 356**
Poor relief compared with
    Continental
    Europe, 357
Prohibition, 54
**Population, 358**
  in Britain, 10, 12,
    113, 60–62, 257,
    260, 348; Europe,
    323, 351, 369, 370,
    Census of population
    first in 1790 in US,
    360; England 1801;
    France, 520; in
    America, 18, 27; in
    China, 107–112; in
    India, 249, 252, 253;
    in Ireland, 280, 281;
    and Malthus, 306
    *et seq*
Ports, *see* **Seaports**
Portugal, 157
**Poverty, 361**
  In Africa, 220; in
    India, 253; and the
    Poor Laws, 357;
    problems of
    international com-
    parisons, 147–8, 366

**Prices and Inflation, 367**
  in Britain, 2,  62, 64,
    66; and in business
    cycles, 73, 74, 100;
    in America, 16, 18,
    75; in Europe, 75,
    113, 522; in India,
    248, 249; in Russia,
    410; 413, 415; cost-
    push inflation,
    369; demand-pull
    inflation, 369;
    hyper-inflation, 232,
    522; impact of silver
    from Latin America,
    442; *see also* **Business
    Cycles; Classical
    and Neo Classical
    Economics**
**Productivity, 372**
  in agriculture,
    9, 10; Baumol
    Effect, the, 372;
    in Britain, 68–9;
    and information
    technology, 374–5;
    long view of, 374;
    in services, 428; in
    small firms, 451;
    measurement of,
    372–3; total factor
    (TFP) 372–3
Protection
  in Asia, 219; in Britain,
    12, 63; and economic
    development, 152;
    after World War I,
    66, 218, 233, 236,
    278; disadvantages
    of, 217; *see also*
    **International
    Trade**
**Proto-Industrialization,**
  76, **377**; *see also*
  **Industrious
  Revolution**
public finance; *see also*
  **Taxation**
  in American Civil War,
    16; in early USA 238;
    National Debt in
    Britain, 479
Public choice, economics
  of, 388, 469
Purchasing Power Parities
  (PPPs), 147

Putting out system,
  122; *see also* **Proto-
  Industrialization**

Quesnay, François and the
  Physiocrats, 353–5

**Railways, 380**
  Anglo-French Channel
    Tunnel, 381–2;
    convert from
    coal to oil, 344;
    in India, 250; US
    transcontinental
    lines, 24, 25
Real wages, *see* standards
  of living
Refrigeration, 13, 27
Regional Trade
  Agreements (RTAs),
  279
**Regulation, 386**
  compliance costs of,
    389; deregulation
    in the USA, 388–9;
    efficiency costs of,
    390; Factory Acts,
    260, 387; of road
    transport, 402–3;
    Regulatory Impact
    Assessments, 389
Reparations, *see* Germany
Resale Price Maintenance
  (RPM), 135
Research and development
  (R&D), 503–4
Retailing, *see* **Consumer
  Revolution**
**Ricardo, David, 390**
  and division of
    production, 149, 268;
    and the quantity
    of money, 115; and
    the theory of value,
    155; in economic
    history, 155; Law
    of Comparative
    Cost, 216, 276, 394;
    Schumpeter on,
    394–5; and Malthus,
    7, 234, 306; and
    Marx, 314, 316
**Rice, 395**
**Road Transport, 398**
  Automobiles, 38 *et
    seq*, 402; financing

of, 401, 403;
    horse-drawn buses
    and cabs, 402;
    motorways, 403;
    passenger coach
    services, 399–400;
    regulation, 402;
    suspension of
    vehicles, 400;
    turnpikes, 401;
    wheeled transport,
    origins of, 400
Robber Barons, 200, 504
Robinson–Patman Act, 136
Roberts, Richard, 303
Rock oil, *see* **Oil**
**Rostow, Walt Whitman,
  406**
  criticized by
    Gerschenkron,
    214, 407
Rubber, synthetic, 503
**Russia, 408**
  89, 106; coal, 118,
    120, 121, 264,
    371; electrification
    of, 173; famine,
    199, 231; gas, 213;
    gold, 58, 224; gold
    standard, 227; grain,
    230, 231; migration,
    322; national plans,
    412–4; oil, 344, 345;
    railways, 380, 383–4;
    serfdom, 349, 408–90

Sarbanes-Oxley, 7, 86, 142
Savery, Thomas, 256, 471
**Schumpeter, Joseph
  Aloisius, 418**
  and banking, 331;
    and monopoly, 30;
    dynamic model of
    capitalism, 150; on
    Keynes view of Great
    Depression, 420; on
    Smith, Adam, 453
Science and technology,
  258
Scientific management, *see*
  **Taylor, Frederick W.**
**Seaports, 421**
  Containerization, 423;
    Antwerp, 382, 423;
    Hong Kong, 424;
    Liverpool, 422;

Seaports – *continued*
London, 421–2; New
York, 501; Rotterdam,
423; Singapore, 424
Seaton, John, 284
Separation of ownership
and control,
76–7; 128–9; *see
also* **Corporate
Governance**
Serfs, *see* **Peasantry and
Serfdom**
**Service Sector, 425**
definition of, 425–6;
productivity in, 428
Sherman Act, *see*
**Anti-Trust**
**Shipping, 429**
cabotage restrictions,
435; containerization,
436; convergence of
commodity prices,
434; English East
India fleet; 191; flags
of convenience, 435;
freight rates, 433;
large crude carriers,
436; piracy, 430;
sailing vessels, share
of world tonnage,
432; steamships,
431–2, 472; Panama
canal, 434; Suez
Canal, 250, 344,
432, 434 438; US and
Royal Navies' switch
to oil, 434
Shockley, William, 177
Silicon Valley, *see*
**Electronics**
**Silk, 437**
beginnings in China,
437; early attempts
to found industry
in Britain, 438;
mechanization of
production, 439;
properties of, 437;
Silk Road, 438; in
France, 438, 439; in
India, 440; in USA
439, 440
**Silver, 441** *see also*
**Bimetallic system**
coinage in China,
442; 'Free Silver'

Movement in US,
444, 445; Spanish
exploitation of mines
in Latin America,
442
**Slavery, 441**
abolition of, 158
efficiency of plantation
system, 447–8;
as a factor in the
industrialization of
Europe, 259, 447–8;
in the American
Civil War, 15–16;
and Classical
Economists, 446
Sloan, Alfred, 42
**Small and Medium
Enterprises, 449**
and accounting, 6, 7;
and Chandler, 197,
451; in capitalism, 92;
business population,
economic
history of, 450–1;
imperfections in
capital markets, 451;
family businesses,
451–2; in industrial
districts, 254; and
Marshall, Alfred,
451; productivity in,
451; promotion by
governments, 452; in
proto-industry, 378;
in retailing, 136, 138
**Smith, Adam, 453;**
*see also* **Classical
and Neo-Classical
Economics**
Theory of value,
454–5; self interest,
455–6; allocation
of resources, 456;
imperfections
of markets, 456;
landowners, 457; wage
earners, 457; capital,
458; intervention in
markets justified in
specific areas, 459;
taxation, 459, 484
Smith, Francis Pettit, 431
**South Africa, 460**
Afrikaners, 461, 463;
apartheid system,

414–15; becomes
a Republic, 464;
Britain occupies
Cape, 461; discovery
of diamonds and
gold, 462; gold
mining, 462, 464;
labour issues,
462–3; agriculture
and industry,
463–4; platinum,
464; Republics
of Transvaal and
Orange Free State,
461; Union of 461
South-East Asia (SEA) 36
Spain
industrial revolution,
264; exploitation
of silver in Latin
America, 442
Stages of growth
theories, 51, 214, 407
**Standards of Living**
in colonial
America, 18
during industrial
revolutions, 28, 62–3,
259–260, 266, 265–6;
human height as
an indicator of, *see*
**Anthropometric
History**
State-chartered trading
companies *see* Dutch
East India company,
**English East India
Company**
**State, Rise of, 466**
accounts for increased
share of expenditure
and employment,
467; government
expenditure as per
cent of GDP, 480;
civil service reform,
470; efficiency costs
of, 467; impact
of broadening
franchise, 469;
intervention in
industry, 468;
necessity for strong
government, 468;
transfers, costs of,
468–9;

State, Rise of – *continued*
  power of state, 470;
    public choice
    economics, 469; wars
    lead to racheting-
    up of state share in
    national
    income, 480
Steam Power, 470
  condensers, 471;
    impact on economic
    development, 473;
    on farms, 472; in
    Continental
    Europe, 473
Stop-Go in Britain, 67
Stubblefield, Nathan, 490
Suez Canal, 250, 344, 432,
    434 438
Sugar, 474
  and slavery, 474–5;
    beet, 475–6; in
    Brazil, 474; in
    Carribean, 474–5;
    plantation system,
    474–5; in Cuba,
    475–6; saturation of
    demand, 476; trade
    agreements, 476;
    use of indentured
    workers, 475;
Switzerland, 525

Taxation, 478
  in colonial America,
    20; in Britain higher
    than in France in
    18th century, 479;
    compliance costs of,
    389; customs duties,
    478; death duties,
    479; excise taxes,
    478; income tax, 479;
    fiscal activism, 480;
    Land Tax, 478; local,
    481–2; Pay-As-You-
    Earn, 480; Purchase
    Tax, 480; Reagan and
    Thatcher reforms
    in, 483; in Russia,
    409; sales taxes in
    USA, 483; Selective
    Employment Tax,
    426, 480; evasion
    of, 481; shift of

  burden from capital
    to labour, 483; Value
    Added Tax (VAT),
    480–1; wars lead to
    permanent increases
    in, 480; Window
    Tax, 478
Taylor, Frederick W. 305,
    484
Telecommunications,
    486
  information society,
    490–1; mobile
    (wireless) technology,
    487, 490; state
    monopolies of, 487,
    490
Telford, Thomas, 400
Telegraph, *see*
    **Telecommunications**
Tesla, Nikola, 172
Third Industrial
    Revolution, 176
Thomas, Sidney
    Gilchrist, 285
Thomas, Percy Gilchrist,
    285
Thompson, Edward
    Palmer, 491
Tinkers, *see* **Pedlars**
Tokyo Stock Exchange,
    (TSE) 84
Torrens, Robert, 115
Total Factor Productivity,
    (TFP)
  defined, 37, 372–3
Trade Unions, 492
  density in Britain,
    493; legal
    constraints on,
    495; role in Britain
    and Germany
    contrasted, 495,
    496; in USA, 502
Truck Acts, 132
Townsend Acts, 20
Treaty of Paris, 17, 24
Transnational
    Corporations (TNCs),
    *see* **Multinational
    Enterprises**
Treaty Ports in China,
    109, 439
Treaty of Versailles, 45;
    159, 296, 522

Trevithick, Richard, 380,
    472
Truck Acts
Turbines, *see* **Jet Engines**
Turnpikes, 258, 401

U form companies,
    *see* **Business
    Management**
United States (USA)
    498, *see also* esp.
    **American Civil
    War, American War
    of Independence,
    American Westward
    Expansion
    Hamilton,
    Alexander, New Deal**
  Aviation industry, 44
    *et seq*; 292; as supplier
    of raw cotton, 145;
    as supplier of wheat,
    230, 231; banking,
    330–2, 334; bimetallic
    system, 58–9;
    colonization by, 159;
    economic growth,
    500, 501, 504;
    148–9; education,
    167; gas, 211–12;
    Great Depression,
    232, 233, 502;
    incorporation, 127 *et
    seq*; industrialization,
    498–500; industrial
    revolution, 264;
    gold-dollar link
    abandoned, 225; gold
    standard, 227, 228,
    229; inequality, 269,
    270–1; innovation
    system, 502–4;
    Interstate Commerce
    Commission (ICC),
    385; land area,
    changes in, 24,
    500; machine tool
    industry, 303–5;
    multinational
    companies, 337;
    native Americans,
    26–7; National
    Industrial Recovery
    Act, 341; nuclear
    energy, 175;

**United States (USA)**
– *continued*
oil industry, 343–5;
population, 501,
505; ports, 425;
poverty line,
364; productivity
performance, 374–6;
racial minorities,
505–6, 238; railways,
25, 384–5, 501;
retailing, 136–7; river
transport, 501; road
transport, 404–5;
silver mining and
coinage, 443, 444,
445; Smoot–Hawley
Act, 231, 232, 278;
steamships, 472;
steel industry, 283,
285, 287; sub-prime
credit crisis, 334;
taxation, 239, 482–3;
telecommunications,
487, 488–90; trade
unions, 494, 495,
502; universities, 498;
wheat production,
230; slavery, 15,
446 *et seq*; small
business, 452, 504;
social problems of,
industrialization, 502;
South, the, 499–500;
sugar importation,
476; unincorporated
enterprises, 129;
Urbanization, 151, 501
Universal banking, 331
**Usury, 506**

**Veblin, Thorstein Bunde,**
509
Verbruggen, Jan, 302
Volta, Alessandro, 171

Watson, Thomas J., and
son, 178–9, 489
Watt, James, 256, 302,
471, 473
**Weber, Max, 512**
**Wedgwood, Josiah, 516**
Weimar Government, *see*
Germany
Welfare State, 57, 361
Welsbach, Baron Von, 211
**Western Europe, 518**
controversy over level
of development
before the industrial
revolution, 148–9;
economic weight cf.
USA 526; emergence
of enlarged European
Community, 525–6;
GDP per capita in,
520; technology cf.
USA, 524; unification
of grain market, 230
Westinghouse, George,
172
Wheat, 12
Wheatstone, Charles, 487
Whitney, Eli, 145, 304
Whittle, Frank, *see* **Jet**
**Engines**
Whitworth, Joseph, 303
Wholesaling, origins of,
132
Wilkinson, John, 257,
302, 472
'Wizard of Oz" and 'Free
Silver' Movement,
445
Women, *see* **Employment**
**of Women and**
**Children**
Worcester, Marquis of,
470
**Wool and Wool Textiles,**
**527**

**World War I, 529**
aircraft production,
45; allies superior
in resources to the
Central Powers,
532; Britain more
dependent on
international trade,
532; causes of, 529;
combatants, the, 529;
conscription, 531;
destruction human
and physical, 532–3;
horses and lances
employed, 530;
impact of war on
growth, 532; levels of
GDP per capita, 531;
long term effects of,
533; reparations, 534;
USA enters, 530
**World War II, 535**
agriculture, 539–40;
aircraft production,
45–6; armed forces
and equipment, 536;
costs of the, 540;
death toll and physical
destruction, 535;
economic warfare,
539; economic weight
of combatants, 536;
finance, 537–8; led
to greater role for
government, 538–9;
living standards, 537;
long-term economic
impact of, 540–1;
resource policies,
538–9; technical
innovations, 541

Zaibatsu, *see* Japan
Zollverein Customs Area,
*see* Germany